CONTENTS

Acknowledgements

We are grateful to all those teachers and students who have contributed to the development of the *Collins French School Dictionary* by advising us on how to tailor it to their needs. We also gratefully acknowledge the help of the examining boards.

Collins French School Dictionary

Published by Collins
An imprint of HarperCollins Publishers
Westerhill Road
Bishopbriggs
Glasgow G64 2QT

Fourth Edition 2015

10 9 8 7 6 5 4

ISBN 978-0-00-756935-9

www.collinsdictionary.com
www.collins.co.uk/dictionaries

Typeset by Davidson Publishing Solutions, Glasgow

Printed in Italy by Grafica Veneta S.p.A.

A catalogue record for this book is available from the British Library.

If you would like to comment on any aspect of this book, please contact us at the given address or online.
E-mail: dictionaries@harpercollins.co.uk

facebook.com/collinsdictionary

@collinsdict

Acknowledgements
We would like to thank those authors and publishers who kindly gave permission for copyright material to be used in the Collins Corpus. We would also like to thank Times Newspapers Ltd for providing valuable data.

EDITOR
Susie Beattie

CONTRIBUTORS
Val McNulty
Phyllis Buchanan
Maggie Seaton

FOR THE PUBLISHER
Gerry Breslin
Helen Newstead
Ruth O'Donovan
Sheena Shanks

TECHNICAL SUPPORT
Thomas Callan
Agnieszka Urbanowicz

USING THIS DICTIONARY

The *Collins French School Dictionary* is designed specifically for anyone starting to learn French, and has been carefully researched with teachers and students. It is very straightforward, with an accessible layout that is easy on the eye, guiding students quickly to the right translation. It also offers essential help on French culture.

This section gives useful tips on how to use the *Collins French School Dictionary* effectively.

▷ Make sure you look in the right side of the dictionary

There are two sides in a bilingual dictionary. Here, the **French–English** side comes first, and the second part is **English–French**. At the top of each page there is a reminder of which side of the dictionary you have open. The middle pages of the book have a blue border so you can see where one side finishes and the other one starts.

▷ Finding the word you want

To help you find a word more quickly, use the **alphabet tabs** down the side of the page, then look at the words in **blue** at the top of pages. They show the first and last words on the two pages where the dictionary is open.

▷ Make sure you use the right part of speech

Some entries are split into several parts of speech. For example '**glue**' can either be a noun ("Can I borrow your **glue**?") or a verb ("**Glue** this into your exercise book"). Parts of speech within an entry are separated by a black triangle ▶ and are given on a new line. They are given in their abbreviated form (*n* for noun, *adj* for adjective, etc). For the full list of abbreviations, look at page viii.

> **glue** *n* colle *f*
> ▶ *vb* coller [**28**]

▷ **Choosing the right translation**

The main translation of a word is underlined and is shown after the part of speech. If there is more than one main translation for a word, each one is numbered. You may also sometimes find bracketed words in *italics* which give you some context. They help you to choose the translation you want.

> **pool** *n* ❶ *(puddle)* flaque *f* ❷ *(pond)* étang *m* ❸ *(for swimming)* piscine *f* ❹ *(game)* billard américain *m* ...

Often you will see phrases in *italics*, preceded by a white triangle ▷. These are examples of the word being used in context.

> **numérique** *adj* digital ▷ *un appareil photo numérique* a digital camera

Phrases in **bold type** are phrases which are particularly common and important. Sometimes these phrases have a completely different translation.

> **chausson** *nm* slipper; **un chausson aux pommes** an apple turnover

Once you have found the right translation, remember that you may need to adapt the French word you have found. You may need to make a **noun** plural, or make an **adjective** feminine or plural. Remember that the feminine form is given for nouns and adjectives, and that irregular plural forms are given also.

> **dancer** *n* danseur *m*, danseuse *f*
> **horse** *n* cheval *m* (*pl* chevaux)
> **salty** *adj* salé(e)

You may also need to adapt the **verb**. Verbs are given in the infinitive form, but you may want to use them in the present, past or future tense. To do this, use the **verb tables** in the last section of the dictionary. All French verbs on both sides are followed by a number in square brackets. This number corresponds to a page number in the Verb Tables at the back of the dictionary.

In the following example, **imprimer** follows the same pattern as **donner**, shown on page **28** in the Verb Tables.

imprimer *vb* [**28**] to print

▷ Find out more

In the *Collins French School Dictionary*, you will find lots of extra information about the French language. These **usage notes** help you understand how the language works, draw your attention to false friends (words which look similar but have a different meaning), and give you some word-for-word translations.

te *pron*

> **te** changes to **t'** before a vowel and most words beginning with 'h'.

librairie *nf* bookshop

> Be careful! **librairie** does not mean **library**.

chauve-souris (*pl* **chauves-souris**) *nf* (*animal*) bat

> Word for word, this means 'bald mouse'.

You can also find out more about life in France and French-speaking countries by reading the **cultural notes**.

half-term *n* petites vacances *fpl*

> There are two half-term holidays in France: **les vacances de la Toussaint** (in October/November) and **les vacances de février** (in February).

▷ Remember!

Never take the first translation you see without looking at the others. Always look to see if there is more than one translation, or more than one part of speech.

ABBREVIATIONS USED IN THIS DICTIONARY

abbr	abbreviation
adj	adjective
adv	adverb
art	article
conj	conjunction
excl	exclamation
f	feminine
n	noun
nf	feminine noun
nm	masculine noun
nmf	masculine and feminine noun
nm/f	masculine or feminine noun
npl	plural noun
num	number
prep	preposition
pron	pronoun
vb	verb

SYMBOLS

▷	example
▶	new part of speech
❷	new meaning
[29]	verb table number (see Verb Tables section at the back of the dictionary)
accident	Key words which you need for your GCSE or other exams of a similar level are highlighted in light blue throughout both sides of the dictionary to help you find them more easily.

Note that to help you decide whether to use **le**, **la** or **l'** in front of a word starting with 'h', the article is given for all the nouns in letter **H** on the **French–English** side of the dictionary.

TIME

Quelle heure est-il? **What time is it?**
Il est… **It's…**

une heure

une heure dix

une heure et quart

une heure et demie

deux heures moins vingt

deux heures moins le quart

À quelle heure? **At what time?**

à minuit

à midi

à une heure (de l'après-midi)

à huit heures (du soir)

In French times are often given using the 24-hour clock.

à onze heures quinze (11h15)

à vingt heures quarante-cinq (20h45)

DATES

▷ Days of the Week

lundi	Monday
mardi	Tuesday
mercredi	Wednesday
jeudi	Thursday
vendredi	Friday
samedi	Saturday
dimanche	Sunday

▷ Months of the Year

janvier	January	**juillet**	July
février	February	**août**	August
mars	March	**septembre**	September
avril	April	**octobre**	October
mai	May	**novembre**	November
juin	June	**décembre**	December

▷ Quand?	▷ When?
en février	in February
le 1er décembre	on 1 December
le premier décembre	on the first of December
en 2015	in 2015
en deux mille quinze	in two thousand and fifteen

▷ Quel jour sommes nous?	▷ What day is it?
Nous sommes le...	**It's...**
dimanche 1er octobre *or*	Sunday 1 October *or*
dimanche premier octobre	Sunday, the first of October
lundi 10 février *or*	Monday, 10 February *or*
lundi dix février	Monday, the tenth of February

▷ Cardinal numbers

1	un (une)	21	vingt et un (une)
2	deux	22	vingt-deux
3	trois	30	trente
4	quatre	40	quarante
5	cinq	50	cinquante
6	six	60	soixante
7	sept	70	soixante-dix
8	huit	71	soixante et onze
9	neuf	72	soixante-douze
10	dix	80	quatre-vingts
11	onze	81	quatre-vingt-un (-une)
12	douze	90	quatre-vingt-dix
13	treize	91	quatre-vingt-onze
14	quatorze	100	cent
15	quinze	101	cent un (une)
16	seize	200	deux cents
17	dix-sept	201	deux cent un (une)
18	dix-huit	300	trois cents
19	dix-neuf	1000	mille
20	vingt	1,000,000	un million

▷ Fractions

1/2	un demi, une demie	1/5	un cinquième
1/3	un tiers	0.5	zéro virgule cinq (0,5)
2/3	deux tiers	10%	dix pour cent
1/4	un quart	100%	cent pour cent
3/4	trois quarts		

NUMBERS

▷ Ordinal numbers

1st	premier (1er), première (1re)
2nd	deuxième (2e *or* 2ème)
3rd	troisième (3e *or* 3ème)
4th	quatrième (4e *or* 4ème)
5th	cinquième (5e *or* 5ème)
6th	sixième (6e *or* 6ème)
7th	septième (7e *or* 7ème)
8th	huitième (8e *or* 8ème)
9th	neuvième (9e *or* 9ème)
10th	dixième (10e *or* 10ème)
11th	onzième (11e *or* 11ème)
12th	douzième (12e *or* 12ème)
13th	treizième (13e *or* 13ème)
14th	quatorzième (14e *or* 14ème)
15th	quinzième (15e *or* 15ème)
16th	seizième (16e *or* 16ème)
17th	dix-septième (17e *or* 17ème)
18th	dix-huitième (18e *or* 18ème)
19th	dix-neuvième (19e *or* 19ème)
20th	vingtième (20e *or* 20ème)
21st	vingt et unième (21e *or* 21ème)
22nd	vingt-deuxième (22e *or* 22ème)
30th	trentième (30e *or* 30ème)
100th	centième (100e *or* 100ème)
101st	cent-unième (101e *or* 101ème)
1000th	millième (1000e *or* 1000ème)

a *vb* *see* **avoir**

> **a** should not be confused with the preposition **à**.

Il a beaucoup d'amis. He has a lot of friends.; **Il a mangé des frites.** He had some chips.; **Il a neigé pendant la nuit.** It snowed during the night.; **il y a (1)** there is ▷ *Il y a un bon film à la télé.* There's a good film on TV. **(2)** there are ▷ *Il y a beaucoup de monde.* There are lots of people.

à *prep*

> **à** should not be confused with the verb form **a**. See also **au (=à + le)** and **aux (=à + les)**.

❶ at ▷ *être à la maison* to be at home ▷ *à trois heures* at 3 o'clock ❷ in ▷ *être à Paris* to be in Paris ▷ *habiter au Portugal* to live in Portugal ▷ *habiter à la campagne* to live in the country ▷ *au printemps* in the spring ▷ *au mois de juin* in June ❸ to ▷ *aller à Paris* to go to Paris ▷ *aller au Portugal* to go to Portugal ▷ *aller à la campagne* to go to the country ▷ *donner quelque chose à quelqu'un* to give something to somebody ▷ *Cette veste appartient à Marie.* This jacket belongs to Marie. ▷ *Je n'ai rien à faire.* I've got nothing to do.; **Ce livre est à Paul.** This book is Paul's.; **Cette voiture est à nous.** This car is ours. ❹ by ▷ *à bicyclette* by bicycle ▷ *être payé à l'heure* to be paid by the hour; **à pied** on foot; **C'est à côté de chez moi.** It's near my house.; **C'est à dix kilomètres d'ici.** It's 10 kilometres from here.; **C'est à dix minutes d'ici.** It's 10 minutes from here.; **cent kilomètres à l'heure** 100 kilometres an hour; **À bientôt!** See you soon! ▷ *À demain!* See you tomorrow! ▷ *À samedi!* See you on Saturday! ▷ *À tout à l'heure!* See you later!

abandonner *vb* **[28]** ❶ to abandon ❷ to give up ▷ *J'ai décidé d'abandonner la natation.* I've decided to give up swimming.

abeille *nf* bee

abîmer *vb* **[28]** to damage; **s'abîmer** to get damaged

abonnement *nm* ❶ season ticket ❷ *(to magazine)* subscription

s'**abonner** *vb* **[28]** **s'abonner à une revue** to take out a subscription to a magazine; **être abonné sur**

Twitter to be on Twitter
abord *nm* **d'abord** first
aboyer *vb* [**53**] to bark
abri *nm* shelter; **être à l'abri** to be under cover; **se mettre à l'abri** to shelter
abricot *nm* apricot
s' **abriter** *vb* [**28**] to shelter
absence *nf* absence; **Il est passé pendant ton absence.** He came while you were away.
absent, e *adj* absent
absolument *adv* absolutely
accélérateur *nm* accelerator
accélérer *vb* [**34**] to accelerate
accent *nm* accent ▷ *Il a l'accent de Marseille.* He has a Marseilles accent.; **un accent aigu** an acute accent; **un accent grave** a grave accent; **un accent circonflexe** a circumflex
accentuer *vb* [**28**] to stress
accepter *vb* [**28**] to accept; **accepter de faire quelque chose** to agree to do something
accès *nm* access ▷ *avoir accès à quelque chose* to have access to something; **'Accès aux quais'** 'To the trains'
accessoire *nm* ❶ accessory ❷ prop
accident *nm* accident; **par accident** by chance
accompagner *vb* [**28**] to accompany
accomplir *vb* [**38**] to carry out ▷ *Il n'a pas réussi à accomplir cette tâche.* He didn't manage to carry out this task.
accord *nm* agreement; **être d'accord** to agree ▷ *Tu es d'accord avec moi?* Do you agree with me?; **se mettre d'accord** to come to an agreement; **D'accord!** OK!
accordéon *nm* accordion
accoudoir *nm* armrest
accrochage *nm* collision
accrocher *vb* [**28**] **accrocher quelque chose à (1)** to hang something on ▷ *Il a accroché sa veste au portemanteau.* He hung his jacket on the coat rack. **(2)** to hitch something up to ▷ *Ils ont accroché la remorque à leur voiture.* They hitched the trailer up to their car.; **s'accrocher à quelque chose** to get caught on something ▷ *Sa jupe s'est accrochée aux ronces.* Her skirt got caught on the brambles.
s' **accroupir** *vb* [**38**] to squat down
accueil *nm* welcome; **Elle s'occupe de l'accueil des visiteurs.** She's in charge of looking after visitors.; **'Accueil'** 'Reception'
accueillant, e *adj* welcoming
accueillir *vb* [**22**] to welcome
accumuler *vb* [**28**] to accumulate; **s'accumuler** to pile up
accusation *nf* accusation
accusé *nm* accused; **un accusé de réception** an acknowledgement of receipt
accusée *nf* accused
accuser *vb* [**28**] to accuse ▷ *accuser quelqu'un de quelque chose* to accuse somebody of something
achat *nm* purchase; **faire des achats** to do some shopping
acheter *vb* [**1**] to buy ▷ *J'ai acheté des*

gâteaux à la pâtisserie. I bought some cakes at the cake shop.; **acheter quelque chose à quelqu'un (1)** to buy something for somebody ▷ *Qu'est-ce que tu lui as acheté pour son anniversaire?* What did you buy him for his birthday? **(2)** to buy something from somebody ▷ *J'ai acheté des œufs au fermier.* I bought some eggs from the farmer.

acide *adj* acid
▶ *nm* acid

acier *nm* steel

acné *nf* acne

acquérir *vb* [**2**] to acquire

acquis *vb see* **acquérir**

acquitter *vb* [**28**] to acquit ▷ *L'accusé a été acquitté.* The accused was acquitted.

acte *nm* act; **un acte de naissance** a birth certificate

acteur *nm* actor

actif (*f* **active**) *adj* active; **la population active** the working population

action *nf* action; **une bonne action** a good deed

s' **activer** *vb* [**28**] ❶ to bustle about ▷ *Elle s'activait à préparer le repas.* She bustled about preparing the meal. ❷ to get moving ▷ *Allez! Active-toi!* Come on! Get moving!

activité *nf* activity

actrice *nf* actress

actualité *nf* current events; **un problème d'actualité** a topical issue; **les actualités** the news

actuel (*f* **actuelle**) *adj* present; **à l'heure actuelle** at the present time

Be careful! **actuel** does not mean **actual**.

actuellement *adv* at present

Be careful! **actuellement** does not mean **actually**.

adaptateur *nm* adaptor

addition *nf* ❶ addition ❷ bill ▷ *L'addition, s'il vous plaît!* Can we have the bill, please?

additionner *vb* [**28**] to add up

adhérent *nm* member

adhérente *nf* member

adhésif (*f* **adhésive**) *adj* **le ruban adhésif** sticky tape

adieu *excl* farewell!

adjectif *nm* adjective

admettre *vb* [**47**] ❶ to admit ▷ *Il refuse d'admettre qu'il s'est trompé.* He won't admit that he made a mistake. ❷ to allow ▷ *Les chiens ne sont pas admis dans le restaurant.* Dogs are not allowed in the restaurant.

administration *nf* administration; **l'Administration** the Civil Service

admirable *adj* wonderful

admirateur *nm* admirer

admiratrice *nf* admirer

admirer *vb* [**28**] to admire

admis *vb see* **admettre**

adolescence *nf* adolescence

adolescent *nm* teenager

adolescente *nf* teenager

adopter *vb* [**28**] to adopt

adorable *adj* lovely

adorer *vb* [**28**] to love ▷ *Elle adore le*

chocolat. She loves chocolate. ▷ *J'adore jouer au tennis*. I love playing tennis.

adresse *nf* address; **une adresse web** a Web address; **mon adresse électronique** my email address

adresser *vb* [**28**] **adresser la parole à quelqu'un** to speak to someone; **s'adresser à quelqu'un** **(1)** to speak to somebody ▷ *C'est à toi que je m'adresse*. It's you I'm speaking to. **(2)** to go and see somebody ▷ *Adressez-vous au patron*. Go and see the boss. **(3)** to be aimed at somebody ▷ *Ce film s'adresse surtout aux enfants*. This film is aimed mainly at children.

adulte *nmf* adult

adverbe *nm* adverb

adversaire *nmf* opponent

aérien (*f* **aérienne**) *adj* **une compagnie aérienne** an airline

aérobic *nm* aerobics

aérogare *nf* terminal

aéroglisseur *nm* hovercraft

aéroport *nm* airport

affaire *nf* ❶ case ▷ *une affaire de drogue* a drugs case ❷ business ▷ *Son affaire marche bien*. His business is doing well.; **une bonne affaire** a real bargain; **Ça fera l'affaire.** This will do nicely.; **avoir affaire à quelqu'un** to deal with somebody

affaires *nfpl* ❶ things ▷ *Va chercher tes affaires!* Go and get your things! ❷ business ▷ *Les affaires marchent bien en ce moment*. Business is good at the moment.; **un homme d'affaires** a businessman

affection *nf* affection

affectueusement *adv* affectionately

affectueux (*f* **affectueuse**) *adj* affectionate

affiche *nf* poster

afficher *vb* [**28**] to put up ▷ *Ils ont affiché les résultats dehors*. They've put the results up outside.; **'Défense d'afficher'** 'Post no bills'

affilée: **d'affilée** *adv* at a stretch

affirmation *nf* assertion

affirmer *vb* [**28**] to claim ▷ *Il a affirmé que c'était la vérité*. He claimed it was the truth.; **s'affirmer** to assert oneself ▷ *Il est trop timide, il faut qu'il s'affirme*. He's too shy, he should assert himself.

affluence *nf* **les heures d'affluence** the rush hour

s' **affoler** *vb* [**28**] to panic ▷ *Ne t'affole pas!* Don't panic!

affranchir *vb* [**38**] to stamp

affreux (*f* **affreuse**) *adj* awful

affronter *vb* [**28**] to face ▷ *L'Allemagne affrontera l'Italie en finale*. Germany will face Italy in the final.

afin de *conj* **afin de faire quelque chose** so as to do something ▷ *Je me suis levé très tôt afin d'être prêt à temps*. I got up very early so as to be ready on time.

afin que *conj* so that

> **afin que** is followed by a verb in the subjunctive.

▷ *Il m'a téléphoné afin que je sois prêt à temps*. He phoned me so that I'd be ready on time.

africain, e *adj, nm/f* African; **un Africain** *(man)* an African; **une Africaine** *(woman)* an African

Afrique *nf* Africa; **en Afrique (1)** in Africa **(2)** to Africa; **l'Afrique du Sud** South Africa

agacer *vb* **[12] agacer quelqu'un** to get on somebody's nerves ▷ *Tu m'agaces avec tes questions!* You're getting on my nerves with all your questions!

âge *nm* age; **Quel âge as-tu?** How old are you?

âgé, e *adj* old; **les personnes âgées** elderly people

agence *nf* ❶ agency ▷ *l'agence pour l'emploi* the employment agency; **une agence de voyages** a travel agency ❷ office; **une agence immobilière** an estate agent's

agenda *nm* diary ▷ *J'ai perdu mon agenda.* I have lost my diary.

> Be careful! The French word **agenda** does not mean **agenda**.

s' **agenouiller** *vb* **[28]** to kneel down

agent *nm* **un agent de police** a police officer; **un agent d'entretien** a cleaner

agglomération *nf* town; **l'agglomération parisienne** Greater Paris

aggraver *vb* **[28]** to make worse; **s'aggraver** to worsen

agir *vb* **[38]** to act ▷ *Il a agi par vengeance.* He acted out of vengeance.; **Il s'agit de ...** It's about ... ▷ *Il s'agit du club de sport.* It's about the sports club. ▷ *De quoi s'agit-il?* What is it about?; **Il s'agit de faire attention.** We must be careful.

agité, e *adj* ❶ restless ❷ rough; **un sommeil agité** broken sleep

agiter *vb* **[28]** to shake ▷ *Agitez la bouteille.* Shake the bottle.

agneau (*pl* **agneaux**) *nm* lamb

agrafe *nf (for papers)* staple

agrafeuse *nf* stapler

agrandir *vb* **[38]** ❶ to enlarge ▷ *J'ai fait agrandir mes photos.* I've had my photos enlarged. ❷ to extend ▷ *Ils ont agrandi leur jardin.* They've extended their garden.; **s'agrandir** to expand ▷ *Leur magasin s'est agrandi.* Their shop has expanded.

agréable *adj* nice

agréer *vb* **[18] Veuillez agréer, Monsieur, l'expression de mes sentiments les meilleurs. Jean Ormal.** Yours sincerely, Jean Ormal.

agressif (*f* **agressive**) *adj* aggressive

agressivité *nf* aggression; **faire preuve d'agressivité envers quelqu'un** to be aggressive to somebody; **l'agressivité au volant** road rage

agricole *adj* agricultural; **une exploitation agricole** a farm

agriculteur *nm* farmer ▷ *Il est agriculteur.* He's a farmer.

agricultrice *nf* farmer

agriculture *nf* farming

ai *vb see* **avoir**; **J'ai deux chats.**

I have two cats.; **J'ai bien dormi.** I slept well.

aide *nf* ❶ help; **À l'aide!** Help! ❷ aid; **à l'aide de** using

aider *vb* [**28**] to help

aide-soignant (*pl* **aides-soignants**) *nm* auxiliary nurse

aide-soignante (*pl* **aides-soignantes**) *nf* auxiliary nurse

aie *vb see* **avoir**

aïe *excl* ouch!

aigre *adj* sour

aigu (*f* **aiguë**) *adj (pain)* sharp; **e accent aigu** e acute

aiguille *nf* needle; **les aiguilles d'une montre** the hands of a watch

ail *nm* garlic

aile *nf* wing

aille *vb see* **aller**

ailleurs *adv* somewhere else; **partout ailleurs** everywhere else; **nulle part ailleurs** nowhere else; **d'ailleurs** besides

aimable *adj* kind

aimant *nm* magnet

aimer *vb* [**28**] ❶ to love ▷ *Elle aime ses enfants.* She loves her children. ❷ to like ▷ *Tu aimes le chocolat?* Do you like chocolate? ▷ *J'aime bien ce garçon.* I like this boy. ▷ *J'aime bien jouer au tennis.* I like playing tennis. ▷ *J'aimerais aller en Grèce.* I'd like to go to Greece.; **J'aimerais mieux ne pas y aller.** I'd rather not go.

aîné, e *adj* elder ▷ *mon frère aîné* my big brother

aîné *nm* oldest child ▷ *C'est l'aîné.* He's the oldest child.

aînée *nf* oldest child

ainsi *adv* in this way; **C'est ainsi qu'il a réussi.** That's how he succeeded.; **ainsi que** as well as; **et ainsi de suite** and so on

air *nm* ❶ air; **prendre l'air** to get some fresh air ❷ tune ▷ *Elle a joué un air au piano.* She played a tune on the piano.; **Elle a l'air fatiguée.** She looks tired.; **Il a l'air d'un clown.** He looks like a clown.

aire de jeux *nf* playground

aire de repos *nf (on motorway)* rest area

aise *nf* **être à l'aise** to be at ease; **être mal à l'aise** to be ill at ease; **se mettre à l'aise** to make oneself comfortable

ait *vb see* **avoir**

ajouter *vb* [**28**] to add

alarme *nf* alarm

Albanie *nf* Albania

album *nm* album

alcool *nm* alcohol ▷ *Je ne bois pas d'alcool.* I don't drink alcohol.

alcoolisé, e *adj* alcoholic; **une boisson non alcoolisée** a soft drink

alentours *nmpl* **dans les alentours** in the area; **aux alentours de Paris** in the Paris area; **aux alentours de cinq heures** around 5 o'clock

algèbre *nf* algebra

Alger *n* Algiers

Algérie *nf* Algeria

algérien (*f* **algérienne**) *adj, nm/f* Algerian; **un Algérien** *(man)* an Algerian; **une Algérienne** *(woman)* an Algerian

algue *nf* seaweed

aliment *nm* food

alimentation *nf* ❶ groceries ▷ *le rayon alimentation du supermarché* the grocery department in the supermarket ❷ diet ▷ *Elle a une alimentation saine.* She has a healthy diet.

allée *nf* ❶ path ❷ *(in street names)* drive

allégé, e *adj* low-fat

Allemagne *nf* Germany; **en Allemagne (1)** in Germany **(2)** to Germany

allemand, e *adj, n* German ▷ *Elle parle allemand.* She speaks German.; **un Allemand** *(man)* a German; **une Allemande** *(woman)* a German; **les Allemands** the Germans

aller *vb* [3] to go ▷ *Je suis allé à Londres.* I went to London. ▷ *Je vais me fâcher.* I'm going to get angry.; **s'en aller** to go away ▷ *Je m'en vais demain.* I'm going tomorrow.; **aller bien à quelqu'un** to suit somebody ▷ *Cette robe te va bien.* This dress suits you.; **Allez! Dépêche-toi!** Come on! Hurry up!; **Comment allez-vous? — Je vais bien.** How are you? — I'm fine.; **Comment ça va? — Ça va bien.** How are you? — I'm fine.; **aller mieux** to be better ▶ *nm* ❶ outward journey ❷ *(ticket)* single; **un aller simple** a single; **un aller retour (1)** a return ticket **(2)** a round trip

allergique *adj* **allergique à** allergic to

allô *excl* hello! ▷ *Allô! Je voudrais parler à Monsieur Simon.* Hello! I'd like to speak to Mr Simon.

> **allô** is only used when talking to someone on the phone.

allocation *nf* allowance; **les allocations chômage** unemployment benefit

s' **allonger** *vb* [45] to lie down ▷ *Il s'est allongé sur son lit.* He lay down on his bed.

allumer *vb* [28] ❶ to switch on ▷ *Tu peux allumer la lumière?* Can you put the light on? ▷ *Allume la radio.* Switch on the radio. ❷ to light ▷ *Elle a allumé une cigarette.* She lit a cigarette.; **s'allumer** *(light)* to come on ▷ *La lumière s'est allumée.* The light came on.

allumette *nf* match ▷ *une boîte d'allumettes* a box of matches

allure *nf* ❶ speed ❷ look ▷ *avoir une drôle d'allure* to look odd

allusion *nf* reference

alors *adv* ❶ then ▷ *Tu as fini? Alors je m'en vais.* Have you finished? I'm going then. ❷ so ▷ *Alors je lui ai dit de partir.* So I told him to leave.; **Et alors?** So what? ❸ at that time; **alors que (1)** as ▷ *Il est arrivé alors que je partais.* He arrived just as I was leaving. **(2)** while ▷ *Alors que je travaillais dur, lui se reposait.* While I was working hard, he was resting.

Alpes *nfpl* Alps

alphabet *nm* alphabet

alphabétique *adj* alphabetical

alpinisme *nm* mountaineering

alpiniste *nmf* mountaineer

Alsace *nf* Alsace
amande *nf* almond; **la pâte d'amandes** marzipan
amant *nm* lover
amateur (*f* **amatrice**) *adj* amateur
amateur *nm* amateur; **en amateur** as a hobby; **C'est un amateur de musique.** He's a music lover.
amatrice *nf* amateur
ambassade *nf* embassy
ambassadeur *nm* ambassador
ambiance *nf* atmosphere; **la musique d'ambiance** background music
ambitieux (*f* **ambitieuse**) *adj* ambitious
ambition *nf* ambition; **Il a beaucoup d'ambition.** He's very ambitious.
ambulance *nf* ambulance
âme *nf* soul
amélioration *nf* improvement
améliorer *vb* [**28**] to improve; **s'améliorer** to improve ▷ *Le temps s'améliore.* The weather's improving.
amende *nf* fine
amener *vb* [**43**] to bring ▷ *Qu'est-ce qui t'amène?* What brings you here? ▷ *Est-ce que je peux amener un ami?* Can I bring a friend?
amer (*f* **amère**) *adj* bitter
américain, e *adj, nm/f* American; **un Américain** *(man)* an American; **une Américaine** *(woman)* an American
Amérique *nf* America; **en Amérique (1)** in America **(2)** to America; **l'Amérique du Nord** North America; **l'Amérique du Sud** South America
ami *nm* friend; **C'est son petit ami.** He's her boyfriend.
amical, e (*mpl* **amicaux**) *adj* friendly
amicalement *adv* in a friendly way; **Amicalement, Pierre.** *(in letter)* Best wishes, Pierre.
amie *nf* friend; **C'est sa petite amie.** She's his girlfriend.
amitié *nf* friendship; **Fais mes amitiés à Paul.** Give my regards to Paul.; **Amitiés, Christèle.** *(in letter)* Best wishes, Christèle.
amour *nm* love; **faire l'amour** to make love
amoureux (*f* **amoureuse**) *adj* in love ▷ *être amoureux de quelqu'un* to be in love with somebody
amour-propre *nm* self-esteem
amphithéâtre *nm* lecture theatre
amplement *adv* **Nous avons amplement le temps.** We have plenty of time.
ampoule *nf* ❶ light bulb ❷ blister
amusant, e *adj* amusing
amuse-gueule *nmpl* party nibbles
amuser *vb* [**28**] to amuse; **s'amuser (1)** to play ▷ *Les enfants s'amusent dehors.* The children are playing outside. **(2)** to enjoy oneself ▷ *On s'est bien amusés.* We really enjoyed ourselves.
an *nm* year; **le premier de l'an** New Year's Day; **le nouvel an** New Year
analyse *nf* ❶ analysis ❷ *(medical)* test

ananas *nm* pineapple
ancêtre *nmf* ancestor
anchois *nm* anchovy
ancien (*f* **ancienne**) *adj* ❶ former ▷ *C'est une ancienne élève.* She's a former pupil. ❷ old ▷ *notre ancienne voiture* our old car ❸ antique
ancre *nf* anchor
Andorre *nf* Andorra
âne *nm* donkey
ange *nm* angel; **être aux anges** to be over the moon
angine *nf* throat infection
anglais, e *adj, n* English ▷ *Est-ce que vous parlez anglais?* Do you speak English?; **un Anglais** an Englishman; **une Anglaise** an Englishwoman; **les Anglais** the English
angle *nm* ❶ angle ❷ corner
Angleterre *nf* England; **en Angleterre (1)** in England ▷ *J'habite en Angleterre.* I live in England. **(2)** to England ▷ *Je suis allée en Angleterre le mois dernier.* I went to England last month.
anglo- *prefix* anglo-; **les îles Anglo-Normandes** the Channel Islands
anglophone *adj* English-speaking
angoissé, e *adj* stressed
animal (*pl* **animaux**) *nm* animal
animateur *nm* ❶ host ❷ youth leader
animatrice *nf* ❶ host ❷ youth leader
animé, e *adj* lively ▷ *Cette rue est très animée.* This is a very lively street.; **un dessin animé** a cartoon
anis *nm* aniseed
anneau (*pl* **anneaux**) *nm* ring
année *nf* year
anniversaire *nm* ❶ birthday ❷ anniversary
annonce *nf* advert; **les petites annonces** the small ads
annoncer *vb* [12] to announce ▷ *Ils ont annoncé leurs fiançailles.* They've announced their engagement.
annuaire *nm* phone book
annuel (*f* **annuelle**) *adj* annual
annuler *vb* [28] to cancel
anonyme *adj* anonymous
anorak *nm* anorak
ANPE *nf* (= *Agence nationale pour l'emploi*) job centre
Antarctique *nm* Antarctic
antenne *nf* ❶ aerial; **antenne parabolique** satellite dish; **être à l'antenne** to be on the air ❷ antenna
antibiotique *nm* antibiotic
antidépresseur *nm* antidepressant
antigel *nm* antifreeze
Antilles *nfpl* West Indies; **aux Antilles (1)** in the West Indies **(2)** to the West Indies
antipathique *adj* unpleasant
antiquaire *nmf* antique dealer
antiquité *nf* antique; **pendant l'antiquité** in classical times
antiseptique *adj* antiseptic ▶ *nm* antiseptic
antivirus *nm* antivirus (program)
antivol *nm* ❶ (*on bike*) lock ❷ (*on car*) steering lock
anxieux (*f* **anxieuse**) *adj* anxious

août *nm* August; **en août** in August
apercevoir *vb* [**67**] to see ▷ *J'aperçois la côte.* I can see the shore.; **s'apercevoir de quelque chose** to notice something; **s'apercevoir que ...** to notice that ...
apéritif *nm* aperitif
apparaître *vb* [**56**] to appear
appareil *nm* device; **un appareil dentaire** *(for teeth)* a brace; **les appareils ménagers** domestic appliances; **un appareil photo** a camera; **Qui est à l'appareil?** *(on phone)* Who's speaking?
apparemment *adv* apparently
apparence *nf* appearance
apparition *nf* appearance
appartement *nm* flat
appartenir *vb* [**83**] **appartenir à quelqu'un** to belong to somebody
apparu *vb see* **apparaître**
appel *nm* ❶ cry ▷ *un appel au secours* a cry for help ❷ phone call; **faire appel à quelqu'un** to appeal to somebody; **faire l'appel** *(in school)* to call the register; **faire un appel de phares** to flash one's headlights
appeler *vb* [**4**] to call; **s'appeler** to be called ▷ *Elle s'appelle Muriel.* Her name's Muriel. ▷ *Comment tu t'appelles?* What's your name?
appendicite *nf* appendicitis
appétissant, e *adj* appetizing
appétit *nm* appetite; **Bon appétit!** Enjoy your meal!
applaudir *vb* [**38**] *(applaud)* to clap
applaudissements *nmpl* applause *sg*
appliquer *vb* [**28**] ❶ to apply ❷ to enforce ▷ *appliquer la loi* to enforce the law; **s'appliquer** to apply oneself
apporter *vb* [**28**] to bring
apprécier *vb* [**19**] to appreciate
appréhender *vb* [**28**] to dread ▷ *J'appréhende cette réunion.* I'm dreading this meeting.
apprendre *vb* [**65**] ❶ to learn ▷ *apprendre quelque chose par cœur* to learn something by heart; **apprendre à faire quelque chose** to learn to do something ▷ *J'apprends à faire la cuisine.* I'm learning to cook. ❷ to hear ▷ *J'ai appris son départ.* I heard that she had left.; **apprendre quelque chose à quelqu'un (1)** to teach somebody something ▷ *Ma mère m'a appris l'anglais.* My mother taught me English. **(2)** to tell somebody something ▷ *Jean-Pierre m'a appris la nouvelle.* Jean-Pierre told me the news.
apprentissage *nm* learning
appris *vb see* **apprendre**
approbation *nf* approval
approcher *vb* [**28**] **approcher de** to approach ▷ *Nous approchons de Paris.* We are approaching Paris.; **s'approcher de** to come closer to ▷ *Ne t'approche pas, j'ai la grippe!* Don't get too close to me, I've got flu!
approprié, e *adj* suitable
approuver *vb* [**28**] to approve of ▷ *Je n'approuve pas ses méthodes.* I don't approve of his methods.

approximatif (*f* **approximative**) *adj* ❶ approximate ❷ rough
appui *nm* support
appuyer *vb* [53] ❶ to press ▷ *appuyer sur un bouton* to press a button ❷ to lean ▷ *Elle a appuyé son vélo contre la porte.* She leaned her bike against the door.; **s'appuyer** to lean ▷ *Elle s'est appuyée contre le mur.* She leaned against the wall.
après *prep, adv* ❶ after ▷ *après le déjeuner* after lunch ▷ *après son départ* after he had left ❷ afterwards ▷ *aussitôt après* immediately afterwards; **après coup** afterwards ▷ *J'y ai repensé après coup.* I thought about it again afterwards.; **d'après** according to ▷ *D'après lui, c'est une erreur.* According to him, that's a mistake.; **après tout** after all
après-demain *adv* the day after tomorrow
après-midi *nmf* afternoon
après-rasage *nm* aftershave
aquarium *nm* aquarium
arabe *adj, nmf* ❶ Arab ❷ Arabic ▷ *Il parle arabe.* He speaks Arabic.; **un Arabe** *(man)* an Arab; **une Arabe** *(woman)* an Arab
Arabie Saoudite *nf* Saudi Arabia
araignée *nf* spider
arbitre *nm* ❶ referee ❷ umpire
arbre *nm* tree; **un arbre généalogique** a family tree
arbuste *nm* shrub
arc *nm* bow
arc-en-ciel (*pl* **arcs-en-ciel**) *nm* rainbow
archéologie *nf* archaeology
archéologue *nmf* archaeologist
archipel *nm* archipelago
architecte *nmf* architect
architecture *nf* architecture
Arctique *nm* Arctic
ardoise *nf* slate
arène *nf* bullring; **des arènes romaines** a Roman amphitheatre; **l'arène politique** the political arena
arête *nf* fish bone
argent *nm* ❶ silver ❷ money ▷ *Je n'ai plus d'argent.* I haven't got any more money.; **l'argent de poche** pocket money; **l'argent liquide** cash
argentin, e *adj, nm/f* Argentinian; **un Argentin** *(man)* an Argentinian; **une Argentine** *(woman)* an Argentinian
Argentine *nf* Argentina
argile *nf* clay
argot *nm* slang
arme *nf* weapon; **une arme à feu** a firearm
armée *nf* army; **l'armée de l'air** the Air Force
armistice *nm* armistice
armoire *nf* wardrobe
armure *nf* armour
arnaquer *vb* [28] *(informal)* to con
arobase *nf* @ symbol
aromatisé, e *adj* flavoured
arôme *nm* ❶ aroma ❷ *(added to food)* flavouring
arpenter *vb* [28] to pace up and down ▷ *Il arpentait le couloir.* He was pacing up and down the corridor.

arrache-pied: **d'arrache-pied** *adv* furiously

arracher *vb* [**28**] ❶ to take out ▷ *Le dentiste m'a arraché une dent.* The dentist took one of my teeth out. ❷ to tear out ▷ *Arrachez la page.* Tear the page out. ❸ to pull up ▷ *Elle a arraché les mauvaises herbes.* She pulled up the weeds.; **arracher quelque chose à quelqu'un** to snatch something from somebody

arranger *vb* [**45**] ❶ to arrange ▷ *arranger des fleurs dans un vase* to arrange flowers in a vase ❷ to suit ▷ *Ça m'arrange de partir plus tôt.* It suits me to leave earlier.; **s'arranger** to come to an agreement; **Je vais m'arranger pour venir.** I'll organize things so that I can come.; **Ça va s'arranger.** Things will work themselves out.

arrestation *nf* arrest

arrêt *nm* stop; **sans arrêt** **(1)** non-stop **(2)** continually

arrêter *vb* [**28**] ❶ to stop; **Arrête!** Stop it!; **arrêter de faire quelque chose** to stop doing something ❷ to switch off ▷ *Il a arrêté le moteur.* He switched the engine off. ❸ to arrest ▷ *Mon voisin a été arrêté.* My neighbour's been arrested.; **s'arrêter** to stop ▷ *Elle s'est arrêtée devant une vitrine.* She stopped in front of a shop window.; **s'arrêter de faire quelque chose** to stop doing something ▷ *s'arrêter de fumer* to stop smoking

arrhes *nfpl* deposit *sg* ▷ *verser des arrhes* to pay a deposit

arrière *nm* back; **à l'arrière** at the back; **en arrière** behind ▶ *adj* back ▷ *le siège arrière* the back seat

arrière-grand-mère (*pl* **arrière-grands-mères**) *nf* great-grandmother

arrière-grand-père (*pl* **arrière-grands-pères**) *nm* great-grandfather

arrivée *nf* arrival

arriver *vb* [**5**] ❶ to arrive ▷ *J'arrive à l'école à huit heures.* I arrive at school at 8 o'clock. ❷ to happen ▷ *Qu'est-ce qui est arrivé à Christian?* What happened to Christian?; **arriver à faire quelque chose** to manage to do something ▷ *J'espère que je vais y arriver.* I hope I'll manage it.; **Il m'arrive de dormir jusqu'à midi.** I sometimes sleep till midday.

arrogant, e *adj* arrogant

arrondissement *nm* district

Paris, Lyons and Marseilles are divided into numbered districts called **arrondissements**.

arroser *vb* [**28**] to water ▷ *Daphne arrose ses tomates.* Daphne is watering her tomatoes.; **Ils ont arrosé leur victoire.** They had a drink to celebrate their victory.

arrosoir *nm* watering can

art *nm* art

artère *nf* ❶ artery ❷ thoroughfare

artichaut *nm* artichoke

article *nm* ❶ article ❷ item

articulation *nf* joint

articuler *vb* [**28**] to pronounce clearly
artificiel (*f* **artificielle**) *adj* artificial
artisan *nm* self-employed craftsman
artiste *nmf* ❶ artist ❷ performer
artistique *adj* artistic
as *vb see* **avoir**; **Tu as de beaux cheveux.** You've got nice hair.
▸ *nm* ace
ascenseur *nm* lift
Ascension *nf* Ascension
asiatique *adj* Asiatic
Asie *nf* Asia; **en Asie (1)** in Asia **(2)** to Asia
aspect *nm* appearance
asperge *nf* asparagus
aspirateur *nm* vacuum cleaner; **passer l'aspirateur** to vacuum
aspirine *nf* aspirin
assaisonner *vb* [**28**] to season
assassin *nm* murderer
assassiner *vb* [**28**] to murder
assembler *vb* [**28**] to assemble; **s'assembler** to gather ▷ *Une foule énorme s'était assemblée.* A huge crowd had gathered.
s' **asseoir** *vb* [**6**] to sit down ▷ *Asseyez-vous!* Sit down! ▷ *Assieds-toi!* Sit down!
assez *adv* ❶ enough; **J'en ai assez!** I've had enough! ❷ quite ▷ *Il faisait assez beau.* The weather was quite nice.
assiette *nf* plate; **une assiette anglaise** assorted cold meats
assis, e *adj* sitting
▸ *vb see* **asseoir**
assistance *nf* ❶ audience ❷ aid ▷ *l'assistance humanitaire* humanitarian aid ❸ assistance
assistant *nm* assistant; **un assistant social** a social worker
assistante *nf* assistant
assister *vb* [**28**] **assister à un accident** to witness an accident; **assister à un cours** to attend a class; **assister à un concert** to be at a concert
association *nf* association
associé *nm (in business)* partner
associée *nf (in business)* partner
s' **associer** *vb* [**19**] to go into partnership
assommer *vb* [**28**] to knock out ▷ *Il l'a assommé avec une bouteille.* He knocked him out with a bottle.
Assomption *nf* Assumption
assorti, e *adj* ❶ matching ❷ assorted; **être assorti à quelque chose** to match something
assortiment *nm* assortment
assurance *nf* ❶ insurance ❷ confidence
assurer *vb* [**28**] ❶ to insure ▷ *La maison est assurée.* The house is insured. ▷ *être assuré contre quelque chose* to be insured against something ❷ to assure ▷ *Je t'assure que c'est vrai!* I assure you it's true!; **s'assurer de quelque chose** to make sure of something ▷ *Il s'est assuré que la porte était fermée.* He made sure the door was shut.
asthme *nm* asthma
astronaute *nmf* astronaut

astronomie *nf* astronomy
astucieux (*f* **astucieuse**) *adj* clever
atelier *nm* ❶ workshop ❷ *(artist's)* studio
Athènes *n* Athens
athlète *nmf* athlete
athlétisme *nm* athletics
Atlantique *nm* Atlantic
atlas *nm* atlas
atmosphère *nf* atmosphere
atomique *adj* atomic
atout *nm* ❶ asset ❷ trump card
atroce *adj* terrible
attachant, e *adj* lovable
attacher *vb* [**28**] to tie up ▷ *Elle a attaché ses cheveux avec un élastique.* She tied her hair up with an elastic band.; **s'attacher à quelqu'un** to become attached to somebody; **une poêle qui n'attache pas** a non-stick frying pan
attaquer *vb* [**28**] to attack
atteindre *vb* [**60**] to reach
attendant: **en attendant** *adv* in the meantime
attendre *vb* [**7**] to wait ▷ *attendre quelqu'un* to wait for someone; **attendre un enfant** to be expecting a baby; **s'attendre à** to expect ▷ *Je m'attends à une surprise.* I'm expecting a surprise.

> Be careful! **attendre** does not mean **to attend**.

attentat *nm* **un attentat à la bombe** a terrorist bombing
attente *nf* wait; **la salle d'attente** the waiting room
attentif (*f* **attentive**) *adj* attentive
attention *nf* attention; **faire attention** to be careful; **Attention!** Watch out!
attentionné, e *adj* thoughtful
atterrir *vb* [**38**] to land
atterrissage *nm (of plane)* landing
attirant, e *adj* attractive
attirer *vb* [**28**] to attract ▷ *attirer l'attention de quelqu'un* to attract somebody's attention; **s'attirer des ennuis** to get into trouble ▷ *Si tu continues, tu vas t'attirer des ennuis.* If you keep on like that, you'll get yourself into trouble.
attitude *nf* attitude
attraction *nf* **un parc d'attractions** an amusement park
attraper *vb* [**28**] to catch
attrayant, e *adj* attractive
attrister *vb* [**28**] to sadden
au *prep see* **à**

> **au** is the contracted form of **à + le**.

▷ *au printemps* in the spring
aube *nf* dawn ▷ *à l'aube* at dawn
auberge *nf* inn; **une auberge de jeunesse** a youth hostel
aubergine *nf* aubergine
aucun, e *adj, pron* ❶ no ▷ *Il n'a aucun ami.* He's got no friends. ❷ none ▷ *Aucun d'entre eux n'est venu.* None of them came.; **sans aucun doute** without any doubt
au-delà *adv* **au-delà de** beyond
au-dessous *adv* ❶ downstairs ▷ *Ils habitent au-dessous.* They live downstairs. ❷ underneath; **au-dessous de** under
au-dessus *adv* ❶ upstairs ▷ *J'habite au-dessus.* I live upstairs. ❷ above;

au-dessus de above
audiovisuel (*f* **audiovisuelle**) *adj* audiovisual
auditeur *nm (to radio)* listener
auditrice *nf (to radio)* listener
augmentation *nf* rise
augmenter *vb* [**28**] to increase
aujourd'hui *adv* today
auparavant *adv* first
auquel (*mpl* **auxquels**, *fpl* **auxquelles**) *pron*

auquel is the contracted form of **à** + **lequel**.

▷ *l'homme auquel j'ai parlé* the man I spoke to
aura, aurai, auras, aurez, aurons, auront *vb see* **avoir**
aurore *nf* daybreak
ausculter *vb* [**28**] **Le médecin l'a ausculté.** The doctor listened to his chest.
aussi *adv* ❶ too ▷ *Dors bien. — Toi aussi.* Sleep well. — You too. ❷ also ▷ *Je parle anglais et aussi allemand.* I speak English and also German.; **aussi ... que** as ... as ▷ *aussi grand que moi* as big as me
aussitôt *adv* straight away; **aussitôt que** as soon as
Australie *nf* Australia; **en Australie (1)** in Australia **(2)** to Australia
australien (*f* **australienne**) *adj, nm/f* Australian; **un Australien** *(man)* an Australian; **une Australienne** *(woman)* an Australian
autant *adv* **autant de (1)** so much **(2)** so many; **autant ... que (1)** as much ... as **(2)** as many ... as; **d'autant plus que** all the more since; **d'autant moins que** even less since
auteur *nm* author
auto *nf* car
autobus *nm* bus
autocar *nm* coach
autocollant, e *adj* self-adhesive; **une enveloppe autocollante** a self-seal envelope
▶ *nm* sticker
auto-école *nf* driving school
automatique *adj* automatic
automne *nm* autumn; **en automne** in autumn
automobile *adj* **une course automobile** a motor race
▶ *nf* car
automobiliste *nmf* motorist
autoradio *nm* car radio
autorisation *nf* ❶ permission ❷ permit
autoriser *vb* [**28**] to give permission for ▷ *Il m'a autorisé à en parler.* He's given me permission to talk about it.
autoritaire *adj* authoritarian
autorité *nf* authority
autoroute *nf* motorway
auto-stop *nm* **faire de l'auto-stop** to hitchhike
auto-stoppeur *nm* hitchhiker
autour *adv* around
autre *adj, pron* other ▷ *J'ai d'autres projets.* I've got other plans.; **autre chose** something else; **autre part** somewhere else; **un autre** another ▷ *Tu veux un autre morceau de gâteau?*

Would you like another piece of cake?; **l'autre** the other; **d'autres** others; **les autres** the others; **ni l'un ni l'autre** neither of them; **entre autres** among other things

autrefois *adv* in the old days

autrement *adv* ❶ differently ❷ otherwise; **autrement dit** in other words

Autriche *nf* Austria; **en Autriche** **(1)** in Austria **(2)** to Austria

autrichien (*f* **autrichienne**) *adj, nm/f* Austrian; **un Autrichien** *(man)* an Austrian; **une Autrichienne** *(woman)* an Austrian

autruche *nf* ostrich

aux *prep see* **à**

> **aux** is the contracted form of **à** + **les**.

▷ *J'ai dit aux enfants d'aller jouer.* I told the children to go and play.

auxquelles *pron pl*

> **auxquelles** is the contracted form of **à** + **lesquelles**.

▷ *les revues auxquelles il est abonné* the magazines to which he subscribes

auxquels *pron pl*

> **auxquels** is the contracted form of **à** + **lesquels**.

▷ *les enfants auxquels il a parlé* the children he spoke to

avaient, avais, avait *vb see* **avoir**; **Il y avait beaucoup de monde.** There were lots of people.

avalanche *nf* avalanche

avaler *vb* [**28**] to swallow

avance *nf* **être en avance** to be early; **à l'avance** beforehand; **d'avance** in advance

avancé, e *adj* advanced; **bien avancé** well under way

avancer *vb* [**12**] ❶ to move forward ❷ to bring forward ▷ *La date de l'examen a été avancée.* The date of the exam has been brought forward. ❸ to put forward ▷ *Il a avancé sa montre d'une heure.* He put his watch forward an hour. ❹ *(watch)* to be fast ▷ *Ma montre avance d'une heure.* My watch is an hour fast. ❺ to lend ▷ *Peux-tu m'avancer dix euros?* Can you lend me 10 euros?

avant *prep, adj* ❶ before ▷ *avant qu'il ne pleuve* before it rains ▷ *avant de partir* before leaving ❷ front ▷ *le siège avant* the front seat; **avant tout** above all

▶ *nm* front; **à l'avant** in front; **en avant** forward

avantage *nm* advantage

avant-bras (*pl* **avant-bras**) *nm* forearm

avant-dernier (*f* **avant-dernière**, *mpl* **avant-derniers**) *adj* last but one

avant-hier *adv* the day before yesterday

avare *adj* miserly

▶ *nmf* miser

avec *prep* with ▷ *avec mon père* with my father; **Et avec ça?** *(in shop)* Anything else?

avenir *nm* future; **à l'avenir** in future; **dans un proche avenir** in the near future

aventure *nf* adventure

avenue *nf* avenue
averse *nf (of rain)* shower
avertir *vb* [**38**] to warn; **avertir quelqu'un de quelque chose** to warn somebody about something
avertissement *nm* warning
aveugle *adj* blind
avion *nm* plane; **aller en avion** to fly; **par avion** by airmail
aviron *nm* rowing
avis *nm* ❶ opinion; **à mon avis** in my opinion ❷ notice; **changer d'avis** to change one's mind
avocat *nm* ❶ lawyer ❷ avocado
avocate *nf* lawyer
avoine *nf* oats
avoir *vb* [**8**] ❶ to have ▷ *Ils ont deux enfants.* They have two children. ▷ *Il a les yeux bleus.* He's got blue eyes. ▷ *J'ai déjà mangé.* I've already eaten.; **On t'a bien eu!** *(informal)* You've been had! ❷ to be ▷ *Il a trois ans.* He's three.; **il y a (1)** there is ▷ *Il y a quelqu'un à la porte.* There's somebody at the door. **(2)** there are ▷ *Il y a des chocolats sur la table.* There are some chocolates on the table. **(3)** ago ▷ *Je l'ai rencontré il y a deux ans.* I met him two years ago.; **Qu'est-ce qu'il y a?** What's the matter?; **Il n'y a qu'à partir plus tôt.** We'll just have to leave earlier.
avortement *nm* abortion
avouer *vb* [**28**] to admit
avril *nm* April; **en avril** in April
ayez, ayons *vb see* **avoir**

b

baby-foot *nm* table football
baby-sitting *nm* **faire du baby-sitting** to babysit
bac *nm* = **baccalauréat**
baccalauréat *nm* A levels

The French **baccalauréat**, or **bac** for short, is taken at the age of 17 or 18. Students have to sit one of a variety of set subject combinations, rather than being able to choose any combination of subjects they want. If you pass you have the right to a place at university.

bâcler *vb* [**28**] to botch up
bagage *nm* luggage; **faire ses bagages** to pack; **les bagages à main** hand luggage
bagarre *nf* fight
se **bagarrer** *vb* [**28**] to fight

bagnole *nf (informal)* car
bague *nf* ring
baguette *nf* ❶ stick of French bread ❷ chopstick; **une baguette magique** a magic wand
baie *nf* bay
baignade *nf* **'baignade interdite'** 'no swimming'
se **baigner** *vb* [**28**] to go swimming ▷ *Si on allait se baigner?* Shall we go swimming?
baignoire *nf (bathtub)* bath
bâiller *vb* [**28**] to yawn
bain *nm* bath ▷ *prendre un bain* to take a bath ▷ *prendre un bain de soleil* to sunbathe
baiser *nm* kiss
baisse *nf* fall; **être en baisse** to be falling; **revoir les chiffres à la baisse** to revise figures downwards
baisser *vb* [**28**] ❶ to turn down ▷ *Il fait moins froid, tu peux baisser le chauffage.* It's not so cold, you can turn down the heating. ❷ to fall ▷ *Le prix des CD a baissé.* The price of CDs has fallen.; **se baisser** to bend down
bal *nm* dance
balade *nf (informal)* walk
se **balader** *vb* [**28**] *(informal)* to wander around
baladeur *nm*
balai *nm* broom
balance *nf (for weighing)* scales *pl*; **la Balance** Libra
se **balancer** *vb* [**12**] to swing
balançoire *nf* swing
balayer *vb* [**59**] ❶ to sweep ❷ to sweep up
balayeur *nm* roadsweeper
balbutier *vb* [**19**] to stammer
balcon *nm* balcony
baleine *nf* whale
balle *nf* ❶ ball ▷ *une balle de tennis* a tennis ball ❷ bullet
ballerine *nf* ❶ ballet dancer ❷ ballet shoe
ballet *nm* ballet
ballon *nm* ❶ ball ▷ *lancer le ballon* to throw the ball; **un ballon de foot** a football ❷ balloon
balnéaire *adj* **une station balnéaire** a seaside resort
banal, e *adj* ❶ commonplace ❷ hackneyed
banane *nf* ❶ banana ❷ bumbag
banc *nm* bench
bancaire *adj* **une carte bancaire** a bank card
bandage *nm* bandage
bande *nf* ❶ gang ▷ *une bande de voyous* a gang of louts ❷ bunch ▷ *C'est une bande d'idiots!* They are a bunch of idiots! ❸ bandage; **une bande dessinée** a comic strip

Comic strips are very popular in France with people of all ages.

une bande magnétique a tape; **la bande sonore** the sound track; **Elle fait toujours bande à part.** She always keeps to herself.
bandeau (*pl* **bandeaux**) *nm* headband
bander *vb* [**28**] to bandage ▷ *L'infirmière lui a bandé la jambe.* The nurse bandaged his leg.
bandit *nm* bandit
banlieue *nf* suburbs; **les lignes de**

banlieue suburban lines; **les trains de banlieue** commuter trains

banque *nf* bank

banquet *nm* dinner

banquette *nf* seat

banquier *nm* banker

baptême *nm* christening; **C'était mon baptême de l'air.** It was the first time I had flown.

baquet *nm* tub

bar *nm* bar

baraque *nf (informal)* house

barbant, e *adj (informal)* boring

barbare *adj* barbaric

barbe *nf* beard ▷ *Il porte la barbe.* He's got a beard.; **Quelle barbe!** *(informal)* What a drag!; **la barbe à papa** candyfloss

barbecue *nm* barbecue

barbouiller *vb* [**28**] to daub ▷ *Les murs étaient barbouillés de graffitis.* The walls were daubed with graffiti.; **J'ai l'estomac barbouillé.** *(informal)* I'm feeling queasy.

barbu, e *adj* bearded

barder *vb* [**28**] *(informal)* **Ça va barder!** There's going to be trouble!

baromètre *nm* barometer

barque *nf* rowing boat

barrage *nm* dam; **un barrage de police** a police roadblock

barre *nf (metal)* bar

barreau (*pl* **barreaux**) *nm (on window)* bar

barrer *vb* [**28**] to block ▷ *Il y a un tronc d'arbre qui barre la route.* There's a tree trunk blocking the road.; **se barrer** *(informal)* to clear off ▷ *Barre-toi!* Clear off!

barrette *nf* hair slide

barrière *nf* fence

bar-tabac (*pl* **bars-tabacs**) *nm*

A **bar-tabac** is a bar which also sells cigarettes and stamps; you can tell a **bar-tabac** by the red diamond-shaped sign outside it.

bas (*f* **basse**) *adj, adv* low ▷ *parler à voix basse* to speak in a low voice; **en bas (1)** down ▷ *Ça me donne le vertige de regarder en bas.* I get dizzy if I look down. **(2)** (down) at the bottom ▷ *Son nom est tout en bas.* His name is down at the bottom. **(3)** downstairs ▷ *Elle habite en bas.* She lives downstairs.

▸ *nm* ❶ bottom ▷ *en bas de la page* at the bottom of the page ❷ stocking

bas-côté *nm* verge

bascule *nf* **un fauteuil à bascule** a rocking chair

base *nf* base; **de base** basic; **à base de** made from; **une base de données** a database

basilic *nm* basil

basket *nm* basketball

baskets *nfpl* trainers ▷ *une paire de baskets* a pair of trainers

basque *adj, n* Basque ▷ *Elle parle basque.* She speaks Basque.; **un Basque** *(man)* a Basque; **une Basque** *(woman)* a Basque

basse *adj f see* **bas**

basse-cour (*pl* **basses-cours**) *nf* farmyard

bassin *nm* ❶ pond ❷ pelvis

bassine *nf (for washing)* bowl

a **b** c d e f g h i j k l m n o p q r s t u v w x y z

bas-ventre *nm* lower abdomen
bataille *nf* battle
bateau (*pl* **bateaux**) *nm* boat
bateau-mouche (*pl* **bateaux-mouches**) *nm* pleasure boat
bâti, e *adj* **bien bâti** well-built
bâtiment *nm* building
bâtir *vb* [**38**] to build
bâton *nm* stick
battement *nm* **J'ai dix minutes de battement.** I've got ten minutes free.
batterie *nf* ❶ battery ❷ drums; **la batterie de cuisine** the pots and pans
batteur *nm* drummer
battre *vb* [**9**] to beat ▷ *Quand je le vois, mon cœur bat plus vite.* When I see him, my heart beats faster.; **se battre** to fight ▷ *Je me bats souvent avec mon frère.* I fight a lot with my brother.; **battre les cartes** to shuffle the cards; **Battre les blancs en neige.** Beat the egg whites until stiff.; **battre son plein** to be in full swing
bavard, e *adj* talkative
bavarder *vb* [**28**] to chat
baver *vb* [**28**] to dribble
baveux (*f* **baveuse**) *adj* runny
bavure *nf* blunder
bazar *nm* general store; **Quel bazar!** *(informal)* What a mess!
BCBG *adj* (= *bon chic bon genre*) posh
BD (*pl* **BD**) *nf* (= *bande dessinée*) comic strip
béant, e *adj* gaping
beau (*f* **belle**, *mpl* **beaux**) *adj, adv*

> The masculine singular form **beau** changes to **bel** before a vowel and most words beginning with 'h'.

❶ lovely ❷ beautiful ❸ good-looking ❹ handsome; **Il fait beau aujourd'hui.** It's a nice day today.; **J'ai beau essayer, je n'y arrive pas.** However hard I try, I just can't do it.
beaucoup *adv* ❶ a lot ▷ *Il boit beaucoup.* He drinks a lot. ❷ much ▷ *Elle n'a pas beaucoup d'argent.* She hasn't got much money.; **beaucoup de** a lot of; **J'ai eu beaucoup de chance.** I was very lucky.
beau-fils (*pl* **beaux-fils**) *nm* ❶ son-in-law ❷ stepson
beau-frère (*pl* **beaux-frères**) *nm* brother-in-law
beau-père (*pl* **beaux-pères**) *nm* ❶ father-in-law ❷ stepfather
beauté *nf* beauty
beaux-arts *nmpl* fine arts
beaux-parents *nmpl* in-laws
bébé *nm* baby
bec *nm* beak
bécane *nf* *(informal)* bike
bêche *nf* spade
bêcher *vb* [**28**] to dig ▷ *Il bêchait son jardin.* He was digging the garden.
bégayer *vb* [**59**] to stammer
beige *adj* beige
beignet *nm* fritter
bel *adj m* *see* **beau**
belge *adj, nmf* Belgian; **un Belge** *(man)* a Belgian; **une Belge** *(woman)* a Belgian

Belgique *nf* Belgium; **en Belgique** **(1)** in Belgium **(2)** to Belgium
bélier *nm* ram; **le Bélier** Aries
belle *adj f see* **beau**
belle-famille (*pl* **belles-familles**) *nf* in-laws
belle-fille (*pl* **belles-filles**) *nf* ❶ daughter-in-law ❷ stepdaughter
belle-mère (*pl* **belles-mères**) *nf* ❶ mother-in-law ❷ stepmother
belle-sœur (*pl* **belles-sœurs**) *nf* sister-in-law
bénédiction *nf* blessing
bénéfice *nm* profit
bénévole *adj* voluntary ▷ *du travail bénévole* voluntary work
bénir *vb* [**38**] to bless
bénit, e *adj* consecrated; **l'eau bénite** holy water
béquille *nf* crutch
berceau (*pl* **berceaux**) *nm* cradle
bercer *vb* [**12**] to rock
berceuse *nf* lullaby
béret *nm* beret
berge *nf* (*of river*) bank
berger *nm* shepherd
bergère *nf* shepherdess
besoin *nm* need; **avoir besoin de quelque chose** to need something ▷ *J'ai besoin d'argent.* I need some money.; **une famille dans le besoin** a needy family
bétail *nm* livestock
bête *adj* stupid
▶ *nf* animal
bêtise *nf* **faire une bêtise** to do something stupid; **dire des bêtises** to talk nonsense
béton *nm* concrete; **un alibi en béton** a cast-iron alibi
betterave *nf* beetroot
beur *nmf* (*informal*)

A **beur** is a young person of North African origin born in France.

beurre *nm* butter
beurrer *vb* [**28**] to butter
Beyrouth *n* Beirut
bibelot *nm* ornament
biberon *nm* baby's bottle
Bible *nf* Bible
bibliothécaire *nmf* librarian
bibliothèque *nf* ❶ library ❷ bookcase
bic® *nm* Biro®
biche *nf* doe
bicyclette *nf* bicycle
bidet *nm* bidet
bidon *nm* can
▶ *adj* (*informal*) phoney
bidonville *nm* shanty town
Biélorussie *nf* Belarus
bien *adj, adv* ❶ well ▷ *Daphne travaille bien.* Daphne works well. ▷ *Je ne me sens pas bien.* I don't feel well. ❷ good ▷ *Ce restaurant est vraiment bien.* This restaurant is really good. ❸ quite; **Je veux bien le faire.** I'm quite willing to do it.; **bien mieux** much better; **J'espère bien y aller.** I very much hope to go. ❹ right; **C'est bien fait pour lui!** It serves him right!
▶ *nm* ❶ good; **faire du bien à quelqu'un** to do somebody good ❷ possession
bien-être *nm* well-being

bienfaisance *nf* charity; **une œuvre de bienfaisance** a charity

bien que *conj* although

> **bien que** is followed by a verb in the subjunctive.

▷ *Il fait assez chaud bien qu'il n'y ait pas de soleil.* It's quite warm although there's no sun.

bien sûr *adv* of course

bientôt *adv* soon

bienvenu *nm* **Vous êtes le bienvenu!** You're welcome!

bienvenue *nf* welcome ▷ *Bienvenue à Paris!* Welcome to Paris!

bière *nf* beer; **la bière blonde** lager; **la bière brune** brown ale; **la bière pression** draught beer

bifteck *nm* steak

bigoudi *nm (in hair)* roller

bijou (*pl* **bijoux**) *nm* jewel

bijouterie *nf* jeweller's

bijoutier *nm* jeweller

bilan *nm* **faire le bilan de quelque chose** to assess something

bilingue *adj* bilingual

billard *nm* billiards; **le billard américain** pool

bille *nf (toy)* marble

billet *nm* ❶ ticket ▷ *un billet d'avion* a plane ticket ❷ banknote ▷ *un billet de dix euros* a 10 euro note

biographie *nf* biography

biologie *nf* biology

biologique *adj* ❶ organic ❷ biological

Birmanie *nf* Burma

bis *adv* ▷ *Il habite au douze bis rue des Fleurs.* He lives at 12A rue des Fleurs.
▶ *nm* encore

biscotte *nf (sold in packets)* toasted bread

biscuit *nm* biscuit; **un biscuit de Savoie** a sponge cake

bise *nf (informal)* kiss ▷ *Grosses bises de Bretagne.* Love and kisses from Brittany.; **faire la bise à quelqu'un** to give somebody a peck on the cheek

> Between girls and boys, and between girls, the normal French way of saying hello and goodbye is with kisses, usually one on each cheek. Boys shake hands with each other instead.

bisou *nm (informal)* kiss

bissextile *adj* **une année bissextile** a leap year

bistrot *nm (informal)* café

> Cafés in France sell both alcoholic and non-alcoholic drinks.

bizarre *adj* strange

blague *nf (informal)* ❶ joke ▷ *raconter une blague* to tell a joke; **Sans blague!** No kidding! ❷ trick

blaguer *vb* [**28**] *(informal)* to joke

blaireau (*pl* **blaireaux**) *nm* ❶ badger ❷ shaving brush

blâmer *vb* [**28**] to blame

Blanc *nm* white man

blanc (*f* **blanche**) *adj* ❶ white ▷ *un chemisier blanc* a white blouse ❷ blank ▷ *une page blanche* a blank page
▶ *nm* ❶ white ❷ white wine; **un blanc d'œuf** an egg white; **un blanc de poulet** a chicken breast

Blanche *nf* white woman
blanche *adj f see* **blanc**
blanchisserie *nf* laundry
blé *nm* wheat
blessé, e *adj* injured
blessé *nm* injured person
blessée *nf* injured person
blesser *vb* [**28**] ❶ to injure ▷ *Il a été blessé dans un accident de voiture.* He was injured in a car accident. ❷ to hurt ▷ *Il a fait exprès de le blesser.* He hurt him on purpose.; **se blesser** to hurt oneself
blessure *nf* injury
bleu, e *adj* ❶ blue; **bleu marine** navy blue ❷ *(steak)* very rare ▶ *nm* ❶ blue ❷ bruise
bleuet *nm* cornflower
bloc *nm* pad; **le bloc opératoire** the operating theatre
bloc-notes (*pl* **blocs-notes**) *nm* note pad
blog *nm* blog
bloguer *vb* [**28**] to blog
blond, e *adj* blond; **blond cendré** ash blond
bloquer *vb* [**28**] to block ▷ *bloquer le passage* to block the way; **être bloqué dans un embouteillage** to be stuck in a traffic jam
se **blottir** *vb* [**38**] to huddle
blouse *nf* overall
blouson *nm* jacket
bob *nm* cotton sunhat
bobine *nf* reel
bocal (*pl* **bocaux**) *nm* jar
bœuf *nm* ❶ ox ❷ beef
bof *excl (informal)* **Le film t'a plu? — Bof! C'était pas terrible!** Did you like the film? — Well ... it wasn't that great!; **Comment ça va? — Bof! Pas terrible.** How is it going? — Oh ... not too well actually.
bohémien *nm* gipsy
bohémienne *nf* gipsy
boire *vb* [**10**] to drink; **boire un coup** *(informal)* to have a drink
bois *nm* wood; **en bois** wooden; **avoir la gueule de bois** *(informal)* to have a hangover
boisson *nf* drink
boîte *nf* ❶ box ▷ *une boîte d'allumettes* a box of matches; **une boîte aux lettres** a letter box; **une boîte postale** a PO Box ❷ tin; **une boîte de conserve** a tin; **en boîte** tinned; **une boîte de nuit** a night club; **sortir en boîte** to go clubbing
boiter *vb* [**28**] to limp
bol *nm* bowl; **en avoir ras le bol** *(informal)* to be fed up
bombarder *vb* [**28**] to bomb
bombe *nf* ❶ bomb ❷ aerosol
bon (*f* **bonne**) *adj, adv* ❶ good ▷ *un bon restaurant* a good restaurant ▷ *Le tabac n'est pas bon pour la santé.* Smoking isn't good for you. ▷ *être bon en maths* to be good at maths; **sentir bon** to smell nice; **Bon anniversaire!** Happy birthday!; **Bon courage!** Good luck!; **Bon voyage!** Have a good trip!; **Bon week-end!** Have a nice weekend!; **Bonne chance!** Good luck!; **Bonne journée!** Have a nice day!; **Bonne nuit!** Good

night!; **Bonne année!** Happy New Year!; **Bonnes vacances!** Have a good holiday! ❷ right ▷ *Il est arrivé au bon moment.* He arrived at the right moment. ▷ *Ce n'est pas la bonne réponse.* That's not the right answer.; **Il fait bon aujourd'hui.** It's nice today.; **de bonne heure** early; **bon marché** cheap ▷ *Les fraises ne sont pas bon marché en hiver.* Strawberries aren't cheap in winter.; **Ah bon?** Really? ▷ *Je pars aux États-Unis la semaine prochaine. — Ah bon?* I'm going to the States next week. — Really?; **J'aimerais vraiment que tu viennes! — Bon, d'accord.** I'd really like you to come! — OK then, I will.; **Est-ce que ce yaourt est encore bon?** Is this yoghurt still OK?
▶ *nm* voucher ▷ *un bon d'achat* a voucher; **pour de bon (1)** for good ▷ *Il est parti pour de bon.* He's gone for good. **(2)** for real ▷ *Cette fois, on le fait pour de bon.* Let's do it for real this time.

bonbon *nm* sweet

bondé, e *adj* crowded

bondir *vb* [**38**] to leap

bonheur *nm* happiness; **porter bonheur** to bring luck

bonhomme (*pl* **bonshommes**) *nm* **un bonhomme de neige** a snowman

bonjour *excl* ❶ hello! ▷ *Donne le bonjour à tes parents de ma part.* Say hello to your parents for me. ❷ good morning! ❸ good afternoon!

> **bonjour** is used in the morning and afternoon; in the evening **bonsoir** is used instead.

C'est simple comme bonjour! It's easy as pie!

bonne *adj f see* **bon**

bonnet *nm* hat; **un bonnet de bain** a bathing cap

bonsoir *excl* good evening!

bonté *nf* kindness

bord *nm* ❶ edge ❷ side; **au bord de la mer** at the seaside; **au bord de l'eau** by the water; **monter à bord** to go on board; **être au bord des larmes** to be on the verge of tears

bordeaux *nm* Bordeaux wine; **du bordeaux rouge** claret
▶ *adj* burgundy

border *vb* [**28**] ❶ to line ▷ *une route bordée d'arbres* a tree-lined street ❷ to trim ▷ *un col bordé de dentelle* a collar trimmed with lace ❸ to tuck up ▷ *Sa mère vient la border tous les soirs.* Her mother comes and tucks her up every night.

bordure *nf* border; **une villa en bordure de mer** a villa right by the sea

borne *nf* (*of computer*) terminal

Bosnie *nf* Bosnia; **la Bosnie-Herzégovine** Bosnia-Herzegovina

bosse *nf* bump

bosser *vb* [**28**] (*informal*) to work; **bosser un examen** to study for an exam

bossu *nm* hunchback

botanique *adj* botanic
▶ *nf* botany

botte *nf* ❶ boot ▷ *une paire de bottes*

a pair of boots; **les bottes en caoutchouc** Wellington boots ❷ bunch ▷ *une botte de radis* a bunch of radishes
bottin® *nm* phone book
bouc *nm* ❶ goatee beard ❷ billy goat; **un bouc émissaire** a scapegoat
bouche *nf* mouth; **le bouche à bouche** the kiss of life; **une bouche d'égout** a manhole; **une bouche de métro** an entrance to the underground
bouchée *nf* mouthful; **une bouchée à la reine** a chicken vol-au-vent
boucher *vb* [**28**] ❶ to fill ▷ *boucher un trou* to fill a hole ❷ to block ▷ *L'évier est bouché.* The sink is blocked. ▷ *J'ai le nez bouché.* My nose is blocked.
▶ *nm* butcher
bouchère *nf* butcher
boucherie *nf* butcher's
bouchon *nm* ❶ *(of plastic bottle)* top ❷ *(of wine bottle)* cork ❸ hold-up
boucle *nf (of hair)* curl; **une boucle d'oreille** an earring
bouclé, e *adj* curly
bouclier *nm* shield
bouddhiste *nmf* Buddhist
bouder *vb* [**28**] to sulk
boudin *nm* **le boudin noir** black pudding; **le boudin blanc** white pudding
boue *nf* mud
bouée *nf* buoy; **une bouée de sauvetage** a life buoy
boueux (*f* **boueuse**) *adj* muddy
bouffe *nf (informal)* food
bouffée *nf* **une bouffée d'air frais** a breath of fresh air
bouffer *vb* [**28**] *(informal)* to eat
bougeoir *nm* candlestick
bouger *vb* [**45**] to move
bougie *nf* candle
bouillabaisse *nf* fish soup
bouillant, e *adj* ❶ boiling ❷ piping hot
bouillir *vb* [**11**] to boil ▷ *L'eau bout.* The water's boiling.; **Je bous d'impatience.** I'm bursting with impatience.
bouilloire *nf* kettle
bouillon *nm* stock
bouillotte *nf* hot-water bottle
boulanger *nm* baker
boulangère *nf* baker
boulangerie *nf* baker's
boule *nf* ball; **une boule de neige** a snowball; **jouer aux boules** to play bowls
boulevard *nm* boulevard
bouleverser *vb* [**28**] ❶ to move deeply ❷ to shatter ▷ *La mort de son ami l'a bouleversé.* He was shattered by the death of his friend. ❸ to turn upside down ▷ *Cette rencontre a bouleversé sa vie.* This meeting turned his life upside down.
boulot *nm (informal)* ❶ job ❷ work
boum *nf (informal)* party
bouquet *nm* bunch of flowers
bouquin *nm (informal)* book
bouquiner *vb* [**28**] *(informal)* to read
bourdonner *vb* [**28**] to buzz
bourg *nm* small market town

bourgeois, e *adj* middle-class
bourgeon *nm* bud
Bourgogne *nf* Burgundy
bourré, e *adj* **bourré de** stuffed with; **être bourré** *(informal)* to be plastered
bourreau (*pl* **bourreaux**) *nm* executioner; **C'est un véritable bourreau de travail.** He's a real workaholic.
bourrer *vb* [**28**] to stuff
bourse *nf* grant; **la Bourse** the Stock Exchange
bous *vb see* **bouillir**
bousculade *nf* crush
bousculer *vb* [**28**] ❶ to jostle ▷ *être bousculé par la foule* to be jostled by the crowd ❷ to rush ▷ *Je n'aime pas qu'on me bouscule.* I don't like to be rushed.
boussole *nf* compass
bout *vb see* **bouillir**
▶ *nm* ❶ end ▷ *Elle habite au bout de la rue.* She lives at the end of the street. ❷ tip ▷ *le bout du nez* the tip of the nose ❸ bit; **un bout de papier** a scrap of paper; **au bout de** after; **Elle est à bout.** She's at the end of her tether.
bouteille *nf* bottle; **une bouteille de gaz** a gas cylinder
boutique *nf* shop
bouton *nm* ❶ button ❷ *(on skin)* spot ❸ bud; **un bouton d'or** a buttercup
bowling *nm* ❶ tenpin bowling ❷ bowling alley
boxe *nf* boxing
boxeur *nm* boxer
bracelet *nm* bracelet
bracelet-montre (*pl* **bracelets-montres**) *nm* wristwatch
brancard *nm* stretcher
brancardier *nm* stretcher-bearer
branche *nf* branch
branché, e *adj (informal)* trendy
brancher *vb* [**28**] ❶ to connect ▷ *Le téléphone est branché?* Is the phone connected? ❷ to plug in ▷ *L'aspirateur n'est pas branché.* The hoover isn't plugged in.
bras *nm* arm
brasse *nf* breaststroke
brasserie *nf* café-restaurant
brave *adj* nice
bravo *excl* bravo!
break *nm* estate car
brebis *nf* ewe; **le fromage de brebis** sheep's cheese
bref (*f* **brève**) *adj, adv* short; **en bref** in brief; **... bref, ça s'est bien terminé.** ... to cut a long story short, it turned out all right in the end.
Brésil *nm* Brazil
Bretagne *nf* Brittany
bretelle *nf* strap; **les bretelles** braces
breton (*f* **bretonne**) *adj, nm/f* Breton ▷ *Ils parlent breton.* They speak Breton.; **un Breton** *(man)* a Breton; **une Bretonne** *(woman)* a Breton; **les Bretons** the Bretons
brève *adj f see* **bref**
brevet *nm* certificate
brevet des collèges *nm*

- The **brevet des collèges** is an exam you take at the end of **collège**, at the age of 15.

bricolage *nm* do-it-yourself
bricole *nf (informal)* **J'ai acheté une bricole pour le bébé de Sabine.** I've bought a little something for Sabine's baby.; **J'ai encore quelques bricoles à faire avant de partir.** I've still got a few things to do before I go.
bricoler *vb* [**28**] to do DIY ▷ *Pascal aime bricoler.* Pascal loves doing DIY.
bricoleur *nm* DIY enthusiast
bricoleuse *nf* DIY enthusiast
bridge *nm (game)* bridge
brièvement *adv* briefly
brigade *nf (of police)* squad
brillamment *adv* brilliantly
brillant, e *adj* ❶ brilliant ❷ shiny
briller *vb* [**28**] to shine
brin *nm* **un brin d'herbe** a blade of grass; **un brin de muguet** a sprig of lily of the valley
brindille *nf* twig
brioche *nf* brioche bun
brique *nf* brick
briquet *nm* cigarette lighter
brise *nf* breeze
se **briser** *vb* [**28**] to break ▷ *Le vase s'est brisé en mille morceaux.* The vase broke into a thousand pieces.
Britannique *nmf* Briton; **les Britanniques** the British
britannique *adj* British
brocante *nf* junk
brocanteur *nm* dealer in second-hand goods
broche *nf* brooch; **à la broche** spit-roasted
brochette *nf* skewer; **les brochettes d'agneau** lamb kebabs
brochure *nf* brochure
broder *vb* [**28**] to embroider
broderie *nf* embroidery
bronchite *nf* bronchitis
bronze *nm* bronze
bronzer *vb* [**28**] to get a tan ▷ *Il est bien bronzé.* He's got a good tan.; **se bronzer** to sunbathe
brosse *nf* brush; **une brosse à cheveux** a hairbrush; **une brosse à dents** a toothbrush; **Il est coiffé en brosse.** He's got a crew cut.
brosser *vb* [**28**] to brush; **se brosser les dents** to brush one's teeth ▷ *Je me brosse les dents tous les soirs.* I brush my teeth every night.
brouette *nf* wheelbarrow
brouillard *nm* fog
brouillon *nm* first draft
broussailles *nfpl* undergrowth *sg*
brouter *vb* [**28**] *(animals)* to graze
broyer *vb* [**53**] to crush; **broyer du noir** to be down in the dumps
brugnon *nm* nectarine
bruit *nm* ❶ noise ▷ *faire du bruit* to make a noise; **sans bruit** without a sound ❷ rumour
brûlant, e *adj* ❶ blazing ❷ boiling hot
brûlé *nm* smell of burning
brûler *vb* [**28**] to burn; **se brûler** to burn oneself
brûlure *nf* burn; **des brûlures d'estomac** heartburn
brume *nf* mist

brumeux (*f* **brumeuse**) *adj* misty
brun, e *adj* brown; **Elle est brune.** She's got dark hair.
brushing *nm* blow-dry
brusque *adj* abrupt; **d'un ton brusque** brusquely
brusquer *vb* [**28**] to rush
brut, e *adj* **le champagne brut** dry champagne; **le pétrole brut** crude oil; **son salaire brut** his gross salary
brutal, e (*mpl* **brutaux**) *adj* brutal
brutaliser *vb* [**28**] to knock about ▷ *Il a été brutalisé par la police.* He was treated roughly by the police.
Bruxelles *n* Brussels
bruyamment *adv* noisily
bruyant, e *adj* noisy
bruyère *nf* heather
bu *vb see* **boire**
bûche *nf* log; **la bûche de Noël** the Yule log

la bûche de Noël is what is usually eaten in France instead of Christmas pudding.

bûcheron *nm* woodcutter
budget *nm* budget
buffet *nm* ❶ sideboard ❷ buffet ▷ *un buffet de gare* a station buffet
buisson *nm* bush
Bulgarie *nf* Bulgaria
bulle *nf* bubble
bulletin *nm* ❶ bulletin; **le bulletin d'informations** the news bulletin ❷ report; **le bulletin météorologique** the weather report; **un bulletin de salaire** a pay slip; **un bulletin de vote** a ballot paper
bureau (*pl* **bureaux**) *nm* ❶ desk ❷ office; **un bureau de change** a bureau de change; **le bureau de poste** the post office; **le bureau de tabac** the tobacconist's; **le bureau de vote** the polling station
bus *vb see* **boire**
▶ *nm* bus
buste *nm* bust
but *vb see* **boire**
▶ *nm* ❶ aim; **Quel est le but de votre visite?** What's the reason for your visit?; **dans le but de** with the intention of ❷ goal ▷ *marquer un but* to score a goal
butane *nm* Calor gas®
butin *nm* loot
buvais, buvait *vb see* **boire**
buvard *nm* blotter

C

c' *pron see* **ce**

ça *pron* ❶ this ▷ *Est-ce que vous pouvez me donner un peu de ça?* Can you give me a bit of this? ❷ that ▷ *Regarde ça là-bas.* Look at that over there. ❸ it ▷ *Ça ne fait rien.* It doesn't matter.; **Comment ça va?** How are you?; **Ça alors!** Well, well!; **C'est ça.** That's right.; **Ça y est!** That's it!

çà *adv* **çà et là** here and there

cabane *nf* hut

cabillaud *nm* cod

cabine *nf (on a ship)* cabin; **une cabine d'essayage** a fitting room; **une cabine téléphonique** a phone box

cabinet *nm (of doctor, dentist)* surgery; **une chambre avec cabinet de toilette** a room with washing facilities

cabinets *nmpl* toilet *sg*

câble *nm* cable; **la télévision par câble** cable television

cabosser *vb* [**28**] to dent

cacahuète *nf* peanut; **le beurre de cacahuète** peanut butter

cacao *nm* cocoa; **le beurre de cacao** cocoa butter

cache-cache *nm* **jouer à cache-cache** to play hide-and-seek

cachemire *nm* cashmere

cache-nez (*pl* **cache-nez**) *nm* long woollen scarf

cacher *vb* [**28**] to hide ▷ *J'ai caché les cadeaux sous le lit.* I hid the presents under the bed.; **se cacher** to hide

cachet *nm* ❶ tablet; **un cachet d'aspirine** an aspirin ❷ *(for performer)* fee; **le cachet de la poste** the postmark

cachette *nf* hiding place; **en cachette** on the sly

cachot *nm* dungeon

cactus *nm* cactus

cadavre *nm* corpse

Caddie® *nm* supermarket trolley

cadeau (*pl* **cadeaux**) *nm* present ▷ *un cadeau d'anniversaire* a birthday present ▷ *un cadeau de Noël* a Christmas present; **faire un cadeau à quelqu'un** to give somebody a present

cadenas *nm* padlock

cadet (*f* **cadette**) *adj* ❶ *(brother, sister)* younger ❷ *(son, daughter)* youngest

cadet *nm* youngest ▷ *C'est le cadet*

de la famille. He's the youngest of the family.

cadette *nf* youngest

cadre *nm* ❶ frame ❷ surroundings ❸ executive ▷ *un cadre supérieur* a senior executive

cafard *nm* cockroach; **avoir le cafard** *(informal)* to be feeling down

café *nm* ❶ coffee ▷ *un café au lait* a white coffee ▷ *un café crème* a strong white coffee ❷ café

Cafés in France sell both alcoholic and non-alcoholic drinks.

café-tabac (*pl* **cafés-tabacs**) *nm*

A **café-tabac** is a bar which also sells cigarettes and stamps; you can tell a **café-tabac** by the red diamond-shaped sign outside it.

cafétéria *nf* cafeteria

cafetière *nf* ❶ coffee maker ❷ coffeepot

cage *nf* cage; **la cage d'escalier** the stairwell

cagoule *nf* balaclava

cahier *nm* exercise book

caille *nf* quail

caillou (*pl* **cailloux**) *nm* pebble

caisse *nf* ❶ box ❷ till ▷ *le ticket de caisse* the till receipt ❸ checkout

caissier *nm* cashier

cake *nm* fruit cake

calcul *nm* ❶ calculation ❷ arithmetic

calculatrice *nf* calculator

calculer *vb* [**28**] to work out ▷ *J'ai calculé combien ça allait coûter.* I worked out how much it was going to cost.

calculette *nf* pocket calculator

cale *nf* wedge

calé, e *adj (informal)*; **Elle est calée en histoire.** She's really good at history.

caleçon *nm* ❶ boxer shorts ❷ leggings

calendrier *nm* calendar

calepin *nm* notebook

caler *vb* [**28**] to stall

câlin, e *adj* cuddly
▸ *nm* cuddle

calmant *nm* tranquillizer

calme *adj* ❶ quiet ❷ calm
▸ *nm* peace and quiet

calmer *vb* [**28**] to soothe; **se calmer** to calm down ▷ *Calme-toi!* Calm down!

calorie *nf* calorie

camarade *nmf* friend; **un camarade de classe** a school friend

cambriolage *nm* burglary

cambrioler *vb* [**28**] to burgle

cambrioleur *nm* burglar

camelote *nf (informal)* junk

caméra *nf (cinema, TV)* camera; **une caméra numérique** a digital camera

caméscope® *nm* camcorder

camion *nm* lorry

camionnette *nf* van

camionneur *nm* lorry driver

camomille *nf* camomile tea

camp *nm* camp

campagne *nf* ❶ country; **à la campagne** in the country ❷ campaign

camper *vb* [**28**] to camp

campeur *nm* camper
campeuse *nf* camper
camping *nm* camping ▷ *faire du camping* to go camping; **un (terrain de) camping** a campsite
Canada *nm* Canada; **au Canada** (1) in Canada (2) to Canada
canadien (*f* **canadienne**) *adj, nm/f* Canadian; **un Canadien** *(man)* a Canadian; **une Canadienne** *(woman)* a Canadian
canal (*pl* **canaux**) *nm* canal
canapé *nm* ❶ sofa ❷ open sandwich
canard *nm* duck
canari *nm* canary
cancer *nm* cancer; **le Cancer** Cancer
candidat *nm* ❶ *(in exam, election)* candidate ❷ *(for job)* applicant
candidature *nf* **poser sa candidature à un poste** to apply for a job
caneton *nm* duckling
canette *nf* **une canette de bière** a small bottle of beer
caniche *nm* poodle
canicule *nf* scorching heat
canif *nm* penknife
caniveau (*pl* **caniveaux**) *nm* gutter
canne *nf* walking stick; **une canne à pêche** a fishing rod
cannelle *nf* cinnamon
canoë *nm* ❶ canoe ❷ canoeing
canon *nm* ❶ gun ❷ cannon
canot *nm* dinghy; **un canot de sauvetage** a lifeboat
cantatrice *nf* opera singer
cantine *nf* canteen
caoutchouc *nm* rubber; **des bottes en caoutchouc** Wellington boots
cap *nm (land)* cape
capable *adj* **Elle est capable de marcher pendant des heures.** She can walk for hours.; **Il est capable de changer d'avis au dernier moment.** He's capable of changing his mind at the last minute.
cape *nf (garment)* cape
capitaine *nm* captain
capitale *nf* capital
capot *nm (of car)* bonnet
capote *nf (informal)* condom
câpre *nf (food)* caper
caprice *nm* **faire des caprices** to make a fuss
capricieux (*f* **capricieuse**) *adj* **un enfant capricieux** an awkward child
Capricorne *nm* Capricorn
captivant, e *adj* fascinating
captivité *nf* captivity
capturer *vb* [**28**] to capture
capuche *nf* hood
capuchon *nm (of pen)* cap
capucine *nf* nasturtium
car *nm* coach ▷ *un car scolaire* a school bus
▶ *conj* because ▷ *Réfléchis bien car c'est important.* Think carefully because it's important.
carabine *nf* rifle
caractère *nm* personality; **Il a bon caractère.** He's good-natured.; **Elle a mauvais caractère.** She's

bad-tempered.; **Il n'a pas un caractère facile.** He isn't easy to get on with.

caractéristique *adj* characteristic
▶ *nf* characteristic

carafe *nf* jug

Caraïbes *nfpl* Caribbean Islands

caramel *nm* ❶ caramel ❷ toffee

caravane *nf* caravan

carbonique *adj* **le gaz carbonique** carbon dioxide

carburant *nm* fuel

cardiaque *adj* **une crise cardiaque** a heart attack; **Ma tante est cardiaque.** My aunt has heart trouble.

cardigan *nm* cardigan

cardiologue *nmf* heart specialist

carême *nm* Lent

caresse *nf* stroke

caresser *vb* [**28**] to stroke

carie *nf* tooth decay

caritatif (*f* **caritative**) *adj* **une organisation caritative** a charity

carnaval *nm* carnival

carnet *nm* ❶ notebook ❷ book ▷ *un carnet d'adresses* an address book ▷ *un carnet de chèques* a cheque book ▷ *un carnet de timbres* a book of stamps ▷ *un carnet de tickets* a book of tickets

In the Paris metro it is cheaper to buy tickets in a book of ten, known as a **carnet**.

mon carnet de notes my school report

carotte *nf* carrot

carré, e *adj* square; **un mètre carré** a square metre
▶ *nm* square

carreau (*pl* **carreaux**) *nm* ❶ check ❷ *(on floor, wall)* tile ❸ pane ❹ *(cards)* diamonds

carrefour *nm* junction

carrelage *nm* tiled floor

carrément *adv* ❶ completely ❷ straight out

carrière *nf* career; **un militaire de carrière** a professional soldier

carrure *nf* build

cartable *nm* satchel

carte *nf* ❶ card; **une carte d'anniversaire** a birthday card; **une carte postale** a postcard; **une carte de vœux** a Christmas card

The French send greetings cards (**les cartes de vœux**) in January rather than at Christmas, with best wishes for the New Year.

une carte de vœux électronique an e-card; **une carte bancaire** a cash card; **une carte bleue**

Carte bleue is a major French debit card.

une carte de crédit a credit card; **une carte de fidélité** a loyalty card; **une carte d'embarquement** a boarding card; **une carte d'identité** an identity card; **une carte de séjour** a residence permit; **une carte téléphonique** a phonecard; **un jeu de cartes (1)** a pack of cards **(2)** a card game ❷ map ▷ *une carte de France* a map of France ▷ *une carte routière* a road map ❸ menu ▷ *la carte des vins* the wine list; **manger à la carte** to eat à la carte ▷ *Nous allons manger à la* *carte*. We'll choose from the à la carte menu.

carton *nm* ❶ cardboard ❷ cardboard box

cartouche *nf* cartridge; **une cartouche de cigarettes** a carton of cigarettes

cas (*pl* **cas**) *nm* case; **ne faire aucun cas de** to take no notice of; **en aucun cas** on no account; **en tout cas** at any rate; **au cas où** in case; **en cas de** in case of

cascade *nf* waterfall

cascadeur *nm* stuntman

case *nf* ❶ *(in board game)* square ❷ *(on form)* box

caserne *nf* barracks

cash *adv* **payer cash** to pay cash

casier *nm* locker

casque *nm* ❶ helmet ❷ headphones

casquette *nf* cap

cassant, e *adj* **Il m'a parlé d'un ton cassant.** He spoke to me curtly.

casse-croûte (*pl* **casse-croûte**) *nm* snack

casse-noix (*pl* **casse-noix**) *nm* nutcrackers

casse-pieds *adj (informal)* **Il est vraiment casse-pieds!** He's a real pain in the neck!

casser *vb* [**28**] to break ▷ *J'ai cassé un verre*. I've broken a glass.; **se casser** to break ▷ *Il s'est cassé la jambe au ski*. He broke his leg when he was skiing.; **se casser la tête** *(informal)* to go to a lot of trouble

casserole *nf* saucepan

casse-tête (*pl* **casse-tête**) *nm* **C'est un vrai casse-tête!** It's a real headache!

cassette *nf* cassette

cassis *nm* blackcurrant

castor *nm* beaver

catalogue *nm* catalogue

catastrophe *nf* disaster

catch *nm* wrestling

catéchisme *nm* catechism

catégorie *nf* category

catégorique *adj* firm

cathédrale *nf* cathedral

catholique *adj* Catholic
▶ *nmf* Catholic

cauchemar *nm* nightmare

cause *nf* cause; **à cause de** because of

causer *vb* [**28**] ❶ to cause ▷ *La tempête a causé beaucoup de dégâts*. The storm caused a lot of damage. ❷ to chat

caution *nf* ❶ bail ❷ deposit

cavalier *nm* ❶ rider ❷ *(at dance)* partner

cavalière *nf* rider

cave *nf* cellar

caverne *nf* cave

CD (*pl* **CD**) *nm* CD

CD-ROM (*pl* **CD-ROM**) *nm* CD-ROM

ce (*f* **cette**, *pl* **ces**) *adj*

> The masculine singular form **ce** changes to **cet** before a vowel and most words beginning with 'h'.

❶ this ▷ *Tu peux prendre ce livre*. You can take this book. ▷ *cet après-midi* this afternoon ▷ *cet hiver* this

winter; **ce livre-ci** this book; **cette voiture-ci** this car ❷ that ▷ *Je n'aime pas du tout ce film.* I don't like that film at all.; **ce livre-là** that book; **cette voiture-là** that car
▶ *pron*

> **ce** changes to **c'** before the vowel in **est**, **était** and **étaient**.

it ▷ *Ce n'est pas facile.* It's not easy.; **c'est (1)** it is ▷ *C'est vraiment trop cher.* It's really too expensive. ▷ *Ouvre, c'est moi!* Open the door, it's me! **(2)** he is ▷ *C'est un peintre du début du siècle.* He's a painter from the turn of the century. **(3)** she is ▷ *C'est une actrice très célèbre.* She's a very famous actress.; **ce sont** they are ▷ *Ce sont des amis de mes parents.* They're friends of my parents'.; **Qui est-ce?** Who is it?; **Qu'est-ce que c'est?** What is it?; **ce qui** what ▷ *C'est ce qui compte.* That's what matters.; **tout ce qui** everything that ▷ *J'ai rangé tout ce qui traînait par terre.* I've tidied up everything that was on the floor.; **ce que** what ▷ *Je vais lui dire ce que je pense.* I'm going to tell him what I think.; **tout ce que** everything ▷ *Tu peux avoir tout ce que tu veux.* You can have everything you want.

ceci *pron* this ▷ *Prends ceci, tu en auras besoin.* Take this, you'll need it.

céder *vb* [**34**] to give in ▷ *Elle a tellement insisté qu'il a fini par céder.* She went on so much that he eventually gave in.; **céder à** to give in to

cédérom *nm* CD-ROM

cédille *nf* cedilla

ceinture *nf* belt; **une ceinture de sauvetage** a lifebelt; **votre ceinture de sécurité** your seatbelt

cela *pron* ❶ it ▷ *Cela dépend.* It depends. ❷ that ▷ *Je n'aime pas cela.* I don't like that.; **C'est cela.** That's right.; **à part cela** apart from that

célèbre *adj* famous

célébrer *vb* [**34**] to celebrate

céleri *nm* **le céleri-rave** celeriac; **le céleri (en branche)** celery

célibataire *adj* single

célibataire *nmf* single person; **un célibataire** a bachelor; **une célibataire** a single woman

celle *pron* see **celui**

celles *pron* see **ceux**

cellule *nf* cell

celui (*f* **celle**, *mpl* **ceux**, *fpl* **celles**) *pron* the one ▷ *Prends celui que tu préfères.* Take the one you like best. ▷ *Je n'ai pas d'appareil photo mais je peux emprunter celui de ma sœur.* I haven't got a camera but I can borrow my sister's. ▷ *Je n'ai pas de webcam mais je peux emprunter celle de mon frère.* I haven't got a webcam but I can borrow my brother's.; **celui-ci** this one; **celle-ci** this one; **celui-là** that one; **celle-là** that one

cendre *nf* ash

cendrier *nm* ashtray

censé, e *adj* **être censé faire quelque chose** to be supposed to do something ▷ *Vous êtes censé arriver à l'heure.* You're supposed to get here on time.

cent *num* a hundred ▷ *cent euros* a hundred euros

cent is spelt with an **-s** when there are two or more hundreds, but not when it is followed by another number, as in 'four hundred and two'.

▷ *trois cents ans* three hundred years ▷ *trois cent cinquante kilomètres* three hundred and fifty kilometres
▶ *nm (currency)* cent

centaine *nf* about a hundred; **des centaines de** hundreds of
centenaire *nm* centenary
centième *adj* hundredth
centilitre *nm* centilitre
centime *nm* ❶ *(one hundredth of a euro)* cent

The euro is divided into 100 **centimes**.

❷ *(one hundredth of a franc)* centime

centimètre *nm* centimetre
central, e (*mpl* **centraux**) *adj* central
centrale *nf* power station
centre *nm* centre; **un centre commercial** a shopping centre; **un centre d'appels** a call centre
centre-ville (*pl* **centres-villes**) *nm* town centre
cependant *adv* however
cercle *nm* circle; **un cercle vicieux** a vicious circle
cercueil *nm* coffin
céréale *nf* cereal; **un pain aux cinq céréales** a multigrain loaf
cérémonie *nf* ceremony
cerf *nm* stag
cerf-volant (*pl* **cerfs-volants**) *nm* kite
cerise *nf* cherry
cerisier *nm* cherry tree
cerné, e *adj* **avoir les yeux cernés** to have shadows under one's eyes
cerner *vb* [**28**] **J'ai du mal à le cerner.** I can't figure him out.
certain, e *adj* ❶ certain ❷ some; **un certain temps** quite some time
certainement *adv* ❶ definitely ❷ of course
certains (*f* **certaines**) *pron pl* ❶ some ▷ *certains d'entre vous* some of you ▷ *certaines de ses amies* some of his friends ❷ some people ▷ *Certains pensent que le film est meilleur que le roman.* Some people think that the film is better than the novel.
certes *adv* certainly
certificat *nm* certificate
cerveau (*pl* **cerveaux**) *nm* brain
cervelle *nf* brain; **se creuser la cervelle** *(informal)* to rack one's brains
ces *adj pl* ❶ these; **ces photos-ci** these photos ❷ those; **ces livres-là** those books
cesse: **sans cesse** *adv* continually ▷ *Elle me dérange sans cesse.* She continually interrupts me.
cesser *vb* [**28**] to stop ▷ *cesser de faire quelque chose* to stop doing something
cessez-le-feu (*pl* **cessez-le-feu**) *nm* ceasefire
c'est-à-dire *adv* that is
cet *adj* *see* **ce**

cette *adj see* **ce**
ceux (*fpl* **celles**) *pron pl* the ones ▷ *Prends ceux que tu préfères.* Take the ones you like best.; **ceux-ci** these ones; **celles-ci** these ones; **ceux-là** those ones; **celles-là** those ones
chacun (*f* **chacune**) *pron* ❶ each ▷ *Il nous a donné un cadeau à chacun.* He gave us each a present. ▷ *Nous avons chacune donné dix euros.* We each gave 10 euros. ❷ everyone ▷ *Chacun fait ce qu'il veut.* Everyone does what they like.
chagrin *nm* **avoir du chagrin** to be very upset
chahut *nm* bedlam
chaîne *nf* ❶ chain ▷ *une chaîne en or* a gold chain ❷ *(on TV)* channel ▷ *Le film passe sur quelle chaîne?* Which channel is the film on?; **une chaîne hi-fi** a hi-fi system; **une chaîne stéréo** a music centre; **travailler à la chaîne** to work on an assembly line
chair *nf* flesh; **en chair et en os** in the flesh; **avoir la chair de poule** to have goose pimples
chaise *nf* chair; **une chaise longue** a deckchair
châle *nm* shawl
chaleur *nf* ❶ heat ❷ warmth
chaleureux (*f* **chaleureuse**) *adj* warm
se **chamailler** *vb* [**28**] *(informal)* to squabble ▷ *Elle se chamaille sans cesse avec son frère.* She's always squabbling with her brother.
chambre *nf* room; **une chambre à coucher** a bedroom; **une chambre d'amis** a spare room; **une chambre à un lit** a single room; **une chambre pour une personne** a single room; **une chambre pour deux personnes** a double room; **'Chambres d'hôte'** 'Bed and Breakfast'
chameau (*pl* **chameaux**) *nm* camel
champ *nm* field
champagne *nm* champagne
champignon *nm* mushroom; **un champignon de Paris** a button mushroom
champion *nm* champion
championnat *nm* championship
chance *nf* ❶ luck; **Bonne chance!** Good luck!; **par chance** luckily; **avoir de la chance** to be lucky ❷ chance
change *nm* exchange
changement *nm* change
changer *vb* [**45**] to change ▷ *Il n'a pas beaucoup changé.* He hasn't changed much.; **se changer** to get changed; **changer de** to change ▷ *Je change de chaussures et j'arrive!* I'll change my shoes and then I'll be ready!; **changer d'avis** to change one's mind ▷ *Appelle-moi si tu changes d'avis.* Give me a ring if you change your mind.; **changer de chaîne** to change the channel
chanson *nf* song
chant *nm* singing; **un chant de Noël** a Christmas carol
chantage *nm* blackmail
chanter *vb* [**28**] to sing

chanteur *nm* singer
chanteuse *nf* singer
chantier *nm* building site
chantonner *vb* [**28**] to hum
chapeau (*pl* **chapeaux**) *nm* hat
chapelle *nf* chapel
chapitre *nm* chapter
chaque *adj* ❶ every ❷ each
char *nm* *(military)* tank
charabia *nm* *(informal)* gibberish
charade *nf* ❶ riddle ❷ charade
charbon *nm* coal; **le charbon de bois** charcoal
charcuterie *nf* ❶ pork butcher's

A **charcuterie** sells cuts of pork and pork products such as sausages, salami and pâté, as well as various cooked dishes and salads.

❷ cold meats
charcutier *nm* pork butcher
chardon *nm* thistle
charger *vb* [**45**] to load; **charger quelqu'un de faire quelque chose** to tell somebody to do something
chariot *nm* *(at supermarket)* trolley
charmant, e *adj* charming
charme *nm* charm
charmer *vb* [**28**] to charm
charrue *nf* plough
chasse *nf* ❶ hunting ❷ shooting; **tirer la chasse d'eau** to flush the toilet
chasse-neige (*pl* **chasse-neige**) *nm* snowplough
chasser *vb* [**28**] ❶ to hunt ▷ *Mon père chasse le lapin.* My father hunts rabbits. ❷ to chase away ▷ *Ils ont chassé les cambrioleurs.* They chased away the robbers. ❸ to get rid of
chasseur *nm* hunter
chat *nm* ❶ cat ❷ chat
châtaigne *nf* chestnut
châtaignier *nm* chestnut tree
châtain *adj* brown
château (*pl* **châteaux**) *nm* ❶ castle; **un château fort** a castle ❷ palace
chaton *nm* kitten
chatouiller *vb* [**28**] to tickle
chatouilleux (*f* **chatouilleuse**) *adj* ticklish
chatte *nf* *(female)* cat
chatter *vb* [**28**] *(on the internet)* to chat
chaud, e *adj* ❶ warm; **avoir chaud** to be warm ❷ hot ▷ *Il fait chaud aujourd'hui.* It's hot today.
chauffage *nm* heating; **le chauffage central** central heating
chauffe-eau (*pl* **chauffe-eau**) *nm* water heater
chauffer *vb* [**28**] to heat ▷ *Je vais mettre de l'eau à chauffer pour faire du thé.* I'm going to heat some water to make tea.
chauffeur *nm* driver
chaume *nm* **un toit de chaume** a thatched roof
chaussée *nf* road surface
chausser *vb* [**28**] **Vous chaussez du combien?** What size shoe do you take?
chaussette *nf* sock
chausson *nm* slipper; **un chausson aux pommes** an apple turnover
chaussure *nf* shoe; **les**

chaussures de ski ski boots

chauve *adj* bald

chauve-souris (*pl* **chauves-souris**) *nf* *(animal)* bat

Word for word, this means 'bald mouse'.

chef *nm* ❶ head; **le chef de l'État** the Head of State ❷ boss; **un chef d'entreprise** a company director ❸ chef; **un chef d'orchestre** a conductor

chef-d'œuvre (*pl* **chefs-d'œuvre**) *nm* masterpiece

chemin *nm* ❶ path ❷ way; **en chemin** on the way; **le chemin de fer** the railway

cheminée *nf* ❶ chimney ❷ fireplace

chemise *nf* ❶ shirt; **une chemise de nuit** a nightdress ❷ folder

chemisier *nm* blouse

chêne *nm* oak

chenil *nm* kennels

chenille *nf* caterpillar

chèque *nm* cheque; **les chèques de voyage** traveller's cheques

chéquier *nm* cheque book

cher (*f* **chère**) *adj, adv* ❶ dear ▷ *Chère Mélusine ...* Dear Mélusine ... ❷ expensive ▷ *C'est trop cher.* It's too expensive. ▷ *coûter cher* to be expensive

chercher *vb* **[28]** ❶ to look for ▷ *Je cherche mes clés.* I'm looking for my keys. ❷ to look up ▷ *chercher un mot dans le dictionnaire* to look up a word in the dictionary; **aller chercher (1)** to go to get ▷ *Elle est allée chercher du pain.* She's gone to get some bread. **(2)** to pick up ▷ *J'irai te chercher à la gare.* I'll pick you up at the station.

chercheur *nm* scientist

chercheuse *nf* scientist

chère *adj f see* **cher**

chéri, e *adj* darling ▷ *ma petite fille chérie* my darling daughter

chéri *nm* darling; **mon chéri** darling

chérie *nf* darling

cheval (*pl* **chevaux**) *nm* horse; **un cheval de course** a racehorse; **à cheval** on horseback; **faire du cheval** to go riding

chevalier *nm* knight

chevalière *nf* signet ring

chevalin, e *adj* **une boucherie chevaline** a horsemeat butcher's

chevaux *nmpl see* **cheval**

chevet *nm* **une table de chevet** a bedside table; **une lampe de chevet** a bedside lamp

cheveux *nmpl* hair *sg* ▷ *Elle a les cheveux courts.* She's got short hair.

cheville *nf* ankle

chèvre *nf* goat; **le fromage de chèvre** goat's cheese

chevreau (*pl* **chevreaux**) *nm* *(animal, leather)* kid

chèvrefeuille *nm* honeysuckle

chevreuil *nm* ❶ roe deer ❷ venison

chewing-gum *nm* chewing gum

chez *prep* **chez Pierre (1)** at Pierre's house **(2)** to Pierre's house; **chez moi (1)** at my house ▷ *Mes amis sont restés chez moi.* My friends stayed at my house. **(2)** to my house ▷ *Allons chez moi.* Let's go to my house.; **Je**

rentre chez moi. I'm going home.; **chez le dentiste (1)** at the dentist's ▷ *J'ai rendez-vous chez le dentiste demain matin.* I've got an appointment at the dentist's tomorrow morning. **(2)** to the dentist's ▷ *Je vais chez le dentiste.* I'm going to the dentist's.

chic *adj* ❶ smart ❷ nice

chicorée *nf* endive

chien *nm* dog; **'Attention, chien méchant'** 'Beware of the dog'

chienne *nf (dog)* bitch

chiffon *nm* cloth

chiffonner *vb* [**28**] to crease

chiffre *nm* figure; **les chiffres romains** Roman numerals

chignon *nm (in hair)* bun

Chili *nm* Chile

chimie *nf* chemistry

chimique *adj* chemical; **les produits chimiques** chemicals

Chine *nf* China

chinois, e *adj, n* Chinese ▷ *Il apprend le chinois.* He's learning Chinese.; **un Chinois** *(man)* a Chinese; **une Chinoise** *(woman)* a Chinese; **les Chinois** the Chinese

chiot *nm* puppy

chips *nfpl* crisps

chirurgical, e (*mpl* **chirurgicaux**) *adj* **une intervention chirurgicale** an operation

chirurgie *nf* surgery; **la chirurgie esthétique** plastic surgery

chirurgien *nm* surgeon

choc *nm* shock; **Elle est encore sous le choc.** She's still in shock.

chocolat *nm* chocolate; **un chocolat chaud** a hot chocolate; **le chocolat à croquer** dark chocolate

chœur *nm* choir

choisir *vb* [**38**] to choose

choix *nm* ❶ choice; **avoir le choix** to have the choice ❷ selection

chômage *nm* unemployment; **être au chômage** to be unemployed

chômeur *nm* unemployed person

chômeuse *nf* unemployed woman

choquer *vb* [**28**] to shock

chorale *nf* choir

chose *nf* thing; **C'est peu de chose.** It's nothing really.

chou (*pl* **choux**) *nm* cabbage; **les choux de Bruxelles** Brussels sprouts; **un chou à la crème** a choux bun

chouchou *nm (informal)* teacher's pet

choucroute *nf (with sausages and ham)* sauerkraut

chouette *nf* owl
▶ *adj (informal)* brilliant

chou-fleur (*pl* **choux-fleurs**) *nm* cauliflower

chrétien (*f* **chrétienne**) *adj* Christian

Christ *nm* Christ

chronologique *adj* chronological

chronomètre *nm* stopwatch

chronométrer *vb* [**34**] to time

chrysanthème *nm* chrysanthemum

Chrysanthemums are strongly associated with funerals in France.

chuchoter *vb* [**28**] to whisper
chut *excl* shh!
chute *nf* fall; **faire une chute** to fall; **une chute d'eau** a waterfall; **la chute des cheveux** hair loss; **les chutes de neige** snowfalls
Chypre *n* Cyprus
-ci *adv* **ce livre-ci** this book; **ces bottes-ci** these boots
cible *nf* target
ciboulette *nf* chives
cicatrice *nf* scar
se **cicatriser** *vb* [**28**] to heal up ▷ *Cette plaie s'est vite cicatrisée.* This wound has healed up quickly.
ci-contre *adv* opposite
ci-dessous *adv* below
ci-dessus *adv* above
cidre *nm* cider
ciel *nm* ❶ sky ❷ heaven
cierge *nm (in church)* candle
cigale *nf* cicada
cigare *nm* cigar
cigarette *nf* cigarette
cigogne *nf* stork
ci-joint *adv* attached ▷ *Veuillez trouver ci-joint mon curriculum vitae.* Please find attached my CV.
cil *nm* eyelash
ciment *nm* cement
cimetière *nm* cemetery
cinéaste *nmf* film-maker
cinéma *nm* cinema
cinq *num* five ▷ *Il a cinq ans.* He's five.; **le cinq février** the fifth of February
cinquantaine *nf* about fifty; **Il a la cinquantaine.** He's in his fifties.
cinquante *num* fifty ▷ *Il a cinquante ans.* He's fifty.; **cinquante et un** fifty-one; **cinquante-deux** fifty-two
cinquième *adj* fifth
▶ *nf* year 8
In French secondary schools, years are counted from the **sixième** (youngest) to **première** and **terminale** (oldest).
cintre *nm* coat hanger
cirage *nm* shoe polish
circonflexe *adj* **un accent circonflexe** a circumflex
circonstance *nf* circumstance
circulation *nf* ❶ traffic ❷ circulation
circuler *vb* [**28**] to run ▷ *Il n'y a qu'un bus sur trois qui circule.* Only one bus in three is running.
cire *nf* wax
ciré *nm* oilskin jacket
cirer *vb* [**28**] *(shoes, floor)* to polish
cirque *nm* circus
ciseaux *nmpl* **une paire de ciseaux** a pair of scissors
citadin *nm* city dweller
citation *nf* quotation
cité *nf* estate ▷ *J'habite dans une cité.* I live on an estate.; **une cité universitaire** halls of residence; **une cité-dortoir** a dormitory town
citer *vb* [**28**] to quote
citoyen *nm* citizen
citoyenne *nf* citizen
citoyenneté *nf* citizenship
citron *nm* lemon; **un citron vert** a lime; **un citron pressé** a fresh lemon juice
citronnade *nf* still lemonade
citrouille *nf* pumpkin

civet *nm* stew
civil, e *adj* civilian; **en civil** in civilian clothes
civilisation *nf* civilization
civique *adj* **l'instruction civique** PSHE
clair, e *adj, adv* ❶ light ❷ *(water)* clear; **voir clair** to see clearly; **le clair de lune** moonlight
clairement *adv* clearly
clairière *nf* clearing
clandestin, e *adj* **un passager clandestin** a stowaway
claque *nf* slap
claquer *vb* [**28**] ❶ to bang ▷ *On entend des volets qui claquent*. You can hear shutters banging. ❷ to slam ▷ *Elle est partie en claquant la porte*. She left, slamming the door behind her.
claquettes *nfpl* **faire des claquettes** to tap-dance
clarinette *nf* clarinet
classe *nf* ❶ class ❷ classroom
classer *vb* [**28**] to arrange ▷ *Les livres sont classés par ordre alphabétique*. The books are arranged in alphabetical order.
classeur *nm* ring binder
classique *adj* ❶ classical ❷ classic
clavier *nm (of computer, typewriter)* keyboard
clé *nf* ❶ key ❷ clef
clef *nf* = **clé**
client *nm* customer
cliente *nf* customer
clientèle *nf* customers
cligner *vb* [**28**] **cligner des yeux** to blink
clignotant *nm* indicator
climat *nm* climate
climatisation *nf* air conditioning
climatisé, e *adj* air-conditioned
clin d'œil (*pl* **clins d'œil**) *nm* wink; **en un clin d'œil** in a flash
clinique *nf* private hospital
cliquer *vb* [**28**] to click ▷ *cliquer sur une icône* to click on an icon
clochard *nm* tramp
cloche *nf* bell
clocher *nm* ❶ church tower ❷ steeple
clone *nm* clone
cloner *vb* [**28**] to clone
clou *nm* nail; **un clou de girofle** a clove
clown *nm* clown
club *nm* club
cobaye *nm* guinea pig
coca *nm* Coke®
cocaïne *nf* cocaine
coccinelle *nf* ladybird
cocher *vb* [**28**] to tick ▷ *Cochez la bonne réponse*. Tick the right answer.
cochon (*f* **cochonne**) *adj (informal)* dirty
▶ *nm* pig; **un cochon d'Inde** a guinea pig
cocktail *nm* ❶ cocktail ❷ cocktail party
coco *nm* **une noix de coco** a coconut
cocorico *excl* ❶ cock-a-doodle-doo! ❷ three cheers for France!

The symbol of France is the cockerel and so **cocorico!** is sometimes used as an expression of French national pride.

cocotte *nf (pan)* casserole; **une cocotte-minute®** a pressure cooker

code *nm* code; **le code de la route** the highway code; **le code postal** the postcode

cœur *nm* heart; **avoir bon cœur** to be kind-hearted; **la dame de cœur** the queen of hearts; **avoir mal au cœur** to feel sick; **par cœur** by heart ▷ *apprendre quelque chose par cœur* to learn something by heart

coffre *nm* ❶ *(of car)* boot ❷ *(furniture)* chest

coffre-fort (*pl* **coffres-forts**) *nm* safe

coffret *nm* **un coffret à bijoux** a jewellery box

cognac *nm* brandy

se **cogner** *vb* [**28**] **se cogner à quelque chose** to bang into something

coiffé, e *adj* **Tu es bien coiffée.** Your hair looks nice.

coiffer *vb* [**28**] **se coiffer** to do one's hair

coiffeur *nm* hairdresser

coiffure *nf* hairstyle; **un salon de coiffure** a hairdresser's

coin *nm* corner ▷ *au coin de la rue* on the corner of the street; **Tu habites dans le coin?** Do you live near here?; **Je ne suis pas du coin.** I'm not from here.; **le bistrot du coin** the local pub

coincé, e *adj* ❶ stuck ❷ stuffy

coincer *vb* [**12**] to jam ▷ *La porte est coincée.* The door's jammed.

coïncidence *nf* coincidence

col *nm* ❶ collar ❷ *(of mountain)* pass

colère *nf* anger; **Je suis en colère.** I'm angry.; **se mettre en colère** to get angry

colin *nm* hake

colique *nf* diarrhoea

colis *nm* parcel

collaborer *vb* [**28**] to collaborate

collant, e *adj* ❶ sticky ❷ clingy ▸ *nm* tights

colle *nf* ❶ glue ❷ detention; **Je n'en sais rien: tu me poses une colle.** I really don't know: you've got me there.

collecte *nf (of money)* collection

collection *nf* collection

collectionner *vb* [**28**] to collect

collège *nm* secondary school

In France pupils go to a **collège** between the ages of 11 and 15, and then to a **lycée** until the age of 18.

collégien *nm* schoolboy

collégienne *nf* schoolgirl

collègue *nmf* colleague

coller *vb* [**28**] ❶ to stick ▷ *Il y a un chewing-gum collé sous la chaise.* There's a bit of chewing gum stuck under the chair. ▷ *Ce timbre ne colle plus.* This stamp won't stick on. ❷ to press ▷ *J'ai collé mon oreille au mur.* I pressed my ear against the wall.

collier *nm* ❶ necklace ❷ *(of dog, cat)* collar

colline *nf* hill

collision *nf* crash

colombe *nf* dove

colonie *nf* **aller en colonie de**

vacances to go to summer camp
colonne *nf* column; **la colonne vertébrale** the spine
colorant *nm* colouring
coloris *nm* colour
coma *nm* coma ▷ *être dans le coma* to be in a coma
combat *nm* fighting; **un combat de boxe** a boxing match
combattant *nm* **un ancien combattant** a war veteran
combattre *vb* [9] to fight
combien *adv* ❶ how much ▷ *Vous en voulez combien? Un kilo?* How much do you want? One kilo?; **C'est combien?** How much is that? ▷ *Combien est-ce que ça coûte?* How much does it cost? ▷ *Combien ça fait?* How much does it come to? ❷ how many ▷ *Tu en veux combien? Deux?* How many do you want? Two?; **combien de (1)** how much ▷ *Combien de purée est-ce que je vous sers?* How much mashed potato shall I give you? **(2)** how many ▷ *Combien de personnes as-tu invitées?* How many people have you invited?; **combien de temps** how long ▷ *Combien de temps est-ce que tu seras absente?* How long will you be away?; **Il y a combien de temps?** How long ago? ▷ *Il est parti il y a combien de temps?* How long ago did he leave?; **On est le combien aujourd'hui? — On est le vingt.** What's the date today? — It's the 20th.
combinaison *nf* ❶ combination ❷ *(petticoat)* slip; **une combinaison de plongée** a wetsuit; **une combinaison de ski** a ski suit
comble *nm* **Alors ça, c'est le comble!** That's the last straw!
comédie *nf* comedy; **une comédie musicale** a musical
comédien *nm* actor
comédienne *nf* actress
comestible *adj* edible
comique *adj* comical ▶ *nmf* comedian
comité *nm* committee
commandant *nm (of ship, plane)* captain
commande *nf* order; **être aux commandes** to be at the controls
commander *vb* [28] ❶ to order ▷ *J'ai commandé une robe sur catalogue.* I've ordered a dress from a catalogue. ❷ to give orders ▷ *C'est moi qui commande ici, pas vous!* I give the orders here, not you!
comme *conj, adv* ❶ like ▷ *Il est comme son père.* He's like his father. ❷ for ▷ *Qu'est-ce que tu veux comme dessert?* What would you like for pudding? ❸ as ▷ *J'ai travaillé comme serveuse cet été.* I worked as a waitress this summer. ▷ *Faites comme vous voulez.* Do as you like.; **comme ça** like this ▷ *Ça se plie comme ça.* You fold it like this.; **comme il faut** properly ▷ *Mets le couvert comme il faut!* Set the table properly!; **Comme tu as grandi!** How you've grown!; **Regarde comme c'est beau!** Look, isn't it

lovely!; **comme ci comme ça** so-so

commencement *nm* beginning

commencer *vb* [**12**] to start ▷ *Les cours commencent à huit heures.* Lessons start at 8 o'clock.

comment *adv* how; **Comment allez-vous?** How are you?; **Comment dit-on 'pomme' en anglais?** How do you say 'pomme' in English?; **Comment s'appelle-t-il?** What's his name?; **Comment?** What did you say?

commentaire *nm* comment

commérages *nmpl* gossip *sg*

commerçant *nm* shopkeeper

commerce *nm* ❶ trade ▷ *le commerce extérieur* foreign trade; **le commerce électronique** e-commerce ❷ business ▷ *Il fait des études de commerce.* He's studying business. ❸ shop ▷ *tenir un commerce* to have a shop; **On trouve ça dans le commerce.** You can find it in the shops.

commercial, e (*mpl* **commerciaux**) *adj* **un centre commercial** a shopping centre

commettre *vb* [**47**] to commit

commissaire *nmf* police superintendent

commissariat *nm* police station

commissions *nfpl* shopping *sg*

commode *nf* chest of drawers ▶ *adj* handy; **Son père n'est pas commode.** His father is a difficult character.

commun, e *adj* shared; **en commun** in common; **les transports en commun** public transport; **mettre quelque chose en commun** to share something

communauté *nf* community

communication *nf* communication; **une communication téléphonique** a telephone call

communion *nf* communion

communiquer *vb* [**28**] to communicate

communiste *adj* communist

compact, e *adj* compact; **un disque compact** a compact disc

compagne *nf* ❶ companion ❷ *(living together)* partner

compagnie *nf* company; **une compagnie d'assurances** an insurance company; **une compagnie aérienne** an airline

compagnon *nm* ❶ companion ❷ *(living together)* partner

comparaison *nf* comparison

comparer *vb* [**28**] to compare

compartiment *nm (on train)* compartment

compas *nm (for drawing circles)* compass

compatible *adj* compatible

compétence *nf* competence

compétent, e *adj* competent

compétitif (*f* **compétitive**) *adj* competitive

compétition *nf* competition; **avoir l'esprit de compétition** to be competitive

complet (*f* **complète**) *adj* ❶ complete ❷ full; **'complet'** 'no vacancies'; **le pain complet**

wholemeal bread
▶ *nm (for man)* suit
complètement *adv* completely
compléter *vb* [**34**] to complete
▷ *Complétez les phrases suivantes.* Complete the following sentences.
complexe *adj* complex
complexé, e *adj* hung up
complication *nf* complication
complice *nmf* accomplice
compliqué, e *adj* complicated
complot *nm* plot
comportement *nm* behaviour
comporter *vb* [**28**] ❶ to consist of
▷ *Le château comporte trois parties.* The castle consists of three parts. ❷ to have ▷ *Ce modèle comporte un écran couleur.* This model has a colour screen.; **se comporter** to behave
composer *vb* [**28**] *(music, text)* to compose; **composer un numéro** to dial a number; **se composer de** to consist of
compositeur *nm* composer
composition *nf* test
compostage *nm* date stamping
composter *vb* [**28**] to punch
▷ *N'oublie pas de composter ton billet avant de monter dans le train.* Remember to punch your ticket before you get on the train.

In France you have to punch your ticket on the platform to validate it before getting onto the train.

compote *nf* stewed fruit; **la compote de prunes** stewed plums
compréhensible *adj* understandable
compréhensif (*f* **compréhensive**) *adj* understanding

Be careful! **compréhensif** does not mean **comprehensive**.

compréhension *nf*
❶ comprehension ❷ sympathy
▷ *Elle a fait preuve de beaucoup de compréhension à mon égard.* She showed a lot of sympathy for me.
comprendre *vb* [**65**] ❶ to understand ▷ *Je ne comprends pas ce que vous dites.* I don't understand what you're saying. ❷ to include ▷ *Le forfait ne comprend pas la location des skis.* The price doesn't include ski hire.
comprimé *nm* tablet
compris, e *adj* included ▷ *Le service n'est pas compris.* Service is not included.; **y compris** including; **non compris** excluding; **cent euros tout compris** 100 euros all-inclusive
compromettre *vb* [**47**] to compromise
compromis *nm* compromise
comptabilité *nf* accounting
comptable *nmf* accountant
comptant *adv* **payer comptant** to pay cash
compte *nm* account; **Le compte est bon.** That's the right amount.; **tenir compte de (1)** to take into account **(2)** to take notice of; **travailler à son compte** to be self-employed; **en fin de compte** all things considered

compter *vb* [**28**] to count
compte rendu (*pl* **comptes rendus**) *nm* report
compteur *nm* meter
comptoir *nm* bar
se **concentrer** *vb* [**28**] to concentrate
conception *nf* design
concernant *prep* regarding
concerner *vb* [**28**] to concern ▷ *en ce qui me concerne* as far as I'm concerned; **Je ne me sens pas concerné.** I don't feel it's anything to do with me.
concert *nm* concert
concierge *nmf* caretaker
conclure *vb* [**13**] to conclude
conclusion *nf* conclusion
concombre *nm* cucumber
concorder *vb* [**28**] to tally ▷ *Les dates concordent.* The dates tally.
concours *nm* ❶ competition ❷ *(for a job or a place in a school)* competitive exam
concret (*f* **concrète**) *adj* concrete
conçu *vb* designed ▷ *Ces appartements sont très mal conçus.* These flats are very badly designed.
concurrence *nf* competition
concurrent *nm* competitor
condamner *vb* [**28**] ❶ to sentence ▷ *condamner à mort* to sentence to death ❷ to condemn ▷ *Le gouvernement a condamné cette décision.* The government condemned this decision.
condition *nf* condition; **à condition que** provided that; **les conditions de travail** working conditions
conditionnel *nm* conditional tense
conducteur *nm* driver
conductrice *nf* driver
conduire *vb* [**23**] to drive ▷ *Est-ce que tu sais conduire?* Can you drive?; **se conduire** to behave ▷ *Il s'est mal conduit.* He behaved badly.
conduite *nf* behaviour
conférence *nf* ❶ lecture ❷ conference
se **confesser** *vb* [**28**] to go to confession
confettis *nmpl* confetti
confiance *nf* ❶ trust; **avoir confiance en quelqu'un** to trust somebody ❷ confidence; **Tu peux avoir confiance. Il sera à l'heure.** You don't need to worry. He'll be on time.; **confiance en soi** self-confidence
confiant, e *adj* confident
confidences *nfpl* **faire des confidences à quelqu'un** to confide in someone
confidentiel (*f* **confidentielle**) *adj* confidential
confier *vb* [**19**] **se confier à quelqu'un** to confide in somebody ▷ *Elle s'est confiée à sa meilleure amie.* She confided in her best friend.
confirmer *vb* [**28**] to confirm
confiserie *nf* sweet shop
confisquer *vb* [**28**] to confiscate
confit, e *adj* **des fruits confits** crystallized fruits
confiture *nf* jam; **la confiture**

d'oranges marmalade
conflit *nm* conflict
confondre *vb* [**69**] to mix up ▷ *On le confond souvent avec son frère.* People often mix him up with his brother.
confort *nm* comfort; **tout confort** with all mod cons
confortable *adj* comfortable
confus, e *adj* ❶ unclear ❷ embarrassed
confusion *nf* ❶ confusion ❷ embarrassment
congé *nm* holiday; **en congé** on holiday; **un congé de maladie** sick leave
congélateur *nm* freezer
congeler *vb* [**1**] to freeze
conjonction *nf* conjunction
conjonctivite *nf* conjunctivitis
conjugaison *nf* conjugation
connaissance *nf* ❶ knowledge ❷ acquaintance; **perdre connaissance** to lose consciousness; **faire la connaissance de quelqu'un** to meet somebody
connaître *vb* [**14**] to know ▷ *Je ne connais pas du tout cette région.* I don't know this area at all.; **Ils se sont connus à Nantes.** They first met in Nantes.; **s'y connaître en quelque chose** to know about something ▷ *Je ne m'y connais pas beaucoup en musique classique.* I don't know much about classical music.
se **connecter** *vb* [**28**] to log on
connu, e *adj* well-known
conquérir *vb* [**2**] to conquer
consacrer *vb* [**28**] to devote ▷ *Il consacre beaucoup de temps à ses enfants.* He devotes a lot of time to his children.
conscience *nf* conscience; **prendre conscience de** to become aware of
consciencieux (*f* **consciencieuse**) *adj* conscientious
conscient, e *adj* conscious
consécutif (*f* **consécutive**) *adj* consecutive
conseil *nm* advice; **un conseil** a piece of advice
conseiller *vb* [**28**] ❶ to advise ▷ *Il a été mal conseillé.* He has been badly advised. ❷ to recommend ▷ *Il m'a conseillé ce livre.* He recommended this book to me.
▶ *nm* ❶ *(political)* councillor ❷ adviser ▷ *le conseiller d'orientation* the careers adviser
consentement *nm* consent
consentir *vb* [**77**] to agree ▷ *consentir à quelque chose* to agree to something
conséquence *nf* consequence; **en conséquence** consequently
conséquent (*f* **conséquente**) *adj* **par conséquent** consequently
conservatoire *nm* school of music
conserve *nf* tin; **une boîte de conserve** a tin; **les conserves** tinned food; **en conserve** tinned
conserver *vb* [**28**] to keep ▷ *J'ai conservé toutes ses lettres.* I've kept all her letters.; **se conserver** to keep ▷ *Ce pain se conserve plus d'une*

semaine. This bread will keep for more than a week.

considérable *adj* considerable

considération *nf* **prendre quelque chose en considération** to take something into consideration

considérer *vb* [**34**] **considérer que** to believe that ▷ *Je considère que le gouvernement devrait investir davantage dans l'éducation.* I believe that the government should invest more money in education.

consigne *nf* left-luggage office; **une consigne automatique** a left-luggage locker

consistant, e *adj* substantial

consister *vb* [**28**] **consister à** to consist of; **En quoi consiste votre travail?** What does your job involve?

console de jeu *nf* games console

consoler *vb* [**28**] to console

consommateur *nm* ❶ consumer ❷ *(in café)* customer

consommation *nf* ❶ consumption ❷ drink

consommer *vb* [**28**] ❶ to use ▷ *Ces grosses voitures consomment beaucoup d'essence.* These big cars use a lot of petrol. ❷ to have a drink ▷ *Est-ce qu'on peut consommer à la terrasse?* Can we have drinks outside?

consonne *nf* consonant

constamment *adv* constantly

constant, e *adj* constant

constater *vb* [**28**] to notice

constipé, e *adj* constipated

constitué, e *adj* **être constitué de** to consist of

constituer *vb* [**28**] to make up ▷ *les États qui constituent la Fédération russe* the states which make up the Russian Federation

construction *nf* building; **une maison en construction** a house being built

construire *vb* [**23**] to build ▷ *Ils font construire une maison neuve.* They're having a new house built.

consulat *nm* consulate

consultation *nf* **les heures de consultation** surgery hours

consulter *vb* [**28**] ❶ to consult ▷ *Il vaut toujours mieux consulter un médecin.* It's always best to consult a doctor. ❷ to see patients ▷ *Le docteur ne consulte pas le samedi.* The doctor doesn't see patients on Saturdays.

contact *nm* contact; **Il a le contact facile.** He's very approachable.; **garder le contact avec quelqu'un** to keep in touch with somebody

contacter *vb* [**28**] to get in touch with ▷ *Je te contacterai dès que j'aurai des nouvelles.* I'll get in touch with you as soon as I have some news.

contagieux (*f* **contagieuse**) *adj* infectious

contaminer *vb* [**28**] to contaminate

conte de fées (*pl* **contes de fées**) *nm* fairy tale

contempler *vb* [**28**] to gaze at

contemporain, e *adj* contemporary; **un auteur**

contemporain a modern writer

contenir *vb* [**83**] to contain ▷ *un portefeuille contenant de l'argent* a wallet containing money

content, e *adj* glad ▷ *Je suis content que tu sois venu.* I'm glad you've come.; **content de** pleased with

contenter *vb* [**28**] to please ▷ *Il est difficile à contenter.* He's hard to please.; **Je me contente de peu.** I can make do with very little.

contesté, e *adj* controversial

continent *nm* continent

continu, e *adj* continuous; **faire la journée continue** to work without taking a full lunch break

continuellement *adv* constantly

continuer *vb* [**28**] to carry on ▷ *Continuez sans moi!* Carry on without me! ▷ *Il ne veut pas continuer ses études.* He doesn't want to carry on studying.; **continuer à faire quelque chose** to go on doing something ▷ *Ils ont continué à regarder la télé sans me dire bonjour.* They went on watching TV without saying hello to me.; **continuer de faire quelque chose** to keep on doing something ▷ *Il continue de fumer malgré son asthme.* He keeps on smoking, despite his asthma.

contourner *vb* [**28**] to go round ▷ *La route contourne la ville.* The road goes round the town.

contraceptif *nm* contraceptive

contraception *nf* contraception

contractuel *nm* traffic warden

contradiction *nf* contradiction; **par esprit de contradiction** just to be awkward

contraire *nm* opposite; **au contraire** on the contrary

contrarier *vb* [**19**] ❶ to annoy ▷ *Il avait l'air contrarié.* He looked annoyed. ❷ to upset ▷ *Est-ce que tu serais contrariée si je ne venais pas?* Would you be upset if I didn't come?

contraste *nm* contrast

contrat *nm* contract

contravention *nf* parking ticket

contre *prep* ❶ against ▷ *Ne mets pas ton vélo contre le mur.* Don't put your bike against the wall. ▷ *Tu es pour ou contre ce projet?* Are you for or against this plan? ❷ for ▷ *échanger quelque chose contre quelque chose* to swap something for something; **par contre** on the other hand

contrebande *nf* smuggling; **des produits de contrebande** smuggled goods

contrebasse *nf* double bass

contrecœur: **à contrecœur** *adv* reluctantly

contredire *vb* [**27**] to contradict ▷ *Il ne supporte pas d'être contredit.* He can't stand being contradicted.

contre-indication *nf* **'Contre-indication en cas d'eczéma'** 'Not to be used by people with eczema'

contresens *nm* mistranslation

contretemps *nm* **Désolé d'être en retard: j'ai eu un contretemps.** Sorry I'm late: I was held up.

contribuer *vb* [**28**] **contribuer à** to

contribute to ▷ *Est-ce que tu veux contribuer au cadeau pour Marie?* Do you want to contribute to Marie's present?

contrôle *nm* ❶ control ▷ *le contrôle des passeports* passport control ❷ check; **un contrôle d'identité** an identity check; **le contrôle des billets** ticket inspection ❸ test ▷ *un contrôle antidopage* a drugs test; **le contrôle continu** continuous assessment

contrôler *vb* [**28**] to check ▷ *Personne n'a contrôlé mon billet.* Nobody checked my ticket.

contrôleur *nm* ticket inspector

controversé, e *adj* controversial

convaincre *vb* [**86**] ❶ to persuade ▷ *Il a essayé de me convaincre de rester.* He tried to persuade me to stay. ❷ to convince ▷ *Tu n'as pas l'air convaincu.* You don't look convinced.

convalescence *nf* convalescence

convenable *adj* decent; **Ce n'est pas convenable.** It's bad manners.

convenir *vb* [**89**] **convenir à** to suit ▷ *Est-ce que cette date te convient?* Does this date suit you?; **convenir de** to agree on ▷ *Nous avons convenu d'une date.* We've agreed on a date.

conventionné, e *adj* **un médecin conventionné** a Health Service doctor

All doctors in France charge for treatment, but patients of Health Service doctors get their money refunded by the government.

convenu, e *adj* agreed

conversation *nf* conversation

convocation *nf* notification

convoquer *vb* [**28**] **convoquer quelqu'un à une réunion** to invite somebody to a meeting

cool *adj (informal)* cool

coopération *nf* co-operation

coopérer *vb* [**34**] to co-operate

coordonnées *nfpl* contact details

copain *nm (informal)* ❶ friend ❷ boyfriend

copie *nf* ❶ copy ❷ paper ▷ *Il a des copies à corriger ce week-end.* He's got some papers to mark this weekend.

copier *vb* [**19**] to copy; **copier-coller** to copy and paste

copieux (*f* **copieuse**) *adj* hearty

copine *nf (informal)* ❶ friend ❷ girlfriend

coq *nm* cockerel

coque *nf (of boat)* hull; **un œuf à la coque** a soft-boiled egg

coquelicot *nm* poppy

coqueluche *nf* whooping cough

coquillage *nm* ❶ shellfish ❷ shell

coquille *nf* shell; **une coquille d'œuf** an eggshell; **une coquille Saint-Jacques** a scallop

coquin, e *adj* cheeky

cor *nm* horn

corbeau (*pl* **corbeaux**) *nm* crow

corbeille *nf* ❶ basket ❷ *(of a computer)* recycle bin; **une corbeille à papier** a wastepaper basket

corde *nf* ❶ rope ❷ *(of violin, tennis racket)* string; **une corde à linge**

a clothes line
cordonnerie *nf* shoe repair shop
cordonnier *nm* cobbler
coriace *adj* tough
corne *nf* horn
cornemuse *nf* bagpipes
cornet *nm* **un cornet de frites** a bag of chips; **un cornet de glace** an ice cream cone
cornichon *nm* gherkin
Cornouailles *nf* Cornwall
corps *nm* body
correct, e *adj* ❶ correct ❷ reasonable ▷ *un salaire correct* a reasonable salary
correction *nf* correction
correspondance *nf* ❶ correspondence; **un cours par correspondance** a correspondence course ❷ *(train, plane)* connection
correspondant *nm* penfriend
correspondre *vb* [**69**] to correspond; **Faites correspondre les phrases.** Match the sentences together.
corridor *nm* corridor
corriger *vb* [**45**] to mark ▷ *Vous pouvez corriger mon test?* Can you mark my test?
corsage *nm* blouse
corse *adj, nmf* Corsican; **un Corse** *(man)* a Corsican; **une Corse** *(woman)* a Corsican
corvée *nf* chore
costaud, e *adj* brawny
costume *nm* ❶ *(man's)* suit ❷ *(theatre)* costume
côte *nf* ❶ coastline; **la Côte d'Azur** the French Riviera ❷ hill ❸ rib ❹ chop; **une côte de bœuf** a rib of beef; **côte à côte** side by side
côté *nm* side; **à côté de (1)** next to ▷ *Le café est à côté du sucre.* The coffee's next to the sugar. **(2)** next door to ▷ *Il habite à côté de chez moi.* He lives next door to me.; **de l'autre côté** on the other side; **De quel côté est-il parti?** Which way did he go?; **mettre quelque chose de côté** to save something
côtelette *nf* chop
cotisation *nf* ❶ *(to club, union)* subscription ❷ *(to pension, national insurance)* contributions; **cotisations sociales** social security contributions
coton *nm* cotton; **le coton hydrophile** cotton wool
Coton-tige® (*pl* **Cotons-tiges**) *nm* cotton bud
cou *nm* neck
couchant *adj* **le soleil couchant** the setting sun
couche *nf* ❶ layer ▷ *la couche d'ozone* the ozone layer ❷ *(of paint, varnish)* coat ❸ nappy
couché, e *adj* ❶ lying down ▷ *Il était couché sur le tapis.* He was lying on the carpet. ❷ in bed ▷ *Il est déjà couché.* He's already in bed.
coucher *nm* **un coucher de soleil** a sunset
se **coucher** *vb* [**28**] ❶ to go to bed ❷ *(sun)* to set
couchette *nf* ❶ *(on train)* couchette ❷ *(on boat)* bunk
coude *nm* elbow

coudre *vb* [**15**] ❶ to sew ▷ *J'aime coudre.* I like sewing. ❷ to sew on ▷ *Il ne sait même pas coudre un bouton.* He can't even sew a button on.

couette *nf* duvet

couettes *nfpl* bunches

couler *vb* [**28**] ❶ to run ▷ *Ne laissez pas couler les robinets.* Don't leave the taps running. ❷ to flow ▷ *La rivière coulait lentement.* The river was flowing slowly. ❸ to leak ▷ *Mon stylo coule.* My pen's leaking. ❹ to sink ▷ *Le bateau a coulé.* The boat sank.

couleur *nf* colour; **Tu as pris des couleurs.** You've got a tan.

couleuvre *nf* grass snake

coulisses *nfpl (in theatre)* wings; **dans les coulisses** behind the scenes

couloir *nm* corridor

coup *nm* ❶ knock ▷ *donner un coup à quelque chose* to give something a knock ❷ blow; **Il m'a donné un coup!** He hit me!; **un coup de pied** a kick; **un coup de poing** a punch ❸ shock; **un coup de feu** a shot; **un coup de fil** *(informal)* a ring; **donner un coup de main à quelqu'un** to give somebody a hand; **un coup d'œil** a quick look; **attraper un coup de soleil** to get sunburnt; **un coup de téléphone** a phone call; **un coup de tonnerre** a clap of thunder; **boire un coup** *(informal)* to have a drink; **après coup** afterwards; **à tous les coups** *(informal)* every time; **du premier coup** first time; **sur le coup** at first

coupable *adj* guilty
▶ *nmf* culprit

coupe *nf (sport)* cup; **une coupe de cheveux** a haircut; **une coupe de champagne** a glass of champagne

coupe-ongle (*pl* **coupe-ongles**) *nm* nail clippers

couper *vb* [**28**] ❶ to cut ❷ to turn off ▷ *couper le courant* to turn off the electricity ❸ to take a short-cut ▷ *On peut couper par la forêt.* We could take a short-cut through the woods.; **couper l'appétit** to spoil one's appetite; **se couper** to cut oneself ▷ *Je me suis coupé le doigt avec une boîte de conserve.* I cut my finger on a tin.; **couper la parole à quelqu'un** to interrupt somebody

couple *nm* couple

couplet *nm* verse

coupure *nf* cut; **une coupure de courant** a power cut

cour *nf* ❶ yard ▷ *la cour de l'école* the school yard ❷ court

courage *nm* courage

courageux (*f* **courageuse**) *adj* brave

couramment *adv* ❶ fluently ❷ commonly

courant, e *adj* ❶ common ❷ standard
▶ *nm* ❶ *(of river)* current; **un courant d'air** a draught ❷ power ▷ *une panne de courant* a power cut; **Je le ferai dans le courant de la semaine.** I'll do it some time during the week.; **être au courant de quelque chose** to know about

something; **mettre quelqu'un au courant de quelque chose** to tell somebody about something; **Tu es au courant?** Have you heard about it?; **se tenir au courant de quelque chose** to keep up with something

coureur *nm* runner; **un coureur à pied** a runner; **un coureur cycliste** a racing cyclist; **un coureur automobile** a racing driver

coureuse *nf* runner

courgette *nf* courgette

courir *vb* [16] to run ▷ *Elle a traversé la rue en courant.* She ran across the street.; **courir un risque** to run a risk

couronne *nf* crown

courons, courez *vb see* **courir**

courriel *nm* email

courrier *nm* mail; **N'oublie pas de poster le courrier.** Don't forget to post the letters.; **le courrier électronique** email

Be careful! The French word **courrier** does not mean **courier**.

courroie *nf* **la courroie du ventilateur** fan belt

cours *nm* ❶ lesson ▷ *un cours d'espagnol* a Spanish lesson ❷ course ▷ *un cours intensif* a crash course ❸ rate; **au cours de** during

course *nf* ❶ running ▷ *la course de fond* long-distance running ❷ race ▷ *une course hippique* a horse race ❸ shopping ▷ *J'ai juste une course à faire.* I've just got a bit of shopping to do.; **faire les courses** to go shopping

court, e *adj* short
▶ *nm* **un court de tennis** a tennis court

couru *vb see* **courir**

couscous *nm* couscous

couscous is a spicy North African dish made with meat, vegetables and steamed semolina.

cousin *nm* cousin

cousine *nf* cousin

coussin *nm* cushion

coût *nm* cost

couteau (*pl* **couteaux**) *nm* knife

coûter *vb* [28] to cost ▷ *Est-ce que ça coûte cher?* Does it cost a lot?; **Combien ça coûte?** How much is it?

coûteux (*f* **coûteuse**) *adj* expensive

coutume *nf* custom

couture *nf* ❶ sewing; **faire de la couture** to sew ❷ seam

couturier *nm* fashion designer

couturière *nf* dressmaker

couvercle *nm* ❶ *(of pan)* lid ❷ *(of tube, jar, spray can)* top

couvert, e *adj* ❶ covered; **couvert de** covered with ❷ *(sky)* overcast
▶ *vb see* **couvrir**
▶ *nm* **mettre le couvert** to lay the table

couverts *nmpl* cutlery *sg*

couverture *nf* blanket

couvre-lit *nm* bedspread

couvrir *vb* [55] to cover ▷ *Le chien est revenu couvert de boue.* The dog came back covered with mud.; **se couvrir (1)** to wrap up ▷ *Couvre-toi* *bien: il fait très froid dehors.* Wrap up well: it's very cold outside. **(2)** to cloud over ▷ *Le ciel se couvre.* The sky's clouding over.

crabe *nm* crab

cracher *vb* [**28**] to spit

crachin *nm* drizzle

craie *nf* chalk

craindre *vb* [**17**] to fear ▷ *Tu n'as rien à craindre.* You've got nothing to fear.

crainte *nf* fear; **de crainte de** for fear of

craintif (*f* **craintive**) *adj* timid

crampe *nf* cramp

cran *nm (in belt)* hole; **avoir du cran** *(informal)* to have guts

crâne *nm* skull

crâner *vb* [**28**] *(informal)* to show off

crapaud *nm* toad

craquer *vb* [**28**] ❶ to creak ▷ *Le plancher craque.* The floor creaks. ❷ to burst ▷ *Ma fermeture éclair a craqué.* My zip's burst. ❸ to crack up ▷ *Je vais finir par craquer!* *(informal)* I'm going to crack up at this rate!; **Quand j'ai vu cette robe, j'ai craqué!** *(informal)* When I saw that dress, I couldn't resist it!

crasse *nf* filth

cravate *nf* tie

crawl *nm* crawl

crayon *nm* pencil ▷ *un crayon de couleur* a coloured pencil; **un crayon feutre** a felt-tip pen

création *nf* creation

crèche *nf* ❶ nursery ❷ nativity scene

crédit *nm* credit

créer *vb* [**18**] to create

crémaillère *nf* **pendre la crémaillère** to have a house-warming party

crème *nf* cream; **la crème anglaise** custard; **la crème Chantilly** whipped cream; **la crème fouettée** whipped cream; **une crème caramel** a crème caramel; **une crème au chocolat** a chocolate dessert
▶ *nm* white coffee

crémerie *nf* cheese shop

crémeux (*f* **crémeuse**) *adj* creamy

crêpe *nf* pancake

crêperie *nf* pancake restaurant

crépuscule *nm* dusk

cresson *nm* watercress

Crète *nf* Crete

creuser *vb* [**28**] *(a hole)* to dig; **Ça creuse!** That gives you a real appetite!; **se creuser la cervelle** *(informal)* to rack one's brains

creux (*f* **creuse**) *adj* hollow

crevaison *nf* puncture

crevé, e *adj* ❶ punctured ▷ *un pneu crevé* a puncture ❷ knackered

crever *vb* [**43**] ❶ *(balloon)* to burst ❷ *(motorist)* to have a puncture ▷ *J'ai crevé sur l'autoroute.* I had a puncture on the motorway.; **Je crève de faim!** *(informal)* I'm starving!; **Je crève de froid!** *(informal)* I'm freezing!

crevette *nf* prawn; **une crevette rose** a prawn; **une crevette grise** a shrimp

cri *nm* ❶ scream ❷ call; **C'est le dernier cri.** It's the latest fashion.

criard, e *adj (colours)* garish
cric *nm (for car)* jack
crier *vb* [**19**] to shout; **crier de douleur** to scream with pain
crime *nm* ❶ crime ❷ murder
criminel *nm* ❶ criminal ❷ murderer
crin *nm* horsehair
crinière *nf* mane
criquet *nm* grasshopper
crise *nf* ❶ crisis; **la crise économique** the recession ❷ attack ▷ *une crise d'asthme* an asthma attack ▷ *une crise cardiaque* a heart attack; **une crise de foie** an upset stomach; **piquer une crise de nerfs** to go hysterical; **avoir une crise de fou rire** to have a fit of the giggles
cristal (*pl* **cristaux**) *nm* crystal
critère *nm* criterion
critique *adj* critical
▶ *nm* critic
▶ *nf* ❶ criticism ❷ review
critiquer *vb* [**28**] to criticize
Croatie *nf* Croatia
crochet *nm* ❶ hook ❷ detour ▷ *faire un crochet* to make a detour ❸ crochet
crocodile *nm* crocodile
croire *vb* [**20**] to believe; **croire que** to think that ▷ *Tu crois qu'il fera meilleur demain?* Do you think the weather will be better tomorrow?; **croire à quelque chose** to believe in something; **croire en Dieu** to believe in God
crois *vb see* **croire**
croîs *vb see* **croître**
croisement *nm* crossroads
croiser *vb* [**28**] **J'ai croisé Anne-Laure dans la rue.** I bumped into Anne-Laure in the street.; **croiser les bras** to fold one's arms; **croiser les jambes** to cross one's legs; **se croiser** to pass each other
croisière *nf* cruise
croissance *nf* growth
croissant *nm* croissant
croit *vb see* **croire**
croître *vb* [**21**] to grow
croix *nf* cross; **la Croix-Rouge** the Red Cross
croque-madame (*pl* **croque-madame**) *nm* toasted ham and cheese sandwich with fried egg on top
croque-monsieur (*pl* **croque-monsieur**) *nm* toasted ham and cheese sandwich
croquer *vb* [**28**] to munch; **le chocolat à croquer** plain chocolate
croquis *nm* sketch
crotte *nf* **une crotte de chien** dog dirt
crottin *nm* ❶ manure ❷ small goat's cheese
croustillant, e *adj* crusty
croûte *nf* ❶ *(of bread)* crust; **en croûte** in pastry ❷ *(of cheese)* rind ❸ *(on skin)* scab
croûton *nm* ❶ *(end of loaf)* crust ❷ crouton
croyons, croyez *vb see* **croire**
CRS *nmpl* French riot police
cru, e *adj* raw; **le jambon cru** Parma ham
▶ *vb see* **croire**

crû *vb see* **croître**
cruauté *nf* cruelty
cruche *nf* jug
crudités *nfpl* assorted raw vegetables
cruel (*f* **cruelle**) *adj* cruel
crustacés *nmpl* shellfish
cube *nm* cube; **un mètre cube** a cubic metre
cueillette *nf* picking
cueillir *vb* [**22**] *(flowers, fruit)* to pick
cuiller *nf* spoon; **une cuiller à café** a teaspoon; **une cuiller à soupe** a soup spoon
cuillerée *nf* spoonful
cuir *nm* leather; **le cuir chevelu** the scalp
cuire *vb* [**23**] to cook ▷ *cuire quelque chose à feu vif* to cook something on a high heat; **cuire quelque chose au four** to bake something; **cuire quelque chose à la vapeur** to steam something; **faire cuire** to cook ▷ *'Faire cuire pendant une heure'* 'Cook for one hour'; **bien cuit** well done; **trop cuit** overdone
cuisine *nf* ❶ kitchen ❷ cooking; **faire la cuisine** to cook
cuisiné, e *adj* **un plat cuisiné** a ready-made meal
cuisiner *vb* [**28**] to cook ▷ *J'aime beaucoup cuisiner.* I love cooking.
cuisinier *nm* cook
cuisinière *nf* ❶ cook ❷ cooker
cuisse *nf* thigh; **une cuisse de poulet** a chicken leg
cuisson *nf* cooking ▷ *'une heure de cuisson'* 'cooking time: one hour'
cuit *vb see* **cuire**
cuivre *nm* copper
culot *nm (informal)* cheek
culotte *nf* knickers
culpabilité *nf* guilt
cultivateur *nm* farmer
cultivatrice *nf* farmer
cultivé, e *adj* cultured
cultiver *vb* [**28**] to grow ▷ *Il cultive la vigne.* He grows grapes.; **cultiver la terre** to farm the land
culture *nf* ❶ farming ❷ education; **la culture physique** physical education
culturisme *nm* body-building
curé *nm* parish priest
cure-dent *nm* toothpick
curieux (*f* **curieuse**) *adj* curious
curiosité *nf* curiosity
curriculum vitae *nm* CV
curseur *nm* cursor
cuvette *nf* bowl
CV *nm (= curriculum vitae)* CV
cybercafé *nm* internet café
cyclable *adj* **une piste cyclable** a cycle track
cycle *nm* cycle
cyclisme *nm* cycling
cycliste *nmf* cyclist
cyclomoteur *nm* moped
cyclone *nm* hurricane
cygne *nm* swan

d

d' *prep, art* see **de**

dactylo *nf* ❶ typist ▷ *Elle est dactylo.* She's a typist. ❷ typing

daim *nm* suede

dame *nf* ❶ lady ❷ *(in cards, chess)* queen

dames *nfpl* draughts

Danemark *nm* Denmark

danger *nm* danger; **être en danger** to be in danger; **'Danger de mort'** 'Extremely dangerous'

dangereux (*f* **dangereuse**) *adj* dangerous

danois, e *adj, n* Danish ▷ *Il parle danois.* He speaks Danish.; **un Danois** *(man)* a Dane; **une Danoise** *(woman)* a Dane; **les Danois** the Danish

dans *prep* ❶ in ▷ *Il est dans sa chambre.* He's in his bedroom. ▷ *dans deux mois* in two months' time ❷ into ▷ *Il est entré dans mon bureau.* He came into my office. ❸ out of ▷ *On a bu dans des verres en plastique.* We drank out of plastic glasses.

danse *nf* ❶ dance; **la danse classique** ballet ❷ dancing

danser *vb* [**28**] to dance

danseur *nm* dancer

danseuse *nf* dancer

date *nf* date; **un ami de longue date** an old friend

dater *vb* [**28**] **dater de** to date from

datte *nf (fruit)* date

dauphin *nm* dolphin

davantage *adv* **davantage de** more

de *prep, art*

> See also **du (=de + le)** and **des (=de + les)**. **de** changes to **d'** before a vowel and most words beginning with 'h'.

❶ of ▷ *le toit de la maison* the roof of the house ▷ *la voiture de Paul* Paul's car ▷ *la voiture d'Hélène* Hélène's car ▷ *deux bouteilles de vin* two bottles of wine ▷ *un litre d'essence* a litre of petrol; **un bébé d'un an** a one-year-old baby; **un billet de cinquante euros** a 50-euro note ❷ from ▷ *de Londres à Paris* from London to Paris ▷ *Il vient de Londres.* He comes from London. ▷ *une lettre de Victor* a letter from Victor ❸ by ▷ *augmenter de dix euros* to increase by ten euros

> You use **de** to form expressions with the meaning of 'some' and 'any'.

Je voudrais de l'eau. I'd like some water.; **du pain et de la confiture** bread and jam; **Il n'a pas de famille.** He hasn't got any family.; **Il n'y a plus de biscuits.** There aren't any more biscuits.

dé *nm* ❶ dice ❷ thimble

dealer *nm (informal)* drug-pusher

déballer *vb* [**28**] to unpack

débardeur *nm* tank top

débarquer *vb* [**28**] to disembark ▷ *Nous avons dû débarquer à Marseille.* We had to disembark at Marseilles.; **débarquer chez quelqu'un** *(informal)* to descend on somebody

débarras *nm* junk room; **Bon débarras!** Good riddance!

débarrasser *vb* [**28**] to clear ▷ *Tu peux débarrasser la table, s'il te plaît?* Can you clear the table please?; **se débarrasser de quelque chose** to get rid of something ▷ *Je me suis débarrassé de mon vieux frigo.* I got rid of my old fridge.

débat *nm* debate

se **débattre** *vb* [**9**] to struggle

débile *adj* crazy

débordé, e *adj* **être débordé** to be snowed under

déborder *vb* [**28**] *(river)* to overflow; **déborder d'énergie** to be full of energy

débouché *nm* job prospect

déboucher *vb* [**28**] ❶ *(sink, pipe)* to unblock ❷ *(bottle)* to open; **déboucher sur** to lead into ▷ *La rue débouche sur une place.* The street leads into a square.

debout *adv* ❶ standing up ▷ *Il a mangé ses céréales debout.* He ate his cereal standing up. ❷ upright ▷ *Mets les livres debout sur l'étagère.* Put the books upright on the shelf. ❸ up ▷ *Tu es déjà debout?* Are you up already?; **Debout!** Get up!

déboutonner *vb* [**28**] to unbutton

débraillé, e *adj* sloppily dressed

débrancher *vb* [**28**] to unplug

débris *nm* **des débris de verre** bits of glass

débrouillard, e *adj* streetwise

se **débrouiller** *vb* [**28**] to manage ▷ *C'était difficile, mais je ne me suis pas trop mal débrouillé.* It was difficult, but I managed OK.; **Débrouille-toi tout seul.** Sort things out for yourself.

début *nm* beginning ▷ *au début* at the beginning; **début mai** in early May

débutant *nm* beginner

débuter *vb* [**28**] to start

décaféiné, e *adj* decaffeinated

décalage horaire *nm (between time zones)* time difference

décalquer *vb* [**28**] to trace

décapiter *vb* [**28**] to behead

décapotable *adj* convertible

décapsuler *vb* [**28**] **décapsuler une bouteille** to take the top off a bottle

décapsuleur *nm* bottle-opener

décéder *vb* [**34**] to die ▷ *Son père est décédé il y a trois ans.* His father died three years ago.

décembre *nm* December; **en décembre** in December

décemment *adv* decently
décent, e *adj* decent
déception *nf* disappointment
décerner *vb* [**28**] to award
décès *nm* death
décevant, e *adj* disappointing
décevoir *vb* [**67**] to disappoint
décharger *vb* [**45**] to unload
se **déchausser** *vb* [**28**] to take off one's shoes
déchets *nmpl* waste *sg*
déchiffrer *vb* [**28**] to decipher
déchirant, e *adj* heart-rending
déchirer *vb* [**28**] ❶ *(clothes)* to tear ❷ to tear up ▷ *déchirer une lettre* to tear up a letter ❸ to tear out ▷ *déchirer une page d'un livre* to tear a page out of a book; **se déchirer** to tear ▷ *se déchirer un muscle* to tear a muscle
déchirure *nf (rip)* tear; **une déchirure musculaire** a torn muscle
décidé, e *adj* determined; **C'est décidé.** It's decided.
décidément *adv* certainly
décider *vb* [**28**] to decide; **décider de faire quelque chose** to decide to do something; **se décider** to make up one's mind ▷ *Elle n'arrive pas à se décider.* She can't make up her mind.
décisif (*f* **décisive**) *adj* decisive
décision *nf* decision
déclaration *nf* statement; **faire une déclaration de vol** to report something as stolen
déclarer *vb* [**28**] to declare ▷ *déclarer la guerre à un pays* to declare war on a country; **se déclarer** to break out ▷ *Le feu s'est déclaré dans la cantine.* The fire broke out in the canteen.
déclencher *vb* [**28**] *(alarm, explosion)* to set off; **se déclencher** to go off
déclic *nm* click
décoiffé, e *adj* **Elle était toute décoiffée.** Her hair was in a real mess.
décollage *nm (of plane)* takeoff
décollé, e *adj* **avoir les oreilles décollées** to have sticking-out ears
décoller *vb* [**28**] ❶ to unstick ▷ *décoller une étiquette* to unstick a label; **se décoller** to come unstuck ❷ to take off ▷ *L'avion a décollé avec dix minutes de retard.* The plane took off ten minutes late.
décolleté, e *adj* low-cut ▶ *nm* **un décolleté plongeant** a plunging neckline
se **décolorer** *vb* [**28**] to fade ▷ *Ce T-shirt s'est décoloré au lavage.* This T-shirt has faded in the wash.; **se faire décolorer les cheveux** to have one's hair bleached
décombres *nmpl* rubble *sg*
se **décommander** *vb* [**28**] to cry off ▷ *Elle devait venir mais elle s'est décommandée à la dernière minute.* She was supposed to be coming, but she cried off at the last minute.
déconcerté, e *adj* disconcerted
décongeler *vb* [**1**] to thaw
se **déconnecter** *vb* [**28**] to log out
déconseiller *vb* [**28**] **déconseiller à quelqu'un de faire quelque**

chose to advise somebody not to do something ▷ *Je lui ai déconseillé d'y aller.* I advised him not to go.; **C'est déconseillé.** It's not recommended.

décontenancé, e *adj* disconcerted

décontracté, e *adj* relaxed; **s'habiller décontracté** to dress casually

se **décontracter** *vb* [**28**] to relax ▷ *Il est allé faire du footing pour se décontracter.* He went jogging to relax.

décor *nm* décor

décorateur *nm* interior decorator

décoration *nf* decoration

décorer *vb* [**28**] to decorate

décors *nmpl* ❶ *(in play)* scenery *sg* ❷ *(in film)* set

décortiquer *vb* [**28**] to shell; **des crevettes décortiquées** peeled shrimps

découdre *vb* [**15**] to unpick; **se découdre** to come unstitched

découper *vb* [**28**] ❶ to cut out ▷ *J'ai découpé cet article dans le journal.* I cut this article out of the paper. ❷ *(meat)* to carve

décourageant, e *adj* discouraging

décourager *vb* [**45**] to discourage; **se décourager** to get discouraged; **Ne te décourage pas!** Don't give up!

décousu, e *adj* unstitched

découvert *nm* overdraft

découverte *nf* discovery

découvrir *vb* [**55**] to discover

décrire *vb* [**30**] to describe

décrocher *vb* [**28**] ❶ to take down ▷ *Tu peux m'aider à décrocher les rideaux?* Can you help me take down the curtains? ❷ to pick up the phone ▷ *Il a décroché et a composé le numéro.* He picked up the phone and dialled the number.; **décrocher le téléphone** to take the phone off the hook

déçu *vb* disappointed

dédaigneux (*f* **dédaigneuse**) *adj* disdainful

dédain *nm* disdain

dedans *adv* inside; **là-dedans (1)** in there ▷ *J'ai trouvé les clés là-dedans.* I found the keys in there. **(2)** in that ▷ *Il y a du vrai là-dedans.* There's some truth in that.

dédicacé, e *adj* **un exemplaire dédicacé** a signed copy

dédier *vb* [**19**] to dedicate

déduire *vb* [**23**] to take off ▷ *Tu as déduit les vingt euros que je te devais?* Did you take off the twenty euros I owed you?; **J'en déduis qu'il m'a menti.** That means he must have been lying.

défaire *vb* [**36**] to undo; **défaire sa valise** to unpack; **se défaire** to come undone

défaite *nf* defeat

défaut *nm* fault

défavorable *adj* unfavourable

défavorisé, e *adj* underprivileged

défectueux (*f* **défectueuse**) *adj* faulty

défendre *vb* [**88**] ❶ to forbid; **défendre à quelqu'un de faire**

quelque chose to forbid somebody to do something ▷ *Sa mère lui a défendu de le revoir.* Her mother forbade her to see him again. ❷ to defend ▷ *défendre quelqu'un* to defend somebody

défendu, e *adj* forbidden ▷ *C'est défendu.* It's forbidden.

défense *nf* ❶ defence; **'défense de fumer'** 'no smoking' ❷ *(of elephant)* tusk

défi *nm* challenge; **d'un air de défi** defiantly; **sur un ton de défi** defiantly

défier *vb* [**19**] ❶ to challenge ▷ *Je te défie de trouver un meilleur exemple.* I challenge you to find a better example. ❷ to dare ▷ *Il m'a défié d'aller à l'école en pyjama.* He dared me to go to school in my pyjamas.

défigurer *vb* [**28**] to disfigure

défilé *nm* ❶ parade; **un défilé de mode** a fashion show ❷ march

défiler *vb* [**28**] to march

définir *vb* [**38**] to define

définitif (*f* **définitive**) *adj* final; **en définitive** in the end

définitivement *adv* for good

déformer *vb* [**28**] to stretch ▷ *Ne tire pas sur ton pull, tu vas le déformer.* Don't pull at your sweater, you'll stretch it.; **se déformer** to stretch ▷ *Ce T-shirt s'est déformé au lavage.* This T-shirt has stretched in the wash.

se **défouler** *vb* [**28**] to unwind

dégagé, e *adj* **d'un air dégagé** casually; **sur un ton dégagé** casually

dégager *vb* [**45**] ❶ to free ▷ *Ils ont mis une heure à dégager les victimes.* They took an hour to free the victims. ❷ to clear ▷ *des gouttes qui dégagent le nez* drops to clear your nose; **Ça se dégage.** *(weather)* It's clearing up.

se **dégarnir** *vb* [**38**] to go bald

dégâts *nmpl* damage

dégel *nm* thaw

dégeler *vb* [**1**] to thaw

dégivrer *vb* [**28**] ❶ to defrost ❷ to de-ice

dégonfler *vb* [**28**] to let down ▷ *Quelqu'un a dégonflé mes pneus.* Somebody let down my tyres.; **se dégonfler** *(informal)* to chicken out

dégouliner *vb* [**28**] to trickle

dégourdi, e *adj* smart

dégourdir *vb* [**38**] **se dégourdir les jambes** to stretch one's legs

dégoût *nm* disgust; **avec dégoût** disgustedly

dégoûtant, e *adj* disgusting

dégoûté, e *adj* disgusted; **être dégoûté de tout** to be sick of everything

dégoûter *vb* [**28**] to disgust; **dégoûter quelqu'un de quelque chose** to put somebody off something ▷ *Ça m'a dégoûté de la viande.* That put me off meat.

se **dégrader** *vb* [**28**] to deteriorate

degré *nm* degree; **de l'alcool à 90 degrés** surgical spirit

dégringoler *vb* [**28**] ❶ to rush down ▷ *Il a dégringolé l'escalier.* He rushed down the stairs. ❷ to collapse ▷ *Elle a fait dégringoler la* *pile de livres.* She knocked over the stack of books.

déguisement *nm* disguise

déguiser *vb* [**28**] **se déguiser en quelque chose** to dress up as something ▷ *Elle s'était déguisée en vampire.* She was dressed up as a vampire.

dégustation *nf* tasting

déguster *vb* [**28**] ❶ *(food, wine)* to taste ❷ to enjoy

dehors *adv* outside ▷ *Je t'attends dehors.* I'll wait for you outside.; **jeter quelqu'un dehors** to throw somebody out; **en dehors de** apart from

déjà *adv* ❶ already ▷ *J'ai déjà fini.* I've already finished. ❷ before ▷ *Tu es déjà venu en France?* Have you been to France before?

déjeuner *vb* [**28**] to have lunch ▶ *nm* lunch

délai *nm* ❶ extension ❷ time limit

> Be careful! **délai** does not mean **delay**.

délasser *vb* [**28**] to relax ▷ *La lecture délasse.* Reading's relaxing.; **se délasser** to relax ▷ *J'ai pris un bain pour me délasser.* I had a bath to relax.

délavé, e *adj* faded

délégué *nm* representative ▷ *les délégués de classe* the class representatives

> In French schools, each class elects two representatives or **délégués de classe**, one boy and one girl.

déléguée *nf* representative

déléguer *vb* [**34**] to delegate

délibéré, e *adj* deliberate

délicat, e *adj* ❶ delicate ❷ tricky ❸ tactful ❹ thoughtful

délicatement *adv* ❶ gently ❷ tactfully

délice *nm* delight; **Ce gâteau est un vrai délice.** This cake's a real treat.

délicieux (*f* **délicieuse**) *adj* delicious

délinquance *nf* crime

délinquant *nm* criminal

délirer *vb* [**28**] **Mais tu délires!** *(informal)* You're crazy!

délit *nm* criminal offence

délivrer *vb* [**28**] *(prisoner)* to set free

deltaplane *nm* hang-glider; **faire du deltaplane** to go hang-gliding

demain *adv* tomorrow; **À demain!** See you tomorrow!

demande *nf* request; **une demande en mariage** an offer of marriage; **'demandes d'emploi'** 'situations wanted'

demandé, e *adj* **très demandé** very much in demand

demander *vb* [**28**] ❶ to ask for ▷ *J'ai demandé la permission.* I've asked for permission. ❷ to require ▷ *un travail qui demande beaucoup de temps* a job that requires a lot of time; **se demander** to wonder ▷ *Je me demande à quelle heure il va venir.* I wonder what time he'll come.

> Be careful! **demander** does not mean **to demand**.

demandeur d'asile *nm* asylum seeker

demandeur d'emploi *nm* job-seeker
démangeaison *nf* itching
démanger *vb* [**45**] to itch ▷ *Ça me démange.* It itches.
démaquillant *nm* make-up remover
démaquiller *vb* [**28**] **se démaquiller** to remove one's make-up
démarche *nf* ❶ walk ❷ step ▷ *faire les démarches nécessaires pour obtenir quelque chose* to take the necessary steps to obtain something
démarrer *vb* [**28**] *(car)* to start
démêler *vb* [**28**] to untangle
déménagement *nm* move; **un camion de déménagement** a removal van
déménager *vb* [**45**] to move house
déménageur *nm* removal man
dément, e *adj* crazy
démentiel (*f* **démentielle**) *adj* insane
demeurer *vb* [**28**] to live
demi, e *adj, adv* half ▷ *Il a trois ans et demi.* He's three and a half.; **Il est trois heures et demie.** It's half past three.; **Il est midi et demi.** It's half past twelve.; **à demi endormi** half-asleep
▶ *nm* half pint of beer; **Un demi, s'il vous plaît!** A beer please!
demi-baguette *nf* half a baguette
demi-cercle *nm* semicircle
demi-douzaine *nf* half-dozen
demie *nf* half-hour ▷ *Le bus passe à la demie.* The bus comes by on the half-hour.
demi-écrémé, e *adj* semi-skimmed
demi-finale *nf* semi-final
demi-frère *nm* half-brother
demi-heure *nf* half an hour ▷ *dans une demi-heure* in half an hour
demi-journée *nf* half-day
demi-litre *nm* half litre
demi-livre *nf* half-pound
demi-pension *nf* half board ▷ *Cet hôtel propose des tarifs raisonnables en demi-pension.* This hotel has reasonable rates for half board.
demi-pensionnaire *nmf* **être demi-pensionnaire** to have school lunches
demi-sel *adj* **du beurre demi-sel** slightly salted butter
demi-sœur *nf* half-sister
démission *nf* resignation; **donner sa démission** to resign
démissionner *vb* [**28**] to resign
demi-tarif *nm* ❶ half-price ❷ half-fare
demi-tour *nm* **faire demi-tour** to turn back
démocratie *nf* democracy
démocratique *adj* democratic
démodé, e *adj* old-fashioned
demoiselle *nf* young lady; **une demoiselle d'honneur** a bridesmaid
démolir *vb* [**38**] to demolish
démon *nm* devil
démonter *vb* [**28**] ❶ *(tent)* to take down ❷ *(machine)* to take apart
démontrer *vb* [**28**] to show
dénoncer *vb* [**12**] to denounce; **se dénoncer** to give oneself up

dénouement *nm* outcome
densité *nf* density
dent *nf* tooth ▷ *une dent de lait* a milk tooth ▷ *une dent de sagesse* a wisdom tooth
dentaire *adj* dental
dentelle *nf* lace
dentier *nm* denture
dentifrice *nm* toothpaste
dentiste *nmf* dentist
déodorant *nm* deodorant
dépannage *nm* **un service de dépannage** a breakdown service
dépanner *vb* [**28**] ❶ to fix ▷ *Il a dépanné la voiture en cinq minutes.* He fixed the car in five minutes. ❷ to help out ▷ *Il m'a prêté dix euros pour me dépanner. (informal)* He lent me 10 euros to help me out.
dépanneuse *nf* breakdown lorry
départ *nm* departure; **Je lui téléphonerai la veille de son départ.** I'll phone him the day before he leaves.
département *nm* ❶ department ❷ administrative area
France is divided into 96 **départements**, administrative areas rather like counties.
dépasser *vb* [**58**] ❶ to overtake ❷ to pass ▷ *Nous avons dépassé Dijon.* We've passed Dijon. ❸ *(sum, limit)* to exceed
dépaysé, e *adj* **se sentir un peu dépaysé** to feel a bit lost
se **dépêcher** *vb* [**28**] to hurry ▷ *Dépêche-toi!* Hurry up!
dépendre *vb* [**88**] **dépendre de** to depend on ▷ *Ça dépend du temps.* It depends on the weather.; **dépendre de quelqu'un** to be dependent on somebody; **Ça dépend.** It depends.
dépenser *vb* [**28**] *(money)* to spend
dépensier (*f* **dépensière**) *adj* **Il est dépensier.** He's a big spender.; **Elle n'est pas dépensière.** She's not exactly extravagant.
dépilatoire *adj* **une crème dépilatoire** a hair-removing cream
dépit *nm* **en dépit de** in spite of
déplacé, e *adj* uncalled-for
déplacement *nm* trip
déplacer *vb* [**12**] ❶ to move ▷ *Tu peux m'aider à déplacer la table?* Can you help me move the table? ❷ to put off ▷ *déplacer un rendez-vous* to put off an appointment; **se déplacer (1)** to travel around ▷ *Il se déplace beaucoup pour son travail.* He travels around a lot for his work. **(2)** to get around ▷ *Il a du mal à se déplacer.* He has difficulty getting around.; **se déplacer une vertèbre** to slip a disc
déplaire *vb* [**62**] **Cela me déplaît.** I dislike this.
déplaisant, e *adj* unpleasant
dépliant *nm* leaflet
déplier *vb* [**19**] to unfold
déposer *vb* [**28**] ❶ to leave ▷ *J'ai déposé mon sac à la consigne.* I left my bag at the left-luggage office. ❷ to put down ▷ *Déposez le paquet sur la table.* Put the parcel down on the table.; **déposer quelqu'un** to drop somebody off
dépourvu, e *adj* **prendre**

quelqu'un au dépourvu to take somebody by surprise
dépression *nf* depression; **faire de la dépression** to be suffering from depression; **faire une dépression** to have a breakdown
déprimant, e *adj* depressing
déprimer *vb* [**28**] to get depressed ▷ *Ce genre de temps me déprime.* This kind of weather makes me depressed.
depuis *prep, adv* ❶ since ▷ *Il habite Paris depuis 2003.* He's been living in Paris since 2003.; **depuis que** since ❷ for ▷ *Il habite Paris depuis cinq ans.* He's been living in Paris for five years.; **Depuis combien de temps?** How long? ▷ *Depuis combien de temps est-ce que vous le connaissez?* How long have you known him?; **Depuis quand?** How long? ▷ *Depuis quand est-ce que vous le connaissez?* How long have you known him?
député *nm* Member of Parliament
députée *nf* Member of Parliament
déraciner *vb* [**28**] to uproot
dérangement *nm* **en dérangement** out of order
déranger *vb* [**45**] ❶ to bother ▷ *Excusez-moi de vous déranger.* I'm sorry to bother you.; **Ne vous dérangez pas, je vais répondre au téléphone.** You stay there, I'll answer the phone. ❷ to mess up ▷ *Ne dérange pas mes livres, s'il te plaît.* Don't mess up my books, please.
déraper *vb* [**28**] to skid
dermatologue *nmf* dermatologist
dernier (*f* **dernière**) *adj* ❶ last ▷ *la dernière fois* the last time ❷ latest ▷ *le dernier film de Spielberg* Spielberg's latest film; **en dernier** last
dernièrement *adv* recently
dérouler *vb* [**28**] ❶ to unroll ❷ to unwind; **se dérouler** to take place; **Tout s'est déroulé comme prévu.** Everything went as planned.
derrière *adv, prep* behind ▶ *nm* ❶ back ▷ *la porte de derrière* the back door ❷ backside
des *art*

> **des** is the contracted form of **de + les**.

❶ some ▷ *Tu veux des chips?* Would you like some crisps?

> **des** is sometimes not translated.

▷ *J'ai des cousins en France.* I have cousins in France. ❷ any ▷ *Tu as des frères?* Have you got any brothers? ▷ *la fin des vacances* the end of the holidays ▷ *la voiture des Durand* the Durands' car ▷ *Il arrive des États-Unis.* He's arriving from the United States.
dès *prep* as early as; **dès le mois de novembre** from November; **dès le début** right from the start; **Il vous appellera dès son retour.** He'll call you as soon as he gets back.; **dès que** as soon as ▷ *Il m'a reconnu dès qu'il m'a vu.* He recognized me as soon as he saw me.
désabusé, e *adj* disillusioned
désaccord *nm* disagreement

désagréable *adj* unpleasant
désaltérer *vb* [**34**] **L'eau gazeuse désaltère bien.** Sparkling water is very thirst-quenching.; **se désaltérer** to quench one's thirst
désapprobateur (*f* **désapprobatrice**) *adj* disapproving
désastre *nm* disaster
désavantage *nm* disadvantage
désavantager *vb* [**45**] **désavantager quelqu'un** to put somebody at a disadvantage
descendre *vb* [**24**] ❶ to go down ▷ *Je suis tombé en descendant l'escalier.* I fell as I was going down the stairs. ❷ to come down ▷ *Attends en bas; je descends!* Wait downstairs; I'm coming down! ❸ to get down ▷ *Vous pouvez descendre ma valise, s'il vous plaît?* Can you get my suitcase down, please? ❹ to get off ▷ *Nous descendons à la prochaine station.* We're getting off at the next station.
descente *nf* way down ▷ *Je t'attendrai au bas de la descente.* I'll wait for you at the bottom of the hill.; **une descente de police** a police raid
description *nf* description
déséquilibré, e *adj* unbalanced
déséquilibrer *vb* [**28**] **déséquilibrer quelqu'un** to throw somebody off balance
désert, e *adj* deserted; **une île déserte** a desert island
▶ *nm* desert
déserter *vb* [**28**] to desert
désertique *adj* desert ▷ *une région désertique* a desert region
désespéré, e *adj* desperate
désespérer *vb* [**34**] to despair ▷ *Il ne faut pas désespérer.* Don't despair.
désespoir *nm* despair
déshabiller *vb* [**28**] to undress; **se déshabiller** to get undressed
déshériter *vb* [**28**] to disinherit; **les déshérités** the underprivileged
déshydraté, e *adj* dehydrated
désigner *vb* [**28**] to choose ▷ *On l'a désignée pour remettre le prix.* She was chosen to present the prize.; **désigner quelque chose du doigt** to point at something
désinfectant *nm* disinfectant
désinfecter *vb* [**28**] to disinfect
désintéressé, e *adj* ❶ unselfish ▷ *un acte désintéressé* an unselfish action ❷ impartial ▷ *un conseil désintéressé* impartial advice
désintéresser *vb* [**28**] **se désintéresser de quelque chose** to lose interest in something
désir *nm* ❶ wish ▷ *Vos désirs sont des ordres.* Your wish is my command. ❷ will ▷ *le désir de réussir* the will to succeed ❸ desire
désirer *vb* [**28**] to want ▷ *Vous désirez? (in shop)* What would you like?
désobéir *vb* [**38**] **désobéir à quelqu'un** to disobey somebody
désobéissant, e *adj* disobedient
désobligeant, e *adj* unpleasant
désodorisant *nm* air freshener
désolé, e *adj* sorry; **Désolé!** Sorry!

désopilant, e *adj* hilarious
désordonné, e *adj* untidy
désordre *nm* untidiness; **Quel désordre!** What a mess!; **en désordre** untidy
désormais *adv* from now on
desquelles *pron pl*

desquelles is the contracted form of **de** + **lesquelles**.

▷ *des négociations au cours desquelles les patrons ont fait des concessions* negotiations during which the employers made concessions
desquels *pron pl*

desquels is the contracted form of **de** + **lesquels**.

▷ *les lacs au bord desquels nous avons campé* the lakes on the banks of which we camped
dessécher *vb* [**34**] to dry out ▷ *Le soleil dessèche la peau.* The sun dries your skin out.
desserrer *vb* [**28**] to loosen
dessert *nm* pudding
dessin *nm* drawing; **un dessin animé** *(film)* a cartoon; **un dessin humoristique** *(drawing)* a cartoon
dessinateur *nm* **un dessinateur industriel** a draughtsman
dessiner *vb* [**28**] to draw
dessous *adv* underneath; **en dessous** underneath; **par-dessous** underneath; **là-dessous** under there; **ci-dessous** below ▷ *Complétez les phrases ci-dessous.* Complete the sentences below.; **au-dessous de** below
▶ *nm* underneath; **les voisins du dessous** the downstairs neighbours; **les dessous** underwear
dessous-de-plat (*pl* **dessous-de-plat**) *nm* tablemat
dessus *adv* on top; **par-dessus** over; **au-dessus** above ▷ *la taille au-dessus* the size above ▷ *au-dessus du lit* above the bed; **là-dessus** **(1)** on there ▷ *Tu peux écrire là-dessus.* You can write on there. **(2)** with that ▷ *'Je démissionne!' Là-dessus, il est parti.* 'I resign!' With that, he left.; **ci-dessus** above ▷ *l'exemple ci-dessus* the example above
▶ *nm* top; **les voisins du dessus** the upstairs neighbours; **avoir le dessus** to have the upper hand
destinataire *nmf* addressee
destination *nf* destination; **les passagers à destination de Paris** passengers travelling to Paris
destiné, e *adj* intended; **Elle était destinée à faire ce métier.** She was destined to go into that job.
destruction *nf* destruction
détachant *nm* stain remover
détacher *vb* [**28**] to undo; **se détacher** **(1)** to come off ▷ *La poignée de la porte s'est détachée.* The door handle came off. **(2)** to break away ▷ *Un wagon s'est détaché du reste du train.* A carriage broke away from the rest of the train.
détail *nm* detail; **en détail** in detail
détective *nm* detective
déteindre *vb* [**60**] *(in wash)* to fade
détendre *vb* [**88**] to relax ▷ *La*

lecture, ça me détend. I find reading relaxing.; **se détendre** to relax ▷ *Il est allé prendre un bain pour se détendre.* He's gone to have a bath to relax.

détente *nf* relaxation

détenu *nm* prisoner

détenue *nf* prisoner

se **détériorer** *vb* [**28**] to deteriorate

déterminé, e *adj* ❶ determined ❷ specific ▷ *un but déterminé* a specific aim

détestable *adj* horrible

détester *vb* [**28**] to hate

détonation *nf* bang

détour *nm* detour; **Ça vaut le détour.** It's worth the trip.

détournement *nm* **un détournement d'avion** a hijacking

détrempé, e *adj* waterlogged

détritus *nmpl* litter *sg*

détruire *vb* [**23**] to destroy

dette *nf* debt

deuil *nm* **être en deuil** to be in mourning

deux *num* two ▷ *Elle a deux ans.* She's two.; **deux fois** twice; **deux-points** colon; **tous les deux** both; **le deux février** the second of February

deuxième *adj* second ▷ *au deuxième étage* on the second floor

deuxièmement *adv* secondly

devais, devait, devaient *vb see* **devoir**

dévaliser *vb* [**28**] to rob

devant *adv, prep* ❶ in front ❷ in front of; **passer devant** to go past
▶ *nm* front ▷ *le devant de la maison* the front of the house; **les pattes de devant** the front legs

développement *nm* development; **les pays en voie de développement** developing countries

développer *vb* [**28**] to develop; **se développer** to develop

devenir *vb* [**25**] to become

devez *vb see* **devoir**

déviation *nf* diversion

deviez *vb see* **devoir**

deviner *vb* [**28**] to guess

devinette *nf* riddle

devions *vb see* **devoir**

dévisager *vb* [**45**] **dévisager quelqu'un** to stare at somebody

devise *nf* currency

dévisser *vb* [**28**] to unscrew

dévoiler *vb* [**28**] to unveil

devoir *vb* [**26**] ❶ to have to ▷ *Je dois partir.* I've got to go. ❷ must ▷ *Tu dois être fatigué.* You must be tired. ❸ to be due to ▷ *Le nouveau centre commercial doit ouvrir en mai.* The new shopping centre is due to open in May.; **devoir quelque chose à quelqu'un** to owe somebody something ▷ *Combien est-ce que je vous dois?* How much do I owe you?
▶ *nm* ❶ exercise; **les devoirs** homework; **un devoir sur table** a written test ❷ duty

devons *vb see* **devoir**

dévorer *vb* [**28**] to devour

dévoué, e *adj* devoted

devra, devrai, devras, devrez, devrons, devront *vb see* **devoir**

diabète *nm* diabetes
diabétique *adj* diabetic
diable *nm* devil
diabolo *nm* fruit cordial and lemonade; **un diabolo menthe** a mint cordial and lemonade
diagonal, e (*mpl* **diagonaux**) *adj* diagonal
diagonale *nf* diagonal; **en diagonale** diagonally
diagramme *nm* diagram
dialecte *nm* dialect
dialogue *nm* dialogue
diamant *nm* diamond
diamètre *nm* diameter
diapo *nf (informal) (image)* slide
diapositive *nf* slide
diarrhée *nf* diarrhoea
dictateur *nm* dictator
dictature *nf* dictatorship
dictée *nf* dictation
dicter *vb* [**28**] to dictate
dictionnaire *nm* dictionary
diététique *adj* **un magasin diététique** a health food shop
dieu (*pl* **dieux**) *nm* god; **Dieu** God ▷ *Mon Dieu!* Oh my God!
différé *nm* **une émission en différé** a recording
différence *nf* difference; **la différence d'âge** the age difference; **à la différence de** unlike
différent, e *adj* ❶ different ❷ various; **différent de** different from
difficile *adj* difficult
difficilement *adv* **faire quelque chose difficilement** to have trouble doing something; **Je pouvais difficilement refuser.** It was difficult for me to refuse.
difficulté *nf* difficulty ▷ *avec difficulté* with difficulty; **élève en difficulté (scolaire)** a student who is struggling
digérer *vb* [**34**] to digest
digestif *nm* after-dinner liqueur
digne *adj* **digne de** worthy of ▷ *digne de confiance* trustworthy
dignité *nf* dignity
dilemme *nm* dilemma
diluer *vb* [**28**] to dilute
dimanche *nm* ❶ Sunday ▷ *Aujourd'hui, on est dimanche.* It's Sunday today. ❷ on Sunday; **le dimanche** on Sundays; **tous les dimanches** every Sunday; **dimanche dernier** last Sunday; **dimanche prochain** next Sunday
diminuer *vb* [**28**] to decrease
diminutif *nm* pet name
diminution *nf* ❶ reduction ❷ decrease
dinde *nf (meat)* turkey
dindon *nm (bird)* turkey
dîner *nm (evening meal)* dinner ▶ *vb* [**28**] *(evening meal)* to have dinner
dingue *adj (informal)* crazy
diplomate *adj* diplomatic ▶ *nmf* diplomat
diplomatie *nf* diplomacy
diplôme *nm* qualification
diplômé, e *adj* qualified
dire *vb* [**27**] ❶ to say ▷ *Il a dit qu'il ne viendrait pas.* He said he wouldn't come.; **on dit que ...** they say

that ... ❷ to tell; **dire quelque chose à quelqu'un** to tell somebody something ▷ *Elle m'a dit la vérité.* She told me the truth.; **On dirait qu'il va pleuvoir.** It looks as if it's going to rain.; **se dire quelque chose** to think something ▷ *Quand je l'ai vu, je me suis dit qu'il avait vieilli.* When I saw him, I thought to myself that he'd aged.; **Est-ce que ça se dit?** Can you say that?; **Ça ne me dit rien.** **(1)** That doesn't appeal to me. **(2)** It doesn't ring a bell.

direct, e *adj* direct; **en direct** live

directement *adv* straight

directeur *nm* ❶ headteacher ❷ manager

direction *nf* ❶ management ❷ direction

directrice *nf* manager ▷ *Elle est directrice commerciale.* She's a sales manager.

dirent *vb see* **dire**

dirigeant *nm* leader

dirigeante *nf* leader

diriger *vb* [**45**] to manage ▷ *Il dirige une petite entreprise.* He manages a small company.; **se diriger vers** to head for ▷ *Il se dirigeait vers la gare.* He was heading for the station.

dis *vb see* **dire**; **Dis-moi la vérité!** Tell me the truth!; **dis donc** hey ▷ *Dis donc, tu te souviens de Sam?* Hey, do you remember Sam?

disaient, disais, disait *vb see* **dire**

discothèque *nf (club)* disco

discours *nm* speech

discret (*f* **discrète**) *adj* discreet

discrimination *nf* discrimination

discussion *nf* discussion

discutable *adj* debatable

discuter *vb* [**28**] ❶ to talk ▷ *Nous avons discuté pendant des heures.* We talked for hours. ❷ to argue ▷ *C'est ce que j'ai décidé, alors ne discutez pas!* That's what I've decided, so don't argue!

disent, disiez, disions *vb see* **dire**

disons *vb see* **dire** let's say ▷ *C'est à, disons, une demi-heure à pied.* It's half an hour's walk, say.

disparaître *vb* [**56**] to disappear; **faire disparaître quelque chose** **(1)** to make something disappear **(2)** to get rid of something

disparition *nf* disappearance; **une espèce en voie de disparition** an endangered species

disparu, e *adj* **être porté disparu** to be reported missing

dispensaire *nm* community clinic

dispensé, e *adj* **être dispensé de quelque chose** to be excused something ▷ *Elle est dispensée de gymnastique.* She's excused gym.

disperser *vb* [**28**] to break up ▷ *La police a dispersé les manifestants.* The police broke up the demonstrators.; **se disperser** to break up ▷ *Une fois l'ambulance partie, la foule s'est dispersée.* Once the ambulance had left, the crowd broke up.

disponible *adj* available

disposé, e *adj* **être disposé à faire quelque chose** to be willing to do

something ▷ *Il était disposé à m'aider.* He was willing to help me.
disposer *vb* [**28**] **disposer de quelque chose** to have access to something ▷ *Je dispose d'un ordinateur.* I have access to a computer.
disposition *nf* **prendre ses dispositions** to make arrangements; **avoir quelque chose à sa disposition** to have something at one's disposal; **Je suis à votre disposition.** I am at your service.; **Je tiens ces livres à votre disposition.** The books are at your disposal.
dispute *nf* argument
se **disputer** *vb* [**28**] to argue
disquaire *nm* record dealer
disque *nm* record; **un disque compact** a compact disc; **le disque dur** hard disk
disséminé, e *adj* scattered
disséquer *vb* [**34**] to dissect
dissertation *nf* essay
dissimuler *vb* [**28**] to conceal
se **dissiper** *vb* [**28**] to clear ▷ *Le brouillard va se dissiper dans l'après-midi.* The fog will clear during the afternoon.
dissolvant *nm* nail polish remover
dissoudre *vb* [**70**] to dissolve; **se dissoudre** to dissolve
dissuader *vb* [**28**] **dissuader quelqu'un de faire quelque chose** to dissuade somebody from doing something
distance *nf* distance
distillerie *nf* distillery
distingué, e *adj* distinguished
distinguer *vb* [**28**] to distinguish
distraction *nf* entertainment
distraire *vb* [**85**] **Va voir un film, ça te distraira.** Go and see a film, it'll take your mind off things.
distrait, e *adj* absent-minded
distribuer *vb* [**28**] ❶ to give out ▷ *Distribue les livres, s'il te plaît.* Give out the books, please. ❷ *(cards)* to deal
distributeur *nm* **un distributeur automatique** a vending machine; **un distributeur de billets** a cash machine
dit, e *adj* known as ▷ *Pierre, dit Pierrot* Pierre, known as Pierrot
▶ *vb see* **dire**
dites *vb see* **dire**; **Dites-moi ce que vous pensez.** Tell me what you think.; **dites donc** hey ▷ *Dites donc, vous, là-bas!* Hey, you there!
divers, e *adj* diverse; **pour diverses raisons** for various reasons
se **divertir** *vb* [**38**] to enjoy oneself
divin, e *adj* divine
diviser *vb* [**28**] to divide ▷ *Quatre divisé par deux égale deux.* 4 divided by 2 equals 2.
divorcé *nm* divorcee
divorcer *vb* [**12**] to get divorced
dix *num* ten ▷ *Elle a dix ans.* She's ten.; **le dix février** the tenth of February
dix-huit *num* eighteen ▷ *Elle a dix-huit ans.* She's eighteen. ▷ *à dix-huit heures* at 6 p.m.
dixième *adj* tenth

dix-neuf *num* nineteen ▷ *Elle a dix-neuf ans.* She's nineteen. ▷ *à dix-neuf heures* at 7 p.m.

dix-sept *num* seventeen ▷ *Elle a dix-sept ans.* She's seventeen. ▷ *à dix-sept heures* at 5 p.m.

dizaine *nf* about ten

do *nm* ❶ C ❷ do

docteur *nm* doctor

document *nm* document

documentaire *nm* documentary

documentaliste *nmf* librarian

documentation *nf* documentation

documenter *vb* [**28**] **se documenter sur quelque chose** to gather information on something

dodu, e *adj* plump

doigt *nm* finger; **les doigts de pied** the toes

dois, doit, doivent *vb see* **devoir**

domaine *nm* ❶ estate ▷ *Il possède un immense domaine en Normandie.* He owns a huge estate in Normandy. ❷ field ▷ *La chimie n'est pas mon domaine.* Chemistry's not my field.

domestique *adj* domestic; **les animaux domestiques** pets ▶ *nmf* servant

domicile *nm* place of residence; **à domicile** at home ▷ *Il travaille à domicile.* He works at home.

domicilié, e *adj* **'domicilié à: ...'** 'address: ...'

dominer *vb* [**28**] to dominate; **se dominer** to control oneself

dominos *nmpl* dominoes

dommage *nm* damage; **C'est dommage.** It's a shame.

dompter *vb* [**28**] to tame

dompteur *nm* animal tamer

don *nm* ❶ donation ❷ gift; **Elle a le don de m'énerver.** She's got a knack of getting on my nerves.

donc *conj* so

donjon *nm (of castle)* keep

données *nfpl* data

donner *vb* [**28**] ❶ to give; **donner quelque chose à quelqu'un** to give somebody something ▷ *Elle m'a donné son adresse.* She gave me her address.; **Ça m'a donné faim.** That made me feel hungry. ❷ to give away; **donner sur quelque chose** to overlook something ▷ *une fenêtre qui donne sur la mer* a window overlooking the sea

dont *pron* ❶ of which ▷ *deux livres, dont l'un est en anglais* two books, one of which is in English ▷ *le prix dont il est si fier* the prize he's so proud of ❷ of whom ▷ *trois candidats, dont deux parlent italien* three candidates, two of whom speak Italian ▷ *la fille dont je t'ai parlé* the girl I told you about

doré, e *adj* golden

dorénavant *adv* from now on

dorloter *vb* [**28**] to pamper

dormir *vb* [**29**] ❶ to sleep ▷ *Tu as bien dormi?* Did you sleep well? ❷ to be asleep ▷ *Tu dors?* Are you asleep?

dortoir *nm* dormitory

dos *nm* back; **faire quelque chose dans le dos de quelqu'un** to do something behind somebody's back; **de dos** from behind; **nager le dos crawlé** to swim backstroke; **'voir au dos'** 'see over'

dose *nf* dose

dossier *nm* ❶ file ▷ *une pile de dossiers* a stack of files ❷ report ▷ *un bon dossier scolaire* a good school report ❸ *(in magazine)* feature ❹ *(of chair)* back

douane *nf* customs

douanier *nm* customs officer

double *nm* **le double** twice as much; **en double** in duplicate; **le double messieurs** *(tennis)* the men's doubles

double-cliquer *vb* [**28**] to double-click ▷ *double-cliquer sur une icône* to double-click on an icon

doubler *vb* [**28**] ❶ to double ▷ *Le prix a doublé en dix ans.* The price has doubled in 10 years. ❷ to overtake ▷ *Il est dangereux de doubler sur cette route.* It's dangerous to overtake on this road.; **un film doublé** a dubbed film

douce *adj f see* **doux**

doucement *adv* ❶ gently ❷ slowly ▷ *Je ne comprends pas, parle plus doucement.* I don't understand, speak more slowly.

douceur *nf* ❶ softness ❷ gentleness; **L'avion a atterri en douceur.** The plane made a smooth landing.

douche *nf* shower; **les douches** the shower room; **prendre une douche** to have a shower

se **doucher** *vb* [**28**] to have a shower

doué, e *adj* talented; **être doué en quelque chose** to be good at something

douillet (*f* **douillette**) *adj* ❶ cosy ❷ soft

douleur *nf* pain

douloureux (*f* **douloureuse**) *adj* painful

doute *nm* doubt; **sans doute** probably

douter *vb* [**28**] to doubt; **douter de quelque chose** to have doubts about something ▷ *Je doute de sa sincérité.* I have my doubts about his sincerity.; **se douter de quelque chose** to suspect something; **Je m'en doutais.** I suspected as much.

douteux (*f* **douteuse**) *adj* ❶ dubious ❷ suspicious-looking

Douvres *n* Dover

doux (*f* **douce**, *mpl* **doux**) *adj* ❶ soft ▷ *un tissu doux* soft material ❷ sweet ▷ *du cidre doux* sweet cider ❸ mild ▷ *Il fait doux aujourd'hui.* It's mild today. ❹ gentle ▷ *C'est quelqu'un de très doux.* He's a very gentle person.; **en douce** on the quiet

douzaine *nf* dozen; **une douzaine de personnes** about twelve people

douze *num* twelve ▷ *Il a douze ans.* He's twelve.; **le douze février** the twelfth of February

douzième *adj* twelfth ▷ *au douzième étage* on the twelfth floor

dragée *nf* sugared almond

draguer *vb* [**28**] *(informal)* **draguer quelqu'un** to chat somebody up;

se faire draguer to get chatted up
dragueur *nm (informal) (person)* flirt
dramatique *adj* tragic; **l'art dramatique** drama
drame *nm (incident)* drama; **Ça n'est pas un drame si tu ne viens pas.** It's not the end of the world if you don't come.
drap *nm (for bed)* sheet
drapeau (*pl* **drapeaux**) *nm* flag
dressé, e *adj* trained
dresser *vb* [**28**] ❶ to draw up ▷ *dresser une liste* to draw up a list ❷ to train ▷ *dresser un chien* to train a dog; **dresser l'oreille** to prick up one's ears
drogue *nf* drug; **les drogues douces** soft drugs; **les drogues dures** hard drugs
drogué *nm* drug addict
droguer *vb* [**28**] **droguer quelqu'un** to drug somebody; **se droguer** to take drugs
droguerie *nf* hardware shop
droit, e *adj, adv* ❶ right ▷ *le côté droit* the right-hand side ❷ straight ▷ *Tiens-toi droite!* Stand up straight!; **tout droit** straight on ▶ *nm* ❶ right ▷ *les droits de l'homme* human rights; **avoir le droit de faire quelque chose** to be allowed to do something ❷ law ▷ *un étudiant en droit* a law student
droite *nf* right ▷ *sur votre droite* on your right; **à droite (1)** on the right ▷ *la troisième rue à droite* the third street on the right **(2)** to the right ▷ *à droite de la fenêtre* to the right of the window; **Tournez à droite.** Turn right.; **la voie de droite** the right-hand lane; **la droite** *(in politics)* the right
droitier (*f* **droitière**) *adj* right-handed
drôle *adj* funny; **un drôle de temps** funny weather
drôlement *adv (informal)* really
du *art*

> **du** is the contracted form of **de** + **le**.

❶ some ▷ *Tu veux du fromage?* Would you like some cheese? ❷ any ▷ *Tu as du chocolat?* Have you got any chocolate? ❸ of the ▷ *la porte du garage* the door of the garage ▷ *la femme du directeur* the headmaster's wife
dû (*f* **due**, *mpl* **dus**) *adj* **dû à** due to ▶ *vb see* **devoir**; **Nous avons dû nous arrêter.** We had to stop.
duc *nm* duke
duchesse *nf* duchess
dupe *adj* **Elle me ment mais je ne suis pas dupe.** She lies to me but I'm not taken in by that.
duquel (*mpl* **desquels**, *fpl* **desquelles**) *pron*

> **duquel** is the contracted form of **de** + **lequel**.

▷ *l'homme duquel il parle* the man he is talking about
dur, e *adj, adv* hard
durant *prep* ❶ during ▷ *durant la nuit* during the night ❷ for ▷ *durant des années* for years
durée *nf* length; **pour une durée de quinze jours** for a period of two

weeks; **de courte durée** short; **de longue durée** long
durement *adv* harshly
durer *vb* [**28**] to last
dureté *nf* harshness
DVD *nm* DVD
dynamique *adj* dynamic
dyslexique *adj* dyslexic

eau (*pl* **eaux**) *nf* water; **l'eau minérale** mineral water; **l'eau plate** still water; **tomber à l'eau** to fall through
ébahi, e *adj* amazed
éblouir *vb* [**38**] to dazzle
éboueur *nm* dustman
ébouillanter *vb* [**28**] to scald
écaille *nf (of fish)* scale
s'**écailler** *vb* [**28**] to flake
écart *nm* gap; **à l'écart de** away from
écarté, e *adj* remote; **les bras écartés** arms outstretched; **les jambes écartées** legs apart
écarter *vb* [**28**] *(arms, legs)* to open wide; **s'écarter** to move ▷ *Ils se sont écartés pour le laisser passer.* They moved to let him pass.
échafaudage *nm* scaffolding

échalote *nf* shallot
échange *nm* exchange
échanger *vb* [**45**] to swap ▷ *Je t'échange ce timbre contre celui-là.* I'll swap you this stamp for that one.
échantillon *nm* sample
échapper *vb* [**28**] **échapper à** to escape from ▷ *Le prisonnier a réussi à échapper à la police.* The prisoner managed to escape from the police.; **s'échapper** to escape ▷ *Il s'est échappé de prison.* He escaped from prison.; **l'échapper belle** to have a narrow escape ▷ *Nous l'avons échappé belle.* We had a narrow escape.
écharde *nf* splinter of wood
écharpe *nf* scarf
s' **échauffer** *vb* [**28**] *(before exercise)* to warm up
échec *nm* failure
échecs *nmpl* chess *sg*
échelle *nf* ❶ ladder ❷ *(of map)* scale
échevelé, e *adj* dishevelled
écho *nm* echo
échouer *vb* [**28**] **échouer à un examen** to fail an exam
éclabousser *vb* [**28**] to splash
éclair *nm* flash of lightning; **un éclair au chocolat** a chocolate éclair
éclairage *nm* lighting
éclaircie *nf* bright interval
éclairer *vb* [**28**] **Cette lampe éclaire bien.** This lamp gives a good light.
éclat *nm* ❶ *(of glass)* piece ❷ *(of sun, colour)* brightness; **des éclats de rire** roars of laughter
éclatant, e *adj* brilliant
éclater *vb* [**28**] ❶ *(tyre, balloon)* to burst; **éclater de rire** to burst out laughing; **éclater en sanglots** to burst into tears ❷ to break out ▷ *La Seconde Guerre mondiale a éclaté en 1939.* The Second World War broke out in 1939.
écœurant, e *adj* sickly
écœurer *vb* [**28**] **Tous ces mensonges m'écœurent.** All these lies make me sick.
école *nf* school ▷ *aller à l'école* to go to school ▷ *une école publique* a state school ▷ *une école maternelle* a nursery school

The **école maternelle** is a state school for 2–6 year-olds.

écolier *nm* schoolboy
écolière *nf* schoolgirl
écologie *nf* ecology
écologique *adj* ecological
économie *nf* ❶ economy ❷ economics ▷ *un cours d'économie* an economics class
économies *nfpl* savings; **faire des économies** to save up
économique *adj* ❶ economic ❷ economical
économiser *vb* [**28**] to save
économiseur d'écran *nm* screen saver
écorce *nf* ❶ *(of tree)* bark ❷ *(of orange, lemon)* peel
s' **écorcher** *vb* [**28**] **Je me suis écorché le genou.** I've grazed my knee.
écossais, e *adj, nm/f* ❶ Scottish; **un Écossais** *(man)* a Scot; **une**

Écossaise *(woman)* a Scot; **les Écossais** the Scots ❷ tartan
Écosse *nf* Scotland; **en Écosse** **(1)** in Scotland **(2)** to Scotland
s'**écouler** *vb* [**28**] ❶ *(water)* to flow out ❷ to pass ▷ *Le temps s'écoule trop vite.* Time passes too quickly.
écouter *vb* [**28**] to listen to ▷ *J'aime écouter de la musique.* I like listening to music.; **Écoute-moi!** Listen!
écouteur *nm (of phone)* earpiece
écran *nm* screen; **le petit écran** television; **l'écran total** sunblock
écraser *vb* [**28**] ❶ to crush ▷ *Écrasez une gousse d'ail.* Crush a clove of garlic. ❷ to run over ▷ *Mon chien s'est fait écraser par une voiture.* My dog got run over by a car.; **s'écraser** to crash ▷ *L'avion s'est écrasé dans le désert.* The plane crashed in the desert.
écrémé, e *adj* skimmed
écrevisse *nf* crayfish
écrire *vb* [**30**] to write ▷ *Nous nous écrivons régulièrement.* We write to each other regularly.; **Ça s'écrit comment?** How do you spell that?
écrit *nm* written paper; **par écrit** in writing
écriteau (*pl* **écriteaux**) *nm* notice
écriture *nf* writing
écrivain *nm* writer
écrou *nm (metal)* nut
s'**écrouler** *vb* [**28**] to collapse
écru, e *adj* off-white
écureuil *nm* squirrel
écurie *nf* stable
Édimbourg *n* Edinburgh
éditer *vb* [**28**] to publish
éditeur *nm* publisher
édition *nf* ❶ edition ❷ publishing
édredon *nm* eiderdown
éducateur *nm (of people with special needs)* teacher
éducatif (*f* **éducative**) *adj* educational
éducation *nf* ❶ education ❷ upbringing
éducatrice *nf (of people with special needs)* teacher
éduquer *vb* [**28**] to educate
effacer *vb* [**12**] to rub out
effarant, e *adj* amazing
effectivement *adv* indeed

Be careful! **effectivement** does not mean **effectively**.

effectuer *vb* [**28**] ❶ to make ❷ to do
effervescent, e *adj* effervescent
effet *nm* effect; **faire de l'effet** to take effect; **Ça m'a fait un drôle d'effet de le revoir.** It gave me a strange feeling to see him again.; **en effet** yes indeed
efficace *adj* ❶ efficient ❷ effective ▷ *un médicament efficace* an effective medicine
s'**effondrer** *vb* [**28**] to collapse
s'**efforcer** *vb* [**12**] **s'efforcer de faire quelque chose** to try hard to do something
effort *nm* effort
effrayant, e *adj* frightening
effrayer *vb* [**59**] to frighten
effronté, e *adj* cheeky
effroyable *adj* horrifying
égal, e (*mpl* **égaux**) *adj* equal; **Ça m'est égal.** **(1)** I don't mind.

(2) I don't care.
également *adv* also
égaler *vb* [**28**] to equal
égalité *nf* equality; **être à égalité** to be level
égard *nm* **à cet égard** in this respect
égarer *vb* [**28**] to mislay ▷ *J'ai égaré mes clés.* I've mislaid my keys.; **s'égarer** to get lost ▷ *Ils se sont égarés dans la forêt.* They got lost in the forest.
église *nf* church
égoïsme *nm* selfishness
égoïste *adj* selfish
égout *nm* sewer
égratignure *nf* scratch
Égypte *nf* Egypt
égyptien (*f* **égyptienne**) *adj* Egyptian
eh *excl* hey!; **eh bien** well
élan *nm* **prendre de l'élan** to gather speed
s' **élancer** *vb* [**12**] to hurl oneself
élargir *vb* [**38**] to widen
élastique *nm* rubber band
électeur *nm* *(man)* voter
élection *nf* election
électrice *nf* *(woman)* voter
électricien *nm* electrician
électricité *nf* electricity ▷ *une facture d'électricité* an electricity bill
électrique *adj* electric
électronique *adj* electronic ▶ *nf* electronics
élégant, e *adj* smart
élémentaire *adj* elementary
éléphant *nm* elephant
élevage *nm* cattle rearing; **un élevage de porcs** a pig farm; **un élevage de poulets** a chicken farm; **les truites d'élevage** farmed trout
élevé, e *adj* high; **être bien élevé** to have good manners; **être mal élevé** to have bad manners
élève *nmf* pupil
élever *vb* [**43**] ❶ to bring up ▷ *Il a été élevé par sa grand-mère.* He was brought up by his grandmother. ❷ to breed ▷ *Son oncle élève des chevaux.* His uncle breeds horses.; **élever la voix** to raise one's voice; **s'élever à** to come to
éleveur *nm* breeder
éliminatoire *adj* **une note éliminatoire** a fail mark; **une épreuve éliminatoire** *(sport)* a qualifying round
éliminer *vb* [**28**] to eliminate
élire *vb* [**44**] to elect
elle *pron* ❶ she ▷ *Elle est institutrice.* She is a primary school teacher. ❷ her ▷ *Vous pouvez avoir confiance en elle.* You can trust her. ❸ it ▷ *Prends cette chaise: elle est plus confortable.* Take this chair: it's more comfortable.

elle is also used for emphasis. ▷ *Elle, elle est toujours en retard!* Oh, SHE's always late!; **elle-même** herself ▷ *Elle l'a choisi elle-même.* She chose it herself.

elles *pron pl* they ▷ *Où sont Anne et Rachel? — Elles sont allées au cinéma.* Where are Anne and Rachel? — They've gone to the cinema.; **elles-mêmes** themselves

élogieux (*f* **élogieuse**) *adj* complimentary
éloigné, e *adj* distant
s' **éloigner** *vb* [**28**] to go far away ▷ *Ne vous éloignez pas: le dîner est bientôt prêt!* Don't go far away: dinner will soon be ready!; **Vous vous éloignez du sujet.** You are getting off the point.
Élysée *nm* Élysée Palace
The **Élysée** is the residence of the French president.
e-mail *nm* email
emballage *nm* **le papier d'emballage** wrapping paper
emballer *vb* [**28**] to wrap; **s'emballer** (*informal*) to get excited ▷ *Il s'est emballé pour ce projet.* He got really excited about this plan.
embarquement *nm* boarding
embarras *nm* embarrassment; **Vous n'avez que l'embarras du choix.** The only problem is choosing.
embarrassant, e *adj* embarrassing
embarrasser *vb* [**28**] to embarrass ▷ *Cela m'embarrasse de vous demander encore un service.* I feel embarrassed to ask you to do something more for me.
embaucher *vb* [**28**] to take on ▷ *L'entreprise vient d'embaucher cinquante ouvriers.* The firm has just taken on fifty workers.
embêtant, e *adj* annoying
embêtements *nmpl* trouble *sg*
embêter *vb* [**28**] to bother; **s'embêter** to be bored ▷ *Qu'est-ce qu'on s'embête ici!* Isn't it boring here!
embouteillage *nm* traffic jam
embrasser *vb* [**28**] to kiss ▷ *Ils se sont embrassés.* They kissed each other.
s' **embrouiller** *vb* [**28**] to get confused ▷ *Il s'embrouille dans ses explications.* He gets confused when he explains things.
émerveiller *vb* [**28**] to dazzle
émeute *nf* riot
émigrer *vb* [**28**] to emigrate
émission *nf* programme ▷ *une émission de télévision* a TV programme
s' **emmêler** *vb* [**28**] to get tangled
emménager *vb* [**45**] to move in ▷ *Nous venons d'emménager dans une nouvelle maison.* We've just moved into a new house.
emmener *vb* [**43**] to take ▷ *Ils m'ont emmené au cinéma pour mon anniversaire.* They took me to the cinema for my birthday.
émoticon *nm* (*computing*) smiley
émotif (*f* **émotive**) *adj* emotional
émotion *nf* emotion
émouvoir *vb* [**31**] to move ▷ *Sa lettre l'a beaucoup émue.* She was deeply moved by his letter.
emparer *vb* [**28**] **s'emparer de** to grab ▷ *Il s'est emparé de ma valise.* He grabbed my case.
empêchement *nm* **Nous avons eu un empêchement de dernière minute.** We were held up at the last minute.
empêcher *vb* [**28**] to prevent ▷ *Le*

café le soir m'empêche de dormir. Coffee at night keeps me awake.; **Il n'a pas pu s'empêcher de rire.** He couldn't help laughing.

empereur *nm* emperor

s'**empiffrer** *vb* [**28**] *(informal)* to stuff one's face

empiler *vb* [**28**] to pile up

empirer *vb* [**28**] to worsen ▷ *La situation a encore empiré.* The situation got even worse.

emplacement *nm* site

emploi *nm* ❶ use; **le mode d'emploi** directions for use ❷ job; **un emploi du temps** a timetable

employé *nm* employee; **un employé de bureau** an office worker

employée *nf* employee

employer *vb* [**53**] ❶ to use ▷ *Quelle méthode employez-vous?* What method do you use? ❷ to employ ▷ *L'entreprise emploie dix ingénieurs.* The firm employs ten engineers.

employeur *nm* employer

empoisonner *vb* [**28**] to poison

emporter *vb* [**28**] to take ▷ *N'emportez que le strict nécessaire.* Only take the bare minimum.; **plats à emporter** take-away meals; **s'emporter** to lose one's temper ▷ *Je m'emporte facilement.* I'm quick to lose my temper.

empreinte *nf* footprint; **l'empreinte carbone** carbon footprint; **une empreinte digitale** a fingerprint

s'**empresser** *vb* [**28**] **s'empresser de faire quelque chose** to be quick to do something

emprisonner *vb* [**28**] to imprison

emprunt *nm* loan

emprunter *vb* [**28**] to borrow; **emprunter quelque chose à quelqu'un** to borrow something from somebody ▷ *Je peux t'emprunter dix euros?* Can I borrow ten euros from you?

ému, e *adj* touched

en *prep, pron* ❶ in ▷ *Il habite en France.* He lives in France. ▷ *La mariée est en blanc.* The bride is in white. ▷ *Je le verrai en mai.* I'll see him in May. ❷ to ▷ *Je vais en France cet été.* I'm going to France this summer. ❸ by ▷ *C'est plus rapide en voiture.* It's quicker by car. ❹ made of ▷ *C'est en verre.* It's made of glass. ▷ *un collier en argent* a silver necklace ❺ while ▷ *Il s'est coupé le doigt en ouvrant une boîte de conserve.* He cut his finger while opening a tin.; **Elle est sortie en courant.** She ran out.

> When **en** is used with **avoir** and **il y a**, it is not translated in English.

▷ *Est-ce que tu as un dictionnaire? — Oui, j'en ai un.* Have you got a dictionary? — Yes, I've got one. ▷ *Combien d'élèves y a-t-il dans ta classe? — Il y en a trente.* How many pupils are there in your class? — There are 30.

> **en** is also used with verbs and expressions normally followed by **de** to avoid repeating the same word.

▷ *Si tu as un problème, tu peux m'en parler.* If you've got a problem, you can talk to me about it. ▷ *Est-ce que tu peux me rendre ce livre? J'en ai besoin.* Can you give me back that book? I need it. ▷ *Il a un beau jardin et il en est très fier.* He's got a beautiful garden and is very proud of it.; **J'en ai assez.** I've had enough.

encaisser *vb* [**28**] *(money)* to cash

enceinte *adj f* pregnant

enchanté, e *adj* delighted; **Enchanté!** Pleased to meet you!

encombrant, e *adj* bulky

encombrer *vb* [**28**] to clutter

encore *adv* ❶ still ▷ *Il est encore au travail.* He's still at work. ❷ even ❸ again ▷ *Il m'a encore demandé de l'argent.* He asked me for money again.; **encore une fois** once again; **pas encore** not yet

encourager *vb* [**45**] to encourage

encre *nf* ink

encyclopédie *nf* encyclopaedia

endive *nf* chicory

endommager *vb* [**45**] to damage

endormi, e *adj* asleep

endormir *vb* [**29**] to deaden ▷ *Cette piqûre sert à endormir le nerf.* This injection is to deaden the nerve.; **s'endormir** to go to sleep

endroit *nm* place; **à l'endroit** **(1)** the right way out **(2)** the right way up

endurant, e *adj (person)* tough

endurcir *vb* [**38**] to toughen up; **s'endurcir** to become hardened

endurer *vb* [**28**] to endure

énergie *nf* ❶ energy ❷ power; **avec énergie** vigorously

énergique *adj* energetic; **des mesures énergiques** strong measures

énerver *vb* [**28**] **Il m'énerve!** He gets on my nerves!; **Ce bruit m'énerve.** This noise gets on my nerves.; **s'énerver** to get worked up; **Ne t'énerve pas!** Take it easy!

enfance *nf* childhood ▷ *Je le connais depuis l'enfance.* I've known him since I was a child.

enfant *nmf* child

enfer *nm* hell

s'**enfermer** *vb* [**28**] **Il s'est enfermé dans sa chambre.** He shut himself up in his bedroom.

enfiler *vb* [**28**] ❶ to put on ▷ *J'ai rapidement enfilé un pull avant de sortir.* I quickly put on a sweater before going out. ❷ to thread ▷ *J'ai du mal à enfiler cette aiguille.* I am having difficulty threading this needle.

enfin *adv* at last

enflé, e *adj* swollen

enfler *vb* [**28**] to swell

enfoncer *vb* [**12**] **Il marchait, les mains enfoncées dans les poches.** He was walking with his hands thrust into his pockets.; **s'enfoncer** to sink

s'**enfuir** *vb* [**39**] to run off

engagement *nm* commitment

engager *vb* [**45**] *(person)* to take on

s'**engager** *vb* [**45**] to commit oneself ▷ *Le Premier ministre s'est engagé à combattre le chômage.* The

Prime Minister has committed himself to fighting unemployment.; **Il s'est engagé dans l'armée à dix-huit ans.** He joined the army when he was 18.

engelures *nfpl* chilblains

engin *nm* device

Be careful! The French word **engin** does not mean **engine**.

s' **engourdir** *vb* [**38**] to go numb

engueuler *vb* [**28**] *(informal)* **engueuler quelqu'un** to tell somebody off

énigme *nf* riddle

s' **enivrer** *vb* [**28**] to get drunk

enjamber *vb* [**28**] to stride over ▷ *enjamber une barrière* to stride over a fence

enlèvement *nm* kidnapping

enlever *vb* [**43**] ❶ to take off ▷ *Enlève donc ton manteau!* Take off your coat! ❷ to kidnap

enneigé, e *adj* snowed up

ennemi *nm* enemy

ennui *nm* ❶ boredom ❷ problem ▷ *avoir des ennuis* to have problems

ennuyer *vb* [**53**] to bother ▷ *J'espère que cela ne vous ennuie pas trop.* I hope it doesn't bother you too much.; **s'ennuyer** to be bored

ennuyeux (*f* **ennuyeuse**) *adj* ❶ boring ❷ awkward

énorme *adj* huge

énormément *adv* **Il a énormément grossi.** He's put on an awful lot of weight.; **Il y a énormément de neige.** There's an enormous amount of snow.

enquête *nf* ❶ investigation ❷ survey

enquêter *vb* [**28**] to investigate ▷ *La police enquête actuellement sur le crime.* The police are currently investigating the crime.

enrageant, e *adj* infuriating

enrager *vb* [**45**] to be furious

enregistrement *nm* recording; **l'enregistrement des bagages** baggage check-in

enregistrer *vb* [**28**] ❶ to record ▷ *Ils viennent d'enregistrer un nouvel album.* They've just recorded a new album. ❷ to check in ▷ *Vous pouvez enregistrer plusieurs valises.* You can check in several cases.

s' **enrhumer** *vb* [**28**] to catch a cold ▷ *Je suis enrhumé.* I've got a cold.

s' **enrichir** *vb* [**38**] to get rich

enrouler *vb* [**28**] to wind ▷ *Enroulez le fil autour de la bobine.* Wind the thread round the bobbin.

enseignant *nm* teacher

enseignante *nf* teacher

enseignement *nm* ❶ education ▷ *les réformes de l'enseignement* education reforms ❷ teaching ▷ *l'enseignement des langues étrangères* the teaching of foreign languages

enseigner *vb* [**28**] to teach

ensemble *adv* together ▷ *tous ensemble* all together
▶ *nm* outfit; **l'ensemble de** the whole of; **dans l'ensemble** on the whole

ensoleillé, e *adj* sunny

ensuite *adv* then

entamer *vb* [**28**] to start ▷ *Qui a*

entamé le gâteau? Who's started the cake?

s' **entasser** *vb* [**28**] to cram ▷ *Ils se sont tous entassés dans ma voiture.* They all crammed into my car.

entendre *vb* [**88**] ❶ to hear ▷ *Je ne t'entends pas.* I can't hear you.; **J'ai entendu dire qu'il est dangereux de nager ici.** I've heard that it's dangerous to swim here. ❷ to mean ▷ *Qu'est-ce que tu entends par là?* What do you mean by that?; **s'entendre** to get on ▷ *Il s'entend bien avec sa sœur.* He gets on well with his sister.

entendu, e *adj* **C'est entendu!** Agreed!; **bien entendu** of course

enterrement *nm (burial)* funeral

enterrer *vb* [**28**] to bury

entêté, e *adj* stubborn

s' **entêter** *vb* [**28**] to persist ▷ *Il s'entête à refuser de voir le médecin.* He persists in refusing to go to the doctor.

enthousiasme *nm* enthusiasm

s' **enthousiasmer** *vb* [**28**] to get enthusiastic ▷ *Il s'enthousiasme facilement.* He gets very enthusiastic about things.

entier (*f* **entière**) *adj* whole ▷ *Il a mangé une quiche entière.* He ate a whole quiche.; **le lait entier** full fat milk

entièrement *adv* completely

entorse *nf* sprain ▷ *Il s'est fait une entorse à la cheville.* He's sprained his ankle.

entourer *vb* [**28**] to surround

entracte *nm* interval

entraînement *nm* training

entraîner *vb* [**28**] ❶ to lead ▷ *Il se laisse facilement entraîner par les autres.* He's easily led. ❷ to train ▷ *Il entraîne l'équipe de France depuis cinq ans.* He's been training the French team for five years. ❸ to involve ▷ *Un mariage entraîne beaucoup de dépenses.* A wedding involves a lot of expense.; **s'entraîner** to train ▷ *Il s'entraîne au foot tous les samedis matins.* He does football training every Saturday morning.

entraîneur *nm* trainer

entre *prep* between ▷ *Il est assis entre son père et son oncle.* He's sitting between his father and his uncle.; **entre eux** among themselves; **l'un d'entre eux** one of them

entrecôte *nf* rib steak

entrée *nf* ❶ entrance ❷ *(of meal)* starter ▷ *Qu'est ce que vous prenez comme entrée?* What would you like for the starter?

entreprendre *vb* [**65**] to start on ▷ *Elle a entrepris des démarches pour adopter un enfant.* She's started on the procedures for adopting a child.

entrepreneur *nm* contractor

entreprise *nf* firm

entrer *vb* [**32**] ❶ to come in ▷ *Entrez donc!* Come on in! ❷ to go in ▷ *Ils sont tous entrés dans la maison.* They all went into the house.; **entrer à l'hôpital** to go into hospital; **entrer des données** to enter data

entre-temps *adv* meanwhile

entretien *nm* ❶ maintenance ❷ interview
entrevue *nf* interview
entrouvert, e *adj* half open
envahir *vb* [**38**] to invade
enveloppe *nf* envelope
envelopper *vb* [**28**] to wrap
envers *prep* towards ▷ *Il est bien disposé envers elle.* He's well disposed towards her.
▶ *nm* **à l'envers** inside out
envie *nf* **avoir envie de faire quelque chose** to feel like doing something ▷ *J'avais envie de pleurer.* I felt like crying. ▷ *J'ai envie d'aller aux toilettes.* I want to go to the toilet.; **Cette glace me fait envie.** I fancy some of that ice cream.
envier *vb* [**19**] to envy
environ *adv* about ▷ *C'est à soixante kilomètres environ.* It's about 60 kilometres.
environnement *nm* environment
environs *nmpl* area *sg* ▷ *Il y a beaucoup de choses intéressantes à voir dans les environs.* There are a lot of interesting things to see in the area.; **aux environs de dix-neuf heures** around 7 p.m.
envisager *vb* [**45**] to consider
s' **envoler** *vb* [**28**] ❶ to fly away ▷ *Le papillon s'est envolé.* The butterfly flew away. ❷ to blow away ▷ *Toutes mes feuilles de cours se sont envolées.* All my lecture notes blew away.
envoyer *vb* [**33**] to send ▷ *Ma tante m'a envoyé une carte pour mon anniversaire.* My aunt sent me a card for my birthday.; **envoyer quelqu'un chercher quelque chose** to send somebody to get something ▷ *Sa mère l'a envoyé chercher du pain.* His mother sent him to get some bread.; **envoyer un e-mail à quelqu'un** to send somebody an email
épais (*f* **épaisse**) *adj* thick
épaisseur *nf* thickness
épatant, e *adj (informal)* great
épaule *nf* shoulder
épée *nf* sword
épeler *vb* [**4**] to spell ▷ *Est-ce que vous pouvez épeler votre nom, s'il vous plaît?* Can you spell your name, please?
épice *nf* spice
épicé, e *adj* spicy
épicerie *nf* grocer's shop
épicier *nm* grocer
épidémie *nf* epidemic
épiler *vb* [**28**] **s'épiler les jambes** to wax one's legs; **s'épiler les sourcils** to pluck one's eyebrows
épinards *nmpl* spinach *sg*
épine *nf* thorn
épingle *nf* pin; **une épingle de sûreté** a safety pin
épisode *nm* episode
éplucher *vb* [**28**] to peel
éponge *nf* sponge
époque *nf* time ▷ *à cette époque de l'année* at this time of year; **à l'époque** at that time
épouse *nf* wife
épouser *vb* [**28**] to marry
épouvantable *adj* awful
épouvante *nf* terror; **un film**

d'épouvante a horror film
épouvanter *vb* [**28**] to terrify
époux *nm* husband; **les nouveaux époux** the newly-weds
épreuve *nf* ❶ test ▷ *une épreuve écrite* a written test ❷ *(sport)* event
éprouver *vb* [**28**] to feel ▷ *Qu'est-ce que vous avez éprouvé à ce moment-là?* What did you feel at that moment?
EPS *nf* (= *éducation physique et sportive*) PE (= *physical education*)
épuisé, e *adj* exhausted
épuiser *vb* [**28**] to wear out ▷ *Ce travail m'a complètement épuisé.* This job has completely worn me out.; **s'épuiser** to wear oneself out ▷ *Il s'épuise à garder un jardin impeccable.* He wears himself out keeping his garden immaculate.
Équateur *nm* Ecuador
équateur *nm* equator
équation *nf* equation
équerre *nf* set square
équilibre *nm* balance ▷ *J'ai failli perdre l'équilibre.* I nearly lost my balance.
équilibré, e *adj* well-balanced
équipage *nm* crew
équipe *nf* team
équipé, e *adj* **bien équipé** well-equipped
équipement *nm* equipment
équipements *nmpl* facilities ▷ *les équipements sportifs* sports facilities
équitation *nf* riding
équivalent *nm* equivalent
erreur *nf* mistake; **faire erreur** to be mistaken
es *vb see* **être**; **Tu es très gentille.** You're very kind.
escabeau (*pl* **escabeaux**) *nm* stepladder
escalade *nf* climbing
escalader *vb* [**28**] to climb
escale *nf* **faire escale** to stop off
escalier *nm* stairs
escargot *nm* snail
esclavage *nm* slavery
esclave *nmf* slave
escrime *nf* fencing
escroc *nm* crook
espace *nm* space; **espace de travail** workspace
s'**espacer** *vb* [**12**] to become less frequent ▷ *Ses visites se sont peu à peu espacées.* His visits became less and less frequent.
espadrille *nf* rope-soled sandal
Espagne *nf* Spain; **en Espagne** **(1)** in Spain **(2)** to Spain
espagnol, e *adj, n* Spanish ▷ *J'apprends l'espagnol.* I'm learning Spanish.; **un Espagnol** *(man)* a Spaniard; **une Espagnole** *(woman)* a Spaniard
espèce *nf* ❶ sort ❷ species ▷ *une espèce en voie de disparition* an endangered species; **Espèce d'idiot!** You idiot!
espèces *nfpl* cash *sg*
espérer *vb* [**34**] to hope; **J'espère bien.** I hope so. ▷ *Tu penses avoir réussi? — Oui, j'espère bien.* Do you think you've passed? — Yes, I hope so.
espiègle *adj* mischievous
espion *nm* spy
espionnage *nm* spying; **un roman**

d'espionnage a spy novel

espoir *nm* hope

esprit *nm* mind ▷ *Ça ne m'est pas venu à l'esprit.* It didn't cross my mind.; **avoir de l'esprit** to be witty

esquimau® (*pl* **esquimaux**) *nm* ice lolly

essai *nm* attempt; **prendre quelqu'un à l'essai** to take somebody on for a trial period

essayer *vb* [**59**] ❶ to try ▷ *Essaie de rentrer de bonne heure.* Try to come home early. ❷ to try on ▷ *Essaie ce pull: il devrait bien t'aller.* Try this sweater on: it ought to look good on you.

essence *nf* petrol

essentiel (*f* **essentielle**) *adj* essential; **Tu es là: c'est l'essentiel.** You're here: that's the main thing.

s' **essouffler** *vb* [**28**] to get out of breath

essuie-glace *nm* windscreen wiper

essuyer *vb* [**53**] to wipe; **essuyer la vaisselle** to dry the dishes; **s'essuyer** to dry oneself ▷ *Vous pouvez vous essuyer les mains avec cette serviette.* You can dry your hands on this towel.

est *vb see* **être**; **Elle est merveilleuse.** She's marvellous.
▸ *adj* ❶ east ❷ eastern
▸ *nm* east; **vers l'est** eastwards; **à l'est de Paris** east of Paris; **l'Europe de l'Est** Eastern Europe; **le vent d'est** the east wind

est-ce que *adv* **Est-ce que c'est cher?** Is it expensive?; **Quand est-ce qu'il part?** When is he leaving?

esthéticienne *nf* beautician

estime *nf* **J'ai beaucoup d'estime pour elle.** I think a lot of her.

estimer *vb* [**28**] **estimer quelqu'un** to have great respect for somebody; **estimer que** to consider that ▷ *J'estime que c'est de sa faute.* I consider that it's his fault.

estivant *nm* holiday-maker

estomac *nm* stomach

Estonie *nf* Estonia

estrade *nf* platform

et *conj* and

établir *vb* [**38**] to establish; **s'établir à son compte** to set up in business

établissement *nm* establishment; **un établissement scolaire** a school

étage *nm* floor ▷ *au premier étage* on the first floor; **à l'étage** upstairs

étagère *nf* shelf

étaient *vb see* **être**

étain *nm* tin

étais, était *vb see* **être**; **Il était très jeune.** He was very young.

étalage *nm* display

étaler *vb* [**28**] to spread

étanche *adj* ❶ watertight ❷ *(watch)* waterproof

étang *nm* pond

étant *vb see* **être**; **Mes revenus étant limités ...** My income being limited ...

étape *nf* stage; **faire étape** to stop off

État *nm (nation)* state
état *nm* condition ▷ *en mauvais état* in poor condition; **remettre quelque chose en état** to repair something; **le bureau d'état civil** the registry office
États-Unis *nmpl* United States; **aux États-Unis (1)** in the United States **(2)** to the United States
été *vb see* **être**; **Il a été licencié.** He's been made redundant.
▶ *nm* summer; **en été** in the summer
éteindre *vb* **[60]** ❶ to switch off ▷ *Éteins la lumière.* Switch the light off. ❷ *(cigarette)* to put out
étendre *vb* **[88]** to spread ▷ *Elle a étendu une nappe propre sur la table.* She spread a clean cloth on the table.; **étendre le linge** to hang out the washing; **s'étendre** to lie down ▷ *Je vais m'étendre cinq minutes.* I'm going to lie down for five minutes.
éternité *nf* **J'ai attendu une éternité chez le médecin.** I waited for ages at the doctor's.
éternuer *vb* **[28]** to sneeze
êtes *vb see* **être**; **Vous êtes en retard.** You're late.
étiez *vb see* **être**
étinceler *vb* **[4]** to sparkle
étions *vb see* **être**
étiquette *nf* label
s' **étirer** *vb* **[28]** to stretch ▷ *Elle s'est étirée paresseusement.* She stretched lazily.
étoile *nf* star; **une étoile de mer** a starfish; **une étoile filante** a shooting star; **dormir à la belle étoile** to sleep under the stars
étonnant, e *adj* amazing
étonner *vb* **[28]** to surprise ▷ *Cela m'étonnerait que le colis soit déjà arrivé.* I'd be surprised if the parcel had arrived yet.
étouffer *vb* **[28]** **On étouffe ici: ouvre donc les fenêtres.** It's stifling in here: open the windows.; **s'étouffer** to choke ▷ *Ne mange pas si vite: tu vas t'étouffer!* Don't eat so fast: you'll choke!
étourderie *nf* absent-mindedness; **une erreur d'étourderie** a slip
étourdi, e *adj* scatterbrained
étourdissement *nm* **avoir des étourdissements** to feel dizzy
étrange *adj* strange
étranger *(f* **étrangère***)* *adj* foreign; **une personne étrangère** a stranger
étranger *nm* ❶ foreigner ❷ stranger; **à l'étranger** abroad
étrangère *nf* ❶ foreigner ❷ stranger
étrangler *vb* **[28]** to strangle; **s'étrangler** to choke ▷ *s'étrangler avec quelque chose* to choke on something
être *nm* **un être humain** a human being
▶ *vb* **[35]** ❶ to be ▷ *Je suis heureux.* I'm happy. ▷ *Il est dix heures.* It's 10 o'clock. ❷ to have ▷ *Il n'est pas encore arrivé.* He hasn't arrived yet.
étrennes *nfpl* **Nous avons donné des étrennes à la gardienne.** We

gave the caretaker a New Year gift.

étroit, e *adj* narrow; **être à l'étroit** to be cramped

étude *nf* study; **faire des études** to be studying ▷ *Il fait des études de droit.* He's studying law.

étudiant *nm* student

étudiante *nf* student

étudier *vb* [19] to study

étui *nm* case ▷ *un étui à lunettes* a glasses case

eu *vb see* **avoir**; **J'ai eu une bonne note.** I got a good mark.

euh *excl* er ▷ *Euh ... je ne m'en souviens pas.* Er ... I can't remember.

euro *nm* euro

Europe *nf* Europe; **en Europe (1)** in Europe **(2)** to Europe

européen (*f* **européenne**) *adj* European

eux *pron pl* them ▷ *Je pense souvent à eux.* I often think of them.

eux is also used for emphasis. ▷ *Elle a accepté l'invitation, mais eux, ils ont refusé.* She accepted the invitation, but THEY refused.

évacuer *vb* [28] to evacuate

s'**évader** *vb* [28] to escape

évangile *nm* gospel

s'**évanouir** *vb* [38] to faint

s'**évaporer** *vb* [28] to evaporate

évasif (*f* **évasive**) *adj* evasive

évasion *nf* escape

éveillé, e *adj* ❶ awake ▷ *Il est resté éveillé toute la nuit.* He stayed awake all night. ❷ bright ▷ *C'est un enfant très éveillé pour son âge.* He's very bright for his age.

s'**éveiller** *vb* [28] to awaken

événement *nm* event

éventail *nm (hand-held)* fan; **un large éventail de prix** a wide range of prices

éventualité *nf* **dans l'éventualité d'un retard** in the event of a delay

éventuel (*f* **éventuelle**) *adj* possible

Be careful! **éventuel** does not mean **eventual**.

éventuellement *adv* possibly

Be careful! **éventuellement** does not mean **eventually**.

évêque *nm* bishop

évidemment *adv* ❶ obviously ❷ of course

évidence *nf* **C'est une évidence.** It's quite obvious.; **de toute évidence** obviously; **être en évidence** to be clearly visible; **mettre en évidence** to reveal

évident, e *adj* obvious

évier *nm* sink

éviter *vb* [28] to avoid

évolué, e *adj* advanced

évoluer *vb* [28] to progress ▷ *La chirurgie esthétique a beaucoup évolué.* Cosmetic surgery has progressed a great deal.; **Il a beaucoup évolué.** He has come on a great deal.

évolution *nf* ❶ development ❷ evolution

évoquer *vb* [28] to mention ▷ *Il a évoqué divers problèmes dans son discours.* He mentioned various problems in his speech.

exact, e *adj* ❶ right ❷ exact

exactement *adv* exactly

ex aequo *adj* **Ils sont arrivés ex aequo.** They finished neck and neck.

exagérer *vb* **[34]** ❶ to exaggerate ▷ *Vous exagérez!* You're exaggerating! ❷ to go too far ▷ *Ça fait trois fois que tu arrives en retard: tu exagères!* That's three times you've been late: you really go too far sometimes!

examen *nm* exam; **un examen médical** a medical

examiner *vb* **[28]** to examine

exaspérant, e *adj* infuriating

exaspérer *vb* **[34]** to infuriate

excédent *nm* **l'excédent de bagages** excess baggage

excéder *vb* **[34]** to exceed ▷ *un contrat dont la durée n'excède pas deux ans* a contract for a period not exceeding two years; **excéder quelqu'un** to drive somebody mad ▷ *Les cris des enfants l'excédaient.* The noise of the children was driving her mad.

excellent, e *adj* excellent

excentrique *adj* eccentric

excepté *prep* except ▷ *Toutes les chaussures excepté les sandales sont en solde.* All the shoes except sandals are reduced.

exception *nf* exception; **à l'exception de** except

exceptionnel (*f* **exceptionnelle**) *adj* exceptional

excès *nm* **faire des excès** to overindulge; **les excès de vitesse** speeding

excessif (*f* **excessive**) *adj* excessive

excitant, e *adj* exciting ▶ *nm* stimulant

excitation *nf* excitement

exciter *vb* **[28]** to excite ▷ *Il était tout excité à l'idée de revoir ses cousins.* He was all excited about seeing his cousins again.; **s'exciter** *(informal)* to get excited ▷ *Ne t'excite pas trop vite: ça ne va peut-être pas marcher!* Don't get excited too soon: it may not work!

exclamation *nf* exclamation

exclu, e *adj* **Il n'est pas exclu que ...** It's not impossible that ...

exclusif (*f* **exclusive**) *adj* exclusive

excursion *nf* ❶ trip ❷ walk ▷ *une excursion dans la montagne* a walk in the hills

excuse *nf* ❶ excuse ❷ apology ▷ *présenter ses excuses* to offer one's apologies; **un mot d'excuse** a note ▷ *Vous devez apporter un mot d'excuse signé par vos parents.* You have to bring a note signed by your parents.

excuser *vb* **[28]** to excuse; **Excusez-moi. (1)** Sorry. ▷ *Excusez-moi, je ne vous avais pas vu.* Sorry, I didn't see you. **(2)** Excuse me. ▷ *Excusez-moi, est-ce que vous avez l'heure?* Excuse me, have you got the time?; **s'excuser** to apologize

exécuter *vb* **[28]** ❶ to execute ▷ *Le prisonnier a été exécuté à l'aube.* The prisoner was executed at dawn. ❷ to perform ▷ *Le pianiste va maintenant exécuter une valse de Chopin.* The pianist is now going to

perform a waltz by Chopin.
exemplaire *nm* copy
exemple *nm* example ▷ *donner l'exemple* to set an example; **par exemple** for example
s' **exercer** *vb* [**12**] to practise
exercice *nm* exercise
exhiber *vb* [**28**] to show off ▷ *Il aime bien exhiber ses décorations.* He likes showing off his medals.; **s'exhiber** to expose oneself
exhibitionniste *nm* flasher
exigeant, e *adj* hard to please
exiger *vb* [**45**] ❶ to demand ▷ *Le propriétaire exige d'être payé immédiatement.* The landlord is demanding to be paid immediately. ❷ to require ▷ *Ce travail exige beaucoup de patience.* This job requires a lot of patience.
exil *nm* exile
exister *vb* [**28**] to exist ▷ *Ça n'existe pas.* It doesn't exist.
exotique *adj* exotic; **un yaourt aux fruits exotiques** a tropical fruit yoghurt
expédier *vb* [**19**] to send ▷ *expédier un colis* to send a parcel
expéditeur *nm* sender
expédition *nf* expedition; **l'expédition du courrier** the dispatch of the mail
expérience *nf* ❶ experience ❷ experiment
expérimenter *vb* [**28**] to test ▷ *Ces produits de beauté n'ont pas été expérimentés sur des animaux.* These cosmetics have not been tested on animals.
expert *nm* expert
expirer *vb* [**28**] ❶ *(document, passport)* to expire ❷ *(time allowed)* to run out ❸ *(person)* to breathe out
explication *nf* explanation; **une explication de texte** *(of a text)* a critical analysis
expliquer *vb* [**28**] to explain ▷ *Il m'a expliqué comment faire.* He explained to me how to do it.; **Ça s'explique.** It's understandable.
exploit *nm* achievement
exploitation *nf* exploitation; **une exploitation agricole** a farm
exploiter *vb* [**28**] to exploit
explorer *vb* [**28**] to explore
exploser *vb* [**28**] to explode
explosif *nm* explosive
explosion *nf* explosion
exportateur *nm* exporter
exportation *nf* export
exporter *vb* [**28**] to export
exposé *nm* talk ▷ *un exposé sur l'environnement* a talk on the environment
exposer *vb* [**28**] ❶ to show ▷ *Il expose ses peintures dans une galerie d'art.* He shows his paintings in a private art gallery. ❷ to expose ▷ *N'exposez pas la pellicule à la lumière.* Do not expose the film to light. ❸ to set out ▷ *Il nous a exposé les raisons de son départ.* He set out the reasons for his departure.; **s'exposer au soleil** to stay out in the sun
exposition *nf* exhibition
exprès *adv* ❶ on purpose

❷ specially

express *nm* ❶ *(coffee)* espresso ❷ fast train

expression *nf* ❶ expression ❷ phrase

exprimer *vb* [**28**] to express; **s'exprimer** to express oneself

exquis, e *adj* exquisite

extérieur, e *adj* outside ▶ *nm* outside; **à l'extérieur** outside ▷ *Les toilettes sont à l'extérieur.* The toilet is outside.

externat *nm* day school

externe *nmf* day pupil

extincteur *nm* fire extinguisher

extra *adj* excellent

extraire *vb* [**85**] to extract

extrait *nm* extract

extraordinaire *adj* extraordinary

extravagant, e *adj* extravagant

extrême *adj* extreme ▶ *nm* extreme

extrêmement *adv* extremely

Extrême-Orient *nm* the Far East

extrémité *nf* end ▷ *La gare est à l'autre extrémité de la ville.* The station is at the other end of the town.

f

F *abbr (currency in Switzerland and many former French colonies)* franc

fa *nm* F

fabrication *nf* manufacture

fabriquer *vb* [**28**] to make ▷ *fabriqué en France* made in France; **Qu'est-ce qu'il fabrique?** *(informal)* What's he up to?

fac *nf (informal)* university; **à la fac** at university

face *nf* **face à face** face to face; **en face de** opposite ▷ *Le bus s'arrête en face de chez moi.* The bus stops opposite my house.; **faire face à quelque chose** to face something; **Pile ou face? — Face.** Heads or tails? — Heads.

fâché, e *adj* angry; **être fâché contre quelqu'un** to be angry with somebody; **être fâché avec**

quelqu'un to be on bad terms with somebody

se **fâcher** *vb* [**28**] **se fâcher contre quelqu'un** to lose one's temper with somebody; **se fâcher avec quelqu'un** to fall out with somebody

facile *adj* easy; **facile à faire** easy to do

facilement *adv* easily

facilité *nf* **un logiciel d'une grande facilité d'utilisation** a very user-friendly piece of software; **Il a des facilités en langues.** He has a gift for languages.

Be careful! **facilité** does not mean **facility**.

façon *nf* way ▷ *De quelle façon?* In what way?; **de toute façon** anyway

facteur *nm* postman

facture *nf* bill ▷ *une facture de gaz* a gas bill

facultatif (*f* **facultative**) *adj* optional

faculté *nf* faculty; **avoir une grande faculté de concentration** to have great powers of concentration

fade *adj* tasteless

faible *adj* weak; **Il est faible en maths.** He's not very good at maths.

faiblesse *nf* weakness

faïence *nf* pottery

faillir *vb* [**12**] **J'ai failli tomber.** I nearly fell down.

faillite *nf* bankruptcy; **une entreprise en faillite** a bankrupt business; **faire faillite** to go bankrupt

faim *nf* hunger; **avoir faim** to be hungry

fainéant, e *adj* lazy

faire *vb* [**36**] ❶ to make ▷ *Je vais faire un gâteau pour ce soir.* I'm going to make a cake for tonight. ▷ *Ils font trop de bruit.* They're making too much noise. ❷ to do ▷ *Qu'est-ce que tu fais?* What are you doing? ▷ *Il fait de l'italien.* He's doing Italian. ❸ to play ▷ *Il fait du piano.* He plays the piano. ❹ to be ▷ *Qu'est-ce qu'il fait chaud!* Isn't it hot! ▷ *Espérons qu'il fera beau demain.* Let's hope it'll be nice weather tomorrow.; **Ça ne fait rien.** It doesn't matter.; **Ça fait cinquante-trois euros en tout.** That makes fifty-three euros in all.; **Ça fait trois ans qu'il habite à Paris.** He's lived in Paris for three years.; **faire tomber** to knock over ▷ *Le chat a fait tomber le vase.* The cat knocked over the vase.; **faire faire quelque chose** to get something done ▷ *Je dois faire réparer ma voiture.* I've got to get my car repaired.; **Je vais me faire couper les cheveux.** I'm going to get my hair cut.; **Ne t'en fais pas!** Don't worry!

fais, faisaient, faisais, faisait *vb see* **faire**

faisan *nm* pheasant

faisiez, faisions, faisons, fait *vb see* **faire**

fait *nm* fact; **un fait divers** a news item; **au fait** by the way; **en fait** actually

faites *vb see* **faire**
falaise *nf* cliff
falloir *vb* [**37**] *see* **faut**; **faudra**; **faudrait**
famé, e *adj* **un quartier mal famé** a rough area
fameux (*f* **fameuse**) *adj* **Ce n'est pas fameux.** It's not great.
familial, e (*mpl* **familiaux**) *adj* family; **les allocations familiales** child benefit
familier (*f* **familière**) *adj* familiar
famille *nf* ❶ family ▷ *une famille nombreuse* a big family ❷ relatives ▷ *Il a de la famille à Paris.* He's got relatives in Paris.
famine *nf* famine
fanatique *adj* fanatical ▶ *nmf* fanatic
fanfare *nf* brass band
fantaisie *adj* **des bijoux fantaisie** costume jewellery
fantastique *adj* fantastic
fantôme *nm* ghost
farce *nf* ❶ *(for chicken, turkey)* stuffing ❷ practical joke
farci, e *adj* stuffed ▷ *des tomates farcies* stuffed tomatoes
farine *nf* flour
fascinant, e *adj* fascinating
fasciner *vb* [**28**] to fascinate
fascisme *nm* fascism
fasse, fassent, fasses, fassiez, fassions *vb see* **faire**; **Pourvu qu'il fasse beau demain!** Let's hope it'll be fine tomorrow!
fatal, e *adj* fatal; **C'était fatal.** It was bound to happen.
fatalité *nf* fate
fatigant, e *adj* tiring
fatigue *nf* tiredness
fatigué, e *adj* tired
se **fatiguer** *vb* [**28**] to get tired
fauché, e *adj (informal)* hard up
faudra *vb*

> **faudra** is the future tense of **falloir**.

Il faudra qu'on soit plus rapide. We'll have to be quicker.
faudrait *vb*

> **faudrait** is the conditional tense of **falloir**.

Il faudrait qu'on fasse attention. We ought to be careful.
se **faufiler** *vb* [**28**] **Il s'est faufilé à travers la foule.** He made his way through the crowd.
faune *nf* wildlife
fausse *adj see* **faux**
faut *vb*

> **faut** is the present tense of **falloir**.

Il faut faire attention. You've got to be careful.; **Nous n'avons pas le choix, il faut y aller.** We've no choice, we've got to go.; **Il faut que je parte.** I've got to go.; **Il faut du courage pour faire ce métier.** It takes courage to do that job.; **Il me faut de l'argent.** I need money.
faute *nf* ❶ mistake ▷ *faire une faute* to make a mistake ❷ fault ▷ *Ce n'est pas de ma faute.* It's not my fault.; **sans faute** without fail
fauteuil *nm* armchair; **un fauteuil roulant** a wheelchair
faux (*f* **fausse**) *adj, adv* untrue;

faire un faux pas to trip; **Il chante faux.** He sings out of tune.
▶ *nm* fake ▷ *Ce tableau est un faux.* This painting is a fake.
faveur *nf* favour
favori (*f* **favorite**) *adj* favourite
favoriser *vb* [**28**] to favour
fax *nm* fax
faxer *vb* [**28**] to fax; **faxer un document à quelqu'un** to fax somebody a document
fée *nf* fairy
feignant, e *adj (informal)* lazy
félicitations *nfpl* congratulations
féliciter *vb* [**28**] to congratulate
femelle *nf (animal)* female
féminin, e *adj* ❶ female ▷ *les personnages féminins du roman* the female characters in the novel ❷ feminine ▷ *Elle est très féminine.* She's very feminine. ❸ women's ▷ *Elle joue dans l'équipe féminine de France.* She plays in the French women's team.
féministe *adj* feminist
femme *nf* ❶ woman ❷ wife; **une femme au foyer** a housewife; **une femme de ménage** a cleaning woman; **une femme de chambre** a chambermaid
se **fendre** *vb* [**88**] to crack
fenêtre *nf* window
fenouil *nm* fennel
fente *nf* slot
fer *nm* iron; **un fer à cheval** a horseshoe; **un fer à repasser** an iron
fera, ferai, feras, ferez *vb see* **faire**
férié, e *adj* **un jour férié** a public holiday
feriez, ferions *vb see* **faire**
ferme *adj* firm
▶ *nf* farm
fermé, e *adj* ❶ closed ▷ *La pharmacie est fermée.* The chemist's is closed. ❷ off ▷ *Est-ce que le gaz est fermé?* Is the gas off?
fermer *vb* [**28**] ❶ to close ▷ *Ferme la fenêtre.* Close the window. ❷ to turn off ▷ *As-tu bien fermé le robinet?* Have you turned the tap off?; **fermer à clé** to lock ▷ *N'oublie pas de fermer la porte à clé!* Don't forget to lock the door!
fermeture *nf* **les heures de fermeture** closing times; **une fermeture éclair®** a zip
fermier *nm* farmer
fermière *nf* ❶ *(woman)* farmer ❷ farmer's wife
féroce *adj* fierce
ferons, feront *vb see* **faire**
fesses *nfpl* buttocks
festival *nm* festival
festivités *nfpl* festivities
fête *nf* ❶ party; **faire la fête** to party ❷ name day ▷ *C'est sa fête aujourd'hui.* It's his name day today.; **une fête foraine** a funfair; **la Fête Nationale** Bastille Day; **les fêtes de fin d'année** the festive season
fêter *vb* [**28**] to celebrate
feu (*pl* **feux**) *nm* ❶ fire ▷ *prendre feu* to catch fire ▷ *faire du feu* to make a fire; **Au feu!** Fire!; **un feu de joie** a bonfire ❷ traffic light ▷ *un feu rouge*

a red light ▷ *Tournez à gauche aux feux.* Turn left at the lights.; **Avez-vous du feu?** Have you got a light? ❸ heat ▷ *... mijoter à feu doux* ... simmer over a gentle heat; **un feu d'artifice** a firework display

feuillage *nm* leaves

feuille *nf* ❶ leaf ▷ *des feuilles mortes* fallen leaves ❷ sheet ▷ *une feuille de papier* a sheet of paper; **une feuille de maladie** a claim form for medical expenses

feuilleté, e *adj* **de la pâte feuilletée** flaky pastry

feuilleter *vb* [**41**] to leaf through

feuilleton *nm* serial

feutre *nm* felt; **un stylo-feutre** a felt-tip pen

fève *nf* broad bean

février *nm* February; **en février** in February

fiable *adj* reliable

fiançailles *nfpl* engagement *sg*

fiancé, e *adj* **être fiancé à quelqu'un** to be engaged to somebody

se **fiancer** *vb* [**12**] to get engaged

ficelle *nf* ❶ string ❷ *(bread)* thin baguette

fiche *nf* form

se **ficher** *vb* [**28**] *(informal)* **Je m'en fiche!** I don't care!; **Quoi, tu n'as fait que ça? Tu te fiches de moi!** You've only done that much? You can't be serious!

fichier *nm* file

fichu, e *adj (informal)* **Ce parapluie est fichu.** This umbrella's knackered.

fidèle *adj* faithful

fier (*f* **fière**) *adj* proud

fierté *nf* pride

fièvre *nf* fever

fiévreux (*f* **fiévreuse**) *adj* feverish

figue *nf* fig

figure *nf* ❶ face ▷ *Il a reçu le ballon en pleine figure.* The ball hit him smack in the face. ❷ *(illustration)* figure ▷ *Voir figure 2.1, page 32.* See figure 2.1, page 32.

fil *nm* thread; **le fil de fer** wire; **un coup de fil** a phone call

file *nf (of people, objects)* line; **une file d'attente** a queue; **à la file** one after the other; **en file indienne** in single file

filer *vb* [**28**] to speed along; **File dans ta chambre!** Off to your room with you!

filet *nm* net

fille *nf* ❶ girl ▷ *C'est une école de filles.* It's a girls' school. ❷ daughter ▷ *C'est leur fille aînée.* She's their oldest daughter.

fillette *nf* little girl

filleul *nm* godson

filleule *nf* goddaughter

film *nm* film; **un film policier** a thriller; **un film d'aventures** an adventure film; **un film d'épouvante** a horror film; **le film alimentaire** Clingfilm®

fils *nm* son

fin *nf* end ▷ *À la fin, il a réussi à se décider.* In the end he managed to make up his mind.; **'Fin'** 'The End'; **Il sera en vacances fin juin.** He'll be on holiday at the end of June.;

en fin de journée at the end of the day; **en fin de compte** when all's said and done; **sans fin** endless ▶ *adj* fine; **des fines herbes** mixed herbs

finale *nf* final

finalement *adv* ❶ at last ▷ *Nous sommes finalement arrivés.* At last we arrived. ❷ after all ▷ *Finalement, tu avais raison.* You were right after all.

fini, e *adj* finished

finir *vb* [**38**] to finish ▷ *Le cours finit à onze heures.* The lesson finishes at 11 o'clock.; **Il a fini par se décider.** He made up his mind in the end.

finlandais, e *adj, nm/f* Finnish ▷ *Ils parlent finlandais.* They speak Finnish.; **un Finlandais** *(man)* a Finn; **une Finlandaise** *(woman)* a Finn; **les Finlandais** the Finns

Finlande *nf* Finland

firme *nf* firm

fis *vb see* **faire**

fissure *nf* crack

fit *vb see* **faire**

fixe *adj* ❶ steady ▷ *Il n'a pas d'emploi fixe.* He hasn't got a steady job. ❷ set ▷ *Il mange toujours à heures fixes.* He always eats at set times.; **un menu à prix fixe** a set menu

fixer *vb* [**28**] ❶ to fix ▷ *Nous avons fixé une heure pour nous retrouver.* We fixed a time to meet. ❷ to stare at ▷ *Ne fixe pas les gens comme ça!* Don't stare at people like that!

flacon *nm* bottle

flageolet *nm* small haricot bean

flamand, e *adj, nm/f* Flemish ▷ *Il parle flamand chez lui.* He speaks Flemish at home.; **les Flamands** the Dutch-speaking Belgians

flambé, e *adj* **des bananes flambées** flambéed bananas

flamme *nf* flame; **en flammes** on fire

flan *nm* baked custard

flâner *vb* [**28**] to stroll

flaque *nf (of water)* puddle

flash (*pl* **flashes**) *nm (of camera)* flash; **un flash d'information** a newsflash

flatter *vb* [**28**] to flatter

flèche *nf* arrow

fléchettes *nfpl* darts

fleur *nf* flower

fleuri, e *adj* ❶ full of flowers ❷ flowery

fleurir *vb* [**38**] to flower ▷ *Cette plante fleurit en automne.* This plant flowers in autumn.

fleuriste *nmf* florist

fleuve *nm* river

flic *nm (informal)* cop

flipper *nm* pinball machine

flirter *vb* [**28**] to flirt

flocon *nm* flake

flotter *vb* [**28**] to float

flou, e *adj* blurred

fluor *nm* **le dentifrice au fluor** fluoride toothpaste

flûte *nf* flute; **une flûte à bec** a recorder; **Flûte!** *(informal)* Heck!

foi *nf* faith

foie *nm* liver; **une crise de foie** a stomach upset

foin *nm* hay; **le rhume des foins** hay fever

foire *nf* fair
fois *nf* time ▷ *la première fois* the first time ▷ *à chaque fois* each time ▷ *Deux fois deux font quatre.* 2 times 2 is 4.; **une fois** once; **deux fois** twice ▷ *deux fois plus de gens* twice as many people; **une fois que** once; **à la fois** at once ▷ *Je ne peux pas faire deux choses à la fois.* I can't do two things at once.
folie *nf* madness; **faire une folie** to be extravagant
folklorique *adj* folk
folle *adj f see* **fou**
foncé, e *adj* dark
foncer *vb* [**12**] *(informal)* **Je vais foncer à la boulangerie.** I'm just going to dash to the baker's.
fonction *nf* function; **une voiture de fonction** a company car
fonctionnaire *nmf* civil servant
fonctionner *vb* [**28**] to work
fond *nm* ❶ bottom ▷ *Mon porte-monnaie est au fond de mon sac.* My purse is at the bottom of my bag. ❷ end ▷ *Les toilettes sont au fond du couloir.* The toilets are at the end of the corridor.; **dans le fond** all things considered
fonder *vb* [**28**] to found
fondre *vb* [**69**] to melt; **fondre en larmes** to burst into tears
fondu, e *adj* **du beurre fondu** melted butter
font *vb see* **faire**
fontaine *nf* fountain
foot *nm* football
football *nm* football
footballeur *nm* footballer
footing *nm* jogging
forain, e *adj* **une fête foraine** a funfair
▸ *nm* fairground worker
force *nf* strength; **à force de** by ▷ *Il a grossi à force de manger autant.* He got fat by eating so much.; **de force** by force
forcé, e *adj* forced; **C'est forcé.** *(informal)* It's inevitable.
forcément *adv* **Ça devait forcément arriver.** That was bound to happen.; **pas forcément** not necessarily
forêt *nf* forest
forfait *nm* all-in price; **C'est compris dans le forfait.** It's included in the price.
forgeron *nm* blacksmith
formalité *nf* formality
format *nm* size
formation *nf* training; **la formation continue** continuing education; **Il a une formation d'ingénieur.** He is a trained engineer.
forme *nf* shape; **être en forme** to be in good shape; **Je ne suis pas en forme aujourd'hui.** I'm not feeling too good today.; **Tu as l'air en forme.** You're looking well.
formellement *adv* strictly
former *vb* [**28**] ❶ to form ❷ to train
formidable *adj* great
formulaire *nm* form
fort, e *adj, adv* ❶ strong ▷ *Le café est trop fort.* The coffee's too strong. ❷ good ▷ *Il est très fort en espagnol.* He's very good at Spanish. ❸ loud

▷ *Est-ce vous pouvez parler plus fort?* Can you speak louder?; **frapper fort** to hit hard
fortifiant *nm (medicine)* tonic
fortune *nf* fortune; **de fortune** makeshift
forum de discussion *nm (for discussion)* forum
fossé *nm* ditch
fou (*f* **folle**) *adj* mad; **Il y a un monde fou sur la plage!** *(informal)* There are loads of people on the beach!; **attraper le fou rire** to get the giggles
foudre *nf* lightning
foudroyant, e *adj* instant
fouet *nm* whisk
fougère *nf* fern
fouiller *vb* [**28**] to rummage
fouillis *nm* mess ▷ *Il y a du fouillis dans sa chambre.* His bedroom is a mess.
foulard *nm* scarf
foule *nf* crowd; **une foule de** masses of
se **fouler** *vb* [**28**] **se fouler la cheville** to sprain one's ankle
four *nm* oven ▷ *un four à micro-ondes* a microwave oven
fourchette *nf* fork
fourmi *nf* ant; **avoir des fourmis dans les jambes** to have pins and needles

Word for word, this means 'to have ants in one's legs'.

fourneau (*pl* **fourneaux**) *nm* stove
fourni, e *adj (beard, hair)* thick
fournir *vb* [**38**] to supply
fournisseur *nm* supplier; **un fournisseur d'accès à Internet** an internet service provider
fournitures *nfpl* **les fournitures scolaires** school stationery
fourré, e *adj* filled
fourrer *vb* [**28**] *(informal)* to put ▷ *Où as-tu fourré mon sac?* Where have you put my bag?
fourre-tout (*pl* **fourre-tout**) *nm* holdall
fourrure *nf* fur
foyer *nm* home; **un foyer de jeunes** a youth club
fracture *nf* fracture
fragile *adj* fragile
fragilité *nf* fragility
fraîche *adj f see* **frais**
fraîcheur *nf* ❶ cool ❷ freshness
frais (*f* **fraîche**) *adj* ❶ fresh ▷ *des œufs frais* fresh eggs ❷ chilly ▷ *Il fait un peu frais ce soir.* It's a bit chilly this evening. ❸ cool ▷ *des boissons fraîches* cool drinks; **'servir frais'** 'serve chilled'; **mettre au frais** to put in a cool place
▶ *nmpl* expenses
fraise *nf* strawberry
framboise *nf* raspberry
franc (*f* **franche**) *adj* frank
▶ *nm* franc

The **franc** is the unit of currency in Switzerland and many former French colonies.

français, e *adj, n* French ▷ *Il parle français couramment.* He speaks French fluently.; **un Français** a Frenchman; **une Française** a Frenchwoman; **les Français** the French

France *nf* France; **en France (1)** in France ▷ *Je suis né en France.* I was born in France. **(2)** to France ▷ *Je pars en France pour Noël.* I'm going to France for Christmas.
franche *adj f see* **franc**
franchement *adv* ❶ frankly ❷ really
franchir *vb* [**38**] to get over
franchise *nf* frankness
francophone *adj* French-speaking
frange *nf* fringe
frangipane *nf* almond cream
frapper *vb* [**28**] to strike ▷ *Il l'a frappée au visage.* He struck her in the face.
fredonner *vb* [**28**] to hum
freezer *nm* freezing compartment
frein *nm* brake; **le frein à main** handbrake
freiner *vb* [**28**] to brake
frêle *adj* frail
frelon *nm* hornet
frémir *vb* [**38**] shudder
fréquemment *adv* frequently
fréquent, e *adj* frequent
fréquenté, e *adj* busy ▷ *une rue très fréquentée* a very busy street; **un bar mal fréquenté** a rough pub
fréquenter *vb* [**28**] *(person)* to see ▷ *Je ne le fréquente pas beaucoup.* I don't see him often.
frère *nm* brother
friand *nm* **un friand au fromage** a cheese puff
friandise *nf* sweet
fric *nm (informal)* cash
frigidaire® *nm* refrigerator
frigo *nm (informal)* fridge
frileux (*f* **frileuse**) *adj* **être frileux** to feel the cold ▷ *Je suis très frileuse.* I really feel the cold.
frimer *vb* [**28**] *(informal)* to show off
fringues *nfpl (informal)* clothes
fripé, e *adj* crumpled
frire *vb* [**80**] **faire frire** to fry
frisé, e *adj* curly
frisson *nm* shiver
frissonner *vb* [**28**] to shiver
frit, e *adj* fried
frites *nfpl* chips
friture *nf* ❶ fried food ❷ fried fish
froid, e *adj* cold
▶ *nm* cold; **Il fait froid.** It's cold.; **avoir froid** to be cold ▷ *Est-ce que tu as froid?* Are you cold?
se **froisser** *vb* [**28**] ❶ to crease ▷ *Ce tissu se froisse très facilement.* This material creases very easily. ❷ to take offence ▷ *Paul se froisse très facilement.* Paul's very quick to take offence.; **se froisser un muscle** to strain a muscle
frôler *vb* [**28**] ❶ to brush against ▷ *Le chat m'a frôlé au passage.* The cat brushed against me as it went past. ❷ to narrowly avoid ▷ *Nous avons frôlé la catastrophe.* We narrowly avoided disaster.
fromage *nm* cheese
froment *nm* wheat; **une crêpe de froment** *(made with wheat flour)* a pancake
froncer *vb* [**12**] **froncer les sourcils** to frown
front *nm* forehead
frontière *nf* border
frotter *vb* [**28**] to rub ▷ *se frotter les*

a b c d e f g h i j k l m n o p q r s t u v w x y z

yeux to rub one's eyes; **frotter une allumette** to strike a match

fruit *nm* fruit; **un fruit** a piece of fruit; **les fruits de mer** seafood

fruité, e *adj* fruity

frustrer *vb* [**28**] to frustrate

fugue *nf* **faire une fugue** to run away

fuir *vb* [**39**] ❶ to flee ▷ *fuir devant un danger* to flee from danger ❷ to drip ▷ *Le robinet fuit.* The tap's dripping.

fuite *nf* ❶ leak ❷ *(escape)* flight; **être en fuite** to be on the run

fumé, e *adj* smoked ▷ *du saumon fumé* smoked salmon

fumée *nf* smoke

fumer *vb* [**28**] to smoke

fumeur *nm* smoker

fur *nm* **au fur et à mesure** as you go along ▷ *Je vérifie mon travail au fur et à mesure.* I check my work as I go along.; **au fur et à mesure que** as ▷ *Je réponds à mon courrier au fur et à mesure que je le reçois.* I answer my mail as I receive it.

furet *nm* ferret

fureur *nf* fury; **faire fureur** to be all the rage

furieux (*f* **furieuse**) *adj* furious

furoncle *nm (on skin)* boil

fus *vb see* **être**

fuseau (*pl* **fuseaux**) *nm* ski pants

fusée *nf* rocket

fusil *nm* gun

fut *vb see* **être**

futé, e *adj* crafty

futur *nm* future

g

gâcher *vb* [**28**] to waste ▷ *Je n'aime pas gâcher la nourriture.* I don't like to waste food.

gâchis *nm* waste

gaffe *nf* **faire une gaffe** to do something stupid; **Fais gaffe!** *(informal)* Watch out!

gage *nm (in a game)* forfeit

gagnant *nm* winner

gagner *vb* [**28**] to win ▷ *Qui a gagné?* Who won?; **gagner du temps** to save time; **Il gagne bien sa vie.** He makes a good living.

gai, e *adj* cheerful

gaieté *nf* cheerfulness

galerie *nf* gallery; **une galerie marchande** a shopping arcade; **une galerie de jeux d'arcade** an amusement arcade

galet *nm* pebble

galette *nf* ❶ round flat cake; **une galette de blé noir** a buckwheat pancake ❷ biscuit ▷ *des galettes pur beurre* shortbread biscuits; **la galette des Rois**

A **galette des Rois** is a cake eaten on Twelfth Night containing a figurine. The person who finds it is the king (or queen) and gets a paper crown. They then choose someone else to be their queen (or king).

Galles *nf* **le pays de Galles** Wales; **le prince de Galles** the Prince of Wales

gallois, e *adj, n* Welsh; **un Gallois** a Welshman; **une Galloise** a Welshwoman; **les Gallois** the Welsh

galop *nm* gallop

galoper *vb* [**28**] to gallop

gamin *nm (informal)* kid

gamine *nf (informal)* kid

gamme *nf (in music)* scale; **une gamme de produits** a range of products

gammée *adj* **la croix gammée** the swastika

gant *nm* glove; **un gant de toilette** a face cloth

garage *nm* garage

garagiste *nmf* ❶ garage owner ❷ mechanic

garantie *nf* guarantee

garantir *vb* [**38**] to guarantee

garçon *nm* boy; **un vieux garçon** a bachelor

garde *nm* ❶ *(in prison)* warder ❷ security man; **un garde du corps** a bodyguard
▶ *nf* ❶ guarding ❷ guard; **être de garde** to be on duty ▷ *La pharmacie de garde ce week-end est ...* The duty chemist this weekend is ...; **mettre en garde** to warn

garde-côte (*pl* **garde-côtes**) *nm* coastguard

garder *vb* [**28**] ❶ to keep ▷ *Tu as gardé toutes ses lettres?* Have you kept all his letters? ❷ to look after ▷ *Je garde ma nièce samedi après-midi.* I'm looking after my niece on Saturday afternoon. ❸ to guard ▷ *Ils ont pris un gros chien pour garder la maison.* They got a big dog to guard the house.; **garder le lit** to stay in bed; **se garder** to keep ▷ *Ces crêpes se gardent bien.* These pancakes keep well.

garderie *nf* nursery

garde-robe *nf (clothes)* wardrobe

gardien *nm* ❶ caretaker ❷ *(in a museum)* attendant; **un gardien de but** a goalkeeper

gare *nf* station ▷ *la gare routière* the bus station
▶ *excl* **Gare aux serpents!** Watch out for snakes!

garer *vb* [**28**] to park; **se garer** to park

garni, e *adj* **un plat garni** *(vegetables, chips, rice etc)* a dish served with accompaniments

gars *nm (informal)* guy

gaspiller *vb* [**28**] to waste

gâteau (*pl* **gâteaux**) *nm* cake; **les gâteaux secs** biscuits

gâter *vb* [**28**] to spoil ▷ *Il aime gâter*

ses petits-enfants. He likes to spoil his grandchildren.; **se gâter** to go bad; **Le temps va se gâter.** The weather's going to break.

gauche *adj* left ▷ *le côté gauche* the left-hand side
▶ *nf* left ▷ *sur votre gauche* on your left; **à gauche (1)** on the left ▷ *la deuxième rue à gauche* the second street on the left **(2)** to the left ▷ *à gauche de l'armoire* to the left of the cupboard; **Tournez à gauche.** Turn left.; **la voie de gauche** the left-hand lane; **la gauche** *(in politics)* the left

gaucher (*f* **gauchère**) *adj* left-handed

gaufre *nf* waffle

gaufrette *nf* wafer

Gaulois *nm* Gaul ▷ *Astérix le Gaulois* Asterix the Gaul

gaulois, e *adj* Gallic

gaz *nm* gas

gazeux (*f* **gazeuse**) *adj* **une boisson gazeuse** a fizzy drink; **de l'eau gazeuse** sparkling water

gazole *nm (fuel)* diesel

gazon *nm* lawn

géant *nm* giant

gel *nm* frost

gelée *nf* ❶ jelly ❷ frost

geler *vb* [**43**] to freeze; **Il a gelé cette nuit.** There was a frost last night.

gélule *nf (containing medicine)* capsule

Gémeaux *nmpl* Gemini

gémir *vb* [**38**] to moan

gênant, e *adj* awkward

gencive *nf (in mouth)* gum

gendarme *nm* police officer

gendarmerie *nf* ❶ police force ❷ police station

gendre *nm* son-in-law

gêné, e *adj* embarrassed

gêner *vb* [**28**] ❶ to bother ▷ *Je ne voudrais pas vous gêner.* I don't want to bother you. ❷ to feel awkward ▷ *Son regard la gênait.* The way he was looking at her made her feel awkward.

général, e (*mpl* **généraux**) *adj* general; **en général** usually
▶ *nm* general

généralement *adv* generally

généraliste *nmf* family doctor

génération *nf* generation

généreux (*f* **généreuse**) *adj* generous

générosité *nf* generosity

genêt *nm (bush)* broom

génétique *nf* genetics

génétiquement *adv* genetically ▷ *les aliments génétiquement modifiés* GM foods

Genève *n* Geneva

génial, e (*mpl* **géniaux**) *adj (informal)* great

genou (*pl* **genoux**) *nm* knee

genre *nm* kind

gens *nmpl* people

gentil (*f* **gentille**) *adj* ❶ nice ❷ kind

gentillesse *nf* kindness

gentiment *adv* ❶ nicely ❷ kindly

géographie *nf* geography

géométrie *nf* geometry

gérant *nm* manager

gérer *vb* [**34**] to manage

germain, e *adj* **un cousin germain** a first cousin
geste *nm* gesture; **Ne faites pas un geste!** Don't move!
gestion *nf* management
gestionnaire de site *nmf* webmaster
gifle *nf* slap across the face
gifler *vb* [28] to slap across the face
gigantesque *adj* gigantic
gigot *nm* leg of lamb
gilet *nm* ❶ waistcoat ❷ cardigan; **un gilet de sauvetage** a life jacket
gingembre *nm* ginger
girafe *nf* giraffe
gitan *nm* gipsy
gitane *nf* gipsy
gîte *nm* **un gîte rural** a holiday house
glace *nf* ❶ ice ❷ ice cream ▷ *une glace à la fraise* a strawberry ice cream ❸ mirror
glacé, e *adj* ❶ icy ❷ iced ▷ *un thé glacé* an iced tea
glacial, e (*mpl* **glaciaux**) *adj* icy
glaçon *nm* ice cube
glissant, e *adj* slippery
glisser *vb* [28] ❶ to slip ❷ to be slippery
global, e (*mpl* **globaux**) *adj* total
gloire *nf* glory
godasse *nf* (*informal*) shoe
goéland *nm* seagull
golf *nm* ❶ golf ❷ golf course
golfe *nm* gulf; **le golfe de Gascogne** the Bay of Biscay
gomme *nf* rubber
gommer *vb* [28] to rub out
gonflé, e *adj* ❶ (*arm, finger, stomach*) swollen ❷ (*ball, tyre*) inflated; **Il est gonflé!** (*informal*) He's got a nerve!
gonfler *vb* [28] ❶ to blow up ▷ *gonfler un ballon* to blow up a balloon ❷ to pump up ▷ *gonfler un pneu* to pump up a tyre
gorge *nf* ❶ throat ▷ *J'ai mal à la gorge.* I've got a sore throat. ❷ gorge ▷ *les gorges du Tarn* the Tarn gorges
gorgée *nf* sip
gorille *nm* gorilla
gosse *nmf* (*informal*) kid
goudron *nm* tar
gouffre *nm* chasm; **Cette voiture est un vrai gouffre!** This car eats up money!
gourde *nf* water bottle
gourmand, e *adj* greedy
gourmandise *nf* greed
gousse *nf* **une gousse d'ail** a clove of garlic
goût *nm* taste
goûter *vb* [28] ❶ to taste ❷ (*in the afternoon*) to have a snack ▷ *Les enfants goûtent généralement vers quatre heures.* The children usually have a snack around 4 o'clock.
▶ *nm* afternoon snack
goutte *nf* drop
gouvernement *nm* government
gouverner *vb* [28] to govern
grâce *nf* **grâce à** thanks to
gracieux (*f* **gracieuse**) *adj* graceful
gradins *nmpl* (*in stadium*) terraces
graduel (*f* **graduelle**) *adj* gradual
graffiti *nmpl* graffiti *sg*
grain *nm* grain; **un grain de**

beauté a beauty spot; **un grain de café** a coffee bean; **un grain de raisin** a grape
graine *nf* seed
graisse *nf* fat
grammaire *nf* grammar
gramme *nm* gram
grand, e *adj, adv* ❶ tall ▷ *Il est grand pour son âge.* He's tall for his age. ❷ big ▷ *C'est sa grande sœur.* She's his big sister.; **une grande personne** a grown-up ❸ long ▷ *un grand voyage* a long journey; **les grandes vacances** the summer holidays ❹ great ▷ *C'est un grand ami à moi.* He's a great friend of mine.; **un grand magasin** a department store; **une grande surface** a hypermarket; **les grandes écoles** *(at university level)* top ranking colleges; **au grand air** out in the open air; **grand ouvert** wide open
grand-chose *pron* **pas grand-chose** not much
Grande-Bretagne *nf* Britain
grandeur *nf* size
grandir *vb* **[38]** to grow ▷ *Il a beaucoup grandi.* He's grown a lot.
grand-mère (*pl* **grands-mères**) *nf* grandmother
grand-peine: **à grand-peine** *adv* with great difficulty
grand-père (*pl* **grands-pères**) *nm* grandfather
grands-parents *nmpl* grandparents
grange *nf* barn
grappe *nf* **une grappe de raisin** a bunch of grapes
gras (*f* **grasse**) *adj* ❶ *(food)* fatty ❷ greasy ❸ oily; **faire la grasse matinée** to have a lie-in
gratis *adj, adv* free
gratte-ciel (*pl* **gratte-ciel**) *nm* skyscraper
gratter *vb* **[28]** ❶ to scratch ❷ to be itchy
gratuit, e *adj* free ▷ *entrée gratuite* entrance free
grave *adj* ❶ serious ❷ deep ▷ *Il a une voix grave.* He's got a deep voice.; **Ce n'est pas grave.** It doesn't matter.
gravement *adv* seriously
graveur *nm* **un graveur de CD** a CD burner
grec (*f* **grecque**) *adj, nm/f* Greek ▷ *J'apprends le grec.* I'm learning Greek.; **un Grec** *(man)* a Greek; **une Grecque** *(woman)* a Greek; **les Grecs** the Greeks
Grèce *nf* Greece; **en Grèce (1)** in Greece **(2)** to Greece
grêle *nf* hail
grêler *vb* **[28]** **Il grêle.** It's hailing.
grelotter *vb* **[28]** to shiver
grenade *nf* ❶ pomegranate ❷ grenade
grenier *nm* attic
grenouille *nf* frog
grève *nf* ❶ strike; **en grève** on strike; **faire grève** to be on strike ❷ shore
gréviste *nmf* striker
grièvement *adv* **grièvement blessé** seriously injured
griffe *nf* ❶ claw ❷ label

griffer *vb* [**28**] to scratch ▷ *Le chat m'a griffé.* The cat scratched me.
grignoter *vb* [**28**] to nibble
grillade *nf* grilled food
grille *nf* ❶ wire fence ❷ metal gate
grille-pain (*pl* **grille-pain**) *nm* toaster
griller *vb* [**28**] ❶ to toast; **du pain grillé** toast ❷ to grill ▷ *des saucisses grillées* grilled sausages
grimace *nf* **faire des grimaces** to make faces
grimper *vb* [**28**] to climb
grincer *vb* [**12**] to creak
grincheux (*f* **grincheuse**) *adj* grumpy
grippe *nf* flu; **avoir la grippe** to have flu
grippé, e *adj* **être grippé** to have flu
gris, e *adj* grey
Groenland *nm* Greenland
grogner *vb* [**28**] ❶ to growl ❷ to complain
gronder *vb* [**28**] to tell off; **se faire gronder** to get a telling-off ▷ *Tu vas te faire gronder par ton père!* You're going to get a telling-off from your father!
gros (*f* **grosse**) *adj* ❶ big ▷ *une grosse pomme* a big apple ❷ fat ▷ *Je suis trop grosse pour porter ça!* I'm too fat to wear that!
groseille *nf* **la groseille rouge** redcurrant; **la groseille à maquereau** gooseberry
grossesse *nf* pregnancy
grossier (*f* **grossière**) *adj* rude; **une erreur grossière** a bad mistake
grossir *vb* [**38**] to put on weight ▷ *Il a beaucoup grossi.* He's put on a lot of weight.
grosso modo *adv* roughly
grotte *nf* cave
groupe *nm* group
grouper *vb* [**28**] to group; **se grouper** to gather ▷ *Nous nous sommes groupés autour du feu.* We gathered round the fire.
guépard *nm* cheetah
guêpe *nf* wasp
guérir *vb* [**38**] to recover ▷ *Il est maintenant complètement guéri.* He's now completely recovered.
guérison *nf* recovery
guerre *nf* war ▷ *la Deuxième Guerre mondiale* the Second World War
guetter *vb* [**28**] to look out for
gueule *nf* mouth; **Ta gueule!** *(rude)* Shut your face!; **avoir la gueule de bois** *(informal)* to have a hangover
gueuler *vb* [**28**] *(informal)* to bawl
guichet *nm (in bank, booking office)* counter
guide *nm* guide
guider *vb* [**28**] to guide
guidon *nm* handlebars
guillemets *nmpl* inverted commas
guirlande *nf* tinsel; **des guirlandes en papier** paper chains
guitare *nf* guitar
gym *nf (informal)* PE
gymnase *nm* gym
gymnastique *nf* gymnastics

habile *adj* skilful
habillé, e *adj* ❶ dressed ▷ *Il n'est pas encore habillé.* He's not dressed yet. ❷ smart ▷ *Cette robe fait très habillé.* This dress looks very smart.
s' **habiller** *vb* [**28**] ❶ to get dressed ▷ *Je me suis rapidement habillé.* I got dressed quickly. ❷ to dress up ▷ *Est-ce qu'il faut s'habiller pour la réception?* Do you have to dress up to go to the party?
habitant *nm* inhabitant
habiter *vb* [**28**] to live ▷ *Il habite à Montpellier.* He lives in Montpellier.
habits *nmpl* clothes
habitude *nf* habit; **avoir l'habitude de quelque chose** to be used to something; **d'habitude** usually; **comme d'habitude** as usual
habituel (*f* **habituelle**) *adj* usual
s' **habituer** *vb* [**28**] **s'habituer à quelque chose** to get used to something
hachis *nm* mince; **le hachis Parmentier** shepherd's pie
haie *nf* hedge
haine *nf* hatred
haïr *vb* [**40**] to hate
haleine *nf* breath ▷ *être hors d'haleine* to be out of breath
halles *nfpl* covered market *sg*
halte *nf* stop; **Halte!** Stop!
haltérophilie *nf* weightlifting
hamburger *nm* hamburger
hameçon *nm* fish hook
hamster *nm* hamster
hanche *nf* hip
handball *nm* handball
handicapé *nm* disabled man
handicapée *nf* disabled woman
harcèlement *nm* harassment
hareng *nm* herring; **un hareng saur** a kipper
haricot *nm* bean; **les haricots verts** runner beans; **les haricots blancs** haricot beans
harmonica *nm* mouth organ
harpe *nf* harp
hasard *nm* coincidence; **au hasard** at random; **par hasard** by chance; **à tout hasard (1)** just in case **(2)** on the off chance
hâte *nf* **à la hâte** hurriedly; **J'ai hâte de te voir.** I can't wait to see you.
hausse *nf* ❶ increase ❷ rise
hausser *vb* [**28**] **hausser les épaules** to shrug one's shoulders

haut, e *adj, adv* ❶ high ▷ *une haute montagne* a high mountain ❷ aloud ▷ *penser tout haut* to think aloud ▶ *nm* top; **un mur de trois mètres de haut** a wall 3 metres high; **en haut (1)** upstairs **(2)** at the top

hauteur *nf* height

haut-parleur (*pl* **haut-parleurs**) *nm* loudspeaker

hebdomadaire *nm (magazine)* weekly

hébergement *nm* accommodation

héberger *vb* [**45**] to put up ▷ *Mon cousin a dit qu'il nous hébergerait.* My cousin said he would put us up.

hein? *excl* eh? ▷ *Hein? Qu'est-ce que tu dis?* Eh? What did you say?

hélas *adv* unfortunately

hélicoptère *nm* helicopter

hémorragie *nf* haemorrhage

herbe *nf* grass; **les herbes de Provence** mixed herbs

hérisson *nm* hedgehog

hériter *vb* [**28**] to inherit

héritier *nm* heir

héritière *nf* heiress

hermétique *adj* airtight

héroïne *nf* ❶ heroine ❷ *(drug)* heroin

héros *nm* hero

hésitation *nf* hesitation

hésiter *vb* [**28**] to hesitate; **J'ai hésité entre le pull vert et le cardigan jaune.** I couldn't decide between the green pullover and the yellow cardigan.; **sans hésiter** without hesitating

heure *nf* ❶ hour ▷ *Le trajet dure six heures.* The journey lasts six hours. ❷ time ▷ *Vous avez l'heure?* Have you got the time?; **Quelle heure est-il?** What time is it?; **À quelle heure?** What time?; **deux heures du matin** 2 o'clock in the morning; **être à l'heure** to be on time; **une heure de français** a period of French

heureusement *adv* luckily

heureux (*f* **heureuse**) *adj* happy

heurter *vb* [**28**] to hit

hexagone *nm* hexagon; **l'Hexagone** France

France is often referred to as **l'Hexagone** because of its six-sided shape.

hibou (*pl* **hiboux**) *nm* owl

hier *adv* yesterday; **avant-hier** the day before yesterday

hi-fi *nf* stereo; **une chaîne hi-fi** a stereo system

hippique *adj* **un club hippique** a riding centre; **un concours hippique** a horse show

hippopotame *nm* hippopotamus

hirondelle *nf (bird)* swallow

histoire *nf* ❶ history ▷ *un cours d'histoire* a history lesson ❷ story ▷ *C'est l'histoire de deux enfants.* It's the story of two children.; **Ne fais pas d'histoires!** Don't make a fuss!

historique *adj* historic

hiver *nm* winter; **en hiver** in winter

HLM *nmf (= habitation à loyer modéré)* council flat; **des HLM** council housing

hockey *nm* hockey; **le hockey sur glace** ice hockey

hollandais, e *adj, n* Dutch ▷ *J'apprends le hollandais.* I'm learning Dutch.; **un Hollandais** a Dutch man; **une Hollandaise** a Dutch woman; **les Hollandais** the Dutch

Hollande *nf* Holland; **en Hollande** **(1)** in Holland **(2)** to Holland

homard *nm* lobster

homéopathique *adj* homeopathic

hommage *nm* tribute

homme *nm* man; **un homme d'affaires** a businessman

homosexuel (*f* **homosexuelle**) *adj* homosexual

Hongrie *nf* Hungary

hongrois, e *adj, n* Hungarian

honnête *adj* honest

honnêteté *nf* honesty

honneur *nm* honour

honte *nf* shame; **avoir honte de quelque chose** to be ashamed of something

hôpital (*pl* **hôpitaux**) *nm* hospital

hoquet *nm* **avoir le hoquet** to have hiccups

horaire *nm* timetable; **les horaires de train** the train timetable

horizon *nm* horizon

horizontal, e (*mpl* **horizontaux**) *adj* horizontal

horloge *nf* clock

horreur *nf* horror ▷ *un film d'horreur* a horror film; **avoir horreur de** to hate ▷ *J'ai horreur du chou.* I hate cabbage.

horrible *adj* horrible

hors *prep* **hors de** out of ▷ *Elle est hors de danger maintenant.* She's out of danger now.; **hors taxes** duty-free

hors-d'œuvre (*pl* **hors-d'œuvre**) *nm (food)* starter

hospitalier (*f* **hospitalière**) *adj* hospitable; **les services hospitaliers** hospital services

hospitalité *nf* hospitality

hostile *adj* hostile

hôte *nmf* ❶ host ❷ guest

hôtel *nm* hotel; **l'hôtel de ville** the town hall

hôtesse *nf* hostess; **une hôtesse de l'air** a stewardess

housse *nf* cover ▷ *une housse de couette* a quilt cover ▷ *une housse de téléphone* a phone cover

houx *nm* holly

huile *nf* oil; **l'huile solaire** suntan oil

huit *num* eight ▷ *Il a huit ans.* He's eight.; **le huit février** the eighth of February; **dans huit jours** in a week's time

huitaine *nf* **une huitaine de jours** about a week

huitième *adj* eighth ▷ *au huitième étage* on the eighth floor

huître *nf* oyster

humain, e *adj* human ▶ *nm* human being

humeur *nf* mood ▷ *Il est de bonne humeur.* He's in a good mood.

humide *adj* damp

humilier *vb* [**19**] to humiliate

humoristique *adj* humorous; **des dessins humoristiques** cartoons

humour *nm* humour ▷ *Il n'a pas beaucoup d'humour.* He hasn't got much of a sense of humour.

hurler *vb* [**28**] ❶ to howl ❷ to scream

hutte *nf* hut

hydratant, e *adj* **une crème hydratante** a moisturizing cream

hygiène *nf* hygiene

hygiénique *adj* hygienic; **une serviette hygiénique** a sanitary towel; **le papier hygiénique** toilet paper

hymne *nm* **l'hymne national** the national anthem

hypermarché *nm* hypermarket

hypermétrope *adj* long-sighted

hypocrite *adj* hypocritical

hypothèse *nf* hypothesis

I

iceberg *nm* iceberg

ici *adv* here ▷ *Les assiettes sont ici.* The plates are here.; **La mer monte parfois jusqu'ici.** The sea sometimes comes in as far as this.; **Jusqu'ici nous n'avons eu aucun problème avec la voiture.** So far we haven't had any problems with the car.

icône *nf* icon

idéal, e (*mpl* **idéaux**) *adj* ideal

idée *nf* idea

identifiant *nm (on a computer)* login

identifier *vb* [**19**] to identify

identique *adj* identical

identité *nf* identity; **une pièce d'identité** a form of identification

idiot, e *adj* ❶ stupid ❷ silly

idiot *nm* idiot

idiote *nf* idiot

ignoble *adj* horrible
ignorant, e *adj* ignorant
ignorer *vb* [**28**] ❶ not to know ▷ *J'ignore son nom.* I don't know his name. ❷ to ignore ▷ *Il m'a complètement ignoré.* He completely ignored me.
il *pron* ❶ he ▷ *Il est parti ce matin de bonne heure.* He left early this morning. ❷ it ▷ *Méfie-toi de ce chien: il mord.* Be careful of that dog: it bites. ▷ *Il pleut.* It's raining.
île *nf* island; **les îles Anglo-Normandes** the Channel Islands; **les îles Britanniques** the British Isles; **les îles Féroé** the Faroe Islands
illégal, e (*mpl* **illégaux**) *adj* illegal
illimité, e *adj* unlimited
illisible *adj* illegible
illuminer *vb* [**28**] to floodlight
illusion *nf* illusion
illustration *nf* illustration
illustré, e *adj* illustrated ▶ *nm* comic
illustrer *vb* [**28**] to illustrate
ils *pron pl* they ▷ *Ils nous ont appelés hier soir.* They phoned us last night.
image *nf* picture
imagination *nf* imagination
imaginer *vb* [**28**] to imagine
imbécile *nmf* idiot
imitation *nf* imitation
imiter *vb* [**28**] to imitate
immatriculation *nf* **une plaque d'immatriculation** *(of car)* a numberplate
immédiat *nm* **dans l'immédiat** for the moment
immédiatement *adv* immediately
immense *adj* ❶ huge ❷ tremendous
immeuble *nm* block of flats
immigration *nf* immigration
immigré *nm* immigrant
immigrée *nf* immigrant
immobile *adj* motionless
immobilier (*f* **immobilière**) *adj* **une agence immobilière** an estate agent's
immobiliser *vb* [**28**] to immobilize
immunisé, e *adj* immunized
impact *nm* impact
impair, e *adj* odd
impardonnable *adj* unforgivable
impasse *nf* cul-de-sac
impatience *nf* impatience
impatient, e *adj* impatient
impeccable *adj* ❶ immaculate ❷ perfect
imper *nm (informal)* mac
impératif *nm* imperative
impératrice *nf* empress
imperméable *nm* raincoat
impertinent, e *adj* cheeky
impitoyable *adj* merciless
impliquer *vb* [**28**] to mean ▷ *Son silence implique qu'il est d'accord.* His silence means he agrees.; **être impliqué dans** to be involved in ▷ *Il est impliqué dans un scandale financier.* He's involved in a financial scandal.
impoli, e *adj* rude
importance *nf* importance
important, e *adj* ❶ important ❷ considerable

importation *nf* import
importer *vb* [**28**] *see also* **n'importe** ❶ *(goods)* to import ❷ to matter ▷ *Peu importe.* It doesn't matter.
imposant, e *adj* imposing
imposer *vb* [**28**] to impose; **La direction leur impose des horaires impossibles.** The managers are making them work ridiculous hours.
impossible *adj* impossible ▶ *nm* **Nous ferons l'impossible pour finir à temps.** We'll do our utmost to finish on time.
impôt *nm* tax
imprécis, e *adj* imprecise
impression *nf* impression
impressionnant, e *adj* impressive
impressionner *vb* [**28**] to impress
imprévisible *adj* unpredictable
imprévu, e *adj* unexpected
imprimante *nf (for computer)* printer
imprimé, e *adj* printed
imprimer *vb* [**28**] to print
impropre *adj* **impropre à la consommation** unfit for human consumption
improviser *vb* [**28**] to improvise
improviste *adv* **arriver à l'improviste** to arrive unexpectedly
imprudence *nf* carelessness; **Ne fais pas d'imprudences!** Don't do anything silly!
imprudent, e *adj* ❶ unwise ❷ careless
impuissant, e *adj* helpless
impulsif (*f* **impulsive**) *adj* impulsive
inabordable *adj* prohibitive
inaccessible *adj* inaccessible
inachevé, e *adj* unfinished
inadmissible *adj* intolerable
inanimé, e *adj* unconscious
inaperçu, e *adj* **passer inaperçu** to go unnoticed
inattendu, e *adj* unexpected
inattention *nf* **une faute d'inattention** a careless mistake
inaugurer *vb* [**28**] *(an exhibition)* to open
incapable *adj* incapable
incassable *adj* unbreakable
incendie *nm* fire ▷ *un incendie de forêt* a forest fire
incertain, e *adj* ❶ uncertain ❷ unsettled ▷ *Le temps est incertain.* The weather is unsettled.
incident *nm* incident
inciter *vb* [**28**] **inciter quelqu'un à faire quelque chose** to encourage somebody to do something
inclure *vb* [**13**] to enclose ▷ *Veuillez inclure une enveloppe timbrée libellée à votre adresse.* Please enclose a stamped addressed envelope.; **jusqu'au dix mars inclus** until 10th March inclusive
incohérent, e *adj* incoherent
incollable *adj* **être incollable sur quelque chose** *(informal)* to know everything there is to know about something; **le riz incollable** non-stick rice
incolore *adj* colourless
incompétent, e *adj* incompetent

incompris, e *adj* misunderstood
inconnu *nm* stranger; **l'inconnu** the unknown
inconsciemment *adv* unconsciously
inconscient, e *adj* ❶ unconscious ❷ unaware
incontestable *adj* indisputable
incontournable *adj* inevitable
inconvénient *nm* disadvantage; **si vous n'y voyez pas d'inconvénient** if you have no objection
incorrect, e *adj* ❶ incorrect ❷ rude
incroyable *adj* incredible
inculper *vb* [**28**] **inculper de** to charge with
Inde *nf* India
indécis, e *adj* ❶ indecisive ❷ undecided
indéfiniment *adv* indefinitely
indélicat, e *adj* tactless
indemne *adj* unharmed
indemniser *vb* [**28**] to compensate
indépendamment *adv* independently; **indépendamment de** irrespective of
indépendance *nf* independence
indépendant, e *adj* independent
index *nm* ❶ index finger ❷ *(in book)* index
indicatif (*f* **indicative**) *adj* **à titre indicatif** for your information ▸ *nm* ❶ dialling code ❷ *(of verb)* indicative ❸ *(of TV programme)* theme tune
indications *nfpl* instructions
indice *nm* clue
indien (*f* **indienne**) *adj, nm/f* Indian; **un Indien** *(man)* an Indian; **une Indienne** *(woman)* an Indian
indifférence *nf* indifference
indifférent, e *adj* indifferent
indigène *nmf* native
indigeste *adj* indigestible
indigestion *nf* indigestion
indigne *adj* unworthy
indigner *vb* [**28**] **s'indigner de quelque chose** to get indignant about something
indiqué, e *adj* advisable
indiquer *vb* [**28**] to point out ▷ *Il m'a indiqué la mairie.* He pointed out the town hall.
indirect, e *adj* indirect
indiscipliné, e *adj* unruly
indiscret (*f* **indiscrète**) *adj* indiscreet
indispensable *adj* indispensable
indisposé, e *adj* indisposed; **être indisposée** to be having one's period
individu *nm* individual
individuel (*f* **individuelle**) *adj* individual; **Vous aurez une chambre individuelle.** You'll have a room of your own.
indolore *adj* painless
Indonésie *nf* Indonesia
indulgent, e *adj* indulgent; **Elle est trop indulgente avec son fils.** She's not firm enough with her son.
industrie *nf* industry
industriel (*f* **industrielle**) *adj* industrial ▸ *nm* industrialist

inédit, e *adj* unpublished
inefficace *adj* ❶ *(treatment)* ineffective ❷ inefficient
inégal, e (*mpl* **inégaux**) *adj* ❶ unequal ❷ uneven
inévitable *adj* unavoidable; **C'était inévitable!** That was bound to happen!
inexact, e *adj* inaccurate
in extremis *adv* **Il a réussi à attraper son train in extremis.** He just managed to catch his train.; **Ils ont évité un accident in extremis.** They avoided an accident by the skin of their teeth.
infarctus *nm* coronary
infatigable *adj* indefatigable
infect, e *adj (meal)* revolting
s'**infecter** *vb* [**28**] to go septic
infection *nf* infection
inférieur, e *adj* lower
infernal, e (*mpl* **infernaux**) *adj* terrible
infini *nm* **à l'infini** indefinitely
infinitif *nm* infinitive
infirme *nmf* person with a disability
infirmerie *nf* medical room
infirmier *nm* nurse
inflammable *adj* inflammable
influence *nf* influence
influencer *vb* [**12**] to influence
informaticien *nm* computer scientist
informaticienne *nf* computer scientist
informations *nfpl* ❶ *(on TV)* news ▷ *les informations de vingt heures* the 8 o'clock news ❷ information ▷ *Je voudrais quelques informations, s'il vous plaît.* I'd like some information, please.; **une information** a piece of information
informatique *nf* computing
informer *vb* [**28**] to inform; **s'informer** to find out
infuser *vb* [**28**] ❶ *(tea)* to brew ❷ *(herbal tea)* to infuse
infusion *nf* herbal tea
ingénieur *nmf* engineer
ingrat, e *adj* ungrateful
ingrédient *nm* ingredient
inhabituel (*f* **inhabituelle**) *adj* unusual
inhumain, e *adj* inhuman
initial, e (*mpl* **initiaux**) *adj* initial
initiale *nf* initial
initiation *nf* introduction
initiative *nf* initiative ▷ *avoir de l'initiative* to have initiative
injecter *vb* [**28**] to inject
injection *nf* injection
injure *nf* ❶ insult ❷ abuse
injurier *vb* [**19**] to insult
injurieux (*f* **injurieuse**) *adj (language)* abusive
injuste *adj* unfair
innocent, e *adj* innocent
innombrable *adj* innumerable
innover *vb* [**28**] to break new ground
inoccupé, e *adj* empty ▷ *un appartement inoccupé* an empty flat
inoffensif (*f* **inoffensive**) *adj* harmless
inondation *nf* flood
inoubliable *adj* unforgettable
inoxydable *adj* **l'acier inoxydable**

stainless steel

inquiet (*f* **inquiète**) *adj* worried

inquiétant, e *adj* worrying

s' **inquiéter** *vb* [**34**] to worry ▷ *Ne t'inquiète pas!* Don't worry!

inquiétude *nf* anxiety

insatisfait, e *adj* dissatisfied

inscription *nf (for school, course)* registration

s' **inscrire** *vb* [**30**] **s'inscrire à** **(1)** to join ▷ *Je me suis inscrit au club de tennis.* I've joined the tennis club. **(2)** to register ▷ *N'attends pas trop pour t'inscrire à la fac.* Don't leave it too long to register at the university.

insecte *nm* insect

insensible *adj* insensitive

insigne *nm* badge

insignifiant, e *adj* insignificant

insister *vb* [**28**] to insist; **N'insiste pas!** Don't keep on!

insolation *nf* sunstroke

insolent, e *adj* cheeky

insouciant, e *adj* carefree

insoutenable *adj* unbearable

inspecter *vb* [**28**] to inspect

inspecteur *nm* inspector

inspection *nf* inspection

inspirer *vb* [**28**] ❶ to inspire; **s'inspirer de** to take one's inspiration from ❷ to breathe in ▷ *Inspirez! Expirez!* Breathe in! Breathe out!

instable *adj* ❶ *(piece of furniture)* unsteady ❷ *(person)* unstable

installations *nfpl* facilities

installer *vb* [**28**] ❶ *(shelves)* to put up ❷ *(gas, telephone)* to install; **s'installer** to settle in; **Installez-vous, je vous en prie.** Have a seat, please.

instant *nm* moment ▷ *pour l'instant* for the moment

instantané, e *adj* instant ▷ *du café instantané* instant coffee

instinct *nm* instinct

institut *nm* institute

instituteur *nm* primary school teacher

institution *nf* institution

institutrice *nf* primary school teacher

instruction *nf* ❶ instruction ❷ education

s' **instruire** *vb* [**23**] to educate oneself

instruit, e *adj* educated

instrument *nm* instrument ▷ *un instrument de musique* a musical instrument

insuffisant, e *adj* insufficient; **'travail insuffisant'** *(on school report)* 'must try harder'

insuline *nf* insulin

insultant, e *adj* insulting

insulte *nf* insult

insulter *vb* [**28**] to insult

insupportable *adj* unbearable

intact, e *adj* intact

intégral, e (*mpl* **intégraux**) *adj* **le texte intégral** unabridged version; **un remboursement intégral** a full refund

intégrisme *nm* fundamentalism

intelligence *nf* intelligence

intelligent, e *adj* intelligent

intense *adj* intense

intensif (*f* **intensive**) *adj* intensive; **un cours intensif** a crash course
intention *nf* intention; **avoir l'intention de faire quelque chose** to intend to do something
interdiction *nf* **'interdiction de stationner'** 'no parking'; **'interdiction de fumer'** 'no smoking'
interdire *vb* [**27**] to forbid
interdit, e *adj* forbidden
intéressant, e *adj* interesting; **On lui a fait une offre intéressante.** They made him an attractive offer.; **On trouve des CD à des prix très intéressants dans ce magasin.** You can get very cheap CDs in this shop.
intéresser *vb* [**28**] to interest; **s'intéresser à** to be interested in
intérêt *nm* interest; **avoir intérêt à faire quelque chose** to do well to do something
intérieur *nm* inside
interlocuteur *nm* **son interlocuteur** the man he's speaking to
intermédiaire *nm* intermediary; **par l'intermédiaire de** through
internat *nm* boarding school
international, e (*mpl* **internationaux**) *adj* international
internaute *nmf* internet user
interne *nmf* boarder
Internet *nm* internet ▷ *sur Internet* on the internet
interphone *nm* intercom
interprète *nmf* interpreter
interpréter *vb* [**34**] to interpret
interrogatif (*f* **interrogative**) *adj* interrogative
interrogation *nf* ❶ question ❷ test ▷ *une interrogation écrite* a written test
interrogatoire *nm* questioning; **C'est un interrogatoire ou quoi?** Am I being cross-examined?
interroger *vb* [**45**] to question
interrompre *vb* [**75**] to interrupt
interrupteur *nm* switch
interruption *nf* interruption; **sans interruption** without stopping
intervalle *nm* interval; **dans l'intervalle** in the meantime
intervenir *vb* [**89**] ❶ to intervene ❷ to take action ▷ *La police est intervenue.* The police took action.
intervention *nf* intervention; **une intervention chirurgicale** a surgical operation
interview *nf* (*on radio, TV*) interview
intestin *nm* intestine
intime *adj* intimate; **un journal intime** a diary
intimider *vb* [**28**] to intimidate
intimité *nf* **dans l'intimité** in private; **Le mariage a eu lieu dans l'intimité.** The wedding ceremony was private.
intitulé, e *adj* entitled
intolérable *adj* intolerable
intoxication *nf* **une intoxication alimentaire** food poisoning
Intranet *nm* Intranet

intransigeant, e *adj* uncompromising
intrigue *nf (of book, film)* plot
introduction *nf* introduction
introduire *vb* [**23**] to introduce
intuition *nf* intuition
inusable *adj* hard-wearing
inutile *adj* useless
invalide *nmf* person with a disability
invasion *nf* invasion
inventer *vb* [**28**] ❶ to invent ❷ to make up ▷ *inventer une excuse* to make up an excuse
inventeur *nm* inventor
invention *nf* invention
inverse *adj* **dans l'ordre inverse** in reverse order; **en sens inverse** in the opposite direction
▶ *nm* reverse; **Tu t'es trompé, c'est l'inverse.** You've got it wrong, it's the other way round.
investissement *nm* investment
invisible *adj* invisible
invitation *nf* invitation
invité *nm* guest
inviter *vb* [**28**] to invite
involontaire *adj* unintentional
invraisemblable *adj* unlikely
ira, irai, iraient, irais *vb see* **aller**; **J'irai demain au supermarché.** I'll go to the supermarket tomorrow.
Irak *nm* Iraq
Iran *nm* Iran
iras, irez *vb see* **aller**
irlandais, e *adj, n* Irish; **un Irlandais** an Irishman; **une Irlandaise** an Irishwoman; **les Irlandais** the Irish
Irlande *nf* Ireland; **en Irlande (1)** in Ireland **(2)** to Ireland; **la République d'Irlande** the Irish Republic; **l'Irlande du Nord** Northern Ireland
ironie *nf* irony
ironique *adj* ironical
irons, iront *vb see* **aller**; **Nous irons à la plage cet après-midi.** We'll go to the beach this afternoon.
irrationnel (*f* **irrationnelle**) *adj* irrational
irréel (*f* **irréelle**) *adj* unreal
irrégulier (*f* **irrégulière**) *adj* irregular
irrésistible *adj* irresistible
irritable *adj* irritable
irriter *vb* [**28**] to irritate
islamique *adj* Islamic
Islande *nf* Iceland
isolé, e *adj* isolated
Israël *nm* Israel
israélien (*f* **israélienne**) *adj, nm/f* Israeli; **un Israélien** *(man)* an Israeli; **une Israélienne** *(woman)* an Israeli; **les Israéliens** the Israelis
issue *nf* **une voie sans issue** a dead end; **l'issue de secours** emergency exit
Italie *nf* Italy; **en Italie (1)** in Italy **(2)** to Italy
italien (*f* **italienne**) *adj, n* Italian ▷ *J'apprends l'italien.* I'm learning Italian.; **un Italien** *(man)* an Italian; **une Italienne** *(woman)* an Italian; **les Italiens** the Italians

itinéraire *nm* route
IUT *nm* (= *Institut universitaire de technologie*) *(at university level)* institute of technology
ivre *adj* drunk
ivrogne *nmf* drunkard

j' *pron see* **je**
jalousie *nf* jealousy
jaloux (*f* **jalouse**) *adj* jealous
jamais *adv* ❶ never ▷ *Il ne boit jamais d'alcool.* He never drinks alcohol. ❷ ever

> Phrases with **jamais** meaning 'ever' are followed by a verb in the subjunctive.

▷ *C'est la plus belle chose que j'aie jamais vue.* It's the most beautiful thing I've ever seen.
jambe *nf* leg
jambon *nm* ham; **le jambon cru** Parma ham
jambonneau (*pl* **jambonneaux**) *nm* knuckle of ham
janvier *nm* January; **en janvier** in January
Japon *nm* Japan; **au Japon (1)** in

Japan **(2)** to Japan

japonais, e *adj, n* Japanese ▷ *Elle parle japonais.* She speaks Japanese.; **un Japonais** *(man)* a Japanese; **une Japonaise** *(woman)* a Japanese; **les Japonais** the Japanese

jardin *nm* garden ▷ *un jardin potager* a vegetable garden

jardinage *nm* gardening

jardinier *nm* gardener

jaune *adj* yellow
▶ *nm* yellow; **un jaune d'œuf** an egg yolk

jaunir *vb* [**38**] to turn yellow

jaunisse *nf* jaundice

Javel *n* **l'eau de Javel** bleach

jazz *nm* jazz

J.-C. *abbr (= Jésus-Christ)* **44 avant J.-C.** 44 BC; **115 après J.-C.** 115 AD

je *pron*

> **je** changes to **j'** before a vowel and most words beginning with 'h'.

I ▷ *Je t'appellerai ce soir.* I'll phone you this evening. ▷ *J'arrive!* I'm coming! ▷ *J'hésite.* I'm not sure.

jean *nm* jeans

jeannette *nf* Brownie

Jésus-Christ *nm* Jesus Christ

jet *nm* ❶ *(of water)* jet; **un jet d'eau** a fountain ❷ jet plane

jetable *adj* disposable

jetée *nf* jetty

jeter *vb* [**41**] ❶ to throw ▷ *Il a jeté son sac sur le lit.* He threw his bag onto the bed. ❷ to throw away ▷ *Ils ne jettent jamais rien.* They never throw anything away.; **jeter un coup d'œil** to have a look

jeton *nm (in board game)* counter

jeu *(pl* **jeux***)* *nm* game ▷ *Les enfants jouaient à un jeu.* The children were playing a game.; **un jeu d'arcade** an arcade video game; **un jeu de cartes (1)** a pack of cards **(2)** a card game; **un jeu de mots** a pun; **un jeu de société** a board game; **un jeu électronique** an electronic game; **les jeux sur ordinateur** computer gaming; **les jeux sur téléphone portable** mobile gaming; **les jeux vidéo** video games; **en jeu** at stake ▷ *Des vies humaines sont en jeu.* Human lives are at stake.

jeudi *nm* ❶ Thursday ▷ *Aujourd'hui, nous sommes jeudi.* It's Thursday today. ❷ on Thursday; **le jeudi** on Thursdays; **tous les jeudis** every Thursday; **jeudi dernier** last Thursday; **jeudi prochain** next Thursday

jeun: **à jeun** *adv* on an empty stomach

jeune *adj* young ▷ *un jeune homme* a young man; **une jeune fille** a girl
▶ *nmf* young person ▷ *les jeunes* young people

jeunesse *nf* youth

job *nm (informal)* job

jogging *nm* ❶ jogging ❷ tracksuit

joie *nf* joy

joindre *vb* [**42**] ❶ to put together ▷ *On va joindre les deux tables.* We're going to put the two tables together. ❷ to contact ▷ *Vous pouvez le joindre chez lui.* You can contact him at home.

joint, e *adj* **une pièce jointe** *(in email)* an attachment

joli, e *adj* pretty

jonc *nm* rush

jonquille *nf* daffodil

joue *nf* cheek

jouer *vb* [**28**] ❶ to play; **jouer de** *(instrument)* to play ▷ *Il joue de la guitare et du piano.* He plays the guitar and the piano.; **jouer à** *(sport, game)* to play ▷ *Elle joue au tennis.* She plays tennis. ▷ *jouer aux cartes* to play cards ❷ to act ▷ *Je trouve qu'il joue très bien dans ce film.* I think he acts very well in this film.; **On joue Hamlet au Théâtre de la Ville.** Hamlet is on at the Théâtre de la Ville.

jouet *nm* toy

joueur *nm* player; **être mauvais joueur** to be a bad loser

joueuse *nf* player

jour *nm* day; **Il fait jour.** It's daylight.; **mettre quelque chose à jour** to update something; **le jour de l'An** New Year's Day; **un jour de congé** a day off; **un jour férié** a public holiday; **dans huit jours** in a week; **dans quinze jours** in a fortnight

journal (*pl* **journaux**) *nm* ❶ newspaper; **le journal télévisé** the television news ❷ diary

journalier (*f* **journalière**) *adj* daily

journalisme *nm* journalism

journaliste *nmf* journalist

journée *nf* day

joyeux (*f* **joyeuse**) *adj* happy; **Joyeux anniversaire!** Happy birthday!; **Joyeux Noël!** Merry Christmas!

judo *nm* judo

juge *nm* judge

juger *vb* [**45**] to judge

juif (*f* **juive**) *adj, nm/f* Jewish; **un Juif** *(man)* a Jew; **une Juive** *(woman)* a Jew

juillet *nm* July; **en juillet** in July

juin *nm* June; **en juin** in June

jumeau (*pl* **jumeaux**) *nm* twin

jumeler *vb* [**4**] to twin ▷ *Saint-Brieuc est jumelée avec Aberystwyth.* Saint-Brieuc is twinned with Aberystwyth.

jumelle *nf* twin

jumelles *nfpl* binoculars

jument *nf* mare

jungle *nf* jungle

jupe *nf* skirt

jurer *vb* [**28**] to swear ▷ *Je jure que c'est vrai!* I swear it's true!

juridique *adj* legal

jury *nm* jury

jus *nm* juice; **un jus de fruit** a fruit juice

jusqu'à *prep* ❶ as far as ▷ *Nous avons marché jusqu'au village.* We walked as far as the village. ❷ until ▷ *Il fait généralement chaud jusqu'à la mi-août.* It's usually hot until mid-August.; **jusqu'à ce que** until; **jusqu'à présent** so far

jusque *prep* as far as ▷ *Je l'ai raccompagnée jusque chez elle.* I went with her as far as her house.

juste *adj, adv* ❶ fair ▷ *Il est sévère, mais juste.* He's strict but fair.

❷ tight ▷ *Cette veste est un peu juste.* This jacket is a bit tight.; **juste assez** just enough; **chanter juste** to sing in tune

justement *adv* just

justesse *nf* **de justesse** only just

justice *nf* justice

justifier *vb* [**19**] to justify

juteux (*f* **juteuse**) *adj* juicy

juvénile *adj* youthful

kaki *adj* khaki

kangourou *nm* kangaroo

karaté *nm* karate

kermesse *nf* fair

kidnapper *vb* [**28**] to kidnap

kilo *nm* kilo

kilogramme *nm* kilogram

kilomètre *nm* kilometre

kinésithérapeute *nmf* physiotherapist

kiosque *nm* **un kiosque à journaux** a news stand

kit *nm* kit ▷ *en kit* in kit form ▷ *un kit mains libres* a hands-free kit

klaxon *nm* *(of car)* horn

klaxonner *vb* [**28**] to sound the horn

km *abbr* (= *kilomètre*) km (= *kilometre*)

KO *adj* knocked out; **mettre quelqu'un KO** to knock somebody out; **Je suis complètement KO.** *(informal)* I'm completely knackered.

K-way® *nm* cagoule

l

l' *art, pron see* **la**; **le**

la *art, pron*

> **la** changes to **l'** before a vowel and most words beginning with 'h'.

❶ the ▷ *la maison* the house ▷ *l'actrice* the actress ▷ *l'herbe* the grass ❷ her ▷ *Je la connais depuis longtemps.* I've known her for a long time. ❸ it ▷ *C'est une bonne émission: je la regarde tous les jours.* It's a good programme: I watch it every day. ❹ one's; **se mordre la langue** to bite one's tongue ▷ *Je me suis mordu la langue.* I've bitten my tongue.; **six euros la douzaine** six euros a dozen

▸ *nm* ❶ A ▷ *en la bémol* in A flat ❷ la ▷ *sol, la, si, do* so, la, ti, do

là *adv* ❶ there ▷ *Ton livre est là, sur la*

table. Your book's there, on the table. ❷ here ▷ *Elle n'est pas là*. She isn't here.; **C'est là que ... (1)** That's where ... ▷ *C'est là que je suis né*. That's where I was born. **(2)** That's when ... ▷ *C'est là que j'ai réalisé que je m'étais trompé*. That's when I realized that I had made a mistake.

là-bas *adv* over there

labo *nm (informal)* lab

laboratoire *nm* laboratory

labourer *vb* [**28**] to plough

labyrinthe *nm* maze

lac *nm* lake

lacer *vb* [**12**] *(shoes)* to do up

lacet *nm* lace; **des chaussures à lacets** lace-up shoes

lâche *adj* ❶ loose ▷ *Le nœud est trop lâche*. The knot's too loose. ❷ cowardly; **Il est lâche.** He's a coward.
▸ *nmf* coward

lâcher *vb* [**28**] ❶ to let go of ▷ *Il n'a pas lâché ma main de tout le film*. He didn't let go of my hand until the end of the film. ❷ to drop ▷ *Il a été tellement surpris qu'il a lâché son verre*. He was so surprised that he dropped his glass. ❸ to fail ▷ *Les freins ont lâché*. The brakes failed.

lâcheté *nf* cowardice

lacrymogène *adj* **le gaz lacrymogène** tear gas

lacune *nf* gap

là-dedans *adv* in there

là-dessous *adv* ❶ under there ❷ behind it

là-dessus *adv* on there

là-haut *adv* up there

laid, e *adj* ugly

laideur *nf* ugliness

lainage *nm* woollen garment

laine *nf* wool; **une laine polaire** *(jacket)* a fleece

laïque *adj* **une école laïque** a state school

laisse *nf* lead ▷ *Tenez votre chien en laisse*. Keep your dog on a lead.

laisser *vb* [**28**] ❶ to leave ▷ *J'ai laissé mon parapluie à la maison*. I've left my umbrella at home. ❷ to let ▷ *Laisse-le parler*. Let him speak.; **Il se laisse aller.** He's letting himself go.

laisser-aller *nm* carelessness

lait *nm* milk; **un café au lait** a white coffee

laitue *nf* lettuce

lambeaux *nmpl* **en lambeaux** tattered

lame *nf* blade

lamelle *nf* thin strip

lamentable *adj* appalling

se **lamenter** *vb* [**28**] to moan

lampadaire *nm* standard lamp

lampe *nf* lamp; **une lampe de poche** a torch

lance *nf* spear

lancement *nm* launch

lancer *vb* [**12**] ❶ to throw ▷ *Lance-moi le ballon!* Throw me the ball! ❷ to launch ▷ *Ils viennent de lancer un nouveau modèle*. They've just launched a new model.; **se lancer dans** to embark on ▷ *Il s'est lancé là-dedans sans bien réfléchir*. He embarked on it without thinking properly.

▸ *nm* **le lancer de poids** putting the shot
lancinant, e *adj* **une douleur lancinante** a shooting pain
landau *nm* pram
lande *nf* moor
langage *nm* language
langouste *nf* crayfish
langue *nf* ❶ tongue; **sa langue maternelle** his mother tongue ❷ language ▷ *une langue étrangère* a foreign language
lanière *nf* strap
lapin *nm* rabbit
laps *nm* **un laps de temps** a space of time
laque *nf* hair spray
laquelle (*pl* **lesquelles**) *pron f* ❶ which ▷ *Laquelle de ces photos préfères-tu?* Which of these photos do you prefer? ❷ whom ▷ *la personne à laquelle vous faites référence* the person to whom you are referring

laquelle is often not translated in English.

▷ *la personne à laquelle je pense* the person I'm thinking of
lard *nm* streaky bacon
lardons *nmpl* chunks of bacon
large *adj, adv* wide; **voir large** to allow a bit extra
▸ *nm* **cinq mètres de large** 5 m wide; **le large** the open sea; **au large de** off the coast of
largement *adv* **Vous avez largement le temps.** You have plenty of time.; **C'est largement suffisant.** That's ample.
largeur *nf* width
larme *nf* tear
laryngite *nf* laryngitis
laser *nm* laser; **une platine laser** a compact disc player; **un disque laser** a compact disc
lasser *vb* [**28**] **se lasser de** to get tired of
latin *nm* Latin
laurier *nm* laurel tree ▷ *une feuille de laurier* a bay leaf
lavable *adj* washable
lavabo *nm* washbasin
lavage *nm* wash
lavande *nf* lavender
lave-linge (*pl* **lave-linge**) *nm* washing machine
laver *vb* [**28**] to wash; **se laver** to wash ▷ *se laver les mains* to wash one's hands
laverie *nf* **une laverie automatique** a launderette
lave-vaisselle (*pl* **lave-vaisselle**) *nm* dishwasher
le *art, pron*

le changes to **l'** before a vowel and most words beginning with 'h'.

❶ the ▷ *le livre* the book ▷ *l'arbre* the tree ▷ *l'hélicoptère* the helicopter ❷ him ▷ *Daniel est un vieil ami: je le connais depuis plus de vingt ans.* Daniel is an old friend: I've known him for over 20 years. ❸ it ▷ *Où est mon stylo? Je ne le trouve plus.* Where's my pen? I can't find it. ❹ one's; **se laver le visage** to wash one's face ▷ *Évitez de vous laver le visage avec du savon.* Avoid washing

your face with soap.; **dix euros le kilo** 10 euros a kilo; **Il est arrivé le douze mai.** He arrived on 12 May.
lécher *vb* [**34**] to lick
lèche-vitrine *nm* **faire du lèche-vitrine** to go window-shopping
leçon *nf* lesson
lecteur *nm* ❶ reader ❷ *(at a university)* foreign language assistant; **un lecteur de CD** a CD player; **un lecteur de DVD** a DVD player; **un lecteur MP3** an MP3 player
lectrice *nf* ❶ reader ❷ *(at a university)* foreign language assistant
lecture *nf* reading

> Be careful! The French word **lecture** does not mean **lecture**.

légal, e (*mpl* **légaux**) *adj* legal
légende *nf* ❶ legend ❷ *(of map)* key ❸ *(of picture)* caption
léger (*f* **légère**) *adj* ❶ light ❷ slight; **à la légère** thoughtlessly
légèrement *adv* ❶ lightly ❷ slightly ▷ *Il est légèrement plus grand que son frère.* He's slightly taller than his brother.
législatives *nfpl* general election *sg*
légume *nm* vegetable
lendemain *nm* next day ▷ *le lendemain de son arrivée* the day after he arrived; **le lendemain matin** the next morning
lent, e *adj* slow
lentement *adv* slowly
lenteur *nf* slowness
lentille *nf* ❶ contact lens ❷ lentil
léopard *nm* leopard
lequel (*f* **laquelle**, *mpl* **lesquels**, *fpl* **lesquelles**) *pron* ❶ which ▷ *Lequel de ces films as-tu préféré?* Which of the films did you prefer? ❷ whom ▷ *l'homme avec lequel elle a été vue pour la dernière fois* the man with whom she was last seen

> **lequel** is often not translated in English.

▷ *le garçon avec lequel elle est sortie* the boy she went out with
les *art, pron* ❶ the ▷ *les arbres* the trees ❷ them ▷ *Elle les a invités à dîner.* She invited them to dinner. ❸ one's; **se brosser les dents** to brush one's teeth ▷ *Elle s'est brossé les dents.* She brushed her teeth.; **dix euros les cinq** 10 euros for 5
lesbienne *nf* lesbian
lesquels (*f* **lesquelles**) *pron pl* ❶ which ▷ *Lesquelles de ces photos préfères-tu?* Which of the photos do you prefer? ❷ whom ▷ *les personnes avec lesquelles il est associé* the people with whom he is in partnership

> **lesquels** is often not translated in English.

▷ *les gens chez lesquels nous avons dîné* the people we had dinner with
lessive *nf* ❶ washing powder ❷ washing; **faire la lessive** to do the washing
leste *adj* nimble
Lettonie *nf* Latvia
lettre *nf* letter
lettres *nfpl* arts ▷ *la faculté de lettres*

the Faculty of Arts

leur *adj, pron* ❶ their ▷ *leur ami* their friend ❷ them ▷ *Je leur ai dit la vérité.* I told them the truth.; **le leur** theirs ▷ *Ma voiture est rouge, la leur est bleue.* My car's red, theirs is blue.

leurs (*f* **leurs**) *adj pl, pron pl* their ▷ *leurs amis* their friends; **les leurs** theirs ▷ *tes livres et les leurs* your books and theirs

levé, e *adj* **être levé** to be up ▷ *Est-ce qu'il est levé?* Is he up?

levée *nf (of mail)* collection

lever *vb* [**43**] to raise; **Levez la main!** Put your hand up!; **lever les yeux** to look up; **se lever (1)** to get up ▷ *Il se lève tous les jours à six heures.* He gets up at 6 o'clock every day. ▷ *Lève-toi!* Get up! **(2)** to rise ▷ *Le soleil se lève actuellement à cinq heures.* At the moment the sun rises at 5 o'clock. **(3)** to stand up ▷ *Levez-vous!* Stand up!

▶ *nm* **le lever du soleil** sunrise

levier *nm* lever

lèvre *nf* lip

lévrier *nm* greyhound

levure *nf* yeast; **la levure chimique** baking powder

lexique *nm* word list

lézard *nm* lizard

liaison *nf* affair

libellule *nf* dragonfly

libérer *vb* [**34**] to free; **se libérer** to find time

liberté *nf* freedom; **mettre en liberté** to release

libraire *nmf* bookseller

librairie *nf* bookshop

Be careful! **librairie** does not mean **library**.

libre *adj* ❶ free ▷ *Tu es libre de faire ce que tu veux.* You are free to do as you wish. ▷ *Est-ce que cette place est libre?* Is this seat free?; **Avez-vous une chambre de libre?** Have you got a free room? ❷ clear ▷ *La route est libre: vous pouvez traverser.* The road is clear: you can cross.

libre-service (*pl* **libres-services**) *nm* self-service store

Libye *nf* Libya

licence *nf* ❶ degree ❷ licence

licencié *nm* graduate

licenciée *nf* graduate

licenciement *nm* redundancy

licencier *vb* [**19**] to make redundant

liège *nm* cork; **un bouchon en liège** *(for bottle)* a cork

lien *nm* ❶ connection; **un lien de parenté** a family tie ❷ *(in computing)* link

lier *vb* [**19**] **lier conversation avec quelqu'un** to get into conversation with somebody; **se lier avec quelqu'un** to make friends with somebody

lierre *nm* ivy

lieu (*pl* **lieux**) *nm* place; **avoir lieu** to take place ▷ *La cérémonie a eu lieu dans la salle des fêtes.* The ceremony took place in the village hall.; **au lieu de** instead of

lièvre *nm* hare

ligne *nf* ❶ *(phone, train)* line ▷ *la ligne de bus numéro six* the number 6 bus; **en ligne** *(computing)* online

❷ figure ▷ *C'est mauvais pour la ligne.* It's bad for your figure.
ligoter *vb* [**28**] to tie up
ligue *nf* league
lilas *nm* lilac
limace *nf* slug
lime *nf* **une lime à ongles** a nail file
limitation *nf* **la limitation de vitesse** the speed limit
limite *nf* ❶ *(of property, football pitch)* boundary ❷ limit; **À la limite, on pourrait prendre le bus.** At a pinch we could go by bus.; **la date limite** the deadline; **la date limite de vente** the sell-by date
limiter *vb* [**28**] to limit
limonade *nf* lemonade
lin *nm* linen
linge *nm* ❶ linen ❷ washing ▷ *laver le linge* to do the washing; **du linge de corps** underwear
lingerie *nf* *(women's)* underwear
lion *nm* lion; **le Lion** Leo
lionne *nf* lioness
liqueur *nf* liqueur
liquide *adj* liquid
▸ *nm* liquid; **payer quelque chose en liquide** to pay cash for something
lire *vb* [**44**] to read ▷ *Tu as lu 'Madame Bovary'?* Have you read 'Madame Bovary'?
lis, lisent, lisez *vb* *see* **lire**; **Je lis beaucoup.** I read a lot.
lisible *adj* legible
lisse *adj* smooth
liste *nf* list; **faire la liste de** to make a list of
lit *nm* bed ▷ *un grand lit* a double bed ▷ *aller au lit* to go to bed; **faire son lit** to make one's bed; **un lit de camp** a campbed
▸ *vb* *see* **lire**
literie *nf* bedding
litière *nf* ❶ *(for cat)* litter ❷ *(of caged pet)* bedding
litre *nm* litre
littéraire *adj* **une œuvre littéraire** a work of literature
littérature *nf* literature
littoral (*pl* **littoraux**) *nm* coast
Lituanie *nf* Lithuania
livraison *nf* delivery; **la livraison des bagages** baggage reclaim
livre *nm* book; **un livre de poche** a paperback

> Word for word, **livre de poche** means 'pocket book'.

▸ *nf* pound

> The French **livre** is 500 grams.

▷ *une livre de beurre* a pound of butter; **la livre sterling** the pound sterling
livrer *vb* [**28**] to deliver
livret *nm* booklet; **le livret scolaire** the school report book
livreur *nm* delivery man
local, e (*mpl* **locaux**) *adj* local
▸ *nm* premises
locataire *nmf* ❶ tenant ❷ lodger
location *nf* **location de voitures** car rental; **location de skis** ski hire

> Be careful! The French word **location** does not mean **location**.

locomotive *nf* locomotive
loge *nf* dressing room

logement *nm* ❶ housing ❷ accommodation
loger *vb* [**45**] to stay; **trouver à se loger** to find somewhere to live
logiciel *nm* software
logique *adj* logical
▶ *nf* logic
loi *nf* law
loin *adv* ❶ far ▷ *La gare n'est pas très loin d'ici.* The station is not very far from here. ❷ far off ▷ *Noël n'est plus tellement loin.* Christmas isn't far off now. ❸ a long time ago ▷ *Les vacances paraissent déjà tellement loin!* The holidays already seem such a long time ago!; **au loin** in the distance; **de loin (1)** from a long way away ▷ *On voit l'église de loin.* You can see the church from a long way away. **(2)** by far ▷ *C'est de loin l'élève la plus brillante.* She is by far the brightest pupil.; **C'est plus loin que la gare.** It's further on than the station.
lointain, e *adj* distant
▶ *nm* **dans le lointain** in the distance
loir *nm* dormouse; **dormir comme un loir** to sleep like a log
loisirs *nmpl* ❶ free time *sg* ▷ *Qu'est-ce que vous faites pendant vos loisirs?* What do you do in your free time? ❷ hobby
Londonien *nm* Londoner
Londres *n* London; **à Londres (1)** in London **(2)** to London
long (*f* **longue**) *adj* long
▶ *nm* **un bateau de trois mètres de long** a boat 3 m long; **tout le long de** all along; **marcher de long en large** to walk up and down
longer *vb* [**45**] **La route longe la forêt.** The road runs along the edge of the forest.; **Nous avons longé la Seine à pied.** We walked along the Seine.
longtemps *adv* a long time; **pendant longtemps** for a long time; **mettre longtemps à faire quelque chose** to take a long time to do something
longue *nf* **à la longue** in the end
longuement *adv* at length
longueur *nf* length; **à longueur de journée** all day long
look *nm* look
loques *nfpl* **être en loques** to be torn to bits
lors de *prep* during
lorsque *conj* when
lot *nm* prize; **le gros lot** the jackpot
loterie *nf* ❶ lottery ❷ raffle
lotion *nf* lotion; **une lotion après-rasage** an aftershave; **une lotion démaquillante** cleansing milk
lotissement *nm* housing estate
loto *nm* lottery; **le loto sportif** the pools
loubard *nm* (*informal*) lout
louche *adj* fishy
▶ *nf* ladle
loucher *vb* [**28**] to squint
louer *vb* [**28**] ❶ to let; **'à louer'** 'to let' ❷ to rent ▷ *Je loue un petit appartement au centre-ville.* I rent a little flat in the centre of town. ❸ to hire ▷ *Nous allons louer une*

voiture. We're going to hire a car. ❹ to praise

loup *nm* wolf

loupe *nf* magnifying glass

louper *vb* [**28**] *(informal)* to miss

lourd, e *adj* heavy
▶ *adv (weather)* close

loutre *nf* otter

loyauté *nf* loyalty

loyer *nm* rent

lu *vb see* **lire**

lucarne *nf* skylight

luge *nf* sledge

lugubre *adj* gloomy

lui *pron* ❶ him ▷ *Il a été très content du cadeau que je lui ai offert.* He was very pleased with the present I gave him. ▷ *C'est bien lui!* It's definitely him! ▷ *J'ai pensé à lui toute la journée.* I thought about him all day long. ❷ to him ▷ *Mon père est d'accord: je lui ai parlé ce matin.* My father said yes: I spoke to him this morning. ❸ her ▷ *Elle a été très contente du cadeau que je lui ai offert.* She was very pleased with the present I gave her. ❹ to her ▷ *Ma mère est d'accord: je lui ai parlé ce matin.* My mother said yes: I spoke to her this morning. ❺ it ▷ *Qu'est-ce que tu donnes à ton chat? — Je lui donne de la viande crue.* What do you give your cat? — I give it raw meat.
lui is also used for emphasis. ▷ *Lui, il est toujours en retard!* Oh him, he's always late!; **lui-même** himself ▷ *Il a construit son bateau lui-même.* He built his boat himself.

lumière *nf* light; **la lumière du jour** daylight

lumineux (*f* **lumineuse**) *adj* **une enseigne lumineuse** a neon sign

lunatique *adj* temperamental

lundi *nm* ❶ Monday ▷ *Aujourd'hui, nous sommes lundi.* It's Monday today. ❷ on Monday; **le lundi** on Mondays; **tous les lundis** every Monday; **lundi dernier** last Monday; **lundi prochain** next Monday; **le lundi de Pâques** Easter Monday

lune *nf* moon; **la lune de miel** honeymoon

lunettes *nfpl* glasses; **des lunettes de soleil** sunglasses; **des lunettes de plongée** swimming goggles

lutte *nf* ❶ fight ❷ wrestling

lutter *vb* [**28**] to fight

luxe *nm* luxury; **de luxe** luxury

luxueux (*f* **luxueuse**) *adj* luxurious

lycée *nm* secondary school; **lycée technique** technical college

In France pupils go to a **collège** between the ages of 11 and 15, and then to a **lycée** until the age of 18.

lycéen *nm* secondary school pupil

lycéenne *nf* secondary school pupil

M. *abbr* (= *Monsieur*) Mr ▷ *M. Bernard* Mr Bernard
m' *pron see* **me**
ma *adj f* my ▷ *ma mère* my mother ▷ *ma montre* my watch
macaronis *nmpl* macaroni *sg*
Macédoine *nf* Macedonia
macédoine *nf* **la macédoine de fruits** fruit salad; **la macédoine de légumes** mixed vegetables
mâcher *vb* [**28**] to chew
machin *nm (informal)* thingy
machinalement *adv* **Elle a regardé sa montre machinalement.** She looked at her watch without thinking.
machine *nf* machine; **une machine à laver** a washing machine; **une machine à écrire** a typewriter; **une machine à coudre** a sewing machine; **une machine à sous** a fruit machine
machiste *nm* male chauvinist
macho *nm (informal)* male chauvinist pig
mâchoire *nf* jaw
mâchonner *vb* [**28**] to chew
maçon *nm* bricklayer
Madame (*pl* **Mesdames**) *nf* ❶ Mrs ▷ *Madame Legall* Mrs Legall ❷ lady ▷ *Occupez-vous de Madame.* Could you look after this lady? ❸ Madam ▷ *Madame, ... (in letter)* Dear Madam, ...
Mademoiselle (*pl* **Mesdemoiselles**) *nf* ❶ Miss ▷ *Mademoiselle Martin* Miss Martin ❷ Madam ▷ *Mademoiselle, ... (in letter)* Dear Madam, ...
magasin *nm* shop; **faire les magasins** to go shopping
magazine *nm* magazine
magicien *nm* magician
magie *nf* magic ▷ *un tour de magie* a magic trick
magique *adj* magic ▷ *une baguette magique* a magic wand
magistral, e (*mpl* **magistraux**) *adj* **un cours magistral** *(at university)* a lecture
magnétique *adj* magnetic
magnétophone *nm* tape recorder; **un magnétophone à cassettes** a cassette recorder
magnétoscope *nm* video recorder
magnifique *adj* superb
mai *nm* May; **en mai** in May
maigre *adj* ❶ skinny ❷ *(meat)* lean ❸ *(cheese, yoghurt)* low-fat

maigrir *vb* **[38]** to lose weight
maillot de bain *nm* ❶ swimsuit ❷ swimming trunks
main *nf* hand; **serrer la main à quelqu'un** to shake hands with somebody; **se serrer la main** to shake hands; **sous la main** to hand
main-d'œuvre *nf* workforce; **la main-d'œuvre immigrée** immigrant labour
maintenant *adv* ❶ now ▷ *Qu'est-ce que tu veux faire maintenant?* What do you want to do now? ❷ nowadays
maintenir *vb* **[83]** to maintain; **se maintenir** to hold
maire *nm* mayor
mairie *nf* town hall
mais *conj* but ▷ *C'est cher mais de très bonne qualité.* It's expensive, but very good quality.
maïs *nm* ❶ maize ❷ sweetcorn
maison *nf* house; **une maison des jeunes** a youth club; **des maisons mitoyennes (1)** semi-detached houses **(2)** terraced houses; **à la maison (1)** at home ▷ *Je serai à la maison cet après-midi.* I'll be at home this afternoon. **(2)** home ▷ *Elle est rentrée à la maison.* She's gone home.
▶ *adj* home-made
maître *nm* ❶ *(in primary school)* teacher ❷ *(of dog)* master; **un maître d'hôtel** *(in restaurant)* a head waiter; **un maître nageur** a lifeguard
maîtresse *nf* ❶ *(in primary school)* teacher ❷ mistress
maîtrise *nf* master's degree; **la maîtrise de soi** self-control
maîtriser *vb* **[28]** **se maîtriser** to control oneself
majestueux (*f* **majestueuse**) *adj* majestic
majeur, e *adj* **être majeur** to be 18 ▷ *Tu feras ce que tu voudras quand tu seras majeure.* You can do what you like once you're 18. ▷ *Elle sera majeure en août.* She will be 18 in August.; **la majeure partie** most ▷ *la majeure partie de mon salaire* most of my salary
majorité *nf* majority; **la majorité et l'opposition** the government and the opposition
Majorque *nf* Majorca
majuscule *nf* capital letter
mal *adv, adj* ❶ badly ❷ wrong ▷ *C'est mal de mentir.* It's wrong to tell lies.; **aller mal** to be ill; **pas mal** quite good
▶ *nm* ❶ ache ▷ *J'ai mal à la tête.* I've got a headache. ▷ *J'ai mal aux dents.* I've got toothache. ▷ *J'ai mal au dos.* My back hurts. ▷ *Est-ce que vous avez mal à la gorge?* Have you got a sore throat?; **Ça fait mal.** It hurts.; **Où est-ce que tu as mal?** Where does it hurt?; **faire mal à quelqu'un** to hurt somebody; **se faire mal** to hurt oneself ▷ *Je me suis fait mal au bras.* I hurt my arm.; **se donner du mal pour faire quelque chose** to go to a lot of trouble to do something; **avoir le mal de mer** to be seasick; **avoir le**

mal du pays to be homesick ❷ evil; **dire du mal de quelqu'un** to speak ill of somebody

malade *adj* ill; **tomber malade** to fall ill
▶ *nmf* patient

maladie *nf* illness

maladif (*f* **maladive**) *adj* sickly

maladresse *nf* clumsiness

maladroit, e *adj* clumsy

malaise *nm* **avoir un malaise** to feel faint; **Son arrivée a créé un malaise parmi les invités.** Her arrival made the guests feel uncomfortable.

malchance *nf* bad luck

mâle *adj* male

malédiction *nf* curse

mal en point *adj* **Il avait l'air mal en point quand je l'ai vu hier soir.** He didn't look too good when I saw him last night.

malentendu *nm* misunderstanding

malfaiteur *nm* criminal

mal famé, e (*mpl* **mal famés**) *adj* **un quartier mal famé** a seedy area

malgache *adj* from Madagascar

malgré *prep* in spite of; **malgré tout** all the same

malheur *nm* tragedy; **faire un malheur** *(informal)* to be a smash hit

malheureusement *adv* unfortunately

malheureux (*f* **malheureuse**) *adj* miserable

malhonnête *adj* dishonest

malice *nf* mischief

malicieux (*f* **malicieuse**) *adj* mischievous

> Be careful! **malicieux** does not mean **malicious**.

malin (*f* **maligne**) *adj* crafty; **C'est malin!** *(informal)* That's clever!

malle *nf* trunk

malodorant, e *adj* foul-smelling

malpropre *adj* dirty

malsain, e *adj* unhealthy

Malte *nm* Malta

maltraiter *vb* [**28**] to ill-treat; **des enfants maltraités** battered children

malveillant, e *adj* malicious

maman *nf* mum

mamie *nf* granny

mammifère *nm* mammal

manche *nf* ❶ *(of clothes)* sleeve ❷ *(of game)* leg; **la Manche** the Channel
▶ *nm (of pan)* handle

mandarine *nf* mandarin orange

manège *nm* merry-go-round

manette *nf* lever

mangeable *adj* edible

manger *vb* [**45**] to eat

mangue *nf* mango

maniaque *adj* fussy

manie *nf* ❶ obsession; **avoir la manie de** to be obsessive about ❷ habit

manier *vb* [**19**] to handle

maniéré, e *adj* affected

manière *nf* way; **de manière à** so as to; **de toute manière** in any case

manières *nfpl* ❶ manners ❷ fuss
▷ *Ne fais pas de manières: mange ta*

soupe! Don't make a fuss: eat your soup!

manifestant *nm* demonstrator

manifestation *nf* demonstration

manifester *vb* [**28**] to demonstrate

manipuler *vb* [**28**] ❶ to handle ❷ to manipulate

mannequin *nmf* model

manœuvrer *vb* [**28**] to manœuvre

manque *nm* **le manque de** lack of

manqué, e *adj* **un garçon manqué** a tomboy

manquer *vb* [**28**] to miss ▷ *Il manque des pages à ce livre.* There are some pages missing from this book.; **Mes parents me manquent.** I miss my parents.; **Ma sœur me manque.** I miss my sister.; **Il manque encore dix euros.** We are still 10 euros short.; **manquer de** to lack; **Il a manqué se tuer.** He nearly got killed.

manteau (*pl* **manteaux**) *nm* coat

manuel (*f* **manuelle**) *adj* manual ▸ *nm* ❶ textbook ❷ handbook

maquereau (*pl* **maquereaux**) *nm* mackerel

maquette *nf* model

maquillage *nm* make-up

se **maquiller** *vb* [**28**] to put on one's make-up

marais *nm* marsh

marbre *nm* marble

marchand *nm* ❶ shopkeeper; **un marchand de journaux** a newsagent ❷ stallholder *(in market)*

marchander *vb* [**28**] to haggle

marchandise *nf* goods

marche *nf* ❶ step ▷ *Fais attention à la marche!* Mind the step! ❷ walking ▷ *La marche me fait du bien.* Walking does me good.; **être en état de marche** to be in working order; **Ne montez jamais dans un train en marche.** Never try to get onto a moving train.; **mettre en marche** to start; **la marche arrière** reverse gear; **faire marche arrière** to reverse ❸ march ▷ *une marche militaire* a military march

marché *nm* market; **un marché aux puces** a flea market; **le marché noir** the black market

marcher *vb* [**28**] ❶ to walk ▷ *Elle marche cinq kilomètres par jour.* She walks 5 kilometres every day. ❷ to run ▷ *Le métro marche normalement aujourd'hui.* The underground is running normally today. ❸ to work ▷ *Est-ce que l'ascenseur marche?* Is the lift working? ❹ to go well; **Alors les études, ça marche?** *(informal)* How are you getting on at school?; **faire marcher quelqu'un** to pull somebody's leg

marcheur *nm* walker

mardi *nm* ❶ Tuesday ▷ *Aujourd'hui, nous sommes mardi.* It's Tuesday today. ❷ on Tuesday; **le mardi** on Tuesdays; **tous les mardis** every Tuesday; **mardi dernier** last Tuesday; **mardi prochain** next Tuesday; **Mardi gras** Shrove Tuesday

mare *nf* pond
marécage *nm* marsh
marée *nf* tide; **une marée noire** an oil slick
margarine *nf* margarine
marge *nf* margin
mari *nm* husband
mariage *nm* ❶ marriage ❷ wedding
marié, e *adj* married
marié *nm* bridegroom; **les mariés** the bride and groom
mariée *nf* bride
se **marier** *vb* [**19**] to marry
marin, e *adj* sea; **un pull marin** a sailor's jersey
▶ *nm* sailor
marine *adj* **bleu marine** navy-blue
▶ *nf* navy; **la marine nationale** the French navy
marionnette *nf* puppet
marketing *nm* marketing
marmelade *nf* stewed fruit; **la marmelade de pommes** stewed apple; **la marmelade d'oranges** marmalade
marmite *nf* cooking pot
marmonner *vb* [**28**] to mumble
Maroc *nm* Morocco
marocain, e *adj, nm/f* Moroccan
maroquinerie *nf* leather goods shop
marquant, e *adj* significant
marque *nf* ❶ mark ▷ *des marques de doigts* fingermarks ❷ make ▷ *De quelle marque est ton jean?* What make are your jeans? ❸ brand ▷ *une grande marque de cognac* a well-known brand of cognac; **l'image de marque** the public image ▷ *Le ministre tient à son image de marque.* The minister cares about his public image.; **une marque déposée** a registered trademark; **À vos marques! Prêts! Partez!** Ready, steady, go!
marquer *vb* [**28**] ❶ to mark ❷ to score ▷ *L'équipe irlandaise a marqué dix points.* The Irish team scored ten points. ❸ to celebrate ▷ *On va sortir au restaurant pour marquer ton anniversaire.* We'll eat out to celebrate your birthday.
marraine *nf* godmother
marrant, e *adj (informal)* funny
marre *adv (informal)*; **en avoir marre de quelque chose** to be fed up with something
se **marrer** *vb* [**28**] *(informal)* to have a good laugh
marron *nm* chestnut ▷ *la crème de marrons* chestnut purée
▶ *adj* brown
marronnier *nm* chestnut tree
mars *nm* March; **en mars** in March
marteau (*pl* **marteaux**) *nm* hammer
martyriser *vb* [**28**] to batter
masculin, e *adj* ❶ men's ▷ *la mode masculine* men's fashion ❷ masculine ▷ *'Chat' est un nom masculin.* 'Chat' is a masculine noun.
masque *nm* mask
massacre *nm* massacre
massacrer *vb* [**28**] to massacre
massage *nm* massage
masse *nf* **une masse de** *(informal)*

masses of; **produire en masse** to mass-produce; **venir en masse** to come en masse

masser *vb* [**28**] to massage; **se masser** to gather

massif (*f* **massive**) *adj* ❶ *(gold, silver, wood)* solid ❷ massive ▷ *une dose massive d'antibiotiques* a massive dose of antibiotics ❸ mass ▷ *des départs massifs* a mass exodus

mat, e *adj* matt; **être mat** *(chess)* to be checkmate

match *nm* match; **le match aller** the first leg; **le match retour** the second leg; **faire match nul** to draw

matelas *nm* mattress; **un matelas pneumatique** an air bed

matelassé, e *adj* quilted

matelot *nm* sailor

matériaux *nmpl* materials

matériel *nm* ❶ equipment ❷ gear

maternel (*f* **maternelle**) *adj* motherly; **ma grand-mère maternelle** my mother's mother; **mon oncle maternel** my mother's brother

maternelle *nf* nursery school

The **maternelle** is a state school for 2–6 year-olds.

maternité *nf* **le congé de maternité** maternity leave

mathématiques *nfpl* mathematics

maths *nfpl (informal)* maths

matière *nf* subject ▷ *Le latin est une matière facultative.* Latin is an optional subject.; **sans matières grasses** fat-free; **les matières premières** raw materials

matin *nm* morning ▷ *à trois heures du matin* at 3 o'clock in the morning; **Je suis du matin.** I'm at my best in the morning.; **de bon matin** early in the morning

matinal, e (*mpl* **matinaux**) *adj* morning; **être matinal** to be up early

matinée *nf* morning

matou *nm* tomcat

matrimonial, e (*mpl* **matrimoniaux**) *adj* **une agence matrimoniale** a marriage bureau

maudire *vb* [**46**] to curse

maudit, e *adj (informal)* blasted

maussade *adj* sullen

mauvais, e *adj, adv* ❶ bad ▷ *une mauvaise note* a bad mark; **Il fait mauvais.** The weather's bad.; **être mauvais en** to be bad at ▷ *Je suis mauvais en allemand.* I'm bad at German. ❷ poor ▷ *Il est en mauvaise santé.* His health is poor.; **Tu as mauvaise mine.** You don't look well. ❸ wrong ▷ *Vous avez fait le mauvais numéro.* You've dialled the wrong number.; **des mauvaises herbes** weeds; **sentir mauvais** to smell

maux *nmpl* **des maux de ventre** stomachache; **des maux de tête** headache

maximal, e (*mpl* **maximaux**) *adj* maximum

maximum *nm* maximum; **au maximum (1)** as much as one can **(2)** at the very most

mayonnaise *nf* mayonnaise
mazout *nm* fuel oil
me *pron*

me changes to **m'** before a vowel and most words beginning with 'h'.

❶ me ▷ *Elle me téléphone tous les jours.* She phones me every day. ▷ *Il m'attend depuis une heure.* He's been waiting for me for an hour. ❷ to me ▷ *Il me parle en allemand.* He talks to me in German. ❸ myself ▷ *Je vais me préparer quelque chose à manger.* I'm going to make myself something to eat.

With reflexive verbs, **me** is often not translated.

▷ *Je me lève à sept heures tous les matins.* I get up at 7 every morning.
mec *nm (informal)* guy
mécanicien *nm* mechanic
mécanique *nf* ❶ mechanics ❷ *(of watch, clock)* mechanism
mécanisme *nm* mechanism
méchamment *adv* nastily
méchanceté *nf* nastiness
méchant, e *adj* nasty; **'Attention, chien méchant'** 'Beware of the dog'
mèche *nf (of hair)* lock
mécontent, e *adj* **mécontent de** unhappy with
mécontentement *nm* displeasure
médaille *nf* medal
médecin *nm* doctor
médecine *nf (subject)* medicine
médias *nmpl* media *sg*
médical, e (*mpl* **médicaux**) *adj* medical; **passer une visite médicale** to have a medical
médicament *nm (drug)* medicine
médiéval, e (*mpl* **médiévaux**) *adj* medieval
médiocre *adj* poor
Méditerranée *nf* Mediterranean
méditerranéen (*f* **méditerranéenne**) *adj* Mediterranean
méduse *nf* jellyfish
méfiance *nf* mistrust
méfiant, e *adj* mistrustful
se **méfier** *vb* [**19**] **se méfier de quelqu'un** to distrust somebody
mégarde *nf* **par mégarde** by mistake
mégot *nm* cigarette end
meilleur, e *adj, adv, n* better; **le meilleur** the best; **le meilleur des deux** the better of the two; **meilleur marché** cheaper
mél *nm* email
mélancolique *adj* melancholy
mélange *nm* mixture
mélanger *vb* [**45**] ❶ to mix ❷ to muddle up
mêlée *nf* scrum
mêler *vb* [**28**] **se mêler** to mix; **Mêle-toi de ce qui te regarde!** *(informal)* Mind your own business!
mélodie *nf* melody
melon *nm* melon
membre *nm* ❶ limb ❷ member ▷ *un membre de la famille* a member of the family
mémé *nf (informal)* granny
même *adj, adv, pron* ❶ same; **en même temps** at the same time;

moi-même myself ▷ *Je l'ai fait moi-même.* I did it myself.; **toi-même** yourself; **eux-mêmes** themselves ❷ even ▷ *Il n'a même pas pleuré.* He didn't even cry.
mémoire *nf* memory
menace *nf* threat
menacer *vb* [**12**] to threaten
ménage *nm* housework; **une femme de ménage** a cleaning woman
ménager (*f* **ménagère**) *adj* **les travaux ménagers** housework
ménagère *nf* housewife
mendiant *nm* beggar
mendier *vb* [**19**] to beg
mener *vb* [**43**] to lead; **Cela ne vous mènera à rien!** That will get you nowhere!
méningite *nf* meningitis
menottes *nfpl* handcuffs
mensonge *nm* lie
mensualité *nf* monthly payment
mensuel (*f* **mensuelle**) *adj* monthly
mensurations *nfpl* measurements
mentalité *nf* mentality
menteur *nm* liar
menteuse *nf* liar
menthe *nf* mint
mention *nf* grade
mentionner *vb* [**28**] to mention
mentir *vb* [**77**] to lie ▷ *Tu mens!* You're lying!
menton *nm* chin
menu, e *adj, adv* ❶ slim ▷ *Elle est menue.* She's slim. ❷ very fine ▷ *Les oignons doivent être coupés menu.* The onions have to be cut up very fine.
▶ *nm* menu ▷ *le menu du jour* today's menu
menuiserie *nf* woodwork
menuisier *nm* joiner
mépris *nm* contempt
méprisant, e *adj* contemptuous
mépriser *vb* [**28**] to despise
mer *nf* ❶ sea; **au bord de la mer** at the seaside; **la mer du Nord** the North Sea ❷ tide
mercerie *nf* ❶ haberdashery ❷ haberdasher's shop
merci *excl* thank you ▷ *Merci de m'avoir raccompagné.* Thank you for taking me home.; **merci beaucoup** thank you very much
mercredi *nm* ❶ Wednesday ▷ *Aujourd'hui, nous sommes mercredi.* It's Wednesday today. ❷ on Wednesday; **le mercredi** on Wednesdays; **tous les mercredis** every Wednesday; **mercredi dernier** last Wednesday; **mercredi prochain** next Wednesday
mère *nf* mother
merguez *nf* spicy sausage
méridional, e (*mpl* **méridionaux**) *adj* southern
meringue *nf* meringue
mériter *vb* [**28**] to deserve
merlan *nm* whiting
merle *nm* blackbird
merveille *nf* **Cet ordinateur est une vraie merveille!** This computer's really wonderful!; **à merveille** wonderfully
merveilleux (*f* **merveilleuse**) *adj*

marvellous

mes *adj pl* my ▷ *mes parents* my parents

Mesdames *nfpl* ladies

Mesdemoiselles *nfpl* ladies

mesquin, e *adj* mean

message *nm* message; **un message SMS** a text message

messagerie *nf* **une messagerie vocale** voice mail; **la messagerie électronique** email

messe *nf* mass

messieurs *nmpl* gentlemen; **Messieurs, ...** *(in letter)* Dear Sirs, ...

mesure *nf* ❶ measurement; **sur mesure** tailor-made ❷ measure; **au fur et à mesure** as one goes along; **être en mesure de faire quelque chose** to be in a position to do something

mesurer *vb* [**28**] to measure; **Il mesure un mètre quatre-vingts.** He's 1 m 80 tall.

met *vb see* **mettre**

métal (*pl* **métaux**) *nm* metal

métallique *adj* metallic

météo *nf* weather forecast

méthode *nf* ❶ method ❷ tutor ▷ *une méthode de guitare* a guitar tutor

métier *nm* job

mètre *nm* metre; **un mètre ruban** a tape measure

métro *nm* underground

mets *vb see* **mettre**

metteur en scène (*pl* **metteurs en scène**) *nm (of film or play)* director

mettre *vb* [**47**] ❶ to put ▷ *Où est-ce que tu as mis les clés?* Where have you put the keys? ❷ to put on ▷ *Je mets mon manteau et j'arrive.* I'll put on my coat and then I'll be ready. ❸ to wear ▷ *Elle ne met pas souvent de jupe.* She doesn't often wear a skirt. ❹ to take ▷ *Combien de temps as-tu mis pour aller à Lille?* How long did it take you to get to Lille?; **mettre en marche** to start; **Vous pouvez vous mettre là.** You can sit there.; **se mettre au lit** to get into bed; **se mettre en maillot de bain** to put on one's swimsuit; **se mettre à** to start

meuble *nm* piece of furniture

meublé *nm* ❶ furnished flat ❷ furnished room

meubler *vb* [**28**] to furnish

meurtre *nm* murder

meurtrier *nm* murderer

meurtrière *nf* murderess

Mexico *n* Mexico City

Mexique *nm* Mexico

mi *nm* ❶ E ▷ *mi bémol* E flat ❷ mi ▷ *do, ré, mi ...* do, re, mi ...

mi- *prefix* ❶ half- ▷ *mi-clos* half-shut ❷ mid- ▷ *à la mi-janvier* in mid-January

miauler *vb* [**28**] to mew

miche *nf* loaf

mi-chemin: **à mi-chemin** *adv* halfway

micro *nm* microphone

microbe *nm* germ

micro-ondes *nm* microwave oven

micro-ordinateur *nm* microcomputer

microscope *nm* microscope

midi *nm* ❶ midday ▷ *à midi* at midday; **midi et demi** half past twelve ❷ lunchtime ▷ *On a bien mangé à midi.* We had a good meal at lunchtime.; **le Midi** the South of France
mie *nf* breadcrumbs
miel *nm* honey
mien *pron m* **le mien** mine
mienne *pron f* **la mienne** mine
miennes *pron fpl* **les miennes** mine
miens *pron mpl* **les miens** mine
miette *nf (of bread, cake)* crumb
mieux *adv, adj, n* better; **Il vaut mieux que tu appelles ta mère.** You'd better phone your mother.; **le mieux** the best; **faire de son mieux** to do one's best; **de mieux en mieux** better and better; **au mieux** at best
mignon (*f* **mignonne**) *adj* sweet
migraine *nf* migraine
mijoter *vb* [**28**] to simmer
milieu (*pl* **milieux**) *nm* ❶ middle; **au milieu de** in the middle of; **au beau milieu de** in the middle of ❷ background ▷ *le milieu familial* the family background ❸ environment ▷ *le milieu marin* the marine environment
militaire *adj* military
▶ *nm* serviceman; **un militaire de carrière** a professional soldier
mille *num* a thousand ▷ *mille euros* a thousand euros ▷ *deux mille personnes* two thousand people
millefeuille *nm* vanilla slice
millénaire *nm* millennium
milliard *nm* billion
milliardaire *nmf* billionaire
millier *nm* thousand; **par milliers** by the thousand
milligramme *nm* milligram
millimètre *nm* millimetre
million *nm* million
millionnaire *nmf* millionaire
mime *nmf* mime artist
mimer *vb* [**28**] to mimic
minable *adj* ❶ shabby ❷ pathetic
mince *adj* ❶ thin ❷ slim; **Mince alors!** *(informal)* Oh bother!
minceur *nf* ❶ thinness ❷ slimness
mine *nf* ❶ expression ❷ look ▷ *Tu as bonne mine.* You look well. ▷ *Il a mauvaise mine.* He doesn't look well. ▷ *Elle avait une mine fatiguée.* She was looking tired. ❸ appearance ▷ *Il ne faut pas juger les gens d'après leur mine.* You shouldn't judge people by their appearance. ❹ *(of pencil)* lead ❺ mine ▷ *une mine de charbon* a coal mine; **faire mine de faire quelque chose** to pretend to do something ▷ *Elle a fait mine de le croire.* She pretended to believe him.
minéral, e (*mpl* **minéraux**) *adj* mineral
minéralogique *adj* **une plaque minéralogique** a number plate
minet *nm* pussycat
minette *nf (female)* pussycat
mineur, e *adj* minor
mineur *nm* ❶ boy under 18; **les mineurs** the under-18s ❷ miner
mineure *nf* girl under 18
minijupe *nf* miniskirt
minimal, e (*mpl* **minimaux**) *adj*

minimum
minimum *nm* minimum; **au minimum** at the very least
ministère *nm* ministry
ministre *nm* minister
Minitel® *nm*

- **Minitel** was a system for getting information online which pre-dated the internet.

minorité *nf* minority
Minorque *nf* Minorca
minuit *nm* midnight ▷ *à minuit et quart* at a quarter past midnight
minuscule *adj* tiny
▶ *nf* small letter
minute *nf* minute; **à la minute** just this minute
minutieux (*f* **minutieuse**) *adj* meticulous; **C'est un travail minutieux.** It's a fiddly job.
mirabelle *nf* small yellow plum
miracle *nm* miracle
miroir *nm* mirror
mis, e *adj* **bien mis** well turned out
▶ *vb see* **mettre**
miser *vb* [**28**] *(informal)* to bank on
misérable *adj* shabby-looking
misère *nf* extreme poverty; **un salaire de misère** starvation wages
missionnaire *nmf* missionary
mit *vb see* **mettre**
mi-temps *nf* ❶ *(of match)* half ▷ *la première mi-temps* the first half ❷ half-time; **travailler à mi-temps** to work part-time
mitraillette *nf* submachine gun
mixte *adj* **une école mixte** a mixed school
Mlle (*pl* **Mlles**) *abbr* (= *Mademoiselle*) Miss ▷ *Mlle Renoir* Miss Renoir
Mme (*pl* **Mmes**) *abbr* (= *Madame*) Mrs ▷ *Mme Leroy* Mrs Leroy
mobile *nm* ❶ motive ❷ mobile phone
mobilier *nm* furniture
mobylette® *nf* moped
moche *adj (informal)* ❶ awful ❷ rotten
mode *nf* fashion
▶ *nm* **le mode d'emploi** directions for use; **le mode de vie** the way of life
modèle *nm* ❶ model ❷ *(of clothes)* style
modéré, e *adj* moderate
moderne *adj* modern
moderniser *vb* [**28**] to modernize
modeste *adj* modest
modestie *nf* modesty
moelleux (*f* **moelleuse**) *adj* soft
mœurs *nfpl* social attitudes; **l'évolution des mœurs** changing attitudes
moi *pron* me ▷ *Coucou, c'est moi!* Hello, it's me!; **Moi, je pense que tu as tort.** I personally think you're wrong.; **à moi** mine ▷ *Ce livre n'est pas à moi.* This book isn't mine. ▷ *un ami à moi* a friend of mine
moi-même *pron* myself
moindre *adj* **le moindre** the slightest
moine *nm* monk
moineau (*pl* **moineaux**) *nm* sparrow
moins *adv, prep* ❶ less ▷ *Ça coûte moins de deux cents euros.* It costs

less than 200 euros. ❷ fewer ▷ *Il y a moins de gens aujourd'hui.* There are fewer people today.; **Il est cinq heures moins dix.** It's 10 to 5. ❸ minus ▷ *quatre moins trois* 4 minus 3; **le moins** the least; **de moins en moins** less and less; **Il a trois ans de moins que moi.** He's three years younger than me.; **au moins** at least; **à moins que** unless

> **à moins que** is followed by a verb in the subjunctive.

▷ *Je te retrouverai à dix heures à moins que le train n'ait du retard.* I'll meet you at 10 o'clock unless the train's late.

mois *nm* month

moisi *nm* **Ça sent le moisi.** It smells musty.

moisir *vb* [**38**] to go mouldy

moisson *nf* harvest

moite *adj* sweaty

moitié *nf* half ▷ *Il a mangé la moitié du gâteau.* He ate half the cake.; **la moitié du temps** half the time; **à la moitié de** halfway through ▷ *Elle est partie à la moitié du film.* She left halfway through the film.; **à moitié** half ▷ *Ton verre est encore à moitié plein.* Your glass is still half-full. ▷ *Ce sac était à moitié prix.* This bag was half-price.; **partager moitié moitié** to go halves ▷ *On partage moitié moitié, d'accord?* We'll go halves, OK?

molaire *nf* back tooth

Moldavie *nf* Moldova

molle *adj f see* **mou**

mollet *nm (of leg)* calf
▸ *adj* **un œuf mollet** a soft-boiled egg

môme *nmf (informal)* kid

moment *nm* moment; **en ce moment** at the moment; **pour le moment** for the moment; **au moment où** just as; **à ce moment-là (1)** at that point **(2)** in that case; **à tout moment (1)** at any moment **(2)** constantly; **sur le moment** at the time; **par moments** at times

momentané, e *adj* momentary

momie *nf (Egyptian)* mummy

mon (*f* **ma**, *pl* **mes**) *adj* my ▷ *mon ami* my friend

monarchie *nf* monarchy

monastère *nm* monastery

monde *nm* world; **Il y a du monde.** There are a lot of people.; **beaucoup de monde** a lot of people; **peu de monde** not many people

mondial, e (*mpl* **mondiaux**) *adj* ❶ world ▷ *la population mondiale* the world population ❷ world-wide

moniteur *nm* ❶ instructor ❷ monitor

monitrice *nf* instructor

monnaie *nf* **une pièce de monnaie** a coin; **avoir de la monnaie** to have change; **rendre la monnaie à quelqu'un** to give somebody their change

monotone *adj* monotonous

Monsieur (*pl* **Messieurs**) *nm* ❶ Mr ▷ *Monsieur Dupont* Mr Dupont

❷ man ▷ *Il y a un monsieur qui veut te voir.* There's a man to see you. ❸ Sir ▷ *Monsieur, ... (in letter)* Dear Sir, ...
monstre *nm* monster
▶ *adj* **Nous avons un travail monstre.** We've got a terrific amount of work.
mont *nm* mount; **le mont Everest** Mount Everest; **le mont Blanc** Mont Blanc
montagne *nf* mountain; **les montagnes russes** roller coaster
montagneux (*f* **montagneuse**) *adj* mountainous
montant, e *adj* ❶ rising ▷ *la marée montante* the rising tide ❷ high
monter *vb* [**48**] ❶ to go up ▷ *Elle a du mal à monter les escaliers.* She has difficulty going upstairs. ❷ to assemble ▷ *Est-ce que ces étagères sont difficiles à monter?* Are these shelves difficult to assemble?; **monter dans** to get on; **monter sur** to stand on; **monter à cheval** to ride
montre *nf* watch
montrer *vb* [**28**] to show
monture *nf (of glasses)* frames
monument *nm* monument
se **moquer** *vb* [**28**] **se moquer de** **(1)** to make fun of **(2)** *(informal)* not to care about
moquette *nf* fitted carpet
moqueur (*f* **moqueuse**) *adj* mocking
moral *nm* **Elle a le moral.** She's in good spirits.; **J'ai le moral à zéro.** I'm feeling really down.
morale *nf* moral; **faire la morale à quelqu'un** to lecture somebody
morceau (*pl* **morceaux**) *nm* piece
mordre *vb* [**49**] to bite
mordu, e *adj* **Il est mordu de jazz.** *(informal)* He's crazy about jazz.
morgue *nf* mortuary
morse *nm* walrus
morsure *nf* bite
mort *nf* death
mort, e *adj* dead; **Il était mort de peur.** He was scared to death.; **Je suis morte de fatigue.** I'm dead tired.
mortel (*f* **mortelle**) *adj* ❶ deadly ❷ fatal
morue *nf* cod
Moscou *n* Moscow
mosquée *nf* mosque
mot *nm* ❶ word ▷ *mot à mot* word for word; **des mots croisés** a crossword; **le mot de passe** the password ❷ note
motard *nm* ❶ biker ❷ *(informal)* motorcycle cop
moteur *nm* engine; **un bateau à moteur** a motor boat; **un moteur de recherche** a search engine
motif *nm* pattern; **sans motif** for no reason
motivé, e *adj* motivated
moto *nf* motorbike
motocycliste *nmf* motorcyclist
mou (*f* **molle**) *adj* ❶ soft ❷ lethargic
mouche *nf* fly; **prendre la mouche** to get into a huff
se **moucher** *vb* [**28**] to blow one's nose
moucheron *nm* midge
mouchoir *nm* handkerchief; **un**

mouchoir en papier a tissue
moudre *vb* [**50**] to grind
moue *nf* pout; **faire la moue** to pout
mouette *nf* seagull
moufle *nf* mitt
mouillé, e *adj* wet
mouiller *vb* [**28**] to get wet; **se mouiller** to get wet
moulant, e *adj* figure-hugging
moule *nf* mussel
▶ *nm* **un moule à gâteaux** a cake tin
moulin *nm* mill
moulu *vb see* **moudre**
mourir *vb* [**51**] to die; **mourir de faim** to starve to death; **Je meurs de faim!** I'm starving!; **mourir de froid** to die of exposure; **Je meurs de froid!** I'm freezing!; **mourir d'envie de faire quelque chose** to be dying to do something
mousse *nf* ❶ moss ❷ *(on beer)* froth ❸ *(of soap, shampoo)* lather ❹ mousse ▷ *une mousse au chocolat* a chocolate mousse; **la mousse à raser** shaving foam
mousseux (*f* **mousseuse**) *adj* **un vin mousseux** a sparkling wine
moustache *nf* moustache; **les moustaches** *(of a cat)* whiskers
moustique *nm* mosquito
moutarde *nf* mustard
mouton *nm* ❶ sheep ❷ mutton
mouvement *nm* movement
mouvementé, e *adj* eventful
moyen (*f* **moyenne**) *adj* ❶ average ❷ medium ▷ *Elle est de taille moyenne.* She's of medium height.; **le Moyen Âge** the Middle Ages
▶ *nm* way ▷ *Quel est le meilleur moyen de le convaincre?* What's the best way of convincing him?; **Je n'en ai pas les moyens.** I can't afford it.; **un moyen de transport** a means of transport; **par tous les moyens** by every possible means
moyenne *nf* **avoir la moyenne** to get a pass mark; **en moyenne** on average; **la moyenne d'âge** the average age
Moyen-Orient *nm* Middle East
muet (*f* **muette**) *adj (not speaking)* dumb; **un film muet** a silent film
muguet *nm* lily of the valley
multiple *adj* numerous
multiplier *vb* [**19**] to multiply
municipal, e (*mpl* **municipaux**) *adj* **la bibliothèque municipale** the public library
municipalité *nf* town council
munir *vb* [**38**] **munir quelqu'un de** to equip someone with; **se munir de** to equip oneself with
munitions *nfpl* ammunition *sg*
mur *nm* wall
mûr, e *adj* ❶ *(fruit)* ripe ❷ *(person)* mature
mûre *nf* bramble
mûrir *vb* [**38**] ❶ to ripen ❷ to make mature ▷ *Cette expérience l'a beaucoup mûrie.* That experience has made her much more mature.
murmurer *vb* [**28**] to whisper
muscade *nf* nutmeg
muscat *nm* ❶ muscat grape ❷ *(wine)* muscatel
muscle *nm* muscle

musclé, e *adj* muscular
museau (*pl* **museaux**) *nm* muzzle
musée *nm* museum
musical, e (*mpl* **musicaux**) *adj* musical; **avoir l'oreille musicale** to be musical
music-hall *nm* variety
musicien *nm* musician
musique *nf* music
musulman, e *adj, nm/f* Muslim; **un musulman** *(man)* a Muslim; **une musulmane** *(woman)* a Muslim
mutation *nf* transfer
myope *adj* short-sighted
mystère *nm* mystery
mystérieux (*f* **mystérieuse**) *adj* mysterious
mythe *nm* myth

n

n' *pron see* **ne**
nage *nf* **traverser une rivière à la nage** to swim across a river; **être en nage** to be sweating profusely
nageoire *nf* fin
nager *vb* [**45**] to swim
nageur *nm* swimmer
naïf (*f* **naïve**) *adj* naïve
naissance *nf* birth; **votre date de naissance** your date of birth
naître *vb* [**52**] to be born; **Il est né en 1992.** He was born in 1992.
naïve *adj f see* **naïf**
nana *nf (informal)* girl
nappe *nf* tablecloth
narine *nf* nostril
natal, e *adj* native
natation *nf* swimming; **faire de la natation** to go swimming

nation *nf* nation
national, e (*mpl* **nationaux**) *adj* national; **la fête nationale espagnole** the national day of Spain
nationale *nf* main road
nationalité *nf* nationality
natte *nf* plait
nature *nf* nature
▶ *adj* plain
naturel (*f* **naturelle**) *adj* natural
naturellement *adv* of course
naufrage *nm* shipwreck
nautique *adj* water; **les sports nautiques** water sports; **le ski nautique** water-skiing
navet *nm* turnip
navette *nf* shuttle; **faire la navette** to commute
navigateur *nm (on computer)* browser
navigation *nf* **La navigation est interdite ici.** Boats are not allowed here.
naviguer *vb* [**28**] to sail
navire *nm* ship
ne *adv*

> **ne** is combined with words such as **pas, personne, plus** and **jamais** to form negative phrases.

▷ *Je ne peux pas venir.* I can't come.

> **ne** changes to **n'** before a vowel and most words beginning with 'h'.

▷ *Je n'ai pas d'argent.* I haven't got any money.

> **ne** is sometimes not translated.

▷ *C'est plus loin que je ne le croyais.* It's further than I thought.
né *vb see* **naître** born ▷ *Elle est née en 1980.* She was born in 1980.
néanmoins *adv* nevertheless
nécessaire *adj* necessary
nectar *nm* **le nectar d'abricot** apricot drink
néerlandais, e *adj, nm/f* Dutch ▷ *Manon parle néerlandais.* Manon speaks Dutch.; **un Néerlandais** a Dutchman; **une Néerlandaise** a Dutchwoman; **les Néerlandais** the Dutch
négatif (*f* **négative**) *adj* negative
▶ *nm (of photo)* negative
négligé, e *adj* scruffy
négliger *vb* [**45**] to neglect
négocier *vb* [**19**] to negotiate
neige *nf* snow; **un bonhomme de neige** a snowman
neiger *vb* [**45**] to snow
nénuphar *nm* water lily
néon *nm* neon
néo-zélandais, e *adj, nm/f* New Zealand; **un Néo-Zélandais** *(man)* a New Zealander; **une Néo-Zélandaise** *(woman)* a New Zealander
nerf *nm* nerve; **taper sur les nerfs de quelqu'un** to get on somebody's nerves
nerveux (*f* **nerveuse**) *adj* nervous
nervosité *nf* nervousness
n'est-ce pas *adv*

> **n'est-ce pas** is used to check that something is true.

▷ *Nous sommes le douze aujourd'hui, n'est-ce pas?* It's the 12th today, isn't it? ▷ *Elle aura dix-huit ans en octobre, n'est-ce pas?* She'll be 18 in October, won't she?

Net *nm* the Net

net (*f* **nette**) *adj, adv* ❶ clear ❷ net ▷ *Poids net: 500 g.* Net weight: 500 g. ❸ flatly ▷ *Il a refusé net de nous aider.* He flatly refused to help us.; **s'arrêter net** to stop dead

nettement *adv* much

nettoyage *nm* cleaning; **le nettoyage à sec** dry cleaning

nettoyer *vb* [**53**] to clean

neuf (*f* **neuve**) *adj* new
▶ *num* nine ▷ *Claire a neuf ans.* Claire's nine.; **le neuf février** the ninth of February

neutre *adj* neutral

neuve *adj f see* **neuf**

neuvième *adj* ninth

neveu (*pl* **neveux**) *nm* nephew

nez *nm* nose; **se trouver nez à nez avec quelqu'un** to come face to face with somebody

ni *conj* **ni ... ni ...** neither ... nor ...

niche *nf* kennel

nid *nm* nest

nièce *nf* niece

nier *vb* [**19**] to deny

n'importe *adv* **n'importe quel** any old; **n'importe qui** anybody; **n'importe quoi** anything; **Tu dis n'importe quoi.** You're talking rubbish.; **n'importe où** anywhere; **Ne laisse pas tes affaires n'importe où.** Don't leave your things lying everywhere.; **n'importe quand** any time; **n'importe comment** any old how

niveau (*pl* **niveaux**) *nm* ❶ level ❷ standard; **le niveau de vie** the standard of living

noble *adj* noble

noblesse *nf* nobility

noce *nf* wedding; **un repas de noce** a wedding reception; **leurs noces d'or** their golden wedding anniversary

nocif (*f* **nocive**) *adj* harmful

nocturne *adj* ❶ nocturnal ❷ by night ▷ *Découvrez le Paris nocturne!* Discover Paris by night!
▶ *nf* late-night opening

Noël *nm* Christmas; **Joyeux Noël!** Merry Christmas!

nœud *nm* ❶ knot ❷ bow; **un nœud papillon** a bow tie

> Word for word, this means 'a butterfly bow'.

Noir *nm* black man

noir, e *adj* ❶ black ▷ *une robe noire* a black dress ❷ dark ▷ *Il fait noir dehors.* It's dark outside.
▶ *nm* dark ▷ *J'ai peur du noir.* I'm afraid of the dark.; **le travail au noir** moonlighting

Noire *nf* black woman

noisette *nf* hazelnut

noix (*pl* **noix**) *nf* walnut; **une noix de coco** a coconut; **les noix de cajou** cashew nuts; **une noix de beurre** a knob of butter

nom *nm* ❶ name; **mon nom de famille** my surname; **son nom de jeune fille** her maiden name ❷ *(in grammar)* noun

nombre *nm* number

nombreux (*f* **nombreuse**) *adj*

❶ many ❷ large ▷ *une famille nombreuse* a large family; **peu nombreux** few

nombril *nm* navel

nommer *vb* [**28**] ❶ to name ❷ to appoint

non *adv* no; **non seulement** not only; **Moi non plus.** Neither do I.

non alcoolisé, e *adj* non-alcoholic

non-fumeur *nm* non-smoker; **une voiture non-fumeurs** a no-smoking carriage

nord *nm* north; **vers le nord** northwards; **au nord de Paris** north of Paris; **l'Afrique du Nord** North Africa; **le vent du nord** the north wind

▶ *adj* ❶ north; **le pôle Nord** the North Pole ❷ northern

nord-est *nm* north-east

nord-ouest *nm* north-west

normal, e (*mpl* **normaux**) *adj* ❶ normal ❷ natural ▷ *C'est tout à fait normal.* It's perfectly natural.; **Vous trouvez que c'est normal?** Does that seem right to you?

normalement *adv* normally; **Normalement, elle doit arriver à huit heures.** She's supposed to arrive at 8 o'clock.

normand, e *adj* **un village normand** a village in Normandy; **la côte normande** the coast of Normandy

Normandie *nf* Normandy

Norvège *nf* Norway

norvégien (*f* **norvégienne**) *adj, nm/f* Norwegian ▷ *Elle parle norvégien.* She speaks Norwegian.; **un Norvégien** *(man)* a Norwegian; **une Norvégienne** *(woman)* a Norwegian

nos *adj pl* our ▷ *Où sont nos affaires?* Where are our things?

notaire *nm* solicitor

note *nf* ❶ note ▷ *J'ai pris des notes pendant la conférence.* I took notes at the lecture. ❷ mark ▷ *Vincent a de bonnes notes en maths.* Vincent's got good marks in maths. ❸ bill ▷ *Il n'a pas payé sa note.* He didn't pay his bill.

noter *vb* [**28**] to make a note of

notions *nfpl* basics

notre (*pl* **nos**) *adj* our ▷ *Voici notre maison.* Here's our house.

nôtre *pron* **le nôtre** ours

nôtres *pron pl* **les nôtres** ours

nouer *vb* [**28**] to tie

nouilles *nfpl* noodles

nounours *nm* teddy bear

nourrir *vb* [**38**] to feed

nourriture *nf* food

nous *pron pl* ❶ we ▷ *Nous avons deux enfants.* We have two children. ❷ us ▷ *Viens avec nous.* Come with us.; **nous-mêmes** ourselves

nouveau (*f* **nouvelle**, *mpl* **nouveaux**) *adj* new ▷ *Elle a une nouvelle voiture.* She's got a new car.

> The masculine singular form **nouveau** changes to **nouvel** before a vowel and most words beginning with 'h'.

▷ *le nouvel élève dans ma classe* The

new boy in my class; **le nouvel an** New Year
▶ *nm* new pupil; **de nouveau** again
nouveau-né *nm* newborn child
nouveauté *nf* novelty
nouvel, nouvelle *adj see* **nouveau**
nouvelle *nf* ❶ news ❷ short story; **les nouvelles** the news; **avoir des nouvelles de quelqu'un** to hear from somebody
Nouvelle-Zélande *nf* New Zealand
novembre *nm* November; **en novembre** in November
noyau (*pl* **noyaux**) *nm* *(of fruit)* stone
noyer *nm* walnut tree
se **noyer** *vb* **[53]** to drown
nu, e *adj* ❶ naked ❷ bare
nuage *nm* cloud; **un nuage de lait** a drop of milk
nuageux (*f* **nuageuse**) *adj* cloudy
nucléaire *adj* nuclear
nudiste *nmf* nudist
nuit *nf* night; **Il fait nuit.** It's dark.; **cette nuit** tonight; **Bonne nuit!** Good night!; **de nuit** by night
nul (*f* **nulle**) *adj* rubbish ▷ *Ce film est nul.* *(informal)* This film's rubbish.; **être nul** to be no good ▷ *Je suis nul en maths.* I'm no good at maths.; **un match nul** *(in sport)* a draw; **nulle part** nowhere
numérique *adj* digital ▷ *un appareil photo numérique* a digital camera
numéro *nm* number; **mon numéro de téléphone** my phone number; **le numéro de compte** the account number
nu-pieds *adj, adv* barefoot
nuque *nf* nape of the neck
nylon *nm* nylon

a b c d e f g h i j k l m n o p q r s t u v w x y z

O

obéir *vb* [**38**] to obey; **obéir à quelqu'un** to obey somebody
obéissant, e *adj* obedient
objet *nm* object; **les objets de valeur** valuables; **les objets trouvés** the lost property office
obligatoire *adj* compulsory
obliger *vb* [**45**] **obliger quelqu'un à faire quelque chose** to force somebody to do something; **Je suis bien obligé d'accepter.** I can't really refuse.
obscur, e *adj* dark
obscurité *nf* darkness
obsédé *nm* sex maniac; **un obsédé sexuel** a sex maniac
obséder *vb* [**34**] to obsess
observation *nf* comment
observer *vb* [**28**] ❶ to watch ▷ *Il observait les canards sur le lac.* He watched the ducks on the lake. ❷ to observe
obstacle *nm* ❶ obstacle ❷ *(in show jumping)* fence; **une course d'obstacles** an obstacle race
obstiné, e *adj* stubborn
obtenir *vb* [**83**] ❶ to get ▷ *Ils ont obtenu cinquante pour cent des voix.* They got 50% of the votes. ❷ to achieve ▷ *Nous avons obtenu de bons résultats.* We achieved good results.
occasion *nf* ❶ opportunity ❷ occasion ❸ bargain; **d'occasion** second-hand
Occident *nm* West ▷ *en Occident* in the West
occidental, e (*mpl* **occidentaux**) *adj* western; **les pays occidentaux** the West
occupation *nf* occupation
occupé, e *adj* ❶ busy ❷ taken ▷ *Est-ce que cette place est occupée?* Is this seat taken? ❸ engaged ▷ *Les toilettes sont occupées.* The toilet's engaged.
occuper *vb* [**28**] to occupy; **s'occuper de quelque chose (1)** to be in charge of something **(2)** to deal with something; **On s'occupe de vous?** *(in a shop)* Are you being attended to?
océan *nm* ocean
octobre *nm* October; **en octobre** in October
odeur *nf* smell
odieux (*f* **odieuse**) *adj* horrible
œil (*pl* **yeux**) *nm* eye; **à l'œil** *(informal)* for free

œillet *nm* carnation
œuf *nm* egg; **un œuf à la coque** a soft-boiled egg; **un œuf dur** a hard-boiled egg; **un œuf au plat** a fried egg; **les œufs brouillés** scrambled eggs; **un œuf de Pâques** an Easter egg
œuvre *nf* work; **une œuvre d'art** a work of art
offert *vb see* **offrir**
office *nm* **un office du tourisme** a tourist office
officiel (*f* **officielle**) *adj* official
officier *nm* officer
offre *nf* offer; **'offres d'emploi'** 'situations vacant'
offrir *vb* [**54**] **offrir quelque chose** (**1**) to offer something ▷ *Elle lui a offert à boire.* She offered him a drink. (**2**) to give something ▷ *Il lui a offert des roses.* He gave her roses.; **s'offrir quelque chose** to treat oneself to something
oie *nf* goose
oignon *nm* onion
oiseau (*pl* **oiseaux**) *nm* bird
olive *nf* olive
olympique *adj* **les Jeux olympiques** the Olympic Games
ombre *nf* ❶ shade ❷ shadow; **l'ombre à paupières** eye shadow
omelette *nf* omelette
omnibus *nm* local train
on *pron* ❶ we ▷ *On va à la plage demain.* We're going to the beach tomorrow. ❷ someone ▷ *On m'a volé mon sac.* Someone has stolen my bag.; **On m'a dit d'attendre.** I was told to wait.; **On vous demande au téléphone.** There's a phone call for you. ❸ you ▷ *On peut visiter le château en été.* You can visit the castle in the summer.
oncle *nm* uncle
onde *nf* (*on radio*) wave
ongle *nm* nail; **se couper les ongles** to cut one's nails
ont *vb see* **avoir**; **Ils ont beaucoup d'argent.** They've got lots of money.; **Elles ont passé de bonnes vacances.** They had a good holiday.
ONU *nf* (= *Organisation des Nations Unies*) UN (= *United Nations*)
onze *num* eleven ▷ *Elle a onze ans.* She's eleven.; **le onze février** the eleventh of February
onzième *adj* eleventh
opéra *nm* opera
opération *nf* operation
opérer *vb* [**34**] to operate on ▷ *Elle a été opérée de l'appendicite.* She was operated on for appendicitis.; **se faire opérer** to have an operation
opinion *nf* opinion
opposé, e *adj* opposite; **être opposé à quelque chose** to be opposed to something
▶ *nm* the opposite
opposer *vb* [**28**] **opposer quelqu'un à quelqu'un** to pit somebody against somebody; **s'opposer** to conflict ▷ *Ces deux points de vue s'opposent.* These two points of view conflict.; **s'opposer à quelque chose** to oppose something
opposition *nf* opposition; **par**

opposition à as opposed to; **faire opposition à un chèque** to stop a cheque
opticien *nm* optician
optimiste *adj* optimistic
option *nf* option; **une matière à option** an optional subject
or *nm* gold ▷ *un bracelet en or* a gold bracelet
▶ *conj* and yet ▷ *Il était sûr de gagner, or il a perdu.* He was sure he would win, and yet he lost.
orage *nm* thunderstorm
orageux (*f* **orageuse**) *adj* stormy
oral, e (*mpl* **oraux**) *adj* **une épreuve orale** an oral exam; **à prendre par voie orale** to be taken orally
▶ *nm (exam)* oral
orange *nf (fruit)* orange
▶ *adj (in colour)* orange
orchestre *nm* ❶ orchestra ❷ band
ordinaire *adj* ❶ ordinary ❷ standard
▶ *nm* two-star (petrol); **sortir de l'ordinaire** to be out of the ordinary
ordinateur *nm* computer
ordonnance *nf* prescription
ordonné, e *adj* tidy
ordonner *vb* [**28**] **ordonner à quelqu'un de faire quelque chose** to order somebody to do something
ordre *nm* order; **dans l'ordre** in order; **mettre en ordre** to tidy up; **jusqu'à nouvel ordre** until further notice
ordures *nfpl* rubbish *sg*; **jeter quelque chose aux ordures** to throw something in the bin
oreille *nf* ear
oreiller *nm* pillow
oreillons *nmpl* mumps
organe *nm (in body)* organ
organisateur *nm* organizer
organisation *nf* organization
organiser *vb* [**28**] to organize; **s'organiser** to get organized
organisme *nm (organization)* body
orgue *nm* organ
orgueilleux (*f* **orgueilleuse**) *adj* proud
Orient *nm* East ▷ *en Orient* in the East
oriental, e (*mpl* **orientaux**) *adj* ❶ oriental ❷ eastern
orientation *nf* orientation; **avoir le sens de l'orientation** to have a good sense of direction; **l'orientation professionnelle** careers advice
originaire *adj* **Elle est originaire de Paris.** She's from Paris.
original, e (*mpl* **originaux**) *adj* original
▶ *nm* original; **un vieil original** an old eccentric
origine *nf* origin; **à l'origine** originally
orphelin *nm* orphan
orteil *nm* toe
orthographe *nf* spelling
os *nm* bone
oser *vb* [**28**] to dare; **oser faire quelque chose** to dare to do something
otage *nm* hostage
ôter *vb* [**28**] ❶ to take off ▷ *Elle a ôté*

son manteau. She took off her coat. ❷ to take away

ou *conj* or; **ou ... ou ...** either ... or ...; **ou bien** or else ▷ *On pourrait aller au cinéma ou bien rentrer directement.* We could go to the cinema or else go straight home.

où *pron, adv* ❶ where ▷ *Où est Nick?* Where's Nick? ▷ *Où allez-vous?* Where are you going? ▷ *Je sais où il est.* I know where he is. ❷ that ▷ *Le jour où il est parti, tout le monde a pleuré.* The day that he left, everyone cried.; **Par où allons-nous passer?** Which way are we going to go?

ouate *nf* cotton wool

oublier *vb* [19] ❶ to forget ▷ *N'oublie pas de fermer la porte.* Don't forget to shut the door. ❷ to leave ▷ *J'ai oublié mon sac chez Sabine.* I left my bag at Sabine's.

ouest *nm* west; **à l'ouest de Paris** west of Paris; **vers l'ouest** westwards; **l'Europe de l'Ouest** Western Europe; **le vent d'ouest** the west wind
▶ *adj* ❶ west ❷ western

ouf *excl* phew!

oui *adv* yes

ouragan *nm* hurricane

ourlet *nm* seam

ours *nm* bear; **un ours en peluche** a teddy bear

outil *nm* tool

outré, e *adj* outraged

ouvert, e *adj* ❶ open ▷ *Le magasin est ouvert.* The shop's open. ❷ on ▷ *Il a laissé le robinet ouvert.* He left the tap on.; **avoir l'esprit ouvert** to be open-minded
▶ *vb see* **ouvrir**

ouverture *nf* opening

ouvre-boîte *nm* tin opener

ouvre-bouteille *nm* bottle-opener

ouvreuse *nf* usherette

ouvrier *nm* worker

ouvrière *nf* worker

ouvrir *vb* [55] to open ▷ *Ouvrez!* Open up! ▷ *Elle a ouvert la porte.* She opened the door.; **s'ouvrir** to open

ovale *adj* oval

ovni *nm* (= *objet volant non identifié*) UFO

oxygène *nm* oxygen

ozone *nm* ozone

P

Pacifique *nm* Pacific
pacifiste *nm* pacifist
pagaille *nf* mess *sg*
page *nf* page; **la page d'accueil** *(on internet)* the home page
paie *nf* wages
paiement *nm* payment
paillasson *nm* doormat
paille *nf* straw
pain *nm* ❶ bread ❷ loaf; **le pain complet** wholemeal bread; **le pain d'épice** gingerbread; **le pain de mie** sandwich loaf; **le pain grillé** toast
pair, e *adj* even ▷ *un nombre pair* an even number; **une jeune fille au pair** an au pair
paire *nf* pair
paisible *adj* peaceful
paix *nf* peace; **faire la paix (1)** to make peace ▷ *Les deux pays ont fait la paix.* The two countries have made peace with each other. **(2)** to make it up ▷ *Laure a fait la paix avec son frère.* Laure made it up with her brother.; **avoir la paix** to have peace and quiet ▷ *J'aimerais bien avoir la paix.* I'd like to have a bit of peace and quiet.; **Fiche-moi la paix!** *(informal)* Leave me alone!
palais *nm* ❶ palace ❷ *(in mouth)* palate
pâle *adj* pale
Palestine *nf* Palestine
pâleur *nf* paleness
palier *nm* landing
pâlir *vb* [**38**] to go pale
palme *nf (for swimming)* flipper
palmé, e *adj* webbed
palmier *nm* palm tree
palpitant, e *adj* thrilling
pamplemousse *nm* grapefruit
panaché *nm* shandy
pancarte *nf* sign
pané, e *adj* fried in breadcrumbs
panier *nm* basket
panique *nf* panic
paniquer *vb* [**28**] to panic
panne *nf* breakdown; **être en panne** to have broken down; **tomber en panne** to break down; **une panne de courant** a power cut
panneau (*pl* **panneaux**) *nm* sign; **panneau d'affichage (1)** advertising hoarding **(2)** *(in station)* arrivals and departures board **(3)** *(on internet)* bulletin board

panorama *nm* panorama
pansement *nm* ❶ *(bandage)* dressing ❷ sticking plaster
pantalon *nm* trousers *pl*; **un pantalon de ski** a pair of ski pants
panthère *nf* panther
pantoufle *nf* slipper
PAO *abbr (= publication assistée par ordinateur)* DTP *(= desktop publishing)*
paon *nm* peacock
papa *nm* dad
pape *nm* pope
papeterie *nf* stationer's
papi *nm (informal)* granddad
papier *nm* paper; **Vos papiers, s'il vous plaît.** Your identity papers, please.; **les papiers d'identité** identity papers; **le papier à lettres** writing paper; **le papier hygiénique** toilet paper; **le papier peint** wallpaper
papillon *nm* butterfly
paquebot *nm* liner
pâquerette *nf* daisy
Pâques *nm* Easter; **les œufs de Pâques** Easter eggs

In France, Easter eggs are said to be brought by the Easter bells or **cloches de Pâques** which fly from Rome and drop them in people's gardens.

paquet *nm* ❶ packet ❷ parcel
paquet-cadeau (*pl* **paquets-cadeaux**) *nm* gift-wrapped parcel
par *prep* ❶ by ▷ *L'Amérique a été découverte par Christophe Colomb.* America was discovered by Christopher Columbus.; **deux par deux** two by two ❷ with ▷ *Son nom commence par un H.* His name begins with H. ❸ out of ▷ *Elle regardait par la fenêtre.* She was looking out of the window. ❹ via ▷ *Nous sommes passés par Lyon pour aller à Grenoble.* We went via Lyons to Grenoble. ❺ through ▷ *Il faut passer par la douane avant de prendre l'avion.* You have to go through customs before boarding the plane. ❻ per ▷ *Prenez trois cachets par jour.* Take three tablets per day.; **par ici (1)** this way ▷ *Il faut passer par ici pour y arriver.* You have to go this way to get there. **(2)** round here ▷ *Il y a beaucoup de touristes par ici.* There are lots of tourists round here.; **par-ci, par-là** here and there
parachute *nm* parachute
parachutiste *nmf* parachutist
paradis *nm* heaven
parages *nmpl* **dans les parages** in the area
paragraphe *nm* paragraph
paraître *vb* **[56]** ❶ to seem ▷ *Ça paraît incroyable.* It seems unbelievable. ❷ to look ▷ *Elle paraît plus jeune que son frère.* She looks younger than her brother.; **il paraît que** it seems that
parallèle *nm* parallel
▶ *nf* parallel line
paralysé, e *adj* paralysed
parapluie *nm* umbrella
parasol *nm* parasol
parc *nm* ❶ park; **un parc d'attractions** an amusement park ❷ grounds

parce que *conj* because ▷ *Il n'est pas venu parce qu'il n'avait pas de voiture.* He didn't come because he didn't have a car.

parcmètre *nm* parking meter

parcourir *vb* [**16**] ❶ to cover ▷ *Gavin a parcouru cinquante kilomètres à vélo.* Gavin covered 50 kilometres on his bike. ❷ to glance through ▷ *J'ai parcouru le journal d'aujourd'hui.* I glanced through today's newspaper.

parcours *nm* journey

par-dessous *adv* underneath

pardessus *nm* overcoat

par-dessus *adv, prep* ❶ on top ❷ over ▷ *Elle a sauté par-dessus le mur.* She jumped over the wall.; **en avoir par-dessus la tête** to have had enough

pardon *nm* forgiveness ▶ *excl* ❶ sorry! ▷ *Oh, pardon! J'espère que je ne vous ai pas fait mal.* Oh, sorry! I hope I didn't hurt you.; **demander pardon à quelqu'un** to apologize to somebody; **Je vous demande pardon.** I'm sorry. ❷ excuse me! ▷ *Pardon, madame! Pouvez-vous me dire où se trouve la poste?* Excuse me! Could you tell me where the post office is? ❸ pardon? ▷ *Pardon? Je n'ai pas compris ce que vous avez dit.* Pardon? I didn't understand what you said.

pardonner *vb* [**28**] to forgive

pare-brise (*pl* **pare-brise**) *nm* windscreen

pare-chocs *nm* bumper

pareil (*f* **pareille**) *adj* ❶ the same ▷ *Ces deux maisons ne sont pas pareilles.* These two houses aren't the same. ❷ like that ▷ *J'aime bien sa voiture. J'en voudrais une pareille.* I like his car. I'd like one like that. ❸ such ▷ *Je refuse d'écouter des bêtises pareilles.* I won't listen to such nonsense.; **sans pareil** unequalled

parenthèse *nf* bracket

parents *nmpl* ❶ *(mother and father)* parents ❷ relatives

paresse *nf* laziness

paresseux (*f* **paresseuse**) *adj* lazy

parfait, e *adj* perfect

parfaitement *adv* perfectly

parfois *adv* sometimes

parfum *nm* ❶ perfume ❷ flavour

parfumé, e *adj* ❶ fragrant ❷ flavoured

parfumerie *nf* perfume shop

pari *nm* bet

parier *vb* [**19**] to bet

Paris *n* Paris; **à Paris (1)** in Paris **(2)** to Paris

parisien (*f* **parisienne**) *adj, nm/f* ❶ Parisian ❷ Paris ▷ *le métro parisien* the Paris metro; **un Parisien** *(man)* a Parisian; **une Parisienne** *(woman)* a Parisian

parking *nm* car park

> Be careful! The French word **parking** does not mean **parking**.

parlement *nm* parliament

parler *vb* [**28**] ❶ to speak ▷ *Vous parlez français?* Do you speak French? ❷ to talk ▷ *Nous étions en train de parler quand le directeur est* *entré.* We were talking when the headmaster came in.; **parler de quelque chose à quelqu'un** to tell somebody about something

parmi *prep* among ▷ *Ils étaient parmi les meilleurs de la classe.* They were among the best pupils in the class.

paroi *nf* wall

paroisse *nf* parish

parole *nf* ❶ speech ❷ word; **les paroles** lyrics

parquet *nm (wooden)* floor

parrain *nm* godfather

parrainer *vb* [**28**] to sponsor ▷ *Cette entreprise parraine notre équipe de rugby.* This firm is sponsoring our rugby team.

pars *vb see* **partir**

part *nf* ❶ share ❷ piece ▷ *une part de gâteau* a piece of cake; **prendre part à quelque chose** to take part in something; **de la part de (1)** on behalf of **(2)** from; **à part** except

partager *vb* [**45**] ❶ to share ▷ *Ils partagent un appartement.* They share a flat. ❷ to divide ▷ *Janet a partagé le gâteau en quatre.* Janet divided the cake into four.

partenaire *nmf* partner

parti *nm* party

participant *nm* participant

participation *nf* participation

participe *nm* participle; **le participe passé** the past participle; **le participe présent** the present participle

participer *vb* [**28**] **participer à quelque chose (1)** to take part in something ▷ *André va participer à la course.* André is going to take part in the race. **(2)** to contribute to something ▷ *Je voudrais participer aux frais.* I would like to contribute to the cost.

particularité *nf* characteristic

particulier (*f* **particulière**) *adj* ❶ private ▷ *une maison particulière* a private house ❷ distinctive ❸ particular; **en particulier (1)** particularly **(2)** in private

particulièrement *adv* particularly

partie *nf* ❶ part ▷ *Une partie du groupe partira en Italie.* Part of the group will go to Italy. ❷ game ▷ *une partie de cartes* a game of cards; **en partie** partly; **en grande partie** largely; **faire partie de** to be part of

partiel (*f* **partielle**) *adj* partial

partir *vb* [**57**] to go ▷ *Je lui ai téléphoné mais il était déjà parti.* I phoned him but he'd already gone.; **partir en vacances** to go on holiday; **partir de** to leave ▷ *Il est parti de Nice à sept heures.* He left Nice at 7.

partition *nf (in music)* score

partout *adv* everywhere

paru *vb see* **paraître**

parution *nf* publication

parvenir *vb* [**89**] **parvenir à faire quelque chose** to manage to do something; **faire parvenir quelque chose à quelqu'un** to send something to somebody

pas *adv* **ne ... pas** not ▷ *Il ne pleut pas.* It's not raining. ▷ *Elle n'est pas*

venue. She didn't come.; **Vous viendrez à notre soirée, n'est-ce pas?** You're coming to our party, aren't you?; **pas moi** not me; **pas du tout** not at all; **pas mal** not bad; **pas mal de** quite a lot of
▶ *nm* ❶ pace ❷ step ❸ footstep; **au pas** at walking pace; **faire les cent pas** to pace up and down

passage *nm* passage; **Il a été éclaboussé au passage de la voiture.** He was soaked by a passing car.; **de passage** passing through; **un passage à niveau** a level crossing; **un passage clouté** a pedestrian crossing; **un passage protégé** a pedestrian crossing; **un passage souterrain** a subway

passager (*f* **passagère**) *adj* temporary

passager *nm* passenger; **un passager clandestin** a stowaway

passagère *nf* passenger

passant *nm* passer-by

passé, e *adj* ❶ last ▷ *Je l'ai vu la semaine passée.* I saw him last week. ❷ past ▷ *Il est minuit passé.* It's past midnight.
▶ *nm* ❶ past ❷ past tense; **le passé composé** the perfect tense; **le passé simple** the past historic

passeport *nm* passport

passer *vb* [**58**] ❶ to cross ▷ *Nous avons passé la frontière belge.* We crossed the Belgian border. ❷ to go through ▷ *Il faut passer la douane en sortant.* You have to go through customs on the way out. ❸ to spend ▷ *Ils passent toujours leurs vacances au Danemark.* They always spend their holidays in Denmark. ❹ to take ▷ *Gordon a passé ses examens la semaine dernière.* Gordon took his exams last week.

> Be careful! **passer un examen** does not mean **to pass an exam**.

❺ to pass ▷ *Passe-moi le sel, s'il te plaît.* Pass me the salt, please. ❻ to show ▷ *On passe 'Le Kid' au cinéma cette semaine.* They're showing 'The Kid' at the cinema this week. ❼ to call in ▷ *Je passerai chez vous ce soir.* I'll call in this evening.; **passer à la radio** to be on the radio; **passer à la télévision** to be on the television; **Ne quittez pas, je vous passe Madame Chevalier.** Hold on please, I'm putting you through to Mrs Chevalier.; **passer par** to go through ▷ *Ils sont passés par Paris pour aller à Tours.* They went through Paris to get to Tours.; **en passant** in passing; **laisser passer** to let through ▷ *Il m'a laissé passer.* He let me through.; **se passer** **(1)** to take place ▷ *Cette histoire se passe au Moyen Âge.* This story takes place in the Middle Ages. **(2)** to go ▷ *Comment se sont passés tes examens?* How did your exams go? **(3)** to happen ▷ *Que s'est-il passé? Un accident?* What happened? Was there an accident?; **Qu'est-ce qui se passe? Pourquoi est-ce qu'elle pleure?** What's the matter? Why is she crying?; **se passer de** to do without

passerelle *nf* ❶ *(over river)* footbridge ❷ *(onto plane, boat)* gangway
passe-temps *nm* pastime
passif (*f* **passive**) *adj* passive ▸ *nm* passive
passion *nf* passion
passionnant, e *adj* fascinating
passionné, e *adj* keen; **Il est passionné de voile.** He's a sailing fanatic.
passionner *vb* [**28**] **Son travail le passionne.** He's passionate about his work.; **se passionner pour quelque chose** to have a passion for something
passoire *nf* sieve
pastèque *nf* watermelon
pasteur *nm (priest)* minister
pastille *nf* cough sweet
patate *nf (informal)* potato; **une patate douce** a sweet potato
pâte *nf* ❶ pastry ❷ dough ❸ cake mixture; **la pâte à crêpes** pancake batter; **la pâte à modeler** Plasticine®; **la pâte d'amandes** marzipan
pâté *nm* pâté; **un pâté de maisons** *(of houses)* a block
paternel (*f* **paternelle**) *adj* **ma grand-mère paternelle** my father's mother; **mon oncle paternel** my father's brother
pâtes *nfpl* pasta *sg*
patience *nf* patience
patient, e *adj* patient
patient *nm* patient
patiente *nf* patient
patienter *vb* [**28**] to wait ▷ *Veuillez patienter un instant, s'il vous plaît.* Please wait a moment.
patin *nm* ❶ skate ❷ skating; **les patins à glace** ice skates; **les patins en ligne** Rollerblades®; **les patins à roulettes** roller skates
patinage *nm* skating; **le patinage artistique** figure skating
patiner *vb* [**28**] to skate
patineur *nm* skater
patinoire *nf* ice rink
pâtisserie *nf* cake shop; **faire de la pâtisserie** to bake; **les pâtisseries** cakes
pâtissier *nm* confectioner
patrie *nf* homeland
patron *nm* ❶ boss ❷ *(for dressmaking)* pattern
patronne *nf* boss; **Elle est patronne de café.** She runs a café.
patronner *vb* [**28**] to sponsor ▷ *Le festival est patronné par des entreprises locales.* The festival is sponsored by local businesses.
patrouille *nf* patrol
patte *nf* ❶ *(of dog, cat)* paw ❷ *(of bird, animal)* leg
paumer *vb* [**28**] *(informal)* to lose ▷ *J'ai paumé mes clés.* I've lost my keys.
paupière *nf* eyelid
pause *nf* ❶ break ▷ *une pause de midi* a lunch break ❷ pause
pauvre *adj* poor
pauvreté *nf* poverty
pavé, e *adj* cobbled
pavillon *nm* house
payant, e *adj* paying; **C'est payant.** You have to pay.

paye *nf* wages
payer *vb* [**59**] ❶ to pay for ▷ *Combien as-tu payé ta voiture?* How much did you pay for your car?; **J'ai payé ce T-shirt vingt euros.** I paid 20 euros for this T-shirt. ❷ to pay ▷ *Elle a été payée aujourd'hui.* She got paid today.; **faire payer quelque chose à quelqu'un** to charge somebody for something ▷ *Il me l'a fait payer dix euros.* He charged me 10 euros for it.; **payer quelque chose à quelqu'un** to buy somebody something ▷ *Allez, je vous paye un verre.* Come on, I'll buy you a drink.
pays *nm* country; **du pays** local
paysage *nm* landscape
paysan *nm* farmer
Pays-Bas *nmpl* Netherlands; **aux Pays-Bas (1)** in the Netherlands **(2)** to the Netherlands
pays de Galles *nm* Wales; **au pays de Galles (1)** in Wales **(2)** to Wales
PC *nm* PC (= *personal computer*) ▶ *abbr* (= *Parti communiste*) Communist Party
PDG *nm* (= *président-directeur général*) MD (= *managing director*)
péage *nm* ❶ toll ▷ *Nous avons payé vingt euros de péage.* We paid a toll of 20 euros. ❷ tollbooth
French motorways charge a toll.
peau (*pl* **peaux**) *nf* skin
Peau-Rouge (*pl* **Peaux-Rouges**) *nmf* Red Indian
péché *nm* sin
pêche *nf* ❶ peach ❷ fishing; **aller à la pêche** to go fishing; **la pêche à la ligne** angling
pêcher *vb* [**28**] ❶ to fish for ▷ *Ils sont partis pêcher la truite.* They've gone fishing for trout. ❷ to catch ▷ *Jacques a pêché deux saumons.* Jacques caught two salmon.
pêcheur *nm* fisherman; **un pêcheur à la ligne** an angler
pédagogique *adj* educational
pédale *nf* pedal
pédalo *nm* pedalo
pédestre *adj* **une randonnée pédestre** a ramble
peigne *nm* comb
peigner *vb* [**28**] to comb ▷ *Elle peigne sa poupée.* She's combing her doll's hair.; **se peigner** to comb one's hair
peignoir *nm* dressing gown; **un peignoir de bain** a bathrobe
peindre *vb* [**60**] to paint
peine *nf* trouble; **avoir de la peine à faire quelque chose** to have trouble doing something; **se donner de la peine** to make a real effort; **prendre la peine de faire quelque chose** to go to the trouble of doing something; **faire de la peine à quelqu'un** to upset somebody; **ce n'est pas la peine** there's no point; **à peine (1)** hardly **(2)** only just
peintre *nm* painter
peinture *nf* ❶ painting ❷ paint; **'peinture fraîche'** 'wet paint'
pêle-mêle *adv* higgledy-piggledy
peler *vb* [**43**] to peel
pelle *nf* ❶ shovel ❷ spade
pellicule *nf* film

pellicules *nfpl* dandruff *sg*
pelote *nf* ball
pelouse *nf* lawn
peluche *nf* **un animal en peluche** a soft toy
penchant *nm* **avoir un penchant pour quelque chose** to have a liking for something
pencher *vb* [**28**] to tilt ▷ *Ce tableau penche vers la droite.* The picture's tilting to the right.; **se pencher** (**1**) to lean over ▷ *Françoise s'est penchée sur son cahier.* Françoise leant over her exercise book. (**2**) to bend down ▷ *Il s'est penché pour ramasser sa casquette.* He bent down to pick his cap up. (**3**) to lean out ▷ *Annick s'est penchée par la fenêtre.* Annick leant out of the window.
pendant *prep* during ▷ *Ça s'est passé pendant l'été.* It happened during the summer.; **pendant que** while
pendentif *nm* pendant
penderie *nf* *(for hanging clothes)* wardrobe
pendre *vb* [**88**] to hang ▷ *Il a pendu sa veste dans l'armoire.* He hung his jacket in the wardrobe.; **pendre quelqu'un** to hang somebody ▷ *L'assassin a été pendu.* The murderer was hanged.
pendule *nf* clock
pénétrer *vb* [**34**] ❶ to enter ▷ *Ils ont pénétré dans la maison en passant par le jardin.* They entered the house through the garden. ❷ to penetrate ▷ *L'armée a pénétré sur le territoire ennemi.* The army penetrated enemy territory.
pénible *adj* hard; **Il est vraiment pénible.** He's a real nuisance.
péniblement *adv* with difficulty
péniche *nf* barge
pénis *nm* penis
pénombre *nf* half-light
pensée *nf* thought
penser *vb* [**28**] to think ▷ *Je pense que Yann a eu raison de partir.* I think Yann was right to leave.; **penser à quelque chose** to think about something; **faire penser quelqu'un à quelque chose** to remind someone of something ▷ *Cette photo me fait penser à la Grèce.* This photo reminds me of Greece.; **faire penser quelqu'un à faire quelque chose** to remind someone to do something ▷ *Fais-moi penser à téléphoner à Claire.* Remind me to phone Claire.; **penser faire quelque chose** to be planning to do something ▷ *Ils pensent partir en Espagne en juillet.* They're planning to go to Spain in July.
pension *nf* ❶ boarding school ❷ pension ❸ boarding house; **la pension complète** full board
pensionnaire *nmf* boarder
pensionnat *nm* boarding school
pente *nf* slope; **en pente** sloping
Pentecôte *nf* Whitsun
pépin *nm* ❶ pip ❷ problem ▷ *avoir un pépin (informal)* to have a slight problem
perçant, e *adj* ❶ sharp ▷ *Il a une vue perçante.* He has very sharp eyes.

❷ piercing ▷ *un cri perçant* a piercing cry
percer *vb* [**12**] to pierce ▷ *Elle s'est fait percer les oreilles.* She's had her ears pierced.
percuter *vb* [**28**] to smash into
perdant *nm* loser
perdre *vb* [**61**] to lose ▷ *Cécile a perdu ses clés.* Cécile's lost her keys.; **J'ai perdu mon chemin.** I've lost my way.; **perdre un match** to lose a match; **perdre du temps** to waste time ▷ *J'ai perdu beaucoup de temps ce matin.* I've wasted a lot of time this morning.; **se perdre** to get lost ▷ *Je me suis perdu en route.* I got lost on the way here.
perdu *vb see* **perdre**
père *nm* father; **le père Noël** Father Christmas
perfectionné, e *adj* sophisticated
perfectionner *vb* [**28**] to improve ▷ *Elle a besoin de perfectionner son anglais.* She needs to improve her English.
périmé, e *adj* out-of-date; **Ces yaourts sont périmés.** These yoghurts are past their use-by date.
période *nf* period
périodique *adj* periodic
périphérique *adj* outlying ▶ *nm* ring road
perle *nf* pearl
permanence *nf* **assurer une permanence** to operate a basic service; **être de permanence** to be on duty; **en permanence** permanently
permanent, e *adj* ❶ permanent ❷ continuous
permanente *nf* perm
permettre *vb* [**47**] to allow; **permettre à quelqu'un de faire quelque chose** to allow somebody to do something ▷ *Sa mère lui permet de sortir le soir.* His mother allows him to go out at night.
permis *nm* permit; **le permis de conduire** driving licence; **un permis de séjour** a residence permit; **un permis de travail** a work permit
permission *nf* permission; **avoir la permission de faire quelque chose** to have permission to do something; **être en permission** *(from the army)* to be on leave
Pérou *nm* Peru
perpétuel (*f* **perpétuelle**) *adj* perpetual
perplexe *adj* puzzled
perroquet *nm* parrot
perruche *nf* budgie
perruque *nf* wig
persil *nm* parsley
personnage *nm* ❶ figure ▷ *les grands personnages de l'histoire de France* the important figures in French history ❷ character ▷ *le personnage principal du film* the main character in the film
personnalité *nf* ❶ personality ❷ prominent figure
personne *nf* person ▷ *une personne âgée* an elderly person; **en personne** in person ▶ *pron* ❶ nobody ▷ *Il n'y a personne à*

la maison. There's nobody at home. ❷ anybody ▷ *Elle ne veut voir personne.* She doesn't want to see anybody.

personnel (*f* **personnelle**) *adj* personal
▸ *nm* staff; **le service du personnel** the personnel department

personnellement *adv* personally

perspective *nf* prospect; **perspectives d'avenir** prospects; **en perspective (1)** in prospect **(2)** in perspective

persuader *vb* [**28**] to persuade; **persuader quelqu'un de faire quelque chose** to persuade somebody to do something

perte *nf* ❶ loss ❷ waste

perturber *vb* [**28**] to disrupt

pèse-personne *nm* bathroom scales *pl*

peser *vb* [**43**] to weigh ▷ *Elle pèse cent kilos.* She weighs 100 kilos.

pessimiste *adj* pessimistic

pétale *nm* petal

pétanque *nf*

> **pétanque** is a type of bowls played in France, especially in the south.

pétard *nm* firecracker

péter *vb* [**34**] *(rude)* to fart

pétillant, e *adj* sparkling

petit, e *adj* ❶ small ▷ *Sonia habite une petite ville.* Sonia lives in a small town. ❷ little ▷ *Elle a une jolie petite maison.* She has a nice little house.; **petit à petit** bit by bit; **un petit ami** a boyfriend; **une petite amie** a girlfriend; **le petit déjeuner** breakfast ▷ *prendre le petit déjeuner* to have breakfast; **un petit pain** a bread roll; **les petites annonces** the small ads; **des petits pois** garden peas; **les petits** *(of animal)* young

petite-fille (*pl* **petites-filles**) *nf* granddaughter

petit-fils (*pl* **petits-fils**) *nm* grandson

petits-enfants *nmpl* grandchildren

pétrole *nm* oil

> Be careful! **pétrole** does not mean **petrol**.

peu *adv, n* not much; **un peu** a bit; **un petit peu** a little bit; **peu de (1)** not many **(2)** not much; **à peu près (1)** more or less **(2)** about; **peu à peu** little by little; **peu avant** shortly before; **peu après** shortly afterwards; **de peu** only just

peuple *nm* people

peur *nf* fear; **avoir peur de** to be afraid of; **avoir peur de faire quelque chose** to be frightened of doing something; **faire peur à quelqu'un** to frighten somebody

peureux (*f* **peureuse**) *adj* fearful

peut *vb see* **pouvoir**; **Il ne peut pas venir.** He can't come.

peut-être *adv* perhaps; **peut-être que** perhaps

peuvent, peux *vb see* **pouvoir**; **Je ne peux pas le faire.** I can't do it.

p. ex. *abbr* (= *par exemple*) e.g.

phare *nm* ❶ lighthouse ▷ *On voit le phare depuis le pont du bateau.* You can see the lighthouse from the ship's deck. ❷ headlight ▷ *Elle a laissé ses phares allumés.* She left her headlights on.

pharmacie *nf* chemist's

Chemists' shops in France are identified by a special green cross outside the shop.

pharmacien *nm* pharmacist

phasme *nm* stick insect

phénomène *nm* phenomenon

philosophie *nf* philosophy

phoque *nm (animal)* seal

photo *nf* photograph; **en photo** in photographs; **prendre quelqu'un en photo** to take a photo of somebody; **une photo d'identité** a passport photograph

photocopie *nf* photocopy

photocopier *vb* [**19**] to photocopy

photocopieuse *nf* photocopier

photographe *nmf* photographer

photographie *nf* ❶ photography ❷ photograph

photographier *vb* [**19**] to photograph

phrase *nf* sentence

physique *adj* physical
▶ *nm* **Il a un physique agréable.** He's quite good-looking.
▶ *nf* physics

pianiste *nmf* pianist

piano *nm* piano

pic *nm* peak; **à pic (1)** vertically ▷ *La falaise tombe à pic dans la mer.* The cliff drops vertically into the sea. **(2)** just at the right time ▷ *Tu es arrivé à pic.* You arrived just at the right time.

pièce *nf* ❶ room ▷ *Mon lit est au centre de la pièce.* My bed is in the middle of the room.; **un cinq-pièces** a five-roomed flat ❷ play ▷ *On joue une pièce de Shakespeare au théâtre.* There's a play by Shakespeare on at the theatre. ❸ part ▷ *Il faut changer une pièce du moteur.* There's an engine part which needs changing. ❹ coin ▷ *des pièces d'un euro* some one-euro coins; **cinquante euros pièce** 50 euros each ▷ *J'ai acheté ces T-shirts dix euros pièce.* I bought these T-shirts for ten euros each.; **un maillot une pièce** a one-piece swimsuit; **un maillot deux-pièces** a bikini; **Avez-vous une pièce d'identité?** Have you got any identification?; **une pièce jointe** an email attachment

pied *nm* foot; **à pied** on foot; **avoir pied** to be able to touch the bottom

pied-noir (*pl* **pieds-noirs**) *nm*

A **pied-noir** is a French person born in Algeria; most of them moved to France during the Algerian war in the 1950s.

piège *nm* trap; **prendre quelqu'un au piège** to trap somebody

piéger *vb* [**66**] to trap; **un colis piégé** a parcel bomb; **une voiture piégée** a car bomb

pierre *nf* stone; **une pierre précieuse** a precious stone

piéton *nm* pedestrian

piétonnier (*f* **piétonnière**) *adj* **une rue piétonnière** a pedestrianized

street; **un quartier piétonnier** a pedestrianized area
pieuvre *nf* octopus
pigeon *nm* pigeon
piger *vb* [**45**] *(informal)* to understand
pile *nf* ❶ pile ▷ *Il y a une pile de disques sur la table.* There's a pile of records on the table. ❷ battery ▷ *La pile de ma montre est usée.* The battery in my watch has run out.
▶ *adv* **à deux heures pile** at two on the dot; **jouer à pile ou face** to toss up; **Pile ou face?** Heads or tails?
pilote *nm* pilot; **un pilote de course** a racing driver; **un pilote de ligne** an airline pilot
piloter *vb* [**28**] *(a plane)* to fly
pilule *nf* pill; **prendre la pilule** to be on the pill
piment *nm* chilli
pin *nm* pine
pinard *nm (informal)* wine
pince *nf* ❶ *(tool)* pliers *pl* ❷ *(of crab)* pincer; **une pince à épiler** tweezers; **une pince à linge** a clothes peg
pinceau (*pl* **pinceaux**) *nm* paintbrush
pincée *nf* **une pincée de sel** a pinch of salt
pincer *vb* [**12**] to pinch
pingouin *nm* penguin
ping-pong *nm* table tennis
pintade *nf* guinea fowl
pion *nm* ❶ *(in chess)* pawn ❷ *(in draughts)* piece ❸ *(man)* supervisor

In French secondary schools, the teachers are not responsible for supervising the pupils outside class. This job is done by people called **pions** or **surveillants**.

pionne *nf (woman)* supervisor
pipe *nf* pipe
piquant, e *adj* ❶ prickly ❷ spicy
pique *nm* spades *pl*
▶ *nf* cutting remark
pique-nique *nm* picnic
piquer *vb* [**28**] ❶ to bite ▷ *Nous avons été piqués par les moustiques.* We were bitten by mosquitoes. ❷ to burn ▷ *Cette sauce me pique la langue.* This sauce is burning my tongue. ❸ to steal ▷ *On m'a piqué mon porte-monnaie. (informal)* I've had my purse stolen.; **se piquer** to prick oneself
piquet *nm* ❶ post ❷ peg ▷ *Il nous manque un des piquets de la tente.* One of our tent pegs is missing.
piqûre *nf* ❶ injection ❷ bite ❸ sting
pirate *nm* pirate; **un pirate informatique** a hacker
pire *adj, n* worse; **le pire** the worst; **le pire de** the worst of
piscine *nf* swimming pool
pisser *vb* [**28**] *(informal)* to have a pee
pistache *nf* pistachio
piste *nf* ❶ lead ▷ *La police est sur une piste.* The police are following a lead. ❷ runway ❸ ski run; **une piste artificielle** a dry ski slope; **la piste de danse** the dance floor; **une piste cyclable** a cycle lane

pistolet *nm* pistol
pistonner *vb* [**28**] **Il a été pistonné pour avoir ce travail.** They pulled some strings to get him this job.
pitié *nf* pity; **Il me fait pitié.** I feel sorry for him.; **avoir pitié de quelqu'un** to feel sorry for somebody
pittoresque *adj* picturesque
pizza *nf* pizza
placard *nm* cupboard
place *nf* ❶ place ❷ square ❸ space ▷ *Il ne reste plus de place pour se garer.* There's no more space to park. ❹ seat ▷ *Il y a vingt places assises.* There are 20 seats.; **remettre quelque chose en place** to put something back in its place; **sur place** on the spot; **à la place** instead; **à la place de** instead of
placer *vb* [**12**] ❶ to seat ▷ *Nous étions placés à côté du directeur.* We were seated next to the manager. ❷ to invest ▷ *Il a placé ses économies en Bourse.* He invested his money on the Stock Exchange.
plafond *nm* ceiling
plage *nf* beach
plaie *nf* wound
plaindre *vb* [**17**] **plaindre quelqu'un** to feel sorry for somebody ▷ *Je te plains.* I feel sorry for you.; **se plaindre** to complain ▷ *Il n'arrête pas de se plaindre.* He never stops complaining.; **se plaindre à quelqu'un** to complain to somebody; **se plaindre de quelque chose** to complain about something
plaine *nf (level area)* plain
plainte *nf* complaint; **porter plainte** to lodge a complaint
plaire *vb* [**62**] **Ce cadeau me plaît beaucoup.** I like this present a lot.; **Ce film plaît beaucoup aux jeunes.** The film is very popular with young people.; **Ça t'a plu d'aller en Italie?** Did you enjoy going to Italy?; **Elle lui plaît.** He fancies her.; **s'il te plaît** please; **s'il vous plaît** please
plaisanter *vb* [**28**] to joke
plaisanterie *nf* joke
plaisir *nm* pleasure; **faire plaisir à quelqu'un** to please somebody
plaît *vb see* **plaire**
plan *nm* plan; **un plan de la ville** a street map; **au premier plan** in the foreground
planche *nf* plank; **une planche à repasser** an ironing board; **une planche à roulettes** a skateboard; **une planche à voile** a sailboard
plancher *nm* floor
planer *vb* [**28**] ❶ to glide ▷ *L'avion planait dans le ciel.* The plane was gliding in the sky. ❷ to have one's head in the clouds ▷ *Ce garçon plane complètement.* *(informal)* He's not with us at all.
planète *nf* planet
plante *nf* plant
planter *vb* [**28**] ❶ to plant ❷ to hammer in ▷ *Jean-Pierre a planté un clou dans le mur.* Jean-Pierre hammered a nail into the wall. ❸ to pitch ▷ *André a planté sa tente au bord du lac.* André pitched his

tent next to the lake.; **Ne reste pas planté là!** Don't just stand there!; **se planter** *(informal)* to fail

plaque *nf* (metal) plate; **une plaque de verglas** a patch of ice; **une plaque de chocolat** a bar of chocolate

plaqué, e *adj* **plaqué or** gold-plated; **plaqué argent** silver-plated

plaquer *vb* [**28**] *(informal)* ❶ to ditch ▷ *Elle a plaqué son copain.* She ditched her boyfriend. ❷ to pack in ▷ *Il a plaqué son boulot.* He packed in his job.

plaquette *nf* **une plaquette de chocolat** a bar of chocolate; **une plaquette de beurre** a pack of butter

plastique *nm* plastic

plat, e *adj* flat; **être à plat ventre** to be lying face down; **l'eau plate** still water
▶ *nm* ❶ dish ❷ course ▷ *le plat principal* the main course; **un plat cuisiné** a pre-cooked meal; **le plat de résistance** the main course; **le plat du jour** the dish of the day

platane *nm* plane tree

plateau (*pl* **plateaux**) *nm* ❶ tray; **un plateau de fromages** a selection of cheeses ❷ plateau

platine *nm* platinum
▶ *nf* *(of record player)* turntable; **une platine laser** a CD player

plâtre *nm* plaster

plein, e *adj* full; **à plein temps** full-time; **plein de** *(informal)* lots of; **Il y a plein de gens dans la rue.** The street is full of people.; **en plein air** in the open air; **en pleine nuit** in the middle of the night; **en plein jour** in broad daylight
▶ *nm* **faire le plein** *(petrol tank)* to fill up

pleurer *vb* [**28**] to cry

pleut *vb see* **pleuvoir**

pleuvoir *vb* [**63**] to rain ▷ *Il pleut.* It's raining.

pli *nm* ❶ fold ❷ pleat ❸ crease

pliant, e *adj* folding

plier *vb* [**19**] ❶ to fold ▷ *Elle a plié sa serviette.* She folded her towel. ❷ to bend ▷ *Elle a plié le bras.* She bent her arm.

plomb *nm* ❶ lead ❷ fuse; **l'essence sans plomb** unleaded petrol

plombier *nm* plumber; **Il est plombier.** He's a plumber.

plongée *nf* diving

plongeoir *nm* diving board

plongeon *nm* dive

plonger *vb* [**45**] to dive; **J'ai plongé ma main dans l'eau.** I plunged my hand into the water.; **être plongé dans son travail** to be absorbed in your work; **se plonger dans un livre** to get absorbed in a book

plu *vb see* **plaire**; **pleuvoir**

pluie *nf* rain

plume *nf* feather; **un stylo à plume** a fountain pen

plupart: **la plupart** *pron* most (of them) ▷ *La plupart ont moins de quinze ans.* Most of them are under 15.; **la plupart des** most ▷ *La plupart des gens ont vu ce film.* Most people have seen this film.; **la**

plupart du temps most of the time

pluriel *nm* plural; **au pluriel** in the plural

plus *adv, prep* **ne ... plus (1)** not ... any more ▷ *Je ne veux plus le voir.* I don't want to see him any more. **(2)** no longer ▷ *Il ne travaille plus ici.* He's no longer working here.; **Je n'ai plus de pain.** I've got no bread left.; **plus ... que** more ... than ▷ *Il est plus intelligent que son frère.* He's more intelligent than his brother.; **C'est le plus grand de la famille.** He's the tallest in his family.; **plus ... plus ...** the more ... the more ...; **plus de (1)** more ▷ *Il nous faut plus de pain.* We need more bread. **(2)** more than ▷ *Il y avait plus de dix personnes.* There were more than 10 people.; **de plus** more ▷ *Il nous faut un joueur de plus.* We need one more player.; **en plus** more ▷ *J'ai apporté quelques gâteaux en plus.* I brought a few more cakes.; **de plus en plus** more and more; **un peu plus difficile** a bit more difficult; **plus ou moins** more or less; **Quatre plus deux égalent six.** 4 plus 2 is 6.

plusieurs *pron pl* several ▷ *Elle a acheté plusieurs chemises.* She bought several shirts.

plus-que-parfait *nm* pluperfect

plutôt *adv* ❶ quite ▷ *Elle est plutôt jolie.* She's quite pretty. ❷ rather ▷ *L'eau est plutôt froide.* The water's rather cold. ❸ instead ▷ *Demande-leur plutôt de venir avec toi.* Ask them to come with you instead.; **plutôt que** rather than

pluvieux (*f* **pluvieuse**) *adj* rainy

pneu *nm* tyre

pneumonie *nf* pneumonia

poche *nf* pocket; **l'argent de poche** pocket money; **un livre de poche** a paperback

podcast *nm* podcast

podcaster *vb* [**28**] to podcast

poêle *nf* frying pan; **une poêle à frire** a frying pan

poème *nm* poem

poésie *nf* ❶ poetry ❷ poem

poète *nm* poet

poids *nm* weight; **prendre du poids** to put on weight; **perdre du poids** to lose weight; **un poids lourd** a lorry

poignée *nf* ❶ handful ❷ handle; **une poignée de main** a handshake

poignet *nm* ❶ wrist ❷ *(of shirt)* cuff

poil *nm* ❶ hair ❷ fur; **à poil** *(informal)* stark naked

poilu, e *adj* hairy

poinçonner *vb* [**28**] to punch ▷ *Le contrôleur a poinçonné les billets.* The conductor punched the tickets.

poing *nm* fist; **un coup de poing** a punch

point *nm* ❶ point ▷ *Je ne suis pas d'accord sur ce point.* I don't agree with this point. ▷ *Son point faible, c'est qu'elle est trop gentille.* Her weak point is she's too nice.; **point de vue** point of view ❷ full stop; **être sur le point de faire quelque chose** to be just about to do something ▷ *J'étais sur le point de te* *téléphoner.* I was just about to phone you.; **mettre au point** to finalize; **Ce n'est pas encore au point.** It's not finalized yet.; **à point** medium ▷ *Comment voulez-vous votre steak? — À point.* How would you like your steak? — Medium.; **un point d'exclamation** an exclamation mark; **un point d'interrogation** a question mark; **un point noir** a blackhead

pointe *nf* point; **être à la pointe du progrès** to be in the forefront of progress; **sur la pointe des pieds** on tiptoe; **les heures de pointe** peak hours

pointillé *nm* dotted line

pointu, e *adj* pointed

pointure *nf* size *(of shoes)* ▷ *Quelle est votre pointure?* What size shoes do you take?

point-virgule (*pl* **points-virgules**) *nm* semicolon

poire *nf* pear

poireau (*pl* **poireaux**) *nm* leek

pois *nm* pea; **les petits pois** peas; **les pois chiches** chickpeas; **à pois** spotted

poison *nm* poison

poisson *nm* fish; **les Poissons** Pisces; **Poisson d'avril!** April fool!

Pinning a paper fish to somebody's back is a traditional April fool joke in France.

un poisson rouge a goldfish

poissonnerie *nf* fish shop

poissonnier *nm* fishmonger

poitrine *nf* ❶ chest ❷ bust

poivre *nm (spice)* pepper

poivron *nm (vegetable)* pepper

pôle *nm* pole; **le pôle Nord** the North Pole; **le pôle Sud** the South Pole

poli, e *adj* polite

police *nf* police; **police secours** emergency services; **une police d'assurance** an insurance policy

policier (*f* **policière**) *adj* **un roman policier** a detective novel
▶ *nm* police officer

politesse *nf* politeness

politique *nf* politics ▷ *La politique ne l'intéresse pas du tout.* He's not at all interested in politics.

pollué, e *adj* polluted

polluer *vb* [**28**] to pollute

pollution *nf* pollution

polo *nm* polo shirt

Pologne *nf* Poland

polonais, e *adj, nm/f* Polish ▷ *Elle parle polonais.* She speaks Polish.; **un Polonais** *(man)* a Pole; **une Polonaise** *(woman)* a Pole; **les Polonais** the Poles

Polynésie *nf* Polynesia

pommade *nf* ointment

pomme *nf* apple; **les pommes de terre** potatoes; **les pommes frites** chips; **les pommes vapeur** boiled potatoes

pompe *nf* pump; **une pompe à essence** a petrol pump; **les pompes funèbres** undertakers

pompier *nm* firefighter

pompiste *nm* petrol pump attendant

ponctuel (*f* **ponctuelle**) *adj* ❶ punctual ❷ occasional; **On a**

rencontré quelques problèmes ponctuels. We've had the occasional problem.

pondre *vb* [**69**] *(eggs)* to lay

poney *nm* pony

pont *nm* ❶ bridge ❷ *(of ship)* deck; **faire le pont** to take a long weekend

populaire *adj* ❶ popular ❷ working-class

population *nf* population

porc *nm* ❶ pig ❷ pork

porcelaine *nf* china

port *nm* ❶ harbour ❷ port

portable *adj (telephone)* mobile ▶ *nm* ❶ mobile phone ❷ laptop

portail *nm* gate

portatif (*f* **portative**) *adj* portable

porte *nf* ❶ door; **la porte d'entrée** the front door ❷ gate; **mettre quelqu'un à la porte** to sack somebody

porte-bagages *nm* luggage rack

porte-clés *nm* key ring

portée *nf* **à portée de main** within arm's reach; **hors de portée** out of reach

portefeuille *nm* wallet

portemanteau (*pl* **portemanteaux**) *nm* ❶ coat hanger ❷ coat rack

porte-monnaie (*pl* **porte-monnaie**) *nm* purse

porter *vb* [**28**] ❶ to carry ▷ *Il portait une valise.* He was carrying a suitcase. ❷ to wear ▷ *Elle porte une robe bleue.* She's wearing a blue dress.; **se porter bien** to be well; **se porter mal** to be unwell

porteur *nm* porter

portière *nf (of car)* door

portion *nf* portion

porto *nm (wine)* port

portrait *nm* portrait

portugais, e *adj, n* Portuguese ▷ *Il parle portugais.* He speaks Portuguese.; **un Portugais** *(man)* a Portuguese; **une Portugaise** *(woman)* a Portuguese; **les Portugais** the Portuguese

Portugal *nm* Portugal; **au Portugal (1)** in Portugal **(2)** to Portugal

poser *vb* [**28**] ❶ to put down ▷ *J'ai posé la cafetière sur la table.* I put the coffee pot down on the table. ❷ to pose ▷ *Cela pose un problème.* That poses a problem.; **poser une question à quelqu'un** to ask somebody a question; **se poser** to land

positif (*f* **positive**) *adj* positive

position *nf* position

posséder *vb* [**34**] to own ▷ *Ils possèdent une jolie maison.* They own a lovely house.

possibilité *nf* possibility

possible *adj* possible; **le plus de gens possible** as many people as possible; **le plus tôt possible** as early as possible; **le moins d'argent possible** as little money as possible; **Il travaille le moins possible.** He works as little as possible.; **dès que possible** as soon as possible; **faire son possible** to do all one can

poste *nf* ❶ post ❷ post office;

mettre une lettre à la poste to post a letter
▶ *nm* ❶ post ❷ *(phone)* extension ❸ set ▷ *un poste de radio* a radio set; **un poste de police** a police station

poster *vb* [**28**] to post
▶ *nm* poster

postérieur, e *adj* ❶ later ❷ back

pot *nm* jar; **prendre un pot** *(informal)* to have a drink; **un pot de fleurs** a plant pot

potable *adj* **eau potable** drinking water; **'eau non potable'** 'not drinking water'

potage *nm* soup

potager *nm* vegetable garden

pot-au-feu (*pl* **pot-au-feu**) *nm* beef stew

pot-de-vin (*pl* **pots-de-vin**) *nm* bribe

pote *nm (informal)* mate

poteau (*pl* **poteaux**) *nm* post; **un poteau indicateur** a signpost

potentiel (*f* **potentielle**) *adj* potential

poterie *nf* ❶ pottery ❷ piece of pottery

potier *nm* potter

pou (*pl* **poux**) *nm* louse

poubelle *nf* dustbin

pouce *nm* ❶ thumb ❷ inch; **manger sur le pouce** to have a quick snack

poudre *nf* ❶ powder ❷ face powder; **la poudre à laver** washing powder; **le lait en poudre** powdered milk; **le café en poudre** instant coffee

poulain *nm* foal

poule *nf* hen

poulet *nm* ❶ chicken ❷ cop

pouls *nm* pulse

poumon *nm* lung

poupée *nf* doll

pour *prep* for ▷ *Qu'est-ce que tu veux pour ton petit déjeuner?* What would you like for breakfast?; **pour faire quelque chose** to do something ▷ *Je lui ai téléphoné pour l'inviter.* I phoned him to invite him.; **Pour aller à Strasbourg, s'il vous plaît?** Which way is it to Strasbourg, please?; **pour que** so that

> **pour que** is followed by a verb in the subjunctive.

▷ *Je lui ai prêté mon pull pour qu'elle n'ait pas froid.* I lent her my jumper so that she wouldn't be cold.; **pour cent** per cent

pourboire *nm* tip

pourcentage *nm* percentage

pourquoi *adv, conj* why

pourra, pourras, pourrai, pourrez *vb see* **pouvoir**

pourri, e *adj* rotten

pourrir *vb* [**38**] to go bad ▷ *Ces poires ont pourri.* These pears have gone bad.

pourrons, pourront *vb see* **pouvoir**

poursuite *nf* chase; **se lancer à la poursuite de quelqu'un** to chase after somebody

poursuivre *vb* [**81**] to carry on with ▷ *Ils ont poursuivi leur travail.* They carried on with their work.; **se poursuivre** to go on ▷ *Le concert* *s'est poursuivi très tard*. The concert went on very late.

pourtant *adv* yet; **C'est pourtant facile!** But it's easy!

pourvu (*f* **pourvue**) *adj* **pourvu que ...** let's hope that ...

> **pourvu que** is followed by a verb in the subjunctive.

▷ *Pourvu qu'il ne pleuve pas!* Let's hope it doesn't rain!

pousser *vb* [**28**] ❶ to push ▷ *Ils ont dû pousser la voiture*. They had to push the car. ❷ to grow ▷ *Mes cheveux poussent vite*. My hair grows quickly.; **pousser un cri** to give a cry; **se pousser** to move over ▷ *Pousse-toi, je ne vois rien*. Move over, I can't see a thing.

poussette *nf* pushchair

poussière *nf* ❶ dust ❷ speck of dust

poussiéreux (*f* **poussiéreuse**) *adj* dusty

poussin *nm* chick

pouvoir *vb* [**64**] can ▷ *Je peux lui téléphoner si tu veux*. I can phone her if you want. ▷ *J'ai fait tout ce que j'ai pu*. I did all I could.; **Je n'en peux plus.** I'm exhausted.; **Il se peut que ...** It's possible that ...

> **il se peut que** is followed by a verb in the subjunctive.

▷ *Il se peut que j'y aille*. I might go.
▶ *nm* power

prairie *nf* meadow

pratique *nf* practice
▶ *adj* practical

pratiquement *adv* virtually

pratiquer *vb* [**28**] to practise; **Pratiquez-vous un sport?** Do you do any sport?

pré *nm* meadow

précaution *nf* precaution; **par précaution** as a precaution; **avec précaution** cautiously; **'à manipuler avec précaution'** 'handle with care'

précédemment *adv* previously

précédent, e *adj* previous

précieux (*f* **précieuse**) *adj* precious; **une pierre précieuse** a precious stone; **de précieux conseils** invaluable advice

précipice *nm* ravine

précipitamment *adv* hurriedly

précipitation *nf* haste

se **précipiter** *vb* [**28**] to rush

précis, e *adj* precise; **à huit heures précises** at exactly eight o'clock

précisément *adv* precisely

préciser *vb* [**28**] ❶ to be more specific about ▷ *Pouvez-vous préciser ce que vous voulez dire?* Can you be more specific about what you want to say? ❷ to specify

précision *nf* ❶ precision ❷ detail

préfecture *nf*

> A **préfecture** is the headquarters of a **département**, one of the 96 administrative areas of France.

la préfecture de police the police headquarters

préférable *adj* preferable

préféré, e *adj* favourite

préférence *nf* preference; **de préférence** preferably

préférer *vb* [**34**] to prefer ▷ *Je préfère manger à la cantine*. I prefer to eat in the canteen.; **Je préférerais du thé.** I'd rather have tea.; **préférer quelqu'un à quelqu'un** to prefer somebody to somebody ▷ *Je le préfère à son frère.* I prefer him to his brother.

préhistorique *adj* prehistoric

préjugé *nm* prejudice

premier (*f* **première**) *adj* first ▷ *au premier étage* on the first floor ▷ *C'est notre premier jour de vacances.* It's the first day of our holiday. ▷ *C'est la première fois que je viens ici.* It's the first time I've been here. ▷ *le premier mai* the first of May ▷ *Il est arrivé premier.* He came first.; **le Premier ministre** the Prime Minister

premièrement *adv* firstly

prendre *vb* [**65**] to take ▷ *Prends tes affaires et viens avec moi.* Take your things and come with me.; **prendre quelque chose à quelqu'un** to take something from somebody; **Nous avons pris le train de huit heures.** We took the eight o'clock train.; **Je prends toujours le train pour aller à Paris.** I always go to Paris by train.; **passer prendre** to pick up ▷ *Je dois passer prendre Richard.* I have to pick up Richard.; **prendre à gauche** to turn left ▷ *Prenez à gauche en arrivant au rond-point.* Turn left at the roundabout.; **Il se prend pour Napoléon.** He thinks he's Napoleon.; **s'en prendre à quelqu'un** *(verbally)* to lay into somebody; **s'y prendre** to set about it ▷ *Tu t'y prends mal!* You're setting about it the wrong way!

prénom *nm* first name

préoccupé, e *adj* worried

préparation *nf* preparation

préparer *vb* [**28**] ❶ to prepare ▷ *Elle prépare le dîner.* She's preparing dinner. ❷ to make ▷ *Je vais préparer le café.* I'm going to make the coffee. ❸ to prepare for ▷ *Laure prépare son examen d'économie.* Laure's preparing for her economics exam.; **se préparer** to get ready

préposition *nf* preposition

près *adv* **tout près** nearby; **près de (1)** near (to) **(2)** next to **(3)** nearly; **de près** closely; **à peu de chose près** more or less

présence *nf* ❶ presence ❷ attendance

présent, e *adj* present
▶ *nm* present tense; **à présent** now

présentation *nf* presentation; **faire les présentations** to do the introductions

présenter *vb* [**28**] to present; **présenter quelqu'un à quelqu'un** to introduce somebody to somebody ▷ *Il m'a présenté à sa sœur.* He introduced me to his sister.; **Marc, je te présente Anaïs.** Marc, this is Anaïs.; **se présenter (1)** to introduce oneself ▷ *Elle s'est présentée à ses collègues.* She introduced herself to her colleagues. **(2)** to arise ▷ *Si l'occasion se présente, nous irons en*

Écosse. If the chance arises, we'll go to Scotland. **(3)** to stand ▷ *Monsieur Legros se présente encore aux élections.* Mr Legros is standing for election again.

préservatif *nm* condom

préserver *vb* [**28**] to protect

président *nm* ❶ president ❷ chairman; **le président-directeur général** the chairman and managing director

présider *vb* [**28**] ❶ to chair ❷ to be the guest of honour

presque *adv* nearly; **presque rien** hardly anything; **presque pas** hardly at all; **presque pas de** hardly any

presqu'île *nf* peninsula

presse *nf* press

pressé, e *adj* ❶ in a hurry ❷ urgent; **une orange pressée** a fresh orange juice

presser *vb* [**28**] ❶ to squeeze ▷ *Tu peux me presser un citron?* Can you squeeze me a lemon? ❷ to be urgent ▷ *Est-ce que ça presse?* Is it urgent?; **se presser** to hurry up; **Rien ne presse.** There's no hurry.

pressing *nm* dry-cleaner's

pression *nf* ❶ pressure; **faire pression sur quelqu'un** to put pressure on somebody ❷ *(informal)* draught beer

prêt, e *adj* ready
▶ *nm* loan

prêt-à-porter *nm* ready-to-wear clothes *pl*

prétendre *vb* [**88**] **prétendre que** to claim that ▷ *Il prétend qu'il ne la connaît pas.* He claims he doesn't know her.

Be careful! **prétendre** does not mean **to pretend**.

prétendu, e *adj* so-called

prétentieux (*f* **prétentieuse**) *adj* pretentious

prêter *vb* [**28**] **prêter quelque chose à quelqu'un** to lend something to someone ▷ *Il m'a prêté sa voiture.* He lent me his car.; **prêter attention à quelque chose** to pay attention to something

prétexte *nm* excuse; **sous aucun prétexte** on no account

prétexter *vb* [**28**] to give as an excuse

prêtre *nm* priest

preuve *nf* ❶ evidence ❷ proof; **faire preuve de courage** to show courage; **faire ses preuves** to prove oneself

prévenir *vb* [**89**] **prévenir quelqu'un** to warn somebody ▷ *Je te préviens, il est de mauvaise humeur.* I'm warning you, he's in a bad mood.

prévention *nf* prevention; **des mesures de prévention** preventative measures; **la prévention routière** road safety

prévision *nf* **les prévisions météorologiques** the weather forecast; **en prévision de quelque chose** in anticipation of something

prévoir *vb* [**92**] ❶ to plan ▷ *Nous prévoyons un pique-nique pour dimanche.* We're planning to have a picnic on Sunday.; **Le départ est**

prévu pour dix heures. The departure's scheduled for 10 o'clock. ❷ to allow ▷ *J'ai prévu assez à manger pour quatre.* I allowed enough food for four. ❸ to foresee ▷ *J'avais prévu qu'il serait en retard.* I'd foreseen that he'd be late.; **Je prévois qu'il me faudra une heure de plus.** I reckon on it taking me another hour.

prier *vb* [**19**] to pray to ▷ *Les Grecs priaient Dionysos.* The Greeks prayed to Dionysos.; **prier quelqu'un de faire quelque chose** to ask somebody to do something ▷ *Elle l'a prié de sortir.* She asked him to leave.; **je vous en prie (1)** please do ▷ *Je peux m'asseoir? — Je vous en prie.* May I sit down? — Please do. **(2)** please ▷ *Je vous en prie, ne me laissez pas seule.* Please, don't leave me alone. **(3)** don't mention it ▷ *Merci pour votre aide. — Je vous en prie.* Thanks for your help. — Don't mention it.

prière *nf* prayer; **'prière de ne pas fumer'** 'no smoking please'

primaire *nm* primary education; **l'école primaire** primary school

prime *nf* ❶ bonus ❷ free gift ❸ premium

primevère *nf* primrose

prince *nm* prince

princesse *nf* princess

principal, e (*mpl* **principaux**) *adj* main
▸ *nm* ❶ head teacher ❷ main thing ▷ *Personne n'a été blessé; c'est le principal.* Nobody was injured; that's the main thing.

principe *nm* principle; **pour le principe** on principle; **en principe (1)** as a rule **(2)** in theory

printemps *nm* spring; **au printemps** in spring

priorité *nf* ❶ priority ❷ right of way

pris, e *adj* ❶ taken ▷ *Est-ce que cette place est prise?* Is this seat taken? ❷ busy ▷ *Je serai très pris la semaine prochaine.* I'll be very busy next week.; **avoir le nez pris** to have a stuffy nose; **être pris de panique** to be panic-stricken
▸ *vb see* **prendre**

prise *nf* ❶ plug ❷ socket; **une prise de courant** a power point; **une prise multiple** an adaptor; **une prise de sang** a blood test

prison *nf* prison

prisonnier (*f* **prisonnière**) *adj* captive

prisonnier *nm* prisoner

prisonnière *nf* prisoner

prit *vb see* **prendre**

privé, e *adj* private; **en privé** in private

priver *vb* [**28**] **priver quelqu'un de quelque chose** to deprive somebody of something; **Tu seras privé de dessert!** You won't get any pudding!

prix *nm* ❶ price ❷ prize; **hors de prix** exorbitantly priced; **à aucun prix** not at any price; **à tout prix** at all costs

probable *adj* likely; **C'est peu probable.** That's unlikely.

probablement *adv* probably
problème *nm* problem
procédé *nm* process
procès *nm* trial; **Il est en procès avec son employeur.** He's involved in a lawsuit with his employer.
prochain, e *adj* next; **la prochaine fois** next time; **la semaine prochaine** next week; **À la prochaine!** See you!
prochainement *adv* soon
proche *adj* ❶ near ❷ close; **proche de** near to; **le Proche-Orient** the Middle East
proches *nmpl* close relatives
proclamer *vb* [**28**] to proclaim
procurer *vb* [**28**] **procurer quelque chose à quelqu'un** to get something for somebody; **se procurer quelque chose** to get something
producteur *nm* producer
production *nf* production
produire *vb* [**23**] to produce; **se produire** to take place
produit *nm* product
prof *nmf (informal)* teacher
professeur *nm* ❶ teacher ❷ professor; **un professeur de faculté** a university lecturer
profession *nf* profession; **'sans profession'** 'unemployed'
professionnel (*f* **professionnelle**) *adj* professional
profil *nm* ❶ *(of person)* profile ❷ *(of object)* contours
profit *nm* profit; **tirer profit de quelque chose** to profit from something; **au profit de** in aid of
profiter *vb* [**28**] **profiter de quelque chose** to take advantage of something; **Profitez-en bien!** Make the most of it!
profond, e *adj* deep; **peu profond** shallow
profondeur *nf* depth
programme *nm* ❶ programme ❷ syllabus ❸ program ▷ *un programme informatique* a computer program
programmer *vb* [**28**] ❶ to show ▷ *Ce film est programmé dimanche soir.* The film is showing on Sunday evening. ❷ to program
programmeur *nm* programmer
programmeuse *nf* programmer
progrès *nm* progress
progresser *vb* [**28**] to progress
progressif (*f* **progressive**) *adj* progressive
projecteur *nm* ❶ projector ❷ spotlight
projet *nm* ❶ plan ❷ draft; **un projet de loi** *(in parliament)* a bill
projeter *vb* [**41**] ❶ to plan ▷ *Ils projettent d'acheter une maison.* They're planning to buy a house. ❷ to cast ▷ *une ombre projetée sur le mur* a shadow cast onto the wall; **Elle a été projetée hors de la voiture.** She was thrown out of the car.
prolonger *vb* [**45**] ❶ to prolong ❷ to extend ▷ *Je vais prolonger mon abonnement.* I'm going to extend my subscription.; **se prolonger** to go on ▷ *La réunion s'est prolongée tard.* The meeting went on late.

promenade *nf* walk; **faire une promenade** to go for a walk; **faire une promenade en voiture** to go for a drive; **faire une promenade à vélo** to go for a bike ride

promener *vb* [**43**] to take for a walk ▷ *Cordelia promène son chien tous les jours.* Cordelia takes her dog for a walk every day.; **se promener** to go for a walk

promesse *nf* promise

promettre *vb* [**47**] to promise

promotion *nf* promotion; **être en promotion** to be on special offer

pronom *nm* pronoun

prononcer *vb* [**12**] ❶ to pronounce ▷ *Le russe est difficile à prononcer.* Russian is difficult to pronounce. ❷ to deliver ▷ *prononcer un discours* to deliver a speech; **se prononcer** to be pronounced ▷ *Le 'e' final ne se prononce pas.* The final 'e' isn't pronounced.

prononciation *nf* pronunciation

propagande *nf* propaganda

se **propager** *vb* [**45**] to spread

proportion *nf* proportion

propos *nm* **à propos** by the way; **à propos de quelque chose** about something

proposer *vb* [**28**] **proposer quelque chose à quelqu'un (1)** to suggest something to somebody ▷ *Nous lui avons proposé une promenade en bateau.* We suggested going on a boat ride to him. **(2)** to offer somebody something ▷ *Ils m'ont proposé des chocolats.* They offered me some chocolates.

proposition *nf* offer

propre *adj* ❶ clean ❷ own ▷ *Gordon l'a fabriqué de ses propres mains.* Gordon made it with his own hands.; **propre à** characteristic of ▶ *nm* **recopier quelque chose au propre** to make a fair copy of something

proprement *adv* properly; **le village proprement dit** the village itself; **à proprement parler** strictly speaking

propreté *nf* cleanliness

propriétaire *nm* ❶ owner ❷ landlord ▶ *nf* ❶ owner ❷ landlady

propriété *nf* property

prospectus *nm* leaflet

prospère *adj* prosperous

prostituée *nf* prostitute

protecteur (*f* **protectrice**) *adj* ❶ protective ❷ patronizing

protection *nf* protection

protéger *vb* [**66**] to protect

protéine *nf* protein

protestant, e *adj* Protestant; **Il est protestant.** He's a Protestant.

protestation *nf* protest

protester *vb* [**28**] to protest ▷ *Ils protestent contre leurs conditions de travail.* They're protesting about their working conditions.

prouver *vb* [**28**] to prove

provenance *nf* origin; **un avion en provenance de Berlin** a plane arriving from Berlin

provenir *vb* [**89**] **provenir de (1)** to come from ▷ *Ces tomates proviennent d'Espagne.* These tomatoes come from Spain. **(2)** to be the result of ▷ *Cela provient d'un manque d'organisation.* This is the result of a lack of organization.

proverbe *nm* proverb

province *nf* province; **en province** in the provinces

proviseur *nm (of state secondary school)* headteacher

provision *nf* supply

provisions *nfpl* food

provisoire *adj* temporary

provoquer *vb* [**28**] ❶ to provoke ❷ to cause ▷ *Cet accident a provoqué la mort de quarante personnes.* The accident caused the death of 40 people.

proximité *nf* proximity; **à proximité** nearby

prudemment *adv* ❶ carefully ❷ wisely ❸ cautiously

prudence *nf* caution; **avec prudence** carefully

prudent, e *adj* ❶ careful ❷ wise

prune *nf* plum

pruneau (*pl* **pruneaux**) *nm* prune

psychiatre *nmf* psychiatrist

psychologie *nf* psychology

psychologique *adj* psychological

psychologue *nmf* psychologist

pu *vb see* **pouvoir**; **Je n'ai pas pu venir.** I couldn't come.

pub *nf (informal)* ❶ advertising ❷ adverts

public (*f* **publique**) *adj* public; **une école publique** a state school
▶ *nm* ❶ public ❷ audience; **en public** in public

publicitaire *adj* **une agence publicitaire** an advertising agency; **un film publicitaire** a publicity film

publicité *nf* ❶ advertising ❷ advert; **faire de la publicité pour quelque chose** to publicize something

publier *vb* [**19**] to publish

publique *adj f see* **public**

puce *nf* ❶ flea ❷ chip; **une carte à puce** a smart card

puces *nfpl* flea market *sg*

puer *vb* [**28**] to stink

puéril, e *adj* childish

puis *vb see* **pouvoir**; **Puis-je venir vous voir samedi?** May I come and see you on Saturday?
▶ *adv* then

puisque *conj* since

puissance *nf* power

puissant, e *adj* powerful

puits *nm* well

pull *nm* jumper

pull-over *nm* jumper

pulvérisateur *nm* spray

pulvériser *vb* [**28**] ❶ to pulverize ❷ to spray

punaise *nf* drawing pin

punir *vb* [**38**] to punish ▷ *Il a été puni pour avoir menti.* He was punished for lying.

punition *nf* punishment

pupitre *nm (for pupil)* desk

pur, e *adj* ❶ pure ❷ *(undiluted)* neat; **C'est de la folie pure.** It's sheer madness.

purée *nf* mashed potatoes; **la purée de marrons** chestnut purée

puzzle *nm* jigsaw puzzle

PV *nm* (= *procès-verbal*) parking ticket
pyjama *nm* pyjamas *pl*
pyramide *nf* pyramid
Pyrénées *nfpl* Pyrenees; **dans les Pyrénées** in the Pyrenees

q

QI *nm* (= *quotient intellectuel*) IQ
quai *nm* ❶ quay ❷ platform
qualifié, e *adj* qualified
qualifier *vb* [19] **se qualifier** to qualify ▷ *Bob s'est qualifié pour la demi-finale.* Bob has qualified for the semifinal.
qualité *nf* quality
quand *conj, adv* when ▷ *Quand est-ce que tu pars en vacances?* When are you going on holiday?; **quand même** all the same ▷ *Je ne voulais pas de dessert, mais j'en ai mangé quand même.* I didn't want any dessert, but I had some all the same.
quant à *prep* regarding ▷ *Quant au problème de chauffage ...* Regarding the problem with the heating ... ▷ *Quant à moi, je n'arriverai qu'à dix*

heures. As for me, I won't be arriving till 10 o'clock.

quantité *nf* amount; **des quantités de** a great deal of

quarantaine *nf* about forty; **Elle a la quarantaine.** She's in her forties.

quarante *num* forty; **quarante et un** forty-one; **quarante-deux** forty-two

quart *nm* quarter; **le quart de** a quarter of; **trois quarts** three quarters; **un quart d'heure** a quarter of an hour; **deux heures et quart** a quarter past two; **dix heures moins le quart** a quarter to ten; **Un quart d'eau minérale, s'il vous plaît.** A small bottle of mineral water, please.

quartier *nm* ❶ *(of town)* area; **un cinéma de quartier** a local cinema ❷ piece ▷ *un quartier d'orange* a piece of orange

quartz *nm* **une montre à quartz** a quartz watch

quasi *adv* nearly

quasiment *adv* nearly; **quasiment jamais** hardly ever

quatorze *num* fourteen; **le quatorze février** the fourteenth of February

quatre *num* four ▷ *Il a quatre ans.* He's four.; **le quatre février** the fourth of February; **faire les quatre cents coups** to be a bit wild

quatre-vingts *num* eighty

> **quatre-vingts** is spelt with an **-s** when it is followed by a noun, but not when it is followed by another number.

▷ *quatre-vingts euros* eighty euros ▷ *Elle a quatre-vingt-deux ans.* She's eighty-two.; **quatre-vingt-dix** ninety; **quatre-vingt-onze** ninety-one; **quatre-vingt-quinze** ninety-five; **quatre-vingt-dix-huit** ninety-eight

> Word for word, **quatre-vingts** means 'four twenties'.

quatrième *adj* fourth ▷ *au quatrième étage* on the fourth floor ▶ *nf* year 9 ▷ *Mon frère est en quatrième.* My brother's in year 9.

> In French secondary schools, years are counted from the **sixième** (youngest) to **première** and **terminale** (oldest).

que *conj, pron, adv* ❶ that ▷ *Il sait que tu es là.* He knows that you're here.; **Je veux que tu viennes.** I want you to come. ❷ what ▷ *Que fais-tu?* What are you doing?; **Qu'est-ce que ...?** What ...? ▷ *Qu'est-ce que tu fais?* What are you doing? ▷ *Qu'est-ce que c'est?* What's that?; **plus ... que** more ... than ▷ *Il est plus grand que moi.* He's bigger than me.; **aussi ... que** as ... as ▷ *Elle est aussi jolie que sa sœur.* She's as pretty as her sister.; **ne ... que** only ▷ *Il ne boit que de l'eau.* He only drinks water.; **Qu'il est bête!** He's so silly!

quel (*f* **quelle**) *adj* ❶ who ▷ *Quel est ton chanteur préféré?* Who's your favourite singer? ❷ what ▷ *Quelle heure est-il?* What time is it? ❸ which ▷ *Quel groupe préfères-tu?* Which band do you like best?; **quel que soit (1)** whoever **(2)** whatever

quelle *adj f see* **quel**

quelque *adj, adv* ❶ some ▷ *Il a quelques amis à Paris.* He has some friends in Paris. ❷ a few ▷ *Il reste quelques bouteilles.* There are a few bottles left. ❸ few ▷ *Ils ont fini les quelques bouteilles qui restaient.* They finished the few bottles that were left.; **quelque chose (1)** something ▷ *J'ai quelque chose pour toi.* I've got something for you. **(2)** anything ▷ *Avez-vous quelque chose à déclarer?* Have you got anything to declare?; **quelque part (1)** somewhere **(2)** anywhere

quelquefois *adv* sometimes

quelques-uns (*f* **quelques-unes**) *pron pl* some ▷ *As-tu vu ses films? J'en ai vu quelques-uns.* Have you seen his films? I've seen some of them.

quelqu'un *pron* ❶ somebody ▷ *Il y a quelqu'un à la porte.* There's somebody at the door. ❷ anybody ▷ *Est-ce que quelqu'un a vu mon parapluie?* Has anybody seen my umbrella?

querelle *nf* quarrel

qu'est-ce que *see* **que**

qu'est-ce qui *see* **qui**

question *nf* ❶ question ❷ matter; **Il n'en est pas question.** There's no question of it.; **De quoi est-il question?** What's it about? ▷ *Il est question de l'organisation du concert.* It's about the organization of the concert.; **hors de question** out of the question

questionnaire *nm* questionnaire

questionner *vb* [28] to question

queue *nf* ❶ tail; **faire la queue** to queue; **une queue de cheval** a ponytail ❷ rear ❸ bottom ❹ *(of fruit, leaf)* stalk

qui *pron* ❶ who ▷ *Qui a téléphoné?* Who phoned? ❷ whom ▷ *C'est la personne à qui j'ai parlé hier.* It's the person who I spoke to yesterday. ❸ that ▷ *Donne-moi la veste qui est sur la chaise.* Give me the jacket that's on the chair.; **Qui est-ce qui ...?** Who ...? ▷ *Qui est-ce qui t'emmène au spectacle?* Who's taking you to the show?; **Qui est-ce que ...?** Who ...? ▷ *Qui est-ce que tu as vu à cette soirée?* Who did you see at the party?; **Qu'est-ce qui ...?** What ...? ▷ *Qu'est-ce qui est sur la table?* What's on the table? ▷ *Qu'est-ce qui te prend?* What's the matter with you?; **À qui est ce sac?** Whose bag is this?; **À qui parlais-tu?** Who were you talking to?

quille *nf* **un jeu de quilles** skittles

quincaillerie *nf* ironmonger's (shop)

quinquennat *nm*

le quinquennat is the five-year term of office of the French President.

quinzaine *nf* about fifteen; **une quinzaine de jours** a fortnight

quinze *num* fifteen; **le quinze février** the fifteenth of February; **dans quinze jours** in a fortnight's time

quittance *nf* ❶ receipt ❷ bill

quitter *vb* [28] to leave ▷ *J'ai quitté*

la maison à huit heures. I left the house at 8 o'clock.; **se quitter** to part ▷ *Les deux amis se sont quittés devant le café.* The two friends parted in front of the café.; **Ne quittez pas.** *(on telephone)* Hold the line.

quoi *pron* what? ▷ *À quoi penses-tu?* What are you thinking about?; **Quoi de neuf?** What's new?; **As-tu de quoi écrire?** Have you got anything to write with?; **Je n'ai pas de quoi acheter une voiture.** I can't afford to buy a car.; **Quoi qu'il arrive.** Whatever happens.; **Il n'y a pas de quoi.** Don't mention it.; **Il n'y a pas de quoi s'énerver.** There's no reason for getting worked up.; **En quoi puis-je vous aider?** How may I help you?

quoique *conj* even though

> **quoique** is followed by a verb in the subjunctive.

▷ *Il va l'acheter quoique ce soit cher.* He's going to buy it even though it's expensive.

quotidien (*f* **quotidienne**) *adj* daily; **la vie quotidienne** everyday life

▶ *nm* daily paper

rab *nm (informal) (of meal)* seconds

rabais *nm (in price)* reduction; **au rabais** at a discount

racaille *nf* riff-raff

raccompagner *vb* [28] to take home ▷ *Tu peux me raccompagner?* Can you take me home?

raccourci *nm* shortcut

raccrocher *vb* [28] to hang up *(telephone)*

race *nf* ❶ race ❷ breed; **de race** pedigree

racheter *vb* [1] ❶ to buy another ▷ *J'ai racheté un portefeuille.* I've bought another wallet. ▷ *racheter du lait* to buy more milk ❷ to buy ▷ *Il m'a racheté ma moto.* He bought my bike from me.

racine *nf* root

racisme *nm* racism

raciste *adj* racist
raconter *vb* [**28**] **raconter quelque chose à quelqu'un** to tell somebody about something; **Qu'est-ce que tu racontes?** What are you talking about?
radar *nm* radar
radiateur *nm* radiator; **un radiateur électrique** an electric heater
radin, e *adj (informal)* stingy
radio *nf* ❶ radio ❷ X-ray; **passer une radio** to have an X-ray
radio-réveil (*pl* **radios-réveils**) *nm* clock radio
radis *nm* radish
raffoler *vb* [**28**] **raffoler de** to be crazy about
rafraîchir *vb* [**38**] to cool down; **se rafraîchir (1)** to get cooler ▷ *Le temps se rafraîchit.* The weather's getting cooler. **(2)** to freshen up ▷ *Il a pris une douche pour se rafraîchir.* He had a shower to freshen up.
rafraîchissant, e *adj* refreshing
rage *nf* rabies; **une rage de dents** raging toothache
ragoût *nm* stew
raide *adj* ❶ steep ❷ straight ▷ *Laure a les cheveux raides.* Laure has straight hair. ❸ stiff ❹ flat broke
raie *nf* ❶ *(fish)* skate ❷ *(in hair)* parting
rail *nm* rail
raisin *nm* grapes; **des raisins secs** raisins
raison *nf* reason; **Ce n'est pas une raison.** That's no excuse.; **avoir raison** to be right; **en raison de** because of
raisonnable *adj* sensible
raisonnement *nm* reasoning
rajouter *vb* [**28**] to add
ralentir *vb* [**38**] to slow down
râler *vb* [**28**] *(informal)* to moan
ramassage *nm* **le ramassage scolaire** the school bus service
ramasser *vb* [**28**] ❶ to pick up ▷ *Il a ramassé son crayon.* He picked up his pencil. ❷ to take in ▷ *Il a ramassé les copies.* He took in the exam papers.
rame *nf* ❶ *(of boat)* oar ❷ *(on the underground)* train
rameau (*pl* **rameaux**) *nm* branch; **le dimanche des Rameaux** Palm Sunday
ramener *vb* [**43**] ❶ to bring back ▷ *Je t'ai ramené un souvenir de Grèce.* I've brought you back a present from Greece. ❷ to take home ▷ *Tu me ramènes?* Will you take me home?
ramer *vb* [**28**] to row
rampe *nf* banister
rancune *nf* **garder rancune à quelqu'un** to bear somebody a grudge; **Sans rancune!** No hard feelings!
rancunier (*f* **rancunière**) *adj* vindictive
randonnée *nf* **une randonnée à vélo** a bike ride; **une randonnée pédestre** a ramble; **faire de la randonnée** to go hiking
randonneur *nm* hiker
rang *nm (line)* row
rangée *nf (line)* row

ranger *vb* [**45**] ❶ to put away ▷ *J'ai rangé tes affaires.* I've put your things away. ❷ to tidy up ▷ *Va ranger ta chambre.* Go and tidy up your room.

rap *nm* rap

râper *vb* [**28**] to grate ▷ *le fromage râpé* grated cheese

rapide *adj* ❶ fast ❷ quick

rapidement *adv* quickly

rappel *nm* ❶ *(vaccination)* booster ❷ curtain call

rappeler *vb* [**4**] to call back ▷ *Je te rappelle dans cinq minutes.* I'll call you back in 5 minutes.; **rappeler quelque chose à quelqu'un** to remind somebody of something; **rappeler à quelqu'un de faire quelque chose** to remind somebody to do something; **se rappeler** to remember ▷ *Il s'est rappelé qu'il avait une course à faire.* He remembered he had some shopping to do.

rapport *nm* ❶ report ▷ *Il a écrit un rapport.* He wrote a report. ❷ connection ▷ *Je ne vois pas le rapport.* I can't see the connection.; **par rapport à** in comparison with

rapporter *vb* [**28**] to bring back

rapporteur *nm* telltale

rapprocher *vb* [**28**] ❶ to bring together ▷ *Cet accident a rapproché les deux frères.* The accident brought the two brothers together. ❷ to bring closer ▷ *Il a rapproché le fauteuil de la télé.* He brought the armchair closer to the TV.; **se rapprocher** to come closer ▷ *Rapproche-toi, tu verras mieux.* Come closer, you'll see better.

raquette *nf* ❶ *(tennis)* racket ❷ *(table tennis)* bat

rare *adj* rare

rarement *adv* rarely

ras, e *adj, adv* short; **à ras bords** to the brim; **en avoir ras le bol de quelque chose** *(informal)* to be fed up with something; **un pull ras du cou** a crew-neck jumper

raser *vb* [**28**] to shave off; **se raser** to shave

rasoir *nm* razor
▶ *adj (informal)* dead boring

rassembler *vb* [**28**] to assemble ▷ *Il a rassemblé les enfants dans la cour.* He assembled the children in the playground.; **se rassembler** to gather together

rassurer *vb* [**28**] to reassure; **Je suis rassuré.** I don't need to worry any more.; **se rassurer** to be reassured; **Rassure-toi!** Don't worry!

rat *nm* rat

raté, e *adj* failed

râteau (*pl* **râteaux**) *nm* rake

rater *vb* [**28**] ❶ to miss ▷ *Chantal a raté son train.* Chantal missed her train. ❷ to fail ▷ *J'ai raté mon examen de maths.* I failed my maths exam.

RATP *nf* Paris transport authority

rattacher *vb* [**28**] to tie up again

rattraper *vb* [**28**] ❶ to recapture ❷ to catch up with ▷ *Je vais rattraper Cécile.* I'll catch up with Cécile. ❸ to make up for ▷ *Il faut rattraper le temps perdu.* We must

make up for lost time.; **se rattraper** to make up for it
rature *nf* correction
ravi, e *adj* **être ravi** to be delighted ▷ *Ils étaient ravis de nous voir.* They were delighted to see us. ▷ *Je suis ravi que vous puissiez venir.* I'm delighted that you can come.
se **raviser** *vb* [**28**] to change your mind ▷ *Il allait accepter, mais il s'est ravisé.* He was going to accept, but he changed his mind.
ravissant, e *adj* lovely
rayé, e *adj* striped
rayer *vb* [**59**] ❶ to scratch ❷ to cross off ▷ *Son nom a été rayé de la liste.* His name has been crossed off the list.
rayon *nm* ❶ ray ▷ *un rayon de soleil* a ray of sunshine ❷ radius ❸ shelf ▷ *les rayons d'une bibliothèque* the shelves of a bookcase ❹ department ▷ *le rayon hi-fi vidéo* the hi-fi and video department; **les rayons X** X-rays
rayure *nf* stripe
ré *nm* ❶ D ❷ re
réaction *nf* reaction
réagir *vb* [**38**] to react
réalisateur *nm* director *(of film)*
réaliser *vb* [**28**] ❶ to carry out ▷ *Ils ont réalisé leur projet.* They carried out their plan. ❷ to fulfil ▷ *Il a réalisé son rêve.* He has fulfilled his dream. ❸ to realize ❹ to make ▷ *réaliser un film* to make a film; **se réaliser** to come true
réaliste *adj* realistic
réalité *nf* reality; **en réalité** in fact
rebelle *nm* rebel
rebondir *vb* [**38**] to bounce
rebord *nm* edge; **le rebord de la fenêtre** the window ledge
recaler *vb* [**28**] *(informal)* **J'ai été recalé en maths.** I failed maths.
récemment *adv* recently
récent, e *adj* recent
récepteur *nm* receiver
réception *nf* reception desk
réceptionniste *nmf* receptionist
recette *nf* recipe
recevoir *vb* [**67**] ❶ to receive ▷ *J'ai reçu une lettre.* I received a letter. ❷ to see ▷ *Il a déjà reçu trois clients.* He has already seen three clients. ❸ to have round ▷ *Je reçois des amis à dîner.* I'm having friends round for dinner.; **être reçu à un examen** to pass an exam
rechange *nm* **de rechange** *(battery, bulb)* spare
recharge *nf* refill
réchaud *nm* stove
réchauffer *vb* [**28**] ❶ to reheat ▷ *Je vais réchauffer les légumes.* I'll reheat the vegetables. ❷ to warm up ▷ *Un bon café va te réchauffer.* A nice cup of coffee will warm you up.; **se réchauffer** to warm oneself
recherche *nf* research; **être à la recherche de quelque chose** to be looking for something; **les recherches** search
recherché, e *adj* much sought-after
rechercher *vb* [**28**] to look for ▷ *La police recherche l'assassin.* The police are looking for the killer.
rechute *nf* relapse

récipient *nm* container
récit *nm* story
réciter *vb* [**28**] to recite
réclamation *nf* complaint; **les réclamations** the complaints department
réclame *nf* advert; **en réclame** on special offer
réclamer *vb* [**28**] ❶ to demand ▷ *Nous réclamons la semaine de trente heures.* We demand a 30-hour week. ❷ to complain ▷ *Elles sont toujours en train de réclamer.* They're always complaining about something.
reçois *vb see* **recevoir**
récolte *nf* harvest
récolter *vb* [**28**] ❶ to harvest ❷ to collect ▷ *Ils ont récolté deux cents euros.* They collected 200 euros. ❸ to get ▷ *Il a récolté une amende. (informal)* He got a fine.
recommandé *nm* **en recommandé** by registered mail
recommander *vb* [**28**] to recommend
recommencer *vb* [**12**] ❶ to start again ▷ *Il a recommencé à pleuvoir.* It's started raining again. ❷ to do again ▷ *S'il n'est pas puni, il va recommencer.* If he's not punished he'll do it again.
récompense *nf* reward
récompenser *vb* [**28**] to reward
réconcilier *vb* [**19**] **se réconcilier avec quelqu'un** to make it up with somebody ▷ *Il s'est réconcilié avec sa sœur.* He has made it up with his sister.
reconnaissant, e *adj* grateful
reconnaître *vb* [**14**] ❶ to recognize ▷ *Je ne l'ai pas reconnu.* I didn't recognize him. ❷ to admit ▷ *Je reconnais que j'ai eu tort.* I admit I was wrong.
reconstruire *vb* [**23**] to rebuild
record *nm* record
recouvrir *vb* [**55**] to cover ▷ *La neige recouvre le sol.* The ground is covered in snow.
récréation *nf* break; **la cour de récréation** the playground *(of school)*
rectangle *nm* rectangle
rectangulaire *adj* rectangular
rectifier *vb* [**19**] to correct
reçu *nm* receipt
▶ *vb see* **recevoir**; **J'ai reçu un colis ce matin.** I received a parcel this morning.; **être reçu à un examen** to pass an exam
reculer *vb* [**28**] ❶ to step back ▷ *Il a reculé pour la laisser entrer.* He stepped back to let her in. ❷ to reverse ▷ *J'ai reculé pour laisser passer le camion.* I reversed to let the lorry past. ❸ to postpone ▷ *Ils ont reculé la date du spectacle.* They postponed the show.
reculons: **à reculons** *adv* backwards
récupérer *vb* [**34**] ❶ to get back ▷ *Je vais récupérer ma voiture au garage.* I'm going to get my car back from the garage. ❷ to make up ▷ *J'ai des heures à récupérer.* I've got time to make up. ❸ to recover ▷ *J'ai besoin de récupérer.* I need to recover.

recycler *vb* [**28**] to recycle
rédaction *nf* essay
redemander *vb* [**28**] ❶ to ask again for ▷ *Je vais lui redemander son adresse.* I'll ask him for his address again. ❷ to ask for more ▷ *Je vais redemander des carottes.* I'm going to ask for more carrots.
redescendre *vb* [**24**] to go back down ▷ *Il est redescendu au premier étage.* He went back down to the first floor. ▷ *Elle a redescendu l'escalier.* She went back down the stairs.
rédiger *vb* [**45**] *(an essay)* to write
redoubler *vb* [**28**] to repeat a year ▷ *Il a raté son examen et doit redoubler.* He's failed his exam and will have to repeat the year.
réduction *nf* ❶ reduction ❷ discount
réduire *vb* [**23**] to cut ▷ *Ils ont réduit leurs prix.* They've cut their prices.
réel (*f* **réelle**) *adj* real
réellement *adv* really
refaire *vb* [**36**] ❶ to do again ▷ *Je dois refaire ce rapport.* I've got to do this report again. ❷ to take up again ▷ *Je voudrais refaire de la gym.* I'd like to take up gymnastics again.
réfectoire *nm* refectory
référence *nf* reference; **faire référence à quelque chose** to refer to something; **Ce n'est pas une référence!** That's no recommendation!
réfléchi, e *adj (verb)* reflexive; **C'est tout réfléchi.** My mind's made up.
réfléchir *vb* [**38**] to think ▷ *Il est en train de réfléchir.* He's thinking.; **réfléchir à quelque chose** to think about something
reflet *nm* reflection
refléter *vb* [**34**] to reflect
réflexe *nm* reflex
réflexion *nf* ❶ thought ❷ remark; **réflexion faite** on reflection
refrain *nm* chorus *(of song)*
réfrigérateur *nm* refrigerator
refroidir *vb* [**38**] to cool ▷ *Laissez le gâteau refroidir.* Leave the cake to cool.; **se refroidir** to get colder ▷ *Le temps se refroidit.* It's getting colder.
se **réfugier** *vb* [**19**] to take shelter
refus *nm* refusal; **Ce n'est pas de refus.** I wouldn't say no.
refuser *vb* [**28**] to refuse ▷ *Il a refusé de payer sa part.* He refused to pay his share.; **Je refuse qu'on me parle ainsi!** I won't let anybody talk to me like that!
se **régaler** *vb* [**28**] **Merci beaucoup: je me suis régalé!** Thank you very much: it was absolutely delicious!
regard *nm* look; **Tous les regards se sont tournés vers lui.** All eyes turned towards him.
regarder *vb* [**28**] ❶ to look at ▷ *Il regardait ses photos de vacances.* He was looking at his holiday photos. ❷ to watch ▷ *Je regarde la télévision.* I'm watching television. ❸ to concern ▷ *Ça ne nous regarde pas.* It doesn't concern us.; **ne pas regarder à la dépense** to spare no expense
régime *nm* ❶ régime *(of a country)*

❷ diet; **un régime de bananes** a bunch of bananas
région *nf* region
régional, e (*mpl* **régionaux**) *adj* regional
registre *nm* register
règle *nf* ❶ ruler ❷ rule; **être en règle** to be in order; **les règles** *(menstruation)* period
règlement *nm* rules
régler *vb* [**34**] ❶ to adjust ❷ to tune ▷ *J'ai réglé ma radio sur 476 FM.* I tuned my radio to 476 FM. ❸ to set ▷ *J'ai réglé le thermostat à vingt degrés.* I've set the thermostat to 20 degrees. ❹ to solve ▷ *Le problème est réglé.* The problem's solved. ❺ to settle ▷ *Elle a réglé sa facture.* She's settled her bill.
réglisse *nf* liquorice
règne *nm* reign
régner *vb* [**34**] to reign
regret *nm* regret; **à regret** reluctantly
regretter *vb* [**28**] ❶ to regret; **Je regrette.** I'm sorry. ▷ *Je regrette, je ne peux pas vous aider.* I'm sorry, I can't help you. ❷ to miss ▷ *Je regrette mon ancien travail.* I miss my old job.
regrouper *vb* [**28**] to group together; **se regrouper** to gather together
régulier (*f* **régulière**) *adj* ❶ regular ❷ steady ▷ *à un rythme régulier* at a steady rate ❸ scheduled ▷ *des vols réguliers pour Marseille* scheduled flights to Marseilles
régulièrement *adv* regularly
rein *nm* kidney; **les reins** *(of body)* back
reine *nf* queen
rejoindre *vb* [**42**] to go back to ▷ *J'ai rejoint mes amis.* I went back to my friends.; **Je te rejoins au café.** I'll see you at the café.; **se rejoindre** to meet up ▷ *Elles se sont rejointes une heure après.* They met up an hour later.
relâcher *vb* [**28**] *(prisoner, animal)* to release; **se relâcher** to get slack ▷ *Il se relâche dans son travail.* He is slacking in his work.
relais *nm* relay race; **prendre le relais** to take over
relation *nf* relationship; **les relations franco-britanniques** Anglo-French relations
se **relaxer** *vb* [**28**] to relax
se **relayer** *vb* [**59**] **se relayer pour faire quelque chose** to take it in turns to do something
relevé *nm* **un relevé de compte** a bank statement
relever *vb* [**43**] ❶ to collect ▷ *Je relève les copies dans cinq minutes.* I'll collect the papers in five minutes. ❷ to react to ▷ *Je n'ai pas relevé sa réflexion.* I didn't react to his remark.; **relever la tête** to look up; **se relever** to get up ▷ *Il est tombé mais s'est relevé aussitôt.* He fell, but got up immediately.
religieuse *nf* ❶ nun ❷ choux cream bun
religieux (*f* **religieuse**) *adj* religious
religion *nf* religion

relire *vb* [**44**] ❶ to read over ❷ to read again
remarquable *adj* remarkable
remarque *nf* ❶ remark ❷ comment
remarquer *vb* [**28**] to notice ▷ *J'ai remarqué qu'elle avait l'air triste.* I noticed she was looking sad.; **faire remarquer quelque chose à quelqu'un** to point something out to somebody ▷ *Je lui ai fait remarquer que c'était un peu cher.* I pointed out to him that it was rather expensive.; **Remarquez, il n'est pas si bête que ça.** Mind you, he's not as stupid as all that.; **se remarquer** to be noticeable; **se faire remarquer** to call attention to oneself
remboursement *nm* refund
rembourser *vb* [**28**] to pay back ▷ *Il m'a remboursé l'argent qu'il me devait.* He paid me back the money he owed me.; **'satisfait ou remboursé'** 'satisfaction or your money back'
remède *nm* ❶ medicine ❷ cure
remercier *vb* [**19**] to thank ▷ *Je te remercie pour ton cadeau.* Thank you for your present.; **remercier quelqu'un d'avoir fait quelque chose** to thank somebody for doing something ▷ *Je vous remercie de m'avoir invité.* Thank you for inviting me.
remettre *vb* [**47**] ❶ to put back on ▷ *Il a remis son pull.* He put his sweater back on. ❷ to put back ▷ *Il a remis sa veste dans l'armoire.* He put his jacket back in the wardrobe. ❸ to put off ▷ *J'ai dû remettre mon rendez-vous.* I've had to put my appointment off.; **se remettre** *(from illness)* to recover
remonte-pente *nm* ski-lift
remonter *vb* [**48**] ❶ to go back up ▷ *Il est remonté au premier étage.* He has gone back up to the first floor. ❷ to go up ▷ *Ils ont remonté la pente.* They went up the hill. ❸ to buck up ▷ *Cette nouvelle m'a un peu remontée.* The news bucked me up a bit.; **remonter le moral à quelqu'un** to cheer somebody up
remords *nm* **avoir des remords** to feel remorse
remorque *nf* *(of car)* trailer
remparts *nmpl* city walls
remplaçant *nm* supply teacher
remplacer *vb* [**12**] to replace ▷ *Il remplace le prof de maths.* He's replacing the maths teacher.; **remplacer par** to replace with
rempli, e *adj* busy; **rempli de** full of
remplir *vb* [**38**] ❶ to fill up ▷ *Elle a rempli son verre de vin.* She filled her glass up with wine. ❷ to fill in ▷ *Tu as rempli ton formulaire?* Have you filled in your form?; **se remplir** to fill up
remuer *vb* [**28**] ❶ to move ▷ *Elle a remué le bras.* She moved her arm. ❷ to stir ▷ *Remuez la sauce pendant deux minutes.* Stir the sauce for two minutes.; **se remuer** *(informal)* to go to a lot of trouble ▷ *Ils se sont beaucoup remués pour organiser cette soirée.* They went to a lot of trouble organizing this party.

a b c d e f g h i j k l m n o p q r s t u v w x y z

renard *nm* fox
rencontre *nf* **faire la rencontre de quelqu'un** to meet somebody; **aller à la rencontre de quelqu'un** to go and meet somebody
rencontrer *vb* [**28**] to meet; **se rencontrer** to meet ▷ *Ils se sont rencontrés il y a deux ans.* They met two years ago.
rendez-vous *nm* ❶ appointment ▷ *J'ai rendez-vous chez le coiffeur.* I've got an appointment at the hairdresser's. ▷ *prendre rendez-vous avec quelqu'un* to make an appointment with somebody ❷ date ▷ *Tu sors ce soir? — Oui, j'ai un rendez-vous.* Are you going out tonight? — Yes, I've got a date.; **donner rendez-vous à quelqu'un** to arrange to meet somebody
rendre *vb* [**7**] ❶ to give back ▷ *J'ai rendu ses CD à Christine.* I've given Christine her CDs back. ❷ to take back ▷ *J'ai rendu mes livres à la bibliothèque.* I've taken my books back to the library.; **rendre quelqu'un célèbre** to make somebody famous; **se rendre** to give oneself up ▷ *Le meurtrier s'est rendu à la police.* The murderer gave himself up to the police.; **se rendre compte de quelque chose** to realize something
renfermé *nm* **sentir le renfermé** to smell stuffy
renifler *vb* [**28**] to sniff
renne *nm* reindeer
renommé, e *adj* renowned
renoncer *vb* [**12**] **renoncer à** to give up ▷ *Ils ont renoncé à leur projet.* They've given up their plan.; **renoncer à faire quelque chose** to give up the idea of doing something
renouvelable *adj* renewable
renouveler *vb* [**4**] *(passport, contract)* to renew; **se renouveler** to happen again ▷ *J'espère que ça ne se renouvellera pas.* I hope that won't happen again.
renseignement *nm* piece of information; **les renseignements** **(1)** information ▷ *Il m'a donné des renseignements.* He gave me some information. **(2)** information desk **(3)** directory inquiries
renseigner *vb* [**28**] **renseigner quelqu'un sur quelque chose** to give somebody information about something; **Est-ce que je peux vous renseigner?** Can I help you?; **se renseigner** to find out
rentable *adj* profitable
rentrée *nf* **la rentrée (des classes)** the start of the new school year
rentrer *vb* [**68**] ❶ to come in ▷ *Rentre, tu vas prendre froid.* Come in, you'll catch cold. ❷ to go in ▷ *Elle est rentrée dans le magasin.* She went into the shop. ❸ to get home ▷ *Je suis rentré à sept heures hier soir.* I got home at 7 o'clock last night. ❹ to put away ▷ *Tu as rentré la voiture?* Have you put the car away?; **rentrer dans** to crash into ▷ *Sa voiture est rentrée dans un arbre.* He crashed into a tree.; **rentrer dans l'ordre** to get back to normal

renverse *nf* **tomber à la renverse** to fall backwards

renverser *vb* [**28**] ❶ to knock over ▷ *J'ai renversé mon verre.* I knocked my glass over. ❷ to knock down ▷ *Elle a été renversée par une voiture.* She was knocked down by a car. ❸ to spill ▷ *Il a renversé de l'eau partout.* He has spilt water everywhere.; **se renverser** *(glass, vase)* to fall over

renvoyer *vb* [**33**] ❶ to send back ▷ *Je t'ai renvoyé ton courrier.* I've sent your mail back to you. ❷ to dismiss ▷ *On a renvoyé deux employés.* Two employees have been dismissed.

répandu, e *adj* common; **du vin répandu sur la table** wine spilt on the table; **des papiers répandus sur le sol** papers scattered over the floor

réparateur *nm* repairman

réparation *nf* repair

réparer *vb* [**28**] to repair

repartir *vb* [**57**] to set off again ▷ *Il était là tout à l'heure, mais il est reparti.* He was here a moment ago, but he's gone again.; **repartir à zéro** to start again from scratch

repas *nm* meal; **le repas de midi** lunch; **le repas du soir** dinner

repassage *nm* ironing

repasser *vb* [**28**] ❶ to come back ▷ *Je repasserai demain.* I'll come back tomorrow. ❷ to go back ▷ *Je dois repasser au magasin.* I've got to go back to the shop. ❸ to iron ▷ *J'ai repassé ma chemise.* I've ironed my shirt. ❹ to resit ▷ *Elle doit repasser son examen.* She's got to resit her exam.

repérer *vb* [**34**] to spot ▷ *J'ai repéré deux fautes.* I spotted two mistakes.; **se repérer** to find one's way around ▷ *J'ai du mal à me repérer de nuit.* I have difficulty finding my way around when it's dark.

répertoire *nm* directory

répéter *vb* [**34**] ❶ to repeat ▷ *Elle répète toujours la même chose.* She keeps repeating the same thing. ❷ to rehearse ▷ *Les acteurs répètent une scène.* The actors are rehearsing a scene.; **se répéter** to happen again ▷ *J'espère que cela ne se répétera pas!* I hope this won't happen again!

répétition *nf* ❶ repetition; **des grèves à répétition** repeated strikes ❷ rehearsal; **la répétition générale** the dress rehearsal

répondeur *nm* answering machine

répondre *vb* [**69**] to answer ▷ *répondre à quelqu'un* to answer somebody

réponse *nf* answer

reportage *nm* ❶ report ❷ story

reporter *nm* reporter

repos *nm* rest

reposer *vb* [**28**] to put back down ▷ *Elle a reposé son verre sur la table.* She put her glass back down on the table.; **se reposer** to have a rest ▷ *Tu pourras te reposer demain.* You'll be able to have a rest tomorrow.

repousser *vb* [**28**] ❶ to grow again ▷ *Ses cheveux ont repoussé.* Her hair has grown again. ❷ to postpone ▷ *Le voyage est repoussé.* The trip's been postponed.

reprendre *vb* [**65**] ❶ to take back ▷ *Il a repris son livre.* He's taken his book back. ❷ to go back to ▷ *Elle a repris le travail.* She went back to work. ❸ to start again ▷ *La réunion reprendra à deux heures.* The meeting will start again at 2 o'clock.; **reprendre du pain** to take more bread; **reprendre la route** to set off again; **reprendre son souffle** to get one's breath back

représentant *nm* rep

représentation *nf* performance

représenter *vb* [**28**] to show ▷ *Le tableau représente un enfant et un chat.* The picture shows a child with a cat.; **se représenter** to arise again ▷ *Cette occasion ne se représentera pas.* This opportunity won't arise again.

reproche *nm* **faire des reproches à quelqu'un** to reproach somebody

reprocher *vb* [**28**] **reprocher quelque chose à quelqu'un** to reproach somebody for something; **Qu'est-ce que tu lui reproches?** What have you got against him?

reproduction *nf* reproduction

reproduire *vb* [**23**] to reproduce; **se reproduire** to happen again ▷ *Je te promets que ça ne se reproduira pas!* I promise it won't happen again!

républicain, e *adj* republican

république *nf* republic

répugnant, e *adj* repulsive

réputation *nf* reputation

requin *nm* shark

RER *nm* Greater Paris high-speed train service

réseau (*pl* **réseaux**) *nm* network

réservation *nf* reservation

réserve *nf* stock; **mettre quelque chose en réserve** to put something aside

réservé, e *adj* reserved

réserver *vb* [**28**] ❶ to reserve ▷ *Je voudrais réserver une table.* I'd like to reserve a table. ❷ to book ▷ *Nous avons réservé une chambre.* We've booked a room. ❸ to save ▷ *Je t'ai réservé une part de gâteau.* I've saved you a piece of cake.

réservoir *nm* petrol tank

résidence *nf* block of flats; **une résidence secondaire** a second home

résistant, e *adj* ❶ hard-wearing ❷ robust

résister *vb* [**28**] to resist

résolu, e *adj* **Le problème est résolu.** The problem's solved.

résoudre *vb* [**70**] to solve

respect *nm* respect

respecter *vb* [**28**] to respect

respiration *nf* breathing

respirer *vb* [**28**] to breathe

responsabilité *nf* responsibility

responsable *adj* responsible ▷ *être responsable de quelque chose* to be responsible for something ▶ *nmf* ❶ person in charge ❷ person responsible

ressembler *vb* [**28**] **ressembler à** (**1**) to look like ▷ *Elle ne ressemble pas* *à sa sœur.* She doesn't look like her sister. **(2)** to be like ▷ *Ça ressemble à un conte de fées.* It's like a fairy tale.; **se ressembler (1)** to look alike ▷ *Les deux frères ne se ressemblent pas.* The two brothers don't look alike. **(2)** to be alike ▷ *Ces deux pays ne se ressemblent pas.* These two countries aren't alike.

ressort *nm (metal)* spring

ressortir *vb* **[79]** to go out again

restaurant *nm* restaurant

reste *nm* rest; **un reste de poulet** some left-over chicken; **les restes** the left-overs

rester *vb* **[71]** ❶ to stay ▷ *Je reste à la maison ce week-end.* I'm staying at home this weekend. ❷ to be left ▷ *Il reste du pain.* There's some bread left.; **Il ne me reste plus qu'à ...** I've just got to ... ▷ *Il ne me reste plus qu'à ranger mes affaires.* I've just got to put my things away.; **Restons-en là.** Let's leave it at that.

résultat *nm* result

résumé *nm* summary

résumer *vb* **[28]** to summarize

> Be careful! **résumer** does not mean **to resume**.

se **rétablir** *vb* **[38]** to get well

retard *nm* delay; **avoir du retard** to be late; **être en retard de deux heures** to be two hours late; **prendre du retard** to be delayed

retarder *vb* **[28]** ❶ to be slow ▷ *Ma montre retarde.* My watch is slow. ❷ to put back ▷ *Je dois retarder la pendule d'une heure.* I've got to put the clock back an hour.; **être retardé** to be delayed

retenir *vb* **[83]** ❶ to remember ▷ *Tu as retenu leur adresse?* Do you remember their address? ❷ to book ▷ *J'ai retenu une chambre à l'hôtel.* I've booked a room at the hotel.; **retenir son souffle** to hold one's breath

retenu, e *adj* ❶ reserved ▷ *Cette place est retenue.* This seat is reserved. ❷ held up

retenue *nf* detention

retirer *vb* **[28]** ❶ to withdraw ▷ *Elle a retiré de l'argent.* She withdrew some money. ❷ to take off ▷ *Il a retiré son pull.* He took off his sweater.

retour *nm* return; **être de retour** to be back

retourner *vb* **[72]** ❶ to go back ▷ *Est-ce que tu es retourné à Londres?* Have you been back to London? ❷ to turn over ▷ *Elle a retourné la crêpe.* She turned the pancake over.; **se retourner (1)** to turn round ▷ *Janet s'est retournée.* Janet turned round. **(2)** to turn over ▷ *La voiture s'est retournée.* The car turned over.

retraite *nf* **être à la retraite** to be retired; **prendre sa retraite** to retire

retraité, e *adj* retired

retraité *nm* pensioner

retraitée *nf* pensioner

rétrécir *vb* **[38]** to shrink ▷ *Son pull a rétréci au lavage.* Her sweater shrank in the wash.; **se rétrécir** to get narrower ▷ *La rue se rétrécit.* The street gets narrower.

retrouver *vb* [**28**] ❶ to find ▷ *J'ai retrouvé mon portefeuille.* I've found my wallet. ❷ to meet up with ▷ *Je te retrouve au café à trois heures.* I'll meet you at the café at 3 o'clock.; **se retrouver (1)** to meet up ▷ *Ils se sont retrouvés devant le cinéma.* They met up in front of the cinema. **(2)** to find one's way around ▷ *Je n'arrive pas à me retrouver.* I can't find my way around.

rétroviseur *nm* rear-view mirror

réunion *nf* meeting

se **réunir** *vb* [**38**] to meet ▷ *Ils se sont réunis à cinq heures.* They met at 5 o'clock.

réussi, e *adj* successful; **être réussi** to be a success

réussir *vb* [**38**] to be successful ▷ *Tous ses enfants ont très bien réussi.* All her children are very successful.; **réussir à faire quelque chose** to succeed in doing something; **réussir à un examen** to pass an exam

réussite *nf* success

revanche *nf* return match; **prendre sa revanche** to get one's own back; **en revanche** on the other hand

rêve *nm* dream; **de rêve** fantastic

réveil *nm* alarm clock; **mettre le réveil à huit heures** to set the alarm for eight o'clock

réveille-matin (*pl* **réveille-matin**) *nm* alarm clock

réveiller *vb* [**28**] to wake up ▷ *réveiller quelqu'un* to wake somebody up; **se réveiller** to wake up

réveillon *nm* **le réveillon du Premier de l'an** New Year's Eve celebrations; **le réveillon de Noël** Christmas Eve celebrations

réveillonner *vb* [**28**] ❶ to celebrate New Year's Eve ❷ to celebrate Christmas Eve

revenir *vb* [**73**] to come back ▷ *Reviens vite!* Come back soon!; **Ça revient au même.** It comes to the same thing.; **Ça revient cher.** It costs a lot.; **Je n'en reviens pas!** I can't get over it!; **revenir sur ses pas** to retrace one's steps

revenu *nm* income

rêver *vb* [**28**] to dream; **rêver de quelque chose** to dream of something

réverbère *nm* street lamp

revers *nm* ❶ backhand ❷ *(of jacket)* lapel; **le revers de la médaille** the other side of the coin

revient *vb see* **revenir**

réviser *vb* [**28**] ❶ to revise ▷ *Je dois réviser mon anglais.* I've got to revise my English. ❷ to service ▷ *Je dois faire réviser ma voiture.* I must get my car serviced.

révision *nf* revision

revoir *vb* [**92**] ❶ to see again ▷ *J'ai revu Sophie hier soir.* I saw Sophie again last night. ❷ to revise ▷ *Il est en train de revoir sa géographie.* He's revising his geography.; **au revoir** goodbye

révolution *nf* revolution

revolver *nm* revolver
revue *nf* magazine
rez-de-chaussée *nm* ground floor
Rhin *nm* Rhine
rhinocéros *nm* rhinoceros
Rhône *nm* Rhone
rhubarbe *nf* rhubarb
rhum *nm* rum
rhume *nm* cold; **un rhume de cerveau** a head cold; **le rhume des foins** hay fever
ri *vb see* **rire**; **Nous avons bien ri.** We had a good laugh.
riche *adj* ❶ well-off ❷ rich
rideau (*pl* **rideaux**) *nm* curtain
ridicule *adj* ridiculous
rien *pron* ❶ nothing ▷ *Qu'est-ce que tu as acheté? — Rien.* What have you bought? — Nothing. ▷ *Ça n'a rien à voir.* It has nothing to do with it.; **rien d'intéressant** nothing interesting; **rien d'autre** nothing else; **rien du tout** nothing at all ❷ anything ▷ *Il n'a rien dit.* He didn't say anything.; **rien que (1)** just ▷ *rien que pour lui faire plaisir* just to please him ▷ *Rien que la voiture coûte un million.* The car alone costs a million. **(2)** nothing but ▷ *rien que la vérité* nothing but the truth; **De rien!** Not at all! ▷ *Merci beaucoup! — De rien!* Thank you very much! — Not at all!
▶ *nm* **pour un rien** at the slightest thing ▷ *Il se met en colère pour un rien.* He loses his temper over the slightest thing.; **en un rien de temps** in no time at all
rigoler *vb* [**28**] *(informal)* ❶ to laugh ▷ *Elle a rigolé en le voyant tomber.* She laughed when she saw him fall. ❷ to have fun ▷ *On a bien rigolé hier soir.* We had good fun last night. ❸ to be joking ▷ *Ne te fâche pas, je rigolais.* Don't get upset, I was only joking.; **pour rigoler** for a laugh
rigolo (*f* **rigolote**) *adj (informal)* funny
rincer *vb* [**12**] to rinse
rire *vb* [**74**] to laugh ▷ *Nous avons bien ri.* We had a good laugh.; **pour rire** for a laugh
▶ *nm* laughter
risque *nm* ❶ risk ❷ danger
risqué, e *adj* risky
risquer *vb* [**28**] to risk; **Ça ne risque rien.** It's quite safe.; **Il risque de se tuer.** He could get himself killed.; **C'est ce qui risque de se passer.** That's what might well happen.
rivage *nm* shore
rivière *nf* river
riz *nm* rice
RN *nf (= route nationale)* A road
robe *nf* dress; **une robe de soirée** an evening dress; **une robe de mariée** a wedding dress; **une robe de chambre** a dressing gown
robinet *nm* tap
robot *nm* robot
roche *nf (stone)* rock
rocher *nm* rock
rock *nm (music)* rock
rôder *vb* [**28**] to loiter ▷ *Il y a un homme louche qui rôde autour de l'école.* There's a suspicious man loitering around the school.

a b c d e f g h i j k l m n o p q r s t u v w x y z

rognons *nmpl (in cooking)* kidneys
roi *nm* king; **le jour des Rois** Twelfth Night
rôle *nm* role
rollers *nmpl* Rollerblades®
romain, e *adj* Roman
roman *nm* novel; **un roman policier** a detective story; **un roman d'espionnage** a spy story
romancier *nm* novelist
romantique *adj* romantic
rompre *vb* [75] ❶ to split up ▷ *Paul et Justine ont rompu.* Paul and Justine have split up. ❷ to break off ▷ *Ils ont rompu leurs fiançailles.* They've broken off their engagement.
ronces *nfpl* brambles
ronchonner *vb* [28] *(informal)* to grouse
rond, e *adj* ❶ round ▷ *La Terre est ronde.* The earth is round.; **ouvrir des yeux ronds** to stare in amazement ❷ chubby ▷ *Il a les joues rondes.* He has chubby cheeks. ❸ drunk
▶ *nm* circle; **en rond** in a circle; **tourner en rond** to go round in circles; **Je n'ai plus un rond.** *(informal)* I haven't a penny left.
rondelle *nf* slice
rond-point (*pl* **ronds-points**) *nm* roundabout
ronfler *vb* [28] to snore
rosbif *nm* roast beef
rose *nf* rose
▶ *adj* pink
rosé *nm* rosé (wine)
rosier *nm* rosebush
rôti *nm* roast meat; **un rôti de bœuf** a joint of beef
rôtir *vb* [38] to roast ▷ *faire rôtir quelque chose* to roast something
roue *nf* wheel ▷ *une roue de secours* a spare wheel
rouge *adj* red
▶ *nm* ❶ red ▷ *Le rouge est ma couleur préférée.* Red is my favourite colour. ❷ red wine ▷ *un verre de rouge* a glass of red wine; **passer au rouge** **(1)** to change to red ▷ *Le feu est passé au rouge.* The light changed to red. **(2)** to go through a red light ▷ *Jean-Pierre est passé au rouge.* Jean-Pierre went through a red light.; **un rouge à lèvres** a lipstick

Word for word, this means 'red for lips'.

rougeole *nf* measles
rougir *vb* [38] ❶ to blush ▷ *Il a rougi en me voyant.* He blushed when he saw me. ❷ to flush ▷ *Il a rougi de colère.* He flushed with anger.
rouille *nf* rust
rouillé, e *adj* rusty
rouiller *vb* [28] to go rusty
roulant, e *adj* **un fauteuil roulant** a wheelchair; **une table roulante** a trolley
rouleau (*pl* **rouleaux**) *nm* roll; **un rouleau à pâtisserie** a rolling pin
rouler *vb* [28] ❶ to go ▷ *Le train roulait à 250 km/h.* The train was going at 250 km an hour. ❷ to drive ▷ *Il a roulé sans s'arrêter.* He drove without stopping. ❸ to roll ▷ *Gilles a roulé une cigarette.* Gilles rolled a cigarette. ❹ to roll up ▷ *Il a roulé le*

tapis. He rolled the carpet up. ❺ to con ▷ *Ils se sont fait rouler. (informal)* They were conned.; **Alors, ça roule?** *(informal)* How's it going?

Roumanie *nf* Romania

rouquin *nm (informal)* redhead

rousse *adj f see* **roux**
▶ *nf* redhead

route *nf* ❶ road; **une route nationale** an A road ❷ way ▷ *Je ne connais pas la route.* I don't know the way.; **Il y a trois heures de route.** It's a 3-hour journey.; **en route** on the way; **mettre en route** to start up; **se mettre en route** to set off

routier *nm* ❶ lorry driver ❷ transport café

routine *nf* routine

roux (*f* **rousse**) *adj* ❶ red ❷ red-haired
▶ *nm/f* redhead

royal, e (*mpl* **royaux**) *adj* royal

royaume *nm* kingdom; **le Royaume-Uni** the United Kingdom

ruban *nm* ribbon; **le ruban adhésif** adhesive tape

rubéole *nf* German measles

ruche *nf* hive

rudement *adv (informal)* terribly

rue *nf* street

ruelle *nf* alley

rugby *nm* rugby

rugueux (*f* **rugueuse**) *adj* rough

ruine *nf* ruin

ruiner *vb* [**28**] to ruin

ruisseau (*pl* **ruisseaux**) *nm* stream

rumeur *nf* rumour

rupture *nf* break-up

ruse *nf* trickery

rusé, e *adj* cunning

russe *adj, nmf* Russian ▷ *Il parle russe.* He speaks Russian.; **un Russe** *(man)* a Russian; **une Russe** *(woman)* a Russian; **les Russes** the Russians

Russie *nf* Russia

rythme *nm* ❶ rhythm ❷ pace

S

s' *pron see* **se**

sa *adj f* ❶ his ▷ *Paul est allé voir sa grand-mère.* Paul's gone to see his grandmother. ❷ her ▷ *Elle a embrassé sa mère.* She kissed her mother.

sable *nm* sand; **des sables mouvants** quicksand

sablé *nm* shortbread biscuit

sabot *nm* ❶ clog ❷ *(of horse)* hoof

sac *nm* bag; **un sac de voyage** a travel bag; **un sac de couchage** a sleeping bag; **un sac à main** a handbag; **un sac à dos** a rucksack; **voyager sac au dos** to go backpacking

sachet *nm (of sugar, coffee)* sachet; **du potage en sachet** packet soup; **un sachet de thé** a tea bag

sacoche *nf* bag; **une sacoche de bicyclette** a saddlebag

sacré, e *adj* sacred

sage *adj* ❶ *(well-behaved)* good ❷ *(sensible)* wise

sagesse *nf* wisdom; **une dent de sagesse** a wisdom tooth

Sagittaire *nm* Sagittarius

saignant, e *adj (meat)* rare

saigner *vb* [**28**] to bleed; **saigner du nez** to have a nosebleed

sain, e *adj* healthy; **sain et sauf** safe and sound

saint, e *adj* holy; **la Sainte Vierge** the Blessed Virgin; **le vendredi saint** Good Friday; **la Saint-Sylvestre** New Year's Eve
▶ *nm* saint

sainte *nf* saint

sais *vb see* **savoir**; **Je ne sais pas.** I don't know.

saisir *vb* [**38**] to take hold of; **saisir l'occasion de faire quelque chose** to seize the opportunity to do something

saison *nf* season; **la saison des vendanges** harvest time

sait *vb see* **savoir**; **Il sait que ...** He knows that ...; **On ne sait jamais!** You never know!

salade *nf* ❶ lettuce ❷ salad

saladier *nm* salad bowl

salaire *nm* salary

salami *nm* salami

salarié *nm* salaried employee

salariée *nf* salaried employee

sale *adj* dirty

salé, e *adj* ❶ salty ❷ salted ❸ savoury

saler *vb* [**28**] to put salt in ▷ *J'ai*

oublié de saler la soupe. I forgot to put salt in the soup.
saleté *nf* dirt; **faire des saletés** to make a mess
salir *vb* [**38**] **salir quelque chose** to get something dirty; **se salir** to get oneself dirty
salle *nf* ❶ room ❷ audience ❸ *(in hospital)* ward; **la salle à manger** the dining room; **la salle de séjour** the living room; **la salle de bains** the bathroom; **la salle d'attente** the waiting room; **une salle de classe** a classroom; **la salle des professeurs** the staffroom; **une salle de concert** a concert hall; **la salle d'embarquement** the departure lounge
salon *nm* lounge; **un salon de thé** a tearoom; **un salon de coiffure** a hair salon; **un salon de beauté** a beauty salon
salopette *nf* ❶ dungarees ❷ overalls
saluer *vb* [**28**] **saluer quelqu'un** **(1)** to say hello to somebody ▷ *Je l'ai croisé dans la rue et il m'a salué.* I met him in the street and he said hello. **(2)** to say goodbye to somebody ▷ *Il nous a salués et il est parti.* He said goodbye and left.
salut *excl (informal)* hi!
salutation *nf* greeting
samedi *nm* ❶ Saturday ▷ *Aujourd'hui, nous sommes samedi.* It's Saturday today. ❷ on Saturday; **le samedi** on Saturdays; **tous les samedis** every Saturday; **samedi dernier** last Saturday; **samedi prochain** next Saturday
SAMU *nm* ambulance service
sandale *nf* sandal
sandwich *nm* sandwich
sang *nm* blood; **en sang** covered in blood
sang-froid *nm* **garder son sang-froid** to keep calm; **perdre son sang-froid** to lose one's cool; **faire quelque chose de sang-froid** to do something in cold blood
sanglier *nm* wild boar
sanglot *nm* **éclater en sanglots** to burst into tears
sans *prep* without ▷ *Elle est venue sans son frère.* She came without her brother.; **un pull sans manches** a sleeveless sweater
sans-abri (*pl* **sans-abri**) *nmf* homeless person
sans-gêne *adj* inconsiderate
santé *nf* health; **Santé!** Cheers!
saoudien (*f* **saoudienne**) *adj, nm/f* Saudi Arabian; **un Saoudien** *(man)* a Saudi Arabian; **une Saoudienne** *(woman)* a Saudi Arabian
sapeur-pompier (*pl* **sapeurs-pompiers**) *nm* firefighter; **les sapeurs-pompiers** the fire brigade
sapin *nm* fir tree; **un sapin de Noël** a Christmas tree
Sardaigne *nf* Sardinia
sardine *nf* sardine
satellite *nm* satellite
satisfaire *vb* [**36**] to satisfy
satisfaisant, e *adj* satisfactory
satisfait, e *adj* satisfied
sauce *nf* ❶ sauce ❷ gravy

saucisse *nf* sausage
saucisson *nm* salami
sauf *prep* except ▷ *Tout le monde est venu sauf lui.* Everyone came except him.; **sauf si** unless; **sauf que** except that
saumon *nm* salmon
saur *adj m* **un hareng saur** a kipper
saut *nm* jump; **le saut en longueur** the long jump; **le saut en hauteur** the high jump; **le saut à la perche** the pole vault; **le saut à l'élastique** bungee jumping; **un saut périlleux** a somersault
sauter *vb* [**28**] to jump ▷ *Nous avons sauté par-dessus la barrière.* We jumped over the gate.; **sauter à la corde** to skip *(with a rope)*; **faire sauter quelque chose** to blow something up
sauterelle *nf* grasshopper
sauvage *adj* ❶ wild ▷ *les animaux sauvages* wild animals; **une région sauvage** an unspoiled area ❷ shy ▷ *Il est sauvage.* He's shy.
sauvegarder *vb* [**28**] *(file on computer)* to save
sauver *vb* [**28**] to save; **se sauver (1)** to run away ▷ *Il s'est sauvé à toutes jambes.* He ran away as fast as he could. **(2)** *(informal)* to be off ▷ *Allez, je me sauve!* Right, I'm off.
sauvetage *nm* rescue
sauveur *nm* saviour
savais, savait *vb see* **savoir**; **Je ne savais pas qu'il devait venir.** I didn't know he was going to come.
savant *nm* scientist
savent *vb see* **savoir**; **Ils ne savent pas ce qu'ils veulent.** They don't know what they want.
saveur *nf* flavour
savez *vb see* **savoir**; **Est-ce que vous savez où elle habite?** Do you know where she lives?
savoir *vb* [**76**] to know ▷ *Je ne sais pas où il est allé.* I don't know where he's gone.; **Tu sais nager?** Can you swim?
savon *nm* soap
savonnette *nf* bar of soap
savons *vb see* **savoir**
savoureux (*f* **savoureuse**) *adj* tasty
saxo *nm (informal)* ❶ sax ❷ sax player
▶ *nf (informal)* sax player
scandale *nm* scandal; **faire scandale** to cause a scandal
scandaleux (*f* **scandaleuse**) *adj* outrageous
Scandinave *nmf* Scandinavian
scandinave *adj* Scandinavian
Scandinavie *nf* Scandinavia
scarabée *nm* beetle
scène *nf* scene ▷ *une scène d'amour* a love scene ▷ *la scène du crime* the scene of the crime ▷ *Il m'a fait une scène.* He made a scene.; **une scène de ménage** a domestic row
sceptique *adj* sceptical
schéma *nm* diagram
schématique *adj* **l'explication schématique d'une théorie** the broad outline of a theory; **Cette interprétation est un peu trop schématique.** This interpretation is a bit oversimplified.

scie *nf* saw; **une scie à métaux** a hacksaw
science *nf* science; **Elle est forte en sciences.** She is good at science.; **les sciences physiques** physics; **les sciences naturelles** biology; **les sciences économiques** economics; **les sciences po** *(informal)* politics
science-fiction *nf* science fiction
scientifique *adj* scientific
▸ *nmf* ❶ scientist ❷ science student
scier *vb* [**19**] to saw
scolaire *adj* school ▹ *l'année scolaire* the school year ▹ *les vacances scolaires* the school holidays
Scorpion *nm* Scorpio
Scotch® *nm* adhesive tape
scrupule *nm* scruple
sculpter *vb* [**28**] to sculpt
sculpteur *nm* sculptor
sculpture *nf* sculpture
SDF *nmf* (*= sans domicile fixe*) homeless person; **les SDF** the homeless
se *pron*

> **se** forms part of reflexive constructions.

❶ himself ▹ *Il se regarde dans la glace.* He's looking at himself in the mirror. ❷ herself ▹ *Elle se regarde dans la glace.* She's looking at herself in the mirror. ❸ itself ▹ *Le chien s'est fait mal.* The dog hurt itself. ❹ oneself ▹ *se regarder dans une glace* to look at oneself in a mirror ❺ themselves ▹ *Ils se sont regardés dans la glace.* They looked at themselves in the mirror.

> **se** changes to **s'** before a vowel and most words beginning with 'h'.

▹ *Elle s'admire dans sa nouvelle robe.* She's admiring herself in her new dress. ❻ each other ▹ *Ils s'aiment.* They love each other.
séance *nf* ❶ session ❷ *(at the cinema)* showing
seau (*pl* **seaux**) *nm* bucket
sec (*f* **sèche**) *adj* ❶ dry ❷ dried
sèche-cheveux (*pl* **sèche-cheveux**) *nm* hair dryer
sèche-linge (*pl* **sèche-linge**) *nm* tumble dryer
sécher *vb* [**34**] ❶ to dry ❷ to be stumped ▹ *J'ai complètement séché à l'interrogation de maths. (informal)* I was completely stumped in the maths test.; **se sécher** to dry oneself ▹ *Sèche-toi avec cette serviette.* Dry yourself with this towel.
sécheresse *nf* drought
séchoir *nm* dryer
second, e *adj* second ▹ *Il est arrivé second.* He came second.
second *nm* second floor ▹ *Elle habite au second.* She lives on the second floor.
secondaire *adj* secondary; **des effets secondaires** side effects
seconde *nf* ❶ second ❷ year 11 ❸ second class
secouer *vb* [**28**] to shake ▹ *secouer la tête* to shake one's head
secourir *vb* [**16**] to rescue
secourisme *nm* first aid

secours *nm* help ▷ *Au secours!* Help!; **les premiers secours** first aid; **une sortie de secours** an emergency exit; **la roue de secours** the spare wheel

secret (*f* **secrète**) *adj* secret ▶ *nm* secret

secrétaire *nm* ❶ secretary ❷ writing desk ▶ *nf* secretary

secrétariat *nm* secretary's office

secteur *nm* sector

section *nf (of school)* department

sécu *nf (informal)* Social Security

sécurité *nf* ❶ safety; **être en sécurité** to be safe; **la sécurité routière** road safety; **une ceinture de sécurité** a seatbelt ❷ security; **la sécurité sociale** Social Security; **la sécurité de l'emploi** job security

séduisant, e *adj* attractive

seigle *nm* rye

seigneur *nm* lord; **le Seigneur** the Lord

sein *nm* breast; **au sein de** within

seize *num* sixteen ▷ *Elle a seize ans.* She's sixteen.; **le seize février** the sixteenth of February

seizième *adj* sixteenth

séjour *nm* stay ▷ *J'ai fait un séjour d'une semaine en Italie.* I stayed in Italy for a week.

sel *nm* salt

sélectionner *vb* [**28**] to select

self *nm (informal)* self-service restaurant

self-service *nm* self-service restaurant

selle *nf* saddle

selon *prep* according to ▷ *selon lui* according to him

semaine *nf* week; **en semaine** on weekdays

semblable *adj* similar

semblant *nm* **faire semblant de faire quelque chose** to pretend to do something

sembler *vb* [**28**] to seem ▷ *Le temps semble s'améliorer.* The weather seems to be improving.

semelle *nf* ❶ sole ❷ insole

semoule *nf* semolina

sens *nm* ❶ sense ▷ *avoir le sens de l'humour* to have a sense of humour; **le bon sens** common sense ❷ direction; **sens dessus dessous** upside down; **un sens interdit** a one-way street; **un sens unique** a one-way street

sensation *nf* feeling

sensationnel (*f* **sensationnelle**) *adj* sensational

sensé, e *adj* sensible

sensible *adj* ❶ sensitive ❷ visible

> Be careful! The French word **sensible** does not mean **sensible**.

sensiblement *adv* ❶ visibly ❷ approximately

sentence *nf (judgement)* sentence

sentier *nm* path

sentiment *nm* feeling

sentimental, e (*mpl* **sentimentaux**) *adj* sentimental

sentir *vb* [**77**] ❶ to smell ▷ *Ça sent bon.* That smells good. ▷ *Ça sent mauvais.* It smells bad. ❷ to smell of ▷ *Ça sent les frites ici.* It smells of chips in here. ❸ to taste ▷ *Tu sens l'ail dans le rôti?* Can you taste the garlic in the roast? ❹ to feel ▷ *Ça t'a fait mal? — Non, je n'ai rien senti.* Did it hurt? — No, I didn't feel a thing. ▷ *Je ne me sens pas bien.* I don't feel well.; **Il ne peut pas la sentir.** *(informal)* He can't stand her.

séparé, e *adj* separated

séparément *adv* separately

séparer *vb* [**28**] to separate; **se séparer** to separate

sept *num* seven ▷ *Elle a sept ans.* She's seven.; **le sept février** the seventh of February

septembre *nm* September; **en septembre** in September

septième *adj* seventh

sera, serai, seras, serez *vb see* **être**; **Je serai de retour à dix heures.** I'll be back at 10 o'clock.

série *nf* series

sérieusement *adv* seriously

sérieux (*f* **sérieuse**) *adj* ❶ serious ❷ responsible ▶ *nm* **garder son sérieux** to keep a straight face; **prendre quelque chose au sérieux** to take something seriously; **prendre quelqu'un au sérieux** to take somebody seriously; **Il manque un peu de sérieux.** He's not very responsible.

seringue *nf* syringe

séronégatif (*f* **séronégative**) *adj* HIV-negative

serons, seront *vb see* **être**

séropositif (*f* **séropositive**) *adj* HIV-positive

serpent *nm* snake

serre *nf* greenhouse; **l'effet de serre** the greenhouse effect

serré, e *adj* ❶ tight ▷ *Mon pantalon est trop serré.* My trousers are too tight. ❷ close-fought

serrer *vb* [**28**] **Ce pantalon me serre trop.** These trousers are too tight for me.; **serrer la main à quelqu'un** to shake hands with somebody; **se serrer** to squeeze up ▷ *Serrez-vous un peu pour que je puisse m'asseoir.* Squeeze up a bit so I can sit down.; **serrer quelqu'un dans ses bras** to hug somebody; **'Serrer à droite'** 'Keep right'

serrure *nf* lock

sers, sert *vb see* **servir**

serveur *nm* ❶ *(in café)* waiter ❷ *(computer)* server

serveuse *nf* waitress

serviable *adj* helpful

service *nm* ❶ *(in restaurant)* service ▷ *Le service est compris.* Service is included.; **être de service** to be on duty; **hors service** out of order; **faire le service** *(at table)* to serve ❷ favour ▷ *rendre service à quelqu'un* to do somebody a favour ❸ *(sport)* serve ▷ *Il a un bon service.* He's got a good serve.; **le service militaire** military service; **les services sociaux** the social services; **les services secrets** the secret service

serviette *nf* ❶ towel; **une serviette hygiénique** a sanitary towel ❷ *(napkin)* serviette ❸ briefcase

servir *vb* [**78**] to serve ▷ *On vous sert?*

Are you being served?; **À toi de servir.** *(tennis)* It's your serve.; **se servir** to help oneself ▷ *Servez-vous.* Help yourself.; **se servir de** to use ▷ *Tu te sers souvent de ton vélo?* Do you use your bike a lot?; **servir à quelqu'un** to be of use to somebody; **À quoi ça sert?** What's it for?; **Ça ne sert à rien.** It's no use.

ses *adj pl* ❶ his ▷ *Il est parti voir ses grands-parents.* He's gone to see his grandparents. ❷ her ▷ *Delphine a oublié ses baskets.* Delphine's forgotten her trainers. ❸ its ▷ *la ville et ses alentours* the town and its surroundings

set *nm* ❶ *(on table)* tablemat ❷ *(in tennis)* set

seuil *nm* doorstep

seul, e *adj, adv* ❶ alone ❷ by oneself; **faire quelque chose tout seul** to do something by oneself; **se sentir seul** to feel lonely; **un seul livre** one book only; **Il reste une seule nectarine.** There's only one nectarine left.; **le seul livre que ...** the only book that ...; **le seul** the only one

seulement *adv* only; **non seulement ... mais** not only ... but

sévère *adj* strict

sexe *nm* sex

sexuel (*f* **sexuelle**) *adj* sexual

shampooing *nm* shampoo; **se faire un shampooing** to wash one's hair

short *nm* shorts

si *conj, adv* ❶ if ▷ *si tu veux* if you like ▷ *Je me demande si elle va venir.* I wonder if she'll come. ▷ *si seulement* if only ❷ so ▷ *Elle est si gentille.* She's so kind. ▷ *Tout s'est passé si vite.* Everything happened so fast. ❸ yes ▷ *Tu n'es pas allé à l'école habillé comme ça? — Si.* You didn't go to school dressed like that? — Yes I did.

▶ *nm* ❶ B ▷ *en si bémol* in B flat ❷ ti ▷ *la, si, do* la, ti, do

Sicile *nf* Sicily

sida *nm* AIDS

siècle *nm* century

siège *nm* ❶ *(in vehicle)* seat ❷ head office

sien *pron m* **le sien (1)** his **(2)** hers

sienne *pron f* **la sienne (1)** his **(2)** hers

siennes *pron fpl* **les siennes (1)** his **(2)** hers

siens *pron mpl* **les siens (1)** his **(2)** hers

sieste *nf* nap

siffler *vb* [**28**] to whistle

sifflet *nm* whistle

sigle *nm* acronym

signal (*pl* **signaux**) *nm* signal

signature *nf* signature

signe *nm* sign; **faire un signe de la main** to wave; **faire signe à quelqu'un d'entrer** to beckon to somebody to come in; **les signes du zodiaque** the signs of the zodiac

signer *vb* [**28**] to sign

signet *nm* bookmark

signification *nf* meaning

signifier *vb* [**19**] to mean ▷ *Que*

signifie ce mot? What does this word mean?
silence *nm* silence; **Silence!** Be quiet!
silencieux (*f* **silencieuse**) *adj* ❶ silent ❷ quiet
silhouette *nf* figure
similaire *adj* similar
simple *nm (tennis)* singles
▶ *adj* simple
simplement *adv* simply
simuler *vb* [**28**] to simulate
simultané, e *adj* simultaneous
sincère *adj* sincere
sincèrement *adv* sincerely
sincérité *nf* sincerity
singe *nm* monkey
singulier *nm* singular
sinistre *adj* sinister
sinon *conj* otherwise
sinusite *nf* sinusitis
sirène *nf* mermaid; **la sirène d'alarme** the fire alarm
sirop *nm* syrup; **le sirop contre la toux** cough mixture
site *nm* setting; **un site pittoresque** a beauty spot; **un site touristique** a tourist attraction; **un site archéologique** an archaeological site; **un site Web** a website
sitôt *adv* **sitôt dit, sitôt fait** no sooner said than done; **pas de sitôt** not for a long time
situation *nf* ❶ situation; **la situation de famille** marital status ❷ job
se **situer** *vb* [**28**] to be situated ▷ *Versailles se situe à l'ouest de Paris.* Versailles is situated to the west of Paris.; **bien situé** well situated
six *num* six ▷ *Il a six ans.* He's six.; **le six février** the sixth of February
sixième *adj* sixth ▷ *au sixième étage* on the sixth floor
▶ *nf* year 7 ▷ *Mon frère est en sixième.* My brother's in year 7.

In French secondary schools, years are counted from the **sixième** (youngest) to **première** and **terminale** (oldest).

ski *nm* ❶ ski ❷ skiing; **le ski de fond** cross-country skiing; **le ski nautique** water-skiing; **le ski de piste** downhill skiing; **le ski de randonnée** cross-country skiing
skier *vb* [**19**] to ski
skieur *nm* skier
slip *nm* pants; **un slip de bain** swimming trunks
Slovaquie *nf* Slovakia
Slovénie *nf* Slovenia
SMIC *nm* guaranteed minimum wage
smoking *nm* dinner suit
SNCF *nf* (= *Société nationale des chemins de fer français*) French railways
snob *adj* snobbish
sobre *adj* ❶ sober ❷ plain
social, e (*mpl* **sociaux**) *adj* social
socialiste *nmf* socialist
société *nf* ❶ society ❷ company
sociologie *nf* sociology
socquette *nf* ankle sock
sœur *nf* sister; **une bonne sœur** *(informal)* a nun
soi *pron* oneself ▷ *avoir confiance en*

a b c d e f g h i j k l m n o p q r s t u v w x y z

soi to have confidence in oneself; **rester chez soi** to stay at home; **Ça va de soi.** It goes without saying.

soi-disant (*f* **soi-disante**) *adv, adj* supposedly; **un soi-disant poète** a so-called poet

soie *nf* silk

soif *nf* thirst; **avoir soif** to be thirsty

soigner *vb* [**28**] *(ill person, animal)* to look after

soigneux (*f* **soigneuse**) *adj* careful

soi-même *pron* oneself ▷ *Il vaut mieux le faire soi-même.* It's better to do it oneself.

soin *nm* care; **prendre soin de quelque chose** to take care of something

soins *nmpl* treatment *sg*; **les premiers soins** first aid; **'aux bons soins de Madame Martin'** *(on letter)* 'c/o Mrs Martin'

soir *nm* evening; **à sept heures du soir** at 7 p.m.; **demain soir** tomorrow night; **hier soir** last night

soirée *nf* evening

sois *vb see* **être**; **Sois tranquille!** Don't worry!

soit *conj* **soit ..., soit ...** either ... or ... ▷ *soit lundi, soit mardi* either Monday or Tuesday

soixantaine *nf* about sixty; **Elle a la soixantaine.** She's in her sixties.

soixante *num* sixty; **soixante-dix** seventy; **soixante et onze** seventy-one; **soixante-quinze** seventy-five

soja *nm* soya; **des germes de soja** beansprouts

sol *nm* ❶ floor; **à même le sol** on the floor ❷ soil ❸ G ▷ *sol dièse* G sharp ❹ so ▷ *do, ré, mi, fa, sol ...* do, re, mi, fa, so ...

solaire *adj* solar; **la crème solaire** sun cream

soldat *nm* soldier

solde *nm* **être en solde** to be reduced; **les soldes** the sales ▷ *faire les soldes* to go round the sales

soldé, e *adj* **être soldé** to be reduced ▷ *un article soldé à dix euros* an item reduced to 10 euros

sole *nf (fish)* sole

soleil *nm* sun; **Il y a du soleil.** It's sunny.

solfège *nm* musical theory

solidaire *adj* **être solidaire de quelqu'un** to back somebody up

solide *adj* ❶ *(person)* strong ❷ *(object)* solid

solitaire *adj* solitary ▶ *nmf* loner

solitude *nf* loneliness

solution *nf* solution; **une solution de facilité** an easy way out

sombre *adj* dark

sommaire *nm* summary

somme *nf* sum ▶ *nm* nap

sommeil *nm* sleep; **avoir sommeil** to be sleepy

sommes *vb see* **être**; **Nous sommes en vacances.** We're on holiday.

sommet *nm* summit

somnifère *nm* sleeping pill

somptueux (*f* **somptueuse**) *adj*

sumptuous

son (*f* **sa**, *pl* **ses**) *adj* ❶ his ▷ *son père* his father ▷ *Il a perdu son portefeuille.* He's lost his wallet. ❷ her ▷ *son père* her father ▷ *Elle a perdu son sac.* She's lost her bag.
▶ *nm* ❶ sound ▷ *Le son n'est pas très bon.* The sound's not very good. ▷ *baisser le son* to turn the sound down ❷ bran; **le pain de son** brown bread

sondage *nm* survey; **un sondage d'opinion** an opinion poll

sonner *vb* [**28**] to ring ▷ *Le téléphone a sonné.* The phone rang.

sonnerie *nf* ❶ *(electric)* bell ❷ *(on mobile phone)* ringtone

sonnette *nf* bell

sono *nf (informal)* sound system

sont *vb see* **être**; **Ils sont en vacances.** They're on holiday.

sophistiqué, e *adj* sophisticated

sorcière *nf* witch

sort *nm* ❶ spell; **un mauvais sort** a curse ❷ fate; **tirer au sort** to draw lots

sorte *nf* sort

sortie *nf* way out; **la sortie de secours** the emergency exit; **Attends-moi à la sortie de l'école.** Meet me after school.

sortir *vb* [**79**] ❶ to go out ▷ *J'aime sortir.* I like going out. ❷ to come out ▷ *Elle sort de l'hôpital demain.* She's coming out of hospital tomorrow. ❸ to take out ▷ *Je vais sortir la voiture du garage.* I'll get the car out of the garage.; **sortir avec quelqu'un** to be going out with somebody ▷ *Tu sors avec lui?* Are you going out with him?; **s'en sortir** to manage ▷ *Ne t'en fais pas, tu t'en sortiras.* Don't worry, you'll manage OK.

sottise *nf* **Ne fais pas de sottises.** Don't do anything silly.; **Ne dis pas de sottises.** Don't talk nonsense.

sou *nm* **une machine à sous** a fruit machine; **Je n'ai pas un sou sur moi.** I haven't got a penny on me.; **être près de ses sous** *(informal)* to be tight-fisted

souci *nm* worry; **se faire du souci** to worry

soucieux (*f* **soucieuse**) *adj* worried

soucoupe *nf* saucer; **une soucoupe volante** a flying saucer

soudain, e *adj, adv* ❶ sudden ❷ suddenly

souffle *nm* breath; **à bout de souffle** out of breath

soufflé *nm* soufflé

souffler *vb* [**28**] ❶ to blow ▷ *Le vent soufflait fort.* The wind was blowing hard. ❷ to blow out ▷ *Souffle les bougies!* Blow out the candles!

souffrance *nf* suffering

souffrant, e *adj* unwell

souffrir *vb* [**54**] to be in pain

souhait *nm* wish ▷ *faire un souhait* to make a wish ▷ *Tous nos souhaits de réussite.* All our best wishes for your success. ▷ *les souhaits de bonne année* New Year's wishes; **Atchoum! — À tes souhaits!** Atchoo! — Bless you!

souhaiter *vb* [**28**] to wish

soûl, e *adj (informal)* drunk

soulager *vb* [**45**] to relieve

soulever *vb* [**43**] ❶ to lift ▷ *Je n'arrive pas à soulever cette valise.* I can't lift this suitcase. ❷ to raise

soulier *nm* shoe

souligner *vb* [**28**] to underline

soupçon *nm* suspicion; **un soupçon de** a dash of

soupçonner *vb* [**28**] to suspect

soupe *nf* soup

souper *vb* [**28**] to have supper

soupir *nm* sigh

soupirer *vb* [**28**] to sigh

souple *adj* ❶ *(person)* supple ❷ *(system)* flexible

source *nf* spring

sourcil *nm* eyebrow

sourd, e *adj* deaf

souriant, e *adj* cheerful

sourire *nm* smile ▸ *vb* [**74**] to smile ▷ *sourire à quelqu'un* to smile at somebody

souris *nf* mouse

sournois, e *adj* sly

sous *prep* under; **sous terre** underground; **sous la pluie** in the rain

sous-entendu, e *adj* implied ▸ *nm* insinuation

sous-marin, e *adj* underwater ▸ *nm* submarine

sous-sol *nm* basement

sous-titre *nm* subtitle

sous-titré, e *adj* with subtitles

soustraction *nf* subtraction

sous-vêtements *nmpl* underwear *sg*

soutenir *vb* [**83**] to support; **soutenir que** to maintain that

souterrain, e *adj* underground ▸ *nm* underground passage

soutien *nm* support

soutien-gorge (*pl* **soutiens-gorge**) *nm* bra

souvenir *nm* ❶ memory ❷ souvenir

se **souvenir** *vb* [**83**] **se souvenir de quelque chose** to remember something ▷ *Je ne me souviens pas de son adresse.* I can't remember his address.; **se souvenir que** to remember that ▷ *Je me souviens qu'il neigeait.* I remember it was snowing.

souvent *adv* often

soyez, soyons *vb see* **être**; **Soyons clairs!** Let's be clear about this!

SPA *nf* (= *Société protectrice des animaux*) RSPCA

spacieux (*f* **spacieuse**) *adj* spacious

spaghettis *nmpl* spaghetti *sg*

sparadrap *nm* sticking plaster

speaker *nm* announcer

spécial, e (*mpl* **spéciaux**) *adj* ❶ special; **les effets spéciaux** special effects ❷ peculiar

spécialement *adv* ❶ specially ❷ particularly

se **spécialiser** *vb* [**28**] **se spécialiser dans quelque chose** to specialize in something

spécialiste *nmf* specialist

spécialité *nf* speciality

spécifier *vb* [**19**] to specify

spectacle *nm* show

spectaculaire *adj* spectacular

spectateur *nm* ❶ member of the audience ❷ spectator
spéléologie *nf* potholing
spirituel (*f* **spirituelle**) *adj* ❶ spiritual ❷ witty
splendide *adj* magnificent
spontané, e *adj* spontaneous
sport *nm* sport; **les sports d'hiver** winter sports
▶ *adj* casual
sportif (*f* **sportive**) *adj* ❶ sporty ▷ *Elle est très sportive.* She's very sporty. ❷ sports ▷ *un club sportif* a sports club
sportif *nm* sportsman
sportive *nf* sportswoman
spot *nm* spotlight; **un spot publicitaire** a commercial break
square *nm* public gardens
squelette *nm* skeleton
stable *adj* stable; **un emploi stable** a steady job
stade *nm* stadium
stage *nm* ❶ training course ❷ work experience; **faire un stage en entreprise** to do a work placement

> Be careful! The French word **stage** does not mean **stage**.

stagiaire *nmf* trainee
▶ *adj* trainee ▷ *un professeur stagiaire* a trainee teacher
stand *nm* ❶ *(at exhibition)* stand ❷ *(at fair)* stall
standardiste *nmf* operator
station *nf* **une station de métro** an underground station; **une station de taxis** a taxi rank; **une station de ski** a ski resort
stationnement *nm* parking; **'stationnement interdit'** 'no parking'
stationner *vb* [**28**] to park
station-service (*pl* **stations-service**) *nf* service station
statistique *nf* statistic
steak *nm* steak; **un steak frites** steak and chips; **un steak haché** a hamburger
sténo *nf* shorthand
sténodactylo *nf* shorthand typist
stérile *adj* sterile
stimulant, e *adj* stimulating
stimuler *vb* [**28**] to stimulate
stop *nm* stop sign; **faire du stop** to hitchhike
stopper *vb* [**28**] to stop
store *nm* ❶ *(on window)* blind ❷ awning
strapontin *nm* foldaway seat
stratégie *nf* strategy
stratégique *adj* strategic
stressant, e *adj* stressful
stressé, e *adj* stressed out
strict, e *adj* ❶ *(person)* strict ❷ *(clothes)* severe; **le strict minimum** the bare minimum
strophe *nf* stanza
studieux (*f* **studieuse**) *adj* studious
studio *nm* ❶ studio flat ❷ studio
stupéfait, e *adj* astonished
stupéfiants *nmpl* narcotics
stupéfier *vb* [**19**] to astonish ▷ *Sa réponse m'a stupéfié.* I was astonished by his answer.
stupide *adj* stupid
style *nm* style
styliste *nmf* designer

stylo *nm* pen; **un stylo plume** a fountain pen; **un stylo bille** a ballpoint pen; **un stylo-feutre** a felt-tip pen
su *vb see* **savoir**; **Si j'avais su ...** If I'd known ...
subir *vb* [**38**] *(defeat)* to suffer; **subir une opération** to have an operation
subit, e *adj* sudden
subitement *adv* suddenly
subjectif (*f* **subjective**) *adj* subjective
subjonctif *nm* subjunctive
substituer *vb* [**28**] to substitute ▷ *substituer un mot à un autre* to substitute one word for another
subtil, e *adj* subtle
subvention *nf* subsidy
subventionner *vb* [**28**] to subsidize
succès *nm* success; **avoir du succès** to be successful
successeur *nm* successor
succursale *nf (of company)* branch
sucer *vb* [**12**] to suck
sucette *nf* lollipop
sucre *nm* sugar; **un sucre** a sugar lump; **du sucre en morceaux** lump sugar; **un sucre d'orge** a barley sugar; **du sucre en poudre** caster sugar; **du sucre glace** icing sugar
sucré, e *adj* ❶ sweet ❷ sweetened
sucreries *nfpl* sweet things
sucrier *nm* sugar bowl
sud *nm* south; **vers le sud** southwards; **au sud de Paris** south of Paris; **l'Amérique du Sud** South America; **le vent du sud** the south wind
▶ *adj* ❶ south; **le pôle Sud** the South Pole ❷ southern
sud-africain, e *adj* South African
sud-américain, e *adj* South American
sud-est *nm* south-east
sud-ouest *nm* south-west
Suède *nf* Sweden
suédois, e *adj, n* Swedish ▷ *Ils parlent suédois.* They speak Swedish.; **un Suédois** *(man)* a Swede; **une Suédoise** *(woman)* a Swede; **les Suédois** the Swedes
suer *vb* [**28**] to sweat
sueur *nf* sweat; **en sueur** sweating
suffire *vb* [**80**] to be enough ▷ *Tiens, voilà dix euros. Ça te suffit?* Here's 10 euros. Is that enough for you?; **Ça suffit!** That's enough!
suffisamment *adv* enough
suffisant, e *adj* ❶ sufficient ❷ smug
suffoquer *vb* [**28**] to suffocate
suggérer *vb* [**34**] to suggest
se **suicider** *vb* [**28**] to commit suicide
suis *vb see* **être**; **suivre**; **Je suis écossais.** I'm Scottish.; **Suis-moi.** Follow me.
Suisse *nf* Switzerland ▷ *la Suisse allemande* German-speaking Switzerland ▷ *la Suisse romande* French-speaking Switzerland
suisse *adj, nmf* Swiss ▷ *le franc suisse* the Swiss franc; **un Suisse** a Swiss man; **une Suisse** a Swiss woman
suite *nf* ❶ rest ❷ *(to book, film)*

sequel; **tout de suite** straightaway; **de suite** in succession; **par la suite** subsequently

suivant, e *adj* following; **Au suivant!** Next!

suivre *vb* [81] ❶ to follow ▷ *Il m'a suivie jusque chez moi.* He followed me home. ❷ to do ▷ *Je suis un cours d'anglais à la fac.* I'm doing an English course at college. ❸ to keep up ▷ *Il n'arrive pas à suivre en maths.* He can't keep up in maths.; **'à suivre'** 'to be continued'; **suivre un régime** to be on a diet

sujet *nm* subject; **au sujet de** about; **un sujet de conversation** a topic of conversation; **un sujet d'examen** an examination question; **un sujet de plaisanterie** something to joke about

super *adj* great
▶ *nm (petrol)* super

superficiel (*f* **superficielle**) *adj* superficial

superflu, e *adj* superfluous

supérieur, e *adj* ❶ upper ▷ *la lèvre supérieure* the upper lip ❷ superior ▷ *qualité supérieure* superior quality; **supérieur à** greater than
▶ *nm* superior

supermarché *nm* supermarket

superposé, e *adj* **des lits superposés** bunk beds

superstitieux (*f* **superstitieuse**) *adj* superstitious

suppléant *nm* supply teacher

supplément *nm* **payer un supplément** to pay an additional charge; **Le vin est en supplément.** Wine is extra.; **un supplément de travail** extra work

supplémentaire *adj* additional; **faire des heures supplémentaires** to do overtime

supplice *nm* torture

supplier *vb* [19] **supplier quelqu'un de faire quelque chose** to beg somebody to do something ▷ *Je t'en supplie!* I'm begging you!

supportable *adj* bearable

supporter *vb* [28] *(tolerate)* to stand ▷ *Je ne peux pas la supporter.* I can't stand her.

> Be careful! **supporter** does not mean **to support**.

supposer *vb* [28] to suppose

supprimer *vb* [28] ❶ to cut ▷ *Deux mille emplois ont été supprimés.* Two thousand jobs have been cut. ❷ to cancel ▷ *Le train de Londres a été supprimé.* The train to London has been cancelled. ❸ to get rid of ▷ *Ils ont supprimé les témoins gênants.* They got rid of the awkward witnesses.

sur *prep* ❶ on ▷ *Pose-le sur la table.* Put it down on the table. ❷ in ▷ *une personne sur dix* 1 person in 10 ❸ out of ▷ *J'ai eu onze sur vingt en maths.* I got 11 out of 20 in maths. ❹ by ▷ *quatre mètres sur deux* 4 metres by 2

sûr, e *adj* ❶ sure ▷ *Tu es sûr?* Are you sure?; **sûr et certain** absolutely certain ❷ reliable ❸ safe; **sûr de soi** self-confident

sûrement *adv* certainly

sûreté *nf* **mettre quelque chose en sûreté** to put something in a safe place
surf *nm* surfing
surface *nf* surface; **les grandes surfaces** the supermarkets
surfer *vb* [**28**] to go surfing; **surfer sur le Net** to surf the Net
surgelé, e *adj* frozen
surgelés *nmpl* frozen food *sg*
surhumain, e *adj* superhuman
sur-le-champ *adv* immediately
surlendemain *nm* **le surlendemain de son arrivée** two days after he arrived; **le surlendemain dans la matinée** two days later, in the morning
se **surmener** *vb* [**43**] to work too hard
surmonter *vb* [**48**] to overcome
surnaturel (*f* **surnaturelle**) *adj* supernatural
surnom *nm* nickname
surnommer *vb* [**28**] to nickname
surpeuplé, e *adj* overpopulated
surprenant, e *adj* surprising
surprendre *vb* [**65**] to surprise; **surprendre quelqu'un en train de faire quelque chose** to catch somebody doing something
surpris, e *adj* surprised
surprise *nf* surprise ▷ *faire une surprise à quelqu'un* to give somebody a surprise
sursauter *vb* [**28**] to jump ▷ *J'ai sursauté en entendant mon nom.* I jumped when I heard my name.
surtout *adv* ❶ especially ❷ crucially
surveillant *nm (man)* supervisor

In French secondary schools, the teachers are not responsible for supervising the pupils outside class. This job is done by people called **surveillants** or **pions**.

surveiller *vb* [**28**] ❶ to keep an eye on ❷ to keep a watch on ❸ to supervise; **surveiller un examen** to invigilate an exam; **surveiller sa ligne** to watch one's figure
survêtement *nm* tracksuit
survie *nf* survival
survivant *nm* survivor
survivante *nf* survivor
survivre *vb* [**91**] to survive ▷ *survivre à un accident* to survive an accident
survoler *vb* [**28**] to fly over
sus *adv* **en sus** in addition
susceptible *adj* touchy
suspect, e *adj* suspicious
suspecter *vb* [**28**] to suspect
suspense *nm* suspense; **un film à suspense** a thriller
suture *nf* **un point de suture** a stitch
svelte *adj* slender
SVP *abbr (= s'il vous plaît)* please
sweat *nm* sweatshirt
syllabe *nf* syllable
symbole *nm* symbol
symbolique *adj* symbolic
symboliser *vb* [**28**] to symbolize
symétrique *adj* symmetrical
sympa *adj (informal)* nice
sympathie *nf* **J'ai beaucoup de sympathie pour lui.** I like him a lot.
sympathique *adj* nice

Be careful! **sympathique** does not mean **sympathetic**.

sympathiser *vb* [**28**] to get on well ▷ *Nous avons immédiatement sympathisé avec nos voisins.* We got on well with our neighbours straight away.

symptôme *nm* symptom

synagogue *nf* synagogue

syndicat *nm* trade union; **le syndicat d'initiative** the tourist information office

synonyme *adj* synonymous ▶ *nm* synonym

synthétique *adj* synthetic

Syrie *nf* Syria

syrien (*f* **syrienne**) *adj, nm/f* Syrian

systématique *adj* systematic

système *nm* system

t' *pron see* **te**

ta *adj f* your ▷ *J'ai vu ta sœur hier.* I saw your sister yesterday.

tabac *nm* ❶ tobacco ❷ smoking ▷ *Le tabac est mauvais pour la santé.* Smoking is bad for you.

table *nf* table; **mettre la table** to lay the table; **se mettre à table** to sit down to eat; **À table!** Dinner's ready!; **une table de nuit** a bedside table; **'table des matières'** 'contents'

tableau (*pl* **tableaux**) *nm* painting; **le tableau d'affichage** the notice board; **le tableau noir** the blackboard

tablette *nf* **une tablette de chocolat** a bar of chocolate

tableur *nm* spreadsheet

tablier *nm* apron

tabouret *nm* stool

tache *nf* (*stain*) mark; **des taches de rousseur** freckles

tâche *nf* task

tacher *vb* [**28**] to leave a stain

tâcher *vb* [**28**] **tâcher de faire quelque chose** to try to do something

tact *nm* tact

tactique *nf* tactics; **changer de tactique** to try something different

taie *nf* **une taie d'oreiller** a pillowcase

taille *nf* ❶ waist ❷ height ▷ *un homme de taille moyenne* a man of average height ❸ size ▷ *Avez-vous ma taille?* Have you got my size?

taille-crayon *nm* pencil sharpener

tailleur *nm* ❶ tailor ❷ (*lady's*) suit; **Il est assis en tailleur.** He's sitting cross-legged.

se **taire** *vb* [**82**] to stop talking; **Taisez-vous!** Be quiet!

talon *nm* heel

tambour *nm* drum

Tamise *nf* Thames

tampon *nm* pad; **un tampon hygiénique** a tampon

tamponneuse *adj f* **les autos tamponneuses** dodgems

tandis que *conj* while ▷ *Il a toujours de bonnes notes, tandis que les miennes sont mauvaises.* He always gets good marks, while mine are poor.

tant *adv* so much ▷ *Je l'aime tant!* I love him so much!; **tant de (1)** so much **(2)** so many; **tant que (1)** until **(2)** while; **tant mieux** so much the better; **tant pis** never mind

tante *nf* aunt

tantôt *adv* sometimes

tapage *nm* ❶ racket ❷ fuss

taper *vb* [**28**] to beat down ▷ *Le soleil tape.* The sun's really beating down.; **taper quelqu'un** to hit somebody ▷ *Maman, il m'a tapé!* Mum, he hit me!; **taper sur quelque chose** to bang on something; **taper des pieds** to stamp one's feet; **taper des mains** to clap one's hands; **taper à la machine** to type

tapis *nm* carpet; **le tapis roulant (1)** (*for people*) the Travelator® **(2)** (*in factory*) the conveyor belt **(3)** (*at baggage reclaim*) the carousel; **un tapis de souris** a mouse mat

tapisser *vb* [**28**] to paper

tapisserie *nf* ❶ wallpaper ❷ tapestry

taquiner *vb* [**28**] to tease

tard *adv* late; **plus tard** later on; **au plus tard** at the latest

tardif (*f* **tardive**) *adj* late

tarif *nm* **le tarif des consommations** (*in café*) the price list; **une communication à tarif réduit** an off-peak phone call; **un billet de train à tarif réduit** a concessionary train ticket; **un billet de train à plein tarif** a full-price train ticket; **Est-ce que vous faites un tarif de groupe?** Is there a reduction for groups?

tarte *nf* tart
tartine *nf* slice of bread ▷ *une tartine de confiture* a slice of bread and jam
tartiner *vb* [**28**] to spread; **le fromage à tartiner** cheese spread
tas *nm* heap; **un tas de** *(informal)* loads of
tasse *nf* cup
taureau (*pl* **taureaux**) *nm* bull; **le Taureau** Taurus
taux *nm* rate
taxe *nf* tax; **la boutique hors taxes** the duty-free shop
taxi *nm* taxi
tchèque *adj, nmf* Czech; **la République tchèque** the Czech Republic
te *pron*

te changes to **t'** before a vowel and most words beginning with 'h'.

❶ you ▷ *Je te vois.* I can see you. ▷ *Il t'a vu?* Did he see you? ❷ to you ▷ *Elle t'a parlé?* Did she speak to you? ❸ yourself ▷ *Tu vas te rendre malade.* You'll make yourself sick.

With reflexive verbs, **te** is often not translated.

▷ *Comment tu t'appelles?* What's your name?
technicien *nm* technician
technicienne *nf* technician
technique *adj* technical
▸ *nf* technique
techno *nf* techno music
technologie *nf* technology
teint *nm* complexion
teinte *nf (colour)* shade
teinturier *nm* dry cleaner's
tel (*f* **telle**) *adj* **Il a un tel enthousiasme!** He's got such enthusiasm!; **rien de tel** nothing like; **J'ai tout laissé tel quel.** I left everything as it was.; **tel que** such as
télé *nf* telly ▷ *à la télé* on telly
télécarte *nf* phonecard
télécharger *vb* [**45**] ❶ *(receive)* to download ❷ *(send)* to upload
télécommande *nf* remote control
téléconférence *nf* video conference
télécopie *nf* fax
télégramme *nm* telegram
téléphérique *nm* cable car
téléphone *nm* telephone ▷ *Elle est au téléphone.* She's on the phone.
téléphoner *vb* [**28**] to phone ▷ *Je vais téléphoner à Claire.* I'll phone Claire.
téléréalité *nf* reality TV
télésiège *nm* chairlift
téléski *nm* ski-tow
téléspectateur *nm (TV)* viewer
téléviseur *nm* television set
télévision *nf* television ▷ *à la télévision* on television; **la télévision numérique** digital TV
telle *adj f* **Je n'ai jamais eu une telle peur.** I've never had such a fright.; **telle que** such as
tellement *adv* ❶ so ▷ *Andrew est tellement gentil.* Andrew's so nice. ❷ so much ❸ so many
telles *adj fpl* such
tels *adj mpl* such
témoignage *nm* testimony

témoigner *vb* [**28**] to testify
témoin *nm* witness
température *nf* temperature
tempête *nf* storm
temple *nm* ❶ *(Protestant)* church ❷ *(Hindu, Sikh, Buddhist)* temple
temporaire *adj* temporary
temps *nm* ❶ weather ▷ *Quel temps fait-il?* What's the weather like? ❷ time ▷ *Je n'ai pas le temps.* I haven't got time.; **juste à temps** just in time; **de temps en temps** from time to time; **en même temps** at the same time; **à temps** in time; **à plein temps** full time; **à temps complet** full time; **à temps partiel** part time; **dans le temps** at one time ❸ *(of verb)* tense
tenais, tenait *vb see* **tenir**
tendance *nf* **avoir tendance à faire quelque chose** to tend to do something
tendre *adj* tender
▶ *vb* [**88**] to stretch out ▷ *Ils ont tendu une corde entre deux arbres.* They stretched out a rope between two trees.; **tendre quelque chose à quelqu'un** to hold something out to somebody; **tendre la main** to hold out one's hand; **tendre le bras** to reach out; **tendre un piège à quelqu'un** to set a trap for someone
tendrement *adv* tenderly
tendresse *nf* tenderness
tendu, e *adj* tense
tenir *vb* [**83**] to hold ▷ *Tu peux tenir la lampe, s'il te plaît?* Can you hold the torch, please?; **Tenez votre chien en laisse.** Keep your dog on the lead.; **tenir à quelqu'un** to be attached to somebody; **tenir à faire quelque chose** to be determined to do something ▷ *Elle tient à y aller.* She's determined to go.; **tenir de quelqu'un** to take after somebody ▷ *Il tient de son père.* He takes after his father.; **Tiens, voilà un stylo.** Here's a pen.; **Tiens, c'est Alain là-bas!** Look, that's Alain over there!; **Tiens?** Really?; **se tenir (1)** to stand ▷ *Il se tenait près de la porte.* He was standing by the door. **(2)** to be held ▷ *La foire va se tenir place du marché.* The fair will be held in the market place.; **se tenir droit (1)** to stand up straight ▷ *Tiens-toi droit!* Stand up straight! **(2)** to sit up straight ▷ *Arrête de manger le nez dans ton assiette, tiens-toi droit.* Don't slouch while you're eating, sit up straight.; **Tiens-toi bien!** Behave yourself!
tennis *nm* ❶ tennis; **le tennis de table** table tennis ❷ tennis court; **les tennis** trainers
tentant, e *adj* tempting
tentation *nf* temptation
tentative *nf* attempt
tente *nf* tent
tenter *vb* [**28**] to tempt ▷ *J'ai été tenté de tout abandonner.* I was tempted to give up. ▷ *Ça ne me tente vraiment pas d'aller à la piscine.* I don't really fancy going to the swimming pool.; **tenter de faire quelque chose** to try to do something

tenu *vb see* **tenir**
tenue *nf* clothes; **en tenue de soirée** in evening dress
terme *nm* **à court terme** short-term; **à long terme** long-term
terminale *nf* upper sixth ▷ *Je suis en terminale.* I'm in the upper sixth.
In French secondary schools, years are counted from the **sixième** (youngest) to **première** and **terminale** (oldest).
terminer *vb* [**28**] to finish; **se terminer** to end ▷ *Les vacances se terminent demain.* The holidays end tomorrow.
terminus *nm* terminus
terrain *nm* land; **un terrain de camping** a campsite; **un terrain de football** a football pitch; **un terrain de golf** a golf course; **un terrain de jeu** a playground; **un terrain de sport** a sports ground; **un terrain vague** a piece of waste ground
terrasse *nf* terrace; **Si on s'asseyait en terrasse?** *(at café)* Shall we sit outside?
terre *nf* earth; **la Terre** the Earth; **Elle s'est assise par terre.** She sat on the floor.; **Il est tombé par terre.** He fell down.; **la terre cuite** terracotta; **la terre glaise** clay
terrible *adj* terrible; **pas terrible** *(informal)* nothing special
terrine *nf* pâté
territoire *nm* territory
terrorisé, e *adj* terrified
terrorisme *nm* terrorism
terroriste *nmf* terrorist
tes *adj pl* your ▷ *J'aime bien tes baskets.* I like your trainers.
test *nm* test
testament *nm* will
tester *vb* [**28**] to test
tétanos *nm* tetanus
têtard *nm* tadpole
tête *nf* head; **se laver la tête** to wash one's hair; **la tête la première** headfirst; **tenir tête à quelqu'un** to stand up to somebody; **faire la tête** to sulk; **en avoir par-dessus la tête** to be fed up
têtu, e *adj* stubborn
texte *nm (written work)* text
TGV *nm (= train à grande vitesse)* high-speed train
thé *nm* tea
théâtre *nm* theatre; **faire du théâtre** to act
théière *nf* teapot
thème *nm* ❶ subject ❷ prose *(translation into the foreign language)*
théorie *nf* theory
thermomètre *nm* thermometer
thon *nm* tuna
thune *nf (informal)* dosh
tibia *nm* ❶ shinbone ❷ shin
tic *nm* nervous twitch
ticket *nm* ticket; **le ticket de caisse** the till receipt
tiède *adj* ❶ *(water, air)* warm ❷ *(food, drink)* lukewarm
tien *pron m* **le tien** yours
tienne *pron f* **la tienne** yours
tiennes *pron fpl* **les tiennes** yours
tiens *pron mpl* **les tiens** yours

a b c d e f g h i j k l m n o p q r s t u v w x y z

▸ *vb see* **tenir**

tiers *nm* third; **le tiers-monde** the Third World

tige *nf* stem

tigre *nm* tiger

tilleul *nm* lime tea

timbre *nm* stamp

timbre-poste *nm* postage stamp

timide *adj* shy

timidement *adv* shyly

timidité *nf* shyness

tir *nm* shooting; **le tir à l'arc** archery

tirage *nm* **par tirage au sort** by drawing lots

tire-bouchon *nm* corkscrew

tirelire *nf* money box

tirer *vb* **[28]** ❶ to pull ▷ *Elle a tiré un mouchoir de son sac.* She pulled a handkerchief out of her bag. ▷ *'Tirer'* 'Pull' ❷ to draw ▷ *tirer les rideaux* to draw the curtains ▷ *tirer un trait* to draw a line ▷ *tirer des conclusions* to draw conclusions; **tirer au sort** to draw lots ❸ to fire ▷ *Il a tiré sur les policiers.* He fired at the police.; **Tu t'en tires bien.** You're doing well.

tiret *nm (hyphen)* dash

tiroir *nm* drawer

tisane *nf* herbal tea

tisser *vb* **[28]** to weave

tissu *nm* material; **un sac en tissu** a cloth bag

titre *nm* title; **les gros titres** the headlines; **un titre de transport** a travel ticket

tituber *vb* **[28]** to stagger

TNT *nf (= télévision numérique terrestre)* digital television

toast *nm* ❶ piece of toast ❷ toast ▷ *porter un toast à quelqu'un* to drink a toast to somebody

toboggan *nm* slide

toi *pron* you ▷ *Ça va? — Oui, et toi?* How are you? — Fine, and you? ▷ *J'ai faim, pas toi?* I'm hungry, aren't you?; **Assieds-toi.** Sit down.; **C'est à toi de jouer.** It's your turn to play.; **Est-ce que ce stylo est à toi?** Is this pen yours?

toile *nf* **un pantalon de toile** cotton trousers; **un sac de toile** a canvas bag; **une toile cirée** an oilcloth; **une toile d'araignée** a cobweb

toilette *nf* ❶ wash ▷ *faire sa toilette* to have a wash ❷ outfit

toilettes *nfpl* toilet *sg*

toi-même *pron* yourself ▷ *Tu as fait ça toi-même?* Did you do it yourself?

toit *nm* roof; **un toit ouvrant** a sunroof

tolérant, e *adj* tolerant

tolérer *vb* **[34]** to tolerate

tomate *nf* tomato

tombe *nf* grave

tombeau (*pl* **tombeaux**) *nm* tomb

tombée *nf* **à la tombée de la nuit** at nightfall

tomber *vb* **[84]** to fall ▷ *Attention, tu vas tomber!* Be careful, you'll fall!; **laisser tomber (1)** to drop ▷ *Elle a laissé tomber son stylo.* She dropped her pen. **(2)** to give up ▷ *Il a laissé tomber le piano.* He gave up the piano. **(3)** to let down ▷ *Il ne laisse jamais tomber ses amis.* He never lets his friends down.; **tomber sur quelqu'un** to bump into somebody; **Ça tombe bien.** That's lucky.; **Il tombe de sommeil.** He's asleep on his feet.

ton (*f* **ta**, *pl* **tes**) *adj* your ▷ *C'est ton stylo?* Is this your pen?
▶ *nm* ❶ tone of voice ❷ colour

tonalité *nf* dialling tone

tondeuse *nf* lawnmower

tondre *vb* [**69**] to mow

tonique *adj* fortifying

tonne *nf* tonne

tonneau (*pl* **tonneaux**) *nm* barrel

tonnerre *nm* thunder

tonus *nm* **avoir du tonus** to be energetic

torchon *nm* tea towel

tordre *vb* [**49**] **se tordre la cheville** to twist one's ankle

tordu, e *adj* ❶ bent ❷ crazy ▷ *une histoire complètement tordue* a crazy story

torrent *nm* mountain stream

torse *nm* chest

tort *nm* **avoir tort** to be wrong; **donner tort à quelqu'un** to lay the blame on somebody

torticolis *nm* stiff neck

tortue *nf* tortoise

torture *nf* torture

torturer *vb* [**28**] to torture

tôt *adv* early; **au plus tôt** at the earliest; **tôt ou tard** sooner or later

total, e (*mpl* **totaux**) *adj* total
▶ *nm* total; **au total** in total

totalement *adv* totally

totalité *nf* **la totalité des profs** all the teachers; **la totalité du personnel** the entire staff

touchant, e *adj* touching

toucher *vb* [**28**] ❶ to touch ▷ *Ne touche pas à mes livres!* Don't touch my books!; **Nos deux jardins se touchent.** Our gardens are next to each other. ❷ to feel ▷ *Ce pull a l'air doux. Je peux toucher?* That sweater looks soft. Can I feel it? ❸ to hit ▷ *La balle l'a touché en pleine poitrine.* The bullet hit him right in the chest. ❹ to affect ▷ *Ces nouvelles réformes ne nous touchent pas.* The new reforms don't affect us. ❺ to receive ▷ *Il a touché une grosse somme d'argent.* He received a large sum of money.

toujours *adv* ❶ always ▷ *Il est toujours très gentil.* He's always very nice.; **pour toujours** forever ❷ still ▷ *Quand on est revenus, Pierre était toujours là.* When we got back Pierre was still there.

toupet *nm (informal)* **avoir du toupet** to have a nerve

tour *nf* ❶ tower ▷ *la Tour Eiffel* the Eiffel Tower ❷ tower block
▶ *nm* turn ▷ *C'est ton tour de jouer.* It's your turn to play.; **faire un tour** to go for a walk; **faire un tour en voiture** to go for a drive; **faire un tour à vélo** to go for a ride; **faire le tour du monde** to travel round the world; **à tour de rôle** alternately

tourbillon *nm* whirlpool

tourisme *nm* tourism

touriste *nmf* tourist

touristique *adj* tourist

se **tourmenter** *vb* [**28**] to fret
tournant *nm* ❶ bend ❷ turning point
tournée *nf* ❶ round ▷ *Le facteur commence sa tournée à sept heures du matin.* The postman starts his round at 7 o'clock in the morning. ▷ *Allez, qu'est-ce que vous voulez boire? C'est ma tournée.* Right, what are you drinking? It's my round. ❷ tour ▷ *Il est en tournée aux États-Unis.* He's on tour in the United States.
tourner *vb* [**28**] ❶ to turn ▷ *Tournez à droite au prochain feu.* Turn right at the lights. ❷ to go sour ▷ *Le lait a tourné.* The milk's gone sour.; **mal tourner** to go wrong ▷ *Ça a mal tourné.* It all went wrong.; **tourner le dos à quelqu'un** to have one's back to somebody; **tourner un film** to make a film
tournesol *nm* sunflower
tournevis *nm* screwdriver
tournoi *nm* tournament
tourte *nf* pie
tous *adj pl, pron pl see* **tout**
Toussaint *nf* All Saints' Day
tousser *vb* [**28**] to cough
tout (*f* **toute**, *mpl* **tous**) *adj, adv, pron* ❶ all ▷ *tout le lait* all the milk ▷ *toute la nuit* all night ▷ *tous les livres* all the books ▷ *toute la journée* all day ▷ *tout le temps* all the time ▷ *C'est tout.* That's all.; **Il est tout seul.** He's all alone.; **pas du tout** not at all; **tout de même** all the same ❷ every ▷ *tous les jours* every day; **tout le monde** everybody; **tous les deux** both; **tous les trois** all three ❸ everything ▷ *Il a tout organisé.* He organized everything. ❹ very ▷ *Elle habite tout près.* She lives very close.; **tout en haut** right at the top; **tout droit** straight ahead; **tout d'abord** first of all; **tout à coup** suddenly; **tout à fait** absolutely; **tout à l'heure** **(1)** just now **(2)** in a moment; **tout de suite** straight away; **Il a fait son travail tout en chantant.** He sang as he worked.
toutefois *adv* however
toutes *adj fpl, pron fpl see* **tout**
toux *nf* cough
toxicomane *nmf* drug addict
toxicomanie *nf* drug addiction
TP *nm* (= *travaux pratiques*) practical class
trac *nm* **avoir le trac** to be feeling nervous
tracasser *vb* [**28**] to worry ▷ *La santé de mon père me tracasse.* My dad's health worries me.; **se tracasser** to worry
trace *nf* ❶ trace ❷ mark ▷ *des traces de doigts* finger marks; **des traces de pas** footprints
tracer *vb* [**12**] to draw ▷ *tracer un trait* to draw a line
tracteur *nm* tractor
tradition *nf* tradition
traditionnel (*f* **traditionnelle**) *adj* traditional
traducteur *nm* translator
traduction *nf* translation
traductrice *nf* translator
traduire *vb* [**23**] to translate

trafic *nm* traffic; **le trafic de drogue** drug trafficking
trafiquant *nm* **un trafiquant de drogue** a drug trafficker
tragique *adj* tragic
trahir *vb* [**38**] to betray
trahison *nf* betrayal
train *nm* train; **un train électrique** a train set; **Il est en train de manger.** He's eating.
traîneau (*pl* **traîneaux**) *nm* sledge
traîner *vb* [**28**] ❶ to wander around ▷ *J'ai vu des jeunes qui traînaient en ville.* I saw some young people wandering around town. ❷ to hang about ▷ *Dépêche-toi, ne traîne pas!* Hurry up, don't hang about! ❸ to drag on ▷ *La réunion a traîné jusqu'à midi.* The meeting dragged on till 12 o'clock.; **traîner des pieds** to drag one's feet; **laisser traîner qch** to leave sth lying around
train-train *nm* humdrum routine
traire *vb* [**85**] to milk
trait *nm* ❶ line ▷ *Tracez un trait.* Draw a line. ❷ feature ▷ *Elle a les traits fins.* She has delicate features.; **boire quelque chose d'un trait** to drink something down in one gulp; **un trait d'union** a hyphen
traitement *nm* treatment; **le traitement de texte** word processing
traiter *vb* [**28**] to treat; **Il m'a traité d'imbécile.** He called me an idiot.; **traiter de** to be about ▷ *Cet article traite des sans-abri.* This article is about the homeless.
traiteur *nm* caterer
trajet *nm* ❶ journey ▷ *J'ai une heure de trajet pour aller au travail.* My journey to work takes an hour. ❷ route ▷ *C'est le trajet le plus court.* It's the shortest route.
tramway *nm* tram
tranchant, e *adj* (*knife*) sharp
tranche *nf* slice
tranquille *adj* quiet; **Sois tranquille, il ne va rien lui arriver.** Don't worry, nothing will happen to him.; **Tiens-toi tranquille!** Be quiet!; **Laisse-moi tranquille.** Leave me alone.; **Laisse ça tranquille.** Leave it alone.
tranquillement *adv* quietly; **Je peux travailler tranquillement cinq minutes?** Can I have five minutes to myself to work in peace?
tranquillité *nf* peace and quiet
transférer *vb* [**34**] to transfer
transformer *vb* [**28**] ❶ to transform ❷ to convert ▷ *Ils ont transformé la grange en garage.* They've converted the barn into a garage.; **se transformer en** to turn into
transfusion *nf* **une transfusion sanguine** a blood transfusion
transiger *vb* [**45**] to compromise
transmettre *vb* [**47**] **transmettre quelque chose à quelqu'un** to pass something on to somebody
transpercer *vb* [**12**] to go through ▷ *La pluie a transpercé mes vêtements.* The rain went through my clothes.
transpiration *nf* perspiration

transpirer *vb* [**28**] to perspire
transport *nm* transport; **les transports en commun** public transport
transporter *vb* [**28**] ❶ to carry ▷ *Le train transportait des marchandises.* The train was carrying freight. ❷ to move ▷ *Je ne sais pas comment je vais transporter mes affaires.* I don't know how I'm going to move my stuff.
traumatiser *vb* [**28**] to traumatize
travail (*pl* **travaux**) *nm* ❶ work ▷ *J'ai beaucoup de travail.* I've got a lot of work. ❷ job ▷ *Il a un travail intéressant.* He's got an interesting job.; **Il est sans travail depuis un an.** He has been out of work for a year.; **le travail au noir** moonlighting
travailler *vb* [**28**] to work
travailleur (*f* **travailleuse**) *adj* hard-working
travailleur *nm* worker
travailleuse *nf* worker
travaillistes *nmpl* the Labour Party *sg*
travaux *nmpl* ❶ work *sg* ▷ *des travaux de construction* building work ❷ roadworks; **être en travaux** to be undergoing alterations; **les travaux dirigés** supervised practical work; **les travaux manuels** handicrafts; **les travaux ménagers** housework; **les travaux pratiques** practical work
travers *nm* **en travers de** across; **de travers** crooked; **comprendre de travers** to misunderstand; **J'ai avalé de travers.** Something went down the wrong way.; **à travers** through
traversée *nf* crossing
traverser *vb* [**28**] ❶ to cross ▷ *Traversez la rue.* Cross the street. ❷ to go through ▷ *Nous avons traversé la France pour aller en Espagne.* We went through France on the way to Spain.
traversin *nm* bolster
trébucher *vb* [**28**] to trip up
trèfle *nm* ❶ clover ❷ *(at cards)* clubs
treize *num* thirteen ▷ *Il a treize ans.* He's thirteen.; **le treize février** the thirteenth of February
treizième *adj* thirteenth
tréma *nm* diaeresis
tremblement de terre *nm* earthquake
trembler *vb* [**28**] to shake ▷ *trembler de peur* to shake with fear; **trembler de froid** to shiver
trempé, e *adj* soaking wet; **trempé jusqu'aux os** soaked to the skin
tremper *vb* [**28**] to soak; **tremper sa main dans l'eau** to dip one's hand in the water
tremplin *nm* springboard
trentaine *nf* about thirty; **Il a la trentaine.** He's in his thirties.
trente *num* thirty; **le trente janvier** the thirtieth of January; **trente et un** thirty-one; **trente-deux** thirty-two
trentième *adj* thirtieth
très *adv* very

trésor *nm* treasure
tresse *nf* plait
triangle *nm* triangle
tribu *nf* tribe
tribunal (*pl* **tribunaux**) *nm* court
tricher *vb* [28] to cheat
tricolore *adj* three-coloured; **le drapeau tricolore** the French flag
- **le drapeau tricolore** is the French flag which is blue, white and red.

tricot *nm* ❶ knitting ❷ sweater
tricoter *vb* [28] to knit
trier *vb* [19] to sort out
trimestre *nm* term
trinquer *vb* [28] to clink glasses
triomphe *nm* triumph
triompher *vb* [28] to triumph
tripes *nfpl* tripe
triple *nm* **Ça m'a coûté le triple.** It cost me three times as much.; **Il gagne le triple de mon salaire.** He earns three times my salary.
tripler *vb* [28] to treble
triplés *nmpl* triplets
triste *adj* sad
tristesse *nf* sadness
trognon *nm* core
trois *num* three ▷ *Elle a trois ans.* She's three.; **le trois février** the third of February
troisième *adj* third
▶ *nf* year 10 ▷ *Mon frère est en troisième.* My brother's in year 10.
- In French secondary schools, years are counted from the **sixième** (youngest) to **première** and **terminale** (oldest).

trois-quarts *nmpl* three-quarters
trombone *nm* ❶ trombone ❷ paper clip
trompe *nf* trunk
tromper *vb* [28] to deceive; **se tromper** to make a mistake; **se tromper de jour** to get the wrong day; **Vous vous êtes trompé de numéro.** You've got the wrong number.
trompette *nf* trumpet; **Il a le nez en trompette.** He's got a turned-up nose.
tronc *nm* trunk
trop *adv* ❶ too ▷ *Il conduit trop vite.* He drives too fast. ❷ too much ▷ *J'ai trop mangé.* I've eaten too much.; **trop de (1)** too much **(2)** too many; **trois personnes de trop** 3 people too many
tropique *nm* tropic
trottoir *nm* pavement
trou *nm* hole; **J'ai eu un trou de mémoire.** My mind went blank.
trouble *adj, adv* cloudy; **Sans mes lunettes je vois trouble.** Without my glasses I can't see properly.
troubles *nmpl* **une période de troubles politiques** a period of political instability
trouer *vb* [28] to make a hole in
trouille *nf* **avoir la trouille** (*informal*) to be scared to death
troupe *nf* troop; **une troupe de théâtre** a theatre company
troupeau (*pl* **troupeaux**) *nm* **un troupeau de moutons** a flock of sheep; **un troupeau de vaches** a herd of cows
trousse *nf* pencil case; **une**

trousse de secours a first-aid kit; **une trousse de toilette** a toilet bag

trouver *vb* [**28**] ❶ to find ▷ *Je ne trouve pas mes lunettes.* I can't find my glasses. ❷ to think ▷ *Je trouve que c'est bête.* I think it's stupid.; **se trouver** to be ▷ *Où se trouve la poste?* Where is the post office? ▷ *Nice se trouve dans le sud de la France.* Nice is in the South of France.; **se trouver mal** to pass out

truc *nm (informal)* ❶ thing ▷ *un truc en plastique* a plastic thing ❷ trick

truite *nf* trout

T-shirt *nm* T-shirt

TSVP *abbr (= tournez s'il vous plaît)* PTO *(= please turn over)*

tu *pron* you ▷ *Est-ce que tu as un animal familier?* Have you got a pet?

tuba *nm* ❶ tuba ❷ snorkel

tube *nm* ❶ tube ▷ *un tube de dentifrice* a tube of toothpaste; **un tube de rouge à lèvres** a lipstick ❷ hit ▷ *Ça va être le tube de l'été.* It's going to be this summer's hit.

tuer *vb* [**28**] to kill; **se tuer** to get killed

tue-tête: **à tue-tête** *adv* at the top of one's voice

tuile *nf* tile

tunique *nf* tunic

Tunisie *nf* Tunisia

tunisien (*f* **tunisienne**) *adj, nm/f* Tunisian

tunnel *nm* tunnel; **le tunnel sous la Manche** the Channel Tunnel

turbulent, e *adj* boisterous

turc (*f* **turque**) *adj, nm/f* Turkish ▷ *Il parle turc.* He speaks Turkish.; **un Turc** *(man)* a Turk; **une Turque** *(woman)* a Turk

Turquie *nf* Turkey

tutoyer *vb* [**53**] **tutoyer quelqu'un** to address somebody as 'tu' ▷ *On se tutoie?* Shall we use 'tu' to each other?

tutoyer quelqu'un means to use **tu** when speaking to someone, rather than **vous**. Use **tu** only when talking to one person and when that person is someone of your own age or whom you know well; use **vous** to everyone else. If in doubt use **vous**.

tuyau (*pl* **tuyaux**) *nm* ❶ pipe; **un tuyau d'arrosage** a hosepipe ❷ tip

TVA *nf (= taxe sur la valeur ajoutée)* VAT

tympan *nm* eardrum

type *nm (informal)* guy

typique *adj* typical

tyran *nm* tyrant

tzigane *nmf* gipsy

U

UE *nf* (= *Union européenne*) the EU (= *European Union*)

un (*f* **une**) *art, pron m, adj m* ❶ a ▷ *un garçon* a boy; an ▷ *un œuf* an egg ❷ one ▷ *l'un des meilleurs* one of the best ▷ *un citron et deux oranges* one lemon and two oranges; **l'un ..., l'autre ...** one ..., the other ... ▷ *L'un est grand, l'autre est petit.* One is tall, the other is short.; **les uns ..., les autres ...** some ..., others ... ▷ *Les uns marchaient, les autres couraient.* Some were walking, others were running.; **l'un ou l'autre** either of them ▷ *Prends l'un ou l'autre, ça m'est égal.* Take either of them, I don't mind.; **un par un** one by one

unanime *adj* unanimous

unanimité *nf* **à l'unanimité** unanimously

une *art, pron f, adj f* ❶ a ▷ *une fille* a girl; an ▷ *une pomme* an apple ❷ one ▷ *une pomme et deux bananes* one apple and two bananas ▷ *à une heure du matin* at one in the morning ▷ *l'une des meilleures* one of the best; **l'une ..., l'autre ...** one ..., the other ... ▷ *L'une est grande, l'autre est petite.* One is tall, the other is short.; **les unes..., les autres...** some ..., others ... ▷ *Les unes marchaient, les autres couraient.* Some were walking, others were running.; **l'une ou l'autre** either of them ▷ *Prends l'une ou l'autre, ça m'est égal.* Take either of them, I don't mind.; **une par une** one by one

uni, e *adj* ❶ plain ❷ close-knit

uniforme *nm* uniform

union *nf* union; **l'Union européenne** the European Union

unique *adj* unique; **Il est fils unique.** He's an only child.; **Elle est fille unique.** She's an only child.

uniquement *adv* only

unité *nf* ❶ unity ❷ unit

univers *nm* universe

universitaire *adj* university; **faire des études universitaires** to study at university

université *nf* university

urgence *nf* **C'est une urgence.** It's urgent.; **Il n'y a pas urgence.** It's not urgent.; **le service des urgences** the accident and emergency department; **Il a été transporté d'urgence à l'hôpital.**

He was rushed to hospital.; **Téléphonez d'urgence.** Phone as soon as possible.

urgent, e *adj* urgent

urine *nf* urine

USA *nmpl* USA; **aux USA (1)** in the USA **(2)** to the USA

usage *nm* use; **hors d'usage** out of action

usagé, e *adj* ❶ old ❷ used

usager *nm* user ▷ *les usagers de la route* road users

usé, e *adj* worn

s' **user** *vb* [**28**] to wear out ▷ *Mes baskets se sont usées en quinze jours.* My trainers wore out in two weeks.

usine *nf* factory

ustensile *nm* **un ustensile de cuisine** a kitchen utensil

usuel (*f* **usuelle**) *adj* everyday

utile *adj* useful

utilisation *nf* use

utiliser *vb* [**28**] to use

utilité *nf* use

V

va *vb see* **aller**

vacances *nfpl* holidays ▷ *aller en vacances* to go on holiday ▷ *être en vacances* to be on holiday; **les vacances de Noël** the Christmas holidays; **les vacances de Pâques** the Easter holidays; **les grandes vacances** the summer holidays

vacancier *nm* holiday-maker

vacarme *nm* racket

vaccin *nm* vaccination

vaccination *nf* vaccination

vacciner *vb* [**28**] to vaccinate

vache *nf* cow

▶ *adj (informal)* mean ▷ *Il est vache.* He's a mean sod.

vachement *adv (informal)* really

vagabond *nm* tramp

vagin *nm* vagina

vague *nf (in sea)* wave; **une vague**

de chaleur a heat wave
▸ *adj* vague
vain (*f* **vaine**) *adj* **en vain** in vain
vaincre *vb* [**86**] ❶ to defeat ❷ to overcome
vainqueur *nm* winner
vais *vb see* **aller**; **Je vais écrire à mes cousins.** I'm going to write to my cousins.
vaisseau (*pl* **vaisseaux**) *nm* **un vaisseau spatial** a spaceship; **un vaisseau sanguin** a blood vessel
vaisselle *nf* ❶ washing-up ▹ *Je vais faire la vaisselle.* I'll do the washing-up. ❷ dishes
valable *adj* valid
valet *nm (in card games)* jack
valeur *nf* value; **des objets de valeur** valuables
valider *vb* [**28**] to stamp ▹ *Vous devez faire valider votre billet avant votre départ.* You must get your ticket stamped before you leave.
valise *nf* suitcase; **faire sa valise** to pack
vallée *nf* valley
valoir *vb* [**87**] to be worth ▹ *Ça vaut combien?* How much is it worth?; **Ça vaut mieux.** That would be better. ▹ *Il vaut mieux ne rien dire.* It would be better to say nothing.; **valoir la peine** to be worth it ▹ *Ça vaudrait la peine d'essayer.* It would be worth a try.
vampire *nm* vampire
vandalisme *nm* vandalism
vanille *nf* vanilla
vanité *nf* vanity
vaniteux (*f* **vaniteuse**) *adj* conceited
se **vanter** *vb* [**28**] to boast
vapeur *nf* steam
varappe *nf* rock climbing
variable *adj (weather)* changeable
varicelle *nf* chickenpox
varié, e *adj* varied
varier *vb* [**19**] to vary; **Le menu varie tous les jours.** The menu changes every day.
variété *nf* variety; **une émission de variétés** a television variety show
vas *vb see* **aller**
vase *nm* vase
▸ *nf* mud
vaste *adj* vast
vaudrait, vaut *vb see* **valoir**
vautour *nm* vulture
veau (*pl* **veaux**) *nm* ❶ *(animal)* calf ❷ *(meat)* veal
vécu *vb see* **vivre**; **Il a vécu à Paris pendant dix ans.** He lived in Paris for ten years.
vedette *nf* ❶ star ▹ *une vedette de cinéma* a film star ❷ motor boat; **une vedette de police** a police launch
végétal, e (*mpl* **végétaux**) *adj* vegetable
végétarien (*f* **végétarienne**) *adj* vegetarian
végétation *nf* vegetation
véhicule *nm* vehicle
veille *nf* the day before ▹ *la veille au soir* the previous evening; **la veille de Noël** Christmas Eve; **la veille du jour de l'An** New Year's Eve
veiller *vb* [**28**] to stay up; **veiller**

sur quelqu'un to watch over somebody

veinard, e *adj (informal)* **Qu'est-ce qu'il est veinard!** He's such a lucky devil!

veine *nf* vein; **avoir de la veine** *(informal)* to be lucky

véliplanchiste *nmf* windsurfer

vélo *nm* bike; **un vélo tout-terrain** a mountain bike

vélomoteur *nm* moped

velours *nm* velvet; **le velours côtelé** corduroy

vendanges *nfpl* grape harvest *sg*

vendeur *nm* shop assistant

vendeuse *nf* shop assistant

vendre *vb* [**88**] to sell; **vendre quelque chose à quelqu'un** to sell somebody something; **'à vendre'** 'for sale'

vendredi *nm* ❶ Friday ▷ *Aujourd'hui, nous sommes vendredi.* It's Friday today. ❷ on Friday; **le vendredi** on Fridays; **tous les vendredis** every Friday; **vendredi dernier** last Friday; **vendredi prochain** next Friday; **le Vendredi saint** Good Friday

vénéneux (*f* **vénéneuse**) *adj (plant)* poisonous

vengeance *nf* revenge

se **venger** *vb* [**45**] to get revenge

venimeux (*f* **venimeuse**) *adj (animal)* poisonous

venin *nm* poison

venir *vb* [**89**] to come ▷ *Il viendra demain.* He'll come tomorrow. ▷ *Il est venu nous voir.* He came to see us.; **venir de** to have just ▷ *Je viens de le voir.* I've just seen him.; **faire venir quelqu'un** to call somebody out

vent *nm* wind

vente *nf* sale; **en vente** on sale; **la vente par téléphone** telesales; **une vente aux enchères** an auction

ventilateur *nm (for cooling)* fan

ventre *nm* stomach

venu *vb see* **venir**

ver *nm* worm; **un ver de terre** an earthworm

verbe *nm* verb

verdict *nm* verdict

verger *nm* orchard

verglacé, e *adj* icy

verglas *nm* black ice

véridique *adj* truthful

vérification *nf* check

vérifier *vb* [**19**] to check

véritable *adj* real; **en cuir véritable** made of real leather

vérité *nf* truth

verni, e *adj* varnished; **des chaussures vernies** patent leather shoes

vernir *vb* [**38**] to varnish

vernis *nm* varnish

verra, verrai, verras *vb see* **voir**; **on verra ...** we'll see ...

verre *nm* ❶ glass ▷ *une table en verre* a glass table ▷ *un verre d'eau* a glass of water; **boire un verre** to have a drink ❷ *(of spectacles)* lens ▷ *des verres de contact* contact lenses

verrez, verrons, verront *vb see* **voir**

verrou *nm (on door)* bolt

verrouiller *vb* [**28**] to bolt
verrue *nf* wart
vers *nm* *(of poetry)* line
▶ *prep* ❶ towards ▷ *Il allait vers la gare.* He was going towards the station. ❷ at about ▷ *Il est rentré chez lui vers cinq heures.* He went home at about 5 o'clock.
verse: **à verse** *adv* ▷ *Il pleut à verse.* It's pouring with rain.
Verseau *nm* Aquarius
versement *nm* instalment
verser *vb* [**28**] to pour ▷ *Est-ce que tu peux me verser un verre d'eau?* Could you pour me a glass of water?
version *nf* ❶ version ❷ *(from the foreign language)* translation; **un film en version originale** a film in the original language
verso *nm* *(of sheet of paper)* back; **voir au verso** see overleaf
vert, e *adj* green
vertèbre *nf* vertebra
vertical, e (*mpl* **verticaux**) *adj* vertical
vertige *nm* vertigo
verveine *nf* verbena tea
vessie *nf* bladder
veste *nf* jacket
vestiaire *nm* ❶ *(in theatre, museum)* cloakroom ❷ *(at sports ground)* changing room
vestibule *nm* hall
vêtement *nm* garment; **les vêtements** clothes
vétérinaire *nmf* vet
veuf *nm* widower
veuille, veuillez, veuillons, veulent, veut *vb see* **vouloir**; **Veuillez fermer la porte en sortant.** Please shut the door when you go out.
veuve *nf* widow
veux *vb see* **vouloir**
vexer *vb* [**28**] **vexer quelqu'un** to hurt somebody's feelings; **se vexer** to be offended
viande *nf* meat; **la viande hachée** mince
vibrer *vb* [**28**] to vibrate
vice *nm* vice
vicieux (*f* **vicieuse**) *adj* lecherous
victime *nf* victim
victoire *nf* victory
vide *adj* empty
▶ *nm* vacuum; **avoir peur du vide** to be afraid of heights
vidéo *nf* video
▶ *adj* video ▷ *un jeu vidéo* a video game ▷ *une caméra vidéo* a video camera
vidéoclip *nm* music video
vidéoclub *nm* video shop
vider *vb* [**28**] to empty
vie *nf* life; **être en vie** to be alive
vieil *adj m*

> **vieil** is used in place of **vieux** when the noun begins with a vowel sound.

old ▷ *un vieil arbre* an old tree ▷ *un vieil homme* an old man
vieillard *nm* old man
vieille *adj f see* **vieux**
▶ *nf* old woman; **Eh bien, ma vieille ...** *(informal)* Well, my dear ...
vieillesse *nf* old age
vieillir *vb* [**38**] to age
viendrai, vienne, viens *vb see*

venir; **Je viendrai dès que possible.** I'll come as soon as possible.; **Je voudrais que tu viennes.** I'd like you to come.; **Viens ici!** Come here!

Vierge *nf* Virgo ▷ *Pascal est Vierge.* Pascal is Virgo.; **la Vierge** the Virgin Mary

vierge *adj* ❶ virgin ❷ blank

Viêt-Nam *nm* Vietnam

vietnamien (*f* **vietnamienne**) *adj, nm/f* Vietnamese; **un Vietnamien** *(man)* a Vietnamese; **une Vietnamienne** *(woman)* a Vietnamese; **les Vietnamiens** the Vietnamese

vieux (*f* **vieille**) *adj* old; **un vieux garçon** a bachelor
▶ *nm* old man; **les vieux** old people

vieux jeu *adj* old-fashioned

vif (*f* **vive**) *adj* ❶ *(mentally)* sharp ▷ *Il est très vif.* He's very sharp.; **avoir l'esprit vif** to be quick-witted ❷ crisp ▷ *L'air est plus vif à la campagne qu'en ville.* The air is crisper in the country than in the town. ❸ *(colour)* bright ▷ *un bleu vif* a bright blue; **à vive allure** at a brisk pace; **de vive voix** in person ▷ *Je te le dirai de vive voix.* I'll tell you about it when I see you.

vigne *nf* vine; **des champs de vigne** vineyards

vigneron *nm* wine grower

vignette *nf* tax disc

vignoble *nm* vineyard

vilain, e *adj* ❶ naughty ❷ ugly ▷ *Il n'est pas vilain.* He's not bad-looking.

villa *nf* villa

village *nm* village

villageois *nm* villager

ville *nf* town ▷ *Je vais en ville.* I'm going into town.; **une grande ville** a city

vin *nm* wine

vinaigre *nm* vinegar

vinaigrette *nf* French dressing

vingt *num* twenty; **le vingt février** the twentieth of February; **vingt et un** twenty-one; **vingt-deux** twenty-two

vingtaine *nf* about twenty; **Il a une vingtaine d'années.** He's about twenty.

vingtième *adj* twentieth

viol *nm* rape

violemment *adv* violently

violence *nf* violence

violent, e *adj* violent

violer *vb* **[28]** to rape

violet (*f* **violette**) *adj* purple

violette *nf (flower)* violet

violon *nm* violin

violoncelle *nm* cello

violoniste *nmf* violinist

vipère *nf* viper

virage *nm* bend

virgule *nf* ❶ comma ❷ decimal point

virus *nm* virus

vis *vb see* **vivre**; **Je vis en Écosse.** I live in Scotland.
▶ *nf* screw

visa *nm* visa

visage *nm* face

vis-à-vis de *prep* with regard to ▷ *Ce n'est pas très juste vis-à-vis de lui.*

It's not very fair to him.
viser *vb* [**28**] to aim at
visibilité *nf* visibility
visible *adj* visible
visière *nf (of cap)* peak
visite *nf* visit; **rendre visite à quelqu'un** to visit somebody; **avoir de la visite** to have visitors; **une visite guidée** a guided tour; **une visite médicale** a medical examination
visiter *vb* [**28**] to visit
visiteur *nm* visitor
vison *nm (fur)* mink
vit *vb see* **vivre**
vital, e (*mpl* **vitaux**) *adj* vital
vitamine *nf* vitamin
vite *adv* ❶ quick; **Le temps passe vite.** Time flies. ❷ fast ▷ *Il roule trop vite.* He drives too fast. ❸ soon ▷ *Il va vite oublier.* He'll soon forget.; **Il a vite compris.** He understood immediately.
vitesse *nf* ❶ speed ❷ gear
viticulteur *nm* wine grower
vitrail (*pl* **vitraux**) *nm* stained-glass window
vitre *nf* window
vitrine *nf* shop window
vivant, e *adj* ❶ living ▷ *les êtres vivants* living creatures ❷ lively ▷ *Elle est très vivante.* She's very lively.
vive *adj f see* **vif**
▸ *excl* **Vive le roi!** Long live the king!
vivement *excl* **Vivement les vacances!** Roll on the holidays!
vivre *vb* [**91**] to live ▷ *J'aimerais vivre à l'étranger.* I'd like to live abroad.
vlan *excl* wham!
VO *nf* **un film en VO** a film in the original language
vocabulaire *nm* vocabulary
vocation *nf* vocation
vœu (*pl* **vœux**) *nm* wish ▷ *Meilleurs vœux de bonne année!* Best wishes for the New Year!
vogue *nf* fashion
voici *prep* ❶ this is ▷ *Voici mon frère et voilà ma sœur.* This is my brother and that's my sister. ❷ here is ▷ *Tu as perdu ton stylo? Tiens, en voici un autre.* Have you lost your pen? Here's another one.; **Le voici!** Here he is!
voie *nf* lane ▷ *une route à trois voies* a 3-lane road; **par voie orale** orally ▷ *à prendre par voie orale* to be taken orally; **la voie ferrée** the railway track
voilà *prep* ❶ there is ▷ *Tiens! Voilà Paul.* Look! There's Paul.; **Les voilà!** There they are! ❷ that is ▷ *Voilà ma sœur.* That's my sister.
voile *nf* ❶ sail ❷ sailing; **un bateau à voiles** a sailing boat
▸ *nm* veil
voilier *nm* sailing boat
voir *vb* [**92**] to see ▷ *Venez me voir quand vous serez à Paris.* Come and see me when you're in Paris.; **faire voir quelque chose à quelqu'un** to show somebody something; **se voir** to be obvious ▷ *Est-ce que cette tache se voit?* Does that stain show?; **avoir quelque chose à voir avec** to have something to do with; **Je ne peux vraiment pas la**

voir. *(informal)* I really can't stand her.

voisin *nm* neighbour

voisinage *nm* **dans le voisinage** in the vicinity

voisine *nf* neighbour

voiture *nf* car

voix (*pl* **voix**) *nf* ❶ voice; **à haute voix** aloud ❷ vote

vol *nm* ❶ flight; **à vol d'oiseau** as the crow flies; **le vol à voile** gliding ❷ theft

volaille *nf* poultry

volant *nm* ❶ steering wheel ❷ shuttlecock

volcan *nm* volcano

volée *nf* *(in tennis)* volley; **rattraper une balle à la volée** to catch a ball in mid-air

voler *vb* [**28**] ❶ to fly ▷ *J'aimerais savoir voler.* I'd like to be able to fly. ❷ to steal ▷ *On a volé mon appareil photo.* My camera's been stolen.; **voler quelque chose à quelqu'un** to steal something from somebody; **voler quelqu'un** to rob somebody

volet *nm* shutter

voleur *nm* thief; **Au voleur !** Stop thief!

volley *nm* volleyball

volontaire *nmf* volunteer

volonté *nf* willpower; **la bonne volonté** goodwill; **la mauvaise volonté** lack of goodwill

volontiers *adv* ❶ gladly ❷ please

volume *nm* volume

volumineux (*f* **volumineuse**) *adj* bulky

vomir *vb* [**38**] to vomit

vont *vb see* **aller**

vos *adj pl* your ▷ *Rangez vos jouets, les enfants!* Children, put your toys away!

vote *nm* vote

voter *vb* [**28**] to vote

votre (*pl* **vos**) *adj* your

vôtre *pron* **le vôtre** yours; **À la vôtre!** Cheers!

vôtres *pron pl* **les vôtres** yours

voudra, voudrai, voudrais, voudras, voudrez, voudrons, voudront *vb see* **vouloir**; **Je voudrais ...** I'd like ... ▷ *Je voudrais deux litres de lait, s'il vous plaît.* I'd like two litres of milk, please.

vouloir *vb* [**93**] to want ▷ *Elle veut un vélo pour Noël.* She wants a bike for Christmas. ▷ *Je ne veux pas de dessert.* I don't want any pudding. ▷ *Il ne veut pas venir.* He doesn't want to come. ▷ *On va au cinéma? — Si tu veux.* Shall we go to the cinema? — If you want.; **Je veux bien.** I'll be happy to. ▷ *Je veux bien le faire à ta place si ça t'arrange.* I'd be happy to do it for you if you prefer.; **Voulez-vous une tasse de thé? — Je veux bien.** Would you like a cup of tea? — Yes, please.; **sans le vouloir** without meaning to ▷ *Je l'ai vexé sans le vouloir.* I upset him without meaning to.; **en vouloir à quelqu'un** to be angry with somebody ▷ *Il m'en veut de ne pas l'avoir invité.* He's angry with me for not inviting him.; **vouloir dire** to mean ▷ *Qu'est-ce que ça veut dire?*

What does that mean?

voulu *vb see* **vouloir**

vous *sg, pron pl* ❶ you ▷ *Vous aimez la pizza?* Do you like pizza? ❷ to you ▷ *Je vous écrirai bientôt.* I'll write to you soon. ❸ yourself ▷ *Vous vous êtes fait mal?* Have you hurt yourself?; **vous-même** yourself ▷ *Vous l'avez fait vous-même?* Did you do it yourself?

vouvoyer *vb* [**53**] **vouvoyer quelqu'un** to address somebody as 'vous' ▷ *Est-ce que je dois vouvoyer ta sœur?* Should I use 'vous' to your sister?

vouvoyer quelqu'un means to use **vous** when speaking to someone, rather than **tu**. Use **tu** only when talking to one person and when that person is someone of your own age or whom you know well; use **vous** to everyone else. If in doubt use **vous**.

voyage *nm* journey ▷ *Avez-vous fait bon voyage?* Did you have a good journey?; **Bon voyage!** Have a good trip!

voyager *vb* [**45**] to travel

voyageur *nm* passenger

voyaient, voyais, voyait *vb see* **voir**

voyelle *nf* vowel

voyez, voyiez, voyions *vb see* **voir**

voyons *vb see* **voir** ❶ let's see ▷ *Voyons ce qu'on peut faire.* Let's see what we can do. ❷ come on ▷ *Voyons, sois raisonnable!* Come on, be reasonable!

voyou *nm* hooligan

vrac: **en vrac** *adv* loose

vrai, e *adj* true ▷ *une histoire vraie* a true story ▷ *C'est vrai?* Is that true?; **à vrai dire** to tell the truth

vraiment *adv* really

vraisemblable *adj* likely

VTT *nm (= vélo tout-terrain)* mountain bike

vu *vb see* **voir** ▷ *J'ai vu ce film au cinéma.* I saw this film at the cinema.; **être bien vu** *(person)* to be popular ▷ *Est-ce qu'il est bien vu à l'école?* Is he popular at school?; **C'est mal vu de fumer ici.** They don't like people smoking here.

vue *nf* ❶ eyesight ▷ *J'ai une mauvaise vue.* I've got bad eyesight. ❷ view ▷ *Il y a une belle vue d'ici.* There's a lovely view from here.; **à vue d'œil** visibly

vulgaire *adj* vulgar

W X

wagon *nm* railway carriage
wagon-lit (*pl* **wagons-lits**) *nm* *(on train)* sleeper
wagon-restaurant (*pl* **wagons-restaurants**) *nm* restaurant car
wallon (*f* **wallonne**) *adj, nm/f* *(French-speaking Belgian)* Walloon; **les Wallons** the French-speaking Belgians
Wallonie *nf* French-speaking Belgium
W.-C. *nmpl* toilet *sg*
Web *nm* Web
webcam *nf* webcam
webmaster *nm* webmaster
webzine *nm* webzine
week-end *nm* weekend
western *nm (film)* western
whisky (*pl* **whiskies**) *nm* whisky
wifi *nm* Wi-Fi

xénophobe *adj* prejudiced against foreigners
xénophobie *nf* prejudice against foreigners
xylophone *nm* xylophone

y

y *pron* there ▷ *Nous y sommes allés l'été dernier.* We went there last summer. ▷ *Regarde dans le tiroir: je pense que les clés y sont.* Look in the drawer: I think the keys are in there.

> **y** replaces phrases with **à** in constructions like the ones below:

Je pensais à l'examen. — Mais arrête d'y penser! I was thinking about the exam. — Well, stop thinking about it!; **Je ne m'attendais pas à ça. — Moi, je m'y attendais.** I wasn't expecting that. — I was expecting it.

yaourt *nm* yoghurt

yeux (*sg* **œil**) *nmpl* eyes

yoga *nm* yoga

yoghourt *nm* yoghurt

Yougoslavie *nf* Yugoslavia; **l'ex-Yougoslavie** the former Yugoslavia

youpi *excl* yippee!

yoyo *nm* yo-yo

Z

zapper *vb* [**28**] to channel hop
zèbre *nm* zebra
zéro *nm* zero; **Ils ont gagné trois à zéro.** They won three-nil.
zézayer *vb* [**59**] to lisp ▷ *Il zézaie.* He's got a lisp.
zigzag *nm* **faire des zigzags** to zigzag
zone *nf* zone; **une zone industrielle** an industrial estate; **une zone piétonne** a pedestrian precinct
zoo *nm* zoo
zoologique *adj* zoological
zut *excl* oh heck!

a

a *art*

> Use **un** for masculine nouns, **une** for feminine nouns.

un *m* ▷ *a book* un livre; une *f* ▷ *an apple* une pomme

> You do not translate 'a' when you want to describe somebody's job in French.

▷ *She's a doctor.* Elle est médecin.; **once a week** une fois par semaine; **10 km an hour** dix kilomètres à l'heure; **30 pence a kilo** trente pence le kilo; **a hundred pounds** cent livres

abandon *vb* abandonner [**28**]

abbey *n* abbaye *f*

abbreviation *n* abréviation *f*

ability *n* **to have the ability to do something** être [**35**] capable de faire quelque chose

able *adj* **to be able to do something** être [**35**] capable de faire quelque chose

abolish *vb* abolir [**38**]

abortion *n* avortement *m*; **She had an abortion.** Elle s'est fait avorter.

about *prep, adv* ❶ *(concerning)* à propos de ▷ *I'm phoning you about tomorrow's meeting.* Je vous appelle à propos de la réunion de demain. ❷ *(approximately)* environ ▷ *It takes about 10 hours.* Ça prend dix heures environ.; **about a hundred pounds** une centaine de livres; **at about 11 o'clock** vers onze heures ❸ *(around)* dans ▷ *to walk about the town* se promener dans la ville ❹ sur ▷ *a book about London* un livre sur Londres; **to be about to do something** être [**35**] sur le point de faire quelque chose ▷ *I was about to go out.* J'étais sur le point de sortir.; **to talk about something** parler [**28**] de quelque chose; **What's it about?** De quoi s'agit-il?; **How about going to the cinema?** Et si nous allions au cinéma?

above *prep, adv* ❶ *(higher than)* au-dessus de ▷ *He put his hands above his head.* Il a mis ses mains au-dessus de sa tête.; **the flat above** l'appartement du dessus; **mentioned above** mentionné ci-dessus; **above all** par-dessus tout ❷ *(more than)* plus de ▷ *above 40 degrees* plus de quarante degrés

abroad *adv* à l'étranger ▷ *to go abroad* partir à l'étranger

absence *n* absence *f*
absent *adj* absent(e)
absent-minded *adj* distrait(e) ▷ *She's a bit absent-minded.* Elle est un peu distraite.
absolutely *adv* ❶ *(completely)* tout à fait ▷ *Chantal's absolutely right.* Chantal a tout à fait raison. ❷ absolument ▷ *Do you think it's a good idea? — Absolutely!* Tu trouves que c'est une bonne idée? — Absolument!
abuse *n (misuse)* abus *m*; **to shout abuse at somebody** insulter [**28**] quelqu'un; **the issue of child abuse** la question des enfants maltraités; **the problem of drug abuse** le problème de la drogue ▶ *vb* ❶ maltraiter [**28**] ▷ *abused children* les enfants maltraités *mpl*; **to be abused** *(child, woman)* être [**35**] maltraité ❷ *(insult)* injurier [**19**]; **to abuse drugs** se droguer [**28**]
academic *adj* universitaire ▷ *the academic year* l'année universitaire *f*
academy *n* collège *m* ▷ *a military academy* un collège militaire
accelerate *vb* accélérer [**34**]
accelerator *n* accélérateur *m*
accent *n* accent *m* ▷ *He's got a French accent.* Il a l'accent français.
accept *vb* accepter [**28**]
acceptable *adj* acceptable
access *n* ❶ accès *m* ▷ *He has access to confidential information.* Il a accès à des renseignements confidentiels. ❷ droit de visite *m* ▷ *Her ex-husband has access to the children.* Son ex-mari a le droit de visite.
accessory *n* accessoire *m* ▷ *fashion accessories* les accessoires de mode
accident *n* accident *m* ▷ *to have an accident* avoir un accident; **by accident (1)** *(by mistake)* accidentellement ▷ *The burglar killed him by accident.* Le cambrioleur l'a tué accidentellement. **(2)** *(by chance)* par hasard ▷ *She met him by accident.* Elle l'a rencontré par hasard.
accidental *adj* accidentel (*f* accidentelle)
accommodation *n* logement *m*
accompany *vb* accompagner [**28**]
according to *prep* selon ▷ *According to him, everyone had gone.* Selon lui, tout le monde était parti.
account *n* ❶ compte *m* ▷ *a bank account* un compte en banque; **to do the accounts** tenir [**83**] la comptabilité ❷ *(report)* compte rendu *m* (*pl* comptes rendus) ▷ *He gave a detailed account of what happened.* Il a donné un compte rendu détaillé des événements.; **to take something into account** tenir [**83**] compte de quelque chose; **on account of** à cause de ▷ *We couldn't go out on account of the bad weather.* Nous n'avons pas pu sortir à cause du mauvais temps.
accountant *n* comptable *mf* ▷ *She's an accountant.* Elle est comptable.

accuracy *n* exactitude *f*
accurate *adj* précis(e) ▷ *accurate information* les renseignements précis *mpl*
accurately *adv* avec précision
accuse *vb* **to accuse somebody of something** accuser [**28**] quelqu'un de quelque chose ▷ *The police are accusing her of murder.* La police l'accuse de meurtre.
ace *n* as *m* ▷ *the ace of hearts* l'as de cœur
ache *n* douleur *f*
▶ *vb* **My leg's aching.** J'ai mal à la jambe.
achieve *vb* ❶ *(an aim)* atteindre [**60**] ❷ *(victory)* remporter [**28**]
achievement *n* exploit *m* ▷ *That was quite an achievement.* C'était un véritable exploit.
acid *n* acide *m*
acid rain *n* pluies acides *fpl*
acne *n* acné *f*
acrobat *n* acrobate *mf* ▷ *He's an acrobat.* Il est acrobate.
across *prep, adv* de l'autre côté de ▷ *the shop across the road* la boutique de l'autre côté de la rue; **to walk across the road** traverser [**28**] la rue; **to run across the road** traverser [**28**] la rue en courant; **across from** *(opposite)* en face de ▷ *He sat down across from her.* Il s'est assis en face d'elle.
act *vb* ❶ *(in play, film)* jouer [**28**] ▷ *He acts really well.* Il joue vraiment bien. ❷ *(take action)* agir [**38**] ▷ *The police acted quickly.* La police a agi rapidement.; **She acts as his interpreter.** Elle lui sert d'interprète.
▶ *n (in play)* acte *m* ▷ *in the first act* au premier acte
action *n* action *f* ▷ *The film was full of action.* Il y avait beaucoup d'action dans le film.; **to take firm action against** prendre [**65**] des mesures énergiques contre
active *adj* actif *(f* active) ▷ *He's a very active person.* Il est très actif.; **an active volcano** un volcan en activité
activity *n* activité *f* ▷ *outdoor activities* les activités de plein air
actor *n* acteur *m* ▷ *Brad Pitt is a well-known actor.* Brad Pitt est un acteur connu.
actress *n* actrice *f* ▷ *Julia Roberts is a well-known actress.* Julia Roberts est une actrice connue.
actual *adj* réel *(f* réelle) ▷ *The film is based on actual events.* Le film repose sur des faits réels.; **What's the actual amount?** Quel est le montant exact?

> Be careful not to translate **actual** by **actuel**.

actually *adv* ❶ *(really)* vraiment ▷ *Did it actually happen?* Est-ce que c'est vraiment arrivé? ❷ *(in fact)* en fait ▷ *Actually, I don't know him at all.* En fait, je ne le connais pas du tout.

> Be careful not to translate **actually** by **actuellement**.

AD *abbr* ap. J.-C. (= *après Jésus-Christ)* ▷ *in 800 AD* en huit cents après Jésus-Christ
ad *n* ❶ *(in paper)* annonce *f* ❷ *(on TV, radio)* pub *f*

adapt *vb* adapter [**28**] ▷ *His novel was adapted for television.* Son roman a été adapté pour la télévision.; **to adapt to something** *(get used to)* s'adapter [**28**] à quelque chose ▷ *He adapted to his new school very quickly.* Il s'est adapté très vite à sa nouvelle école.

adaptor *n* adaptateur *m*

add *vb* ajouter [**28**] ▷ *Add two eggs to the mixture.* Ajoutez deux œufs au mélange.

add up *vb* additionner [**28**] ▷ *Add the figures up.* Additionnez les chiffres.

addict *n (drug addict)* drogué *m*, droguée *f*; **Jean-Pierre's a football addict.** Jean-Pierre est un mordu de football.

addicted *adj* **to be addicted to** *(drug)* s'adonner [**28**] à ▷ *She's addicted to heroin.* Elle s'adonne à l'héroïne.; **She's addicted to soap operas.** C'est une mordue des soaps.

addition *n* **in addition** en plus ▷ *He's broken his leg and, in addition, he's caught a cold.* Il s'est cassé la jambe et en plus, il a attrapé un rhume.; **in addition to** en plus de ▷ *There's a postage fee in addition to the repair charge.* Il y a des frais de port en plus du prix de la réparation.

address *n* adresse *f* ▷ *What's your address?* Quelle est votre adresse?

adjective *n* adjectif *m*

adjust *vb* régler [**34**] ▷ *You can adjust the height of the chair.* Tu peux régler la hauteur de la chaise.; **to adjust to something** *(get used to)* s'adapter [**28**] à quelque chose ▷ *He adjusted to his new school very quickly.* Il s'est adapté très vite à sa nouvelle école.

adjustable *adj* réglable

administration *n* administration *f*

admiral *n* amiral *m*

admire *vb* admirer [**28**]

admission *n* entrée *f*; **'admission free'** 'entrée gratuite'

admit *vb* ❶ *(agree)* admettre [**47**] ▷ *I must admit that ...* Je dois admettre que ... ❷ *(confess)* reconnaître [**14**] ▷ *He admitted that he'd done it.* Il a reconnu qu'il l'avait fait.

adolescent *n* adolescent *m*, adolescente *f*

adopt *vb* adopter [**28**] ▷ *Phil was adopted.* Phil a été adopté.

adopted *adj* adoptif (*f* adoptive) ▷ *an adopted son* un fils adoptif

adoption *n* adoption *f*

adore *vb* adorer [**28**]

Adriatic Sea *n* mer Adriatique *f*

adult *n* adulte *mf*; **adult education** l'enseignement pour adultes *m*

advance *vb* ❶ *(move forward)* avancer [**12**] ▷ *The troops are advancing.* Les troupes avancent. ❷ *(progress)* progresser [**28**] ▷ *Technology has advanced a lot.* La technologie a beaucoup progressé.

▶ *n* **in advance** à l'avance ▷ *They*

bought the tickets in advance. Ils ont acheté les billets à l'avance.

advanced *adj* avancé(e)

advantage *n* avantage *m* ▷ *Going to university has many advantages.* Aller à l'université présente de nombreux avantages.; **to take advantage of something** profiter [**28**] de quelque chose ▷ *He took advantage of the good weather to go for a walk.* Il a profité du beau temps pour faire une promenade.; **to take advantage of somebody** exploiter [**28**] quelqu'un ▷ *The company was taking advantage of its employees.* La société exploitait ses employés.

adventure *n* aventure *f*

adverb *n* adverbe *m*

advert, advertisement *n* ❶ *(on TV)* publicité *f* ❷ *(in newspaper)* annonce *f*

advertise *vb* faire [**36**] de la publicité pour ▷ *They're advertising the new model.* Ils font de la publicité pour leur nouveau modèle.; **Jobs are advertised in the paper.** Le journal publie des annonces d'emplois.

advertising *n* publicité *f*

advice *n* conseils *mpl* ▷ *to give somebody advice* donner des conseils à quelqu'un; **a piece of advice** un conseil ▷ *He gave me a good piece of advice.* Il m'a donné un bon conseil.

advise *vb* conseiller [**28**] ▷ *He advised me to wait.* Il m'a conseillé d'attendre. ▷ *He advised me not to go there.* Il m'a conseillé de ne pas y aller.

aerial *n* antenne *f*

aerobics *n* aérobic *f* ▷ *I'm going to aerobics tonight.* Je vais au cours d'aérobic ce soir.

aeroplane *n* avion *m*

aerosol *n* bombe *f*

affair *n* ❶ *(romantic)* aventure *f* ▷ *to have an affair with somebody* avoir une aventure avec quelqu'un ❷ *(event)* affaire *f*

affect *vb* affecter [**1**]

affectionate *adj* affectueux *(f* affectueuse)

afford *vb* avoir [**8**] les moyens d'acheter ▷ *I can't afford a new pair of jeans.* Je n'ai pas les moyens d'acheter un nouveau jean.; **We can't afford to go on holiday.** Nous n'avons pas les moyens de partir en vacances.

afraid *adj* **to be afraid of something** avoir [**8**] peur de quelque chose ▷ *I'm afraid of spiders.* J'ai peur des araignées.; **I'm afraid I can't come.** Je crains de ne pouvoir venir.; **I'm afraid so.** Hélas oui.; **I'm afraid not.** Hélas non.

Africa *n* Afrique *f*; **in Africa** en Afrique

African *n* Africain *m*, Africaine *f* ▶ *adj* africain(e)

after *prep, adv, conj* après ▷ *after dinner* après le dîner ▷ *He ran after me.* Il a couru après moi. ▷ *soon after* peu après; **after I'd had a rest** après m'être reposé; **after having asked** après avoir demandé; **after all** après tout

afternoon *n* après-midi *mf* ▷ *3 o'clock in the afternoon* trois heures de l'après-midi ▷ *this afternoon* cet après-midi ▷ *on Saturday afternoon* samedi après-midi

afters *n* dessert *m*

aftershave *n* après-rasage *m*

afterwards *adv* après ▷ *She left not long afterwards.* Elle est partie peu de temps après.

again *adv* ❶ *(once more)* de nouveau ▷ *They're friends again.* Ils sont de nouveau amis. ❷ *(one more time)* encore une fois ▷ *Can you tell me again?* Tu peux me le dire encore une fois?; **not ... again** ne ... plus ▷ *I won't go there again.* Je n'y retournerai plus.; **Do it again!** Refais-le!; **again and again** à plusieurs reprises

against *prep* contre ▷ *He leant against the wall.* Il s'est appuyé contre le mur. ▷ *I'm against nuclear testing.* Je suis contre les essais nucléaires.

age *n* âge *m* ▷ *at the age of 16* à l'âge de seize ans; **I haven't been to the cinema for ages.** Ça fait une éternité que je ne suis pas allé au cinéma.

agenda *n* ordre du jour *m* ▷ *on the agenda* à l'ordre du jour

> Be careful not to translate **agenda** by the French word **agenda**.

agent *n* agent *m* ▷ *an estate agent* un agent immobilier

aggressive *adj* agressif (*f* agressive)

ago *adv* **two days ago** il y a deux jours; **two years ago** il y a deux ans; **not long ago** il n'y a pas longtemps; **How long ago did it happen?** Il y a combien de temps que c'est arrivé?

agony *n* **to be in agony** souffrir [**54**] le martyre ▷ *He was in agony.* Il souffrait le martyre.

agree *vb* **to agree with** être [**35**] d'accord avec ▷ *I agree with Carol.* Je suis d'accord avec Carol.; **to agree to do something** accepter [**28**] de faire quelque chose ▷ *He agreed to go and pick her up.* Il a accepté d'aller la chercher.; **to agree that ...** admettre [**47**] que ... ▷ *I agree that it's difficult.* J'admets que c'est difficile.; **Garlic doesn't agree with me.** Je ne supporte pas l'ail.

agreement *n* accord *m*; **to be in agreement** être [**35**] d'accord ▷ *Everybody was in agreement with Ray.* Tout le monde était d'accord avec Ray.

agricultural *adj* agricole

agriculture *n* agriculture *f*

ahead *adv* devant ▷ *She looked straight ahead.* Elle regardait droit devant elle.; **ahead of time** en avance; **to plan ahead** organiser [**28**] à l'avance; **The French are 5 points ahead.** Les Français ont cinq points d'avance.; **Go ahead!** Allez-y!

aid *n* **in aid of charity** au profit d'associations caritatives

AIDS *n* sida *m*

aim *vb* **to aim at** braquer [**28**] sur

▷ *He aimed a gun at me.* Il a braqué un revolver sur moi.; **The film is aimed at children.** Le film est destiné aux enfants.; **to aim to do something** avoir [**8**] l'intention de faire quelque chose ▷ *Janice aimed to leave at 5 o'clock.* Janice avait l'intention de partir à cinq heures. ▶ *n* objectif *m* ▷ *The aim of the festival is to raise money.* L'objectif du festival est de collecter des fonds.

air *n* air *m* ▷ *to get some fresh air* prendre l'air; **by air** en avion ▷ *I prefer to travel by air.* Je préfère voyager en avion.

air-conditioned *adj* climatisé(e)

air conditioning *n* climatisation *f*

Air Force *n* armée de l'air *f*

air hostess *n* hôtesse de l'air *f* ▷ *She's an air hostess.* Elle est hôtesse de l'air.

airline *n* compagnie aérienne *f*

airmail *n* **by airmail** par avion

airplane *n (US)* avion *m*

airport *n* aéroport *m*

aisle *n* allée centrale *f*

alarm *n (warning)* alarme *f*; **a fire alarm** une alarme à incendie

alarm clock *n* réveil *m*

album *n* album *m*

alcohol *n* alcool *m*

alcoholic *n* alcoolique *mf* ▷ *He's an alcoholic.* C'est un alcoolique. ▶ *adj* alcoolisé(e) ▷ *alcoholic drinks* des boissons alcoolisées

alert *adj* ❶ *(bright)* vif *(f* vive) ▷ *a very alert baby* un bébé très vif ❷ *(paying attention)* vigilant(e) ▷ *We must stay alert.* Nous devons rester vigilants.

A levels *npl* baccalauréat *msg*

The **baccalauréat** (or **bac** for short) is taken at the age of 17 or 18. Students have to sit one of a variety of set subject combinations, rather than being able to choose any combination of subjects they want. If you pass you have the right to a place at university.

Algeria *n* Algérie *f*; **in Algeria** en Algérie

alien *n (from outer space)* extra-terrestre *mf*

alike *adv* **to look alike** se ressembler [**28**] ▷ *The two sisters look alike.* Les deux sœurs se ressemblent.

alive *adj* vivant(e)

all *adj, pron, adv* tout(e) *(mpl* tous) ▷ *all the time* tout le temps ▷ *I ate all of it.* J'ai tout mangé. ▷ *all day* toute la journée ▷ *all the books* tous les livres ▷ *all the girls* toutes les filles; **All of us went.** Nous y sommes tous allés.; **after all** après tout ▷ *After all, nobody can make us go.* Après tout, personne ne peut nous obliger à y aller.; **all alone** tout seul ▷ *She's all alone.* Elle est toute seule.; **not at all** pas du tout ▷ *I'm not tired at all.* Je ne suis pas du tout fatigué.; **The score is 5 all.** Le score est de cinq partout.

allergic *adj* allergique; **to be allergic to something** être [**35**] allergique à quelque chose ▷ *I'm allergic to cats' hair.* Je suis allergique aux poils de chat.

allergy *n* allergie *f*

allow *vb* **to be allowed to do something** être [**35**] autorisé à faire quelque chose ▷ *He's not allowed to go out at night.* Il n'est pas autorisé à sortir le soir.; **to allow somebody to do something** permettre [**47**] à quelqu'un de faire quelque chose ▷ *His mum allowed him to go out.* Sa mère lui a permis de sortir.

all right *adv* ❶ *(okay)* bien ▷ *Everything turned out all right.* Tout s'est bien terminé.; **Are you all right?** Ça va? ❷ *(not bad)* pas mal ▷ *The film was all right.* Le film n'était pas mal. ❸ *(when agreeing)* d'accord ▷ *We'll talk about it later. — All right.* On en reparlera plus tard. — D'accord.; **Is that all right with you?** Tu es d'accord?

almond *n* amande *f*

almost *adv* presque ▷ *I've almost finished.* J'ai presque fini.

alone *adj, adv* seul(e) ▷ *She lives alone.* Elle habite seule.; **to leave somebody alone** laisser [**28**] quelqu'un tranquille ▷ *Leave her alone!* Laisse-la tranquille!; **to leave something alone** ne pas toucher [**28**] à quelque chose ▷ *Leave my things alone!* Ne touche pas à mes affaires!

along *prep, adv* le long de ▷ *Chris was walking along the beach.* Chris se promenait le long de la plage.; **all along** depuis le début ▷ *He was lying to me all along.* Il m'a menti depuis le début.

aloud *adv* à haute voix ▷ *He read the poem aloud.* Il a lu le poème à haute voix.

alphabet *n* alphabet *m*

Alps *npl* Alpes *fpl*

already *adv* déjà ▷ *Liz had already gone.* Liz était déjà partie.

also *adv* aussi

alter *vb* changer [**45**]

alternate *adj* **on alternate days** tous les deux jours

alternative *n* choix *m* ▷ *You have no alternative.* Tu n'a pas le choix.; **Fruit is a healthy alternative to chocolate.** Les fruits sont plus sains que le chocolat.; **There are several alternatives.** Il y a plusieurs possibilités.
▶ *adj* autre ▷ *They made alternative plans.* Ils ont pris d'autres dispositions.; **an alternative solution** une solution de rechange; **alternative medicine** la médecine douce

alternatively *adv* **Alternatively, we could just stay at home.** On pourrait aussi rester à la maison.

although *conj* bien que

> **bien que** has to be followed by a verb in the subjunctive.

▷ *Although she was tired, she stayed up late.* Bien qu'elle soit fatiguée, elle s'est couchée tard.

altogether *adv* ❶ *(in total)* en tout ▷ *You owe me £20 altogether.* Tu me dois vingt livres en tout.
❷ *(completely)* tout à fait ▷ *I'm not altogether happy with your work.* Je ne suis pas tout à fait satisfait

de votre travail.
aluminium (*US* **aluminum**) *n* aluminium *m*
always *adv* toujours ▷ *He's always moaning.* Il est toujours en train de ronchonner.
am *vb see* **be**
a.m. *abbr* du matin ▷ *at 4 a.m.* à quatre heures du matin
amateur *n* amateur *m*
amaze *vb* **to be amazed** être [**35**] stupéfait ▷ *I was amazed that I managed to do it.* J'étais stupéfait d'avoir réussi.
amazing *adj* ❶ *(surprising)* stupéfiant(e) ▷ *That's amazing news!* C'est une nouvelle stupéfiante! ❷ *(excellent)* exceptionnel (*f* exceptionnelle) ▷ *Vivian's an amazing cook.* Vivian est une cuisinière exceptionnelle.
ambassador *n* ambassadeur *m*, ambassadrice *f*
ambition *n* ambition *f*
ambitious *adj* ambitieux (*f* ambitieuse) ▷ *She's very ambitious.* Elle est très ambitieuse.
ambulance *n* ambulance *f*
amenities *npl* aménagements *mpl*; **The hotel has very good amenities.** L'hôtel est très bien aménagé.
America *n* Amérique *f*; **in America** en Amérique; **to America** en Amérique
American *n* Américain *m*, Américaine *f*; **the Americans** les Américains
▸ *adj* américain(e) ▷ *She's American.* Elle est américaine.
among *prep* parmi ▷ *There were six children among them.* Il y avait six enfants parmi eux.; **We were among friends.** Nous étions entre amis.; **among other things** entre autres
amount *n* ❶ somme *f* ▷ *a large amount of money* une grosse somme d'argent ❷ quantité *f* ▷ *a huge amount of rice* une énorme quantité de riz
amp *n* ❶ *(of electricity)* ampère *m* ❷ *(for hi-fi)* ampli *m*
amplifier *n (for hi-fi)* amplificateur *m*
amuse *vb* amuser [**28**] ▷ *He was most amused by the story.* L'histoire l'a beaucoup amusé.
amusement arcade *n* salle de jeux électroniques *f*
an *art see* **a**
analyse *vb* analyser [**28**]
analysis *n* analyse *f*
ancestor *n* ancêtre *mf*
anchor *n* ancre *f*
ancient *adj* ❶ *(civilization)* antique ▷ *ancient Greece* la Grèce antique ❷ *(custom, building)* ancien (*f* ancienne) ▷ *an ancient monument* un monument ancien
and *conj* et ▷ *you and me* toi et moi; **Please try and come!** Essaie de venir!; **He talked and talked.** Il n'a pas arrêté de parler.; **better and better** de mieux en mieux
angel *n* ange *m*
anger *n* colère *f*
angle *n* angle *m*

angry *adj* en colère ▷ *Dad looks very angry.* Papa a l'air très en colère.; **to be angry with somebody** être [**35**] furieux contre quelqu'un ▷ *Mum's really angry with you.* Maman est vraiment furieuse contre toi.; **to get angry** se fâcher [**28**]

animal *n* animal *m* (*pl* animaux)

ankle *n* cheville *f*

anniversary *n* anniversaire *m* ▷ *a wedding anniversary* un anniversaire de mariage

announce *vb* annoncer [**12**]

announcement *n* annonce *f*

annoy *vb* agacer [**12**] ▷ *He's really annoying me.* Il m'agace vraiment.; **to get annoyed** se fâcher [**28**] ▷ *Don't get so annoyed!* Ne vous fâchez pas!

annoying *adj* agaçant(e) ▷ *It's really annoying.* C'est vraiment agaçant.

annual *adj* annuel (*f* annuelle) ▷ *an annual meeting* une réunion annuelle

anorak *n* anorak *m*

another *adj* un autre (*f* une autre) ▷ *Would you like another piece of cake?* Tu veux un autre morceau de gâteau?

answer *vb* répondre [**69**] à ▷ *Can you answer my question?* Peux-tu répondre à ma question? ▷ *to answer the phone* répondre au téléphone; **to answer the door** aller [**3**] ouvrir ▷ *Can you answer the door please?* Tu peux aller ouvrir s'il te plaît?

▶ *n* ❶ *(to question)* réponse *f* ❷ *(to problem)* solution *f*

answering machine *n* répondeur *m*

ant *n* fourmi *f*

Antarctic *n* Antarctique *f*

anthem *n* **the national anthem** l'hymne national *m*

antibiotic *n* antibiotique *m*

antique *n (furniture)* meuble ancien *m*

antique shop *n* magasin d'antiquités *m*

antiseptic *n* antiseptique *m*

any *adj, pron, adv*

> Use **du**, **de la** or **des** to translate 'any' according to the gender of the French noun that follows it. **du** and **de la** become **de l'** when they're followed by a noun starting with a vowel.

❶ du ▷ *Would you like any bread?* Voulez-vous du pain?; de la ▷ *Would you like any beer?* Voulez-vous de la bière?; de l' ▷ *Have you got any mineral water?* Avez-vous de l'eau minérale?; des ▷ *Have you got any Madonna CDs?* Avez-vous des CD de Madonna?

> If you want to say you haven't got any of something, use **de** whatever the gender of the following noun is. **de** becomes **d'** when it comes before a noun starting with a vowel.

❷ de ▷ *I haven't got any books.* Je n'ai pas de livres.; d' ▷ *I haven't got any money.* Je n'ai pas d'argent. ❸ en

Use **en** where there is no noun after 'any'.

▷ *Sorry, I haven't got any.* Désolé, je n'en ai pas.; **any more** **(1)** *(additional)* encore de ▷ *Would you like any more coffee?* Est-ce que tu veux encore du café? **(2)** *(no longer)* ne ... plus ▷ *I don't love him any more.* Je ne l'aime plus.

anybody *pron* ❶ *(in question)* quelqu'un ▷ *Has anybody got a pen?* Est-ce que quelqu'un a un stylo? ❷ *(no matter who)* n'importe qui ▷ *Anybody can learn to swim.* N'importe qui peut apprendre à nager. ❸ ne ... personne

Use **ne ... personne** in a negative sentence. **ne** comes before the verb, **personne** after it.

▷ *I can't see anybody.* Je ne vois personne.

anyhow *adv* de toute façon

anyone *pron* ❶ *(in question)* quelqu'un ❷ *(no matter who)* n'importe qui ❸ ne ... personne

anything *pron* ❶ *(in question)* quelque chose ▷ *Would you like anything to eat?* Tu veux manger quelque chose? ❷ *(no matter what)* n'importe quoi ▷ *Anything could happen.* Il pourrait arriver n'importe quoi. ❸ ne ... rien

Use **ne ... rien** in a negative sentence. **ne** comes before the verb, **rien** after it.

▷ *I can't hear anything.* Je n'entends rien.

anyway *adv* de toute façon ▷ *He doesn't want to go out and anyway he's not allowed.* Il ne veut pas sortir et de toute façon il n'y est pas autorisé.

anywhere *adv* ❶ *(in question)* quelque part ▷ *Have you seen my coat anywhere?* Est-ce que tu as vu mon manteau quelque part? ❷ n'importe où ▷ *You can buy stamps almost anywhere.* On peut acheter des timbres presque n'importe où. ❸ ne ... nulle part

Use **ne ... nulle part** in a negative sentence. **ne** comes before the verb, **nulle part** after it.

▷ *I can't find it anywhere.* Je ne le trouve nulle part.

apart *adv* **The two towns are 10 kilometres apart.** Les deux villes sont à dix kilomètres l'une de l'autre.; **apart from** à part ▷ *Apart from that, everything's fine.* À part ça, tout va bien.

apartment *n* appartement *m*

apologize *vb* s'excuser **[28]** ▷ *He apologized for being late.* Il s'est excusé de son retard.; **I apologize!** Je vous prie de m'excuser.

apology *n* excuses *fpl*

apostrophe *n* apostrophe *f*

app *n (= application)* appli *f*

apparent *adj* apparent(e)

apparently *adv* apparemment

appeal *vb* lancer **[12]** un appel ▷ *They appealed for help.* Ils ont lancé un appel au secours.; **Greece doesn't appeal to me.** Ça ne me tente pas d'aller en Grèce.; **Does**

that appeal to you? Ça te tente? ▶ *n* appel *m* ▷ *They have launched an appeal.* Ils ont lancé un appel.

appear *vb* ❶ *(come into view)* apparaître [**56**] ▷ *The bus appeared around the corner.* Le bus est apparu au coin de la rue.; **to appear on TV** passer [**58**] à la télé ❷ *(seem)* paraître [**56**] ▷ *She appeared to be asleep.* Elle paraissait dormir.

appendicitis *n* appendicite *f*

appetite *n* appétit *m*

applaud *vb* applaudir [**38**]

applause *n* applaudissements *mpl*

apple *n* pomme *f*; **an apple tree** un pommier

applicant *n* candidat *m*, candidate *f* ▷ *There were a hundred applicants for the job.* Il y avait cent candidats pour ce poste.

application *n* **a job application** une candidature

application form *n* ❶ *(for job)* dossier de candidature *m* ❷ *(for university)* dossier d'inscription *m*

apply *vb* **to apply for a job** poser [**28**] sa candidature à un poste; **to apply to** *(be relevant)* s'appliquer [**28**] à ▷ *This rule doesn't apply to us.* Ce règlement ne s'applique pas à nous.

appointment *n* rendez-vous *m* ▷ *I've got a dental appointment.* J'ai rendez-vous chez le dentiste.

appreciate *vb* être [**35**] reconnaissant de ▷ *I really appreciate your help.* Je vous suis extrêmement reconnaissant de votre aide.

apprentice *n* apprenti *m*, apprentie *f*

approach *vb* ❶ *(get nearer to)* s'approcher [**28**] de ▷ *He approached the house.* Il s'est approché de la maison. ❷ *(tackle)* aborder [**28**] ▷ *to approach a problem* aborder un problème

appropriate *adj* approprié(e) ▷ *That dress isn't very appropriate for an interview.* Cette robe n'est pas très appropriée pour un entretien.

approval *n* approbation *f*

approve *vb* **to approve of** approuver [**28**] ▷ *I don't approve of his choice.* Je n'approuve pas son choix.; **They didn't approve of his girlfriend.** Sa copine ne leur a pas plu.

approximate *adj* approximatif (*f* approximative)

apricot *n* abricot *m*

April *n* avril *m*; **in April** en avril; **April Fools' Day** le premier avril

Pinning a paper fish to somebody's back is a traditional April Fool joke in France.

apron *n* tablier *m*

Aquarius *n* Verseau *m* ▷ *I'm Aquarius.* Je suis Verseau.

Arab *n* Arabe *mf* ▶ *adj* arabe ▷ *the Arab countries* les pays arabes

Arabic *n* arabe *m*

arch *n* arc *m*

archaeologist *n* archéologue *mf* ▷ *He's an archaeologist.* Il est archéologue.

archaeology *n* archéologie *f*

archbishop *n* archevêque *m*
archeologist *n (US)* archéologue *mf*
archeology *n (US)* archéologie *f*
architect *n* architecte *mf* ▷ *She's an architect.* Elle est architecte.
architecture *n* architecture *f*
Arctic *n* Arctique *m*
are *vb see* **be**
area *n* ❶ région *f* ▷ *She lives in the Paris area.* Elle habite dans la région parisienne. ❷ quartier *m* ▷ *My favourite area of Paris is Montmartre.* Montmartre est le quartier de Paris que je préfère. ❸ superficie *f* ▷ *The field has an area of 1500m².* Le champ a une superficie de mille cinq cents mètres carrés.
Argentina *n* Argentine *f*; **in Argentina** en Argentine
Argentinian *adj* argentin(e)
argue *vb* se disputer [**28**] ▷ *They never stop arguing.* Ils n'arrêtent pas de se disputer.
argument *n* **to have an argument** se disputer [**28**] ▷ *They had an argument.* Ils se sont disputés.
Aries *n* Bélier *m* ▷ *I'm Aries.* Je suis Bélier.
arm *n* bras *m*
armchair *n* fauteuil *m*
army *n* armée *f*
around *prep, adv* ❶ autour de ▷ *She wore a scarf around her neck.* Elle portait une écharpe autour du cou. ❷ *(approximately)* environ ▷ *It costs around £100.* Cela coûte environ cent livres. ❸ *(date, time)* vers ▷ *Let's meet at around 8 p.m.* Retrouvons-nous vers vingt heures.; **around here (1)** *(nearby)* près d'ici ▷ *Is there a chemist's around here?* Est-ce qu'il y a une pharmacie près d'ici? **(2)** *(in this area)* dans les parages ▷ *He lives around here.* Il habite dans les parages.
arrange *vb* **to arrange to do something** prévoir [**92**] de faire quelque chose ▷ *They arranged to go out together on Friday.* Ils ont prévu de sortir ensemble vendredi.; **to arrange a meeting** convenir [**89**] d'un rendez-vous ▷ *Can we arrange a meeting?* Pouvons-nous convenir d'un rendez-vous?; **to arrange a party** organiser [**28**] une fête
arrangement *n (plan)* arrangement *m*; **They made arrangements to go out on Friday night.** Ils ont organisé une sortie vendredi soir.
arrest *vb* arrêter [**28**] ▷ *The police have arrested 5 people.* La police a arrêté cinq personnes.
▶ *n* arrestation *f*; **to be under arrest** être [**35**] en état d'arrestation ▷ *You're under arrest!* Vous êtes en état d'arrestation!
arrival *n* arrivée *f*
arrive *vb* arriver [**5**] ▷ *I arrived at 5 o'clock.* Je suis arrivé à cinq heures.
arrow *n* flèche *f*
art *n* art *m*
artery *n* artère *f*
art gallery *n* musée *m*
article *n* article *m* ▷ *a newspaper article* un article de journal
artificial *adj* artificiel (*f* artificielle)

artist *n* artiste *mf* ▷ *She's an artist.* C'est une artiste.
artistic *adj* artistique
as *conj, adv* ❶ *(while)* au moment où ▷ *He came in as I was leaving.* Il est arrivé au moment où je partais. ❷ *(since)* puisque ▷ *As it's Sunday, you can have a lie-in.* Tu peux faire la grasse matinée, puisque c'est dimanche.; **as ... as** aussi ... que ▷ *Pierre's as tall as Michel.* Pierre est aussi grand que Michel.; **twice as ... as** deux fois plus ... que ▷ *Her coat cost twice as much as mine.* Son manteau a coûté deux fois plus cher que le mien.; **as much ... as** autant ... que ▷ *I haven't got as much money as you.* Je n'ai pas autant d'argent que toi.; **as soon as possible** dès que possible ▷ *I'll do it as soon as possible.* Je le ferai dès que possible.; **as from tomorrow** à partir de demain ▷ *As from tomorrow, the shop will be closed on Sundays.* À partir de demain, le magasin sera fermé le dimanche.; **as though** comme si ▷ *She acted as though she hadn't seen me.* Elle a fait comme si elle ne m'avait pas vu.; **as if** comme si; **He works as a waiter in the holidays.** Il travaille comme serveur pendant les vacances.
ashamed *adj* **to be ashamed** avoir [**8**] honte ▷ *You should be ashamed of yourself!* Tu devrais avoir honte!
ashtray *n* cendrier *m*
Asia *n* Asie *f*; **in Asia** en Asie
Asian *n* Asiatique *mf*
▶ *adj* asiatique; **He's Asian.** C'est un Asiatique.
ask *vb* ❶ *(inquire, request)* demander [**28**] ▷ *'Have you finished?' she asked.* 'Tu as fini?' a-t-elle demandé.; **to ask somebody something** demander [**28**] quelque chose à quelqu'un ▷ *He asked her how old she was.* Il lui a demandé quel âge elle avait.; **to ask for something** demander [**28**] quelque chose ▷ *He asked for a cup of tea.* Il a demandé une tasse de thé.; **to ask somebody to do something** demander [**28**] à quelqu'un de faire quelque chose ▷ *She asked him to do the shopping.* Elle lui a demandé de faire les courses.; **to ask about something** se renseigner [**28**] sur quelque chose ▷ *I asked about train times to Leeds.* Je me suis renseigné sur les horaires des trains pour Leeds.; **to ask somebody a question** poser [**28**] une question à quelqu'un ❷ inviter [**28**] ▷ *Have you asked Matthew to the party?* Est-ce que tu as invité Matthew à la fête?; **He asked her out.** *(on a date)* Il lui a demandé de sortir avec lui.
asleep *adj* **to be asleep** dormir [**29**] ▷ *He's asleep.* Il dort.; **to fall asleep** s'endormir [**29**] ▷ *I fell asleep in front of the TV.* Je me suis endormi devant la télé.
asparagus *n* asperges *fpl*
aspirin *n* aspirine *f*
assembly *n*
There is no assembly in French schools.

assignment *n (in school)* devoir *m*
assistance *n* aide *f*
assistant *n* ❶ *(in shop)* vendeur *m*, vendeuse *f* ❷ *(helper)* assistant *m*, assistante *f*
association *n* association *f*
assortment *n* assortiment *m*
assume *vb* supposer [**28**] ▷ *I assume she won't be coming.* Je suppose qu'elle ne viendra pas.
assure *vb* assurer [**28**] ▷ *He assured me he was coming.* Il m'a assuré qu'il viendrait.
asthma *n* asthme *m* ▷ *I've got asthma.* J'ai de l'asthme.
astonished *adj* étonné(e)
astonishing *adj* étonnant(e)
astrology *n* astrologie *f*
astronaut *n* astronaute *mf*
astronomy *n* astronomie *f*
at *prep*

> **à + le** becomes **au**, **à + les** becomes **aux**.

à ▷ *at 4 o'clock* à quatre heures ▷ *at Christmas* à Noël ▷ *at home* à la maison ▷ *at school* à l'école
au ▷ *at the office* au bureau
aux ▷ *at the races* aux courses; **at night** la nuit; **What are you doing at the weekend?** Qu'est-ce que tu fais ce week-end?
▶ *n (@ symbol)* arobase *f*
ate *vb see* **eat**
Athens *n* Athènes; **in Athens** à Athènes
athlete *n* athlète *mf*
athletic *adj* athlétique
athletics *n* athlétisme *m* ▷ *I love athletics.* J'aime l'athlétisme.
Atlantic *n* océan Atlantique *m*
atlas *n* atlas *m*
atmosphere *n* atmosphère *f*
atom *n* atome *m*
atomic *adj* atomique
attach *vb* fixer [**28**] ▷ *He attached a rope to the car.* Il a fixé une corde à la voiture.; **Please find attached ...** Veuillez trouver ci-joint ...
attached *adj* **to be attached to** être [**35**] attaché à ▷ *He's very attached to his family.* Il est très attaché à sa famille.
attachment *n (email)* pièce jointe *f*
attack *vb* attaquer [**28**] ▷ *The dog attacked her.* Le chien l'a attaquée.
▶ *n* attaque *f*
attempt *n* tentative *f* ▷ *She gave up after several attempts.* Elle y a renoncé après plusieurs tentatives.
▶ *vb* **to attempt to do something** essayer [**59**] de faire quelque chose ▷ *I attempted to write a song.* J'ai essayé d'écrire une chanson.
attend *vb* assister [**28**] à ▷ *to attend a meeting* assister à une réunion

> Be careful not to translate **to attend** by **attendre**.

attention *n* **to pay attention to** faire [**36**] attention à ▷ *He didn't pay attention to what I was saying.* Il ne faisait pas attention à ce que je disais.
attic *n* grenier *m*
attitude *n (way of thinking)* attitude *f* ▷ *I really don't like your attitude!* Je n'aime pas du tout ton attitude!
attorney *n (US)* avocat *m*, avocate *f*
attract *vb* attirer [**28**] ▷ *The Lake*

District attracts lots of tourists. La région des lacs attire de nombreux touristes.

attraction *n* attraction *f* ▷ *a tourist attraction* une attraction touristique

attractive *adj* séduisant(e) ▷ *She's very attractive.* Elle est très séduisante.

aubergine *n* aubergine *f*

auction *n* vente aux enchères *f*

audience *n (in theatre)* spectateurs *mpl*

August *n* août *m*; **in August** en août

aunt, aunty *n* tante *f* ▷ *my aunt* ma tante

au pair *n* jeune fille au pair *f* ▷ *She's an au pair.* Elle est jeune fille au pair.

Australia *n* Australie *f*; **in Australia** en Australie; **to Australia** en Australie

Australian *n* Australien *m*, Australienne *f*; **the Australians** les Australiens
▶ *adj* australien (*f* australienne) ▷ *He's Australian.* Il est australien.

Austria *n* Autriche *f*; **in Austria** en Autriche

Austrian *n* Autrichien *m*, Autrichienne *f*; **the Austrians** les Autrichiens
▶ *adj* autrichien (*f* autrichienne) ▷ *She's Austrian.* Elle est autrichienne.

author *n* auteur *m* ▷ *She's a famous author.* C'est un auteur connu.

autobiography *n* autobiographie *f*

autograph *n* autographe *m*

automatic *adj* automatique ▷ *an automatic door* une porte automatique

automatically *adv* automatiquement

autumn *n* automne *m*; **in autumn** en automne

availability *n* disponibilité *f*

available *adj* disponible ▷ *Free brochures are available on request.* Des brochures gratuites sont disponibles sur demande. ▷ *Is Mr Cooke available today?* Est-ce que Monsieur Cooke est disponible aujourd'hui?

avalanche *n* avalanche *f*

avenue *n* avenue *f*

average *n* moyenne *f* ▷ *on average* en moyenne
▶ *adj* moyen (*f* moyenne) ▷ *the average price* le prix moyen

avocado *n* avocat *m*

avoid *vb* éviter [**28**] ▷ *He avoids her when she's in a bad mood.* Il l'évite lorsqu'elle est de mauvaise humeur.; **to avoid doing something** éviter [**28**] de faire quelque chose ▷ *Avoid going out on your own at night.* Évite de sortir seul le soir.

awake *adj* **to be awake** être [**35**] réveillé ▷ *Is she awake?* Elle est réveillée?; **He was still awake.** Il ne dormait pas encore.

award *n* prix *m* ▷ *He's won an award.* Il a remporté un prix.

aware *adj* **to be aware of something** être [**35**] conscient de quelque chose

away *adj, adv (not here)* absent(e) ▷ *André's away today.* André est absent aujourd'hui.; **He's away for a week.** Il est parti pour une semaine.; **The town's 2 kilometres away.** La ville est à deux kilomètres d'ici.; **The coast is 2 hours away by car.** La côte est à deux heures de route.; **Go away!** Va-t'en!; **to put something away** ranger [**45**] quelque chose ▷ *He put the books away in the cupboard.* Il a rangé les livres dans le placard.

away match *n* match à l'extérieur *m*

awful *adj* affreux (*f* affreuse) ▷ *That's awful!* C'est affreux!; **an awful lot of ...** énormément de ...

awkward *adj* ❶ *(difficult to deal with)* délicat(e) ▷ *an awkward situation* une situation délicate ❷ *(embarrassing)* gênant(e) ▷ *an awkward question* une question gênante; **It's a bit awkward for me to come and see you.** Ce n'est pas très pratique pour moi de venir vous voir.

axe *n* hache *f*

baby *n* bébé *m*

babysit *vb* faire [**36**] du baby-sitting

babysitter *n* baby-sitter *mf*

babysitting *n* baby-sitting *m*

bachelor *n* célibataire *m* ▷ *He's a bachelor.* Il est célibataire.

back *n* ❶ *(of person, horse, book)* dos *m* ❷ *(of car, house)* arrière *m* ▷ *in the back* à l'arrière ❸ *(of page)* verso *m* ▷ *on the back* au verso ❹ *(of room, garden)* fond *m* ▷ *at the back* au fond ▶ *adj, adv* arrière ▷ *the back seat* le siège arrière ▷ *the back wheel of my bike* la roue arrière de mon vélo; **the back door** la porte de derrière; **to get back** rentrer [**68**] ▷ *What time did you get back?* À quelle heure est-ce que tu es rentré?; **We went there by bus and walked back.**

Nous y sommes allés en bus et nous sommes rentrés à pied.; **He's not back yet.** Il n'est pas encore rentré.; **to call somebody back** rappeler [**4**] quelqu'un ▷ *I'll call back later.* Je rappellerai plus tard.
▶ *vb (support)* soutenir [**83**] ▷ *I'm backing Nicola Sturgeon.* Je soutiens Nicola Sturgeon.; **to back a horse** parier [**19**] sur un cheval

back out *vb* se désister [**28**] ▷ *They backed out at the last minute.* Ils se sont désistés au dernier moment.

back up *vb* **to back somebody up** soutenir [**83**] quelqu'un

backache *n* mal au dos *m* ▷ *to have backache* avoir mal au dos

backbone *n* colonne vertébrale *f*

backfire *vb (go wrong)* échouer [**28**]

background *n* ❶ *(of picture)* arrière-plan *m* ▷ *a house in the background* une maison à l'arrière-plan; **background noise** les bruits de fond *mpl* ❷ milieu *m* (*pl* milieux) ▷ *his family background* son milieu familial

backhand *n* revers *m*

backing *n (support)* soutien *m*

backpack *n* sac à dos *m*

backpacker *n* ❶ *(globe-trotter)* routard *m*, routarde *f* ❷ *(hill-walker)* randonneur *m*, randonneuse *f*

backside *n* derrière *m*

backstroke *n* dos crawlé *m*

backup *n (support)* soutien *m*; **a backup file** une sauvegarde

backwards *adv* en arrière ▷ *to take a step backwards* faire un pas en arrière; **to fall backwards** tomber [**84**] à la renverse

bacon *n* ❶ *(French type)* lard *m* ❷ *(British type)* bacon *m* ▷ *bacon and eggs* des œufs au bacon

bad *adj* ❶ mauvais(e) ▷ *to be in a bad mood* être de mauvaise humeur; **to be bad at something** être [**35**] mauvais en quelque chose ▷ *I'm really bad at maths.* Je suis vraiment mauvais en maths. ❷ *(serious)* grave ▷ *a bad accident* un accident grave ❸ *(naughty)* vilain(e) ▷ *You bad boy!* Vilain!; **to go bad** *(food)* se gâter [**28**]; **I feel bad about it.** Ça m'ennuie.; **not bad** pas mal ▷ *That's not bad at all.* Ce n'est pas mal du tout.

badge *n* badge *m*

badly *adv* mal ▷ *badly paid* mal payé; **badly wounded** grièvement blessé; **He badly needs a rest.** Il a sérieusement besoin de se reposer.

badminton *n* badminton *m* ▷ *to play badminton* jouer au badminton

bad-tempered *adj* **to be bad-tempered (1)** *(by nature)* avoir [**8**] mauvais caractère ▷ *He's a really bad-tempered person.* Il a vraiment mauvais caractère. **(2)** *(temporarily)* être [**35**] de mauvaise humeur ▷ *He was really bad-tempered yesterday.* Il était vraiment de mauvaise humeur hier.

bag *n* sac *m*; **an old bag** *(person)* une vieille peau

baggage *n* bagages *mpl*

baggage reclaim *n* livraison des bagages *f*

bagpipes *npl* cornemuse *fsg* ▷ *Ed*

plays the bagpipes. Ed joue de la cornemuse.

bake *vb* **to bake a cake** faire [**36**] un gâteau

baked *adj* cuit au four (*f* cuite au four) ▷ *baked potatoes* les pommes de terre cuites au four *fpl*; **baked beans** les haricots blancs en sauce *mpl*

baker *n* boulanger *m*, boulangère *f* ▷ *He's a baker.* Il est boulanger.

bakery *n* boulangerie *f*

balance *n* équilibre *m* ▷ *to lose one's balance* perdre l'équilibre

balanced *adj* équilibré(e)

balcony *n* balcon *m*

bald *adj* chauve

ball *n* ❶ *(tennis, golf, cricket)* balle *f* ❷ *(football, rugby)* ballon *m*

ballet *n* ballet *m* ▷ *We went to a ballet.* Nous sommes allés voir un ballet.; **ballet lessons** les cours de danse *mpl*

ballet dancer *n* danseur classique *m*, danseuse classique *f*

ballet shoes *npl* chaussons de danse *mpl*

balloon *n (for parties)* ballon *m*; **a hot-air balloon** une montgolfière

ballpoint pen *n* stylo à bille *m*

ban *n* interdiction *f*
▶ *vb* interdire [**27**]

banana *n* banane *f* ▷ *a banana skin* une peau de banane

band *n* ❶ *(rock band)* groupe *m* ❷ *(brass band)* fanfare *f*

bandage *n* bandage *m*
▶ *vb* mettre [**47**] un bandage à ▷ *The nurse bandaged his arm.* L'infirmière lui a mis un bandage au bras.

Band-Aid® *n (US)* pansement adhésif *m*

bang *n* ❶ détonation *f* ▷ *I heard a loud bang.* J'ai entendu une forte détonation. ❷ coup *m* ▷ *a bang on the head* un coup sur la tête; **Bang!** Pan!
▶ *vb (part of body)* se cogner [**28**] ▷ *I banged my head.* Je me suis cogné la tête.; **to bang the door** claquer [**28**] la porte; **to bang on the door** cogner [**28**] à la porte

Bangladesh *n* Bangladesh *m*; **from Bangladesh** du Bangladesh

bank *n* ❶ *(financial)* banque *f* ❷ *(of river, lake)* bord *m*

bank account *n* compte en banque *m*

banker *n* banquier *m*

bank holiday *n* jour férié *m*

banknote *n* billet de banque *m*

bar *n* ❶ *(pub)* bar *m* ❷ *(counter)* comptoir *m*; **a bar of chocolate** une tablette de chocolat; **a bar of soap** une savonnette

barbecue *n* barbecue *m*

bare *adj* nu(e)

barefoot *adj, adv* nu-pieds ▷ *The children go around barefoot.* Les enfants se promènent nu-pieds.; **to be barefoot** avoir [**8**] les pieds nus ▷ *She was barefoot.* Elle avait les pieds nus.

barely *adv* à peine ▷ *I could barely hear what she was saying.* J'entendais à peine ce qu'elle disait.

bargain *n* affaire *f* ▷ *It was a bargain!* C'était une affaire!

barge *n* péniche *f*
bark *vb* aboyer [**53**]
barmaid *n* barmaid *f* ▷ *She's a barmaid.* Elle est barmaid.
barman *n* barman *m* ▷ *He's a barman.* Il est barman.
barn *n* grange *f*
barrel *n* tonneau *m* (*pl* tonneaux)
barrier *n* barrière *f*
base *n* base *f*
baseball *n* base-ball *m*; **a baseball cap** une casquette de base-ball
based *adj* **based on** fondé sur
basement *n* sous-sol *m*
bash *vb* **to bash something** taper [**28**] sur quelque chose
▶ *n* **I'll have a bash.** Je vais essayer.
basic *adj* ❶ de base ▷ *It's a basic model.* C'est un modèle de base. ❷ rudimentaire ▷ *The accommodation is pretty basic.* Le logement est plutôt rudimentaire.
basically *adv* tout simplement ▷ *Basically, I just don't like him.* Tout simplement, je ne l'aime pas.
basics *npl* rudiments *mpl*
basin *n* (*washbasin*) lavabo *m*
basis *n* **on a daily basis** quotidiennement; **on a regular basis** régulièrement
basket *n* panier *m*
basketball *n* basket *m*
bass *n* ❶ (*guitar, singer*) basse *f* ▷ *He plays the bass.* Il joue de la basse.; **a bass guitar** une guitare basse ❷ (*on hi-fi*) graves *mpl*
bass drum *n* grosse caisse *f*
bassoon *n* basson *m* ▷ *I play the bassoon.* Je joue du basson.
bat *n* ❶ (*for cricket, rounders*) batte *f* ❷ (*for table tennis*) raquette *f* ❸ (*animal*) chauve-souris *f* (*pl* chauves-souris)
bath *n* ❶ bain *m* ▷ *to have a bath* prendre un bain; **a hot bath** un bain chaud ❷ (*bathtub*) baignoire *f* ▷ *There's a spider in the bath.* Il y a une araignée dans la baignoire.
bathe *vb* se baigner [**28**]
bathroom *n* salle de bains *f*
bath towel *n* serviette de bain *f*
batter *n* pâte à frire *f*
battery *n* ❶ (*for torch, toy*) pile *f* ❷ (*of car*) batterie *f*
battle *n* bataille *f* ▷ *the Battle of Hastings* la bataille de Hastings; **It was a battle, but we managed in the end.** Il a fallu se battre, mais on a fini par y arriver.
bay *n* baie *f*
BC *abbr* (= *before Christ*) av. J.-C. (= *avant Jésus-Christ*) ▷ *in 200 BC* en deux cents avant Jésus-Christ
be *vb* être [**35**] ▷ *I'm tired.* Je suis fatigué. ▷ *I've been ill.* J'ai été malade.; **It's the 28th of October today.** Nous sommes le vingt-huit octobre.; **Have you been to Greece before?** Est-ce que tu es déjà allé en Grèce?; **I've never been to Paris.** Je ne suis jamais allé à Paris.; **to be killed** être [**35**] tué

> When you are saying what somebody's occupation is, you leave out the 'a' in French.

▷ *He's a student.* Il est étudiant.

With certain adjectives, such as 'cold', 'hot', 'hungry' and 'thirsty', use **avoir** instead of **être**.

I'm cold. J'ai froid.; **I'm hungry.** J'ai faim.

When saying how old somebody is, use **avoir** not **être**.

I'm fourteen. J'ai quatorze ans.; **How old are you?** Quel âge as-tu?

When referring to the weather, use **faire**.

It's cold. Il fait froid.; **It's a nice day.** Il fait beau.; **It's too hot.** Il fait trop chaud.

beach *n* plage *f*

bead *n* perle *f*

beak *n* bec *m*

beam *n* rayon *m*

beans *n* ❶ haricots *mpl* ❷ *(baked beans)* haricots blancs à la sauce tomate *mpl*; **broad beans** les fèves *fpl*; **green beans** les haricots verts *mpl*; **kidney beans** les haricots rouges *mpl*

bear *n* ours *m*

▶ *vb* **I can't bear it!** C'est insupportable!

bear up *vb* tenir [**83**] le coup; **Bear up!** Tiens bon!

beard *n* barbe *f*; **He's got a beard.** Il est barbu.; **a man with a beard** un barbu

bearded *adj* barbu(e)

beat *n* rythme *m*

▶ *vb* battre [**9**] ▷ *We beat them 3-0.* On les a battus trois à zéro.; **Beat it!** Fiche le camp! *(informal)*; **to beat somebody up** *(informal)* tabasser [**28**] quelqu'un

beautiful *adj* beau (*f* belle, *mpl* beaux)

beautifully *adv* admirablement

beauty *n* beauté *f*

became *vb see* **become**

because *conj* parce que ▷ *I did it because ...* Je l'ai fait parce que ...; **because of** à cause de ▷ *because of the weather* à cause du temps

become *vb* devenir [**25**] ▷ *He became a famous writer.* Il est devenu un grand écrivain.

bed *n* lit *m* ▷ *in bed* au lit; **to go to bed** aller [**3**] se coucher; **to go to bed with somebody** coucher [**28**] avec quelqu'un

bed and breakfast *n* chambre d'hôte *f* ▷ *We stayed in a bed and breakfast.* Nous avons logé dans une chambre d'hôte.

bedclothes *npl* draps et les couvertures *mpl*

bedding *n* literie *f*

bedroom *n* chambre *f*

bedsit *n* chambre meublée *f*

bedspread *n* dessus-de-lit *m* (*pl* dessus-de-lit)

bedtime *n* **Ten o'clock is my usual bedtime.** Je me couche généralement à dix heures.; **Bedtime!** Au lit!

bee *n* abeille *f*

beef *n* bœuf *m*; **roast beef** le rosbif

beefburger *n* hamburger *m*

been *vb see* **be**

beer *n* bière *f*

beetle *n* scarabée *m*

a **b** c d e f g h i j k l m n o p q r s t u v w x y z

beetroot *n* betterave rouge *f*

before *prep, conj, adv* ❶ avant ▷ *before Tuesday* avant mardi ❷ avant de ▷ *I'll phone before I leave.* J'appellerai avant de partir. ❸ *(already)* déjà ▷ *I've seen this film before.* J'ai déjà vu ce film.; **the day before** la veille; **the week before** la semaine précédente

beforehand *adv* à l'avance

beg *vb* ❶ *(for money)* mendier [**19**] ❷ supplier [**19**] ▷ *He begged me to stop.* Il m'a supplié d'arrêter.

began *vb see* **begin**

beggar *n* mendiant *m*, mendiante *f*

begin *vb* commencer [**12**]; **to begin doing something** commencer [**12**] à faire quelque chose

beginner *n* débutant *m*, débutante *f* ▷ *I'm just a beginner.* Je ne suis qu'un débutant.

beginning *n* début *m* ▷ *in the beginning* au début

begun *vb see* **begin**

behalf *n* **on behalf of somebody** pour quelqu'un

behave *vb* se comporter [**28**] ▷ *He behaved like an idiot.* Il s'est comporté comme un idiot. ▷ *She behaved very badly.* Elle s'est très mal comportée.; **to behave oneself** être [**35**] sage ▷ *Did the children behave themselves?* Est-ce que les enfants ont été sages?; **Behave!** Sois sage!

behaviour (*US* **behavior**) *n* comportement *m*

behind *prep, adv* derrière ▷ *behind the television* derrière la télévision; **to be behind** *(late)* avoir [**8**] du retard ▷ *I'm behind with my revision.* J'ai du retard dans mes révisions.
▶ *n* derrière *m*

beige *adj* beige

Belgian *n* Belge *mf*; **the Belgians** les Belges
▶ *adj* belge ▷ *She's Belgian.* Elle est belge.

Belgium *n* Belgique *f*; **in Belgium** en Belgique

believe *vb* croire [**20**] ▷ *I don't believe you.* Je ne te crois pas.; **to believe in something** croire [**20**] à quelque chose ▷ *Do you believe in ghosts?* Tu crois aux fantômes?; **to believe in God** croire [**20**] en Dieu

bell *n* ❶ *(doorbell)* sonnette *f*; **to ring the bell** sonner [**28**] à la porte ❷ *(in church)* cloche *f* ❸ *(in school)* sonnerie *f* ❹ clochette *f* ▷ *Our cat has a bell on its collar.* Notre chat a une clochette sur son collier.

belong *vb* **to belong to somebody** être [**35**] à quelqu'un ▷ *Who does it belong to?* C'est à qui? ▷ *That belongs to me.* C'est à moi.; **Do you belong to any clubs?** Est-ce que tu es membre d'un club?; **Where does this belong?** Où est-ce que ça va?

belongings *npl* affaires *fpl*

below *prep, adv* ❶ au-dessous de ▷ *below the castle* au-dessous du château ❷ en dessous ▷ *on the floor below* à l'étage en dessous; **10 degrees below freezing** moins dix

belt *n* ceinture *f*

bench *n* ❶ *(seat)* banc *m* ❷ *(for woodwork)* établi *m*

bend *n* ❶ *(in road)* virage *m* ❷ *(in river)* coude *m*
▶ *vb* ❶ *(back)* courber **[28]** ❷ *(leg, arm)* plier **[19]** ▷ *I can't bend my arm.* Je n'arrive pas à plier le bras.; **'do not bend'** 'ne pas plier' ❸ *(object)* tordre **[49]** ▷ *You've bent it.* Tu l'as tordu. ❹ se tordre **[49]** ▷ *It bends easily.* Ça se tord facilement.

bend down *vb* se baisser **[28]**

bend over *vb* se pencher **[28]**

beneath *prep* sous

benefit *n (advantage)* avantage *m*; **unemployment benefit** les allocations chômage
▶ *vb* **He'll benefit from the change.** Le changement lui fera du bien.

bent *vb see* **bend**
▶ *adj* tordu(e) ▷ *a bent fork* une fourchette tordue

beret *n* béret *m*

berth *n* couchette *f*

beside *prep* à côté de ▷ *beside the television* à côté de la télévision; **He was beside himself.** Il était hors de lui.; **That's beside the point.** Cela n'a rien à voir.

besides *adv* en plus ▷ *Besides, it's too expensive.* En plus, c'est trop cher.

best *adj, adv* ❶ meilleur(e) ▷ *He's the best player in the team.* Il est le meilleur joueur de l'équipe.
▷ *Janet's the best at maths.* Janet est la meilleure en maths. ❷ le mieux ▷ *Emma sings best.* C'est Emma qui chante le mieux. ▷ *That's the best I can do.* Je ne peux pas faire mieux.; **to do one's best** faire **[36]** de son mieux ▷ *It's not perfect, but I did my best.* Ça n'est pas parfait, mais j'ai fait de mon mieux.; **to make the best of it** s'en contenter **[28]** ▷ *We'll have to make the best of it.* Il va falloir nous en contenter.

best man *n* garçon d'honneur *m*

bet *n* pari *m* ▷ *to make a bet* faire un pari
▶ *vb* parier **[19]** ▷ *I bet he forgot.* Je parie qu'il a oublié.

better *adj, adv* ❶ meilleur(e) ▷ *This one's better than that one.* Celui-ci est meilleur que celui-là. ▷ *a better way to do it* une meilleure façon de le faire ❷ mieux ▷ *That's better!* C'est mieux comme ça.; **better still** encore mieux ▷ *Go and see her tomorrow, or better still, go today.* Va la voir demain, ou encore mieux, vas-y aujourd'hui.; **to get better** **(1)** *(improve)* s'améliorer **[28]** ▷ *My French is getting better.* Mon français s'améliore. **(2)** *(from illness)* se remettre **[47]** ▷ *I hope you get better soon.* J'espère que tu vas vite te remettre.; **to feel better** se sentir **[77]** mieux ▷ *Are you feeling better now?* Tu te sens mieux maintenant?; **You'd better do it straight away.** Vous feriez mieux de le faire immédiatement.; **I'd better go home.** Je ferais mieux de rentrer.

between *prep* entre ▷ *Stroud is between Oxford and Bristol.* Stroud est entre Oxford et Bristol.
▷ *between 15 and 20 minutes* entre quinze et vingt minutes

beyond *prep* au-delà de ▷ *There was a lake beyond the mountain.* Il y avait un lac au-delà de la montagne.; **beyond belief** incroyable; **beyond repair** irréparable
Bible *n* Bible *f*
bicycle *n* vélo *m*
big *adj* ❶ grand(e) ▷ *a big house* une grande maison ▷ *my big brother* mon grand frère; **He's a big guy.** C'est un grand gaillard. ❷ *(car, animal, book, parcel)* gros (*f* grosse) ▷ *a big car* une grosse voiture
bigheaded *adj* **to be bigheaded** avoir [**8**] la grosse tête
bike *n* vélo *m* ▷ *by bike* en vélo
bikini *n* bikini *m*
bilingual *adj* bilingue
bill *n* ❶ *(in restaurant)* addition *f* ▷ *Can we have the bill, please?* L'addition, s'il vous plaît. ❷ *(for gas, electricity)* facture *f* ❸ *(US)* billet *m* ▷ *a five-dollar bill* un billet de cinq dollars
billiards *n* billard *m* ▷ *to play billiards* jouer au billard
billion *n* milliard *m*
bin *n* poubelle *f*
binoculars *npl* jumelles *fpl*; **a pair of binoculars** des jumelles
biochemistry *n* biochimie *f*
biography *n* biographie *f*
biology *n* biologie *f*
bird *n* oiseau *m* (*pl* oiseaux)
birdwatching *n* **My hobby's birdwatching.** Mon passe-temps favori est d'observer les oiseaux.; **to go birdwatching** aller [**3**] observer les oiseaux
Biro® *n* bic® *m*
birth *n* naissance *f* ▷ *date of birth* la date de naissance
birth certificate *n* acte de naissance *m*
birth control *n* contraception *f*
birthday *n* anniversaire *m* ▷ *When's your birthday?* Quelle est la date de ton anniversaire?; **a birthday cake** un gâteau d'anniversaire; **a birthday card** une carte d'anniversaire; **I'm going to have a birthday party.** Je vais faire une fête pour mon anniversaire.
biscuit *n* gâteau sec *m* (*pl* gâteaux secs)
bishop *n* évêque *m*
bit *vb see* **bite**
▸ *n* morceau *m* (*pl* morceaux) ▷ *Would you like another bit?* Est-ce que tu en veux un autre morceau?; **a bit of (1)** *(piece of)* un morceau de ▷ *a bit of cake* un morceau de gâteau **(2)** *(a little)* un peu de ▷ *a bit of music* un peu de musique; **It's a bit of a nuisance.** C'est ennuyeux.; **a bit** un peu ▷ *a bit too hot* un peu trop chaud; **to fall to bits** se désintégrer [**34**]; **to take something to bits** démonter [**28**] quelque chose; **bit by bit** petit à petit
bite *vb* ❶ *(person, dog)* mordre [**49**] ❷ *(insect)* piquer [**28**] ▷ *I got bitten by mosquitoes.* Je me suis fait piquer par des moustiques.; **to bite one's nails** se ronger [**45**] les ongles
▸ *n* ❶ *(insect bite)* piqûre *f* ❷ *(animal bite)* morsure *f*; **to have a bite to**

eat manger [45] un morceau
bitten *vb see* **bite**
bitter *adj* ❶ amer (*f* amère) ❷ (*weather, wind*) glacial(e) (*mpl* glaciaux) ▷ *It's bitter today.* Il fait un froid glacial aujourd'hui.
▶ *n* bière brune *f*
black *adj* noir(e) ▷ *a black jacket* une veste noire
blackberry *n* mûre *f*
blackbird *n* merle *m*
blackboard *n* tableau noir *m* (*pl* tableaux noirs)
blackcurrant *n* cassis *m*
blackmail *n* chantage *m* ▷ *That's blackmail!* C'est du chantage!
▶ *vb* **to blackmail somebody** faire [36] chanter quelqu'un ▷ *He blackmailed her.* Il l'a fait chanter.
black pudding *n* boudin *m*
blade *n* lame *f*
blame *vb* **Don't blame me!** Ça n'est pas ma faute!; **I blame the police.** À mon avis, c'est la faute de la police.; **He blamed it on my sister.** Il a dit que c'était la faute de ma sœur.
blank *adj* ❶ (*paper*) blanc (*f* blanche) ❷ (*video, page*) vierge; **My mind went blank.** J'ai eu un trou.
▶ *n* blanc *m* ▷ *Fill in the blanks.* Remplissez les blancs.
blanket *n* couverture *f*
blast *n* **a bomb blast** une explosion
blaze *n* incendie *m*
blazer *n* blazer *m*
bleach *n* eau de Javel *f*
bleed *vb* saigner [28] ▷ *My nose is bleeding.* Je saigne du nez.
blender *n* mixer *m*
bless *vb* (*religiously*) bénir [38]; **Bless you!** (*after sneezing*) À tes souhaits!
blew *vb see* **blow**
blind *adj* aveugle
▶ *n* (*for window*) store *m*
blink *vb* cligner [28] des yeux
blister *n* ampoule *f*
blizzard *n* tempête de neige *f*
block *n* immeuble *m* ▷ *He lives in our block.* Il habite dans notre immeuble.; **a block of flats** un immeuble
▶ *vb* bloquer [28]
blog *n* blog *m*
▶ *vb* bloguer [28]
blogger *n* bloggeur *m*, bloggeuse *f*
blonde *adj* blond(e) ▷ *She's got blonde hair.* Elle a les cheveux blonds.
blood *n* sang *m*
blood pressure *n* **to have high blood pressure** faire [36] de la tension
blood test *n* prise de sang *f*
blouse *n* chemisier *m*
blow *n* coup *m*
▶ *vb* (*wind, person*) souffler [28]; **to blow one's nose** se moucher [28]; **to blow a whistle** siffler [28]; **to blow out a candle** éteindre [60] une bougie
blow up *vb* ❶ faire [36] sauter ▷ *The terrorists blew up a police station.* Les terroristes ont fait sauter un commissariat de police. ❷ gonfler [28] ▷ *to blow up a balloon* gonfler un ballon; **The house blew up.** La maison a sauté.

blow-dry *n* brushing *m*; **A cut and blow-dry, please.** Une coupe brushing, s'il vous plaît.
blown *vb see* **blow**
blue *adj* bleu(e) ▷ *a blue dress* une robe bleue; **a blue film** un film pornographique; **It came out of the blue.** C'était complètement inattendu.
blues *npl* blues *msg*
blunder *n* gaffe *f*
blunt *adj* ❶ *(person)* brusque ❷ *(knife)* émoussé(e)
blush *vb* rougir **[38]**
board *n* ❶ *(wooden)* planche *f* ❷ *(blackboard)* tableau *m* (*pl* tableaux) ▷ *on the board* au tableau ❸ *(noticeboard)* panneau *m* (*pl* panneaux) ❹ *(for board games)* jeu *m* (*pl* jeux) ❺ *(for chess)* échiquier *m*; **on board** à bord; **'full board'** 'pension complète'
boarder *n* interne *mf*
board game *n* jeu de société *m* (*pl* jeux de société)
boarding card *n* carte d'embarquement *f*
boarding school *n* pensionnat *m*; **I go to boarding school.** Je suis interne.
boast *vb* se vanter **[28]** ▷ *Stop boasting!* Arrête de te vanter!; **to boast about something** se vanter **[28]** de quelque chose
boat *n* bateau *m* (*pl* bateaux)
body *n* corps *m*
bodybuilding *n* culturisme *m*
bodyguard *n* garde du corps *m*
boil *n* furoncle *m*
▸ *vb* ❶ faire **[36]** bouillir ▷ *to boil some water* faire bouillir de l'eau; **to boil an egg** faire **[36]** cuire un œuf ❷ bouillir **[11]** ▷ *The water's boiling.* L'eau bout. ▷ *The water's boiled.* L'eau a bouilli.
boil over *vb* déborder **[28]**
boiled *adj* à l'eau ▷ *boiled potatoes* des pommes de terre à l'eau; **a boiled egg** un œuf à la coque
boiling *adj* **It's boiling in here!** Il fait une chaleur torride ici!; **boiling hot** torride ▷ *a boiling hot day* une journée torride
bolt *n* ❶ *(on door)* verrou *m* ❷ *(with nut)* boulon *m*
bomb *n* bombe *f*
▸ *vb* bombarder **[28]**
bomber *n* bombardier *m*
bombing *n* attentat à la bombe *m*
bone *n* ❶ *(of human, animal)* os *m* ❷ *(of fish)* arête *f*
bonfire *n* feu *m* (*pl* feux)
bonnet *n (of car)* capot *m*
bonus *n* ❶ *(extra payment)* prime *f* ❷ *(added advantage)* plus *m*
book *n* livre *m*
▸ *vb* réserver **[28]** ▷ *We haven't booked.* Nous n'avons pas réservé.
bookcase *n* bibliothèque *f*
booklet *n* brochure *f*
bookshelf *n* étagère à livres *f*
bookshop *n* librairie *f*
boot *n* ❶ *(of car)* coffre *m* ❷ *(fashion boot)* botte *f* ❸ *(for hiking)* chaussure de marche *f*; **football boots** des chaussures de foot
border *n* frontière *f*
bore *vb see* **bear**

bored *adj* **to be bored** s'ennuyer [**53**] ▷ *I was bored.* Je m'ennuyais.; **to get bored** s'ennuyer [**53**]
boring *adj* ennuyeux (*f* ennuyeuse)
born *adj* **to be born** naître [**52**] ▷ *I was born in 1990.* Je suis né en mille neuf cent quatre-vingt-dix.
borrow *vb* emprunter [**28**] ▷ *Can I borrow your pen?* Je peux emprunter ton stylo?; **to borrow something from somebody** emprunter [**28**] quelque chose à quelqu'un ▷ *I borrowed some money from a friend.* J'ai emprunté de l'argent à un ami.
Bosnia *n* Bosnie *f*
Bosnian *adj* bosniaque
boss *n* patron *m*, patronne *f*
boss around *vb* **to boss somebody around** donner [**28**] des ordres à quelqu'un
bossy *adj* autoritaire
both *adj, pron* tous les deux *mpl*, toutes les deux *fpl* ▷ *We both went.* Nous y sommes allés tous les deux. ▷ *Both of your answers are wrong.* Vos réponses sont toutes les deux mauvaises. ▷ *Both of them have left.* Ils sont partis tous les deux. ▷ *Both of us went.* Nous y sommes allés tous les deux. ▷ *Both Maggie and John are against it.* Maggie et John sont tous les deux contre.; **He speaks both German and Italian.** Il parle allemand et italien.
bother *vb* ❶ *(worry)* tracasser [**28**] ▷ *What's bothering you?* Qu'est-ce qui te tracasse? ❷ *(disturb)* déranger [**45**] ▷ *I'm sorry to bother you.* Je suis désolé de vous déranger.; **no bother** aucun problème; **Don't bother!** Ça n'est pas la peine!; **to bother to do something** prendre [**65**] la peine de faire quelque chose ▷ *He didn't bother to tell me about it.* Il n'a pas pris la peine de m'en parler.
bottle *n* bouteille *f*
bottle bank *n* conteneur à verre *m*
bottle-opener *n* ouvre-bouteille *m*
bottom *n* ❶ *(of container, bag, sea)* fond *m* ❷ *(buttocks)* derrière *m* ❸ *(of page, list)* bas *m*
▶ *adj* inférieur(e) ▷ *the bottom shelf* l'étagère inférieure; **the bottom sheet** le drap de dessous
bought *vb see* **buy**
bounce *vb* rebondir [**38**]
bouncer *n* videur *m*
bound *adj* **He's bound to fail.** Il va sûrement échouer.
boundary *n* frontière *f*
bow *n* ❶ *(knot)* nœud *m* ▷ *to tie a bow* faire un nœud ❷ arc *m* ▷ *a bow and arrows* un arc et des flèches
▶ *vb* faire [**36**] une révérence
bowl *n (for soup, cereal)* bol *m*
▶ *vb (in cricket)* lancer [**12**] la balle
bowling *n* bowling *m*; **to go bowling** jouer [**28**] au bowling; **a bowling alley** un bowling
bow tie *n* nœud papillon *m*
box *n* boîte *f* ▷ *a box of matches* une boîte d'allumettes; **a cardboard box** un carton
boxer *n* boxeur *m*
boxer shorts *npl* caleçon *msg*

boxing *n* boxe *f*
Boxing Day *n* lendemain de Noël *m* ▷ *on Boxing Day* le lendemain de Noël

Word for word, this means 'the day after Christmas'.

boy *n* garçon *m*
boyfriend *n* copain *m* ▷ *Have you got a boyfriend?* Est-ce que tu as un copain?
bra *n* soutien-gorge *m* (*pl* soutiens-gorge)
brace *n* (*on teeth*) appareil *m* ▷ *She wears a brace.* Elle a un appareil.
bracelet *n* bracelet *m*
brackets *npl* **in brackets** entre parenthèses
brain *n* cerveau *m* (*pl* cerveaux)
brainy *adj* intelligent(e)
brake *n* frein *m*
▸ *vb* freiner [**28**]
branch *n* ❶ (*of tree*) branche *f* ❷ (*of bank*) agence *f*
brand *n* marque *f* ▷ *a well-known brand of coffee* une marque de café bien connue
brand-new *adj* tout neuf (*f* toute neuve)
brandy *n* cognac *m*
brass *n* cuivre *m*; **the brass section** les cuivres
brass band *n* fanfare *f*
brave *adj* courageux (*f* courageuse)
Brazil *n* Brésil *m*; **in Brazil** au Brésil
bread *n* pain *m* ▷ *brown bread* le pain complet ▷ *white bread* le pain blanc; **bread and butter** les tartines de pain beurrées *fpl*
break *n* ❶ (*rest*) pause *f* ▷ *to take a break* faire une pause ❷ (*at school*) récréation *f* ▷ *during morning break* pendant la récréation du matin; **the Christmas break** les vacances de Noël; **Give me a break!** Laisse-moi tranquille!
▸ *vb* ❶ casser [**28**] ▷ *Careful, you'll break something!* Attention, tu vas casser quelque chose! ❷ (*get broken*) se casser [**28**] ▷ *Careful, it'll break!* Attention, ça va se casser!; **to break one's leg** se casser [**28**] la jambe ▷ *I broke my leg.* Je me suis cassé la jambe. ▷ *He broke his arm.* Il s'est cassé le bras.; **to break a promise** rompre [**75**] une promesse; **to break a record** battre [**9**] un record; **to break the law** violer [**28**] la loi
break down *vb* tomber [**84**] en panne ▷ *The car broke down.* La voiture est tombée en panne.
break in *vb* entrer [**32**] par effraction
break off *vb* ❶ casser [**28**] ❷ se casser [**28**]
break open *vb* (*door, cupboard*) forcer [**12**]
break out *vb* ❶ (*fire*) se déclarer [**28**] ❷ (*war*) éclater [**28**] ❸ (*prisoner*) s'évader [**28**]; **to break out in a rash** être [**35**] couvert de boutons
break up *vb* ❶ (*crowd*) se disperser [**28**] ❷ (*meeting, party*) se terminer [**28**] ❸ (*couple*) se séparer [**28**]; **to break up a fight** mettre [**47**] fin à une bagarre; **We break up next**

Wednesday. Nos vacances commencent mercredi.

breakdown *n* ❶ *(in vehicle)* panne *f* ▷ *to have a breakdown* tomber en panne ❷ *(mental)* dépression *f* ▷ *to have a breakdown* faire une dépression

breakfast *n* petit déjeuner *m* ▷ *What would you like for breakfast?* Qu'est-ce que vous voulez pour le petit déjeuner?

break-in *n* cambriolage *m*

breast *n (of woman)* sein *m*; **chicken breast** le blanc de poulet

breaststroke *n* brasse *f*

breath *n* haleine *f* ▷ *to have bad breath* avoir mauvaise haleine; **to be out of breath** être [**35**] essoufflé; **to get one's breath back** reprendre [**65**] son souffle

breathe *vb* respirer [**28**]

breathe in *vb* inspirer [**28**]

breathe out *vb* expirer [**28**]

breed *vb (reproduce)* se reproduire [**23**]; **to breed dogs** faire [**36**] de l'élevage de chiens
▶ *n* race *f*

breeze *n* brise *f*

brewery *n* brasserie *f*

bribe *vb* soudoyer [**53**]

brick *n* brique *f* ▷ *a brick wall* un mur en brique

bride *n* mariée *f*

bridegroom *n* marié *m*

bridesmaid *n* demoiselle d'honneur *f*

bridge *n* ❶ pont *m* ▷ *a suspension bridge* un pont suspendu ❷ bridge *m* ▷ *to play bridge* jouer au bridge

brief *adj* bref (*f* brève)

briefcase *n* serviette *f*

briefly *adv* brièvement

briefs *npl* slip *msg*; **a pair of briefs** un slip

bright *adj* ❶ *(colour, light)* vif (*f* vive) ▷ *a bright colour* une couleur vive; **bright blue** bleu vif ▷ *a bright blue car* une voiture bleu vif ❷ intelligent(e) ▷ *He's not very bright.* Il n'est pas très intelligent.

brilliant *adj* ❶ *(wonderful)* génial(e) (*mpl* géniaux) ▷ *Brilliant!* Génial! ❷ *(clever)* brillant(e) ▷ *a brilliant scientist* un savant brillant

bring *vb* ❶ apporter [**28**] ▷ *Bring warm clothes.* Apportez des vêtements chauds. ❷ *(person)* amener [**43**] ▷ *Can I bring a friend?* Est-ce que je peux amener un ami?

bring back *vb* rapporter [**28**]

bring forward *vb* avancer [**12**]

bring up *vb* élever [**43**] ▷ *She brought up 5 children on her own.* Elle a élevé cinq enfants toute seule.

Britain *n* Grande-Bretagne *f*; **in Britain** en Grande-Bretagne; **to Britain** en Grande-Bretagne; **I'm from Britain.** Je suis britannique.; **Great Britain** la Grande-Bretagne

British *adj* britannique; **the British** les Britanniques *mpl*; **the British Isles** les îles Britanniques *fpl*

Brittany *n* Bretagne *f*; **in Brittany** en Bretagne; **to Brittany** en Bretagne; **She's from Brittany.** Elle est bretonne.

broad *adj (wide)* large; **in broad daylight** en plein jour

broadband *n* ADSL *m* ▷ *Do you have broadband?* Tu as l'ADSL?
broadcast *n* émission *f*
▶ *vb* diffuser [**28**] ▷ *The interview was broadcast yesterday.* L'interview a été diffusée hier.; **to broadcast live** retransmettre [**47**] en direct
broccoli *n* brocolis *mpl*
brochure *n* brochure *f*
broke *vb see* **break**
▶ *adj* **to be broke** *(without money)* être [**35**] fauché
broken *adj* cassé(e) ▷ *It's broken.* C'est cassé. ▷ *He's got a broken arm.* Il a le bras cassé.
bronchitis *n* bronchite *f*
bronze *n* bronze *m* ▷ *the bronze medal* la médaille de bronze
brooch *n* broche *f*
broom *n* balai *m*
brother *n* frère *m* ▷ *my brother* mon frère ▷ *my big brother* mon grand frère
brother-in-law *n* beau-frère *m* (*pl* beaux-frères)
brought *vb see* **bring**
brown *adj* ❶ *(clothes)* marron ❷ *(hair)* brun(e) ❸ *(tanned)* bronzé(e); **brown bread** le pain complet
browse *vb (on internet)* parcourir [**16**] le Net
bruise *n* bleu *m*
brush *n* ❶ brosse *f* ❷ *(paintbrush)* pinceau *m* (*pl* pinceaux)
▶ *vb* brosser [**28**]; **to brush one's hair** se brosser [**28**] les cheveux ▷ *I brushed my hair.* Je me suis brossé les cheveux.; **to brush one's teeth** se brosser [**28**] les dents ▷ *I brush my teeth every night.* Je me brosse les dents tous les soirs.
Brussels *n* Bruxelles; **in Brussels** à Bruxelles; **to Brussels** à Bruxelles
Brussels sprouts *npl* choux de Bruxelles *mpl*
bubble *n* bulle *f*
bubble bath *n* bain moussant *m*
bubble gum *n* chewing-gum *m*
bucket *n* seau *m* (*pl* seaux)
buckle *n (on belt, watch, shoe)* boucle *f*
Buddhism *n* bouddhisme *m*
Buddhist *adj* bouddhiste
budgie *n* perruche *f*
buffet *n* buffet *m*
buffet car *n* voiture-bar *f*
bug *n* ❶ *(insect)* insecte *m* ❷ *(infection)* microbe *m* ▷ *There's a bug going round.* Il y a un microbe qui traîne.; **a stomach bug** une gastroentérite ❸ *(in computer)* bug *m*
build *vb* construire [**23**] ▷ *He's building a garage.* Il construit un garage.
build up *vb (increase)* s'accumuler [**28**]
builder *n* ❶ *(owner of firm)* entrepreneur *m* ❷ *(worker)* maçon *m*
building *n* bâtiment *m*
built *vb see* **build**
bulb *n (electric)* ampoule *f*
Bulgaria *n* Bulgarie *f*
bull *n* taureau *m* (*pl* taureaux)
bullet *n* balle *f*
bullfighting *n* tauromachie *f*

bully *n* brute *f* ▷ *He's a big bully.* C'est une brute.
▶ *vb* tyranniser [**28**]

bum *n (bottom)* derrière *m*

bum bag *n* banane *f*

bump *n* ❶ *(lump)* bosse *f* ❷ *(minor accident)* accrochage *m* ▷ *We had a bump.* Nous avons eu un accrochage.

bump into *vb* **to bump into something** rentrer [**68**] dans quelque chose ▷ *I bumped into the table in the dark.* Je suis rentrée dans la table dans le noir.; **to bump into somebody (1)** *(literally)* rentrer [**68**] dans quelqu'un ▷ *He stopped suddenly and I bumped into him.* Il s'est arrêté subitement et je lui suis rentré dedans. **(2)** *(meet by chance)* rencontrer [**28**] par hasard ▷ *I bumped into Jane in the supermarket.* J'ai rencontré Jane par hasard au supermarché.

bumper *n* pare-chocs *m* (*pl* pare-chocs)

bumpy *adj* cahoteux (*f* cahoteuse)

bun *n* petit pain au lait *m*

bunch *n* **a bunch of flowers** un bouquet de fleurs; **a bunch of grapes** une grappe de raisin; **a bunch of keys** un trousseau de clés

bunches *npl* couettes *fpl* ▷ *She has her hair in bunches.* Elle a des couettes.

bungalow *n* bungalow *m*

bunk *n* couchette *f*; **bunk beds** les lits superposés *mpl*

burger *n* hamburger *m*

burglar *n* cambrioleur *m*, cambrioleuse *f*

burglary *n* cambriolage *m*

burgle *vb* cambrioler [**28**] ▷ *Her house was burgled.* Sa maison a été cambriolée.

burn *n* brûlure *f*
▶ *vb* ❶ *(rubbish, documents)* brûler [**28**] ❷ *(food)* faire [**36**] brûler ▷ *I burned the cake.* J'ai fait brûler le gâteau. ❸ *(CD, DVD)* graver [**28**]; **to burn oneself** se brûler [**28**] ▷ *I burned myself on the oven door.* Je me suis brûlé sur la porte du four.; **I've burned my hand.** Je me suis brûlé la main.

burn down *vb* brûler [**28**] ▷ *The factory burned down.* L'usine a brûlé.

burst *vb* éclater [**28**] ▷ *The balloon burst.* Le ballon a éclaté.; **to burst a balloon** faire [**36**] éclater un ballon; **to burst out laughing** éclater [**28**] de rire; **to burst into flames** prendre [**65**] feu; **to burst into tears** fondre [**69**] en larmes

bury *vb* enterrer [**28**]

bus *n* autobus *m* ▷ *a bus stop* un arrêt d'autobus; **the school bus** le car scolaire; **a bus pass** une carte d'abonnement pour le bus; **a bus station** une gare routière; **a bus ticket** un ticket de bus

bush *n* buisson *m*

business *n* ❶ *(firm)* entreprise *f* ▷ *He's got his own business.* Il a sa propre entreprise. ❷ *(commerce)* affaires *fpl* ▷ *He's away on business.* Il est en voyage d'affaires.; **a business trip** un voyage d'affaires; **It's none of my business.** Ça ne me regarde pas.

businessman *n* homme d'affaires *m*

businesswoman *n* femme d'affaires *f*

bust *n (chest)* poitrine *f*

busy *adj* ❶ *(person, phone line)* occupé(e) ❷ *(day, schedule)* chargé(e) ❸ *(shop, street)* très fréquenté(e)

but *conj* mais ▷ *I'd like to come, but I'm busy.* J'aimerais venir mais je suis occupé.

butcher *n* boucher *m* ▷ *He's a butcher.* Il est boucher.

butcher's *n* boucherie *f*

butter *n* beurre *m*

butterfly *n* papillon *m*

button *n* bouton *m*

buy *vb* acheter [1] ▷ *I bought him an ice cream.* Je lui ai acheté une glace.; **to buy something from somebody** acheter [1] quelque chose à quelqu'un ▷ *I bought a watch from him.* Je lui ai acheté une montre.

▶ *n* **It was a good buy.** C'était une bonne affaire.

by *prep* ❶ par ▷ *The thieves were caught by the police.* Les voleurs ont été arrêtés par la police. ❷ de ▷ *a painting by Picasso* un tableau de Picasso ▷ *a book by Balzac* un livre de Balzac ❸ en ▷ *by car* en voiture ▷ *by train* en train ▷ *by bus* en autobus ❹ *(close to)* à côté de ▷ *Where's the bank? — It's by the post office.* Où est la banque? — Elle est à côté de la poste. ❺ *(not later than)* avant ▷ *We have to be there by 4 o'clock.* Nous devons y être avant quatre heures.; **by the time ...** quand ... ▷ *By the time I got there it was too late.* Quand je suis arrivé il était déjà trop tard. ▷ *It'll be ready by the time you get back.* Ça sera prêt quand vous reviendrez.; **That's fine by me.** Ça me va.; **all by himself** tout seul; **all by herself** toute seule; **I did it all by myself.** Je l'ai fait tout seul.; **by the way** au fait

bye *excl* salut!

bypass *n* route de contournement *f*

C

cab *n* taxi *m*
cabbage *n* chou *m* (*pl* choux)
cabin *n* (*on ship*) cabine *f*
cable *n* câble *m*
cable car *n* téléphérique *m*
cable television *n* télévision par câble *f*
cactus *n* cactus *m*
café *n* café *m*

Cafés in France sell both alcoholic and non-alcoholic drinks.

cafeteria *n* cafétéria *f*
cage *n* cage *f*
cagoule *n* K-way® *m*
cake *n* gâteau *m* (*pl* gâteaux)
calculate *vb* calculer [**28**]
calculation *n* calcul *m*
calculator *n* machine à calculer *f*
calendar *n* calendrier *m*
calf *n* ❶ (*of cow*) veau *m* (*pl* veaux) ❷ (*of leg*) mollet *m*
call *n* (*by phone*) appel *m* ▷ *Thanks for your call.* Merci de votre appel.; **a phone call** un coup de téléphone; **to be on call** (*doctor*) être [**35**] de permanence ▷ *He's on call this evening.* Il est de permanence ce soir.

▶ *vb* appeler [**4**] ▷ *I'll tell him you called.* Je lui dirai que vous avez appelé. ▷ *We called the police.* Nous avons appelé la police. ▷ *Everyone calls him Jimmy.* Tout le monde l'appelle Jimmy.; **to be called** s'appeler [**4**] ▷ *What's she called?* Elle s'appelle comment?; **to call somebody names** insulter [**28**] quelqu'un; **He called me an idiot.** Il m'a traité d'idiot.

call back *vb* (*phone again*) rappeler [**4**] ▷ *I'll call back at 6 o'clock.* Je rappellerai à six heures.
call for *vb* passer [**58**] prendre ▷ *I'll call for you at 2.30.* Je passerai te prendre à deux heures et demie.
call off *vb* annuler [**28**] ▷ *The match was called off.* Le match a été annulé.
call box *n* cabine téléphonique *f*
call centre *n* centre d'appels *m*
calm *adj* calme
calm down *vb* se calmer [**28**] ▷ *Calm down!* Calme-toi!
calorie *n* calorie *f*
calves *npl see* **calf**
Cambodia *n* Cambodge *m*; **in Cambodia** au Cambodge
camcorder *n* caméscope *m*

came *vb see* **come**
camel *n* chameau *m* (*pl* chameaux)
camera *n* ❶ *(for photos)* appareil photo *m* (*pl* appareils photo) ❷ *(for filming, TV)* caméra *f*
cameraman *n* caméraman *m*
camp *vb* camper [**28**]
▶ *n* camp *m*; **a camp bed** un lit de camp
campaign *n* campagne *f*
camper *n* ❶ *(person)* campeur *m*, campeuse *f* ❷ *(van)* camping-car *m*
camping *n* camping *m*; **to go camping** faire [**36**] du camping ▷ *We went camping in Cornwall.* Nous avons fait du camping en Cornouailles.
campsite *n* terrain de camping *m*
can *vb* ❶ *(be able to, be allowed to)* pouvoir [**64**] ▷ *I can't come.* Je ne peux pas venir. ▷ *Can I help you?* Est-ce que je peux vous aider? ▷ *You could hire a bike.* Tu pourrais louer un vélo. ▷ *I couldn't sleep because of the noise.* Je ne pouvais pas dormir à cause du bruit.

'can' is sometimes not translated.

▷ *I can't hear you.* Je ne t'entends pas. ▷ *Can you speak French?* Parlez-vous français? ❷ *(have learnt how to)* savoir [**76**] ▷ *I can swim.* Je sais nager.; **That can't be true!** Ce n'est pas possible!; **You could be right.** Vous avez peut-être raison.
▶ *n* ❶ *(tin)* boîte *f*; **a can of beer** une cannette de bière ❷ *(container)* bidon *m* ▷ *a can of petrol* un bidon d'essence
Canada *n* Canada *m*; **in Canada** au Canada; **to Canada** au Canada
Canadian *n* Canadien *m*, Canadienne *f*
▶ *adj* canadien (*f* canadienne)
canal *n* canal *m* (*pl* canaux)
Canaries *npl* **the Canaries** les îles Canaries *fpl*
canary *n* canari *m*
cancel *vb* annuler [**28**] ▷ *The match was cancelled.* Le match a été annulé.
cancer *n* ❶ cancer *m* ▷ *He's got cancer.* Il a le cancer. ❷ Cancer *m* ▷ *I'm Cancer.* Je suis Cancer.
candidate *n* candidat *m*, candidate *f*
candle *n* bougie *f*
candy *n (US)* bonbons *mpl*; **a candy** un bonbon
candyfloss *n* barbe à papa *f*
canned *adj (food)* en conserve
cannot *vb see* **can**
canoe *n* canoë *m*
canoeing *n* **to go canoeing** faire [**36**] du canoë ▷ *We went canoeing.* Nous avons fait du canoë.
can-opener *n* ouvre-boîte *m*
can't *vb see* **can**
canteen *n* cantine *f*
canter *vb* aller [**3**] au petit galop
canvas *n* toile *f*
cap *n* ❶ *(hat)* casquette *f* ❷ *(of bottle, tube)* bouchon *m*
capable *adj* capable
capacity *n* capacité *f*
capital *n* ❶ capitale *f* ▷ *Cardiff is the capital of Wales.* Cardiff est la capitale du pays de Galles.

❷ *(letter)* majuscule *f* ▷ *Write your address in capitals.* Écris ton adresse en majuscules.

capitalism *n* capitalisme *m*

Capricorn *n* Capricorne *m* ▷ *I'm Capricorn.* Je suis Capricorne.

captain *n* capitaine *m* ▷ *She's captain of the hockey team.* Elle est capitaine de l'équipe de hockey.

capture *vb* capturer [**28**]

car *n* voiture *f*; **to go by car** aller [**3**] en voiture ▷ *We went by car.* Nous y sommes allés en voiture.; **a car crash** un accident de voiture

caramel *n* caramel *m*

caravan *n* caravane *f* ▷ *a caravan site* un camping pour caravanes

carbon footprint *n* empreinte carbone *f*

card *n* carte *f*; **a card game** un jeu de cartes

cardboard *n* carton *m*

cardigan *n* cardigan *m*

cardphone *n* téléphone à carte *m*

care *n* soin *m* ▷ *with care* avec soin; **to take care of** s'occuper [**28**] de ▷ *I take care of the children on Saturdays.* Le samedi, je m'occupe des enfants.; **Take care! (1)** *(Be careful!)* Fais attention! **(2)** *(Look after yourself!)* Prends bien soin de toi!

▸ *vb* **to care about** se soucier [**19**] de ▷ *They don't really care about their image.* Ils ne se soucient pas trop de leur image.; **I don't care!** Ça m'est égal! ▷ *She doesn't care.* Ça lui est égal.; **to care for somebody** *(patients, old people)* s'occuper [**28**] de quelqu'un

career *n* carrière *f*; **a careers adviser** un conseiller d'orientation

careful *adj* **Be careful!** Fais attention!

carefully *adv* ❶ soigneusement ▷ *She carefully avoided talking about it.* Elle évitait soigneusement d'en parler. ❷ *(safely)* prudemment ▷ *Drive carefully!* Conduisez prudemment!; **Think carefully!** Réfléchis bien!

careless *adj* ❶ *(work)* peu soigné(e); **a careless mistake** une faute d'inattention ❷ *(person)* peu soigneux (*f* peu soigneuse) ▷ *She's very careless.* Elle est bien peu soigneuse. ❸ imprudent(e) ▷ *a careless driver* un conducteur imprudent

caretaker *n* gardien *m*, gardienne *f*

car-ferry *n* ferry *m*

cargo *n* cargaison *f*

car hire *n* location de voitures *f*

Caribbean *n* ❶ *(islands)* Caraïbes *fpl* ▷ *We're going to the Caribbean.* Nous allons aux Caraïbes.; **He's from the Caribbean.** Il est antillais. ❷ *(sea)* mer des Caraïbes *f*

▸ *adj* antillais(e) ▷ *Caribbean food* la cuisine antillaise

carnation *n* œillet *m*

carnival *n* carnaval *m*

carol *n* **a Christmas carol** un chant de Noël

car park *n* parking *m*

carpenter *n* charpentier *m* ▷ *He's a carpenter.* Il est charpentier.

carpentry *n* menuiserie *f*

carpet *n* ❶ tapis *m* ▷ *a Persian carpet* un tapis persan ❷ *(fitted)* moquette *f*
car rental *n (US)* location de voitures *f*
carriage *n* voiture *f*
carrier bag *n* sac en plastique *m*
carrot *n* carotte *f*
carry *vb* ❶ porter **[28]** ▷ *I'll carry your bag.* Je vais porter ton sac. ❷ transporter **[28]** ▷ *a plane carrying 100 passengers* un avion transportant cent passagers
carry on *vb* continuer **[28]** ▷ *She carried on talking.* Elle a continué à parler.
carry out *vb (orders)* exécuter **[28]**
carrycot *n* nacelle *f*
cart *n* charrette *f*
carton *n (of milk, juice)* brique *f*
cartoon *n* ❶ *(film)* dessin animé *m* ❷ *(in newspaper)* dessin humoristique *m*; **a strip cartoon** une bande dessinée
cartridge *n* cartouche *f*
carve *vb (meat)* découper **[28]**
case *n* ❶ valise *f* ▷ *I've packed my case.* J'ai fait ma valise. ❷ cas *m* (*pl* cas) ▷ *in some cases* dans certains cas; **in that case** dans ce cas ▷ *I don't want it. — In that case, I'll take it.* Je n'en veux pas. — Dans ce cas, je le prends.; **in case** au cas où ▷ *in case it rains* au cas où il pleuvrait; **just in case** à tout hasard ▷ *Take some money, just in case.* Prends de l'argent à tout hasard.
cash *n* argent *m* ▷ *I'm a bit short of cash.* Je suis un peu à court d'argent.; **in cash** en liquide ▷ *£2000 in cash* deux mille livres en liquide; **to pay cash** payer **[59]** comptant; **a cash card** une carte de retrait; **the cash desk** la caisse; **a cash machine** un distributeur de billets; **a cash register** une caisse
cashew *n* noix de cajou *f* (*pl* noix de cajou)
cashier *n* caissier *m*, caissière *f*
cashmere *n* cachemire *m* ▷ *a cashmere sweater* un pull en cachemire
casino *n* casino *m*
cassette *n* cassette *f*; **a cassette player** un lecteur de cassettes; **a cassette recorder** un magnétophone
cast *n* acteurs *mpl* ▷ *the cast of Eastenders* les acteurs de la série Eastenders
castle *n* château *m* (*pl* châteaux)
casual *adj* ❶ décontracté(e) ▷ *casual clothes* les vêtements décontractés ❷ désinvolte ▷ *a casual attitude* une attitude désinvolte ❸ en passant ▷ *It was just a casual remark.* C'était juste une remarque en passant.
casualty *n (in hospital)* urgences *fpl*
cat *n (female)* chat *m*, chatte *f* ▷ *Have you got a cat?* Est-ce que tu as un chat?
catalogue *n* catalogue *m*
catastrophe *n* catastrophe *f*
catch *vb* ❶ attraper **[28]** ▷ *to catch a thief* attraper un voleur ▷ *My cat catches birds.* Mon chat attrape des

oiseaux.; **to catch somebody doing something** attraper [**28**] quelqu'un en train de faire quelque chose ▷ *If they catch you smoking ...* S'ils t'attrapent en train de fumer ...; **to catch a cold** attraper [**28**] un rhume ❷ *(bus, train)* prendre [**65**] ▷ *We caught the last bus.* On a pris le dernier bus. ❸ *(hear)* saisir [**38**] ▷ *I didn't catch his name.* Je n'ai pas saisi son nom.

catch up *vb* rattraper [**28**] son retard ▷ *I've got to catch up: I was off yesterday.* Je dois rattraper mon retard: j'étais absent hier.

catering *n* restauration *f*

cathedral *n* cathédrale *f*

Catholic *adj* catholique ▶ *n* catholique *mf* ▷ *I'm a Catholic.* Je suis catholique.

cattle *npl* bétail *msg*

caught *vb see* **catch**

cauliflower *n* chou-fleur *m* (*pl* choux-fleurs)

cause *n* cause *f* ▶ *vb* provoquer [**28**] ▷ *to cause an accident* provoquer un accident

cautious *adj* prudent(e)

cave *n* grotte *f*

CD *n* CD *m* (*pl* CD)

CD burner *n* graveur de CD *m*

CD player *n* platine laser *f*

CD-ROM *n* CD-ROM *m* (*pl* CD-ROM)

ceiling *n* plafond *m*

celebrate *vb (birthday)* fêter [**28**]

celebrity *n* célébrité *f*

celery *n* céleri *m*

cell *n* cellule *f*

cellar *n* cave *f* ▷ *a wine cellar* une cave à vins

cello *n* violoncelle *m* ▷ *I play the cello.* Je joue du violoncelle.

cell phone *n (US)* téléphone portable *m*

cement *n* ciment *m*

cemetery *n* cimetière *m*

cent *n* cent *m* ▷ *twenty cents* vingt cents

centenary *n* centenaire *m*

center *n (US)* centre *m*

centigrade *adj* centigrade ▷ *20 degrees centigrade* vingt degrés centigrade

centimetre (*US* **centimeter**) *n* centimètre *m*

central *adj* central(e) (*mpl* centraux)

central heating *n* chauffage central *m*

centre *n* centre *m* ▷ *a sports centre* un centre sportif

century *n* siècle *m* ▷ *the 21st century* le vingt et unième siècle

cereal *n* céréales *fpl* ▷ *I have cereal for breakfast.* Je prends des céréales au petit déjeuner.

ceremony *n* cérémonie *f*

certain *adj* certain(e) ▷ *a certain person* une certaine personne ▷ *I'm absolutely certain it was him.* Je suis absolument certain que c'était lui.; **I don't know for certain.** Je n'en suis pas certain.; **to make certain** s'assurer [**28**] ▷ *I made certain the door was locked.* Je me suis assuré que la porte était fermée à clé.

certainly *adv* vraiment ▷ *I certainly*

expected something better. Je m'attendais vraiment à quelque chose de mieux.; **Certainly not!** Certainement pas!; **So it was a surprise? — It certainly was!** C'était donc une surprise? — Ça oui alors!

certificate *n* certificat *m*

chain *n* chaîne *f*

chair *n* ❶ chaise *f* ▷ *a table and 4 chairs* une table et quatre chaises ❷ *(armchair)* fauteuil *m*

chairlift *n* télésiège *m*

chairman *n* président *m*

chalet *n* chalet *m*

chalk *n* craie *f*

challenge *n* défi *m*
▶ *vb* **She challenged me to a race.** Elle m'a proposé de faire la course avec elle.

champagne *n* champagne *m*

champion *n* champion *m*, championne *f*

championship *n* championnat *m*

chance *n* ❶ chance *f* ▷ *Do you think I've got any chance?* Tu crois que j'ai une chance?; **No chance!** Pas question! ❷ occasion *f* ▷ *I'd like to have a chance to travel.* J'aimerais avoir l'occasion de voyager.; **I'll write when I get the chance.** J'écrirai quand j'aurai un moment.; **by chance** par hasard ▷ *We met by chance.* Nous nous sommes rencontrés par hasard.; **to take a chance** prendre [**65**] un risque ▷ *I'm taking no chances!* Je ne veux prendre aucun risque!

change *vb* ❶ changer [**45**] ▷ *The town has changed a lot.* La ville a beaucoup changé. ▷ *I'd like to change £50.* Je voudrais changer cinquante livres. ❷ changer [**45**] de

> Use **changer de** when you change one thing for another.

▷ *You have to change trains in Paris.* Il faut changer de train à Paris. ▷ *I'm going to change my shoes.* Je vais changer de chaussures. ▷ *He wants to change his job.* Il veut changer d'emploi.; **to change one's mind** changer [**45**] d'avis ▷ *I've changed my mind.* J'ai changé d'avis.; **to change gear** changer [**45**] de vitesse ❸ se changer [**45**] ▷ *She changed to go to the party.* Elle s'est changée pour aller à la fête.; **to get changed** se changer [**45**] ▷ *I'm going to get changed.* Je vais me changer. ❹ *(swap)* échanger [**45**] ▷ *Can I change this sweater? It's too small.* Est-ce que je peux échanger ce pull? Il est trop petit.
▶ *n* ❶ changement *m* ▷ *There's been a change of plan.* Il y a eu un changement de programme. ❷ *(money)* monnaie *f* ▷ *I haven't got any change.* Je n'ai pas de monnaie.; **a change of clothes** des vêtements de rechange; **for a change** pour changer ▷ *Let's play tennis for a change.* Si on jouait au tennis pour changer?

changing room *n* ❶ *(in shop)* salon d'essayage *m* ❷ *(for sport)* vestiaire *m*

channel *n (TV)* chaîne *f* ▷ *There's*

football on the other channel. Il y a du football sur l'autre chaîne.; **the Channel** la Manche; **the Channel Islands** les îles Anglo-Normandes *fpl*; **the Channel Tunnel** le tunnel sous la Manche

chaos *n* chaos *m*

chapel *n (part of church)* chapelle *f*

chapter *n* chapitre *m*

character *n* ❶ caractère *m*; **She's quite a character.** C'est un drôle de numéro. ❷ *(in play, film)* personnage *m* ▷ *The character played by Depardieu ...* Le personnage joué par Depardieu ...

characteristic *n* caractéristique *f*

charcoal *n* charbon de bois *m*

charge *n* frais *mpl* ▷ *Is there a charge for delivery?* Est-ce qu'il y a des frais de livraison?; **an extra charge** un supplément; **free of charge** gratuit; **to reverse the charges** appeler [**4**] en PCV. ▷ *I'd like to reverse the charges.* Je voudrais appeler en PCV.; **to be in charge** être [**35**] responsable ▷ *Mrs Munday was in charge of the group.* Madame Munday était responsable du groupe.

▶ *vb* ❶ *(money)* prendre [**65**] ▷ *How much did he charge you?* Combien est-ce qu'il vous a pris? ▷ *They charge £10 an hour.* Ils prennent dix livres de l'heure. ❷ *(with crime)* inculper [**28**] ▷ *The police have charged him with murder.* La police l'a inculpé de meurtre.

charity *n* association caritative *f* ▷ *He gave the money to charity.* Il a donné l'argent à une association caritative.

charm *n* charme *m* ▷ *He's got a lot of charm.* Il a beaucoup de charme.

charming *adj* charmant(e)

chart *n* tableau *m* (*pl* tableaux) ▷ *The chart shows the rise of unemployment.* Le tableau indique la progression du chômage.; **the charts** le hit-parade ▷ *This album is number one in the charts.* Cet album est numéro un au hit-parade.

charter flight *n* charter *m*

chase *vb* pourchasser [**28**]

▶ *n* poursuite *f* ▷ *a car chase* une poursuite en voiture

chat *n* **to have a chat** bavarder [**28**]

▶ *vb* bavarder [**28**]; **to chat somebody up** draguer [**28**] quelqu'un *(informal)* ▷ *He likes to chat up the girls.* Il aime bien draguer les filles.; **She likes chatting online.** Elle aime chatter sur internet.

chatroom *n* forum de discussion *m*

chat show *n* talk-show *m*

chauvinist *n* **a male chauvinist** un machiste

cheap *adj* bon marché ▷ *a cheap T-shirt* un T-shirt bon marché

cheaper *adj* moins cher (*f* moins chère) ▷ *It's cheaper by bus.* C'est moins cher en bus.

cheat *vb* tricher [**28**] ▷ *You're cheating!* Tu triches!

▶ *n* tricheur *m*, tricheuse *f*

check *n* ❶ contrôle *m* ▷ *a security check* un contrôle de sécurité ❷ *(US)* chèque *m* ▷ *to write a check*

faire un chèque ❸ *(US)* addition *f* ▷ *Can we have the check, please?* L'addition, s'il vous plaît.
▶ *vb* vérifier **[19]** ▷ *I'll check the time of the train.* Je vais vérifier l'heure du train. ▷ *Could you check the oil, please?* Pourriez-vous vérifier le niveau d'huile, s'il vous plaît?

check in *vb* ❶ *(at airport)* se présenter **[28]** à l'enregistrement ▷ *Where do we check in?* Où est-ce qu'on doit se présenter à l'enregistrement? ❷ *(in hotel)* se présenter **[28]** à la réception; **I'd like to check in.** Je voudrais prendre ma chambre.

check out *vb (from hotel)* régler **[34]** la note ▷ *Can I check out, please?* Je peux régler la note, s'il vous plaît?

checked *adj (fabric)* à carreaux

checkers *n (US)* dames *fpl* ▷ *to play checkers* jouer aux dames

check-in *n* enregistrement *m*

checkout *n* caisse *f*

check-up *n* examen de routine *m*

cheek *n* ❶ joue *f* ▷ *He kissed her on the cheek.* Il l'a embrassée sur la joue. ❷ culot *m* ▷ *What a cheek!* Quel culot!

cheeky *adj* effronté(e) ▷ *Don't be cheeky!* Ne sois pas effronté!; **a cheeky smile** un sourire malicieux

cheer *n* hourras *mpl*; **to give a cheer** pousser **[28]** des hourras; **Cheers! (1)** *(good health)* À la vôtre! **(2)** *(thanks)* Merci!
▶ *vb* applaudir **[38]**; **to cheer somebody up** remonter **[48]** le moral à quelqu'un ▷ *I was trying to cheer him up.* J'essayais de lui remonter le moral.; **Cheer up!** Ne te laisse pas abattre!

cheerful *adj* gai(e)

cheese *n* fromage *m*

chef *n* chef *m*

chemical *n* produit chimique *m*

chemist *n* ❶ *(dispenser)* pharmacien *m*, pharmacienne *f* ❷ *(shop)* pharmacie *f* ▷ *You get it from the chemist.* C'est vendu en pharmacie.

Chemists' shops in France are identified by a special green cross outside the shop.

❸ *(scientist)* chimiste *mf*

chemistry *n* chimie *f* ▷ *the chemistry lab* le laboratoire de chimie

cheque *n* chèque *m* ▷ *to write a cheque* faire un chèque

chequebook *n* carnet de chèques *m*

cherry *n* cerise *f*

chess *n* échecs *mpl* ▷ *to play chess* jouer aux échecs

chessboard *n* échiquier *m*

chest *n (of person)* poitrine *f* ▷ *his chest measurement* son tour de poitrine; **a chest of drawers** une commode

chestnut *n* marron *m* ▷ *We have turkey with chestnuts.* Nous mangeons de la dinde aux marrons.

chew *vb* mâcher **[28]**

chewing gum *n* chewing-gum *m*

chick *n* poussin *m* ▷ *a hen and her chicks* une poule et ses poussins

chicken *n* poulet *m*
chickenpox *n* varicelle *f*
chickpeas *npl* pois chiches *mpl*
chief *n* chef *m* ▷ *the chief of security* le chef de la sécurité
▶ *adj* principal(e) ▷ *His chief reason for resigning was stress.* La principale raison de sa démission était le stress.
child *n* enfant *mf* ▷ *all the children* tous les enfants
childish *adj* puéril(e)
child minder *n* nourrice *f*
children *npl see* **child**
Chile *n* Chili *m*; **in Chile** au Chili
chill *vb* mettre [**47**] au frais ▷ *Put the wine in the fridge to chill.* Mets le vin au frais dans le réfrigérateur.
chilli *n* piment *m*
chilly *adj* froid(e)
chimney *n* cheminée *f*
chin *n* menton *m*
China *n* Chine *f*; **in China** en Chine
china *n* porcelaine *f* ▷ *a china plate* une assiette en porcelaine
Chinese *n (language)* chinois *m*; **the Chinese** les Chinois
▶ *adj* chinois(e) ▷ *a Chinese restaurant* un restaurant chinois; **a Chinese man** un Chinois; **a Chinese woman** une Chinoise
chip *n* ❶ *(food)* frite *f* ▷ *We bought some chips.* Nous avons acheté des frites. ❷ *(in computer)* puce *f*
chiropodist *n* pédicure *mf* ▷ *He's a chiropodist.* Il est pédicure.
chives *npl* ciboulette *fsg*
chocolate *n* chocolat *m*
▷ *a chocolate cake* un gâteau au chocolat; **hot chocolate** le chocolat chaud
choice *n* choix *m* ▷ *I had no choice.* Je n'avais pas le choix.
choir *n* chorale *f* ▷ *I sing in the school choir.* Je chante dans la chorale de l'école.
choke *vb* s'étrangler [**28**]; **He choked on a fishbone.** Il s'est étranglé avec une arête de poisson.
choose *vb* choisir [**38**] ▷ *It's difficult to choose.* C'est difficile de choisir.
chop *vb* émincer [**12**] ▷ *Chop the onions.* Émincez les oignons.
▶ *n* côte *f* ▷ *a pork chop* une côte de porc
chopsticks *npl* baguettes *fpl*
chose, chosen *vb see* **choose**
Christ *n* Christ *m* ▷ *the birth of Christ* la naissance du Christ
christening *n* baptême *m*
Christian *n* chrétien *m*, chrétienne *f*
▶ *adj* chrétien (*f* chrétienne)
Christian name *n* prénom *m*
Christmas *n* Noël *m* ▷ *Happy Christmas!* Joyeux Noël!; **Christmas Day** le jour de Noël; **Christmas Eve** la veille de Noël; **a Christmas tree** un arbre de Noël; **a Christmas card** une carte de Noël

The French more often send greetings cards (**une carte de vœux**) in January rather than at Christmas, with best wishes for the New Year.

Christmas dinner le repas de Noël

a b c d e f g h i j k l m n o p q r s t u v w x y z

- Most French people have their Christmas meal (**réveillon de Noël**) on the evening of Christmas Eve, though some have a **repas de Noël** on Christmas Day. The French usually have a Yule log (**une bûche de Noël**) for pudding at the Christmas meal.

chunk *n* gros morceau *m (pl* gros morceaux) ▷ *Cut the meat into chunks.* Coupez la viande en gros morceaux.

church *n* église *f* ▷ *I don't go to church every Sunday.* Je ne vais pas à l'église tous les dimanches.; **the Church of England** l'Église anglicane

cider *n* cidre *m*

cigar *n* cigare *m*

cigarette *n* cigarette *f*

cigarette lighter *n* briquet *m*

cinema *n* cinéma *m* ▷ *I'm going to the cinema this evening.* Je vais au cinéma ce soir.

cinnamon *n* cannelle *f*

circle *n* cercle *m*

circular *adj* circulaire

circumflex *n* accent circonflexe *m*

circumstances *npl* circonstances *fpl*

circus *n* cirque *m*

citizen *n* citoyen *m*, citoyenne *f* ▷ *a French citizen* un citoyen français

citizenship *n* citoyenneté *f*

city *n* ville *f*; **the city centre** le centre-ville ▷ *It's in the city centre.* C'est au centre-ville.

civilization *n* civilisation *f*

civil servant *n* fonctionnaire *mf*

civil war *n* guerre civile *f*

claim *vb* ❶ prétendre [**88**] ▷ *He claims to have found the money.* Il prétend avoir trouvé l'argent. ❷ *(receive)* percevoir [**28**] ▷ *She's claiming unemployment benefit.* Elle perçoit des allocations chômage.; **She can't claim unemployment benefit.** Elle n'a pas droit aux allocations chômage.; **to claim on one's insurance** se faire [**36**] rembourser par son assurance ▷ *We claimed on our insurance.* On s'est fait rembourser par notre assurance.
▶ *n (on insurance policy)* demande d'indemnité *f* ▷ *to make a claim* faire une demande d'indemnité

clap *vb (applaud)* applaudir [**38**]; **to clap one's hands** frapper [**28**] dans ses mains ▷ *My dog sits when I clap my hands.* Mon chien s'assoit quand je frappe dans mes mains.

clarinet *n* clarinette *f* ▷ *I play the clarinet.* Je joue de la clarinette.

clash *vb* ❶ *(colours)* jurer [**28**] ▷ *These two colours clash.* Ces deux couleurs jurent. ❷ *(events)* tomber [**84**] en même temps ▷ *The concert clashes with Ann's party.* Le concert tombe en même temps que la soirée d'Ann.

clasp *n (of necklace)* fermoir *m*

class *n* ❶ *(group)* classe *f* ▷ *We're in the same class.* Nous sommes dans la même classe. ❷ *(lesson)* cours *m* ▷ *I go to dancing classes.* Je vais à des cours de danse.

classic *adj* classique ▷ *a classic example* un cas classique
▶ *n (book, film)* classique *m*
classical *adj* classique ▷ *I like classical music.* J'aime la musique classique.
classmate *n* camarade de classe *m*, camarade de classe *f*
classroom *n* classe *f*
classroom assistant *n* aide-éducateur *m*, aide-éducatrice *f*
claw *n* ❶ *(of cat, dog)* griffe *f* ❷ *(of bird)* serre *f* ❸ *(of crab, lobster)* pince *f*
clean *adj* propre ▷ *a clean shirt* une chemise propre
▶ *vb* nettoyer [**53**]
cleaner *n (woman, man)* femme de ménage *f*, agent d'entretien *m*
cleaner's *n* teinturerie *f*
cleansing lotion *n* lotion démaquillante *f*
clear *adj* ❶ clair(e) ▷ *a clear explanation* une explication claire ▷ *It's clear you don't believe me.* Il est clair que tu ne me crois pas. ❷ *(road, way)* libre ▷ *The road's clear now.* La route est libre maintenant.
▶ *vb* ❶ dégager [**45**] ▷ *The police are clearing the road after the accident.* La police dégage la route après l'accident. ❷ *(fog, mist)* se dissiper [**28**] ▷ *The mist cleared.* La brume s'est dissipée.; **to be cleared of a crime** être [**35**] reconnu non coupable d'un crime ▷ *She was cleared of murder.* Elle a été reconnue non coupable du meurtre.; **to clear the table** débarrasser [**28**] la table ▷ *I'll clear the table.* Je vais débarrasser la table.
clear off *vb* filer [**28**] ▷ *Clear off and leave me alone!* File et laisse-moi tranquille!
clear up *vb* ranger [**45**] ▷ *Who's going to clear all this up?* Qui va ranger tout ça?; **I think it's going to clear up.** *(weather)* Je pense que le temps va se lever.
clearly *adv* ❶ clairement ▷ *She explained it very clearly.* Elle l'a expliqué très clairement. ❷ nettement ▷ *You could clearly make out the French coast.* On distinguait nettement la côte française. ❸ distinctement ▷ *to speak clearly* parler distinctement
clementine *n* clémentine *f*
clever *adj* ❶ intelligent(e) ▷ *She's very clever.* Elle est très intelligente. ❷ *(ingenious)* astucieux (*f* astucieuse) ▷ *a clever system* un système astucieux; **What a clever idea!** Quelle bonne idée!
click *n (of door, camera)* petit bruit *m*
▶ *vb (with mouse)* cliquer [**28**] ▷ *to click on an icon* cliquer sur une icône
client *n* client *m*, cliente *f*
cliff *n* falaise *f*
climate *n* climat *m*
climate change *n* changement climatique *m*
climb *vb* ❶ escalader [**28**] ▷ *We're going to climb Snowdon.* Nous allons escalader le Snowdon. ❷ *(stairs)* monter [**48**]

climber *n* grimpeur *m*, grimpeuse *f*
climbing *n* escalade *f*; **to go climbing** faire [**36**] de l'escalade ▷ *We're going climbing in Scotland.* Nous allons faire de l'escalade en Écosse.
Clingfilm® *n* film alimentaire *m*
clinic *n* centre médical *m* (*pl* centres médicaux)
clip *n* ❶ *(for hair)* barrette *f* ❷ *(film)* court extrait *m* ▷ *some clips from Disney's latest film* quelques courts extraits du dernier film Disney
cloakroom *n* ❶ *(for coats)* vestiaire *m* ❷ *(toilet)* toilettes *fpl*
clock *n* ❶ horloge *f* ▷ *the church clock* l'horloge de l'église ❷ *(smaller)* pendule *f*; **an alarm clock** un réveil; **a clock-radio** un radio-réveil
close *adj, adv* ❶ *(near)* près ▷ *The shops are very close.* Les magasins sont tout près.; **close to** près de ▷ *The youth hostel is close to the station.* L'auberge de jeunesse est près de la gare.; **Come closer.** Rapproche-toi. ❷ *(in relationship)* proche ▷ *We're just inviting close relations.* Nous n'invitons que les parents proches. ▷ *She's a close friend of mine.* C'est une proche amie. ❸ *(contest)* très serré(e) ▷ *It's going to be very close.* Ça va être très très serré. ❹ *(weather)* lourd(e) ▷ *It's close this afternoon.* Il fait lourd cet après-midi.
▶ *vb* ❶ fermer [**28**] ▷ *The shops close at 5.30.* Les magasins ferment à cinq heures et demie. ❷ se fermer [**28**] ▷ *The doors close automatically.* Les portes se ferment automatiquement.
closed *adj* fermé(e) ▷ *The bank's closed.* La banque est fermée.
closely *adv (look, examine)* de près
cloth *n (material)* tissu *m*; **a cloth** un chiffon ▷ *Wipe it with a damp cloth.* Nettoyez-le avec un chiffon humide.
clothes *npl* vêtements *mpl* ▷ *new clothes* des vêtements neufs; **a clothes line** un fil à linge; **a clothes peg** une pince à linge
cloud *n* nuage *m*
▶ *adj* **cloud computing** l'informatique dans le cloud
cloudy *adj* nuageux (*f* nuageuse)
clove *n* **a clove of garlic** une gousse d'ail
clown *n* clown *m*
club *n* club *m* ▷ *a golf club* un club de golf; **the youth club** la maison des jeunes; **clubs** *(in cards)* le trèfle ▷ *the ace of clubs* l'as de trèfle
club together *vb* se cotiser [**28**]
clubbing *n* **to go clubbing** sortir [**79**] en boîte
clue *n* indice *m* ▷ *an important clue* un indice important; **I haven't a clue.** Je n'en ai pas la moindre idée.
clumsy *adj* maladroit(e)
clutch *n (of car)* pédale d'embrayage *f*
clutter *n* désordre *m* ▷ *There's too much clutter in here.* Il y a trop de désordre ici.
coach *n* ❶ car *m* ▷ *We went there by coach.* Nous y sommes allés en car.;

the coach station la gare routière; **a coach trip** une excursion en car ❷ *(trainer)* entraîneur *m* ▷ *the French coach* l'entraîneur de l'équipe de France

coal *n* charbon *m*; **a coal mine** une mine de charbon; **a coal miner** un mineur

coarse *adj* ❶ *(surface, fabric)* rugueux (*f* rugueuse) ▷ *The bag was made of coarse cloth.* Le sac était fait d'un tissu rugueux. ❷ *(vulgar)* grossier (*f* grossière) ▷ *coarse language* un langage grossier

coast *n* côte *f* ▷ *It's on the west coast of Scotland.* C'est sur la côte ouest de l'Écosse.

coastguard *n* garde-côte *m* (*pl* garde-côtes)

coat *n* manteau *m* (*pl* manteaux) ▷ *a warm coat* un manteau chaud; **a coat of paint** une couche de peinture

coat hanger *n* cintre *m*

cobweb *n* toile d'araignée *f*

cocaine *n* cocaïne *f*

cockerel *n* coq *m*

cocoa *n* cacao *m* ▷ *a cup of cocoa* une tasse de cacao

coconut *n* noix de coco *f*

code *n* code *m*

coffee *n* café *m*; **A cup of coffee, please.** Un café, s'il vous plaît.

coffee table *n* table basse *f*

coffin *n* cercueil *m*

coin *n* pièce de monnaie *f*; **a 2 euro coin** une pièce de deux euros

coincidence *n* coïncidence *f*

Coke® *n* coca *m* ▷ *a can of Coke®* une cannette de coca

colander *n* passoire *f*

cold *adj* froid(e) ▷ *The water's cold.* L'eau est froide.; **It's cold today.** Il fait froid aujourd'hui.; **to be cold** *(person)* avoir [**8**] froid ▷ *I'm cold.* J'ai froid.

▶ *n* ❶ froid *m* ▷ *I can't stand the cold.* Je ne supporte pas le froid. ❷ rhume *m* ▷ *to catch a cold* attraper un rhume; **to have a cold** avoir [**8**] un rhume ▷ *I've got a bad cold.* J'ai un gros rhume.; **a cold sore** un bouton de fièvre

coleslaw *n* salade de chou cru à la mayonnaise *f*

collapse *vb* s'effondrer [**28**] ▷ *He collapsed.* Il s'est effondré.

collar *n* ❶ *(of coat, shirt)* col *m* ❷ *(for animal)* collier *m*

collarbone *n* clavicule *f* ▷ *I broke my collarbone.* Je me suis cassé la clavicule.

colleague *n* collègue *mf*

collect *vb* ❶ ramasser [**28**] ▷ *The teacher collected the exercise books.* Le professeur a ramassé les cahiers. ▷ *They collect the rubbish on Fridays.* Ils ramassent les ordures le vendredi. ❷ faire [**36**] collection de ▷ *I collect stamps.* Je fais collection de timbres. ❸ aller [**3**] chercher ▷ *Their mother collects them from school.* Leur mère va les chercher à l'école. ❹ faire [**36**] une collecte ▷ *They're collecting for charity.* Ils font une collecte pour une association caritative.

collection *n* ❶ collection *f* ▷ *my*

DVD collection ma collection de DVD ❷ collecte *f* ▷ *a collection for charity* une collecte pour une association caritative ❸ *(of mail)* levée *f* ▷ *Next collection: 5pm* Prochaine levée: 17 heures

collector *n* collectionneur *m*, collectionneuse *f*

college *n* collège *m* ▷ *a technical college* un collège d'enseignement technique

collide *vb* entrer [**32**] en collision

collie *n* colley *m*

collision *n* collision *f*

colon *n (punctuation mark)* deux-points *mpl*

colonel *n* colonel *m*

colour (*US* **color**) *n* couleur *f* ▷ *What colour is it?* C'est de quelle couleur?; **a colour film** *(for camera)* une pellicule en couleur

colourful (*US* **colorful**) *adj* coloré(e)

comb *n* peigne *m*

▶ *vb* **to comb one's hair** se peigner [**28**] ▷ *You haven't combed your hair.* Tu ne t'es pas peigné.

combination *n* combinaison *f*

combine *vb* ❶ allier [**19**] ▷ *The film combines humour with suspense.* Le film allie l'humour au suspense. ❷ concilier [**19**] ▷ *It's difficult to combine a career with a family.* Il est difficile de concilier carrière et vie de famille.

come *vb* ❶ venir [**89**] ▷ *Can I come too?* Est-ce que je peux venir aussi? ▷ *Some friends came to see us.* Quelques amis sont venus nous voir. ▷ *I'll come with you.* Je viens avec toi. ❷ *(arrive)* arriver [**5**] ▷ *I'm coming!* J'arrive! ▷ *They came late.* Ils sont arrivés en retard. ▷ *The letter came this morning.* La lettre est arrivée ce matin.; **Where do you come from?** Tu viens d'où?; **Come on!** Allez!

come back *vb* revenir [**73**] ▷ *Come back!* Reviens!

come down *vb* ❶ *(person, lift)* descendre [**24**] ❷ *(prices)* baisser [**28**]

come in *vb* entrer [**32**] ▷ *Come in!* Entrez!

come out *vb* sortir [**79**] ▷ *I tripped as we came out of the cinema.* J'ai trébuché quand nous sommes sortis du cinéma. ▷ *It's just come out on DVD.* Ça vient de sortir en DVD.; **None of my photos came out.** Mes photos n'ont rien donné.

come round *vb (after faint, operation)* reprendre [**65**] connaissance

come up *vb* monter [**48**] ▷ *Come up here!* Monte!; **to come up to somebody (1)** s'approcher [**28**] de quelqu'un ▷ *She came up to me and kissed me.* Elle s'est approchée de moi et m'a embrassé. **(2)** *(to speak to them)* aborder [**28**] quelqu'un ▷ *A man came up to me and said ...* Un homme m'a abordé et m'a dit ...

comedian *n* comique *m*

comedy *n* comédie *f*

comfortable *adj* ❶ *(bed, chair)* confortable ❷ *(person)* à l'aise ▷ *I'm very comfortable, thanks.* Je suis parfaitement à l'aise, merci.

comic *n (magazine)* illustré *m*
comic strip *n* bande dessinée *f*
comma *n* virgule *f*
command *n* ordre *m*
comment *n* commentaire *m* ▷ *He made no comment.* Il n'a fait aucun commentaire.; **No comment!** Je n'ai rien à dire!
▶ *vb* **to comment on something** faire [**36**] des commentaires sur quelque chose
commentary *n (on TV, radio)* reportage en direct *m*
commentator *n* commentateur sportif *m*, commentatrice sportive *f*
commercial *n* spot publicitaire *m*
commit *vb* **to commit a crime** commettre [**47**] un crime; **to commit oneself** s'engager [**45**] ▷ *I don't want to commit myself.* Je ne veux pas m'engager.; **to commit suicide** se suicider [**28**] ▷ *He committed suicide.* Il s'est suicidé.
committee *n* comité *m*
common *adj* courant(e) ▷ *'Smith' is a very common surname.* 'Smith' est un nom de famille très courant.; **in common** en commun ▷ *We've got a lot in common.* Nous avons beaucoup de choses en commun.
Commons *npl* **the House of Commons** la Chambre des communes
common sense *n* bon sens *m* ▷ *Use your common sense!* Sers-toi de ton bon sens!
communicate *vb* communiquer [**28**]
communication *n* communication *f*
communion *n* communion *f* ▷ *my First Communion* ma première communion
communism *n* communisme *m*
community *n* communauté *f*
commute *vb* faire [**36**] la navette ▷ *She commutes between Liss and London.* Elle fait la navette entre Liss et Londres.
compact disc *n* disque compact *m*; **a compact disc player** une platine laser
company *n* ❶ société *f* ▷ *He works for a big company.* Il travaille pour une grosse société. ❷ compagnie *f* ▷ *an insurance company* une compagnie d'assurance; **to keep somebody company** tenir [**83**] compagnie à quelqu'un ▷ *I'll keep you company.* Je vais te tenir compagnie.
comparatively *adv* relativement
compare *vb* comparer [**28**] ▷ *People always compare him with his brother.* On le compare toujours à son frère.; **compared with** en comparaison de ▷ *Oxford is small compared with London.* Oxford est une petite ville en comparaison de Londres.
comparison *n* comparaison *f*
compartment *n* compartiment *m*
compass *n* boussole *f*
compensation *n* indemnité *f* ▷ *They got £2000 compensation.* Ils ont reçu une indemnité de deux mille livres.

compete *vb* participer [**28**] ▷ *I'm competing in the marathon.* Je participe au marathon.; **to compete for something** se disputer [**28**] quelque chose ▷ *There are 50 students competing for 6 places.* Ils sont cinquante étudiants à se disputer six places.

competent *adj* compétent(e)

competition *n* concours *m* ▷ *a singing competition* un concours de chant

competitive *adj* compétitif (*f* compétitive) ▷ *a very competitive price* un prix très compétitif; **to be competitive** *(person)* avoir [**8**] l'esprit de compétition ▷ *He's a very competitive person.* Il a vraiment l'esprit de compétition.

competitor *n* concurrent *m*, concurrente *f*

complain *vb* se plaindre [**17**] ▷ *I'm going to complain to the manager.* Je vais me plaindre au directeur.

complaint *n* plainte *f* ▷ *There were lots of complaints about the food.* Il y a eu beaucoup de plaintes à propos de la nourriture.

complete *adj* complet (*f* complète)

completely *adv* complètement

complexion *n* teint *m*

complicated *adj* compliqué(e)

compliment *n* compliment *m* ▶ *vb* complimenter [**28**] ▷ *They complimented me on my French.* Ils m'ont complimenté sur mon français.

composer *n* compositeur *m*, compositrice *f*

comprehension *n* ❶ *(understanding)* compréhension *f* ❷ *(school exercise)* exercice de compréhension *m*

comprehensive *adj* complet (*f* complète) ▷ *a comprehensive guide* un guide complet

> Be careful not to translate **comprehensive** by **compréhensif**.

comprehensive school *n* ❶ collège *m* ❷ lycée *m*

> In France pupils go to a **collège** between the ages of 11 and 15, and then to a **lycée** until the age of 18.

compulsory *adj* obligatoire

computer *n* ordinateur *m*

computer game *n* jeu vidéo *m* (*pl* jeux vidéo)

computer programmer *n* programmeur *m*, programmeuse *f* ▷ *She's a computer programmer.* Elle est programmeuse.

computer science *n* informatique *f*

computing *n* informatique *f*

concentrate *vb* se concentrer [**28**] ▷ *I couldn't concentrate.* Je n'arrivais pas à me concentrer.

concentration *n* concentration *f*

concern *n* *(preoccupation)* inquiétude *f* ▷ *They expressed concern about her health.* Ils ont exprimé leur inquiétude concernant sa santé.

concerned *adj* **to be concerned** s'inquiéter [**34**] ▷ *His mother is concerned about him.* Sa mère s'inquiète à son sujet.; **as far as I'm concerned** en ce qui me concerne

concerning *prep* concernant ▷ *For further information concerning the job, contact ...* Pour plus d'informations concernant cet emploi, contacter ...

concert *n* concert *m*

concrete *n* béton *m*

condemn *vb* condamner [**28**] ▷ *The government has condemned the decision.* Le gouvernement a condamné cette décision.

condition *n* ❶ condition *f* ▷ *I'll do it, on one condition ...* Je veux bien le faire, à une condition ... ❷ état *m* ▷ *in bad condition* en mauvais état

conditional *n* conditionnel *m*

conditioner *n (for hair)* baume démêlant *m*

condom *n* préservatif *m*

conduct *vb (orchestra)* diriger [**45**]

conductor *n* chef d'orchestre *m*

cone *n* cornet *m* ▷ *an ice-cream cone* un cornet de glace

conference *n* conférence *f*

confess *vb* avouer [**28**] ▷ *He confessed to the murder.* Il a avoué avoir commis le meurtre.

confession *n* confession *f*

confidence *n* ❶ confiance *f* ▷ *I've got confidence in you.* J'ai confiance en toi. ❷ assurance *f* ▷ *She lacks confidence.* Elle manque d'assurance.

confident *adj* sûr(e) ▷ *I'm confident everything will be okay.* Je suis sûr que tout ira bien.; **She's seems quite confident.** Elle a l'air sûre d'elle.

confidential *adj* confidentiel (*f* confidentielle)

confirm *vb (booking)* confirmer [**28**]

confuse *vb* **to confuse somebody** embrouiller [**28**] les idées de quelqu'un ▷ *Don't confuse me!* Ne m'embrouille pas les idées!

confused *adj* désorienté(e)

confusing *adj* **The traffic signs are confusing.** Les panneaux de signalisation ne sont pas clairs.

confusion *n* confusion *f*

congratulate *vb* féliciter [**28**] ▷ *My aunt congratulated me on my results.* Ma tante m'a félicité pour mes résultats.

congratulations *npl* félicitations *fpl* ▷ *Congratulations on your new job!* Félicitations pour votre nouveau poste!

conjunction *n* conjonction *f*

conjurer *n* prestidigitateur *m*

connection *n* ❶ rapport *m* ▷ *There's no connection between the two events.* Il n'y a aucun rapport entre les deux événements. ❷ *(electrical)* contact *m* ▷ *There's a loose connection.* Il y a un mauvais contact. ❸ *(of trains, planes)* correspondance *f* ▷ *We missed our connection.* Nous avons raté la correspondance.

conscience *n* conscience *f*

conscious *adj* conscient(e)

consciousness *n* connaissance *f*; **to lose consciousness** perdre [**61**] connaissance ▷ *I lost consciousness.*

a b c d e f g h i j k l m n o p q r s t u v w x y z

J'ai perdu connaissance.
consequence *n* conséquence *f* ▷ *What are the consequences for the environment?* Quelles sont les conséquences pour l'environnement?; **as a consequence** en conséquence
consequently *adv* par conséquent
conservation *n* protection *f*
conservative *adj* conservateur (*f* conservatrice); **the Conservative Party** le Parti conservateur
conservatory *n* jardin d'hiver *m*
consider *vb* ❶ considérer [**34**] ▷ *He considers it a waste of time.* Il considère que c'est une perte de temps. ❷ envisager [**45**] ▷ *We considered cancelling our holiday.* Nous avons envisagé d'annuler nos vacances.; **I'm considering the idea.** J'y songe.
considerate *adj* délicat(e)
considering *prep* ❶ étant donné ▷ *Considering we were there for a month ...* Étant donné que nous étions là pour un mois ... ❷ tout compte fait ▷ *I got a good mark, considering.* J'ai eu une bonne note, tout compte fait.
consist *vb* **to consist of** être [**35**] composé de ▷ *The band consists of a singer and a guitarist.* Le groupe est composé d'un chanteur et d'un guitariste.
consonant *n* consonne *f*
constant *adj* constant(e)
constantly *adv* constamment
constipated *adj* constipé(e)
construct *vb* construire [**23**]
construction *n* construction *f*
consult *vb* consulter [**28**]
consumer *n* consommateur *m*, consommatrice *f*
contact *n* contact *m* ▷ *I'm in contact with her.* Je suis en contact avec elle.
▶ *vb* joindre [**42**] ▷ *Where can we contact you?* Où pouvons-nous vous joindre?
contact lenses *npl* verres de contact *mpl*
contain *vb* contenir [**83**]
container *n* récipient *m*
contents *npl* ❶ *(of container)* contenu *msg* ❷ *(of book)* table des matières *fsg*
contest *n* concours *m*
contestant *n* concurrent *m*, concurrente *f*
context *n* contexte *m*
continent *n* continent *m* ▷ *How many continents are there?* Combien y a-t-il de continents?; **the Continent** l'Europe *f* ▷ *I've never been to the Continent.* Je ne suis jamais allé en Europe.
continental breakfast *n* petit déjeuner à la française *m*
continue *vb* ❶ continuer [**28**] ▷ *She continued talking to her friend.* Elle a continué à parler à son amie.
❷ *(after interruption)* reprendre [**65**] ▷ *We continued working after lunch.* Nous avons repris le travail après le déjeuner.
continuous *adj* continu(e); **continuous assessment** le contrôle continu

contraceptive *n* contraceptif *m*
contract *n* contrat *m*
contradict *vb* contredire [**27**]
contrary *n* contraire *m*; **on the contrary** au contraire
contrast *n* contraste *m*
contribute *vb* ❶ *(to success, achievement)* contribuer [**28**] ▷ *The treaty will contribute to world peace.* Le traité va contribuer à la paix dans le monde. ❷ *(share in)* participer [**28**] ▷ *He didn't contribute to the discussion.* Il n'a pas participé à la discussion. ❸ *(give)* donner [**28**] ▷ *She contributed £10.* Elle a donné dix livres.
contribution *n* ❶ contribution *f* ❷ *(to pension, national insurance)* cotisation *f*
control *n* contrôle *m*; **to lose control** *(of vehicle)* perdre [**61**] le contrôle ▷ *He lost control of the car.* Il a perdu le contrôle de son véhicule.; **the controls** *(of machine)* les commandes *fpl*; **to be in control** être [**35**] maître de la situation; **to keep control** *(of people)* se faire [**36**] obéir ▷ *He can't keep control of the class.* Il ne se fait pas obéir de sa classe.; **out of control** *(child, class)* déchaîné
▶ *vb* ❶ *(country, organization)* diriger [**45**] ❷ se faire [**36**] obéir de ▷ *He can't control the class.* Il ne se fait pas obéir de sa classe. ❸ maîtriser [**28**] ▷ *I couldn't control the horse.* Je ne suis pas arrivé à maîtriser le cheval.; **to control oneself** se contrôler [**28**]
controversial *adj* controversé(e) ▷ *a controversial book* un livre controversé
convenient *adj (place)* bien situé(e) ▷ *The hotel's convenient for the airport.* L'hôtel est bien situé par rapport à l'aéroport.; **It's not a convenient time for me.** C'est une heure qui ne m'arrange pas.; **Would Monday be convenient for you?** Est-ce que lundi vous conviendrait?
conventional *adj* conventionnel (*f* conventionnelle)
conversation *n* conversation *f* ▷ *a French conversation class* un cours de conversation française
convert *vb* transformer [**28**] ▷ *We've converted the loft into a spare room.* Nous avons transformé le grenier en chambre d'amis.
convince *vb* persuader [**28**] ▷ *I'm not convinced.* Je n'en suis pas persuadé.
cook *vb* ❶ faire [**36**] la cuisine ▷ *I can't cook.* Je ne sais pas faire la cuisine. ❷ préparer [**28**] ▷ *She's cooking lunch.* Elle est en train de préparer le déjeuner. ❸ faire [**36**] cuire ▷ *Cook the pasta for 10 minutes.* Faites cuire les pâtes pendant dix minutes.; **to be cooked** être [**35**] cuit ▷ *When the potatoes are cooked ...* Lorsque les pommes de terre sont cuites ...
▶ *n* cuisinier *m*, cuisinière *f* ▷ *Matthew's an excellent cook.* Matthew est un excellent cuisinier.
cooker *n* cuisinière *f* ▷ *a gas cooker*

une cuisinière à gaz

cookery *n* cuisine *f*

cookie *n (US)* gâteau sec *m (pl* gâteaux secs)

cooking *n* cuisine *f* ▷ *I like cooking.* J'aime bien faire la cuisine.

cool *adj* ❶ frais *(f* fraîche) ▷ *a cool place* un endroit frais ❷ *(great)* cool ▷ *That's really cool!* C'est vraiment cool!

cooperation *n* coopération *f*

cop *n (informal)* flic *m*

cope *vb* se débrouiller [**28**] ▷ *It was hard, but we coped.* C'était dur, mais nous nous sommes débrouillés.; **to cope with** faire [**36**] face à ▷ *She's got a lot of problems to cope with.* Elle doit faire face à de nombreux problèmes.

copper *n* ❶ cuivre *m* ▷ *a copper bracelet* un bracelet en cuivre ❷ *(informal: police officer)* flic *m*

copy *n* ❶ *(of letter, document)* copie *f* ❷ *(of book)* exemplaire *m*
▶ *vb* copier [**19**] ▷ *The teacher accused him of copying.* Le professeur l'a accusé d'avoir copié.; **to copy and paste** copier-coller [**28**]

core *n (of fruit)* trognon *m* ▷ *an apple core* un trognon de pomme

cork *n* ❶ *(of bottle)* bouchon *m* ❷ *(material)* liège *m* ▷ *a cork table mat* un set de table en liège

corkscrew *n* tire-bouchon *m*

corn *n* ❶ *(wheat)* blé *m* ❷ *(sweetcorn)* maïs *m*; **corn on the cob** l'épi de maïs *m*

corner *n* ❶ coin *m* ▷ *in a corner of the room* dans un coin de la pièce; **the shop on the corner** la boutique au coin de la rue; **He lives just round the corner.** Il habite tout près d'ici. ❷ *(in football)* corner *m*

cornflakes *npl* corn-flakes *mpl*

Cornwall *n* Cornouailles *f*; **in Cornwall** en Cornouailles

corpse *n* cadavre *m*

correct *adj* exact(e) ▷ *That's correct.* C'est exact.; **the correct choice** le bon choix; **the correct answer** la bonne réponse
▶ *vb* corriger [**45**]

correction *n* correction *f*

correctly *adv* correctement

corridor *n* couloir *m*

corruption *n* corruption *f*

Corsica *n* Corse *f*; **in Corsica** en Corse

cosmetics *npl* produits de beauté *mpl*

cosmetic surgery *n* chirurgie esthétique *f*

cost *vb* coûter [**28**] ▷ *It costs too much.* Ça coûte trop cher.
▶ *n* coût *m*; **the cost of living** le coût de la vie; **at all costs** à tout prix

costume *n* costume *m*

cosy *adj* douillet *(f* douillette)

cot *n* lit d'enfant *m*

cottage *n* cottage *m*; **a thatched cottage** une chaumière

cotton *n* coton *m* ▷ *a cotton shirt* une chemise en coton; **cotton wool** le coton hydrophile

couch *n* canapé *m*

cough *vb* tousser [**28**]
▶ *n* toux *f* ▷ *a bad cough* une

mauvaise toux; **I've got a cough.** Je tousse.; **a cough sweet** une pastille

could *vb see* **can**

council *n* conseil *m*

The nearest French equivalent of a local council would be a **conseil municipal**, which administers a **commune**.

He's on the council. Il fait partie du conseil municipal.; **a council estate** une cité HLM; **a council house** une HLM

HLM stands for **habitation à loyer modéré** which means 'low-rent home'.

councillor *n* **She's a local councillor.** Elle fait partie du conseil municipal.

count *vb* compter [**28**]

count on *vb* compter [**28**] sur ▷ *You can count on me.* Tu peux compter sur moi.

counter *n* ❶ *(in shop)* comptoir *m* ❷ *(in post office, bank)* guichet *m* ❸ *(in game)* jeton *m*

country *n* ❶ pays *m* ▷ *the border between the two countries* la frontière entre les deux pays ❷ campagne *f* ▷ *I live in the country.* J'habite à la campagne.; **country dancing** la danse folklorique

countryside *n* campagne *f*

county *n* comté *m*

The nearest French equivalent of a county would be a **département**.

the county council

The nearest French equivalent of a county council would be a **conseil général**, which administers a **département**.

couple *n* couple *m* ▷ *the couple who live next door* le couple qui habite à côté; **a couple** deux ▷ *a couple of hours* deux heures; **Could you wait a couple of minutes?** Pourriez-vous attendre quelques minutes?

courage *n* courage *m*

courgette *n* courgette *f*

courier *n* ❶ *(for tourists)* accompagnateur *m*, accompagnatrice *f* ❷ *(delivery service)* coursier *m* ▷ *They sent it by courier.* Ils l'ont envoyé par coursier.

Be careful not to translate **courier** by **courrier**.

course *n* ❶ cours *m* ▷ *a French course* un cours de français ▷ *to go on a course* suivre un cours ❷ plat *m* ▷ *the main course* le plat principal; **the first course** l'entrée *f* ❸ terrain *m* ▷ *a golf course* un terrain de golf; **of course** bien sûr ▷ *Do you love me? — Of course I do!* Tu m'aimes? — Bien sûr que oui!

court *n* ❶ *(of law)* tribunal *m* (*pl* tribunaux) ▷ *He was in court yesterday.* Il est passé devant le tribunal hier. ❷ *(tennis)* court *m* ▷ *There are tennis and squash courts.* Il y a des courts de tennis et de squash.

courtyard *n* cour *f*

cousin *n* cousin *m*, cousine *f*

cover *n* ❶ *(of book)* couverture *f*

❷ *(of duvet)* housse *f*
▶ *vb* ❶ couvrir [**55**] ▷ *My face was covered with mosquito bites.* J'avais le visage couvert de piqûres de moustique. ❷ prendre [**65**] en charge ▷ *Our insurance didn't cover it.* Notre assurance ne l'a pas pris en charge.; **to cover up a scandal** étouffer [**28**] un scandale

cow *n* vache *f*

coward *n* lâche *m* ▷ *She's a coward.* Elle est lâche.

cowboy *n* cow-boy *m*

crab *n* crabe *m*

crack *n* ❶ *(in wall)* fissure *f* ❷ *(in cup, window)* fêlure *f* ❸ *(drug)* crack *m*; **I'll have a crack at it.** Je vais tenter le coup.
▶ *vb (nut, egg)* casser [**28**]; **to crack a joke** sortir [**79**] une blague

crack down on *vb* être [**35**] ferme avec

cracked *adj (cup, window)* fêlé(e)

cracker *n* ❶ *(biscuit)* cracker *m* ❷ *(Christmas cracker)* papillote *f*

craft *n* travaux manuels *mpl* ▷ *We do craft at school.* Nous avons des cours de travaux manuels à l'école.; **a craft centre** un centre artisanal

crammed *adj* **crammed with** bourré de ▷ *Her bag was crammed with books.* Son sac était bourré de livres.

crane *n (machine)* grue *f*

crash *vb* avoir [**8**] un accident ▷ *He's crashed his car.* Il a eu un accident de voiture.; **The plane crashed.** L'avion s'est écrasé.
▶ *n* ❶ *(of car)* collision *f* ❷ *(of plane)* accident *m*; **a crash helmet** un casque; **a crash course** un cours intensif

crawl *vb (baby)* marcher [**28**] à quatre pattes
▶ *n* crawl *m* ▷ *to do the crawl* nager le crawl

crazy *adj* fou *(f* folle*)*

cream *adj (colour)* crème
▶ *n* crème *f* ▷ *strawberries and cream* les fraises à la crème; **a cream cake** un gâteau à la crème; **cream cheese** le fromage à la crème; **sun cream** la crème solaire

crease *n* pli *m*

creased *adj* froissé(e)

create *vb* créer [**18**]

creative *adj* créatif *(f* créative*)*

creature *n* créature *f*

crèche *n* crèche *f*

credit *n* crédit *m* ▷ *on credit* à crédit

credit card *n* carte de crédit *f*

creeps *npl* **It gives me the creeps.** Ça me donne la chair de poule.

creep up *vb* **to creep up on somebody** s'approcher [**28**] de quelqu'un à pas de loup

crept *vb see* **creep up**

crew *n* ❶ *(of ship, plane)* équipage *m* ❷ équipe *f* ▷ *a film crew* une équipe de tournage

crew cut *n* cheveux en brosse *mpl*

cricket *n* ❶ cricket *m* ▷ *I play cricket.* Je joue au cricket.; **a cricket bat** une batte de cricket ❷ *(insect)* grillon *m*

crime *n* ❶ délit *m* ▷ *Murder is a crime.* Le meurtre est un délit.

❷ *(lawlessness)* criminalité *f*; ▷ *Crime is rising.* La criminalité augmente.

criminal *n* criminel *m*, criminelle *f*
▶ *adj* criminel (*f* criminelle) ▷ *It's criminal!* C'est criminel!; **It's a criminal offence.** C'est un crime puni par la loi.; **to have a criminal record** avoir [**8**] un casier judiciaire

crisis *n* crise *f*

crisp *adj (food)* croquant(e)

crisps *npl* chips *fpl* ▷ *a bag of crisps* un paquet de chips

critical *adj* critique; **a critical remark** une critique

criticism *n* critique *f*

criticize *vb* critiquer [**28**]

Croatia *n* Croatie *f*; **in Croatia** en Croatie

crochet *vb* crocheter [**1**]

crocodile *n* crocodile *m*

crook *n (criminal)* escroc *m*

crop *n* récolte *f* ▷ *a good crop of apples* une bonne récolte de pommes

cross *n* croix *f*
▶ *adj* fâché(e) ▷ *to be cross about something* être fâché à propos de quelque chose
▶ *vb (street, bridge)* traverser [**28**]

cross out *vb* barrer [**28**]

cross over *vb* traverser [**28**]

cross-country *n (race)* cross *m*; **cross-country skiing** le ski de fond

crossing *n* ❶ *(by boat)* traversée *f* ▷ *the crossing from Dover to Calais* la traversée de Douvres à Calais
❷ *(for pedestrians)* passage clouté *m*

crossroads *n* carrefour *m*

crossword *n* mots croisés *mpl* ▷ *I like doing crosswords.* J'aime faire les mots croisés.

crouch down *vb* s'accroupir [**38**]

crow *n* corbeau *m* (*pl* corbeaux)

crowd *n* foule *f*; **the crowd** *(at sports match)* les spectateurs

crowded *adj* bondé(e)

crown *n* couronne *f*

crude *adj (vulgar)* grossier (*f* grossière)

cruel *adj* cruel (*f* cruelle)

cruise *n* croisière *f* ▷ *to go on a cruise* faire une croisière

crumb *n* miette *f*

crush *vb* écraser [**28**]

crutch *n* béquille *f*

cry *n* cri *m* ▷ *He gave a cry of surprise.* Il a poussé un cri de surprise.; **Go on, have a good cry!** Vas-y, pleure un bon coup!
▶ *vb* pleurer [**28**] ▷ *The baby's crying.* Le bébé pleure.

crystal *n* cristal *m* (*pl* cristaux)

cub *n* ❶ *(animal)* petit *m* ❷ *(scout)* louveteau *m* (*pl* louveteaux)

cube *n* cube *m*

cubic *adj* **a cubic metre** un mètre cube

cucumber *n* concombre *m*

cuddle *n* câlin *m* ▷ *Come and give me a cuddle.* Viens me faire un câlin.

cue *n (for snooker, pool)* queue de billard *f*

culture *n* culture *f*

cunning *adj* ❶ *(person)* rusé(e)
❷ *(plan, idea)* astucieux (*f* astucieuse)

cup *n* ❶ tasse *f* ▷ *a china cup* une tasse en porcelaine; **a cup of coffee** un café ❷ *(trophy)* coupe *f*

cupboard *n* placard *m*
cure *vb* guérir [**38**]
▶ *n* remède *m*
curious *adj* curieux (*f* curieuse)
curl *n (in hair)* boucle *f*
curly *adj* ❶ *(loosely curled)* bouclé(e) ❷ *(tightly curled)* frisé(e)
currant *n (dried fruit)* raisin de Corinthe *m*
currency *n* devise *f* ▷ *foreign currency* les devises étrangères
current *n* courant *m* ▷ *The current is very strong.* Le courant est très fort.
▶ *adj* actuel (*f* actuelle) ▷ *the current situation* la situation actuelle
current affairs *npl* actualité *f*
curriculum *n* programme *m*
curriculum vitae *n* curriculum vitae *m*
curry *n* curry *m*
curtain *n* rideau *m* (*pl* rideaux) ▷ *to draw the curtains* tirer les rideaux
cushion *n* coussin *m*
custard *n (for pouring)* crème anglaise *f*
custody *n (of child)* garde *f*
custom *n* coutume *f, m* ▷ *It's an old custom.* C'est une ancienne coutume.
customer *n* client *m*, cliente *f*
customs *npl* douane *fsg*
customs officer *n* douanier *m*, douanière *f*
cut *n* ❶ coupure *f* ▷ *He's got a cut on his forehead.* Il a une coupure au front. ❷ coupe *f* ▷ *a cut and blow-dry* une coupe brushing ❸ *(in price, spending)* réduction *f*
▶ *vb* ❶ couper [**28**] ▷ *I'll cut some bread.* Je vais couper du pain.; **to cut oneself** se couper [**28**] ▷ *I cut my foot on a piece of glass.* Je me suis coupé au pied avec un morceau de verre. ❷ *(price, spending)* réduire [**23**]
cut down *vb (tree)* abattre [**9**]
cut off *vb* couper [**28**] ▷ *The electricity was cut off.* L'électricité a été coupée.
cut up *vb (vegetables, meat)* hacher [**28**]
cute *adj* mignon (*f* mignonne)
cutlery *n* couverts *mpl*
CV *n* C.V. *m*
cyberbullying *n* harcèlement virtuel *m*
cybercafé *n* cybercafé *m*
cycle *vb* faire [**36**] de la bicyclette ▷ *I like cycling.* J'aime faire de la bicyclette.; **I cycle to school.** Je vais à l'école à bicyclette.
▶ *n* bicyclette *f*; **a cycle ride** une promenade à bicyclette; **a cycle lane** une piste cyclable
cycling *n* cyclisme *m*
cyclist *n* cycliste *mf*
cylinder *n* cylindre *m*
Cyprus *n* Chypre; **in Cyprus** à Chypre; **We went to Cyprus.** Nous sommes allés à Chypre.
Czech *n* ❶ *(person)* Tchèque *mf* ❷ *(language)* tchèque *m*
▶ *adj* tchèque; **the Czech Republic** la République tchèque

dad *n* ❶ père *m* ▷ *my dad* mon père ❷ papa *m*

> Use **papa** only when you are talking to your father or using it as his name; otherwise use **père**.

Dad! Papa! ▷ *I'll ask Dad.* Je vais demander à papa.

daffodil *n* jonquille *f*

daft *adj* idiot(e)

daily *adj, adv* ❶ quotidien (*f* quotidienne) ▷ *It's part of my daily routine.* Ça fait partie de mes occupations quotidiennes. ❷ tous les jours ▷ *The pool is open daily.* La piscine est ouverte tous les jours.

dairy products *npl* produits laitiers *mpl*

daisy *n* pâquerette *f*

dam *n* barrage *m*

damage *n* dégâts *mpl* ▷ *The storm did a lot of damage.* La tempête a fait beaucoup de dégâts.
▶ *vb* endommager [**45**]

damp *adj* humide

dance *n* ❶ danse *f* ▷ *The last dance was a waltz.* La dernière danse était une valse. ❷ bal *m* ▷ *Are you going to the dance tonight?* Tu vas au bal ce soir?
▶ *vb* danser [**28**]; **to go dancing** aller [**3**] danser ▷ *Let's go dancing!* Si on allait danser?

dancer *n* danseur *m*, danseuse *f*

dandruff *n* pellicules *fpl*

Dane *n* Danois *m*, Danoise *f*

danger *n* danger *m*; **in danger** en danger ▷ *His life is in danger.* Sa vie est en danger.; **to be in danger of** risquer [**28**] de ▷ *We were in danger of missing the plane.* Nous risquions de rater l'avion.

dangerous *adj* dangereux (*f* dangereuse)

Danish *adj* danois(e)
▶ *n (language)* danois *m*

dare *vb* oser [**28**]; **to dare to do something** oser [**28**] faire quelque chose ▷ *I didn't dare to tell my parents.* Je n'ai pas osé le dire à mes parents.; **I dare say it'll be okay.** Je suppose que ça va aller.

daring *adj* audacieux (*f* audacieuse)

dark *adj* ❶ *(room)* sombre ▷ *It's dark. (inside)* Il fait sombre.; **It's dark outside.** Il fait nuit dehors.; **It's getting dark.** La nuit tombe.
❷ *(colour)* foncé(e) ▷ *She's got dark hair.* Elle a les cheveux foncés.

▷ *a dark green sweater* un pull vert foncé
▶ *n* noir *m* ▷ *I'm afraid of the dark.* J'ai peur du noir.; **after dark** après la tombée de la nuit

darkness *n* obscurité *f* ▷ *The room was in darkness.* La chambre était dans l'obscurité.

darling *n* chéri *m*, chérie *f* ▷ *Thank you, darling!* Merci, chéri!

dart *n* fléchette *f* ▷ *to play darts* jouer aux fléchettes

data *npl* données *fpl*

database *n (on computer)* base de données *f*

date *n* ❶ date *f* ▷ *my date of birth* ma date de naissance; **What's the date today?** Quel jour sommes-nous?; **to have a date with somebody** sortir [**79**] avec quelqu'un ▷ *She's got a date with Ian tonight.* Elle sort avec Ian ce soir.; **out of date (1)** *(passport)* périmé **(2)** *(technology)* dépassé **(3)** *(clothes)* démodé ❷ *(fruit)* datte *f*

daughter *n* fille *f*

daughter-in-law *n* belle-fille *f (pl* belles-filles)

dawn *n* aube *f* ▷ *at dawn* à l'aube

day *n*

> Use **jour** to refer to the whole 24-hour period. **journée** only refers to the time when you are awake.

❶ jour *m* ▷ *We stayed in Nice for three days.* Nous sommes restés trois jours à Nice.; **every day** tous les jours ❷ journée *f* ▷ *I stayed at home all day.* Je suis resté à la maison toute la journée.; **the day before** la veille ▷ *the day before my birthday* la veille de mon anniversaire; **the day after** le lendemain; **the day after tomorrow** après-demain ▷ *We're leaving the day after tomorrow.* Nous partons après-demain.; **the day before yesterday** avant-hier ▷ *He arrived the day before yesterday.* Il est arrivé avant-hier.

dead *adj, adv* ❶ mort(e) ▷ *He was already dead when the doctor came.* Il était déjà mort quand le docteur est arrivé.; **He was shot dead.** Il a été abattu. ❷ *(totally)* absolument ▷ *You're dead right!* Tu as absolument raison!; **dead on time** à l'heure pile ▷ *The train arrived dead on time.* Le train est arrivé à l'heure pile.

dead end *n* impasse *f*

deadline *n* date limite *f* ▷ *The deadline for entries is May 2nd.* La date limite d'inscription est le deux mai.

deaf *adj* sourd(e)

deafening *adj* assourdissant(e)

deal *n* marché *m*; **It's a deal!** Marché conclu!; **a great deal** beaucoup ▷ *a great deal of money* beaucoup d'argent
▶ *vb (cards)* donner [**28**] ▷ *It's your turn to deal.* C'est à toi de donner.; **to deal with something** s'occuper [**28**] de quelque chose ▷ *He promised to deal with it immediately.* Il a promis de s'en occuper immédiatement.

dealer *n* ❶ marchand *m*, marchande *f* ❷ *(of drugs)* dealer *m*
dealt *vb see* **deal**
dear *adj* ❶ cher *(f* chère*)* ▷ *Dear Mrs Duval* Chère Madame Duval; **Dear Sir/Madam** *(in a letter)* Madame, Monsieur ❷ *(expensive)* coûteux *(f* coûteuse*)*
death *n* mort *f* ▷ *after his death* après sa mort; **I was bored to death.** Je me suis ennuyé à mourir.
debate *n* débat *m*
▶ *vb* débattre [**9**]
debt *n* dette *f* ▷ *He's got a lot of debts.* Il a beaucoup de dettes.; **to be in debt** avoir [**8**] des dettes
decade *n* décennie *f*
decaffeinated *adj* décaféiné(e)
deceive *vb* tromper [**28**]
December *n* décembre *m*; **in December** en décembre
decent *adj* convenable ▷ *a decent education* une éducation convenable
decide *vb* ❶ décider [**28**] ▷ *I decided to write to her.* J'ai décidé de lui écrire. ▷ *I decided not to go.* J'ai décidé de ne pas y aller. ❷ se décider [**28**] ▷ *I can't decide.* Je n'arrive pas à me décider.; **to decide on something** se mettre [**47**] d'accord sur quelque chose ▷ *They haven't decided on a name yet.* Ils ne se sont pas encore mis d'accord sur un nom.
decimal *adj* décimal(e) ▷ *the decimal system* le système décimal
decision *n* décision *f*; **to make a decision** prendre [**65**] une décision
deck *n* ❶ *(of ship)* pont *m*; **on deck** sur le pont ❷ *(of cards)* jeu *m (pl* jeux*)*
deckchair *n* chaise longue *f*
declare *vb* déclarer [**28**]
decorate *vb* ❶ décorer [**28**] ▷ *I decorated the cake with glacé cherries.* J'ai décoré le gâteau avec des cerises confites. ❷ *(paint)* peindre [**60**] ❸ *(wallpaper)* tapisser [**28**]
decrease *n* diminution *f*
▷ *a decrease in the number of unemployed* une diminution du nombre de chômeurs
▶ *vb* diminuer [**28**]
dedication *n* ❶ *(commitment)* dévouement *m* ❷ *(in book, on radio)* dédicace *f*
deduct *vb* déduire [**23**]
deep *adj* ❶ *(water, hole, cut)* profond(e) ▷ *Is it deep?* Est-ce que c'est profond?; **How deep is the lake?** Quelle est la profondeur du lac?; **a hole 4 metres deep** un trou de quatre mètres de profondeur ❷ *(layer)* épais *(f* épaisse*)* ▷ *The snow was really deep.* Il y avait une épaisse couche de neige.; **He's got a deep voice.** Il a la voix grave.; **to take a deep breath** respirer [**28**] à fond
deeply *adv (depressed)* profondément
deer *n* ❶ *(red deer)* cerf *m* ❷ *(fallow deer)* daim *m* ❸ *(roe deer)* chevreuil *m*
defeat *n* défaite *f*
▶ *vb* battre [**9**]

defect *n* défaut *m*
defence *n* défense *f*
defend *vb* défendre [**88**]
defender *n* défenseur *m*
define *vb* définir [**38**]
definite *adj* ❶ précis(e) ▷ *I haven't got any definite plans.* Je n'ai pas de projets précis. ❷ net (*f* nette) ▷ *It's a definite improvement.* Cela constitue une nette amélioration. ❸ sûr(e) ▷ *We might go to Spain, but it's not definite.* Nous irons peut-être en Espagne, mais ce n'est pas sûr.; **He was definite about it.** Il a été catégorique.
definitely *adv* vraiment ▷ *He's definitely the best player.* C'est vraiment lui le meilleur joueur.; **He's the best player. — Definitely!** C'est le meilleur joueur. — C'est sûr!; **I definitely think he'll come.** Je suis sûr qu'il va venir.
definition *n* définition *f*
degree *n* ❶ degré *m* ▷ *a temperature of 30 degrees* une température de trente degrés ❷ licence *f* ▷ *a degree in English* une licence d'anglais
delay *vb* ❶ retarder [**28**] ▷ *We decided to delay our departure.* Nous avons décidé de retarder notre départ. ❷ tarder [**28**] ▷ *Don't delay!* Ne tarde pas!; **to be delayed** être [**35**] retardé ▷ *Our flight was delayed.* Notre vol a été retardé.
▶ *n* retard *m* ▷ *There will be delays to trains on the London-Brighton line.* Il y aura des retards sur la ligne Londres-Brighton.

Be careful not to translate **delay** by **délai**.

delete *vb (on computer, tape)* effacer [**12**]
deliberate *adj* délibéré(e)
deliberately *adv* exprès ▷ *She did it deliberately.* Elle l'a fait exprès.
delicate *adj* délicat(e)
delicatessen *n* épicerie fine *f*
delicious *adj* délicieux (*f* délicieuse)
delight *n* **to her delight** à sa plus grande joie
delighted *adj* ravi(e) ▷ *He'll be delighted to see you.* Il sera ravi de vous voir.
deliver *vb* ❶ livrer [**28**] ▷ *I deliver newspapers.* Je livre les journaux. ❷ *(mail)* distribuer [**28**]
delivery *n* livraison *f*
demand *vb* exiger [**45**]

Be careful not to translate **to demand** by **demander**.

▶ *n (for product)* demande *f*
democracy *n* démocratie *f*
democratic *adj* démocratique
demolish *vb* démolir [**38**]
demonstrate *vb* ❶ *(show)* faire [**36**] une démonstration de ▷ *She demonstrated the technique.* Elle a fait une démonstration de la technique. ❷ *(protest)* manifester [**28**] ▷ *to demonstrate against something* manifester contre quelque chose
demonstration *n* ❶ *(of method, technique)* démonstration *f* ❷ *(protest)* manifestation *f*
demonstrator *n (protester)* manifestant *m*, manifestante *f*

denim *n* jean *m* ▷ *a denim jacket* une veste en jean
Denmark *n* Danemark *m*; **in Denmark** au Danemark; **to Denmark** au Danemark
dense *adj* ❶ *(crowd, fog)* dense ❷ *(smoke)* épais (*f* épaisse); **He's so dense!** Il est vraiment bouché!
dent *n* bosse *f*
▸ *vb* cabosser [**28**]
dental *adj* dentaire; **dental floss** le fil dentaire
dentist *n* dentiste *mf* ▷ *Catherine is a dentist.* Catherine est dentiste.
deny *vb* nier [**19**] ▷ *She denied everything.* Elle a tout nié.
deodorant *n* déodorant *m*
depart *vb* partir [**57**]
department *n* ❶ *(in shop)* rayon *m* ▷ *the shoe department* le rayon chaussures ❷ *(in university, school)* département *m* ▷ *the English department* le département d'anglais
department store *n* grand magasin *m*
departure *n* départ *m*
departure lounge *n* hall des départs *m*
depend *vb* **to depend on** dépendre [**88**] de ▷ *The price depends on the quality.* Le prix dépend de la qualité.; **depending on the weather** selon le temps; **It depends.** Ça dépend.
deposit *n* ❶ *(part payment)* arrhes *fpl* ▷ *You have to pay a deposit when you book.* Il faut verser des arrhes lors de la réservation. ❷ *(when hiring something)* caution *f* ▷ *You get the deposit back when you return the bike.* On vous remboursera la caution quand vous ramènerez le vélo. ❸ *(on bottle)* consigne *f*
depressed *adj* déprimé(e) ▷ *I'm feeling depressed.* Je suis déprimé.
depressing *adj* déprimant(e)
depth *n* profondeur *f*
deputy head *n* directeur adjoint *m*, directrice adjointe *f*
descend *vb* descendre [**24**]
describe *vb* décrire [**30**]
description *n* description *f*
desert *n* désert *m*
desert island *n* île déserte *f*
deserve *vb* mériter [**28**]
design *n* ❶ conception *f* ▷ *It's a completely new design.* C'est une conception entièrement nouvelle. ❷ motif *m* ▷ *a geometric design* un motif géométrique; **fashion design** le stylisme
▸ *vb (clothes, furniture)* dessiner [**28**]
designer *n (of clothes)* styliste *mf*; **designer clothes** les vêtements griffés
desire *n* désir *m*
▸ *vb* désirer [**28**]
desk *n* ❶ *(in office)* bureau *m* (*pl* bureaux) ❷ *(for pupil)* pupitre *m* ❸ *(in hotel)* réception *f* ❹ *(at airport)* comptoir *m*
desktop *n (computer)* ordinateur de bureau *m* (*pl* ordinateurs de bureau)
despair *n* désespoir *m*; **I was in despair.** J'étais désespéré.
desperate *adj* désespéré(e)

▷ *a desperate situation* une situation désespérée; **to get desperate** désespérer [**34**] ▷ *I was getting desperate.* Je commençais à désespérer.

desperately *adv* ❶ terriblement ▷ *We're desperately worried.* Nous sommes terriblement inquiets. ❷ désespérément ▷ *He was desperately trying to persuade her.* Il essayait désespérément de la persuader.

despise *vb* mépriser [**28**]

despite *prep* malgré

dessert *n* dessert *m* ▷ *for dessert* comme dessert

destination *n* destination *f*

destroy *vb* détruire [**23**]

destruction *n* destruction *f*

detached house *n* pavillon *m*

detail *n* détail *m* ▷ *in detail* en détail

detailed *adj* détaillé(e)

detective *n* inspecteur de police *m*; **a private detective** un détective privé; **a detective story** un roman policier

detention *n* **to get a detention** être [**35**] consigné

detergent *n* ❶ détergent *m* ❷ *(US)* lessive *f*

determined *adj* déterminé(e); **to be determined to do something** être [**35**] déterminé à faire quelque chose ▷ *She's determined to succeed.* Elle est déterminée à réussir.

detour *n* détour *m*

devastated *adj* anéanti(e) ▷ *I was devastated.* J'étais anéanti.

develop *vb* ❶ développer [**28**] ▷ *to get a film developed* faire développer un film ❷ se développer [**28**] ▷ *Girls develop faster than boys.* Les filles se développent plus vite que les garçons.; **to develop into** se transformer [**28**] en ▷ *The argument developed into a fight.* La dispute s'est transformée en bagarre.; **a developing country** un pays en voie de développement

development *n* développement *m* ▷ *the latest developments* les derniers développements

devil *n* diable *m* ▷ *Poor devil!* Pauvre diable!

devoted *adj* dévoué(e) ▷ *He's completely devoted to her.* Il lui est très dévoué.

diabetes *n* diabète *m*

diabetic *n* diabétique *mf* ▷ *I'm a diabetic.* Je suis diabétique.

diagonal *adj* diagonal(e) (*mpl* diagonaux)

diagram *n* diagramme *m*

dial *vb* *(number)* composer [**28**]

dialling tone *n* tonalité *f*

dialogue *n* dialogue *m*

diamond *n* diamant *m* ▷ *a diamond ring* une bague en diamant; **diamonds** *(at cards)* le carreau *sg*

diaper *n* *(US)* couche *f*

diarrhoea *n* diarrhée *f* ▷ *I've got diarrhoea.* J'ai la diarrhée.

diary *n* ❶ agenda *m* ▷ *I've got her phone number in my diary.* J'ai son numéro de téléphone dans mon agenda. ❷ journal *m* (*pl* journaux) ▷ *I keep a diary.* Je tiens un journal.

dice *n* dé *m*
dictation *n* dictée *f*
dictionary *n* dictionnaire *m*
did *vb see* **do**
die *vb* mourir [**51**] ▷ *He died last year.* Il est mort l'année dernière.; **to be dying to do something** mourir [**51**] d'envie de faire quelque chose ▷ *I'm dying to see you.* Je meurs d'envie de te voir.
diesel *n* ① *(fuel)* gazole *m* ▷ *30 litres of diesel* trente litres de gazole ② *(car)* voiture diesel *f* ▷ *My car's a diesel.* J'ai une voiture diesel.
diet *n* ① alimentation *f* ② *(for slimming)* régime *m* ▷ *I'm on a diet.* Je suis au régime.
▸ *vb* faire [**36**] un régime ▷ *I've been dieting for two months.* Je fais un régime depuis deux mois.
difference *n* différence *f* ▷ *There's not much difference in age between us.* Il n'y a pas une grande différence d'âge entre nous.; **It makes no difference.** Ça revient au même.
different *adj* différent(e) ▷ *Paris is different from London.* Paris est différent de Londres.
difficult *adj* difficile ▷ *It's difficult to choose.* C'est difficile de choisir.
difficulty *n* difficulté *f* ▷ *without difficulty* sans difficulté; **to have difficulty doing something** avoir [**8**] du mal à faire quelque chose
dig *vb* ① *(hole)* creuser [**28**] ② *(garden)* bêcher [**28**]; **to dig something up** déterrer [**28**] quelque chose
digestion *n* digestion *f*
digital camera *n* appareil photo numérique *m*
digital radio *n* radio numérique *f*
digital television *n* télévision numérique *f*
digital watch *n* montre à affichage numérique *f*
dim *adj* ① *(light)* faible ② *(stupid)* limité(e)
dimension *n* dimension *f*
din *n* vacarme *m*
diner *n (US)* snack *m*
dinghy *n* **a rubber dinghy** un canot pneumatique; **a sailing dinghy** un dériveur
dining room *n* salle à manger *f*
dinner *n* ① *(at midday)* déjeuner *m* ② *(in the evening)* dîner *m*
dinner lady *n* la dame de service *f*
dinner party *n* dîner *m*
dinner time *n* ① *(midday)* heure du déjeuner *f* ② *(in the evening)* heure du dîner *f*
dinosaur *n* dinosaure *m*
diploma *n* diplôme *m*
direct *adj, adv* direct(e) ▷ *the most direct route* le chemin le plus direct ▷ *You can't fly to Nice direct from Cork.* Il n'y a pas de vols directs de Cork à Nice.
▸ *vb* ① *(film, programme)* réaliser [**28**] ② *(play, show)* mettre [**47**] en scène
direction *n* direction *f* ▷ *We're going in the wrong direction.* Nous allons dans la mauvaise direction.; **to ask somebody for directions** demander [**28**] son chemin à quelqu'un

director *n* ❶ *(of company)* directeur *m*, directrice *f* ❷ *(of play)* metteur en scène *m* ❸ *(of film, programme)* réalisateur *m*, réalisatrice *f*

directory *n* ❶ *(phone book)* annuaire *m* ❷ *(computing)* répertoire *m*

dirt *n* saleté *f*

dirty *adj* sale; **to get dirty** se salir [**38**]; **to get something dirty** salir [**38**] quelque chose

disabled *adj* handicapé(e)

disadvantage *n* désavantage *m*

disagree *vb* **We always disagree.** Nous ne sommes jamais d'accord.; **I disagree!** Je ne suis pas d'accord!; **He disagrees with me.** Il n'est pas d'accord avec moi.

disagreement *n* désaccord *m*

disappear *vb* disparaître [**56**]

disappearance *n* disparition *f*

disappointed *adj* déçu(e)

disappointment *n* déception *f*

disaster *n* désastre *m*

disastrous *adj* désastreux (*f* désastreuse)

disc *n* disque *m*

discipline *n* discipline *f*

disc jockey *n* disc-jockey *m*

disco *n* soirée disco *f* ▷ *There's a disco at the school tonight.* Il y a une soirée disco à l'école ce soir.

disconnect *vb* ❶ *(electrical equipment)* débrancher [**28**] ❷ *(telephone, water supply)* couper [**28**]

discount *n* réduction *f* ▷ *a discount for students* une réduction pour les étudiants

discourage *vb* décourager [**45**]; **to get discouraged** se décourager [**45**] ▷ *Don't get discouraged!* Ne te décourage pas!

discover *vb* découvrir [**55**]

discrimination *n* discrimination *f* ▷ *racial discrimination* la discrimination raciale

discuss *vb* ❶ discuter [**28**] de ▷ *I'll discuss it with my parents.* Je vais en discuter avec mes parents. ❷ *(topic)* discuter [**28**] sur ▷ *We discussed the problem of pollution.* Nous avons discuté du problème de la pollution.

discussion *n* discussion *f*

disease *n* maladie *f*

disgraceful *adj* scandaleux (*f* scandaleuse)

disguise *vb* déguiser [**28**] ▷ *He was disguised as a police officer.* Il était déguisé en policier.

disgusted *adj* dégoûté(e) ▷ *I was absolutely disgusted.* J'étais complètement dégoûté.

disgusting *adj* ❶ *(food, smell)* dégoûtant(e) ▷ *It looks disgusting.* Ça a l'air dégoûtant. ❷ *(disgraceful)* honteux (*f* honteuse) ▷ *That's disgusting!* C'est honteux!

dish *n* plat *m* ▷ *a vegetarian dish* un plat végétarien; **to do the dishes** faire [**36**] la vaisselle ▷ *He never does the dishes.* Il ne fait jamais la vaisselle.

dishonest *adj* malhonnête

dishwasher *n* lave-vaisselle *m* (*pl* lave-vaisselle)

disinfectant *n* désinfectant *m*
disk *n* disque *m*; **the hard disk** le disque dur
dismal *adj* lugubre
dismiss *vb (employee)* renvoyer **[33]**
disobedient *adj* désobéissant(e)
display *n* étalage *m* ▷ *There was a lovely display of fruit in the window.* Il y avait un superbe étalage de fruits en vitrine.; **to be on display** être **[35]** exposé ▷ *Her best paintings were on display.* Ses meilleurs tableaux étaient exposés.; **a firework display** un feu d'artifice
▶ *vb* ❶ montrer **[28]** ▷ *She proudly displayed her medal.* Elle a montré sa médaille avec fierté. ❷ *(in shop window)* exposer **[28]**
disposable *adj* jetable
disqualify *vb* disqualifier **[19]**; **to be disqualified** être **[35]** disqualifié ▷ *He was disqualified.* Il a été disqualifié.
disrupt *vb* perturber **[28]** ▷ *Protesters disrupted the meeting.* Des manifestants ont perturbé la réunion.
dissolve *vb* dissoudre **[70]**
distance *n* distance *f* ▷ *a distance of 40 kilometres* une distance de quarante kilomètres; **It's within walking distance.** On peut y aller à pied.; **in the distance** au loin
distant *adj* lointain(e) ▷ *in the distant future* dans un avenir lointain
distract *vb* distraire **[85]**
distribute *vb* distribuer **[28]**
district *n* ❶ *(of town)* quartier *m* ❷ *(of country)* région *f*
disturb *vb* déranger **[45]** ▷ *I'm sorry to disturb you.* Je suis désolé de vous déranger.
ditch *n* fossé *m*
▶ *vb (informal)* plaquer **[28]** ▷ *She's just ditched her boyfriend.* Elle vient de plaquer son copain.
dive *n* plongeon *m*
▶ *vb* plonger **[45]**
diver *n* plongeur *m*, plongeuse *f*
diversion *n (for traffic)* déviation *f*
divide *vb* ❶ diviser **[28]** ▷ *Divide the pastry in half.* Divisez la pâte en deux. ▷ *12 divided by 3 is 4.* Douze divisé par trois égale quatre. ❷ se diviser **[28]** ▷ *We divided into two groups.* Nous nous sommes divisés en deux groupes.
diving *n* plongée *f*; **a diving board** un plongeoir
division *n* division *f*
divorce *n* divorce *m*
divorced *adj* divorcé(e) ▷ *My parents are divorced.* Mes parents sont divorcés.
DIY *n* bricolage *m* ▷ *to do DIY* faire du bricolage
dizzy *adj* **to feel dizzy** avoir **[8]** la tête qui tourne ▷ *I feel dizzy.* J'ai la tête qui tourne.
DJ *n* disc-jockey *m*
do *vb* ❶ faire **[36]** ▷ *What are you doing this evening?* Qu'est-ce que tu fais ce soir? ▷ *I do a lot of cycling.* Je fais beaucoup de vélo. ▷ *I haven't done my homework.* Je n'ai pas fait mes devoirs. ▷ *She did it by herself.* Elle l'a fait toute seule. ▷ *I'll do my*

best. Je ferai de mon mieux.; **to do well** marcher [**28**] bien ▷ *The firm is doing well.* L'entreprise marche bien. ▷ *She's doing well at school.* Ses études marchent bien. ❷ *(be enough)* aller [**3**] ▷ *It's not very good, but it'll do.* Ce n'est pas très bon, mais ça ira.; **That'll do, thanks.** Ça ira, merci.

In English 'do' is used to make questions. In French questions are made either with **est-ce que** or by reversing the order of verb and subject.

▷ *Do you like French food?* Est-ce que vous aimez la cuisine française? ▷ *Where does he live?* Où est-ce qu'il habite? ▷ *Do you speak English?* Parlez-vous anglais? ▷ *What do you do in your free time?* Qu'est-ce que vous faites pendant vos loisirs? ▷ *Where did you go for your holidays?* Où es-tu allé pendant tes vacances?

Use **ne ... pas** in negative sentences for 'don't'.

▷ *I don't understand.* Je ne comprends pas. ▷ *Why didn't you come?* Pourquoi n'êtes-vous pas venus?

'do' is not translated when it is used in place of another verb.

▷ *I hate maths. — So do I.* Je déteste les maths. — Moi aussi. ▷ *I didn't like the film. — Neither did I.* Je n'ai pas aimé le film. — Moi non plus. ▷ *Do you like horses? — No I don't.* Est-ce que tu aimes les chevaux? — Non.

Use **n'est-ce pas** to check information.

▷ *You go swimming on Fridays, don't you?* Tu fais de la natation le vendredi, n'est-ce pas? ▷ *The bus stops at the youth hostel, doesn't it?* Le bus s'arrête à l'auberge de jeunesse, n'est-ce pas?; **How do you do?** Enchanté!

do up *vb* ❶ *(shoes)* lacer [**12**] ▷ *Do up your shoes!* Lace tes chaussures! ❷ *(renovate)* retaper [**28**] ▷ *They're doing up an old cottage.* Ils retapent une vieille maison. ❸ *(shirt, cardigan)* boutonner [**28**]; **Do up your zip!** *(on trousers)* Ferme ta braguette!

do without *vb* se passer [**58**] de ▷ *I couldn't do without my computer.* Je ne pourrais pas me passer de mon ordinateur.

doctor *n* médecin *m* ▷ *She's a doctor.* Elle est médecin.

document *n* document *m*

documentary *n* documentaire *m*

dodge *vb (attacker)* échapper [**28**] à

dodgems *npl* autos tamponneuses *fpl* ▷ *to go on the dodgems* aller faire un tour d'autos tamponneuses

does *vb see* **do**

doesn't = **does not**

dog *n* chien *m*, chienne *f* ▷ *Have you got a dog?* Est-ce que tu as un chien?

do-it-yourself *n* bricolage *m*

dole *n* allocations chômage *fpl*; **to be on the dole** toucher [**28**] le chômage ▷ *A lot of people are on the dole.* Beaucoup de gens touchent le chômage.; **to go on the dole**

s'inscrire [30] au chômage
doll *n* poupée *f*
dollar *n* dollar *m*
dolphin *n* dauphin *m*
dominoes *npl* **to have a game of dominoes** faire [36] une partie de dominos
donate *vb* donner [28]
done *vb see* **do**
donkey *n* âne *m*
don't = **do not**
door *n* ❶ porte *f* ▷ *the first door on the right* la première porte à droite ❷ *(of car, train)* portière *f*
doorbell *n* sonnette *f*; **to ring the doorbell** sonner [28]; **Suddenly the doorbell rang.** Soudain, on a sonné.
doorstep *n* pas de la porte *m*
dormitory *n* dortoir *m*
dot *n (on letter 'i', in email address)* point *m*; **on the dot** à l'heure pile ▷ *He arrived at 9 o'clock on the dot.* Il est arrivé à neuf heures pile.
double *adj, adv* double ▷ *a double helping* une double portion; **to cost double** coûter [28] le double ▷ *First-class tickets cost double.* Les billets de première classe coûtent le double.; **a double bed** un grand lit; **a double room** une chambre pour deux personnes; **a double-decker bus** un autobus à impériale
▶ *vb* doubler [28] ▷ *The number of attacks has doubled.* Le nombre d'agressions a doublé.
double bass *n* contrebasse *f* ▷ *I play the double bass.* Je joue de la contrebasse.
double-click *vb* double-cliquer [28] ▷ *to double-click on an icon* double-cliquer sur une icône
double glazing *n* double vitrage *m*
doubles *npl (in tennis)* double *msg* ▷ *to play mixed doubles* jouer en double mixte
doubt *n* doute *m* ▷ *I have my doubts.* J'ai des doutes.
▶ *vb* douter [28] de; **I doubt it.** J'en doute.; **to doubt that** douter [28] que

> **douter que** has to be followed by a verb in the subjunctive.

▷ *I doubt he'll agree.* Je doute qu'il soit d'accord.
doubtful *adj* **to be doubtful about doing something** hésiter [28] à faire quelque chose ▷ *I'm doubtful about going by myself.* J'hésite à y aller tout seul.; **It's doubtful.** Ce n'est pas sûr.; **You sound doubtful.** Tu n'as pas l'air sûr.
dough *n* pâte *f*
doughnut *n* beignet *m* ▷ *a jam doughnut* un beignet à la confiture
Dover *n* Douvres ▷ *We went from Dover to Boulogne.* Nous sommes allés de Douvres à Boulogne.; **in Dover** à Douvres
down *adv, adj, prep* ❶ *(below)* en bas ▷ *His office is down on the first floor.* Son bureau est en bas, au premier étage. ▷ *It's down there.* C'est là-bas. ❷ *(to the ground)* à terre ▷ *He threw down his racket.* Il a jeté sa raquette à terre.; **They live just down the road.** Ils habitent tout à côté.;

to come down descendre [**24**] ▷ *Come down here!* Descends!; **to go down** descendre [**24**] ▷ *The rabbit went down the hole.* Le lapin est descendu dans le terrier.; **to sit down** s'asseoir [**6**] ▷ *Sit down!* Asseyez-vous!; **to feel down** avoir [**8**] le cafard ▷ *I'm feeling a bit down.* J'ai un peu le cafard.; **The computer's down.** L'ordinateur est en panne.

download *vb* télécharger [**45**] ▷ *to download a file* télécharger un fichier
▸ *n* téléchargement *m* ▷ *a free download* un téléchargement gratuit

downstairs *adv, adj* ❶ au rez-de-chaussée ▷ *The bathroom's downstairs.* La salle de bain est au rez-de-chaussée. ❷ du rez-de-chaussée ▷ *the downstairs bathroom* la salle de bain du rez-de-chaussée; **the people downstairs** les voisins du dessous

downtown *adj (US)* dans le centre

doze *vb* sommeiller [**28**]

doze off *vb* s'assoupir [**38**]

dozen *n* douzaine *f* ▷ *two dozen* deux douzaines ▷ *a dozen eggs* une douzaine d'œufs; **I've told you that dozens of times.** Je t'ai dit ça des centaines de fois.

draft *n (US)* courant d'air *m*

drag *vb (thing, person)* traîner [**28**]
▸ *n* **It's a real drag!** *(informal)* C'est la barbe!; **in drag** travesti ▷ *He was in drag.* Il était travesti.

dragon *n* dragon *m*

drain *n* égout *m* ▷ *The drains are blocked.* Les égouts sont bouchés.
▸ *vb (vegetables, pasta)* égoutter [**28**]

drama *n* art dramatique *m* ▷ *Drama is my favourite subject.* L'art dramatique est ma matière préférée.; **drama school** l'école d'art dramatique ▷ *I'd like to go to drama school.* J'aimerais entrer dans une école d'art dramatique.; **Greek drama** le théâtre grec

dramatic *adj* spectaculaire ▷ *a dramatic improvement* une amélioration spectaculaire; **dramatic news** une nouvelle extraordinaire

drank *vb see* **drink**

drapes *npl (US)* rideaux *mpl*

draught *n* courant d'air *m*

draughts *n* dames *fpl* ▷ *to play draughts* jouer aux dames

draw *vb* ❶ dessiner [**28**] ▷ *He's good at drawing.* Il dessine bien.; **to draw a picture** faire [**36**] un dessin; **to draw a picture of somebody** faire [**36**] le portrait de quelqu'un; **to draw a line** tirer [**28**] un trait ❷ *(sport)* faire [**36**] match nul ▷ *We drew 2-2.* Nous avons fait match nul deux à deux.; **to draw the curtains** tirer [**28**] les rideaux; **to draw lots** tirer [**28**] au sort
▸ *n* ❶ *(sport)* match nul *m* ▷ *The game ended in a draw.* La partie s'est soldée par un match nul. ❷ *(in lottery)* tirage au sort *m* ▷ *The draw takes place on Saturday.* Le tirage au sort a lieu samedi.

drawback *n* inconvénient *m*
drawer *n* tiroir *m*
drawing *n* dessin *m*
drawing pin *n* punaise *f*
drawn *vb see* **draw**
dreadful *adj* ❶ terrible ▷ *a dreadful mistake* une terrible erreur ❷ affreux (*f* affreuse) ▷ *The weather was dreadful.* Il a fait un temps affreux.; **I feel dreadful.** Je ne me sens vraiment pas bien.; **You look dreadful.** (*ill*) Tu as une mine affreuse.
dream *vb* rêver [**28**] ▷ *I dreamed I was in Belgium.* J'ai rêvé que j'étais en Belgique.
▶ *n* rêve *m* ▷ *It was just a dream.* Ce n'était qu'un rêve.; **a bad dream** un cauchemar
drench *vb* **to get drenched** se faire [**36**] tremper ▷ *We got drenched.* Nous nous sommes fait tremper.
dress *n* robe *f*
▶ *vb* s'habiller [**28**] ▷ *I got up, dressed, and went downstairs.* Je me suis levé, je me suis habillé et je suis descendu.; **to dress somebody** habiller [**28**] quelqu'un ▷ *She dressed the children.* Elle a habillé les enfants.; **to get dressed** s'habiller [**28**] ▷ *I got dressed quickly.* Je me suis habillé rapidement.
dress up *vb* se déguiser [**28**] ▷ *I dressed up as a ghost.* Je me suis déguisé en fantôme.
dressed *adj* habillé(e) ▷ *I'm not dressed yet.* Je ne suis pas encore habillé.; **She was dressed in a green sweater and jeans.** Elle portait un pull vert et un jean.
dresser *n* (*furniture*) vaisselier *m*
dressing gown *n* robe de chambre *f*
dressing table *n* coiffeuse *f*
drew *vb see* **draw**
dried *vb see* **dry**
drier *n* séchoir *m*
drift *n* **a snow drift** une congère
▶ *vb* ❶ (*boat*) aller [**3**] à la dérive ❷ (*snow*) s'amonceler [**4**]
drill *n* perceuse *f*
▶ *vb* percer [**12**]
drink *vb* boire [**10**] ▷ *What would you like to drink?* Qu'est-ce que vous voulez boire?; **I don't drink.** Je ne bois pas d'alcool.
▶ *n* ❶ boisson *f* ▷ *a cold drink* une boisson fraîche ❷ (*alcoholic*) verre *m* ▷ *They've gone out for a drink.* Ils sont allés prendre un verre.; **to have a drink** prendre [**65**] un verre
drive *n* ❶ tour en voiture *m*; **to go for a drive** aller [**3**] faire un tour en voiture ▷ *We went for a drive in the country.* Nous sommes allés faire un tour à la campagne.; **We've got a long drive tomorrow.** Nous avons une longue route à faire demain. ❷ (*of house*) allée *f* ▷ *He parked his car in the drive.* Il a garé sa voiture dans l'allée.
▶ *vb* ❶ (*a car*) conduire [**23**] ▷ *She's learning to drive.* Elle apprend à conduire. ▷ *Can you drive?* Tu sais conduire? ❷ (*go by car*) aller [**3**] en voiture ▷ *I'd rather drive than take the train.* Je préfère conduire que de prendre le train. ❸ emmener [**43**]

a b c d e f g h i j k l m n o p q r s t u v w x y z

en voiture ▷ *My mother drives me to school.* Ma mère m'emmène à l'école en voiture.; **to drive somebody home** raccompagner [**28**] quelqu'un ▷ *He offered to drive me home.* Il m'a proposé de me raccompagner.; **to drive somebody mad** rendre [**7**] quelqu'un fou ▷ *He drives her mad.* Il la rend folle.

driver *n* ❶ conducteur *m*, conductrice *f* ▷ *She's an excellent driver.* C'est une excellente conductrice. ❷ *(of taxi, bus)* chauffeur *m* ▷ *He's a bus driver.* Il est chauffeur d'autobus.

driver's license *n (US)* permis de conduire *m*

driving instructor *n* moniteur d'auto-école *m* ▷ *He's a driving instructor.* Il est moniteur d'auto-école.

driving lesson *n* leçon de conduite *f*

driving licence *n* permis de conduire *m*

driving test *n* **to take one's driving test** passer [**58**] son permis de conduire ▷ *He's taking his driving test tomorrow.* Il passe son permis de conduire demain.; **She's just passed her driving test.** Elle vient d'avoir son permis.

drop *n* goutte *f* ▷ *a drop of water* une goutte d'eau
▶ *vb* ❶ laisser [**28**] tomber ▷ *I dropped the glass and it broke.* J'ai laissé tomber le verre et il s'est cassé. ▷ *I'm going to drop chemistry.* Je vais laisser tomber la chimie. ❷ déposer [**28**] ▷ *Could you drop me at the station?* Pouvez-vous me déposer à la gare?

drought *n* sécheresse *f*

drove *vb see* **drive**

drown *vb* se noyer [**53**] ▷ *A boy drowned here yesterday.* Un jeune garçon s'est noyé ici hier.

drug *n* ❶ *(medicine)* médicament *m* ▷ *They need food and drugs.* Ils ont besoin de nourriture et de médicaments. ❷ *(illegal)* drogue *f* ▷ *hard drugs* les drogues dures; **to take drugs** se droguer [**28**]; **a drug addict** un drogué ▷ *She's a drug addict.* C'est une droguée.; **a drug pusher** un dealer; **a drug smuggler** un trafiquant de drogue; **the drugs squad** la brigade antidrogue

drugstore *n (US)* drugstore *m*

drum *n* tambour *m* ▷ *an African drum* un tambour africain; **a drum kit** une batterie; **drums** la batterie *sg* ▷ *I play drums.* Je joue de la batterie.

drummer *n (in rock group)* batteur *m*, batteuse *f*

drunk *adj* ivre ▷ *He was drunk.* Il était ivre.
▶ *n* ivrogne *mf* ▷ *The streets were full of drunks.* Les rues étaient pleines d'ivrognes.

dry *adj* ❶ sec *(f* sèche*)* ▷ *The paint isn't dry yet.* La peinture n'est pas encore sèche. ❷ *(weather)* sans pluie ▷ *a long dry period* une longue période sans pluie
▶ *vb* ❶ sécher [**34**] ▷ *The washing will dry quickly in the sun.* Le linge va

sécher vite au soleil.; **to dry one's hair** se sécher [**34**] les cheveux ▷ *I haven't dried my hair yet.* Je ne me suis pas encore séché les cheveux. ❷ *(clothes)* faire [**36**] sécher ▷ *There's nowhere to dry clothes here.* Il n'y a pas d'endroit où faire sécher les vêtements ici.; **to dry the dishes** essuyer [**53**] la vaisselle

dry-cleaner's *n* teinturerie *f*

dryer *n (for clothes)* séchoir *m*; **a tumble dryer** un séchoir à linge; **a hair dryer** un sèche-cheveux

dubbed *adj* doublé(e) ▷ *The film was dubbed into French.* Le film était doublé en français.

duck *n* canard *m*

due *adj, adv* **to be due to do something** devoir [**26**] faire quelque chose ▷ *He's due to arrive tomorrow.* Il doit arriver demain.; **The plane's due in half an hour.** L'avion doit arriver dans une demi-heure.; **When's the baby due?** Le bébé est prévu pour quand?; **due to** à cause de ▷ *The trip was cancelled due to bad weather.* Le voyage a été annulé à cause du mauvais temps.

dug *vb see* **dig**

dull *adj* ❶ ennuyeux (*f* ennuyeuse) ▷ *He's nice, but a bit dull.* Il est sympathique, mais un peu ennuyeux. ❷ *(weather, day)* maussade

dumb *adj* ❶ *(not speaking)* muet (*f* muette) ❷ *(stupid)* bête ▷ *That was a really dumb thing I did!* C'était vraiment bête de ma part!

dummy *n (for baby)* tétine *f*

dump *n* **It's a real dump!** C'est un endroit minable!; **a rubbish dump** une décharge

▶ *vb* ❶ *(waste)* déposer [**28**] ▷ *'no dumping'* 'défense de déposer des ordures' ❷ *(informal)* plaquer [**28**] ▷ *He's just dumped his girlfriend.* Il vient de plaquer sa copine.

dungarees *npl* salopette *fsg*

dungeon *n* cachot *m*

during *prep* pendant ▷ *during the day* pendant la journée

dusk *n* crépuscule *m* ▷ *at dusk* au crépuscule

dust *n* poussière *f*

▶ *vb* épousseter [**41**] ▷ *I dusted the shelves.* J'ai épousseté les étagères.; **I hate dusting!** Je déteste faire les poussières!

dustbin *n* poubelle *f*

dustman *n* éboueur *m* ▷ *He's a dustman.* Il est éboueur.

dusty *adj* poussiéreux (*f* poussiéreuse)

Dutch *n (language)* hollandais *m*; **the Dutch** les Hollandais

▶ *adj* hollandais(e) ▷ *She's Dutch.* Elle est hollandaise.

Dutchman *n* Hollandais *m*

Dutchwoman *n* Hollandaise *f*

duty *n* devoir *m* ▷ *It was his duty to tell the police.* C'était son devoir de prévenir la police.; **to be on duty** **(1)** *(police officer)* être [**35**] de service **(2)** *(doctor, nurse)* être [**35**] de garde

duty-free *adj* hors taxes; **the duty-free shop** la boutique hors taxes

a b c d e f g h i j k l m n o p q r s t u v w x y z

duvet *n* couette *f*
DVD *n* DVD *m* (*pl* DVD) ▷ *I've got that film on DVD.* J'ai ce film en DVD.
DVD player *n* lecteur de DVD *m*
dying *vb see* **die**
dynamic *adj* dynamique
dyslexia *n* dyslexie *f*

each *adj, pron* ❶ chaque ▷ *each day* chaque jour ❷ chacun(e) ▷ *The girls each have their own bedroom.* Les filles ont chacune leur chambre. ▷ *They have 10 points each.* Ils ont dix points chacun. ▷ *He gave each of us £10.* Il nous a donné dix livres à chacun.

Use a reflexive verb to translate 'each other'.

They hate each other. Ils se détestent.; **We wrote to each other.** Nous nous sommes écrit.; **They don't know each other.** Ils ne se connaissent pas.
ear *n* oreille *f*
earache *n* **to have earache** avoir [8] mal aux oreilles
earlier *adv* ❶ tout à l'heure ▷ *I saw him earlier.* Je l'ai vu tout à l'heure.

❷ *(in the morning)* plus tôt ▷ *I ought to get up earlier.* Je devrais me lever plus tôt.

early *adv, adj* ❶ *(early in the day)* tôt ▷ *I have to get up early.* Je dois me lever tôt.; **to have an early night** se coucher [**28**] tôt ❷ *(ahead of time)* en avance ▷ *I came early to get a good seat.* Je suis venu en avance pour avoir une bonne place.

earn *vb* gagner [**28**] ▷ *She earns £5 an hour.* Elle gagne cinq livres de l'heure.

earnings *npl* salaire *msg*

earring *n* boucle d'oreille *f*

earth *n* terre *f*

earthquake *n* tremblement de terre *m*

easily *adv* facilement

east *adj, adv* ❶ est ▷ *the east coast* la côte est; **an east wind** un vent d'est; **east of** à l'est de ▷ *It's east of London.* C'est à l'est de Londres. ❷ vers l'est ▷ *We were travelling east.* Nous allions vers l'est.
▶ *n* est *m* ▷ *in the east* dans l'est

Easter *n* Pâques *f* ▷ *at Easter* à Pâques ▷ *We went to my grandparents' for Easter.* Nous sommes allés chez mes grands-parents à Pâques.

Easter egg *n* œuf de Pâques *m*

eastern *adj* **the eastern part of the island** la partie est de l'île; **Eastern Europe** l'Europe de l'Est

easy *adj* facile

eat *vb* manger [**45**]; **Would you like something to eat?** Est-ce que tu veux manger quelque chose?

e-book *n* livre numérique *m*

echo *n* écho *m*

eco-friendly *adj* respectueux de l'environnement (*f* respectueuse de l'environnement)

ecological *adj* écologique

ecology *n* écologie *f*

economic *adj (profitable)* rentable

economical *adj* ❶ *(person)* économe ❷ *(method, car)* économique

economics *n* économie *f* ▷ *He's studying economics.* Il étudie les sciences économiques.

economy *n* économie *f*

ecstasy *n (drug)* ecstasy *f*; **to be in ecstasy** s'extasier [**19**]

eczema *n* eczéma *m*

edge *n* bord *m*

Edinburgh *n* Édimbourg

editor *n (of newspaper)* rédacteur en chef *m*, rédactrice en chef *f*

education *n* ❶ éducation *f* ▷ *There should be more investment in education.* On devrait investir plus dans l'éducation. ❷ *(teaching)* enseignement *m* ▷ *She works in education.* Elle travaille dans l'enseignement.

educational *adj (experience, toy)* éducatif (*f* éducative) ▷ *It was very educational.* C'était très éducatif.

effect *n* effet *m* ▷ *special effects* les effets spéciaux

effective *adj* efficace

effectively *adv* efficacement

> Be careful not to translate **effectively** by **effectivement**.

efficient *adj* efficace

effort *n* effort *m*
e.g. *abbr* p. ex. (*= par exemple*)
egg *n* œuf *m* ▷ *a hard-boiled egg* un œuf dur ▷ *a fried egg* un œuf sur le plat; **scrambled eggs** les œufs brouillés
egg cup *n* coquetier *m*
eggplant *n (US)* aubergine *f*
Egypt *n* Égypte *f*; **in Egypt** en Égypte
Eiffel Tower *n* tour Eiffel *f*
eight *num* huit ▷ *She's eight.* Elle a huit ans.
eighteen *num* dix-huit ▷ *She's eighteen.* Elle a dix-huit ans.
eighteenth *adj* dix-huitième ▷ *her eighteenth birthday* son dix-huitième anniversaire ▷ *the eighteenth floor* le dix-huitième étage; **the eighteenth of August** le dix-huit août
eighth *adj* huitième ▷ *the eighth floor* le huitième étage; **the eighth of August** le huit août
eighty *num* quatre-vingts
Eire *n* République d'Irlande *f*; **in Eire** en République d'Irlande
either *adv, conj, pron* non plus ▷ *I don't like milk, and I don't like eggs either.* Je n'aime pas le lait, et je n'aime pas les œufs non plus. ▷ *I've never been to Spain. — I haven't either.* Je ne suis jamais allé en Espagne. — Moi non plus.; **either ... or ...** soit ... soit ... ▷ *You can have either ice cream or yoghurt.* Tu peux prendre soit une glace soit un yaourt.; **either of them** l'un ou l'autre ▷ *Take either of them.* Prends l'un ou l'autre.; **I don't like either of them.** Je n'aime ni l'un ni l'autre.
elastic *n* élastique *m*
elastic band *n* élastique *m*
elbow *n* coude *m*
elder *adj* aîné(e) ▷ *my elder sister* ma sœur aînée
elderly *adj* âgé(e)
eldest *adj* aîné(e) ▷ *my eldest sister* ma sœur aînée ▷ *He's the eldest.* C'est l'aîné.
elect *vb* élire [**44**]
election *n* élection *f*
electric *adj* électrique ▷ *an electric fire* un radiateur électrique ▷ *an electric guitar* une guitare électrique; **an electric blanket** une couverture chauffante
electrical *adj* électrique; **an electrical engineer** un ingénieur électricien
electrician *n* électricien *m* ▷ *He's an electrician.* Il est électricien.
electricity *n* électricité *f*
electronic *adj* électronique
electronics *n* électronique *f* ▷ *My hobby is electronics.* Ma passion, c'est l'électronique.
elegant *adj* élégant(e)
elementary school *n (US)* école primaire *f*
elephant *n* éléphant *m*
elevator *n (US)* ascenseur *m*
eleven *num* onze ▷ *She's eleven.* Elle a onze ans.
eleventh *adj* onzième ▷ *the eleventh floor* le onzième étage ▷ *the eleventh of August* le onze août

else *adv* d'autre ▷ *somebody else* quelqu'un d'autre ▷ *nobody else* personne d'autre ▷ *nothing else* rien d'autre; **something else** autre chose; **anything else** autre chose ▷ *Would you like anything else?* Désirez-vous autre chose?; **I don't want anything else.** Je ne veux rien d'autre.; **somewhere else** ailleurs; **anywhere else** autre part

email *n* courrier électronique *m*; **email address** adresse e-mail *f* ▷ *My email address is: ...* Mon adresse e-mail, c'est: ...
▶ *vb* **to email somebody** envoyer [**33**] un e-mail à quelqu'un

embankment *n* talus *m*

embarrassed *adj* gêné(e) ▷ *I was really embarrassed.* J'étais vraiment gêné.

embarrassing *adj* gênant(e) ▷ *It was so embarrassing.* C'était tellement gênant.

embassy *n* ambassade *f* ▷ *the British Embassy* l'ambassade de Grande-Bretagne ▷ *the French Embassy* l'ambassade de France

embroider *vb* broder [**28**]

embroidery *n* broderie *f* ▷ *I do embroidery.* Je fais de la broderie.

emergency *n* urgence *f* ▷ *This is an emergency!* C'est une urgence!; **in an emergency** en cas d'urgence; **an emergency exit** une sortie de secours; **an emergency landing** un atterrissage forcé; **the emergency services** les services d'urgence *mpl*

emigrate *vb* émigrer [**28**]

emotion *n* émotion *f*

emotional *adj (person)* émotif *(f* émotive)

emperor *n* empereur *m*

emphasize *vb* **to emphasize something** insister [**28**] sur quelque chose; **to emphasize that ...** souligner [**28**] que ...

empire *n* empire *m*

employ *vb* employer [**53**] ▷ *The factory employs 600 people.* L'usine emploie six cents personnes.

employee *n* employé *m*, employée *f*

employer *n* employeur *m*

employment *n* emploi *m*

empty *adj* vide
▶ *vb* vider [**28**]; **to empty something out** vider [**28**] quelque chose

encourage *vb* encourager [**45**]; **to encourage somebody to do something** encourager [**45**] quelqu'un à faire quelque chose

encouragement *n* encouragement *m*

encyclopedia *n* encyclopédie *f*

end *n* ❶ fin *f* ▷ *the end of the film* la fin du film; **in the end** en fin de compte ▷ *In the end I decided to stay at home.* En fin de compte j'ai décidé de rester à la maison.; **It turned out all right in the end.** Ça s'est bien terminé. ❷ bout *m* ▷ *at the end of the street* au bout de la rue; **for hours on end** des heures entières
▶ *vb* finir [**38**] ▷ *What time does the film end?* À quelle heure est-ce que

le film finit?; **to end up doing something** finir [**38**] par faire quelque chose ▷ *I ended up walking home.* J'ai fini par rentrer chez moi à pied.

ending *n* fin *f* ▷ *It was an exciting film, especially the ending.* C'était un film passionnant, surtout la fin.

endless *adj* interminable ▷ *The journey seemed endless.* Le voyage a paru interminable.

enemy *n* ennemi *m*, ennemie *f*

energetic *adj (person)* énergique

energy *n* énergie *f*

engaged *adj* ❶ *(busy, in use)* occupé(e) ▷ *I phoned, but it was engaged.* J'ai téléphoné, mais c'était occupé. ❷ *(to be married)* fiancé(e) ▷ *She's engaged to Brian.* Elle est fiancée à Brian.; **to get engaged** se fiancer [**12**]

engagement *n* fiançailles *fpl* ▷ *an engagement ring* une bague de fiançailles

engine *n* moteur *m*

> Be careful not to translate **engine** by **engin**.

engineer *n* ingénieur *m* ▷ *He's an engineer.* Il est ingénieur.

engineering *n* ingénierie *f*

England *n* Angleterre *f*; **in England** en Angleterre; **to England** en Angleterre; **I'm from England.** Je suis anglais.

English *n (language)* anglais *m* ▷ *Do you speak English?* Est-ce que vous parlez anglais?; **the English** les Anglais
▶ *adj* anglais(e) ▷ *I'm English.* Je suis anglais.; **English people** les Anglais

Englishman *n* Anglais *m*

Englishwoman *n* Anglaise *f*

enjoy *vb* aimer [**28**] ▷ *Did you enjoy the film?* Est-ce que vous avez aimé le film?; **to enjoy oneself** s'amuser [**28**] ▷ *I really enjoyed myself.* Je me suis vraiment bien amusé.

enjoyable *adj* agréable

enlargement *n (of photo)* agrandissement *m*

enormous *adj* énorme

enough *pron, adj* assez de ▷ *enough time* assez de temps ▷ *I didn't have enough money.* Je n'avais pas assez d'argent. ▷ *I've had enough!* J'en ai assez!; **big enough** suffisamment grand; **warm enough** suffisamment chaud; **That's enough.** Ça suffit.

enquire *vb* **to enquire about something** se renseigner [**28**] sur quelque chose ▷ *I am going to enquire about train times.* Je vais me renseigner sur les horaires de trains.

enquiry *n* **to make enquiries (about something)** se renseigner [**28**] (sur quelque chose) ▷ *'enquiries'* 'renseignements'

enter *vb* entrer [**32**]; **to enter a room** entrer [**32**] dans une pièce; **to enter a competition** s'inscrire [**30**] à une compétition

entertain *vb (guests)* recevoir [**67**]

entertaining *adj* amusant(e)

enthusiasm *n* enthousiasme *m*

enthusiast *n* **a railway**

enthusiast un passionné des trains; **She's a DIY enthusiast.** C'est une passionnée de bricolage.

enthusiastic *adj* enthousiaste

entire *adj* entier (*f* entière) ▷ *the entire world* le monde entier

entirely *adv* entièrement

entrance *n* entrée *f*; **an entrance exam** un concours d'entrée; **entrance fee** le prix d'entrée

entry *n* entrée *f*; **'no entry' (1)** *(on door)* 'défense d'entrer' **(2)** *(on road sign)* 'sens interdit'; **an entry form** une feuille d'inscription

entry phone *n* interphone *m*

envelope *n* enveloppe *f*

envious *adj* envieux (*f* envieuse)

environment *n* environnement *m*

environmental *adj* écologique

environment-friendly *adj* écologique

envy *n* envie *f*
▸ *vb* envier **[19]** ▷ *I don't envy you!* Je ne t'envie pas!

epileptic *n* épileptique *mf*

episode *n (of TV programme, story)* épisode *m*

equal *adj* égal(e) (*mpl* égaux)
▸ *vb* égaler **[28]**

equality *n* égalité *f*

equalize *vb (in sport)* égaliser **[28]**

equator *n* équateur *m*

equipment *n* équipement *m* ▷ *fishing equipment* l'équipement de pêche ▷ *skiing equipment* l'équipement de ski

equipped *adj* **equipped with** équipé de; **to be well equipped** être **[35]** bien équipé

error *n* erreur *f*

escalator *n* escalier roulant *m*

escape *n (from prison)* évasion *f*
▸ *vb* s'échapper **[28]** ▷ *A lion has escaped.* Un lion s'est échappé.; **to escape from prison** s'évader **[28]** de prison

escort *n* escorte *f* ▷ *a police escort* une escorte de police

especially *adv* surtout ▷ *It's very hot there, especially in the summer.* Il fait très chaud là-bas, surtout en été.

essay *n* dissertation *f* ▷ *a history essay* une dissertation d'histoire

essential *adj* essentiel (*f* essentielle) ▷ *It's essential to bring warm clothes.* Il est essentiel d'apporter des vêtements chauds.

estate *n (housing estate)* cité *f* ▷ *I live on an estate.* J'habite dans une cité.

estate agent *n* agent immobilier *m*

estate car *n* break *m*

estimate *vb* estimer **[28]** ▷ *They estimated it would take three weeks.* Ils ont estimé que cela prendrait trois semaines.

etc *abbr (= et cetera)* etc.

Ethiopia *n* Éthiopie *f*; **in Ethiopia** en Éthiopie

ethnic *adj* ❶ *(racial)* ethnique ▷ *an ethnic minority* une minorité ethnique ❷ *(clothes, music)* folklorique

EU *n (= European Union)* Union européenne *f*

euro *n* euro *m* ▷ *50 euros* 50 euros

Europe *n* Europe *f*; **in Europe** en

Europe; **to Europe** en Europe

European *n (person)* Européen *m*, Européenne *f*
▸ *adj* européen (*f* européenne)

eve *n* **Christmas Eve** la veille de Noël; **New Year's Eve** la Saint-Sylvestre

even *adv* même ▹ *I like all animals, even snakes.* J'aime tous les animaux, même les serpents.; **even if** même si ▹ *I'd never do that, even if you asked me.* Je ne ferais jamais ça, même si tu me le demandais.; **not even** même pas ▹ *He never stops working, not even at the weekend.* Il n'arrête jamais de travailler, même pas le week-end.; **even though** bien que

> **bien que** has to be followed by a verb in the subjunctive.

▹ *He wants to go out, even though it's raining.* Il veut sortir bien qu'il pleuve.; **even more** encore plus ▹ *I liked Boulogne even more than Paris.* J'ai encore plus aimé Boulogne que Paris.
▸ *adj* régulier (*f* régulière) ▹ *an even layer of snow* une couche régulière de neige; **an even number** un nombre pair; **to get even with somebody** prendre [**65**] sa revanche sur quelqu'un ▹ *He wanted to get even with her.* Il voulait prendre sa revanche sur elle.

evening *n* soir *m* ▹ *in the evening* le soir ▹ *yesterday evening* hier soir ▹ *tomorrow evening* demain soir; **all evening** toute la soirée; **Good evening!** Bonsoir!

evening class *n* cours du soir *m* (*pl* cours du soir)

event *n* événement *m*; **a sporting event** une épreuve sportive

eventful *adj* mouvementé(e)

eventual *adj* final(e)

> Be careful not to translate **eventual** by **éventuel**.

eventually *adv* finalement

> Be careful not to translate **eventually** by **éventuellement**.

ever *adv* **Have you ever been to Germany?** Est-ce que tu es déjà allé en Allemagne?; **Have you ever seen her?** Vous l'avez déjà vue?; **I haven't ever done that.** Je ne l'ai jamais fait.; **the best I've ever seen** le meilleur que j'aie jamais vu; **for the first time ever** pour la première fois; **ever since** depuis que ▹ *ever since I met him* depuis que je l'ai rencontré; **ever since then** depuis ce moment-là

every *adj* chaque ▹ *every pupil* chaque élève; **every time** chaque fois ▹ *Every time I see him he's depressed.* Chaque fois que je le vois il est déprimé.; **every day** tous les jours; **every week** toutes les semaines; **every now and then** de temps en temps

everybody *pron* tout le monde ▹ *Everybody had a good time.* Tout le monde s'est bien amusé.

everyone *pron* tout le monde

everything *pron* tout ▹ *You've thought of everything!* Tu as pensé à tout!; **Have you remembered**

everything? Est-ce que tu n'as rien oublié?; **Money isn't everything.** L'argent ne fait pas le bonheur.

everywhere *adv* partout ▷ *I looked everywhere, but I couldn't find it.* J'ai regardé partout, mais je n'ai pas pu le trouver.

evil *adj* mauvais(e)

exact *adj* exact(e)

exactly *adv* exactement ▷ *exactly the same* exactement le même ▷ *Not exactly.* Pas exactement.; **It's exactly 10 o'clock.** Il est dix heures précises.

exaggerate *vb* exagérer [**34**]

exaggeration *n* exagération *f*

exam *n* examen *m* ▷ *a French exam* un examen de français ▷ *the exam results* les résultats des examens *mpl*

examination *n* examen *m*

examine *vb* examiner [**28**] ▷ *He examined her passport.* Il a examiné son passeport.

examiner *n* examinateur *m*, examinatrice *f*

example *n* exemple *m*; **for example** par exemple

excellent *adj* excellent(e) ▷ *Her results were excellent.* Elle a eu d'excellents résultats.; **It was excellent fun.** C'était vraiment super.

except *prep* sauf ▷ *everyone except me* tout le monde sauf moi; **except for** sauf; **except that** sauf que ▷ *The holiday was great, except that it rained.* Les vacances étaient super, sauf qu'il a plu.

exception *n* exception *f*; **to make an exception** faire [**36**] une exception

exchange *vb* échanger [**45**] ▷ *I exchanged the book for a video.* J'ai échangé le livre contre une vidéo.

exchange rate *n* taux de change *m*

excited *adj* excité(e)

exciting *adj* passionnant(e)

exclamation mark *n* point d'exclamation *m*

excuse *n* excuse *f*
▶ *vb* **Excuse me!** Pardon!

exercise *n* exercice *m*; **an exercise bike** un vélo d'appartement; **an exercise book** un cahier

exhausted *adj* épuisé(e)

exhaust fumes *npl* gaz d'échappement *mpl*

exhaust pipe *n* tuyau d'échappement *m*

exhibition *n* exposition *f*

exist *vb* exister [**28**]

exit *n* sortie *f*

expect *vb* ❶ attendre [**7**] ▷ *I'm expecting him for dinner.* Je l'attends pour dîner. ▷ *She's expecting a baby.* Elle attend un enfant. ❷ s'attendre [**7**] à ▷ *I was expecting the worst.* Je m'attendais au pire. ❸ supposer [**28**] ▷ *I expect it's a mistake.* Je suppose qu'il s'agit d'une erreur.

expedition *n* expédition *f*

expel *vb* **to get expelled** *(from school)* se faire [**36**] renvoyer

expenses *npl* frais *mpl*

expensive *adj* cher (*f* chère)

experience *n* expérience *f*

experienced *adj* expérimenté(e)
experiment *n* expérience *f*
expert *n* spécialiste *m*, spécialiste *f* ▷ *He's a computer expert.* C'est un spécialiste en informatique.; **He's an expert cook.** Il cuisine très bien.
expire *vb* expirer [**28**]
explain *vb* expliquer [**28**]
explanation *n* explication *f*
explode *vb* exploser [**28**]
explore *vb (place)* explorer [**28**]
explosion *n* explosion *f*
express *vb* exprimer [**28**]; **to express oneself** s'exprimer [**28**] ▷ *It's hard to express oneself in French.* C'est dur de s'exprimer en français.
expression *n* expression *f* ▷ *It's an English expression.* C'est une expression anglaise.
expressway *n (US)* autoroute urbaine *f*
extension *n* ❶ *(of building)* annexe *f* ❷ *(telephone)* poste *m*; **Extension 3137, please.** Poste trente et un trente-sept, s'il vous plaît.

> In France phone numbers are broken into groups of two digits where possible.

extent *n* **to some extent** dans une certaine mesure
exterior *adj* extérieur(e)
extinct *adj* **to become extinct** disparaître [**56**]; **to be extinct** avoir [**8**] disparu ▷ *The species is almost extinct.* Cette espèce a presque disparu.
extinguisher *n (fire extinguisher)* extincteur *m*
extra *adj, adv* supplémentaire ▷ *an extra blanket* une couverture supplémentaire; **to pay extra** payer [**59**] un supplément; **Breakfast is extra.** Il y a un supplément pour le petit déjeuner.; **It costs extra.** Il y a un supplément.
extraordinary *adj* extraordinaire
extravagant *adj (person)* dépensier (*f* dépensière)
extreme *adj* extrême
extremely *adv* extrêmement
extremist *n* extrémiste *mf*
eye *n* œil *m (pl* yeux) ▷ *I've got green eyes.* J'ai les yeux verts.; **to keep an eye on something** surveiller [**28**] quelque chose
eyebrow *n* sourcil *m*
eyelash *n* cil *m*
eyelid *n* paupière *f*
eyeliner *n* eye-liner *m*
eye shadow *n* ombre à paupières *f*
eyesight *n* vue *f*

fabric *n* tissu *m*
fabulous *adj* formidable ▷ *The show was fabulous.* Le spectacle était formidable.
face *n* ❶ *(of person)* visage *m* ❷ *(of clock)* cadran *m* ❸ *(of cliff)* paroi *f*; **on the face of it** à première vue; **in the face of these difficulties** face à ces difficultés; **face to face** face à face
▶ *vb (place, problem)* faire [**36**] face à; **to face up to something** faire [**36**] face à quelque chose ▷ *You must face up to your responsibilities.* Vous devez faire face à vos responsabilités.
Facebook® *n* Facebook® *m*
▶ *vb* facebooker [**28**]
face cloth *n* gant de toilette *m*

The French traditionally wash with a towelling glove rather than a flannel.

facilities *npl* équipement *msg* ▷ *This school has excellent facilities.* Cette école dispose d'un excellent équipement.; **toilet facilities** les toilettes *fpl*; **cooking facilities** la cuisine équipée *sg*
fact *n* fait *m*; **in fact** en fait
factory *n* usine *f*
fail *vb* ❶ rater [**28**] ▷ *I failed the history exam.* J'ai raté l'examen d'histoire. ❷ échouer [**28**] ▷ *In our class, no one failed.* Dans notre classe, personne n'a échoué. ❸ lâcher [**28**] ▷ *My brakes failed.* Mes freins ont lâché.; **to fail to do something** ne pas faire [**36**] quelque chose ▷ *She failed to return her library books.* Elle n'a pas rendu ses livres à la bibliothèque.
▶ *n* **without fail** sans faute
failure *n* ❶ échec *m* ▷ *feelings of failure* un sentiment d'échec *sg* ❷ raté *m*, ratée *f* ▷ *He's a failure.* C'est un raté. ❸ défaillance *f* ▷ *a mechanical failure* une défaillance mécanique
faint *adj* faible ▷ *His voice was very faint.* Sa voix était très faible.; **to feel faint** se trouver [**28**] mal
▶ *vb* s'évanouir [**38**] ▷ *All of a sudden she fainted.* Tout à coup elle s'est évanouie.
fair *adj* ❶ juste ▷ *That's not fair.* Ce n'est pas juste. ❷ *(hair)* blond(e) ▷ *He's got fair hair.* Il a les cheveux blonds. ❸ *(skin)* clair(e) ▷ *people*

with fair skin les gens qui ont la peau claire ❹ *(weather)* beau (*f* belle) ▷ *The weather was fair.* Il faisait beau. ❺ *(good enough)* assez bon (*f* assez bonne) ▷ *I have a fair chance of winning.* J'ai d'assez bonnes chances de gagner. ❻ *(sizeable)* considérable ▷ *That's a fair distance.* Ça représente une distance considérable.
▶ *n* foire *f* ▷ *They went to the fair.* Ils sont allés à la foire.; **a trade fair** une foire commerciale

fairground *n* champ de foire *m*

fairly *adv* ❶ équitablement ▷ *The cake was divided fairly.* Le gâteau a été partagé équitablement. ❷ *(quite)* assez ▷ *That's fairly good.* C'est assez bien.

fairy *n* fée *f*

fairy tale *n* conte de fées *m*

faith *n* ❶ foi *f* ▷ *the Catholic faith* la foi catholique ❷ confiance *f* ▷ *People have lost faith in the government.* Les gens ont perdu confiance dans le gouvernement.

faithful *adj* fidèle

faithfully *adv* **Yours faithfully ...** *(in letter)* Veuillez agréer mes salutations distinguées ...

fake *n* faux *m* ▷ *The painting was a fake.* Le tableau était un faux.
▶ *adj* faux (*f* fausse) ▷ *She wore fake fur.* Elle portait une fausse fourrure.

fall *n* ❶ chute *f* ▷ *a fall of snow* une chute de neige ▷ *She had a nasty fall.* Elle a fait une mauvaise chute.; **the Niagara Falls** les chutes du Niagara ❷ *(US: autumn)* automne *m*
▶ *vb* ❶ tomber [**84**] ▷ *He tripped and fell.* Il a trébuché et il est tombé. ❷ baisser [**28**] ▷ *Prices are falling.* Les prix baissent.

fall down *vb* ❶ *(person)* tomber [**84**] ▷ *She's fallen down.* Elle est tombée. ❷ *(building)* s'écrouler [**28**] ▷ *The house is slowly falling down.* La maison est en train de s'écrouler.

fall for *vb* ❶ se laisser [**28**] prendre à ▷ *They fell for it.* Ils s'y sont laissé prendre. ❷ tomber [**84**] amoureux de ▷ *She's falling for him.* Elle est en train de tomber amoureuse de lui.

fall off *vb* tomber [**84**] de ▷ *The book fell off the shelf.* Le livre est tombé de l'étagère.

fall out *vb* **to fall out with somebody** se fâcher [**28**] avec quelqu'un ▷ *Sarah's fallen out with her boyfriend.* Sarah s'est fâchée avec son copain.

fall through *vb* tomber [**84**] à l'eau ▷ *Our plans have fallen through.* Nos projets sont tombés à l'eau.

fallen *vb see* **fall**

false *adj* faux (*f* fausse); **a false alarm** une fausse alerte; **false teeth** les fausses dents

fame *n* renommée *f*

familiar *adj* familier (*f* familière) ▷ *a familiar face* un visage familier; **to be familiar with something** bien connaître [**14**] quelque chose ▷ *I'm familiar with his work.* Je connais bien ses œuvres.

family *n* famille *f*; **the Cooke**

family la famille Cooke
famine *n* famine *f*
famous *adj* célèbre
fan *n* ❶ *(hand-held)* éventail *m* ❷ *(electric)* ventilateur *m* ❸ *(of person, band)* fan *mf* ▷ *I'm a fan of Coldplay.* Je suis une fan de Coldplay. ❹ *(of sport)* supporter *mf* ▷ *football fans* les supporters de football
fanatic *n* fanatique *mf*
fancy *vb* **to fancy something** avoir [8] envie de quelque chose ▷ *I fancy an ice cream.* J'ai envie d'une glace.; **to fancy doing something** avoir [8] envie de faire quelque chose; **He fancies her.** Elle lui plaît.
fancy dress *n* déguisement *m* ▷ *He was wearing fancy dress.* Il portait un déguisement.; **a fancy-dress ball** un bal costumé
fantastic *adj* fantastique
far *adj, adv* loin ▷ *Is it far?* Est-ce que c'est loin?; **far from** loin de ▷ *It's not far from London.* Ce n'est pas loin de Londres.; **How far is it?** C'est à quelle distance?; **How far is it to Geneva?** Combien y a-t-il jusqu'à Genève?; **How far have you got?** *(with a task)* Où en êtes-vous?; **at the far end** à l'autre bout ▷ *at the far end of the room* à l'autre bout de la pièce; **far better** beaucoup mieux; **as far as I know** pour autant que je sache
fare *n* ❶ *(on trains, buses)* prix du billet *m* ❷ *(in taxi)* prix de la course *m*; **half fare** le demi-tarif; **full fare** le plein tarif
Far East *n* Extrême-Orient *m*; **in the Far East** en Extrême-Orient
farm *n* ferme *f*
farmer *n* agriculteur *m*, agricultrice *f* ▷ *He's a farmer.* Il est agriculteur.
farmhouse *n* ferme *f*
farming *n* agriculture *f*
fascinating *adj* fascinant(e)
fashion *n* mode *f* ▷ *a fashion show* un défilé de mode; **in fashion** à la mode
fashionable *adj* à la mode ▷ *Jane wears very fashionable clothes.* Jane porte des vêtements très à la mode. ▷ *a fashionable restaurant* un restaurant à la mode
fast *adj, adv* ❶ vite ▷ *He can run fast.* Il sait courir vite. ❷ rapide ▷ *a fast car* une voiture rapide; **That clock's fast.** Cette pendule avance.; **He's fast asleep.** Il est profondément endormi.
fat *adj* gros (*f* grosse)
▶ *n* ❶ *(on meat, in food)* gras *m* ▷ *It's very high in fat.* C'est très gras. ❷ *(for cooking)* matière grasse *f*
fatal *adj* ❶ *(causing death)* mortel (*f* mortelle) ▷ *a fatal accident* un accident mortel ❷ *(disastrous)* fatal(e) ▷ *He made a fatal mistake.* Il a fait une erreur fatale.
father *n* père *m* ▷ *my father* mon père
father-in-law *n* beau-père *m* (*pl* beaux-pères)
faucet *n* *(US)* robinet *m*
fault *n* ❶ *(mistake)* faute *f* ▷ *It's my fault.* C'est de ma faute. ❷ *(defect)* défaut *m* ▷ *There's a fault in this material.* Ce tissu a un défaut.;

a mechanical fault une défaillance mécanique

favour (*US* **favor**) *n* service *m*; **to do somebody a favour** rendre [**7**] service à quelqu'un ▷ *Could you do me a favour?* Tu peux me rendre service?; **to be in favour of something** être [**35**] pour quelque chose ▷ *I'm in favour of nuclear disarmament.* Je suis pour le désarmement nucléaire.

favourite (*US* **favorite**) *adj* favori (*f* favorite) ▷ *Blue's my favourite colour.* Le bleu est ma couleur favorite.
▶ *n* favori *m*, favorite *f* ▷ *Liverpool are favourites to win the Cup.* L'équipe de Liverpool est favorite pour la coupe.

fax *n* fax *m*; **to send somebody a fax** envoyer [**33**] un fax à quelqu'un
▶ *vb* **to fax somebody** envoyer [**33**] un fax à quelqu'un

fear *n* peur *f*
▶ *vb* craindre [**17**] ▷ *You have nothing to fear.* Vous n'avez rien à craindre.

feather *n* plume *f*

feature *n (of person, object)* caractéristique *f* ▷ *an important feature* une caractéristique essentielle

February *n* février *m*; **in February** en février

fed *vb see* **feed**

fed up *adj* **to be fed up of something** en avoir [**8**] marre de quelque chose ▷ *I'm fed up of waiting for him.* J'en ai marre de l'attendre.

feed *vb* donner [**28**] à manger à ▷ *Have you fed the cat?* Est-ce que tu as donné à manger au chat?; **He worked hard to feed his family.** Il travaillait dur pour nourrir sa famille.

feel *vb* ❶ se sentir [**77**] ▷ *I don't feel well.* Je ne me sens pas bien. ▷ *I feel a bit lonely.* Je me sens un peu seul.
❷ sentir [**77**] ▷ *I didn't feel much pain.* Je n'ai presque rien senti.
❸ toucher [**28**] ▷ *The doctor felt his forehead.* Le docteur lui a touché le front.; **I was feeling hungry.** J'avais faim.; **I was feeling cold, so I went inside.** J'avais froid, alors je suis rentré.; **I feel like ...** *(want)* J'ai envie de ... ▷ *Do you feel like an ice cream?* Tu as envie d'une glace?

feeling *n* ❶ *(physical)* sensation *f* ▷ *a burning feeling* une sensation de brûlure ❷ *(emotional)* sentiment *m* ▷ *a feeling of satisfaction* un sentiment de satisfaction

feet *npl see* **foot**

fell *vb see* **fall**

felt *vb see* **feel**

felt-tip pen *n* stylo-feutre *m*

female *adj* ❶ femelle ▷ *a female animal* un animal femelle
❷ féminin(e) ▷ *the female sex* le sexe féminin
▶ *n (animal)* femelle *f*

feminine *adj* féminin(e)

feminist *n* féministe *mf*

fence *n* barrière *f*

fern *n* fougère *f*

ferry *n* ferry *m*

festival *n* festival *m* ▷ *a jazz festival* un festival de jazz

fetch *vb* ❶ aller [**3**] chercher ▷ *Fetch*

the bucket. Va chercher le seau. ❷ *(sell for)* se vendre [**88**] ▷ *His painting fetched £5000*. Son tableau s'est vendu cinq mille livres.

fever *n (temperature)* fièvre *f*

few *adj, pron (not many)* peu de ▷ *few books* peu de livres; **a few** **(1)** quelques ▷ *a few hours* quelques heures **(2)** quelques-uns ▷ *How many apples do you want? — A few*. Tu veux combien de pommes? — Quelques-unes.; **quite a few people** pas mal de monde

fewer *adj* moins de ▷ *There are fewer pupils in this class*. Il y a moins d'élèves dans cette classe.

fiancé *n* fiancé *m* ▷ *He's my fiancé*. C'est mon fiancé.

fiancée *n* fiancée *f* ▷ *She's my fiancée*. C'est ma fiancée.

fiction *n (novels)* romans *mpl*

field *n* ❶ *(in countryside)* champ *m* ▷ *a field of wheat* un champ de blé ❷ *(for sport)* terrain *m* ▷ *a football field* un terrain de football ❸ *(subject)* domaine *m* ▷ *He's an expert in his field*. C'est un expert dans son domaine.

fierce *adj* ❶ féroce ▷ *The dog looked very fierce*. Le chien avait l'air très féroce. ❷ violent(e) ▷ *a fierce attack* une attaque violente

fifteen *num* quinze ▷ *I'm fifteen*. J'ai quinze ans.

fifteenth *adj* quinzième ▷ *the fifteenth floor* le quinzième étage; **the fifteenth of August** le quinze août

fifth *adj* cinquième ▷ *the fifth floor* le cinquième étage; **the fifth of August** le cinq août

fifty *num* cinquante ▷ *He's fifty*. Il a cinquante ans.

fight *n* ❶ bagarre *f* ▷ *There was a fight in the pub*. Il y a eu une bagarre au pub. ❷ lutte *f* ▷ *the fight against cancer* la lutte contre le cancer
▶ *vb* ❶ se battre [**9**] ▷ *They were fighting*. Ils se battaient. ❷ lutter [**28**] contre ▷ *The doctors tried to fight the disease*. Les médecins ont essayé de lutter contre la maladie.

figure *n* ❶ *(number)* chiffre *m* ▷ *Can you give me the exact figures?* Pouvez-vous me donner les chiffres exacts? ❷ *(outline of person)* silhouette *f* ▷ *Hélène saw the figure of a man on the bridge*. Hélène a vu la silhouette d'un homme sur le pont.; **She's got a good figure.** Elle est bien faite.; **I have to watch my figure.** Je dois faire attention à ma ligne. ❸ *(personality)* personnage *m* ▷ *She's an important political figure*. C'est un personnage politique important.

figure out *vb* ❶ calculer [**28**] ▷ *I'll try to figure out how much it'll cost*. Je vais essayer de calculer combien ça va coûter. ❷ voir [**92**] ▷ *I couldn't figure out what it meant*. Je n'arrivais pas à voir ce que ça voulait dire. ❸ cerner [**28**] ▷ *I can't figure him out at all*. Je n'arrive pas du tout à le cerner.

file *n* ❶ *(document)* dossier *m* ▷ *Have we got a file on the suspect?* Est-ce que nous avons un dossier sur le

suspect? ❷ *(folder)* chemise *f* ▷ *She keeps all her letters in a cardboard file.* Elle garde toutes ses lettres dans une chemise en carton. ❸ *(ring binder)* classeur *m* ❹ *(on computer)* fichier *m* ❺ *(for nails, metal)* lime *f*
▶ *vb* ❶ *(papers)* classer **[28]** ❷ *(nails, metal)* limer **[28]** ▷ *to file one's nails* se limer les ongles

fill *vb* remplir **[38]** ▷ *She filled the glass with water.* Elle a rempli le verre d'eau.

fill in *vb* ❶ remplir **[38]** ▷ *Can you fill this form in please?* Est-ce que vous pouvez remplir ce formulaire s'il vous plaît? ❷ boucher **[28]** ▷ *He filled the hole in with soil.* Il a bouché le trou avec de la terre.

fill up *vb* remplir **[38]** ▷ *He filled the cup up to the brim.* Il a rempli la tasse à ras bords.; **Fill it up, please.** *(at petrol station)* Le plein, s'il vous plaît.

film *n* ❶ *(movie)* film *m* ❷ *(for camera)* pellicule *f*

film star *n* vedette de cinéma *f* ▷ *He's a film star.* C'est une vedette de cinéma.

filthy *adj* dégoûtant(e)

final *adj* ❶ *(last)* dernier (*f* dernière) ▷ *our final farewells* nos derniers adieux ❷ *(definite)* définitif (*f* définitive) ▷ *a final decision* une décision définitive; **I'm not going and that's final.** Je n'y vais pas, un point c'est tout.
▶ *n* finale *f* ▷ *Andy Murray is in the final.* Andy Murray va disputer la finale.

finally *adv* ❶ *(lastly)* enfin ▷ *Finally, I would like to say ...* Enfin, je voudrais dire ... ❷ *(eventually)* finalement ▷ *She finally chose the red shoes.* Elle a finalement choisi les chaussures rouges.

find *vb* ❶ trouver **[28]** ▷ *I can't find the exit.* Je ne trouve pas la sortie. ❷ *(something lost)* retrouver **[28]** ▷ *Did you find your pen?* Est-ce que tu as retrouvé ton crayon?

find out *vb* découvrir **[55]** ▷ *I'm determined to find out the truth.* Je suis décidé à découvrir la vérité.; **to find out about (1)** *(make enquiries)* se renseigner **[28]** sur ▷ *Try to find out about the cost of a hotel.* Essaye de te renseigner sur le prix d'un hôtel. **(2)** *(by chance)* apprendre **[65]** ▷ *I found out about their affair.* J'ai appris leur liaison.

fine *adj, adv* ❶ *(very good)* excellent(e) ▷ *He's a fine musician.* C'est un excellent musicien.; **to be fine** aller **[3]** bien ▷ *How are you? — I'm fine.* Comment ça va? — Ça va bien.; **I feel fine.** Je me sens bien.; **The weather is fine today.** Il fait beau aujourd'hui. ❷ *(not coarse)* fin(e) ▷ *She's got very fine hair.* Elle a les cheveux très fins.
▶ *n* ❶ amende *f* ▷ *She got a £50 fine.* Elle a eu une amende de cinquante livres. ❷ *(for traffic offence)* contravention *f* ▷ *I got a fine for speeding.* J'ai eu une contravention pour excès de vitesse.

finger *n* doigt *m*; **my little finger** mon petit doigt

fingernail *n* ongle *m*

finish *n (of race)* arrivée *f* ▷ *We saw the finish of the London Marathon.* Nous avons vu l'arrivée du marathon de Londres.
▸ *vb* ❶ finir **[38]** ▷ *I've finished!* J'ai fini!; **to finish doing something** finir **[38]** de faire quelque chose ❷ terminer **[28]** ▷ *I've finished the book.* J'ai terminé ce livre. ▷ *The film has finished.* Le film est terminé.

Finland *n* Finlande *f*; **in Finland** en Finlande; **to Finland** en Finlande

Finn *n* Finlandais *m*, Finlandaise *f*

Finnish *n (language)* finnois *m*
▸ *adj* finlandais(e)

fire *n* ❶ feu *m (pl* feux) ▷ *He made a fire in the woods.* Il a fait du feu dans les bois.; **to be on fire** être **[35]** en feu ❷ *(accidental)* incendie *m* ▷ *The house was destroyed by fire.* La maison a été détruite par un incendie. ❸ *(heater)* radiateur *m* ▷ *Turn the fire on.* Allume le radiateur.; **the fire brigade** les pompiers *mpl*; **a fire alarm** une alarme à incendie; **a fire engine** une voiture de pompiers; **a fire escape** un escalier de secours; **a fire extinguisher** un extincteur; **a fire station** une caserne de pompiers
▸ *vb (shoot)* tirer **[28]** ▷ *She fired twice.* Elle a tiré deux fois.; **to fire at somebody** tirer **[28]** sur quelqu'un ▷ *The terrorist fired at the crowd.* Le terroriste a tiré sur la foule.; **to fire a gun** tirer **[28]** un coup de feu; **to fire somebody** mettre **[47]** quelqu'un à la porte ▷ *He was fired from his job.* Il a été mis à la porte.

firefighter *n* pompier *m* ▷ *She's a firefighter.* Elle est pompier.

fireplace *n* cheminée *f*

fireworks *npl* feu d'artifice *msg* ▷ *Are you going to see the fireworks?* Est-ce que tu vas voir le feu d'artifice?

firm *adj* ferme ▷ *to be firm with somebody* se montrer ferme avec quelqu'un
▸ *n* entreprise *f* ▷ *He works for a large firm in London.* Il travaille pour une grande entreprise à Londres.

first *adj, adv* ❶ premier *(f* première) ▷ *the first of September* le premier septembre ▷ *the first time* la première fois; **to come first** *(in exam, race)* arriver **[5]** premier ▷ *Rachel came first.* Rachel est arrivée première. ❷ d'abord ▷ *I want to get a job, but first I have to graduate.* Je veux trouver du travail, mais d'abord je dois finir mes études.; **first of all** tout d'abord
▸ *n* premier *m*, première *f* ▷ *She was the first to arrive.* Elle est arrivée la première.; **at first** au début

first aid *n* premiers secours *mpl*; **a first aid kit** une trousse de secours

first-class *adj, adv* ❶ de première classe ▷ *She has booked a first-class ticket.* Elle a réservé un billet de première classe. ❷ excellent(e) ▷ *a first-class meal* un excellent repas; **a first-class stamp**

- In France there is no first-class or second-class postage. However letters cost more to send than postcards, so you have to remember to say what you are sending when buying stamps.

firstly *adv* premièrement ▷ *Firstly, let's see what the book is about.* Premièrement, voyons de quoi parle ce livre.

fir tree *n* sapin *m*

fish *n* poisson *m* ▷ *I caught three fish.* J'ai pêché trois poissons. ▷ *I don't like fish.* Je n'aime pas le poisson.
▶ *vb* pêcher [**28**]; **to go fishing** aller [**3**] à la pêche ▷ *We went fishing in the River Dee.* Nous sommes allés à la pêche sur la Dee.

fisherman *n* pêcheur *m* ▷ *He's a fisherman.* Il est pêcheur.

fishing *n* pêche *f* ▷ *My hobby is fishing.* La pêche est mon passe-temps favori.

fishing boat *n* bateau de pêche *m*

fishing rod *n* canne à pêche *f*

fishing tackle *n* matériel de pêche *m*

fist *n* poing *m*

fit *adj (in condition)* en forme ▷ *He likes to stay fit.* Il aime se maintenir en forme.; **to keep fit** se maintenir [**83**] en forme ▷ *She does aerobics to keep fit.* Elle fait de l'aérobic pour se maintenir en forme.
▶ *n* **to have a fit (1)** *(epileptic)* avoir [**8**] une crise d'épilepsie **(2)** *(be angry)* piquer [**28**] une crise de nerfs ▷ *My Mum will have a fit when she sees the carpet!* Ma mère va piquer une crise de nerfs quand elle va voir la moquette!
▶ *vb* ❶ *(be the right size)* être [**35**] la bonne taille ▷ *Does it fit?* Est-ce que c'est la bonne taille?

> In French you usually specify whether something is too big, small, tight etc.

These trousers don't fit me. **(1)** *(too big)* Ce pantalon est trop grand pour moi. **(2)** *(too small)* Ce pantalon est trop petit pour moi.
❷ *(fix up)* installer [**28**] ▷ *He fitted an alarm in his car.* Il a installé une alarme dans sa voiture. ❸ *(attach)* adapter [**28**] ▷ *She fitted a plug to the hair dryer.* Elle a adapté une prise au sèche-cheveux.

fit in *vb* ❶ *(match up)* correspondre [**69**] ▷ *That story doesn't fit in with the facts.* Cette histoire ne correspond pas aux faits.
❷ *(person)* s'adapter [**28**] ▷ *She fitted in well at her new school.* Elle s'est bien adaptée à sa nouvelle école.

fitted carpet *n* moquette *f*

five *num* cinq ▷ *He's five.* Il a cinq ans.

fix *vb* ❶ *(mend)* réparer [**28**] ▷ *Can you fix my bike?* Est-ce que tu peux réparer mon vélo? ❷ *(decide)* fixer [**28**] ▷ *Let's fix a date for the party.* Fixons une date pour la soirée.
❸ préparer [**28**] ▷ *Janice fixed some food for us.* Janice nous a préparé à manger.

fizzy *adj* gazeux *(f* gazeuse) ▷ *I don't like fizzy drinks.* Je n'aime pas les boissons gazeuses.

flag *n* drapeau *m* (*pl* drapeaux)

flame *n* flamme *f*

flan *n* ❶ *(sweet)* tarte *f* ▷ *a raspberry flan* une tarte aux framboises ❷ *(savoury)* quiche *f* ▷ *a cheese and onion flan* une quiche au fromage et aux oignons

flap *vb* battre [**9**] de ▷ *The bird flapped its wings.* L'oiseau battait des ailes.

flash *n* flash *m* (*pl* flashes) ▷ *Has your camera got a flash?* Est-ce que ton appareil photo a un flash?; **a flash of lightning** un éclair; **in a flash** en un clin d'œil

► *vb* ❶ clignoter [**28**] ▷ *The police car's blue light was flashing.* Le gyrophare de la voiture de police clignotait. ❷ projeter [**41**] ▷ *They flashed a torch in his face.* Ils lui ont projeté la lumière d'une torche en plein visage.; **She flashed her headlights.** Elle a fait un appel de phares.

flask *n (vacuum flask)* thermos *m*

flat *adj* ❶ plat(e) ▷ *flat shoes* des chaussures plates ❷ *(tyre)* crevé(e) ▷ *I've got a flat tyre.* J'ai un pneu crevé.

► *n* appartement *m* ▷ *She lives in a flat.* Elle habite un appartement.

flatter *vb* flatter [**28**]

flavour (*US* **flavor**) *n* ❶ *(taste)* goût *m* ▷ *It has a very strong flavour.* Ça a un goût très fort. ❷ *(variety)* parfum *m* ▷ *Which flavour of ice cream would you like?* Quel parfum de glace est-ce que tu veux?

flew *vb see* **fly**

flexible *adj* flexible ▷ *flexible working hours* les horaires flexibles

flick *vb* appuyer [**53**] sur; **to flick through a book** feuilleter [**41**] un livre

flight *n* vol *m* ▷ *What time is the flight to Paris?* À quelle heure est le vol pour Paris?; **a flight of stairs** un escalier

flight attendant *n* ❶ *(woman)* hôtesse de l'air *f* ❷ *(man)* steward *m*

fling *vb* jeter [**41**] ▷ *He flung the book onto the floor.* Il a jeté le livre par terre.

flippers *n* palmes *fpl*

float *vb* flotter [**28**] ▷ *A leaf was floating on the water.* Une feuille flottait sur l'eau.

flood *n* ❶ inondation *f* ▷ *We had a flood in the kitchen.* On a eu une inondation dans la cuisine. ❷ flot *m* ▷ *He received a flood of letters.* Il a reçu un flot de lettres.

► *vb* inonder [**28**] ▷ *The river has flooded the village.* La rivière a inondé le village.

floor *n* ❶ sol *m* ▷ *a tiled floor* un sol carrelé; **on the floor** par terre ❷ *(storey)* étage *m* ▷ *the first floor* le premier étage; **the ground floor** le rez-de-chaussée; **on the third floor** au troisième étage

floppy disk *n* disquette *f*

florist *n* fleuriste *mf*

flour *n* farine *f*

flow *vb* ❶ *(river)* couler [**28**] ❷ *(flow out)* s'écouler [**28**]

flower *n* fleur *f*

► *vb* fleurir [**38**]

flown *vb see* **fly**

flu *n* grippe *f* ▷ *She's got flu.* Elle a la grippe.

fluent *adj* **He speaks fluent French.** Il parle couramment le français.

flung *vb see* **fling**

flush *n (of toilet)* chasse d'eau *f*
▶ *vb* **to flush the toilet** tirer [**28**] la chasse

flute *n* flûte *f* ▷ *I play the flute.* Je joue de la flûte.

fly *n (insect)* mouche *f*
▶ *vb* ❶ voler [**28**] ▷ *The plane flew through the night.* L'avion a volé toute la nuit. ❷ *(passenger)* aller [**3**] en avion ▷ *He flew from Paris to New York.* Il est allé de Paris à New York en avion.

fly away *vb* s'envoler [**28**] ▷ *The bird flew away.* L'oiseau s'est envolé.

focus *n* **to be out of focus** être [**35**] flou ▷ *The house is out of focus in this photo.* La maison est floue sur cette photo.
▶ *vb* mettre [**47**] au point ▷ *Try to focus the binoculars.* Essaye de mettre les jumelles au point.; **to focus on something (1)** *(with camera, telescope)* régler [**34**] la mise au point sur quelque chose ▷ *The cameraman focused on the bird.* Le caméraman a réglé la mise au point sur l'oiseau. **(2)** *(concentrate)* se concentrer [**28**] sur quelque chose ▷ *Let's focus on the plot of the play.* Concentrons-nous sur l'intrigue de la pièce.

fog *n* brouillard *m*

foggy *adj* **It's foggy.** Il y a du brouillard.; **a foggy day** un jour de brouillard

foil *n (kitchen foil)* papier d'aluminium *m* ▷ *She wrapped the meat in foil.* Elle a enveloppé la viande dans du papier d'aluminium.

fold *n* pli *m*
▶ *vb* plier [**19**] ▷ *He folded the newspaper in half.* Il a plié le journal en deux.; **to fold something up** plier [**19**] quelque chose; **to fold one's arms** croiser [**28**] ses bras ▷ *She folded her arms.* Elle a croisé les bras.

folder *n* ❶ chemise *f* ▷ *She kept all her letters in a folder.* Elle gardait toutes ses lettres dans une chemise. ❷ *(ring binder)* classeur *m*

follow *vb* suivre [**81**] ▷ *She followed him.* Elle l'a suivi.

following *adj* suivant(e) ▷ *the following day* le jour suivant

fond *adj* **to be fond of somebody** aimer [**28**] beaucoup quelqu'un ▷ *I'm very fond of her.* Je l'aime beaucoup.

food *n* nourriture *f*; **We need to buy some food.** Nous devons acheter à manger.; **cat food** la nourriture pour chat; **dog food** la nourriture pour chien

fool *n* idiot *m*, idiote *f*

foot *n* ❶ *(of person)* pied *m* ▷ *My feet are aching.* J'ai mal aux pieds. ❷ *(of animal)* patte *f* ▷ *The dog's foot was injured.* Le chien était blessé à la patte.; **on foot** à pied ❸ *(12 inches)* pied *m*

- In France measurements are in metres and centimetres rather than feet and inches. A foot is about 30 centimetres.

Dave is 6 foot tall. Dave mesure un mètre quatre-vingts.; **That mountain is 5000 feet high.** Cette montagne fait mille six cents mètres de haut.

football *n* ❶ *(game)* football *m* ▷ *I like playing football.* J'aime jouer au football. ❷ *(ball)* ballon *m* ▷ *Paul threw the football over the fence.* Paul a envoyé le ballon par dessus la clôture.

footballer *n* footballeur *m*, footballeuse *f*

footie *n (informal)* foot *m*

footpath *n* sentier *m* ▷ *Jane followed the footpath through the forest.* Jane a suivi le sentier à travers la forêt.

for *prep*

> There are several ways of translating 'for'. Scan the examples to find one that is similar to what you want to say.

❶ pour ▷ *a present for me* un cadeau pour moi ▷ *the train for London* le train pour Londres ▷ *He works for the government.* Il travaille pour le gouvernement. ▷ *I'll do it for you.* Je vais le faire pour toi. ▷ *Can you do it for tomorrow?* Est-ce que vous pouvez le faire pour demain? ▷ *Are you for or against the idea?* Êtes-vous pour ou contre cette idée? ▷ *Oxford is famous for its university.* Oxford est célèbre pour son université.

> When referring to periods of time, use **pendant** for the future and completed actions in the past, and **depuis** (with the French verb in the present tense) for something that started in the past and is still going on.

❷ pendant ▷ *He worked in France for two years.* Il a travaillé en France pendant deux ans. ▷ *She will be away for a month.* Elle sera absente pendant un mois. ▷ *There are roadworks for three kilometres.* Il y a des travaux pendant trois kilomètres. ❸ depuis ▷ *He's been learning French for two years.* Il apprend le français depuis deux ans. ▷ *She's been away for a month.* Elle est absente depuis un mois.

> When talking about amounts of money, you do not translate 'for'.

▷ *I sold it for £5.* Je l'ai vendu cinq livres. ▷ *He paid fifty pence for his ticket.* Il a payé son billet cinquante pence.; **What's the French for 'lion'?** Comment dit-on 'lion' en français?; **It's time for lunch.** C'est l'heure du déjeuner.; **What for?** Pour quoi faire? ▷ *Give me some money! — What for?* Donne-moi de l'argent! — Pour quoi faire?; **What's it for?** Ça sert à quoi?; **for sale** à vendre ▷ *The factory's for sale.* L'usine est en vente.

forbid *vb* défendre **[88]**; **to forbid somebody to do something** défendre **[88]** à quelqu'un de faire

a b c d e f g h i j k l m n o p q r s t u v w x y z

quelque chose ▷ *I forbid you to go out tonight!* Je te défends de sortir ce soir.

forbidden *adj* défendu(e) ▷ *Smoking is strictly forbidden.* Il est strictement défendu de fumer.

force *n* force *f* ▷ *the force of the explosion* la force de l'explosion; **in force** en vigueur ▷ *No-smoking rules are now in force.* Un règlement qui interdit de fumer est maintenant en vigueur.
▶ *vb* forcer [**12**] ▷ *They forced him to open the safe.* Ils l'ont obligé à ouvrir le coffre-fort.

forecast *n* **the weather forecast** la météo

forehead *n* front *m*

foreign *adj* étranger (*f* étrangère)

foreigner *n* étranger *m*, étrangère *f*

forest *n* forêt *f*

forever *adv* ❶ pour toujours ▷ *He's gone forever.* Il est parti pour toujours. ❷ (*always*) toujours ▷ *She's forever complaining.* Elle est toujours en train de se plaindre.

forgave *vb see* **forgive**

forge *vb* contrefaire [**36**] ▷ *She tried to forge his signature.* Elle a essayé de contrefaire sa signature.

forged *adj* faux (*f* fausse) ▷ *forged banknotes* des faux billets

forget *vb* oublier [**19**] ▷ *I've forgotten his name.* J'ai oublié son nom.

forgive *vb* **to forgive somebody** pardonner [**28**] à quelqu'un ▷ *I forgive you.* Je te pardonne.; **to forgive somebody for doing something** pardonner [**28**] à quelqu'un d'avoir fait quelque chose ▷ *She forgave him for forgetting her birthday.* Elle lui a pardonné d'avoir oublié son anniversaire.

forgot, forgotten *vb see* **forget**

fork *n* ❶ (*for eating*) fourchette *f* ❷ (*for gardening*) fourche *f* ❸ (*in road*) bifurcation *f*

form *n* ❶ (*paper*) formulaire *m* ▷ *to fill in a form* remplir un formulaire ❷ (*type*) forme *f* ▷ *I'm against hunting in any form.* Je suis contre la chasse sous toutes ses formes.; **in top form** en pleine forme; **She's in the fourth form.** Elle est en troisième.

formal *adj* ❶ (*occasion*) officiel (*f* officielle) ▷ *a formal dinner* un dîner officiel ❷ (*person*) guindé(e) ❸ (*language*) soutenu(e) ▷ *In English, 'residence' is a formal term.* En anglais, 'residence' est un terme soutenu.; **formal clothes** une tenue habillée; **He's got no formal education.** Il n'a pas fait beaucoup d'études.

former *adj* ancien (*f* ancienne) ▷ *a former pupil* un ancien élève

fortnight *n* **a fortnight** quinze jours ▷ *I'm going on holiday for a fortnight.* Je pars en vacances pendant quinze jours.

fortunate *adj* **to be fortunate** avoir [**8**] de la chance ▷ *He was extremely fortunate to survive.* Il a eu énormément de chance de survivre.; **It's fortunate that I remembered the map.** C'est une chance que j'aie pris la carte.

fortunately *adv* heureusement ▷ *Fortunately, it didn't rain.* Heureusement, il n'a pas plu.

fortune *n* fortune *f* ▷ *Kate earns a fortune!* Kate gagne une fortune!; **to tell somebody's fortune** dire [27] la bonne aventure à quelqu'un

forty *num* quarante ▷ *He's forty.* Il a quarante ans.

forward *adv* **to move forward** avancer [12]
▶ *vb* faire [36] suivre ▷ *He forwarded all Janette's letters.* Il a fait suivre toutes les lettres de Janette.

forward slash *n* barre oblique *f*

foster child *n* enfant adoptif *m*, enfant adoptive *f*

fought *vb see* **fight**

foul *adj* infect(e) ▷ *The weather was foul.* Le temps était infect.
▶ *n* faute *f* ▷ *Ferguson committed a foul.* Ferguson a fait une faute.

fountain *n* fontaine *f*

fountain pen *n* stylo à encre *m*

four *num* quatre ▷ *She's four.* Elle a quatre ans.

fourteen *num* quatorze ▷ *I'm fourteen.* J'ai quatorze ans.

fourteenth *adj* quatorzième ▷ *the fourteenth floor* le quatorzième étage; **the fourteenth of August** le quatorze août

fourth *adj* quatrième ▷ *the fourth floor* le quatrième étage; **the fourth of July** le quatre juillet

fox *n* renard *m*

fragile *adj* fragile

frame *n (for picture)* cadre *m*

France *n* France *f*; **in France** en France; **to France** en France; **He's from France.** Il est français.

frantic *adj* **I was going frantic.** J'étais dans tous mes états.; **to be frantic with worry** être [35] fou d'inquiétude

fraud *n* ❶ *(crime)* fraude *f* ▷ *He was jailed for fraud.* On l'a mis en prison pour fraude. ❷ *(person)* imposteur *m* ▷ *He's not a real doctor, he's a fraud.* Ce n'est pas un vrai médecin, c'est un imposteur.

freckles *npl* taches de rousseur *fpl*

free *adj* ❶ *(free of charge)* gratuit(e) ▷ *a free brochure* une brochure gratuite ❷ *(not busy, not taken)* libre ▷ *Is this seat free?* Est-ce que cette place est libre? ▷ *Are you free after school?* Tu es libre après l'école?
▶ *vb* libérer [34]

freedom *n* liberté *f*

freeway *n (US)* autoroute *f*

freeze *vb* ❶ geler [43] ▷ *The water had frozen.* L'eau avait gelé. ❷ *(food)* congeler [1] ▷ *She froze the rest of the raspberries.* Elle a congelé le reste des framboises.

freezer *n* congélateur *m*

freezing *adj* **It's freezing!** *(informal)* Il fait un froid de canard!; **I'm freezing!** *(informal)* Je suis gelé!; **3 degrees below freezing** moins trois

French *n (language)* français *m* ▷ *Do you speak French?* Est-ce que tu parles français?; **the French** *(people)* les Français
▶ *adj* français(e) ▷ *She's French.* Elle est française.

French beans *npl* haricots verts *mpl*
French fries *npl* frites *fpl*
French kiss *n* baiser profond *m*
Frenchman *n* Français *m*
French windows *npl* porte-fenêtre *fsg* (*pl* portes-fenêtres)
Frenchwoman *n* Française *f*
frequent *adj* fréquent(e) ▷ *frequent showers* des averses fréquentes; **There are frequent buses to the town centre.** Il y a beaucoup de bus pour le centre ville.
fresh *adj* frais (*f* fraîche); **I need some fresh air.** J'ai besoin de prendre l'air.
Friday *n* vendredi *m* ▷ *on Friday* vendredi ▷ *on Fridays* le vendredi ▷ *every Friday* tous les vendredis
fridge *n* frigo *m*
fried *adj* frit(e) ▷ *fried vegetables* des légumes frits; **a fried egg** un œuf sur le plat
friend *n* ami *m*, amie *f*
▶ *vb* ajouter [**28**] comme ami(e) ▷ *I've friended her on Facebook.* Elle est devenue mon amie sur Facebook.
friendly *adj* ❶ gentil (*f* gentille) ▷ *She's really friendly.* Elle est vraiment gentille. ❷ accueillant(e) ▷ *Liverpool is a very friendly city.* Liverpool est une ville très accueillante.
friendship *n* amitié *f*
fright *n* peur *f* ▷ *I got a terrible fright!* Ça m'a fait une peur terrible!
frighten *vb* faire [**36**] peur à ▷ *Horror films frighten him.* Les films d'horreur lui font peur.
frightened *adj* **to be frightened** avoir [**8**] peur ▷ *I'm frightened!* J'ai peur!; **to be frightened of something** avoir [**8**] peur de quelque chose ▷ *Anna's frightened of spiders.* Anna a peur des araignées.
frightening *adj* effrayant(e)
fringe *n* (*of hair*) frange *f* ▷ *She's got a fringe.* Elle a une frange.
frog *n* grenouille *f*; **frogs' legs** les cuisses de grenouille
from *prep* de ▷ *Where do you come from?* D'où venez-vous? ▷ *I come from Perth.* Je viens de Perth.; **from ... to ...** de ... à ... ▷ *He flew from London to Paris.* Il a pris l'avion de Londres à Paris.; **from ... onwards** à partir de ... ▷ *We'll be at home from 7 o'clock onwards.* Nous serons chez nous à partir de sept heures.
front *n* devant *m* ▷ *the front of the house* le devant de la maison; **in front** devant ▷ *the car in front* la voiture de devant; **in front of** devant ▷ *in front of the house* devant la maison ▷ *the car in front of us* la voiture devant nous; **in the front** (*of car*) à l'avant ▷ *I was sitting in the front.* J'étais assis à l'avant.; **at the front of the train** à l'avant du train
▶ *adj* ❶ de devant ▷ *the front row* la rangée de devant ❷ avant ▷ *the front seats of the car* les sièges avant de la voiture; **the front door** la porte d'entrée
frontier *n* frontière *f*
frost *n* gel *m*

frosty *adj* **It's frosty today.** Il gèle aujourd'hui.
frown *vb* froncer [**12**] les sourcils ▷ *He frowned.* Il a froncé les sourcils.
froze *vb see* **freeze**
frozen *adj (food)* surgelé(e) ▷ *frozen chips* des frites surgelées
fruit *n* fruit *m*; **fruit juice** le jus de fruits; **a fruit salad** une salade de fruits
fruit machine *n* machine à sous *f*
frustrated *adj* frustré(e)
fry *vb* faire [**36**] frire ▷ *Fry the onions for 5 minutes.* Faites frire les oignons pendant cinq minutes.
frying pan *n* poêle *f*
fuel *n (for car, aeroplane)* carburant *m* ▷ *to run out of fuel* avoir une panne de carburant
full *adj, adv* ❶ plein(e) ▷ *The tank's full.* Le réservoir est plein. ❷ complet (*f* complète) ▷ *He asked for full details about the job.* Il a demandé des renseignements complets sur le poste.; **your full name** vos nom et prénoms ▷ *My full name is Ian John Marr.* Je m'appelle Ian John Marr.; **I'm full.** *(after meal)* J'ai bien mangé.; **at full speed** à toute vitesse ▷ *He drove at full speed.* Il conduisait à toute vitesse.; **There was a full moon.** C'était la pleine lune.
full stop *n* point *m*
full-time *adj, adv* à plein temps ▷ *She's got a full-time job.* Elle a un travail à plein temps. ▷ *She works full-time.* Elle travaille à plein temps.
fully *adv* complètement ▷ *He hasn't fully recovered from his illness.* Il n'est pas complètement remis de sa maladie.
fumes *npl* fumées *fpl*; **exhaust fumes** les gaz d'échappement *mpl*
fun *adj* marrant(e) ▷ *She's a fun person.* Elle est marrante.
▶ *n* **to have fun** s'amuser [**28**] ▷ *We had great fun playing in the snow.* Nous nous sommes bien amusés à jouer dans la neige.; **for fun** pour rire ▷ *He entered the competition just for fun.* Il a participé à la compétition juste pour rire.; **to make fun of somebody** se moquer [**28**] de quelqu'un ▷ *They made fun of him.* Ils se sont moqués de lui.; **It's fun!** C'est chouette!; **Have fun!** Amuse-toi bien!
funds *npl* fonds *mpl* ▷ *to raise funds* collecter des fonds
funeral *n* enterrement *m*
funfair *n* fête foraine *f*
funny *adj* ❶ *(amusing)* drôle ▷ *It was really funny.* C'était vraiment drôle. ❷ *(strange)* bizarre ▷ *There's something funny about him.* Il est un peu bizarre.
fur *n* ❶ fourrure *f* ▷ *a fur coat* un manteau de fourrure ❷ poil *m* ▷ *the dog's fur* le poil du chien
furious *adj* furieux (*f* furieuse) ▷ *Dad was furious with me.* Papa était furieux contre moi.
furniture *n* meubles *mpl* ▷ *a piece of furniture* un meuble
further *adv, adj* plus loin ▷ *London is further from Manchester than Leeds is.*

Londres est plus loin de Manchester que Leeds.; **How much further is it?** C'est encore loin?

further education *n* enseignement postscolaire *m*

fuse *n* fusible *m* ▷ *The fuse has blown.* Le fusible a sauté.

fuss *n* agitation *f* ▷ *What's all the fuss about?* Qu'est-ce que c'est que toute cette agitation?; **to make a fuss** faire [**36**] des histoires ▷ *He's always making a fuss about nothing.* Il fait toujours des histoires pour rien.

fussy *adj* difficile ▷ *She is very fussy about her food.* Elle est très difficile sur la nourriture.

future *n* ❶ avenir *m* ▷ *What are your plans for the future?* Quels sont vos projets pour l'avenir?; **in future** à l'avenir ▷ *Be more careful in future.* Sois plus prudent à l'avenir. ❷ *(in grammar)* futur *m* ▷ *Put this sentence into the future.* Mettez cette phrase au futur.

g

gain *vb* **to gain weight** prendre [**65**] du poids; **to gain speed** prendre [**65**] de la vitesse

gallery *n* musée *m* ▷ *an art gallery* un musée d'art

gamble *vb* jouer [**28**] ▷ *He gambled £100 at the casino.* Il a joué cent livres au casino.

gambling *n* jeu *m* ▷ *He likes gambling.* Il aime le jeu.

game *n* ❶ jeu *m* (*pl* jeux) ▷ *The children were playing a game.* Les enfants jouaient à un jeu. ❷ *(sport)* match *m* ▷ *a game of football* un match de football; **a game of cards** une partie de cartes

gamer *n* ❶ *(on computer)* joueur sur ordinateur *m*, joueuse sur ordinateur *f* ❷ *(on mobile phone)* joueur sur téléphone portable *m*,

joueuse sur téléphone portable *f*
gang *n* bande *f*
gangster *n* gangster *m*
gap *n* ❶ trou *m* ▷ *There's a gap in the hedge.* Il y a un trou dans la haie. ❷ intervalle *m* ▷ *a gap of four years* un intervalle de quatre ans
gap year *n* année sabbatique avant d'aller à l'université
garage *n* garage *m*
garbage *n* ordures *fpl*
garden *n* jardin *m*
gardener *n* jardinier *m* ▷ *He's a gardener.* Il est jardinier.
gardening *n* jardinage *m* ▷ *Margaret loves gardening.* Margaret aime le jardinage.
garlic *n* ail *m*
garment *n* vêtement *m*
gas *n* ❶ gaz *m*; **a gas cooker** une cuisinière à gaz; **a gas cylinder** une bouteille de gaz; **a gas fire** un radiateur à gaz; **a gas leak** une fuite de gaz ❷ *(US: petrol)* essence *f*
gasoline *n (US)* essence *f*
gate *n* ❶ *(of garden)* portail *m* ❷ *(of field)* barrière *f* ❸ *(at airport)* porte *f*
gather *vb (assemble)* se rassembler [**28**] ▷ *People gathered in front of Buckingham Palace.* Les gens se sont rassemblés devant Buckingham Palace.; **to gather speed** prendre [**65**] de la vitesse ▷ *The train gathered speed.* Le train a pris de la vitesse.
gave *vb see* **give**
gay *adj* homosexuel (*f* homosexuelle)
GCSE *n* brevet des collèges *m*
gear *n* ❶ *(in car)* vitesse *f* ▷ *in first gear* en première vitesse ▷ *to change gear* changer de vitesse ❷ matériel *m* ▷ *camping gear* le matériel de camping; **your sports gear** *(clothes)* tes affaires de sport
gear lever *n* levier de vitesse *m*
gearshift *n (US)* levier de vitesse *m*
geese *npl see* **goose**
gel *n* gel *m*; **hair gel** le gel pour les cheveux
Gemini *n* Gémeaux *mpl* ▷ *I'm Gemini.* Je suis Gémeaux.
gender *n* ❶ *(of person)* sexe *m* ❷ *(of noun)* genre *m*
general *n* général *m* (*pl* généraux) ▶ *adj* général(e) (*mpl* généraux); **in general** en général
general election *n* élections législatives *fpl*
general knowledge *n* connaissances générales *fpl*
generally *adv* généralement ▷ *I generally go shopping on Saturday.* Généralement, je fais mes courses le samedi.
generation *n* génération *f* ▷ *the younger generation* la nouvelle génération
generous *adj* généreux (*f* généreuse) ▷ *That's very generous of you.* C'est très généreux de votre part.
genetically-modified *adj* génétiquement modifié(e)
genetics *n* génétique *f*
Geneva *n* Genève; **in Geneva** à Genève; **to Geneva** à Genève; **Lake Geneva** le lac Léman

a b c d e f g h i j k l m n o p q r s t u v w x y z

genius *n* génie *m* ▷ *She's a genius!* C'est un génie!

gentle *adj* doux (*f* douce)

gentleman *n* monsieur *m* (*pl* messieurs)

gently *adv* doucement

gents *n* toilettes pour hommes *fpl* ▷ *Can you tell me where the gents is, please?* Pouvez-vous me dire où sont les toilettes, s'il vous plaît?; **'gents'** *(on sign)* 'messieurs'

genuine *adj* ❶ *(real)* véritable ▷ *These are genuine diamonds.* Ce sont de véritables diamants. ❷ *(sincere)* sincère ▷ *She's a very genuine person.* C'est quelqu'un de très sincère.

geography *n* géographie *f*

gerbil *n* gerbille *f*

germ *n* microbe *m*

German *n* ❶ *(person)* Allemand *m*, Allemande *f* ❷ *(language)* allemand ▷ *Do you speak German?* Parlez-vous allemand?
▶ *adj* allemand(e)

Germany *n* Allemagne *f*; **in Germany** en Allemagne; **to Germany** en Allemagne

get *vb*

> There are several ways of translating 'get'. Scan the examples to find one that is similar to what you want to say.

❶ *(have, receive)* avoir [**8**] ▷ *I got lots of presents.* J'ai eu beaucoup de cadeaux. ▷ *He got first prize.* Il a eu le premier prix. ▷ *He got good exam results.* Il a eu de bons résultats aux examens. ▷ *How many have you got?* Combien en avez-vous? ❷ *(fetch)* aller [**3**] chercher ▷ *Quick, get help!* Allez vite chercher de l'aide! ❸ *(catch)* attraper [**28**] ▷ *They've got the thief.* Ils ont attrapé le voleur. ❹ *(train, bus)* prendre [**65**] ▷ *I'm getting the bus into town.* Je prends le bus pour aller en ville. ❺ *(understand)* comprendre [**65**] ▷ *I don't get it.* Je ne comprends pas. ❻ *(go)* aller [**3**] ▷ *How do you get to the castle?* Comment est-ce qu'on va au château? ❼ *(arrive)* arriver [**5**] ▷ *He should get here soon.* Il devrait arriver bientôt. ❽ *(become)* devenir [**25**] ▷ *to get old* devenir vieux; **to get something done** faire [**36**] faire quelque chose ▷ *to get one's hair cut* se faire couper les cheveux; **to get something for somebody** trouver [**28**] quelque chose pour quelqu'un ▷ *The librarian got the book for me.* Le bibliothécaire m'a trouvé le livre.; **to have got to do something** devoir [**26**] faire quelque chose ▷ *I've got to tell him.* Je dois le lui dire.

get away *vb* s'échapper [**28**] ▷ *One of the burglars got away.* L'un des cambrioleurs s'est échappé.

get back *vb* ❶ rentrer [**68**] ▷ *What time did you get back?* Tu es rentré à quelle heure? ❷ récupérer [**34**] ▷ *He got his money back.* Il a récupéré son argent.

get in *vb* rentrer [**68**] ▷ *What time did you get in last night?* Tu es rentré à quelle heure hier soir?

get into *vb* monter [**48**] dans ▷ *Sharon got into the car.* Sharon est montée dans la voiture.

get off *vb (vehicle, bike)* descendre [**24**] de ▷ *Isobel got off the train.* Isobel est descendue du train.

get on *vb* ❶ *(vehicle)* monter [**48**] dans ▷ *Phyllis got on the bus.* Phyllis est montée dans le bus. ❷ *(bike)* enfourcher [**28**] ▷ *Carol got on her bike.* Carol a enfourché son vélo.; **to get on with somebody** s'entendre [**88**] avec quelqu'un ▷ *He doesn't get on with his parents.* Il ne s'entend pas avec ses parents. ▷ *We got on really well.* Nous nous sommes très bien entendus.

get out *vb* sortir [**79**] ▷ *Hélène got out of the car.* Hélène est sortie de la voiture. ▷ *Get out!* Sortez!; **to get something out** sortir [**79**] quelque chose ▷ *She got the map out.* Elle a sorti la carte.

get over *vb* se remettre [**47**] ▷ *She never got over his death.* Elle ne s'est jamais remise de sa mort.

get together *vb* se retrouver [**28**] ▷ *Could we get together this evening?* Pourrait-on se retrouver ce soir?

get up *vb* se lever [**43**] ▷ *What time do you get up?* Tu te lèves à quelle heure?

ghost *n* fantôme *m*

giant *adj* énorme ▷ *They ate a giant meal.* Ils ont mangé un énorme repas.
▸ *n* géant *m*, géante *f*

gift *n* ❶ *(present)* cadeau *m (pl* cadeaux) ❷ *(talent)* don *m*; **to have a gift for something** être [**35**] doué pour quelque chose ▷ *Dave has a gift for painting.* Dave est doué pour la peinture.

gin *n* gin *m*

ginger *n* gingembre *m* ▷ *Add a teaspoon of ginger.* Ajoutez une cuillère à café de gingembre.
▸ *adj* roux *(f* rousse) ▷ *Chris has ginger hair.* Chris a les cheveux roux.

giraffe *n* girafe *f*

girl *n* ❶ fille *f* ▷ *They've got a girl and two boys.* Ils ont une fille et deux garçons. ❷ *(young)* petite fille *f* ▷ *a five-year-old girl* une petite fille de cinq ans ❸ *(older)* jeune fille *f* ▷ *a sixteen-year-old girl* une jeune fille de seize ans ▷ *an English girl* une jeune Anglaise

girlfriend *n* ❶ *(lover)* copine *f* ▷ *Damon's girlfriend is called Justine.* La copine de Damon s'appelle Justine. ❷ *(friend)* amie *f* ▷ *She often went out with her girlfriends.* Elle sortait souvent avec ses amies.

give *vb* donner [**28**]; **to give something to somebody** donner [**28**] quelque chose à quelqu'un ▷ *He gave me £10.* Il m'a donné dix livres.; **to give something back to somebody** rendre [**7**] quelque chose à quelqu'un ▷ *I gave the book back to him.* Je lui ai rendu le livre.; **to give way** *(in traffic)* céder [**34**] la priorité

give in *vb* céder [**34**] ▷ *His mum gave in and let him go out.* Sa mère a cédé et l'a laissé sortir.

give out *vb* distribuer [**28**] ▷ *He*

a b c d e f g h i j k l m n o p q r s t u v w x y z

gave out the exam papers. Il a distribué les sujets d'examen.

give up *vb* laisser [**28**] tomber ▷ *I couldn't do it, so I gave up.* Je n'arrivais pas à le faire, alors j'ai laissé tomber.; **to give up doing something** arrêter [**28**] de faire quelque chose ▷ *He gave up smoking.* Il a arrêté de fumer.; **to give oneself up** se rendre [**7**] ▷ *The thief gave himself up.* Le voleur s'est rendu.

glad *adj* content(e) ▷ *She's glad she's done it.* Elle est contente de l'avoir fait.

glamorous *adj* ❶ *(person)* glamour ▷ *She's very glamourous.* Elle est très glamour. ❷ *(job)* prestigieux (*f* prestigieuse); **to have a glamorous lifestyle** vivre [**91**] comme une star

glass *n* verre *m* ▷ *a glass of milk* un verre de lait

glasses *npl* lunettes *fpl* ▷ *Jean-Pierre wears glasses.* Jean-Pierre porte des lunettes.

glider *n* planeur *m*

global *adj* mondial(e) (*mpl* mondiaux); **on a global scale** à l'échelle mondiale

global warming *n* réchauffement de la planète *m*

globe *n* globe *m*

gloomy *adj* ❶ morose ▷ *She looked gloomy when she heard the news.* Elle avait l'air morose quand elle a entendu les nouvelles. ❷ lugubre ▷ *He lives in a small gloomy flat.* Il habite un petit appartement lugubre.

glorious *adj* magnifique

glove *n* gant *m*

glue *n* colle *f*
▸ *vb* coller [**28**]

GM *adj (= genetically modified)* génétiquement modifié(e) ▷ *GM foods* les aliments génétiquement modifiés *mpl*

go *n* **to have a go at doing something** essayer [**59**] de faire quelque chose ▷ *He had a go at making a cake.* Il a essayé de faire un gâteau.; **Whose go is it?** À qui le tour?
▸ *vb* ❶ aller [**3**] ▷ *I'm going to the cinema tonight.* Je vais au cinéma ce soir. ❷ *(leave)* partir [**57**] ▷ *Where's Pierre? — He's gone.* Où est Pierre? — Il est parti. ❸ *(go away)* s'en aller [**3**] ▷ *I'm going now.* Je m'en vais. ❹ *(vehicle)* marcher [**28**] ▷ *My car won't go.* Ma voiture ne marche pas.; **to go home** rentrer [**68**] à la maison ▷ *I go home at about 4 o'clock.* Je rentre à la maison vers quatre heures.; **to go for a walk** aller [**3**] se promener ▷ *Shall we go for a walk?* Si on allait se promener?; **How did it go?** Comment est-ce que ça s'est passé?; **I'm going to do it tomorrow.** Je vais le faire demain.; **It's going to be difficult.** Ça va être difficile.

go after *vb* suivre [**81**] ▷ *Quick, go after them!* Vite, suivez-les!

go ahead *vb* **The meeting will go ahead as planned.** La réunion aura bien lieu comme prévu.; **We'll go ahead with your plan.** Nous allons mettre votre projet à exécution.; **Go ahead!** Vas-y!

go away *vb* s'en aller [**3**] ▷ *Go away!* Allez-vous-en!

go back *vb*

> Use **retourner** in most cases, unless you are entering a building (usually your home) when you would use **rentrer**.

❶ retourner [**72**] ▷ *We went back to the same place.* Nous sommes retournés au même endroit. ❷ rentrer [**68**] ▷ *After the film he went back home.* Il est rentré chez lui après le film.

go by *vb* passer [**58**] ▷ *Two police officers went by.* Deux policiers sont passés.

go down *vb* ❶ *(person)* descendre [**24**] ▷ *to go down the stairs* descendre l'escalier ❷ *(decrease)* baisser [**28**] ▷ *The price of computers has gone down.* Le prix des ordinateurs a baissé. ❸ *(deflate)* se dégonfler [**28**] ▷ *My airbed kept going down.* Mon matelas pneumatique se dégonflait constamment.; **My brother's gone down with flu.** Mon frère a attrapé la grippe.

go for *vb (attack)* attaquer [**28**] ▷ *Suddenly the dog went for me.* Soudain, le chien m'a attaqué.; **Go for it!** *(go on!)* Vas-y, fonce!

go in *vb* entrer [**32**] ▷ *He knocked on the door and went in.* Il a frappé à la porte et il est entré.

go off *vb* ❶ *(bomb)* exploser [**28**] ▷ *The bomb went off.* La bombe a explosé. ❷ *(alarm, gun)* se déclencher [**28**] ▷ *The fire alarm went off.* L'alarme à incendie s'est déclenchée. ❸ *(alarm clock)* sonner [**28**] ▷ *My alarm clock goes off at seven every morning.* Mon réveil sonne à sept heures tous les matins. ❹ *(food)* tourner [**28**] ▷ *The milk's gone off.* Le lait a tourné. ❺ *(go away)* partir [**57**] ▷ *He went off in a huff.* Il est parti de mauvaise humeur.

go on *vb* ❶ *(happen)* se passer [**58**] ▷ *What's going on?* Qu'est-ce qui se passe? ❷ *(carry on)* continuer [**28**] ▷ *The concert went on until 11 o'clock at night.* Le concert a continué jusqu'à onze heures du soir.; **to go on doing something** continuer [**28**] à faire quelque chose ▷ *He went on reading.* Il a continué à lire.; **to go on at somebody** être [**35**] sur le dos de quelqu'un ▷ *My parents always go on at me.* Mes parents sont toujours sur mon dos.; **Go on!** Allez! ▷ *Go on, tell me what the problem is!* Allez, dis-moi quel est le problème!

go out *vb* ❶ *(person)* sortir [**79**] ▷ *Are you going out tonight?* Tu sors ce soir?; **to go out with somebody** sortir [**79**] avec quelqu'un ▷ *Are you going out with him?* Est-ce que tu sors avec lui? ❷ *(light, fire, candle)* s'éteindre [**60**] ▷ *Suddenly the lights went out.* Soudain, les lumières se sont éteintes.

go past *vb* **to go past something** passer [**58**] devant quelque chose ▷ *He went past the shop.* Il est passé devant la boutique.

go round *vb* **to go round a corner** prendre [**65**] un tournant; **to go round to somebody's house** aller [**3**] chez quelqu'un; **to go round a museum** visiter [**28**] un musée; **to go round the shops** faire [**36**] les boutiques; **There's a bug going round.** Il y a un microbe qui circule.

go through *vb* traverser [**28**] ▷ *We went through Paris to get to Rennes.* Nous avons traversé Paris pour aller à Rennes.

go up *vb* ❶ *(person)* monter [**48**] ▷ *to go up the stairs* monter l'escalier ❷ *(increase)* augmenter [**28**] ▷ *The price has gone up.* Le prix a augmenté.; **to go up in flames** s'embraser [**28**] ▷ *The whole factory went up in flames.* L'usine toute entière s'est embrasée.

go with *vb* aller [**3**] avec ▷ *Does this blouse go with that skirt?* Est-ce que ce chemisier va avec cette jupe?

goal *n* but *m* ▷ *to score a goal* marquer un but

goalkeeper *n* gardien de but *m*

goat *n* chèvre *f*; **goat's cheese** le fromage de chèvre

god *n* dieu *m* (*pl* dieux) ▷ *I believe in God.* Je crois en Dieu.

goddaughter *n* filleule *f*

godfather *n* parrain *m*

godmother *n* marraine *f*

godson *n* filleul *m*

goggles *npl* ❶ *(of welder, mechanic etc)* lunettes de protection *fpl* ❷ *(of swimmer)* lunettes de plongée *fpl*

gold *n* or *m* ▷ *a gold necklace* un collier en or

goldfish *n* poisson rouge *m* ▷ *I've got five goldfish.* J'ai cinq poissons rouges.

golf *n* golf *m* ▷ *My dad plays golf.* Mon père joue au golf.; **a golf club** un club de golf

golf course *n* terrain de golf *m*

gone *vb see* **go**

good *adj* ❶ bon (*f* bonne) ▷ *It's a very good film.* C'est un très bon film. ▷ *Vegetables are good for you.* Les légumes sont bons pour la santé.; **to be good at something** être [**35**] bon en quelque chose ▷ *Jane's very good at maths.* Jane est très bonne en maths. ❷ *(kind)* gentil (*f* gentille) ▷ *That's very good of you.* C'est très gentil de votre part. ❸ *(not naughty)* sage ▷ *Be good!* Sois sage!; **for good** pour de bon ▷ *One day he left for good.* Un jour il est parti pour de bon.; **Good morning!** Bonjour!; **Good afternoon!** Bonjour!; **Good evening!** Bonsoir!; **Good night!** Bonne nuit!; **It's no good complaining.** Cela ne sert à rien de se plaindre.

goodbye *excl* au revoir!

Good Friday *n* Vendredi saint *m*

good-looking *adj* beau (*f* belle, *mpl* beaux) ▷ *He's very good-looking.* Il est très beau.

goods *npl (in shop)* marchandises *fpl*; **a goods train** un train de marchandises

google *vb* googler [**28**]

goose *n* oie *f*

gorgeous *adj* ❶ superbe ▷ *She's*

gorgeous! Elle est superbe! ❷ splendide ▷ *The weather was gorgeous.* Il a fait un temps splendide.

gorilla *n* gorille *m*

gossip *n* ❶ *(rumours)* cancans *mpl* ▷ *Tell me the gossip!* Raconte-moi les cancans! ❷ *(woman)* commère *f* ▷ *She's such a gossip!* C'est une vraie commère! ❸ *(man)* bavard *m* ▷ *What a gossip!* Quel bavard! ▶ *vb* ❶ *(chat)* bavarder [**28**] ▷ *They were always gossiping.* Elles étaient tout le temps en train de bavarder. ❷ *(about somebody)* faire [**36**] des commérages ▷ *They gossiped about her.* Elles faisaient des commérages à son sujet.

got *vb see* **get**

gotten *vb (US) see* **get**

government *n* gouvernement *m*

GP *n* médecin généraliste *m*

grab *vb* saisir [**38**]

graceful *adj* élégant(e)

grade *n (at school)* note *f* ▷ *He got good grades in his exams.* Il a eu de bonnes notes à ses examens.

grade school *n (US)* école primaire *f*

gradual *adj* progressif *(f* progressive)

gradually *adv* peu à peu ▷ *We gradually got used to it.* Nous nous y sommes habitués peu à peu.

graffiti *npl* graffiti *mpl*

grain *n* grain *m*

gram *n* gramme *m*

grammar *n* grammaire *f*

grammar school *n* ❶ collège *m* ❷ lycée *m*

In France pupils go to a **collège** between the ages of 11 and 15, and then to a **lycée** until the age of 18. French schools are mostly non-selective.

grammatical *adj* grammatical(e) *(mpl* grammaticaux)

gramme *n* gramme *m* ▷ *500 grammes of cheese* cinq cents grammes de fromage

grand *adj* somptueux *(f* somptueuse) ▷ *Samantha lives in a very grand house.* Samantha habite une maison somptueuse.

grandchild *n* petit-fils *m*, petite-fille *f*; **my grandchildren** mes petits-enfants *mpl*

granddad *n* papi *m* ▷ *my granddad* mon papi

granddaughter *n* petite-fille *f (pl* petites-filles)

grandfather *n* grand-père *m (pl* grands-pères) ▷ *my grandfather* mon grand-père

grandma *n* mamie *f* ▷ *my grandma* ma mamie

grandmother *n* grand-mère *f (pl* grands-mères) ▷ *my grandmother* ma grand-mère

grandpa *n* papi *m* ▷ *my grandpa* mon papi

grandparents *npl* grands-parents *mpl* ▷ *my grandparents* mes grands-parents

grandson *n* petit-fils *m (pl* petits-fils)

granny *n* mamie *f* ▷ *my granny* ma mamie

grape *n* raisin *m*

a b c d e f **g** h i j k l m n o p q r s t u v w x y z

grapefruit *n* pamplemousse *m*
graph *n* graphique *m*
graphics *npl* ❶ *(computer generated)* images de synthèse *fpl* ❷ *(graphic design)* graphisme *mpl* ▷ *I designed the graphics, she wrote the text.* J'ai fait le graphisme, elle a écrit le texte.; **He works in computer graphics.** Il fait de l'infographie.
grass *n* herbe *f* ▷ *The grass is long.* L'herbe est haute.; **to cut the grass** tondre [**69**] le gazon
grasshopper *n* sauterelle *f*
grate *vb* râper [**28**] ▷ *to grate some cheese* râper du fromage
grateful *adj* reconnaissant(e)
grave *n* tombe *f*
gravel *n* gravier *m*
graveyard *n* cimetière *m*
gravy *n* sauce au jus de viande *f*
grease *n* lubrifiant *m*
greasy *adj* gras (*f* grasse) ▷ *He has greasy hair.* Il a les cheveux gras.
great *adj* ❶ génial(e) (*mpl* géniaux) ▷ *That's great!* C'est génial! ❷ grand(e) ▷ *a great mansion* un grand manoir
Great Britain *n* Grande-Bretagne *f*; **in Great Britain** en Grande-Bretagne; **to Great Britain** en Grande-Bretagne; **I'm from Great Britain.** Je suis britannique.
great-grandfather *n* arrière-grand-père *m* (*pl* arrière-grands-pères)
great-grandmother *n* arrière-grand-mère *f* (*pl* arrière-grands-mères)
Greece *n* Grèce *f*; **in Greece** en Grèce; **to Greece** en Grèce
greedy *adj* ❶ *(for food)* gourmand(e) ▷ *I want some more cake. — Don't be so greedy!* Je veux encore du gâteau. — Ne sois pas si gourmand! ❷ *(for money)* avide
Greek *n* ❶ *(person)* Grec *m*, Grecque *f* ❷ *(language)* grec *m*
▶ *adj* grec (*f* grecque) ▷ *She's Greek.* Elle est grecque.
green *adj* ❶ vert(e) ▷ *a green light* un feu vert ▷ *a green salad* une salade verte ❷ *(movement, candidate)* écologiste ▷ *the Green Party* le parti écologiste
▶ *n* vert *m* ▷ *a dark green* un vert foncé; **greens** *(vegetables)* les légumes verts *mpl*; **the Greens** *(party)* les Verts *mpl*
greengrocer's *n* marchand de fruits et légumes *m*
greenhouse *n* serre *f*; **the greenhouse effect** l'effet de serre *m*
Greenland *n* Groenland *m*
greetings card *n* carte de vœux *f*
grew *vb see* **grow**
grey *adj* gris(e) ▷ *She's got grey hair.* Elle a les cheveux gris.; **He's going grey.** Il grisonne.
grey-haired *adj* grisonnant(e)
grid *n* ❶ *(in road)* grille *f* ❷ *(of electricity)* réseau *m* (*pl* réseaux)
grief *n* chagrin *m*
grill *n (of cooker)* gril *m*; **a mixed grill** un assortiment de grillades
▶ *vb* **to grill something** faire [**36**] griller quelque chose

grin *vb* sourire [**74**] ▷ *Dave grinned at me.* Dave m'a souri.
▶ *n* large sourire *m*
grip *vb* saisir [**38**]
grit *n* gravillon *m*
groan *vb* gémir [**38**] ▷ *He groaned with pain.* Il a gémi sous l'effet de la douleur.
▶ *n (of pain)* gémissement *m*
grocer *n* épicier *m* ▷ *He's a grocer.* Il est épicier.
groceries *npl* provisions *fpl*
grocer's *n* épicerie *f*
grocery store *n (US)* épicerie *f*
groom *n (bridegroom)* marié *m* ▷ *the groom and his best man* le marié et son témoin
gross *adj (revolting)* dégoûtant(e) ▷ *It was really gross!* C'était vraiment dégoûtant!
ground *n* ❶ *(earth)* sol *m* ▷ *The ground's wet.* Le sol est mouillé. ❷ *(for sport)* terrain *m* ▷ *a football ground* un terrain de football ❸ *(reason)* raison *f* ▷ *We've got grounds for complaint.* Nous avons des raisons de nous plaindre.; **on the ground** par terre ▷ *We sat on the ground.* Nous nous sommes assis par terre.
ground floor *n* rez-de-chaussée *m*; **on the ground floor** au rez-de-chaussée
group *n* groupe *m*
grow *vb* ❶ *(plant)* pousser [**28**] ▷ *Grass grows quickly.* L'herbe pousse vite. ❷ *(person, animal)* grandir [**38**] ▷ *Haven't you grown!* Comme tu as grandi! ❸ *(increase)* augmenter [**28**] ▷ *The number of unemployed people has grown.* Le nombre de chômeurs a augmenté. ❹ *(cultivate)* faire [**36**] pousser ▷ *My Dad grows potatoes.* Mon père fait pousser des pommes de terre.; **to grow a beard** se laisser [**28**] pousser la barbe; **He's grown out of his jacket.** Sa veste est devenue trop petite pour lui.
grow up *vb* grandir [**38**] ▷ *Oh, grow up!* Ne fais pas l'enfant!
growl *vb* grogner [**28**]
grown *vb see* **grow**
growth *n* croissance *f* ▷ *economic growth* la croissance économique
grudge *n* rancune *f*; **to bear a grudge against somebody** garder [**28**] rancune à quelqu'un
gruesome *adj* horrible
guarantee *n* garantie *f*; **a five-year guarantee** une garantie de cinq ans
▶ *vb* garantir [**38**] ▷ *I can't guarantee he'll come.* Je ne peux pas garantir qu'il viendra.
guard *vb* garder [**28**] ▷ *They guarded the palace.* Ils gardaient le palais.; **to guard against something** protéger [**66**] contre quelque chose
▶ *n (of train)* chef de train *m*; **a security guard** un vigile; **a guard dog** un chien de garde
guess *vb* deviner [**28**] ▷ *Guess what this is?* Devine ce que c'est!; **to guess wrong** se tromper [**28**] ▷ *Janice guessed wrong.* Janice s'est trompée.

▶ *n* supposition *f* ▷ *It's just a guess.* C'est une simple supposition.; **Have a guess!** Devine!

guest *n* ❶ invité *m*, invitée *f* ▷ *We have guests staying with us.* Nous avons des invités. ❷ *(of hotel)* client *m*, cliente *f*

guesthouse *n* petit hôtel *m*

guide *n* ❶ *(book, person)* guide *m* ▷ *We bought a guide to Paris.* Nous avons acheté un guide sur Paris. ▷ *The guide showed us round the castle.* Le guide nous a fait visiter le château. ❷ *(girl guide)* éclaireuse *f*; **the Guides** les Éclaireuses

guidebook *n* guide *m*

guide dog *n* chien d'aveugle *m*

guilty *adj* coupable ▷ *to feel guilty* se sentir coupable ▷ *She was found guilty.* Elle a été reconnue coupable.

guinea pig *n* cobaye *m*

guitar *n* guitare *f* ▷ *I play the guitar.* Je joue de la guitare.

gum *n (sweet)* chewing-gum *m*; **gums** *(in mouth)* les gencives *fpl*

gun *n* ❶ *(small)* revolver *m* ❷ *(rifle)* fusil *m*

gunpoint *n* **at gunpoint** sous la menace d'une arme

guy *n* type *m* ▷ *He's a nice guy.* C'est un type sympa.

gym *n* gym *f* ▷ *I go to the gym every day.* Je vais tous les jours à la gym.; **gym classes** les cours de gym *mpl*

gymnast *n* gymnaste *mf* ▷ *She's a gymnast.* Elle est gymnaste.

gymnastics *n* gymnastique *f* ▷ *to do gymnastics* faire de la gymnastique

gypsy *n* Tzigane *m*, Tzigane *f*

habit *n* habitude *f* ▷ *a bad habit* une mauvaise habitude

had *vb see* **have**

hadn't = **had not**

hail *n* grêle *f*
▶ *vb* grêler [**28**] ▷ *It's hailing.* Il grêle.

hair *n* ❶ cheveux *mpl* ▷ *She's got long hair.* Elle a les cheveux longs.; **to brush one's hair** se brosser [**28**] les cheveux ▷ *I'm brushing my hair.* Je me brosse les cheveux.; **to wash one's hair** se laver [**28**] les cheveux ▷ *I need to wash my hair.* Il faut que je me lave les cheveux.; **to have one's hair cut** se faire [**36**] couper les cheveux ▷ *I've just had my hair cut.* Je viens de me faire couper les cheveux.; **a hair (1)** *(from head)* un cheveu **(2)** *(from body)* un poil ❷ *(fur of animal)* pelage *m*

hairbrush *n* brosse à cheveux *f*

haircut *n* coupe *f*; **to have a haircut** se faire [**36**] couper les cheveux ▷ *I've just had a haircut.* Je viens de me faire couper les cheveux.

hairdresser *n* coiffeur *m*, coiffeuse *f* ▷ *He's a hairdresser.* Il est coiffeur.

hairdresser's *n* coiffeur *m* ▷ *at the hairdresser's* chez le coiffeur

hair dryer *n* sèche-cheveux *m* (*pl* sèche-cheveux)

hair gel *n* gel pour les cheveux *m*

hairgrip *n* pince à cheveux *f*

hair spray *n* laque *f*

hairstyle *n* coiffure *f*

half *n* ❶ moitié *f* ▷ *half of the cake* la moitié du gâteau ❷ *(ticket)* billet demi-tarif *m* ▷ *A half to York, please.* Un billet demi-tarif pour York, s'il vous plaît.; **two and a half** deux et demi; **half an hour** une demi-heure; **half past ten** dix heures et demie; **half a kilo** cinq cents grammes; **to cut something in half** couper [**28**] quelque chose en deux
▶ *adj, adv* ❶ demi(e) ▷ *a half chicken* un demi-poulet ❷ à moitié ▷ *He was half asleep.* Il était à moitié endormi.

half-brother *n* demi-frère *m* (*pl* demi-frères)

half-hour *n* demi-heure *f*

half-price *adj, adv* **at half-price** à moitié prix

half-sister *n* demi-sœur *f* (*pl* demi-sœurs)

half-term *n* petites vacances *fpl*

- There are two half-term holidays in France: **les vacances de la Toussaint** (in October/ November) and **les vacances de février** (in February).

half-time *n* mi-temps *f*

halfway *adv* ❶ à mi-chemin ▷ *halfway between Oxford and London* à mi-chemin entre Oxford et Londres ❷ à la moitié ▷ *halfway through the chapter* à la moitié du chapitre

hall *n* ❶ *(in house)* entrée *f* ❷ salle *f* ▷ *the village hall* la salle des fêtes

Hallowe'en *n* veille de la Toussaint *f*

hallway *n* vestibule *m*

ham *n* jambon *m* ▷ *a ham sandwich* un sandwich au jambon

hamburger *n* hamburger *m*

hammer *n* marteau *m* (*pl* marteaux)

hamster *n* hamster *m*

hand *n* ❶ *(of person)* main *f*; **to give somebody a hand** donner [**28**] un coup de main à quelqu'un ▷ *Can you give me a hand?* Tu peux me donner un coup de main?; **on the one hand ..., on the other hand ...** d'une part ..., d'autre part ... ❷ *(of clock)* aiguille *f*
▶ *vb* passer [**58**] ▷ *He handed me the book.* Il m'a passé le livre.; **to hand something in** rendre [**7**] quelque chose ▷ *He handed his exam paper in.* Il a rendu sa copie d'examen.; **to hand something out** distribuer [**28**] quelque chose ▷ *The teacher handed out the books.* Le professeur a distribué les livres.; **to hand something over** remettre [**47**] quelque chose ▷ *She handed the keys over to me.* Elle m'a remis les clés.

handbag *n* sac à main *m*

handcuffs *npl* menottes *fpl*

handkerchief *n* mouchoir *m*

handle *n* ❶ *(of door)* poignée *f* ❷ *(of cup)* anse *f* ❸ *(of knife)* manche *m* ❹ *(of saucepan)* queue *f*
▶ *vb* **He handled it well.** Il s'en est bien tiré.; **Kath handled the travel arrangements.** Kath s'est occupée de l'organisation du voyage.; **She's good at handling children.** Elle sait bien s'y prendre avec les enfants.

handlebars *npl* guidon *msg*

handmade *adj* fait à la main (*f* faite à la main)

hands-free kit *n (phone)* kit mains libres *m*

handsome *adj* beau (*f* belle, *mpl* beaux) ▷ *He's handsome.* Il est beau.

handwriting *n* écriture *f*

handy *adj* ❶ pratique ▷ *This knife's very handy.* Ce couteau est très pratique. ❷ sous la main ▷ *Have you got a pen handy?* Est-ce que tu as un stylo sous la main?

hang *vb* ❶ accrocher [**28**] ▷ *Mike hung the painting on the wall.* Mike a accroché le tableau au mur. ❷ pendre [**88**] ▷ *They hanged the criminal.* Ils ont pendu le criminel.

hang around *vb* traîner [**28**] ▷ *On Saturdays we hang around in the park.* Le samedi nous traînons dans le parc.

hang on *vb* patienter [**28**] ▷ *Hang on a minute please.* Patientez une minute s'il vous plaît.

hang up *vb* ❶ *(clothes)* accrocher [**28**] ▷ *Hang your jacket up on the hook.* Accrochez votre veste au portemanteau. ❷ *(phone)* raccrocher [**28**] ▷ *Don't hang up!* Ne raccroche pas!; **to hang up on someone** raccrocher [**28**] au nez de quelqu'un ▷ *He always hangs up on me.* Il me raccroche toujours au nez.

hanger *n (coat hanger)* cintre *m*

hangover *n* gueule de bois *f* ▷ *I've got a terrible hangover.* J'ai une gueule de bois terrible.

happen *vb* se passer [**58**] ▷ *What's happened?* Qu'est-ce qui s'est passé?; **as it happens** justement ▷ *As it happens, I don't want to go.* Justement, je ne veux pas y aller.

happily *adv* ❶ joyeusement ▷ *'Don't worry!' he said happily.* 'Ne te fais pas de souci!' dit-il joyeusement. ❷ *(fortunately)* heureusement ▷ *Happily, everything went well.* Heureusement, tout s'est bien passé.

happiness *n* bonheur *m*

happy *adj* heureux (*f* heureuse) ▷ *Janet looks happy.* Janet a l'air heureuse.; **I'm very happy with your work.** Je suis très satisfait de ton travail.; **Happy birthday!** Bon anniversaire!

harassment *n* harcèlement *m* ▷ *police harassment* le harcèlement policier

harbour (*US* **harbor**) *n* port *m*

hard *adj, adv* ❶ dur(e) ▷ *This cheese is very hard.* Ce fromage est très dur. ▷ *He's worked very hard.* Il a travaillé très dur. ❷ difficile ▷ *This question's too hard for me.* Cette question est trop difficile pour moi.

hard disk *n (of computer)* disque dur *m*

hardly *adv* **I've hardly got any money.** Je n'ai presque pas d'argent.; **I hardly know you.** Je te connais à peine.; **hardly ever** presque jamais

hard up *adj* fauché(e)

harm *vb* **to harm somebody** faire [**36**] du mal à quelqu'un ▷ *I didn't mean to harm you.* Je ne voulais pas te faire de mal.; **to harm something** nuire [**23**] à quelque chose ▷ *Chemicals harm the environment.* Les produits chimiques nuisent à l'environnement.

harmful *adj* nocif (*f* nocive) ▷ *harmful chemicals* des produits chimiques nocifs

harmless *adj* inoffensif (*f* inoffensive) ▷ *Most spiders are harmless.* La plupart des araignées sont inoffensives.

has *vb see* **have**

hasn't = **has not**

hat *n* chapeau *m* (*pl* chapeaux)

hate *vb* détester [**28**] ▷ *I hate maths.* Je déteste les maths.

hatred *n* haine *f*

haunted *adj* hanté(e) ▷ *a haunted house* une maison hantée

have *vb* ❶ avoir [**8**] ▷ *Have you got a sister?* Tu as une sœur? ▷ *He's got blue eyes.* Il a les yeux bleus. ▷ *I've got a cold.* J'ai un rhume. ▷ *He's done it, hasn't he?* Il l'a fait, non? ❷ être [**35**]

The perfect tense of some verbs is formed with **être**.

▷ *They have arrived.* Ils sont arrivés. ❸ prendre [**65**] ▷ *He had his breakfast.* Il a pris son petit déjeuner.; **to have got to do something** devoir [**26**] faire quelque chose ▷ *She's got to do it.* Elle doit le faire.; **to have a party** faire [**36**] une fête; **to have one's hair cut** se faire [**36**] couper les cheveux

haven't = **have not**

hay *n* foin *m*

hay fever *n* rhume des foins *m* ▷ *Do you get hay fever?* Est-ce que vous êtes sujet au rhume des foins?

hazelnut *n* noisette *f*

he *pron* il ▷ *He loves dogs.* Il aime les chiens.

head *n* ❶ *(of person)* tête *f* ▷ *The wine went to my head.* Le vin m'est monté à la tête. ❷ *(of private or primary school)* directeur *m*, directrice *f* ❸ *(of state secondary school)* proviseur *m* ❹ *(leader)* chef *m* ▷ *a head of state* un chef d'État; **to have a head for figures** être [**35**] doué pour les chiffres; **Heads or tails? — Heads.** Pile ou face? — Face.

▶ *vb* **to head for something** se diriger [**45**] vers quelque chose ▷ *They headed for the church.* Ils se sont dirigés vers l'église.

headache *n* **I've got a headache.** J'ai mal à la tête.

headlight *n* phare *m*

headline *n* titre *m*

headmaster *n* ❶ *(of private or primary school)* directeur *m* ❷ *(of state secondary school)* proviseur *m*

headmistress *n* ❶ *(of private or primary school)* directrice *f* ❷ *(of state secondary school)* proviseur *m*

headphones *npl* écouteurs *mpl*

headquarters *npl* *(of organization)* siège *msg*

headteacher *n* ❶ *(of private or primary school)* directeur *m*, directrice *f* ❷ *(of state secondary school)* proviseur *m* ▷ *She's a headteacher.* Elle est proviseur.

heal *vb* cicatriser [**28**] ▷ *The wound soon healed.* La blessure a vite cicatrisé.

health *n* santé *f*

healthy *adj* ❶ *(person)* en bonne santé ▷ *Lesley's a healthy person.* Lesley est en bonne santé. ❷ *(climate, food)* sain(e) ▷ *a healthy diet* une alimentation saine

heap *n* tas *m* ▷ *a rubbish heap* un tas d'ordures

hear *vb* ❶ entendre [**88**] ▷ *He heard the dog bark.* Il a entendu le chien aboyer.; **to hear about something** entendre [**88**] parler de quelque chose ❷ *(news)* apprendre [**65**] ▷ *Did you hear the good news?* Est-ce que tu as appris la bonne nouvelle?; **to hear from**

somebody avoir [**8**] des nouvelles de quelqu'un ▷ *I haven't heard from him recently.* Je n'ai pas eu de ses nouvelles récemment.

heart *n* cœur *m*; **to learn something by heart** apprendre [**65**] quelque chose par cœur; **the ace of hearts** l'as de cœur

heart attack *n* crise cardiaque *f*

heartbroken *adj* **to be heartbroken** avoir [**8**] le cœur brisé

heat *n* chaleur *f*
▶ *vb* faire [**36**] chauffer ▷ *Heat gently for 5 minutes.* Faire chauffer à feu doux pendant cinq minutes.

heat up *vb* ❶ *(cooked food)* faire [**36**] réchauffer ▷ *He heated the soup up.* Il a fait réchauffer la soupe. ❷ *(water, oven)* chauffer [**28**] ▷ *The water is heating up.* L'eau chauffe.

heater *n* radiateur *m* ▷ *an electric heater* un radiateur électrique

heather *n* bruyère *f*

heating *n* chauffage *m*

heaven *n* paradis *m*

heavy *adj* ❶ lourd(e) ▷ *This bag's very heavy.* Ce sac est très lourd.; **heavy rain** une grosse averse ❷ *(busy)* chargé(e) ▷ *I've got a very heavy week ahead.* Je vais avoir une semaine très chargée.; **to be a heavy drinker** être [**35**] un gros buveur

he'd = **he would**; **he had**

hedge *n* haie *f*

hedgehog *n* hérisson *m*

heel *n* talon *m*

height *n* ❶ *(of person)* taille *f* ❷ *(of object)* hauteur *f* ❸ *(of mountain)* altitude *f*

held *vb see* **hold**

helicopter *n* hélicoptère *m*

hell *n* enfer *m*

he'll = **he will**; **he shall**

hello *excl* bonjour!

helmet *n* casque *m*

help *vb* aider [**28**] ▷ *Can you help me?* Est-ce que vous pouvez m'aider?; **Help!** Au secours!; **Help yourself!** Servez-vous!; **He can't help it.** Il n'y peut rien.
▶ *n* aide *f* ▷ *Do you need any help?* Vous avez besoin d'aide?

helpful *adj* serviable ▷ *He was very helpful.* Il a été très serviable.

hen *n* poule *f*

her *adj* son *m* ▷ *her father* son père sa *f* ▷ *her mother* sa mère; ses *pl* ▷ *her parents* ses parents

> **sa** becomes **son** before a vowel sound.

her friend (1) *(male)* son ami **(2)** *(female)* son amie

> Do not use **son/sa/ses** with parts of the body.

▷ *She's going to wash her hair.* Elle va se laver les cheveux. ▷ *She's cleaning her teeth.* Elle se brosse les dents. ▷ *She's hurt her foot.* Elle s'est fait mal au pied.
▶ *pron* ❶ la ▷ *I can see her.* Je la vois. l'

> **la** becomes **l'** before a vowel sound.

▷ *I saw her.* Je l'ai vue. ❷ lui

> Use **lui** when 'her' means 'to her'.

▷ *I gave her a book.* Je lui ai donné un livre. ▷ *I told her the truth.* Je lui ai dit la vérité. ❸ elle

Use **elle** after prepositions.

▷ *I'm going with her.* Je vais avec elle.

elle is also used in comparisons.

▷ *I'm older than her.* Je suis plus âgé qu'elle.

herb *n* herbe *f*; **herbs** les fines herbes *fpl* ▷ *What herbs do you use in this sauce?* Quelles fines herbes utilise-t-on pour cette sauce?

here *adv* ici ▷ *I live here.* J'habite ici.; **here is ...** voici ... ▷ *Here's Helen.* Voici Helen. ▷ *Here he is!* Le voici!; **here are ...** voici ... ▷ *Here are the books.* Voici les livres.

hero *n* héros *m* ▷ *He's a real hero!* C'est un véritable héros!

heroin *n* héroïne *f* ▷ *Heroin is a hard drug.* L'héroïne est une drogue dure.; **a heroin addict** un héroïnomane ▷ *She's a heroin addict.* C'est une héroïnomane.

heroine *n* héroïne *f* ▷ *the heroine of the novel* l'héroïne du roman

hers *pron* le sien ▷ *Is this her coat? — No, hers is black.* C'est son manteau? — Non, le sien est noir.
la sienne ▷ *Is this her car? — No, hers is white.* C'est sa voiture? — Non, la sienne est blanche.
les siens ▷ *my parents and hers* mes parents et les siens
les siennes ▷ *my reasons and hers* mes raisons et les siennes; **Is this hers?** C'est à elle? ▷ *This book is hers.* Ce livre est à elle. ▷ *Whose is this? — It's hers.* C'est à qui? — À elle.

herself *pron* ❶ se ▷ *She's hurt herself.* Elle s'est blessée. ❷ *(after preposition)* elle ▷ *She talked mainly about herself.* Elle a surtout parlé d'elle. ❸ elle-même ▷ *She did it herself.* Elle l'a fait elle-même.; **by herself** toute seule ▷ *She doesn't like travelling by herself.* Elle n'aime pas voyager toute seule.

he's = **he is**; **he has**

hesitate *vb* hésiter [**28**]

heterosexual *adj* hétérosexuel (*f* hétérosexuelle)

hi *excl* salut!

hiccups *npl* **to have hiccups** avoir [**8**] le hoquet

hide *vb* se cacher [**28**] ▷ *He hid behind a bush.* Il s'est caché derrière un buisson.; **to hide something** cacher [**28**] quelque chose ▷ *Paula hid the present.* Paula a caché le cadeau.

hide-and-seek *n* **to play hide-and-seek** jouer [**28**] à cache-cache

hi-fi *n* chaîne hi-fi *f* (*pl* chaînes hi-fi)

high *adj, adv* ❶ haut(e) ▷ *It's too high.* C'est trop haut.; **How high is the wall?** Quelle est la hauteur du mur?; **The wall's 2 metres high.** Le mur fait deux mètres de haut. ❷ élevé(e) ▷ *a high price* un prix élevé; **at high speed** à grande vitesse; **It's very high in fat.** C'est très gras.; **She's got a very high voice.** Elle a la voix très aiguë.; **to be high** *(on drugs) (informal)* être [**35**] défoncé; **to get high** *(informal)*

se défoncer [**12**] ▷ *to get high on crack* se défoncer au crack
higher education *n* enseignement supérieur *m*
high-heeled *adj* à hauts talons ▷ *high-heeled shoes* des chaussures à hauts talons
high jump *n (sport)* saut en hauteur *m*
high-rise *n* tour *f* ▷ *I live in a high-rise.* J'habite dans une tour.
high school *n* ❶ collège *m* ❷ lycée *m*
hijack *vb* détourner [**28**]
hijacker *n* pirate de l'air *m*
hiking *n* **to go hiking** faire [**36**] une randonnée
hilarious *adj* hilarant(e) ▷ *It was hilarious!* C'était hilarant!
hill *n* colline *f* ▷ *She walked up the hill.* Elle a gravi la colline.
hill-walking *n* randonnée de basse montagne *f* ▷ *to go hill-walking* faire de la randonnée de basse montagne
him *pron* ❶ le ▷ *I can see him.* Je le vois.
l'

> **le** becomes **l'** before a vowel sound.

▷ *I saw him.* Je l'ai vu. ❷ lui

> Use **lui** when 'him' means 'to him', and after prepositions.

▷ *I gave him a book.* Je lui ai donné un livre. ▷ *I'm going with him.* Je vais avec lui.

> **lui** is also used in comparisons.

▷ *I'm older than him.* Je suis plus âgé que lui.
himself *pron* ❶ se ▷ *He's hurt himself.* Il s'est blessé. ❷ lui ▷ *He talked mainly about himself.* Il a surtout parlé de lui. ❸ lui-même ▷ *He did it himself.* Il l'a fait lui-même.; **by himself** tout seul ▷ *He was travelling by himself.* Il voyageait tout seul.
Hindu *adj* hindou(e) ▷ *a Hindu temple* un temple hindou
hip *n* hanche *f*
hippie *n* hippie *m*, hippie *f*
hippo *n* hippopotame *m*
hire *vb* ❶ louer [**28**] ▷ *to hire a car* louer une voiture ❷ *(person)* engager [**45**] ▷ *They hired a cleaner.* Ils ont engagé une femme de ménage.
▶ *n* location *f*; **car hire** location de voitures; **for hire** à louer
his *adj* son *m* ▷ *his father* son père; sa *f* ▷ *his mother* sa mère; ses *pl* ▷ *his parents* ses parents

> **sa** becomes **son** before a vowel sound.

his friend (1) *(male)* son ami **(2)** *(female)* son amie

> Do not use **son/sa/ses** with parts of the body.

▷ *He's going to wash his hair.* Il va se laver les cheveux. ▷ *He's cleaning his teeth.* Il se brosse les dents. ▷ *He's hurt his foot.* Il s'est fait mal au pied.
▶ *pron* le sien *m* ▷ *Is this his coat? — No, his is black.* C'est son manteau? — Non, le sien est noir.; la sienne *f* ▷ *Is this his car? — No, his is white.* C'est sa voiture? — Non, la sienne est blanche.

les siens *mpl* ▷ *my parents and his* mes parents et les siens les siennes *fpl* ▷ *my reasons and his* mes raisons et les siennes; **Is this his?** C'est à lui? ▷ *This book is his.* Ce livre est à lui. ▷ *Whose is this? — It's his.* C'est à qui? — À lui.

history *n* histoire *f*

hit *vb* ❶ frapper [**28**] ▷ *Andrew hit him.* Andrew l'a frappé. ❷ renverser [**28**] ▷ *He was hit by a car.* Il a été renversé par une voiture. ❸ toucher [**28**] ▷ *The arrow hit the target.* La flèche a touché la cible.; **to hit it off with somebody** bien s'entendre [**88**] avec quelqu'un ▷ *She hit it off with his parents.* Elle s'est bien entendue avec ses parents.
▶ *n* ❶ *(song)* tube *m* ▷ *Madonna's latest hit* le dernier tube de Madonna ❷ *(success)* succès *m* ▷ *The film was a massive hit.* Le film a eu un immense succès.

hitch *n* contretemps *m* ▷ *There's been a slight hitch.* Il y a eu un léger contretemps.

hitchhike *vb* faire [**36**] de l'auto-stop

hitchhiker *n* auto-stoppeur *m*, auto-stoppeuse *f*

hitchhiking *n* auto-stop *m* ▷ *Hitchhiking can be dangerous.* Il peut être dangereux de faire de l'auto-stop.

HIV-negative *adj* séronégatif (*f* séronégative)

HIV-positive *adj* séropositif (*f* séropositive)

hobby *n* passe-temps favori *m* ▷ *What are your hobbies?* Quels sont tes passe-temps favoris?

hockey *n* hockey *m* ▷ *I play hockey.* Je joue au hockey.

hold *vb* ❶ *(hold on to)* tenir [**83**] ▷ *She held the baby.* Elle tenait le bébé. ❷ *(contain)* contenir [**83**] ▷ *This bottle holds one litre.* Cette bouteille contient un litre.; **to hold a meeting** avoir [**8**] une réunion; **Hold the line!** *(on telephone)* Ne quittez pas!; **Hold it!** *(wait)* Attends!; **to get hold of something** *(obtain)* trouver [**28**] quelque chose ▷ *I couldn't get hold of it.* Je n'ai pas réussi à en trouver.

hold on *vb* ❶ *(keep hold)* tenir [**83**] bon ▷ *Hold on! I'll help you get down.* Tiens bon! Je vais t'aider à descendre.; **to hold on to something** se cramponner [**28**] à quelque chose ▷ *He held on to the chair.* Il se cramponnait à la chaise. ❷ *(wait)* attendre [**7**] ▷ *Hold on, I'm coming!* Attends, je viens!; **Hold on!** *(on telephone)* Ne quittez pas!

hold up *vb* **to hold up one's hand** lever [**43**] la main ▷ *Pierre held up his hand.* Pierre a levé la main.; **to hold somebody up** *(delay)* retenir [**83**] quelqu'un ▷ *I was held up at the office.* J'ai été retenu au bureau.; **to hold up a bank** *(rob)* braquer [**28**] une banque *(informal)*

hold-up *n* ❶ *(at bank)* hold-up *m* ❷ *(delay)* retard *m* ❸ *(traffic jam)* bouchon *m*

hole *n* trou *m*

holiday *n* ❶ vacances *fpl* ▷ *our holidays in France* nos vacances en France; **on holiday** en vacances ▷ *to go on holiday* partir en vacances; **the school holidays** les vacances scolaires ❷ *(public holiday)* jour férié *m* ▷ *Next Wednesday is a holiday.* Mercredi prochain est un jour férié. ❸ *(day off)* jour de congé *m* ▷ *He took a day's holiday.* Il a pris un jour de congé.; **a holiday camp** un camp de vacances

Holland *n* Hollande *f*; **in Holland** en Hollande; **to Holland** en Hollande

hollow *adj* creux (*f* creuse)

holly *n* houx *m* ▷ *a sprig of holly* un brin de houx

holy *adj* saint(e)

home *n* maison *f*; **at home** à la maison; **Make yourself at home.** Faites comme chez vous.
▶ *adv* à la maison ▷ *I'll be home at 5 o'clock.* Je serai à la maison à cinq heures.; **to get home** rentrer [**68**] ▷ *What time did he get home?* Il est rentré à quelle heure?

homeland *n* patrie *f*

homeless *adj* sans abri; **the homeless** les sans-abri

home match *n* match à domicile *m*

home page *n* page d'accueil *f*

homesick *adj* **to be homesick** avoir [**8**] le mal du pays

homework *n* devoirs *mpl* ▷ *Have you done your homework?* Est-ce que tu as fait tes devoirs? ▷ *my geography homework* mes devoirs de géographie

homosexual *adj* homosexuel (*f* homosexuelle)
▶ *n* homosexuel *m*, homosexuelle *f*

honest *adj* ❶ *(trustworthy)* honnête ▷ *She's a very honest person.* Elle est très honnête. ❷ *(sincere)* franc (*f* franche) ▷ *He was very honest with her.* Il a été très franc avec elle.

honestly *adv* franchement ▷ *I honestly don't know.* Franchement, je n'en sais rien.

honesty *n* honnêteté *f*

honey *n* miel *m*

honeymoon *n* lune de miel *f*

honour (*US* **honor**) *n* honneur *m*

hood *n* ❶ *(on coat)* capuche *f* ❷ *(US: of car)* capot *m*

hook *n* crochet *m* ▷ *He hung the painting on the hook.* Il a suspendu le tableau au crochet.; **to take the phone off the hook** décrocher [**28**] le téléphone; **a fish-hook** un hameçon

hooligan *n* voyou *m* (*pl* voyoux)

hooray *excl* hourra!

Hoover® *n* aspirateur *m*

hoover *vb* passer [**58**] l'aspirateur ▷ *to hoover the lounge* passer l'aspirateur dans le salon

hope *vb* espérer [**34**] ▷ *I hope he comes.* J'espère qu'il va venir. ▷ *I'm hoping for good results.* J'espère avoir de bons résultats.; **I hope so.** Je l'espère.; **I hope not.** J'espère que non.
▶ *n* espoir *m*; **to give up hope** perdre [**61**] espoir ▷ *Don't give up*

hope! Ne perds pas espoir!

hopefully *adv* avec un peu de chance ▷ *Hopefully he'll make it in time.* Avec un peu de chance, il arrivera à temps.

hopeless *adj* nul (*f* nulle) ▷ *I'm hopeless at maths.* Je suis nul en maths.

horizon *n* horizon *m*

horizontal *adj* horizontal(e) (*mpl* horizontaux)

horn *n* ❶ klaxon *m* ▷ *He sounded his horn.* Il a klaxonné. ❷ cor *m* ▷ *I play the horn.* Je joue du cor.

horoscope *n* horoscope *m*

horrible *adj* horrible ▷ *What a horrible dress!* Quelle robe horrible!

horrifying *adj* effrayant(e)

horror *n* horreur *f*

horror film *n* film d'horreur *m*

horse *n* cheval *m* (*pl* chevaux)

horse-racing *n* courses de chevaux *fpl*

hose *n* tuyau *m* (*pl* tuyaux) ▷ *a garden hose* un tuyau d'arrosage

hospital *n* hôpital *m* (*pl* hôpitaux) ▷ *in hospital* à l'hôpital

hospitality *n* hospitalité *f*

host *n* hôte *m*, hôtesse *f* ▷ *Don't forget to write and thank your hosts.* N'oublie pas d'écrire à tes hôtes pour les remercier.

hostage *n* otage *m*; **to take somebody hostage** prendre [**65**] quelqu'un en otage

hostel *n* *(for refugees, homeless people)* foyer *m*; **a youth hostel** une auberge de jeunesse

hot *adj* ❶ *(warm)* chaud(e) ▷ *a hot bath* un bain chaud ▷ *a hot country* un pays chaud

> When you are talking about a person being hot, you use **avoir chaud**.

▷ *I'm hot.* J'ai chaud.

> When you mean that the weather is hot, you use **faire chaud**.

▷ *It's hot.* Il fait chaud. ❷ *(spicy)* épicé(e) ▷ *a very hot curry* un curry très épicé

hot dog *n* hot-dog *m*

hotel *n* hôtel *m* ▷ *We stayed in a hotel.* Nous avons logé à l'hôtel.

hour *n* heure *f* ▷ *She always takes hours to get ready.* Elle passe toujours des heures à se préparer.; **a quarter of an hour** un quart d'heure; **half an hour** une demi-heure; **two and a half hours** deux heures et demie

hourly *adj, adv* toutes les heures ▷ *There are hourly buses.* Il y a des bus toutes les heures.; **to be paid hourly** être [**35**] payé à l'heure

house *n* maison *f*; **at his house** chez lui; **We stayed at their house.** Nous avons séjourné chez eux.

housewife *n* femme au foyer *f* ▷ *She's a housewife.* Elle est femme au foyer.

housework *n* ménage *m*; **to do the housework** faire [**36**] le ménage

hovercraft *n* aéroglisseur *m*

how *adv* comment ▷ *How are you?* Comment allez-vous?; **How**

many? Combien?; **How many ...?** Combien de ...? ▷ *How many pupils are there in the class?* Combien d'élèves y a-t-il dans la classe?; **How much?** Combien?; **How much ...?** Combien de ...? ▷ *How much sugar do you want?* Combien de sucres voulez-vous?; **How old are you?** Quel âge as-tu?; **How far is it to Edinburgh?** Combien y a-t-il de kilomètres d'ici à Édimbourg?; **How long have you been here?** Depuis combien de temps êtes-vous là?; **How do you say 'apple' in French?** Comment dit-on 'apple' en français?

however *conj* pourtant ▷ *This, however, isn't true.* Pourtant, ce n'est pas vrai.

hug *vb* serrer [**28**] dans ses bras ▷ *He hugged her.* Il l'a serrée dans ses bras.

▶ *n* **to give somebody a hug** serrer [**28**] quelqu'un dans ses bras ▷ *She gave them a hug.* Elle les a serrés dans ses bras.

huge *adj* immense

hum *vb* fredonner [**28**]

human *adj* humain(e) ▷ *the human body* le corps humain

human being *n* être humain *m*

humour (*US* **humor**) *n* humour *m*; **to have a sense of humour** avoir [**8**] le sens de l'humour

hundred *num* **a hundred** cent ▷ *a hundred euros* cent euros; **five hundred** cinq cents; **five hundred and one** cinq cent un; **hundreds of people** des centaines de personnes

hung *vb see* **hang**

Hungarian *n* ❶ *(person)* Hongrois *m*, Hongroise *f* ❷ *(language)* hongrois *m*

▶ *adj* hongrois(e) ▷ *She's Hungarian.* Elle est hongroise.

Hungary *n* Hongrie *f*; **in Hungary** en Hongrie; **to Hungary** en Hongrie

hunger *n* faim *f*

hungry *adj* **to be hungry** avoir [**8**] faim ▷ *I'm hungry.* J'ai faim.

hunt *vb* ❶ *(animal)* chasser [**28**] ▷ *People used to hunt wild boar.* On chassait le sanglier autrefois.; **to go hunting** aller [**3**] à la chasse ❷ *(criminal)* pourchasser [**28**] ▷ *The police are hunting the killer.* La police pourchasse le meurtrier.; **to hunt for something** *(search)* chercher [**28**] quelque chose partout ▷ *I hunted everywhere for that book.* J'ai cherché ce livre partout.

hunting *n* chasse *f* ▷ *I'm against hunting.* Je suis contre la chasse.; **fox-hunting** la chasse au renard

hurdle *n* obstacle *m*

hurricane *n* ouragan *m*

hurry *vb* se dépêcher [**28**] ▷ *Sharon hurried back home.* Sharon s'est dépêchée de rentrer chez elle.; **Hurry up!** Dépêche-toi!

▶ *n* **to be in a hurry** être [**35**] pressé; **to do something in a hurry** faire [**36**] quelque chose en vitesse; **There's no hurry.** Rien ne presse.

hurt *vb* **to hurt somebody** (**1**) *(physically)* faire [**36**] mal à quelqu'un ▷ *You're hurting me!* Tu me fais mal! **(2)** *(emotionally)* blesser [**28**] quelqu'un ▷ *His remarks really hurt me.* Ses remarques m'ont vraiment blessé.; **to hurt oneself** se faire [**36**] mal ▷ *I fell over and hurt myself.* Je me suis fait mal en tombant.; **That hurts.** Ça fait mal. ▷ *It hurts to have a tooth out.* Ça fait mal de se faire arracher une dent.; **My leg hurts.** J'ai mal à la jambe. ▶ *adj* blessé(e) ▷ *Is he badly hurt?* Est-ce qu'il est grièvement blessé? ▷ *I was hurt by what he said.* J'ai été blessé par ce qu'il a dit.; **Luckily, nobody got hurt.** Heureusement, il n'y a pas eu de blessés.

husband *n* mari *m*

hut *n* hutte *f*

hymn *n* cantique *m*

hypermarket *n* hypermarché *m*

hyphen *n* trait d'union *m*

I *pron* ❶ je ▷ *I speak French.* Je parle français.

> **je** changes to **j'** before a vowel and most words beginning with 'h'.

j' ▷ *I love cats.* J'aime les chats. ❷ moi ▷ *Ann and I* Ann et moi

ice *n* ❶ glace *f* ▷ *There was ice on the lake.* Il y avait de la glace sur le lac. ❷ *(on road)* verglas *m*

iceberg *n* iceberg *m*

ice cream *n* glace *f* ▷ *vanilla ice cream* la glace à la vanille

ice cube *n* glaçon *m*

ice hockey *n* hockey sur glace *m*

Iceland *n* Islande *f*; **in Iceland** en Islande; **to Iceland** en Islande

ice rink *n* patinoire *f*

ice-skating *n* patinage sur glace *m*;

to go ice-skating faire [**36**] du patin à glace

icing *n (on cake)* glaçage *m*; **icing sugar** le sucre glace

icon *n* icône *f*

ICT *n* informatique *f*

icy *adj* glacial(e) (*mpl* glaciaux) ▷ *There was an icy wind.* Il y avait un vent glacial.; **The roads are icy.** Il y a du verglas sur les routes.

I'd = **I had**; **I would**

idea *n* idée *f* ▷ *Good idea!* Bonne idée!

ideal *adj* idéal(e) (*mpl* idéaux)

identical *adj* identique

identification *n* identification *f*

identify *vb* identifier [**19**]

identity card *n* carte d'identité *f*

idiot *n* idiot *m*, idiote *f*

idiotic *adj* stupide

i.e. *abbr* c.-à-d. (= *c'est-à-dire*)

if *conj* si ▷ *You can have it if you like.* Tu peux le prendre si tu veux.

s'

si changes to **s'** before **il** and **ils**.

▷ *Do you know if he's there?* Savez-vous s'il est là?; **if only** si seulement ▷ *If only I had more money!* Si seulement j'avais plus d'argent!; **if not** sinon ▷ *Are you coming? If not, I'll go with Mark.* Est-ce que tu viens? Sinon, j'irai avec Mark.

ignore *vb* **to ignore something** ne tenir [**83**] aucun compte de quelque chose ▷ *She ignored my advice.* Elle n'a tenu aucun compte de mes conseils.; **to ignore somebody** ignorer [**28**] quelqu'un ▷ *She saw me, but she ignored me.* Elle m'a vu, mais elle m'a ignoré.; **Just ignore him!** Ne fais pas attention à lui!

ill *adj (sick)* malade; **to be taken ill** tomber [**84**] malade ▷ *She was taken ill while on holiday.* Elle est tombée malade pendant qu'elle était en vacances.

I'll = **I will**

illegal *adj* illégal(e) (*mpl* illégaux)

illness *n* maladie *f*

illusion *n* illusion *f*

illustration *n* illustration *f*

image *n* image *f* ▷ *The company has changed its image.* La société a changé d'image.

imagination *n* imagination *f*

imagine *vb* imaginer [**28**] ▷ *You can imagine how I felt!* Tu peux imaginer ce que j'ai ressenti! ▷ *Is he angry? — I imagine so.* Est-ce qu'il est en colère? — J'imagine que oui.

imitate *vb* imiter [**28**]

imitation *n* imitation *f*

immediate *adj* immédiat(e)

immediately *adv* immédiatement ▷ *I'll do it immediately.* Je vais le faire immédiatement.

immigrant *n* immigré *m*, immigrée *f*

immigration *n* immigration *f*

impatience *n* impatience *f*

impatient *adj* impatient(e); **to get impatient** s'impatienter [**28**] ▷ *People are getting impatient.* Les gens commencent à s'impatienter.

impatiently *adv* avec impatience ▷ *We waited impatiently.* Nous avons attendu avec impatience.

importance *n* importance *f*
important *adj* important(e)
impossible *adj* impossible
impress *vb* impressionner [**28**] ▷ *She's trying to impress you.* Elle essaie de t'impressionner.
impressed *adj* impressionné(e) ▷ *I'm very impressed!* Je suis très impressionné!
impression *n* impression *f* ▷ *I was under the impression that ...* J'avais l'impression que ...
impressive *adj* impressionnant(e)
improve *vb* ❶ *(make better)* améliorer [**28**] ▷ *They have improved the service.* Ils ont amélioré le service. ❷ *(get better)* s'améliorer [**28**] ▷ *My French has improved.* Mon français s'est amélioré.
improvement *n* ❶ *(of condition)* amélioration *f* ▷ *It's a great improvement.* C'est une nette amélioration. ❷ *(of learner)* progrès *m* ▷ *There's been an improvement in his French.* Il a fait des progrès en français.
in *prep, adv*

> There are several ways of translating 'in'. Scan the examples to find one that is similar to what you want to say. For other expressions with 'in', see the verbs 'go', 'come', 'get', 'give' etc.

❶ dans ▷ *in the house* dans la maison ▷ *in the sixties* dans les années soixante ▷ *I'll see you in three weeks.* Je te verrai dans trois semaines. ❷ à ▷ *in the country* à la campagne ▷ *in school* à l'école ▷ *in London* à Londres ▷ *in spring* au printemps ▷ *in a loud voice* à voix haute ▷ *the boy in the blue shirt* le garçon à la chemise bleue ▷ *It was written in pencil.* C'était écrit au crayon. ❸ en ▷ *in French* en français ▷ *in summer* en été ▷ *in town* en ville ▷ *in good condition* en bon état

> When 'in' refers to a country which is feminine, use **en**; when the country is masculine, use **au**; when the country is plural, use **aux**.

▷ *in France* en France ▷ *in Portugal* au Portugal ▷ *in the United States* aux États-Unis ❹ de ▷ *the best pupil in the class* le meilleur élève de la classe ▷ *at 6 in the morning* à six heures du matin; **in the afternoon** l'après-midi; **You look good in that dress.** Tu es jolie avec cette robe.; **in time** à temps ▷ *We arrived in time for dinner.* Nous sommes arrivés à temps pour le dîner.; **in here** ici ▷ *It's hot in here.* Il fait chaud ici.; **in the rain** sous la pluie; **one person in ten** une personne sur dix; **to be in** *(at home, work)* être [**35**] là ▷ *He wasn't in.* Il n'était pas là.; **to ask somebody in** inviter [**28**] quelqu'un à entrer
inbox *n* boîte de réception *f*
include *vb* comprendre [**65**] ▷ *Service is not included.* Le service n'est pas compris.
including *prep* compris ▷ *It will be 200 euros, including tax.* Ça coûtera deux cents euros, toutes taxes

comprises.

income *n* revenu *m*

income tax *n* impôt sur le revenu *m*

inconsistent *adj* incohérent(e)

inconvenient *adj* **That's very inconvenient for me.** Ça ne m'arrange pas du tout.

incorrect *adj* incorrect(e)

increase *n* augmentation *f* ▷ *an increase in road accidents* une augmentation des accidents de la route
▶ *vb* augmenter [**28**]

incredible *adj* incroyable

indeed *adv* vraiment ▷ *It's very hard indeed.* C'est vraiment très difficile.; **Know what I mean? — Indeed I do.** Tu vois ce que je veux dire? — Oui, tout à fait.; **Thank you very much indeed!** Merci beaucoup!

independence *n* indépendance *f*

independent *adj* indépendant(e); **an independent school** une école privée

index *n (in book)* index *m*

index finger *n* index *m*

India *n* Inde *f*; **in India** en Inde; **to India** en Inde

Indian *n (person)* Indien *m*, Indienne *f*; **an American Indian** un Indien d'Amérique
▶ *adj* indien (*f* indienne)

indicate *vb* indiquer [**28**]

indicator *n (on car)* clignotant *m*

indigestion *n* indigestion *f*; **I've got indigestion.** J'ai une indigestion.

individual *adj* individuel (*f* individuelle)

indoor *adj* **an indoor swimming pool** une piscine couverte

indoors *adv* à l'intérieur ▷ *They're indoors.* Ils sont à l'intérieur.; **to go indoors** rentrer [**68**] ▷ *We'd better go indoors.* Nous ferions mieux de rentrer.

industrial *adj* industriel (*f* industrielle)

industrial estate *n* zone industrielle *f*

industry *n* industrie *f* ▷ *the tourist industry* l'industrie du tourisme

inevitable *adj* inévitable

inexperienced *adj* inexpérimenté(e)

infant school *n* **He's just started at infant school.** Il vient d'entrer au cours préparatoire.

CP (cours préparatoire) is the equivalent of first-year infants, and **CE1 (cours élémentaire première année)** the equivalent of second-year infants.

infection *n* infection *f* ▷ *an ear infection* une infection de l'oreille; **a throat infection** une angine

infectious *adj* contagieux (*f* contagieuse) ▷ *It's not infectious.* Ce n'est pas contagieux.

infinitive *n* infinitif *m*

inflation *n* inflation *f*

inform *vb* informer [**28**]; **to inform somebody of something** informer [**28**] quelqu'un de quelque chose ▷ *Nobody informed me of the new plan.* Personne ne m'a informé de ce nouveau projet.

informal *adj* ❶ *(person, party)* décontracté(e) ▷ *'informal dress'* 'tenue décontractée' ❷ *(colloquial)* familier (*f* familière) ▷ *informal language* le langage familier; **an informal visit** une visite non officielle

information *n* renseignements *mpl* ▷ *important information* les renseignements importants; **a piece of information** un renseignement; **Could you give me some information about trains to Paris?** Pourriez-vous me renseigner sur les trains pour Paris?

information office *n* bureau des renseignements *m* (*pl* bureaux des renseignements)

information technology *n* informatique *f*

infuriating *adj* exaspérant(e)

ingredient *n* ingrédient *m*

inherit *vb* hériter [**28**] de ▷ *She inherited her father's house.* Elle a hérité de la maison de son père.

initials *npl* initiales *fpl* ▷ *Her initials are CDT.* Ses initiales sont CDT.

injection *n* piqûre *f*

injure *vb* blesser [**28**]

injured *adj* blessé(e)

injury *n* blessure *f*

ink *n* encre *f*

in-laws *npl* beaux-parents *mpl*

innocent *adj* innocent(e)

insane *adj* fou (*f* folle)

inscription *n* inscription *f*

insect *n* insecte *m*

insect repellent *n* insectifuge *m*

inside *n* intérieur *m* ▶ *adv, prep* à l'intérieur ▷ *inside the house* à l'intérieur de la maison; **to go inside** rentrer [**68**]; **Come inside!** Rentrez!

insist *vb* insister [**28**] ▷ *I didn't want to, but he insisted.* Je ne voulais pas, mais il a insisté.; **to insist on doing something** insister [**28**] pour faire quelque chose ▷ *She insisted on paying.* Elle a insisté pour payer.; **He insisted he was innocent.** Il affirmait qu'il était innocent.

inspector *n (police)* inspecteur *m* ▷ *Inspector Jill Brown* l'inspecteur Jill Brown; **ticket inspector** *(on buses)* le contrôleur

instalment *n* ❶ *(payment)* versement *m* ▷ *to pay in instalments* payer en plusieurs versements ❷ *(episode)* épisode *m*

instance *n* **for instance** par exemple

instant *adj* immédiat(e) ▷ *It was an instant success.* Ça a été un succès immédiat.; **instant coffee** le café instantané

instantly *adv* tout de suite

instead *adv* **instead of (1)** *(followed by noun)* à la place de ▷ *He went instead of Peter.* Il y est allé à la place de Peter. **(2)** *(followed by verb)* au lieu de ▷ *We played tennis instead of going swimming.* Nous avons joué au tennis au lieu d'aller nager.; **The pool was closed, so we played tennis instead.** La piscine était fermée, alors nous avons joué au tennis.

instinct *n* instinct *m*
instruct *vb* **to instruct somebody to do something** donner [**28**] l'ordre à quelqu'un de faire quelque chose ▷ *She instructed us to wait outside.* Elle nous a donné l'ordre d'attendre dehors.
instructions *npl* ❶ instructions *fpl* ▷ *Follow the instructions carefully.* Suivez soigneusement les instructions. ❷ *(booklet)* mode d'emploi *msg* ▷ *Where are the instructions?* Où est le mode d'emploi?
instructor *n* moniteur *m*, monitrice *f* ▷ *a driving instructor* un moniteur d'auto-école
instrument *n* instrument *m* ▷ *Do you play an instrument?* Est-ce que tu joues d'un instrument?
insulin *n* insuline *f*
insult *n* insulte *f*
▶ *vb* insulter [**28**]
insurance *n* assurance *f* ▷ *his car insurance* son assurance automobile; **an insurance policy** une police d'assurance
intelligent *adj* intelligent(e)
intend *vb* **to intend to do something** avoir [**8**] l'intention de faire quelque chose ▷ *I intend to do French at university.* J'ai l'intention d'étudier le français à l'université.
intensive *adj* intensif (*f* intensive)
intention *n* intention *f*
interest *n* intérêt *m* ▷ *to show an interest in something* manifester de l'intérêt pour quelque chose; **What interests do you have?** Quels sont tes centres d'intérêt?; **My main interest is music.** Ce qui m'intéresse le plus c'est la musique.
▶ *vb* intéresser [**28**] ▷ *It doesn't interest me.* Ça ne m'intéresse pas.; **to be interested in something** s'intéresser [**28**] à quelque chose ▷ *I'm not interested in politics.* Je ne m'intéresse pas à la politique.
interesting *adj* intéressant(e)
interior *n* intérieur *m*
interior designer *n* architecte d'intérieur *mf*
international *adj* international(e) (*mpl* internationaux)
internet *n* Internet *m* ▷ *on the internet* sur Internet
internet café *n* cybercafé *m*
internet user *n* internaute *mf*
interpreter *n* interprète *mf*
interrupt *vb* interrompre [**75**]
interruption *n* interruption *f*
interval *n (in play, concert)* entracte *m*
interview *n* ❶ *(on TV, radio)* interview *f* ❷ *(for job)* entretien *m*
▶ *vb (on TV, radio)* interviewer [**28**] ▷ *I was interviewed on the radio.* J'ai été interviewé à la radio.
interviewer *n (on TV, radio)* interviewer *m*
into *prep* ❶ dans ▷ *He got into the car.* Il est monté dans la voiture. ❷ en ▷ *I'm going into town.* Je vais en ville. ▷ *Translate it into French.* Traduisez ça en français.
introduce *vb* présenter [**28**] ▷ *He introduced me to his parents.* Il m'a

présenté à ses parents.
introduction *n (in book)* introduction *f*
invade *vb* envahir [**38**]
invalid *n* malade *mf*
invent *vb* inventer [**28**]
invention *n* invention *f*
investigation *n (police)* enquête *f*
invisible *adj* invisible
invitation *n* invitation *f*
invite *vb* inviter [**28**] ▷ *He's not invited.* Il n'est pas invité.; **to invite somebody to a party** inviter [**28**] quelqu'un à une fête
involve *vb* nécessiter [**28**] ▷ *His job involves a lot of travelling.* Son travail nécessite de nombreux déplacements.; **to be involved in something** *(crime, drugs)* être [**35**] impliqué dans quelque chose; **to be involved with somebody** *(in relationship)* avoir [**8**] une relation avec quelqu'un
iPad® *n* iPad® *m*
iPhone® *n* iPhone® *m*
iPod® *n* iPod® *m*
Iran *n* Iran *m*; **in Iran** en Iran
Iraq *n* Irak *m*; **in Iraq** en Irak
Iraqi *n* Irakien *m*, Irakienne *f*
▸ *adj* irakien (*f* irakienne) ▷ *the Iraqi government* le gouvernement irakien
Ireland *n* Irlande *f*; **in Ireland** en Irlande; **to Ireland** en Irlande; **I'm from Ireland.** Je suis irlandais.
Irish *n (language)* irlandais *m*; **the Irish** *(people)* les Irlandais
▸ *adj* irlandais(e) ▷ *Irish music* la musique irlandaise
Irishman *n* Irlandais *m*
Irishwoman *n* Irlandaise *f*
iron *n* ❶ *(metal)* fer *m* ❷ *(for clothes)* fer à repasser *m*
▸ *vb* repasser [**28**]
ironing *n* repassage *m* ▷ *to do the ironing* faire le repassage
ironing board *n* planche à repasser *f*
irresponsible *adj (person)* irresponsable ▷ *That was irresponsible of him.* C'était irresponsable de sa part.
irritating *adj* irritant(e)
is *vb see* **be**
Islam *n* Islam *m*
Islamic *adj* islamique ▷ *Islamic law* la loi islamique; **Islamic fundamentalists** les intégristes musulmans
island *n* île *f*
isle *n* **the Isle of Man** l'île de Man *f*; **the Isle of Wight** l'île de Wight *f*
isolated *adj* isolé(e)
Israel *n* Israël *m*; **in Israel** en Israël
Israeli *adj* israélien (*f* israélienne)
▸ *n* Israélien *m*, Israélienne *f*
issue *n* ❶ *(matter)* question *f* ▷ *a controversial issue* une question controversée ❷ *(of magazine)* numéro *m*
▸ *vb (equipment, supplies)* distribuer [**28**]
it *pron*

> Remember to check if 'it' stands for a masculine or feminine noun.

❶ il ▷ *Where's my book? — It's on the table.* Où est mon livre? — Il est sur la table.; elle ▷ *When does the pool close? — It closes at 8.* La piscine ferme à quelle heure? — Elle ferme à vingt heures.

> Use **le** or **la** when 'it' is the object of the sentence. **le** and **la** change to **l'** before a vowel and most words beginning with 'h'.

❷ le ▷ *There's a croissant left. Do you want it?* Il reste un croissant. Tu le veux?; la ▷ *I don't want this apple. Take it.* Je ne veux pas de cette pomme. Prends-la.; l' ▷ *It's a good film. Did you see it?* C'est un bon film. L'as-tu vu? ▷ *He's got a new car. — Yes, I saw it.* Il a une nouvelle voiture. — Oui, je l'ai vue.; **It's raining.** Il pleut.; **It's 6 o'clock.** Il est six heures.; **It's Friday tomorrow.** Demain c'est vendredi.; **Who is it? — It's me.** Qui est-ce? — C'est moi.; **It's expensive.** C'est cher.

Italian *n* ❶ *(person)* Italien *m*, Italienne *f* ❷ *(language)* italien *m* ▶ *adj* italien (*f* italienne)

Italy *n* Italie *f*; **in Italy** en Italie; **to Italy** en Italie

itch *vb* **It itches.** Ça me démange.; **My head's itching.** J'ai des démangeaisons à la tête.

itchy *adj* **My arm is itchy.** J'ai des fourmis dans le bras.

it'd = **it had**; **it would**

item *n (object)* article *m*

it'll = **it will**

its *adj*

> Remember to check if 'its' refers to a masculine, feminine or plural noun.

son *m* ▷ *What's its name?* Quel est son nom?; sa *f*; ses *pl*

it's = **it is**; **it has**

itself *pron* se

> **se** changes to **s'** before a vowel and most words beginning with 'h'.

s' ▷ *The heating switches itself off.* Le chauffage s'arrête automatiquement.

I've = **I have**

jack *n* ❶ *(for car)* cric *m* ❷ *(playing card)* valet *m*

jacket *n* veste *f*; **jacket potatoes** les pommes de terre en robe des champs

jail *n* prison *f*; **to go to jail** aller [**3**] en prison
▸ *vb* emprisonner [**28**]

jam *n* confiture *f* ▹ *strawberry jam* la confiture de fraises; **a traffic jam** un embouteillage

jammed *adj* coincé(e) ▹ *The window's jammed.* La fenêtre est coincée.

janitor *n* concierge *m* ▹ *He's a janitor.* Il est concierge.

January *n* janvier *m*; **in January** en janvier

Japan *n* Japon *m*; **in Japan** au Japon; **from Japan** du Japon

Japanese *n* ❶ *(person)* Japonais *m*, Japonaise *f*; **the Japanese** les Japonais ❷ *(language)* japonais *m*
▸ *adj* japonais(e)

jar *n* bocal *m* (*pl* bocaux) ▹ *an empty jar* un bocal vide; **a jar of honey** un pot de miel

javelin *n* javelot *m*

jaw *n* mâchoire *f*

jazz *n* jazz *m*

jealous *adj* jaloux (*f* jalouse)

jeans *npl* jean *msg*

Jello® *n (US)* gelée *f*

jelly *n* gelée *f*

jellyfish *n* méduse *f*

jersey *n (pullover)* pull-over *m*

Jesus *n* Jésus *m*

jet *n (plane)* jet *m*

jetlag *n* **to be suffering from jetlag** être [**35**] sous le coup du décalage horaire

Jew *n* Juif *m*, Juive *f*

jewel *n* bijou *m* (*pl* bijoux)

jeweller (*US* **jeweler**) *n* bijoutier *m*, bijoutière *f* ▹ *He's a jeweller.* Il est bijoutier.

jeweller's shop (*US* **jeweler's shop**) *n* bijouterie *f*

jewellery (*US* **jewelry**) *n* bijoux *mpl*

Jewish *adj* juif (*f* juive)

jigsaw *n* puzzle *m*

job *n* ❶ emploi *m* ▹ *He's lost his job.* Il a perdu son emploi.; **I've got a Saturday job.** Je travaille le samedi. ❷ *(chore, task)* travail *m* (*pl* travaux) ▹ *That was a difficult job.* C'était un travail difficile.

jobless *adj* sans emploi

jockey *n* jockey *m*

jog *vb* faire [**36**] du jogging

jogging *n* jogging *m*; **to go jogging** faire [**36**] du jogging

join *vb* ❶ *(become member of)* s'inscrire [**30**] à ▷ *I'm going to join the ski club.* Je vais m'inscrire au club de ski. ❷ se joindre [**42**] à ▷ *Do you mind if I join you?* Puis-je me joindre à vous?

joiner *n* menuisier *m* ▷ *He's a joiner.* Il est menuisier.

joint *n* ❶ *(in body)* articulation *f* ❷ *(of meat)* rôti *m* ❸ *(drugs)* joint *m*

joke *n* plaisanterie *f* ▷ *to tell a joke* raconter une plaisanterie
▶ *vb* plaisanter [**28**] ▷ *I'm only joking.* Je plaisante.

Jordan *n (country)* Jordanie *f*; **in Jordan** en Jordanie

jotter *n (pad)* bloc-notes *m (pl* blocs-notes)

journalism *n* journalisme *m*

journalist *n* journaliste *mf* ▷ *She's a journalist.* Elle est journaliste.

journey *n* ❶ voyage *m* ▷ *I don't like long journeys.* Je n'aime pas les longs voyages.; **to go on a journey** faire [**36**] un voyage ❷ *(to school, work)* trajet *m* ▷ *The journey to school takes about half an hour.* Il y a une demi-heure de trajet pour aller à l'école.; **a bus journey** un trajet en autobus

joy *n* joie *f*

joystick *n (for computer game)* manette de jeu *f*

judge *n* juge *m* ▷ *She's a judge.* Elle est juge.
▶ *vb* juger [**45**]

judo *n* judo *m* ▷ *My hobby is judo.* Je fais du judo.

jug *n* pot *m*

juggler *n* jongleur *m*, jongleuse *f*

juice *n* jus *m* ▷ *orange juice* le jus d'orange

July *n* juillet *m*; **in July** en juillet

jumble sale *n* vente de charité *f*

jump *vb* sauter [**28**] ▷ *to jump over something* sauter par-dessus quelque chose ▷ *to jump out of the window* sauter par la fenêtre ▷ *to jump off the roof* sauter du toit

jumper *n (pullover)* pull-over *m*

junction *n (of roads)* carrefour *m*

June *n* juin *m*; **in June** en juin

jungle *n* jungle *f*

junior *n* **the juniors** *(in school)* les élèves des petites classes

junior school *n* école primaire *f*

junk *n (old things)* bric-à-brac *m* ▷ *The attic's full of junk.* Le grenier est rempli de bric-à-brac.; **to eat junk food** manger [**45**] n'importe comment; **a junk shop** un magasin de brocante

jury *n* jury *m*

just *adv* juste ▷ *just after Christmas* juste après Noël ▷ *just in time* juste à temps; **just here** ici; **I'm rather busy just now.** Je suis assez occupé en ce moment.; **I did it just now.** Je viens de le faire.; **He's just arrived.** Il vient d'arriver.; **I'm just coming!** J'arrive!; **It's just a suggestion.** Ce n'est qu'une suggestion.

justice *n* justice *f*

K

kangaroo *n* kangourou *m*
karaoke *n* karaoké *m*
karate *n* karaté *m*
kebab *n* ❶ *(shish kebab)* brochette *f* ❷ *(doner kebab)* doner kebab *m*
keen *adj* enthousiaste ▷ *He doesn't seem very keen.* Il n'a pas l'air très enthousiaste.; **She's a keen student.** C'est une étudiante assidue.; **to be keen on something** aimer [**28**] quelque chose ▷ *I'm keen on maths.* J'aime les maths.; **to be keen on somebody** *(fancy them)* être [**35**] très attiré par quelqu'un ▷ *He's keen on her.* Il est très attiré par elle.; **to be keen on doing something** avoir [**8**] très envie de faire quelque chose ▷ *I'm not very keen on going.* Je n'ai pas très envie d'y aller.
keep *vb* ❶ *(retain)* garder [**28**] ▷ *You can keep it.* Tu peux le garder. ❷ *(remain)* rester [**71**] ▷ *Keep still!* Reste tranquille!; **Keep quiet!** Tais-toi!; **I keep forgetting my keys.** J'oublie tout le temps mes clés.
keep on *vb* **to keep on doing something (1)** *(continue)* continuer [**28**] à faire quelque chose ▷ *He kept on reading.* Il a continué à lire. **(2)** *(repeatedly)* ne pas arrêter [**28**] de faire quelque chose ▷ *The car keeps on breaking down.* La voiture n'arrête pas de tomber en panne.
keep out *vb* **'keep out'** 'défense d'entrer'
keep up *vb* se maintenir [**83**] à la hauteur de quelqu'un ▷ *Matthew walks so fast I can't keep up.* Matthew marche tellement vite que je n'arrive pas à me maintenir à sa hauteur.; **I can't keep up with the rest of the class.** Je n'arrive pas à suivre le reste de la classe.
keep-fit *n* gymnastique d'entretien *f*; **I go to keep-fit classes.** Je vais à des cours de gymnastique.
kept *vb see* **keep**
kettle *n* bouilloire *f*
key *n* clé *f*
keyboard *n* clavier *m* ▷ *... with Matt Bellamy on keyboards* ... avec Matt Bellamy aux claviers
kick *n* coup de pied *m*
▸ *vb* **to kick somebody** donner [**28**] un coup de pied à quelqu'un ▷ *He kicked me.* Il m'a donné un coup de pied. ▷ *He kicked the ball hard.* Il a

donné un bon coup de pied dans le ballon.

kick off *vb (in football)* donner [**28**] le coup d'envoi

kick-off *n* coup d'envoi *m* ▷ *The kick-off is at 10 o'clock.* Le coup d'envoi sera donné à dix heures.

kid *n (child)* gosse *mf*
▶ *vb* plaisanter [**28**] ▷ *I'm just kidding.* Je plaisante.

kidnap *vb* kidnapper [**28**]

kidney *n* ❶ *(human)* rein *m* ▷ *He's got kidney trouble.* Il a des problèmes de reins. ❷ *(to eat)* rognon *m* ▷ *I don't like kidneys.* Je n'aime pas les rognons.

kill *vb* tuer [**28**] ▷ *He was killed in a car accident.* Il a été tué dans un accident de voiture.; **Luckily, nobody was killed.** Il n'y a heureusement pas eu de victimes.; **Six people were killed in the accident.** L'accident a fait six morts.; **to kill oneself** se suicider [**28**] ▷ *He killed himself.* Il s'est suicidé.

killer *n* ❶ *(murderer)* meurtrier *m*, meurtrière *f* ▷ *The police are searching for the killer.* La police recherche le meurtrier. ❷ *(assassin)* tueur *m*, tueuse *f* ▷ *a hired killer* un tueur à gages; **Meningitis can be a killer.** La méningite peut être mortelle.

kilo *n* kilo *m* ▷ *10 euros a kilo* dix euros le kilo

kilometre (*US* **kilometer**) *n* kilomètre *m*

kilt *n* kilt *m*

kind *adj* gentil (*f* gentille); **to be kind to somebody** être [**35**] gentil avec quelqu'un; **Thank you for being so kind.** Merci pour votre gentillesse.
▶ *n* sorte *f* ▷ *It's a kind of sausage.* C'est une sorte de saucisse.

kindness *n* gentillesse *f*

king *n* roi *m*

kingdom *n* royaume *m*

kiosk *n (phone box)* cabine téléphonique *f*

kiss *n* baiser *m* ▷ *a passionate kiss* un baiser passionné
▶ *vb* ❶ embrasser [**28**] ▷ *He kissed her passionately.* Il l'a embrassée passionnément. ❷ s'embrasser [**28**] ▷ *They kissed.* Ils se sont embrassés.

kit *n* ❶ *(clothes for sport)* affaires *fpl* ▷ *I've forgotten my gym kit.* J'ai oublié mes affaires de gym. ❷ trousse *f* ▷ *a first aid kit* une trousse de secours; **a drum kit** une batterie; **a sewing kit** un nécessaire à couture

kitchen *n* cuisine *f* ▷ *a fitted kitchen* une cuisine aménagée; **the kitchen units** les éléments de cuisine; **a kitchen knife** un couteau de cuisine

kite *n* cerf-volant *m* (*pl* cerfs-volants)

kitten *n* chaton *m*

knee *n* genou *m* (*pl* genoux) ▷ *He was on his knees.* Il était à genoux.

kneel *vb* s'agenouiller [**28**]

kneel down *vb* s'agenouiller [**28**]

knew *vb see* **know**

a b c d e f g h i j k l m n o p q r s t u v w x y z

knickers *npl* culotte *fsg*; **a pair of knickers** une culotte

knife *n* couteau *m* (*pl* couteaux); **a kitchen knife** un couteau de cuisine; **a sheath knife** un couteau à gaine; **a penknife** un canif

knit *vb* tricoter [**28**]

knitting *n* tricot *m* ▷ *I like knitting.* J'aime faire du tricot.

knives *npl see* **knife**

knob *n (on door, radio, TV, radiator)* bouton *m*

knock *vb* frapper [**28**] ▷ *Someone's knocking at the door.* Quelqu'un frappe à la porte.
▶ *n* coup *m*

knock down *vb* renverser [**28**] ▷ *She was knocked down by a car.* Elle a été renversée par une voiture.

knock out *vb* ❶ *(defeat)* éliminer [**28**] ▷ *They were knocked out early in the tournament.* Ils ont été éliminés au début du tournoi. ❷ *(stun)* assommer [**28**] ▷ *They knocked out the security guard.* Ils ont assommé le vigile.

knot *n* nœud *m*; **to tie a knot in something** faire [**36**] un nœud à quelque chose

know *vb*

Use **savoir** for knowing facts, **connaître** for knowing people and places.

❶ savoir [**76**] ▷ *It's a long way. — Yes, I know.* C'est loin. — Oui, je sais. ▷ *I don't know.* Je ne sais pas. ▷ *I don't know what to do.* Je ne sais pas quoi faire. ▷ *I don't know how to do it.* Je ne sais pas comment faire. ❷ connaître [**14**] ▷ *I know her.* Je la connais. ▷ *I know Paris well.* Je connais bien Paris.; **I don't know any German.** Je ne parle pas du tout allemand.; **to know that ...** savoir [**76**] que ... ▷ *I know that you like chocolate.* Je sais que tu aimes le chocolat. ▷ *I didn't know that your dad was a police officer.* Je ne savais pas que ton père était policier.; **to know about something (1)** *(be aware of)* être [**35**] au courant de quelque chose ▷ *Do you know about the meeting this afternoon?* Tu es au courant de la réunion de cet après-midi? **(2)** *(be knowledgeable about)* s'y connaître [**14**] en quelque chose ▷ *He knows a lot about cars.* Il s'y connaît en voitures. ▷ *I don't know much about computers.* Je ne m'y connais pas bien en informatique.; **to get to know somebody** apprendre [**65**] à connaître quelqu'un; **How should I know?** *(I don't know!)* Comment veux-tu que je le sache?; **You never know!** On ne sait jamais!

knowledge *n* connaissance *f*

known *vb see* **know**

Koran *n* Coran *m*

Korea *n* Corée *f*; **in Korea** en Corée

kosher *adj* kascher

L

lab *n* (= *laboratory*) labo *m*; **a lab technician** un laborantin
label *n* étiquette *f*
laboratory *n* laboratoire *m*
labour *n* **to be in labour** être [35] en train d'accoucher; **the labour market** le marché du travail
lace *n* ❶ *(of shoe)* lacet *m* ❷ dentelle *f* ▷ *a lace collar* un col en dentelle
lad *n* gars *m*
ladder *n* échelle *f*
lady *n* dame *f*; **a young lady** une jeune fille; **Ladies and gentlemen ...** Mesdames, Messieurs ...; **the ladies** les toilettes pour dames *fpl*
ladybird *n* coccinelle *f*
lager *n* bière blonde *f*
laid *vb see* **lay**
laid-back *adj* relaxe
lain *vb see* **lie**
lake *n* lac *m*; **Lake Geneva** le lac Léman
lamb *n* agneau *m* (*pl* agneaux); **a lamb chop** une côtelette d'agneau
lamp *n* lampe *f*
lamppost *n* réverbère *m*
lampshade *n* abat-jour *m* (*pl* abat-jour)
land *n* terre *f*; **a piece of land** un terrain
▶ *vb (plane, passenger)* atterrir [38]
landing *n* ❶ *(of plane)* atterrissage *m* ❷ *(of staircase)* palier *m*
landlady *n* propriétaire *f*
landlord *n* propriétaire *m*
landscape *n* paysage *m*
lane *n* ❶ *(in country)* chemin *m* ❷ *(on motorway)* voie *f*
language *n* langue *f* ▷ *French isn't a difficult language.* Le français n'est pas une langue difficile.; **to use bad language** dire [27] des grossièretés
language laboratory *n* laboratoire de langues *m*
lap *n (sport)* tour de piste *m* ▷ *I ran ten laps.* J'ai fait dix tours de piste en courant.; **on my lap** sur mes genoux
laptop *n (computer)* portable *m*
large *adj* ❶ grand(e) ▷ *a large house* une grande maison ❷ *(person, animal)* gros (*f* grosse) ▷ *a large dog* un gros chien
laser *n* laser *m*
last *adj, adv* ❶ dernier (*f* dernière) ▷ *last Friday* vendredi dernier ▷ *last week* la semaine dernière ▷ *last*

summer l'été dernier ❷ en dernier ▷ *He arrived last.* Il est arrivé en dernier. ❸ pour la dernière fois ▷ *I've lost my bag. —When did you see it last?* J'ai perdu mon sac. — Quand est-ce que tu l'as vu pour la dernière fois? ▷ *When I last saw him, he was wearing a blue shirt.* La dernière fois que je l'ai vu, il portait une chemise bleue.; **the last time** la dernière fois ▷ *the last time I saw her* la dernière fois que je l'ai vue ▷ *That's the last time I take your advice!* C'est la dernière fois que je suis tes conseils!; **last night (1)** *(evening)* hier soir ▷ *I got home at midnight last night.* Je suis rentré à minuit hier soir. **(2)** *(sleeping hours)* la nuit dernière ▷ *I couldn't sleep last night.* J'ai eu du mal à dormir la nuit dernière.; **at last** enfin
▶ *vb* durer [**28**] ▷ *The concert lasts two hours.* Le concert dure deux heures.

lastly *adv* finalement ▷ *Lastly, what time do you arrive?* Finalement, à quelle heure arrives-tu?

late *adj, adv* ❶ en retard ▷ *Hurry up or you'll be late!* Dépêche-toi, sinon tu vas être en retard! ▷ *I'm often late for school.* J'arrive souvent en retard à l'école.; **to arrive late** arriver [**5**] en retard ▷ *She arrived late.* Elle est arrivée en retard. ❷ tard ▷ *I went to bed late.* Je me suis couché tard.; **in the late afternoon** en fin d'après-midi; **in late May** fin mai

lately *adv* ces derniers temps ▷ *I haven't seen him lately.* Je ne l'ai pas vu ces derniers temps.

later *adv* plus tard ▷ *I'll do it later.* Je ferai ça plus tard.; **See you later!** À tout à l'heure!

latest *adj* dernier (*f* dernière) ▷ *their latest album* leur dernier album; **at the latest** au plus tard ▷ *by 10 o'clock at the latest* à dix heures au plus tard

Latin *n* latin *m* ▷ *I do Latin.* Je fais du latin.

Latin America *n* Amérique latine *f*; **in Latin America** en Amérique latine

Latin American *adj* latino-américain(e)

latter *n* second *m*, seconde *f*; **the former ..., the latter ...** le premier ..., le second ... ▷ *The former lives in the US, the latter in Australia.* Le premier habite aux États-Unis, le second en Australie.

laugh *n* rire *m*; **It was a good laugh.** *(it was fun)* On s'est bien amusés.
▶ *vb* rire [**74**]; **to laugh at something** se moquer [**28**] de quelque chose ▷ *They laughed at her.* Ils se sont moqués d'elle.

launch *vb (product, rocket, boat)* lancer [**12**] ▷ *They're going to launch a new model.* Ils vont lancer un nouveau modèle.

Launderette® *n* laverie *f*

Laundromat® *n (US)* laverie *f*

laundry *n (clothes)* linge *m*

lavatory *n* toilettes *fpl*

lavender *n* lavande *f*

law *n* ❶ loi *f* ▷ *The laws are very strict.*

Les lois sont très sévères.; **It's against the law.** C'est illégal. ❷ *(subject)* droit *m* ▷ *My sister's studying law.* Ma sœur fait des études de droit.

lawn *n* pelouse *f*

lawnmower *n* tondeuse à gazon *f*

lawyer *n* avocat *m*, avocate *f* ▷ *My mother's a lawyer.* Ma mère est avocate.

lay *vb*

'lay' is also a form of the verb 'lie'.

mettre [**47**] ▷ *She laid the baby in her cot.* Elle a mis le bébé dans son lit.; **to lay the table** mettre [**47**] la table; **to lay something on** **(1)** *(provide)* organiser [**28**] quelque chose ▷ *They laid on extra buses.* Ils ont organisé un service de bus supplémentaire. **(2)** *(prepare)* préparer [**28**] quelque chose ▷ *They laid on a special meal.* Ils ont préparé un repas soigné.

lay off *vb* licencier [**19**]

lay-by *n* aire de stationnement *f*

layer *n* couche *f* ▷ *the ozone layer* la couche d'ozone

layout *n* ❶ *(of newspaper article)* mise en page *f* ❷ *(of house, buildings)* disposition *f* ▷ *No one likes the new office layout.* Personne n'aime la nouvelle disposition des bureaux.

lazy *adj* paresseux (*f* paresseuse)

lead *n*

This word has two pronunciations. Make sure you choose the right translation.

❶ *(cable)* fil *m* ❷ *(for dog)* laisse *f*; **to be in the lead** être [**35**] en tête ▷ *Our team is in the lead.* Notre équipe est en tête. ❸ *(metal)* plomb *m*

▶ *vb* mener [**43**] ▷ *the street that leads to the station* la rue qui mène à la gare; **to lead the way** montrer [**28**] le chemin; **to lead somebody away** emmener [**43**] quelqu'un ▷ *The police led the man away.* La police a emmené l'homme.

leader *n* ❶ *(of expedition, gang)* chef *m* ❷ *(of political party)* dirigeant *m*, dirigeante *f*

lead-free *adj* **lead-free petrol** de l'essence sans plomb

lead singer *n* chanteur principal *m*, chanteuse principale *f*

leaf *n* feuille *f*

leaflet *n* brochure *f*

league *n* championnat *m* ▷ *They are at the top of the league.* Ils sont en tête du championnat.; **the Premier League** la première division

leak *n* fuite *f* ▷ *a gas leak* une fuite de gaz

▶ *vb* *(pipe, water, gas)* fuir [**39**]

lean *vb* se pencher [**28**]; **to be leaning against something** être [**35**] appuyé contre quelque chose ▷ *The ladder was leaning against the wall.* L'échelle était appuyée contre le mur.; **to lean something against a wall** appuyer [**53**] quelque chose contre un mur ▷ *He leant his bike against the wall.* Il a appuyé son vélo contre le mur.

lean forward *vb* se pencher [**28**] en avant

lean on *vb* **to lean on something** s'appuyer [**53**] contre quelque chose ▷ *He leant on the wall.* Il s'est appuyé contre le mur.

lean out *vb* se pencher [**28**] au dehors; **She leant out of the window.** Elle s'est penchée par la fenêtre.

lean over *vb* se pencher [**28**] ▷ *Don't lean over too far.* Ne te penche pas trop loin.

leap *vb* sauter [**28**] ▷ *They leapt over the stream.* Ils ont sauté pour traverser la rivière.; **He leapt out of his chair when his team scored.** Il s'est levé d'un bond lorsque son équipe a marqué.

leap year *n* année bissextile *f*

learn *vb* apprendre [**65**] ▷ *I'm learning to ski.* J'apprends à skier.

learner *n* **She's a quick learner.** Elle apprend vite.; **French learners** *(people learning French)* ceux qui apprennent le français

learner driver *n* conducteur débutant *m*, conductrice débutante *f*

learnt *vb* *see* **learn**

least *adv, adj, pron* **the least** **(1)** *(followed by noun)* le moins de ▷ *It takes the least time.* C'est ce qui prend le moins de temps. **(2)** *(after a verb)* le moins ▷ *Maths is the subject I like the least.* Les maths sont la matière que j'aime le moins.

When 'least' is followed by an adjective, the translation depends on whether the noun referred to is masculine, feminine or plural.

the least ... (1) le moins ... ▷ *the least expensive hotel* l'hôtel le moins cher **(2)** la moins ... ▷ *the least expensive seat* la place la moins chère **(3)** les moins ... ▷ *the least expensive hotels* les hôtels les moins chers; **It's the least I can do.** C'est le moins que je puisse faire.; **at least (1)** au moins ▷ *It'll cost at least £200.* Ça va coûter au moins deux cents livres. **(2)** du moins ▷ *... but at least nobody was hurt.* ... mais du moins personne n'a été blessé.

leather *n* cuir *m* ▷ *a black leather jacket* un blouson en cuir noir

leave *n* ❶ *(from job)* congé *m* ❷ *(from army)* permission *f* ▷ *My brother is on leave for a week.* Mon frère est en permission pendant une semaine.

▶ *vb* ❶ *(deliberately)* laisser [**28**] ▷ *Don't leave your camera in the car.* Ne laisse pas ton appareil photo dans la voiture. ❷ *(by mistake)* oublier [**19**] ▷ *I've left my book at home.* J'ai oublié mon livre à la maison. ▷ *Make sure you haven't left anything behind.* Vérifiez bien que vous n'avez rien oublié. ❸ *(go)* partir [**57**] ▷ *The bus leaves at 8.* Le car part à huit heures. ▷ *She's just left.* Elle vient de partir. ❹ *(go away from)* quitter [**28**] ▷ *We leave London at six o'clock.* Nous quittons Londres à six heures. ▷ *My sister left home last year.* Ma sœur a quitté la maison l'an dernier.; **to leave somebody alone** laisser [**28**] quelqu'un tranquille ▷ *Leave me alone!* Laisse-moi tranquille!

leave out *vb* mettre [**47**] à l'écart ▷ *As the new girl, I felt really left out.* En tant que nouvelle, je me suis vraiment sentie à l'écart.

leaves *npl see* **leaf**

Lebanon *n* Liban *m*; **in Lebanon** au Liban

lecture *n* ❶ *(public)* conférence *f* ❷ *(at university)* cours magistral *m* (*pl* cours magistraux)

> Be careful not to translate **lecture** by the French word **lecture**.

▶ *vb* ❶ enseigner [**28**] ▷ *She lectures at the technical college.* Elle enseigne au collège technique. ❷ faire [**36**] la morale ▷ *He's always lecturing us.* Il n'arrête pas de nous faire la morale.

lecturer *n* professeur d'université *m* ▷ *She's a lecturer.* Elle est professeur d'université.

led *vb see* **lead**

leek *n* poireau *m* (*pl* poireaux)

left *vb see* **leave**

▶ *adj, adv* ❶ *(not right)* gauche ▷ *my left hand* ma main gauche ❷ à gauche ▷ *Turn left at the traffic lights.* Tournez à gauche aux prochains feux.; **I haven't got any money left.** Il ne me reste plus d'argent.

▶ *n* gauche *f*; **on the left** à gauche ▷ *Remember to drive on the left.* N'oubliez pas de conduire à gauche.

left-hand *adj* **the left-hand side** la gauche ▷ *It's on the left-hand side.* C'est à gauche.

left-handed *adj* gaucher (*f* gauchère)

left-luggage office *n* consigne *f*

leg *n* jambe *f* ▷ *She's broken her leg.* Elle s'est cassé la jambe.; **a chicken leg** une cuisse de poulet; **a leg of lamb** un gigot d'agneau

legal *adj* légal(e) (*mpl* légaux)

leggings *npl* leggings *mpl*

leisure *n* loisirs *mpl* ▷ *What do you do in your leisure time?* Qu'est-ce que tu fais pendant tes loisirs?

leisure centre *n* centre de loisirs *m*

lemon *n* citron *m*

lemonade *n* limonade *f*

lend *vb* prêter [**28**] ▷ *I can lend you some money.* Je peux te prêter de l'argent.

length *n* longueur *f*; **It's about a metre in length.** Ça fait environ un mètre de long.

lens *n* ❶ *(contact lens)* lentille *f* ❷ *(of spectacles)* verre *m* ❸ *(of camera)* objectif *m*

Lent *n* carême *m*

lent *vb see* **lend**

lentil *n* lentille *f*

Leo *n* Lion *m* ▷ *I'm Leo.* Je suis Lion.

leotard *n* justaucorps *m*

lesbian *n* lesbienne *f*

less *pron, adv, adj* ❶ moins ▷ *He's less intelligent than her.* Il est moins intelligent qu'elle. ❷ moins de ▷ *I've* *got less time for hobbies now.* J'ai moins de temps pour les loisirs maintenant.; **less than (1)** *(with amounts)* moins de ▷ *It's less than a kilometre from here.* C'est à moins d'un kilomètre d'ici. ▷ *less than half* moins de la moitié **(2)** *(in comparisons)* moins que ▷ *He spent less than me.* Il a dépensé moins que moi.

lesson *n* ❶ leçon *f* ▷ *a French lesson* une leçon de français ❷ *(class)* cours *m* ▷ *The lessons last forty minutes each.* Chaque cours dure quarante minutes.

let *vb* ❶ *(allow)* laisser [**28**]; **to let somebody do something** laisser [**28**] quelqu'un faire quelque chose ▷ *Let me have a look.* Laisse-moi voir. ▷ *My parents won't let me stay out that late.* Mes parents ne me laissent pas sortir aussi tard.; **to let somebody know** faire [**36**] savoir à quelqu'un ▷ *I'll let you know as soon as possible.* Je vous le ferai savoir dès que possible.; **to let somebody go** lâcher [**28**] quelqu'un ▷ *Let me go!* Lâche-moi!

> To make suggestions using 'let's', you can ask questions beginning with **si on**.

▷ *Let's go to the cinema!* Si on allait au cinéma?; **Let's go!** Allons-y! ❷ *(hire out)* louer [**28**]; **'to let'** 'à louer'

let down *vb* décevoir [**67**] ▷ *I won't let you down.* Je ne vous décevrai pas.

let in *vb* laisser [**28**] entrer ▷ *They wouldn't let me in because I was under 18.* Ils ne m'ont pas laissé entrer parce que j'avais moins de dix-huit ans.

letter *n* lettre *f*

letterbox *n* boîte à lettres *f*

lettuce *n* salade *f*

leukaemia *n* leucémie *f*

level *adj* plan(e) ▷ *A snooker table must be perfectly level.* Un billard doit être parfaitement plan.
▶ *n* niveau *m* (*pl* niveaux) ▷ *The level of the river is rising.* Le niveau de la rivière monte.; **A levels** le baccalauréat

> The French **baccalauréat** (or **bac** for short) is taken at the age of 17 or 18. Students have to sit one of a variety of set subject combinations, rather than being able to choose any combination of subjects they want. If you pass you have the right to a place at university.

level crossing *n* passage à niveau *m*

lever *n* levier *m*

liar *n* menteur *m*, menteuse *f*

liberal *adj (opinions)* libéral(e) (*mpl* libéraux); **the Liberal Democrats** le parti libéral-démocrate

Libra *n* Balance *f* ▷ *I'm Libra.* Je suis Balance.

librarian *n* bibliothécaire *mf* ▷ *She's a librarian.* Elle est bibliothécaire.

library *n* bibliothèque *f*

> Be careful not to translate **library** by **librairie**.

licence (*US* **license**) *n* permis *m*; **a**

driving licence un permis de conduire
lick *vb* lécher [**34**]
lid *n* couvercle *m*
lie *vb (not tell the truth)* mentir [**77**] ▷ *I know she's lying.* Je sais qu'elle ment.; **to lie down** s'allonger [**45**]; **to be lying down** être [**35**] allongé ▷ *He was lying down on the sofa.* Il était allongé sur le canapé.; **to lie on the beach** être [**35**] allongé sur la plage
▸ *n* mensonge *m*; **to tell a lie** mentir [**77**]; **That's a lie!** Ce n'est pas vrai!
lie-in *n* **to have a lie-in** faire [**36**] la grasse matinée ▷ *I have a lie-in on Sundays.* Je fais la grasse matinée le dimanche.
lieutenant *n* lieutenant *m*
life *n* vie *f*
lifebelt *n* bouée de sauvetage *f*
lifeboat *n* canot de sauvetage *m*
lifeguard *n* maître nageur *m*
life jacket *n* gilet de sauvetage *m*
lifestyle *n* style de vie *m*
lift *vb* soulever [**43**] ▷ *It's too heavy, I can't lift it.* C'est trop lourd, je ne peux pas le soulever.
▸ *n* ascenseur *m* ▷ *The lift isn't working.* L'ascenseur est en panne.; **He gave me a lift to the cinema.** Il m'a emmené au cinéma en voiture.; **Would you like a lift?** Est-ce que je peux vous déposer quelque part?
light *adj* ❶ *(not heavy)* léger (*f* légère) ▷ *a light jacket* une veste légère ▷ *a light meal* un repas léger ❷ *(colour)* clair(e) ▷ *a light blue sweater* un pull bleu clair
▸ *n* ❶ lumière *f* ▷ *to switch on the light* allumer la lumière ❷ lampe *f* ▷ *There's a light by my bed.* Il y a une lampe près de mon lit.; **the traffic lights** les feux *mpl*; **Have you got a light?** *(for cigarette)* Avez-vous du feu?
▸ *vb (candle, cigarette, fire)* allumer [**28**]
light bulb *n* ampoule *f*
lighter *n (for cigarettes)* briquet *m*
lighthouse *n* phare *m*
lightning *n* éclairs *mpl*; **a flash of lightning** un éclair
like *vb* ❶ aimer [**28**] ▷ *I don't like mustard.* Je n'aime pas la moutarde. ▷ *I like riding.* J'aime monter à cheval.

> Note that **aimer** also means to love, so make sure you use **aimer bien** for just liking somebody.

❷ aimer [**28**] bien ▷ *I like Paul, but I don't want to go out with him.* J'aime bien Paul, mais je ne veux pas sortir avec lui.; **I'd like ...** Je voudrais ... ▷ *I'd like an orange juice, please.* Je voudrais un jus d'orange, s'il vous plaît. ▷ *Would you like some coffee?* Voulez-vous du café?; **I'd like to ...** J'aimerais ... ▷ *I'd like to wash my hands.* J'aimerais me laver les mains.; **Would you like to go for a walk?** Tu veux aller faire une promenade?; **... if you like** ... si tu veux
▸ *prep* comme ▷ *It's fine like that.*

C'est bien comme ça. ▷ *Do it like this.* Fais-le comme ça. ▷ *a city like Paris* une ville comme Paris; **What's the weather like?** Quel temps fait-il?; **to look like somebody** ressembler [**28**] à quelqu'un ▷ *You look like my brother.* Tu ressembles à mon frère.

likely *adj* probable ▷ *That's not very likely.* C'est peu probable.; **She's likely to come.** Elle viendra probablement.; **She's not likely to come.** Elle ne viendra probablement pas.

lily of the valley *n* muguet *m*

lime *n (fruit)* citron vert *m*

limit *n* limite *f* ▷ *The speed limit is 70 mph.* La vitesse est limitée à cent dix kilomètres à l'heure.

limp *vb* boiter [**28**]

line *n* ❶ ligne *f* ▷ *a straight line* une ligne droite ❷ *(to divide, cancel)* trait *m* ▷ *Draw a line under each answer.* Tirez un trait après chaque réponse. ❸ *(railway track)* voie *f*; **Hold the line, please.** Ne quittez pas.; **It's a very bad line.** La ligne est très mauvaise.

linen *n* lin *m* ▷ *a linen jacket* une veste en lin

lining *n (of jacket, skirt etc)* doublure *f*

link *n* ❶ rapport *m* ▷ *the link between smoking and cancer* le rapport entre le tabagisme et le cancer ❷ *(computing)* lien *m*

▶ *vb* relier [**19**]

lion *n* lion *m*

lip *n* lèvre *f*

lip-read *vb* lire [**44**] sur les lèvres

lipstick *n* rouge à lèvres *m*

> Word for word, this means 'red for lips'.

liquid *n* liquide *m*

liquidizer *n* mixer *m*

list *n* liste *f*

▶ *vb* faire [**36**] une liste de ▷ *List your hobbies!* Fais une liste de tes hobbies!

listen *vb* écouter [**28**] ▷ *Listen to me!* Écoutez-moi!

lit *vb see* **light**

liter *n (US)* litre *m*

literature *n* littérature *f* ▷ *I'm studying English Literature.* J'étudie la littérature anglaise.

litre *n* litre *m*

litter *n* ordures *fpl*

litter bin *n* poubelle *f*

little *adj* petit(e) ▷ *a little girl* une petite fille; **a little** un peu ▷ *How much would you like? — Just a little.* Combien en voulez-vous? — Juste un peu.; **very little** très peu ▷ *We've got very little time.* Nous avons très peu de temps.; **little by little** petit à petit

live *adj* ❶ *(animal)* vivant(e) ❷ *(broadcast)* en direct; **There's live music on Fridays.** Il y a des musiciens qui jouent le vendredi.

▶ *vb* ❶ vivre [**91**] ▷ *I live with my grandmother.* Je vis avec ma grand-mère. ❷ *(reside)* habiter [**28**] ▷ *Where do you live?* Où est-ce que tu habites? ▷ *I live in Edinburgh.* J'habite à Édimbourg.

live on *vb* **to live on something**

vivre [91] de quelque chose ▷ *He lives on benefit.* Il vit de ses indemnités.

live together *vb* ❶ *(as flatmates)* partager [45] un appartement ▷ *She's living with two Greek students.* Elle partage un appartement avec deux étudiants grecs. ❷ vivre [91] ensemble ▷ *My parents aren't living together any more.* Mes parents ne vivent plus ensemble.; **They're not married, they're living together.** Ils ne sont pas mariés, ils vivent en concubinage.

lively *adj* animé(e) ▷ *It was a lively party.* C'était une soirée animée.; **She's got a lively personality.** Elle est pleine de vitalité.

liver *n* foie *m*

lives *npl see* **life**

living *n* **to make a living** gagner [28] sa vie; **What does she do for a living?** Qu'est-ce qu'elle fait dans la vie?

living room *n* salle de séjour *f*

lizard *n* lézard *m*

load *n* **loads of** un tas de ▷ *loads of people* un tas de gens; **You're talking a load of rubbish!** Tu ne dis que des bêtises!
▶ *vb* charger [45] ▷ *a trolley loaded with luggage* un chariot chargé de bagages

loaf *n* pain *m*; **a loaf of bread** un pain

loan *n* prêt *m*
▶ *vb* prêter [28]

loaves *npl see* **loaf**

lobster *n* homard *m*

local *adj* local(e) (*mpl* locaux) ▷ *the local paper* le journal local; **a local call** une communication urbaine

location *n* endroit *m*; ▷ *a hotel set in a beautiful location* un hôtel situé dans un endroit magnifique

> Be careful not to translate **location** by the French word **location**.

loch *n* loch *m*

lock *n* serrure *f* ▷ *The lock is broken.* La serrure est cassée.
▶ *vb* fermer [28] à clé ▷ *Make sure you lock your door.* N'oubliez pas de fermer votre porte à clé.

lock out *vb* **The door slammed and I was locked out.** La porte a claqué et je me suis retrouvé à la porte.

locker *n* casier *m*; **the locker room** le vestiaire; **the left-luggage lockers** la consigne automatique *sg*

lodger *n* locataire *mf*

loft *n* grenier *m*

log *n (of wood)* bûche *f*

log in *vb* se connecter [28]

log off *vb* se déconnecter [28]

log on *vb* se connecter [28]

log out *vb* se déconnecter [28]

logical *adj* logique

lollipop *n* sucette *f*

London *n* Londres; **in London** à Londres; **to London** à Londres; **I'm from London.** Je suis de Londres.

Londoner *n* Londonien *m*, Londonienne *f*

loneliness *n* solitude *f*

lonely *adj* seul(e); **to feel lonely** se

sentir [**77**] seul ▷ *She feels a bit lonely.* Elle se sent un peu seule.

long *adj, adv* long (*f* longue) ▷ *She's got long hair.* Elle a les cheveux longs.; **The room is 6 metres long.** La pièce fait six mètres de long.; **how long?** *(time)* combien de temps? ▷ *How long did you stay there?* Combien de temps êtes-vous resté là-bas?; **I've been waiting a long time.** J'attends depuis longtemps.; **It takes a long time.** Ça prend du temps.; **as long as** si ▷ *I'll come as long as it's not too expensive.* Je viendrai si ce n'est pas trop cher.
▶ *vb* **to long to do something** attendre [**7**] avec impatience de faire quelque chose ▷ *I'm longing to see my boyfriend again.* J'attends avec impatience de revoir mon copain.

longer *adv* **They're no longer going out together.** Ils ne sortent plus ensemble.; **I can't stand it any longer.** Je ne peux plus le supporter.

long jump *n* saut en longueur *m*

loo *n* toilettes *fpl* ▷ *Where's the loo?* Où sont les toilettes?

look *n* **to have a look** regarder [**28**] ▷ *Have a look at this!* Regardez ceci!; **I don't like the look of it.** Ça ne me dit rien.
▶ *vb* ❶ regarder [**28**] ▷ *Look!* Regardez!; **to look at something** regarder [**28**] quelque chose ▷ *Look at the picture.* Regardez cette image. ❷ *(seem)* avoir [**8**] l'air ▷ *She looks surprised.* Elle a l'air surprise. ▷ *That cake looks nice.* Ce gâteau a l'air bon. ▷ *It looks fine.* Ça a l'air bien.; **to look like somebody** ressembler [**28**] à quelqu'un ▷ *He looks like his brother.* Il ressemble à son frère.; **What does she look like?** Comment est-elle physiquement?; **to look forward to something** attendre [**7**] quelque chose avec impatience ▷ *I'm looking forward to the holidays.* J'attends les vacances avec impatience.; **Looking forward to hearing from you ...** J'espère avoir bientôt de tes nouvelles ...; **Look out!** Attention!

look after *vb* s'occuper [**28**] de ▷ *I look after my little sister.* Je m'occupe de ma petite sœur.

look for *vb* chercher [**28**] ▷ *I'm looking for my passport.* Je cherche mon passeport.

look round *vb* ❶ *(look behind)* se retourner [**72**] ▷ *I shouted and he looked round.* J'ai crié et il s'est retourné. ❷ *(have a look)* jeter [**41**] un coup d'œil ▷ *I'm just looking round.* Je jette simplement un coup d'œil.; **to look round a museum** visiter [**28**] un musée; **I like looking round the shops.** J'aime faire les boutiques.

look up *vb* *(word, name)* chercher [**28**] ▷ *Look the word up in the dictionary.* Cherchez le mot dans le dictionnaire.

loose *adj* *(clothes)* ample; **loose change** la petite monnaie

lord *n (feudal)* seigneur *m*; **the House of Lords** la Chambre des lords; **good Lord!** mon Dieu!

lorry *n* camion *m*

lorry driver *n* routier *m* ▷ *He's a lorry driver.* Il est routier.

lose *vb* perdre [**61**] ▷ *I've lost my purse.* J'ai perdu mon porte-monnaie.; **to get lost** se perdre [**61**] ▷ *I was afraid of getting lost.* J'avais peur de me perdre.

loser *n* ❶ perdant *m*, perdante *f*; **to be a bad loser** être [**35**] mauvais perdant ❷ *(pathetic person)* loser *m* ▷ *He's such a loser!* C'est un vrai loser!

loss *n* perte *f*

lost *vb see* **lose**

▶ *adj* perdu(e)

lost-and-found *n (US)* objets trouvés *mpl*

lost property office *n* objets trouvés *mpl*

Word for word, this means 'things that have been found'.

lot *n* **a lot** beaucoup; **a lot of** beaucoup de ▷ *We saw a lot of interesting things.* Nous avons vu beaucoup de choses intéressantes.; **lots of** un tas de ▷ *She's got lots of money.* Elle a un tas d'argent. ▷ *He's got lots of friends.* Il a un tas d'amis.; **What did you do at the weekend? — Not a lot.** Qu'as-tu fait ce week-end? — Pas grand-chose.; **Do you like football? — Not a lot.** Tu aimes le football? — Pas tellement.; **That's the lot.** C'est tout.

lottery *n* loterie *f* ▷ *to win the lottery* gagner à la loterie

loud *adj* fort(e) ▷ *The television is too loud.* La télévision est trop forte.

loudly *adv* fort

loudspeaker *n* haut-parleur *m*

lounge *n* salon *m*

love *n* amour *m*; **to be in love** être [**35**] amoureux ▷ *She's in love with Paul.* Elle est amoureuse de Paul.; **to make love** faire [**36**] l'amour; **Give Delphine my love.** Embrasse Delphine pour moi.; **Love, Rosemary.** Amitiés, Rosemary.

▶ *vb* ❶ *(be in love with)* aimer [**28**] ▷ *I love you.* Je t'aime. ❷ *(like a lot)* aimer [**28**] beaucoup ▷ *Everybody loves her.* Tout le monde l'aime beaucoup. ▷ *I'd love to come.* J'aimerais beaucoup venir. ❸ *(things)* adorer [**28**] ▷ *I love chocolate.* J'adore le chocolat.

lovely *adj* charmant(e) ▷ *What a lovely surprise!* Quelle charmante surprise! ▷ *She's a lovely person.* Elle est charmante.; **It's a lovely day.** Il fait très beau aujourd'hui.; **Is your meal OK? — Yes, it's lovely.** Est-ce que c'est bon? — Oui, c'est délicieux.; **They've got a lovely house.** Ils ont une très belle maison.; **Have a lovely time!** Amusez-vous bien!

lover *n* ❶ *(in relationship)* amant *m*, maîtresse *f* ❷ *(of hobby, wine)* amateur *m* ▷ *an art lover* un amateur d'art

low *adj, adv (price, level)* bas (*f* basse) ▷ *That plane is flying very low.* Cet

avion vole très bas.; **the low season** la basse saison ▷ *in the low season* en basse saison
lower sixth *n* première *f* ▷ *He's in the lower sixth.* Il est en première.
loyalty *n* fidélité *f*
loyalty card *n* carte de fidélité *f*
luck *n* chance *f* ▷ *She hasn't had much luck.* Elle n'a pas eu beaucoup de chance.; **Good luck!** Bonne chance!; **Bad luck!** Pas de chance!
luckily *adv* heureusement
lucky *adj* **to be lucky (1)** *(be fortunate)* avoir [**8**] de la chance ▷ *He's lucky, he's got a job.* Il a de la chance, il a un emploi. **(2)** *(bring luck)* porter [**28**] bonheur ▷ *Black cats are lucky in Britain.* Les chats noirs portent bonheur en Grande-Bretagne.; **a lucky horseshoe** un fer à cheval porte-bonheur
luggage *n* bagages *mpl*
lump *n* ❶ morceau *m* (*pl* morceaux) ▷ *a lump of butter* un morceau de beurre ❷ *(swelling)* bosse *f* ▷ *He's got a lump on his forehead.* Il a une bosse sur le front.
lunch *n* déjeuner *m*; **to have lunch** déjeuner [**28**] ▷ *We have lunch at 12.30.* Nous déjeunons à midi et demi.
lung *n* poumon *m* ▷ *lung cancer* le cancer du poumon
Luxembourg *n* ❶ *(country)* Luxembourg *m*; **in Luxembourg** au Luxembourg; **to Luxembourg** au Luxembourg ❷ *(city)* Luxembourg; **in Luxembourg** à Luxembourg
luxurious *adj* luxueux (*f* luxueuse)
luxury *n* luxe *m* ▷ *It was luxury!* C'était le luxe!; **a luxury hotel** un hôtel de luxe
lying *vb see* **lie**
lyrics *npl (of song)* paroles *fpl*

macaroni *n* macaronis *mpl*
machine *n* machine *f*
machine gun *n* mitrailleuse *f*
machinery *n* machines *fpl*
mad *adj* ❶ *(insane)* fou (*f* folle) ▷ *You're mad!* Tu es fou! ❷ *(angry)* furieux (*f* furieuse) ▷ *She'll be mad when she finds out.* Elle sera furieuse quand elle va s'en apercevoir.; **to be mad about (1)** *(sport, activity)* être [**35**] enragé de ▷ *He's mad about football.* Il est enragé de foot. **(2)** *(person, animal)* adorer [**28**] ▷ *She's mad about horses.* Elle adore les chevaux.
madam *n* madame *f* ▷ *Would you like to order, Madam?* Désirez-vous commander, Madame?
made *vb see* **make**
madness *n* folie *f* ▷ *It's absolute madness.* C'est de la pure folie.
magazine *n* magazine *m*
maggot *n* asticot *m*
magic *adj* ❶ *(magical)* magique ▷ *a magic wand* une baguette magique ❷ *(brilliant)* super ▷ *It was magic!* C'était super!
▶ *n* magie *f*; **a magic trick** un tour de magie; **My hobby is magic.** Je fais des tours de magie.
magician *n (conjurer)* prestidigitateur *m*
magnet *n* aimant *m*
magnifying glass *n* loupe *f*
maid *n (servant)* domestique *f*
maiden name *n* nom de jeune fille *m*
mail *n* ❶ courrier *m* ▷ *Here's your mail.* Voici ton courrier. ❷ *(email)* courrier électronique *m* ▷ *Can I check my mail on your PC?* Je peux consulter mon courrier électronique sur ton PC?; **by mail** par la poste
▶ *vb* **to mail something** *(email)* envoyer [**33**] quelque chose par courrier électronique
mailbox *n (US)* boîte à lettres *f*
mailman *n (US)* facteur *m*
main *adj* principal(e) (*mpl* principaux) ▷ *the main problem* le principal problème; **the main thing is to ...** l'essentiel est de ...
mainly *adv* principalement
main road *n* grande route *f* ▷ *I don't like cycling on main roads.* Je n'aime pas faire du vélo sur les grandes routes.
majesty *n* majesté *f*; **Your Majesty** Votre Majesté

major *adj* majeur(e) ▷ *a major problem* un problème majeur; **in C major** en do majeur

Majorca *n* Majorque *f* ▷ *We went to Majorca in August.* Nous sommes allés à Majorque en août.

majority *n* majorité *f*

make *n* marque *f* ▷ *What make is that car?* De quelle marque est cette voiture?
▶ *vb* ❶ faire [**36**] ▷ *I'm going to make a cake.* Je vais faire un gâteau. ▷ *I make my bed every morning.* Je fais mon lit tous les matins.
❷ *(manufacture)* fabriquer [**28**] ▷ *made in France* fabriqué en France ❸ *(earn)* gagner [**28**] ▷ *He makes a lot of money.* Il gagne beaucoup d'argent.; **to make somebody do something** obliger [**45**] quelqu'un à faire quelque chose ▷ *My mother makes me do my homework.* Ma mère m'oblige à faire mes devoirs.; **to make lunch** préparer [**28**] le repas ▷ *She's making lunch.* Elle prépare le repas.; **to make a phone call** donner [**28**] un coup de téléphone ▷ *I'd like to make a phone call.* J'aimerais donner un coup de téléphone.; **to make fun of somebody** se moquer [**28**] de quelqu'un ▷ *They made fun of him.* Ils se sont moqués de lui.; **What time do you make it?** Quelle heure avez-vous?

make out *vb* ❶ *(read)* déchiffrer [**28**] ❷ *(understand)* comprendre [**65**] ❸ *(claim, pretend)* prétendre [**88**]

make up *vb* ❶ *(invent)* inventer [**28**] ▷ *He made up the whole story.* Il a inventé cette histoire de toutes pièces. ❷ *(after argument)* se réconcilier [**19**] ▷ *They had a quarrel, but soon made up.* Ils se sont disputés, mais se sont vite réconciliés.; **to make oneself up** se maquiller [**28**] ▷ *She spends hours making herself up.* Elle passe des heures à se maquiller.

make-up *n* maquillage *m*

Malaysia *n* Malaisie *f*; **in Malaysia** en Malaisie

male *adj* ❶ *(animals, plants)* mâle ▷ *a male kitten* un chaton mâle ❷ *(person, on official forms)* masculin(e) ▷ *Sex: male.* Sexe : masculin.; **Most football players are male.** La plupart des joueurs de football sont des hommes.; **a male chauvinist** un macho; **a male nurse** un infirmier

malicious *adj* malveillant(e) ▷ *a malicious rumour* une rumeur malveillante

> Be careful not to translate **malicious** by **malicieux**.

mall *n* centre commercial *m*

Malta *n* Malte; **in Malta** à Malte; **to Malta** à Malte

man *n* homme *m* ▷ *an old man* un vieil homme

manage *vb* ❶ *(be in charge of)* diriger [**45**] ▷ *She manages a big store.* Elle dirige un grand magasin. ❷ *(get by)* se débrouiller [**28**] ▷ *It's okay, I can manage.* Ça va, je me débrouille.; **Can you manage**

okay? Tu y arrives?; **to manage to do something** réussir [38] à faire quelque chose ▷ *Luckily I managed to pass the exam.* J'ai heureusement réussi à avoir mon examen.; **I can't manage all that.** *(food)* C'est trop pour moi.

management *n* ❶ *(organization)* gestion *f* ▷ *He's responsible for the management of the company.* Il est responsable de la gestion de la société. ❷ *(people in charge)* direction *f*; **'under new management'** 'changement de direction'

manager *n* ❶ *(of company)* directeur *m*, directrice *f* ❷ *(of shop, restaurant)* gérant *m*, gérante *f* ❸ *(of team, performer)* manager *m*

manageress *n* gérante *f*

mandarin *n (fruit)* mandarine *f*

mango *n* mangue *f*

mania *n* manie *f*

maniac *n* fou *m*, folle *f* ▷ *He drives like a maniac.* Il conduit comme un fou.; **a religious maniac** un fanatique religieux

mankind *n* humanité *f*

manner *n* façon *f* ▷ *She behaves in an odd manner.* Elle se comporte de façon étrange.; **He has a confident manner.** Il a de l'assurance.

manners *npl* manières *fpl* ▷ *good manners* les bonnes manières; **It's bad manners to speak with your mouth full.** Ce n'est pas poli de parler la bouche pleine.

mansion *n* manoir *m*

mantelpiece *n* cheminée *f*

manual *n* manuel *m*

manufacture *vb* fabriquer [28]

manufacturer *n* fabricant *m*

many *adj, pron* beaucoup de ▷ *He hasn't got many friends.* Il n'a pas beaucoup d'amis. ▷ *Were there many people at the concert?* Est-ce qu'il y avait beaucoup de gens au concert?; **very many** beaucoup de ▷ *I haven't got very many CDs.* Je n'ai pas beaucoup de CD.; **Not many.** Pas beaucoup.; **How many?** Combien? ▷ *How many do you want?* Combien en veux-tu?; **how many ...?** combien de ...? ▷ *How many euros do you get for £1?* Combien d'euros a-t-on pour une livre?; **too many** trop ▷ *That's too many.* C'est trop.; **so many** autant ▷ *I didn't know there would be so many.* Je ne pensais pas qu'il y en aurait autant.

map *n* ❶ *(of country, area)* carte *f* ❷ *(of town)* plan *m*

marathon *n* marathon *m* ▷ *the London marathon* le marathon de Londres

marble *n* marbre *m* ▷ *a marble statue* une statue en marbre; **to play marbles** jouer [28] aux billes

March *n* mars *m*; **in March** en mars

march *n (demonstration)* manifestation *f*
▶ *vb* ❶ *(soldiers)* marcher [28] au pas ❷ *(protesters)* défiler [28]

mare *n* jument *f*

margarine *n* margarine *f*

margin *n* marge *f* ▷ *Write notes in*

the margin. Écrivez vos notes dans la marge.

marijuana *n* marijuana *f*

mark *n* ❶ *(in school)* note *f* ▷ *I get good marks for French.* J'ai de bonnes notes en français. ❷ *(stain)* tache *f* ▷ *You've got a mark on your skirt.* Tu as une tache sur ta jupe. ❸ *(former German currency)* mark *m*
▶ *vb* corriger [**45**] ▷ *The teacher hasn't marked my homework yet.* Le professeur n'a pas encore corrigé mon devoir.

market *n* marché *m*

marketing *n* marketing *m*

marmalade *n* confiture d'oranges *f*

marriage *n* mariage *m*

married *adj* marié(e) ▷ *They are not married.* Ils ne sont pas mariés. ▷ *They have been married for 15 years.* Ils sont mariés depuis quinze ans.

marry *vb* épouser [**28**] ▷ *He wants to marry her.* Il veut l'épouser.; **to get married** se marier [**19**] ▷ *My sister's getting married in June.* Ma sœur se marie en juin.

marvellous (*US* **marvelous**) *adj* ❶ excellent(e) ▷ *She's a marvellous cook.* C'est une excellente cuisinière. ❷ superbe ▷ *The weather was marvellous.* Il a fait un temps superbe.

marzipan *n* pâte d'amandes *f*

mascara *n* mascara *m*

masculine *adj* masculin(e)

mashed potatoes *npl* purée *fsg* ▷ *sausages and mashed potatoes* des saucisses avec de la purée

mask *n* masque *m*

mass *n* ❶ multitude *f* ▷ *a mass of books and papers* une multitude de livres et de papiers ❷ *(in church)* messe *f* ▷ *We go to mass on Sunday.* Nous allons à la messe le dimanche.; **the mass media** les médias

massage *n* massage *m*

massive *adj* énorme

master *vb* maîtriser [**28**]

masterpiece *n* chef-d'œuvre *m* (*pl* chefs-d'œuvre)

mat *n* *(doormat)* paillasson *m*; **a table mat** un set de table; **a beach mat** un tapis de plage

match *n* ❶ allumette *f* ▷ *a box of matches* une boîte d'allumettes ❷ *(sport)* match *m* ▷ *a football match* un match de foot
▶ *vb* être [**35**] assorti à ▷ *The jacket matches the trousers.* La veste est assortie au pantalon.; **These colours don't match.** Ces couleurs ne vont pas ensemble.

mate *n* *(informal)* pote *m* ▷ *On Friday night I go out with my mates.* Vendredi soir, je sors avec mes potes.

material *n* ❶ *(cloth)* tissu *m* ❷ *(information, data)* documentation *f* ▷ *I'm collecting material for my project.* Je rassemble une documentation pour mon dossier.; **raw materials** les matières premières *fpl*

mathematics *n* mathématiques *fpl*

maths *n* maths *fpl*

matter *n* question *f* ▷ *It's a matter of life and death.* C'est une question de vie ou de mort.; **What's the matter?** Qu'est-ce qui ne va pas?; **as a matter of fact** en fait
▶ *vb* **it doesn't matter (1)** *(I don't mind)* ça ne fait rien ▷ *I can't give you the money today. — It doesn't matter.* Je ne peux pas te donner l'argent aujourd'hui. — Ça ne fait rien. **(2)** *(it makes no difference)* ça n'a pas d'importance ▷ *It doesn't matter if you're late.* Ça n'a pas d'importance si tu es en retard.; **It matters a lot to me.** C'est très important pour moi.

mattress *n* matelas *m*

mature *adj* mûr(e) ▷ *She's quite mature for her age.* Elle est très mûre pour son âge.

maximum *n* maximum *m*
▶ *adj* maximum ▷ *The maximum speed is 100 km/h.* La vitesse maximum autorisée est de cent kilomètres à l'heure.; **the maximum amount** le maximum

May *n* mai *m*; **in May** en mai; **May Day** le Premier Mai

may *vb* **He may come.** Il va peut-être venir. ▷ *It may rain.* Il va peut-être pleuvoir.; **May I smoke?** Est-ce que je peux fumer?

maybe *adv* peut-être ▷ *maybe not* peut-être pas ▷ *Maybe she's at home.* Elle est peut-être chez elle. ▷ *Maybe he'll change his mind.* Il va peut-être changer d'avis.

mayonnaise *n* mayonnaise *f*

mayor *n* maire *m*

me *pron* ❶ me ▷ *Could you lend me your pen?* Est-ce que tu peux me prêter ton stylo?
m'

> **me** becomes **m'** before a vowel sound.

▷ *Can you help me?* Est-ce que tu peux m'aider? ❷ moi

> **moi** is used in exclamations.

▷ *Me too!* Moi aussi! ▷ *Excuse me!* Excusez-moi! ▷ *Wait for me!* Attends-moi!

> **moi** is also used after prepositions and in comparisons.

▷ *You're after me.* Tu es après moi. ▷ *She's older than me.* Elle est plus âgée que moi.

meal *n* repas *m*

mean *vb* vouloir [**93**] dire ▷ *I don't know what it means.* Je ne sais pas ce que ça veut dire. ▷ *What do you mean?* Qu'est que vous voulez dire? ▷ *That's not what I meant.* Ce n'est pas ce que je voulais dire.; **Which one do you mean?** Duquel veux-tu parler?; **Do you really mean it?** Tu es sérieux?; **to mean to do something** avoir [**8**] l'intention de faire quelque chose ▷ *I didn't mean to offend you.* Je n'avais pas l'intention de vous blesser.
▶ *adj* ❶ *(with money)* radin(e) ▷ *He's too mean to buy Christmas presents.* Il est trop radin pour acheter des cadeaux de Noël. ❷ *(unkind)* méchant(e) ▷ *You're being mean to me.* Tu es méchant avec moi.; **That's a really mean thing to say!**

Ce n'est vraiment pas gentil de dire ça!

meaning *n* sens *m*

meant *vb see* **mean**

meanwhile *adv* pendant ce temps

measles *n* rougeole *f*

measure *vb* ❶ mesurer [**28**] ▷ *I measured the page.* J'ai mesuré la page. ❷ faire [**36**] ▷ *The room measures 3 metres by 4.* La pièce fait trois mètres sur quatre.

measurements *npl* ❶ *(of object)* dimensions *fpl* ▷ *What are the measurements of the room?* Quelles sont les dimensions de la pièce? ❷ *(of body)* mensurations *fpl* ▷ *What are your measurements?* Quelles sont tes mensurations?; **my waist measurement** mon tour de taille; **What's your neck measurement?** Quel est votre tour de cou?

meat *n* viande *f* ▷ *I don't eat meat.* Je ne mange pas de viande.

Mecca *n* La Mecque

mechanic *n* mécanicien *m* ▷ *He's a mechanic.* Il est mécanicien.

medal *n* médaille *f*; **the gold medal** la médaille d'or

media *npl* médias *mpl*

medical *adj* médical(e) (*mpl* médicaux) ▷ *medical treatment* les soins médicaux; **medical insurance** l'assurance maladie; **to have medical problems** avoir [**8**] des problèmes de santé; **She's a medical student.** Elle est étudiante en médecine.
▶ *n* **to have a medical** passer [**58**] une visite médicale

medicine *n* ❶ *(subject)* médecine *f* ▷ *I want to study medicine.* Je veux faire médecine.; **alternative medicine** la médecine douce ❷ *(medication)* médicament *m* ▷ *I need some medicine.* J'ai besoin d'un médicament.

Mediterranean *adj* méditerranéen (*f* méditerranéenne); **the Mediterranean** la Méditerranée

medium *adj* moyen (*f* moyenne) ▷ *a man of medium height* un homme de taille moyenne

medium-sized *adj* de taille moyenne ▷ *a medium-sized town* une ville de taille moyenne

meet *vb* ❶ *(by chance)* rencontrer [**28**] ▷ *I met Paul in the street.* J'ai rencontré Paul dans la rue. ▷ *Have you met him before?* Tu l'as déjà rencontré? ❷ se rencontrer [**28**] ▷ *We met by chance in the shopping centre.* Nous nous sommes rencontrés par hasard dans le centre commercial. ❸ *(by arrangement)* retrouver [**28**] ▷ *I'm going to meet my friends.* Je vais retrouver mes amis. ❹ se retrouver [**28**] ▷ *Let's meet in front of the tourist office.* Retrouvons-nous devant l'office de tourisme.; **I like meeting new people.** J'aime faire de nouvelles connaissances. ❺ *(pick up)* aller [**3**] chercher ▷ *I'll meet you at the station.* J'irai te chercher à la gare.

meet up *vb* se retrouver [**28**] ▷ *What time shall we meet up?* On se retrouve à quelle heure?

meeting *n* ❶ *(for work)* réunion *f* ▷ *a business meeting* une réunion d'affaires ❷ *(socially)* rencontre *f* ▷ *their first meeting* leur première rencontre

mega *adj* **He's mega rich.** *(informal)* Il est hyper-riche.

melon *n* melon *m*

melt *vb* fondre [**69**] ▷ *The snow is melting.* La neige est en train de fondre.

member *n* membre *m*; **a Member of Parliament** un député

memorial *n* monument *m* ▷ *a war memorial* un monument aux morts

memorize *vb* apprendre [**65**] par cœur

memory *n* ❶ *(also for computer)* mémoire *f* ▷ *I haven't got a good memory.* Je n'ai pas une bonne mémoire. ❷ *(recollection)* souvenir *m* ▷ *to bring back memories* rappeler des souvenirs

men *npl see* **man**

mend *vb* réparer [**28**]

mental *adj* ❶ mental(e) *(mpl* mentaux) ▷ *a mental illness* une maladie mentale ❷ *(mad)* fou *(f* folle) ▷ *You're mental!* Tu es fou!

mention *vb* mentionner [**28**]; **Thank you! — Don't mention it!** Merci! — Il n'y a pas de quoi!

menu *n* menu *m* ▷ *Could I have the menu please?* Est-ce que je pourrais avoir le menu s'il vous plaît?

merchant *n* marchand *m* ▷ *a wine merchant* un marchand de vin

meringue *n* meringue *f*

merry *adj* **Merry Christmas!** Joyeux Noël!

merry-go-round *n* manège *m*

mess *n* fouillis *m* ▷ *My bedroom's usually in a mess.* Il y a généralement du fouillis dans ma chambre.

mess about *vb* **to mess about with something** *(interfere with)* tripoter [**28**] quelque chose ▷ *Stop messing about with my computer!* Arrête de tripoter mon ordinateur!; **Don't mess about with my things!** Ne touche pas à mes affaires!

mess up *vb* **to mess something up** mettre [**47**] la pagaille dans quelque chose ▷ *My little brother has messed up my DVDs.* Mon petit frère a mis la pagaille dans mes DVDs.

message *n* message *m*
▶ *vb* envoyer [**33**] un message ▷ *She messaged me on Facebook.* Elle m'a envoyé un message sur Facebook.

messenger *n* messager *m*

messy *adj* ❶ *(dirty)* salissant(e) ▷ *a messy job* un travail salissant ❷ *(untidy)* en désordre ▷ *Your desk is really messy.* Ton bureau est vraiment en désordre. ❸ *(person)* désordonné(e) ▷ *She's so messy!* Elle est tellement désordonnée!; **My writing is terribly messy.** J'ai une écriture de cochon.

met *vb see* **meet**

metal *n* métal *m (pl* métaux)

meter *n* ❶ *(for gas, electricity, taxi)* compteur *m* ❷ *(parking meter)* parcmètre *m* ❸ *(US: unit of measurement)* mètre *m*

method *n* méthode *f*

Methodist *n* méthodiste *mf* ▷ *I'm a Methodist.* Je suis méthodiste.

metre *n* mètre *m*

metric *adj* métrique

Mexico *n* Mexique *m*; **in Mexico** au Mexique; **to Mexico** au Mexique

mice *npl see* **mouse**

microchip *n* puce *f*

microphone *n* microphone *m*

microscope *n* microscope *m*

microwave oven *n* four à micro-ondes *m*

midday *n* midi *m*; **at midday** à midi

middle *n* milieu *m* ▷ *in the middle of the road* au milieu de la route ▷ *in the middle of the night* au milieu de la nuit

middle-aged *adj* d'un certain âge ▷ *a middle-aged man* un homme d'un certain âge; **to be middle-aged** avoir [**8**] la cinquantaine; **She's middle-aged.** Elle a la cinquantaine.

middle-class *adj* de la classe moyenne ▷ *a middle-class family* une famille de la classe moyenne

Middle East *n* Moyen-Orient *m*; **in the Middle East** au Moyen-Orient

middle name *n* deuxième nom *m*

midge *n* moucheron *m*

midnight *n* minuit *m*; **at midnight** à minuit

midwife *n* sage-femme *f* (*pl* sages-femmes) ▷ *She's a midwife.* Elle est sage-femme.

might *vb* ▷ *He might come later.* Il va peut-être venir plus tard. ▷ *She might not have understood.* Elle n'a peut-être pas compris.

migraine *n* migraine *f* ▷ *I've got a migraine.* J'ai la migraine.

mike *n* micro *m*

mild *adj* doux (*f* douce) ▷ *The winters are quite mild.* Les hivers sont assez doux.

mile *n* mille *m* ▷ *It's 5 miles from here.* C'est à huit kilomètres d'ici.

> In France distances are expressed in kilometres. A mile is about 1.6 kilometres.

We walked miles! Nous avons fait des kilomètres à pied!

military *adj* militaire

milk *n* lait *m* ▷ *tea with milk* du thé au lait
▶ *vb* traire [**85**]

milk chocolate *n* chocolat au lait *m*

milkman *n* **He's a milkman.** Il livre le lait à domicile.

> In France milk is not delivered to people's homes.

milk shake *n* milk-shake *m*

millennium *n* millénaire *m* ▷ *the third millennium* le troisième millénaire

millimetre (*US* **millimeter**) *n* millimètre *m*

million *n* million *m*

millionaire *n* millionnaire *m*

mince *n* viande hachée *f*

mind *vb* ❶ garder [**28**] ▷ *Could you mind the baby this afternoon?* Est-ce que tu pourrais garder le bébé cet après-midi? ❷ *(keep an eye on)* surveiller [**28**] ▷ *Could you mind my bags for a few minutes?* Est-ce que vous pourriez surveiller mes bagages pendant quelques minutes?; **Do you mind if I open the window?** Est-ce que je pourrais ouvrir la fenêtre?; **I don't mind.** Ça ne me dérange pas. ▷ *I don't mind the noise.* Le bruit ne me dérange pas.; **Never mind!** Ça ne fait rien!; **Mind that bike!** Attention au vélo!; **Mind the step!** Attention à la marche!

▶ *n* **to make up one's mind** se décider [**28**] ▷ *I haven't made up my mind yet.* Je ne me suis pas encore décidé.; **to change one's mind** changer [**45**] d'avis ▷ *He's changed his mind.* Il a changé d'avis.; **Are you out of your mind?** Tu as perdu la tête?

mine *pron* le mien ▷ *Is this your coat? — No, mine's black.* C'est ton manteau? — Non, le mien est noir. la mienne ▷ *Is this your car? — No, mine's green.* C'est ta voiture? — Non, la mienne est verte. les miens ▷ *her parents and mine* ses parents et les miens les miennes ▷ *Your hands are dirty, mine are clean.* Tes mains sont sales, les miennes sont propres.; **It's mine.** C'est à moi. ▷ *This book is mine.* Ce livre est à moi. ▷ *Whose is this? — It's mine.* C'est à qui? — À moi.

▶ *n* mine *f* ▷ *a coal mine* une mine de charbon ▷ *a land mine* une mine terrestre

miner *n* mineur *m*

mineral water *n* eau minérale *f*

miniature *adj* miniature ▷ *a miniature version* une version miniature

▶ *n* miniature *f*

minibus *n* minibus *m*

minimum *n* minimum *m*

▶ *adj* minimum ▷ *The minimum age for driving is 17.* L'âge minimum pour conduire est dix-sept ans.; **the minimum amount** le minimum

miniskirt *n* mini-jupe *f*

minister *n* ❶ *(in government)* ministre *m* ❷ *(of church)* pasteur *m*

minor *adj* mineur(e) ▷ *a minor problem* un problème mineur; **in D minor** en ré mineur; **a minor operation** une opération bénigne

minority *n* minorité *f*

mint *n* ❶ *(plant)* menthe *f* ▷ *mint sauce* la sauce à la menthe ❷ *(sweet)* bonbon à la menthe *m*

minus *prep* moins ▷ *16 minus 3 is 13.* Seize moins trois égale treize. ▷ *It's minus two degrees outside.* Il fait moins deux dehors.

minute *n* minute *f* ▷ *Wait a minute!* Attends une minute!

▶ *adj* minuscule ▷ *Her flat is minute.* Son appartement est minuscule.

miracle *n* miracle *m*

mirror *n* ❶ *(on wall)* glace *f* ❷ *(in car)* rétroviseur *m*

misbehave *vb* se conduire [**23**] mal

miscellaneous *adj* divers(e)

mischief *n* bêtises *fpl* ▷ *My little sister's always up to mischief.* Ma petite sœur fait constamment des bêtises.

mischievous *adj* coquin(e)

miser *n* avare *mf*

miserable *adj* ❶ *(person)* malheureux (*f* malheureuse) ▷ *You're looking miserable.* Tu as l'air malheureux. ❷ *(weather)* épouvantable ▷ *The weather was miserable.* Il faisait un temps épouvantable.; **to feel miserable** ne pas avoir [**8**] le moral ▷ *I'm feeling miserable.* Je n'ai pas le moral.

misery *n* ❶ *(unhappiness)* tristesse *f* ▷ *All that money brought nothing but misery.* Tout cet argent n'a apporté que de la tristesse. ❷ *(unhappy person)* pleurnicheur *m*, pleurnicheuse *f* ▷ *She's a real misery.* C'est une vraie pleurnicheuse.

Miss *n* ❶ Mademoiselle (*pl* Mesdemoiselles) ❷ *(in address)* Mlle (*pl* Mlles)

miss *vb* ❶ rater [**28**] ▷ *Hurry or you'll miss the bus.* Dépêche-toi ou tu vas rater le bus. ❷ manquer [**28**] ▷ *to miss an opportunity* manquer une occasion; **I miss you.** Tu me manques. ▷ *I'm missing my family.* Ma famille me manque. ▷ *I miss them.* Ils me manquent.

missing *adj* manquant(e) ▷ *the missing part* la pièce manquante; **to be missing** avoir [**8**] disparu ▷ *Two members of the group are missing.* Deux membres du groupe ont disparu.

mist *n* brume *f*

mistake *n* ❶ *(slip)* faute *f* ▷ *a spelling mistake* une faute d'orthographe; **to make a mistake (1)** *(in writing, speaking)* faire [**36**] une faute **(2)** *(get mixed up)* se tromper [**28**] ▷ *I'm sorry, I made a mistake.* Je suis désolé, je me suis trompé. ❷ *(misjudgement)* erreur *f* ▷ *It was a mistake to come.* J'ai fait une erreur en venant.; **by mistake** par erreur ▷ *I took his bag by mistake.* J'ai pris son sac par erreur.

▶ *vb* **He mistook me for my sister.** Il m'a prise pour ma sœur.

mistaken *adj* **to be mistaken** se tromper [**28**] ▷ *If you think I'm coming with you, you're mistaken.* Si tu penses que je vais venir avec toi, tu te trompes.

mistletoe *n* gui *m*

mistook *vb see* **mistake**

misty *adj* brumeux (*f* brumeuse) ▷ *a misty morning* un matin brumeux

misunderstand *vb* mal comprendre [**65**] ▷ *Sorry, I misunderstood you.* Je suis désolé, je t'avais mal compris.

misunderstanding *n* malentendu *m*

misunderstood *vb see* **misunderstand**

mix *n* mélange *m* ▷ *It's a mix of science fiction and comedy.* C'est un mélange de science-fiction et de comédie.; **a cake mix** une préparation pour gâteau

▶ *vb* ❶ mélanger [**45**] ▷ *Mix the flour with the sugar.* Mélangez la farine au sucre. ❷ combiner [**28**] ▷ *He's mixing business with pleasure.* Il combine les affaires et le plaisir.; **to mix with somebody** *(associate)* fréquenter [**28**] quelqu'un; **He doesn't mix much.** Il se tient à l'écart.

mix up *vb (people)* confondre [**69**] ▷ *He always mixes me up with my sister.* Il me confond toujours avec ma sœur.; **The travel agent mixed up the bookings.** L'agence de voyage s'est embrouillée dans les réservations.; **I'm getting mixed up.** Je ne m'y retrouve plus.

mixed *adj* **a mixed salad** une salade composée; **a mixed school** une école mixte; **a mixed grill** un assortiment de grillades

mixer *n* **She's a good mixer.** Elle est très sociable.

mixture *n* mélange *m* ▷ *a mixture of spices* un mélange d'épices; **cough mixture** le sirop pour la toux

mix-up *n* confusion *f*

moan *vb* râler [**28**] ▷ *She's always moaning.* Elle est toujours en train de râler.

mobile *n (phone)* portable *m*

mobile home *n* mobile home *m*

mobile phone *n* portable *m*

mock *vb* ridiculiser [**28**]

▶ *adj* **a mock exam** un examen blanc

model *n* ❶ *(type)* modèle *m* ▷ *His car is the latest model.* Sa voiture est le tout dernier modèle. ❷ *(mock-up)* maquette *f* ▷ *a model of the castle* une maquette du château ❸ *(fashion)* mannequin *m* ▷ *She's a famous model.* C'est un mannequin célèbre.

▶ *adj* **a model plane** un modèle réduit d'avion; **a model railway** un modèle réduit de voie ferrée; **He's a model pupil.** C'est un élève modèle.

▶ *vb* **She was modelling a Lorna Bailey outfit.** Elle présentait une tenue de la collection Lorna Bailey.

modem *n* modem *m*

moderate *adj* modéré(e) ▷ *His views are quite moderate.* Ses opinions sont assez modérées.; **a moderate amount of** un peu de; **a moderate price** un prix raisonnable

modern *adj* moderne

modernize *vb* moderniser [**28**]

modest *adj* modeste

moisturizer *n* ❶ *(cream)* crème hydratante *f* ❷ *(lotion)* lait hydratant *m*

moldy *adj (US)* moisi(e)

mole *n* ❶ *(animal)* taupe *f* ❷ *(on skin)* grain de beauté *m*

moment *n* instant *m* ▷ *Could you wait a moment?* Pouvez-vous attendre un instant? ▷ *in a moment* dans un instant; **at the moment** en ce moment; **any moment now** d'un moment à l'autre ▷ *They'll be arriving any moment now.* Ils vont arriver d'un moment à l'autre.

Monaco *n* Monaco; **in Monaco** à Monaco

monarchy *n* monarchie *f*

Monday *n* lundi *m* ▷ *on Monday*

a b c d e f g h i j k l **m** n o p q r s t u v w x y z

lundi ▷ *on Mondays* le lundi ▷ *every Monday* tous les lundis

money *n* argent *m* ▷ *I need to change some money.* J'ai besoin de changer de l'argent.; **to make money** gagner [**28**] de l'argent

mongrel *n* bâtard *m* ▷ *My dog's a mongrel.* Mon chien est un bâtard.

monitor *n (of computer)* moniteur *m*

monkey *n* singe *m*

monotonous *adj* monotone

monster *n* monstre *m*

month *n* mois *m* ▷ *this month* ce mois-ci ▷ *next month* le mois prochain ▷ *last month* le mois dernier ▷ *every month* tous les mois

monthly *adj* mensuel (*f* mensuelle)

monument *n* monument *m*

mood *n* humeur *f*; **to be in a bad mood** être [**35**] de mauvaise humeur; **to be in a good mood** être [**35**] de bonne humeur

moody *adj* ❶ *(temperamental)* lunatique ❷ *(in a bad mood)* maussade

moon *n* lune *f* ▷ *There's a full moon tonight.* Il y a pleine lune ce soir.

moped *n* cyclomoteur *m*

moral *adj* moral(e) (*mpl* moraux) ▶ *n* morale *f* ▷ *the moral of the story* la morale de l'histoire; **morals** la moralité

more *adj, pron, adv*

> When comparing one amount with another, you usually use **plus**.

❶ plus ▷ *Could you speak more slowly?* Est-ce que vous pourriez parler plus lentement? ▷ *a bit more* un peu plus ▷ *There isn't any more.* Il n'y en a plus.; **more ... than** plus ... que ▷ *He's more intelligent than me.* Il est plus intelligent que moi. ❷ *(followed by noun)* plus de ▷ *I get more homework than you do.* J'ai plus de devoirs que toi. ▷ *I spent more than 500 euros.* J'ai dépensé plus de cinq cents euros.

> When referring to an additional amount, more than there is already, you usually use **encore**.

❸ encore ▷ *Is there any more?* Est-ce qu'il y en a encore? ▷ *Would you like some more?* Vous en voulez encore? ❹ *(followed by noun)* encore de ▷ *Do you want some more tea?* Voulez-vous encore du thé?; **more or less** plus ou moins; **more than ever** plus que jamais

morning *n* matin *m* ▷ *this morning* ce matin ▷ *tomorrow morning* demain matin ▷ *every morning* tous les matins; **in the morning** le matin ▷ *at 7 o'clock in the morning* à sept heures du matin; **a morning paper** un journal du matin

Morocco *n* Maroc *m*; **in Morocco** au Maroc

Moscow *n* Moscou; **in Moscow** à Moscou

Moslem *n* musulman *m*, musulmane *f* ▷ *He's a Moslem.* Il est musulman.

mosque *n* mosquée *f*

mosquito *n* moustique *m*; **a mosquito bite** une piqûre de moustique

most *adv, adj, pron*

Use **la plupart de** when 'most (of)' is followed by a plural noun and **la majeure partie (de)** when 'most (of)' is followed by a singular noun.

❶ la plupart de ▷ *most of my friends* la plupart de mes amis ▷ *most people* la plupart des gens; **most of them** la plupart d'entre eux; **most of the time** la plupart du temps ❷ la majeure partie de ▷ *most of the work* la majeure partie du travail ▷ *most of the night* la majeure partie de la nuit; **the most** le plus ▷ *He's the one who talks the most.* C'est lui qui parle le plus.

When 'most' is followed by an adjective, the translation depends on whether the noun referred to is masculine, feminine or plural.

the most ... (1) les plus ... **(2)** le plus ... ▷ *the most expensive restaurant* le restaurant le plus cher **(3)** la plus ... ▷ *the most expensive seat* la place la plus chère; **to make the most of something** profiter [**28**] au maximum de quelque chose; **at the most** au maximum ▷ *Two hours at the most.* Deux heures au maximum.

moth *n* papillon de nuit *m*

Word for word, this means 'butterfly of the night'.

mother *n* mère *f* ▷ *my mother* ma mère; **mother tongue** la langue maternelle

mother-in-law *n* belle-mère *f* (*pl* belles-mères)

Mother's Day *n* fête des Mères *f*

Mother's Day is usually on the last Sunday of May in France.

motivated *adj* motivé(e) ▷ *He is highly motivated.* Il est très motivé.

motivation *n* motivation *f*

motor *n* moteur *m* ▷ *The boat has a motor.* Le bateau a un moteur.

motorbike *n* moto *f*

motorboat *n* bateau à moteur *m* (*pl* bateaux à moteur)

motorcycle *n* vélomoteur *m*

motorcyclist *n* motard *m*

motorist *n* automobiliste *mf*

motor racing *n* course automobile *f*

motorway *n* autoroute *f* ▷ *on the motorway* sur l'autoroute

mouldy *adj* moisi(e)

mount *vb* ❶ monter [**48**] ▷ *They're mounting a publicity campaign.* Ils montent une campagne publicitaire. ❷ augmenter [**28**] ▷ *Tension is mounting.* La tension augmente.

mount up *vb* ❶ s'accumuler [**28**] ❷ augmenter [**28**]

mountain *n* montagne *f*; **a mountain bike** un VTT (= *vélo tout-terrain*)

mountaineer *n* alpiniste *mf*

mountaineering *n* alpinisme *m* ▷ *I go mountaineering.* Je fais de l'alpinisme.

mountainous *adj* montagneux (*f* montagneuse)

mouse *n (also for computer)* souris *f* ▷ *white mice* des souris blanches

mouse mat *n* tapis de souris *m*
mousse *n* ❶ *(food)* mousse *f* ▷ *chocolate mousse* la mousse au chocolat ❷ *(for hair)* mousse coiffante *f*
moustache *n* moustache *f* ▷ *He's got a moustache.* Il a une moustache.; **a man with a moustache** un moustachu
mouth *n* bouche *f*
mouthful *n* bouchée *f*
mouth organ *n* harmonica *m* ▷ *I play the mouth organ.* Je joue de l'harmonica.
move *n* ❶ tour *m* ▷ *It's your move.* C'est ton tour. ❷ déménagement *m* ▷ *Our move from Oxford to Luton ...* Notre déménagement d'Oxford à Luton ...; **to get a move on** se remuer [**28**] ▷ *Get a move on!* Remue-toi!
▶ *vb* ❶ bouger [**45**] ▷ *Don't move!* Ne bouge pas! ▷ *Could you move your stuff please?* Est-ce que tu peux bouger tes affaires s'il te plaît? ❷ avancer [**12**] ▷ *The car was moving very slowly.* La voiture avançait très lentement. ❸ émouvoir [**31**] ▷ *I was very moved by the film.* J'ai été très émue par ce film.; **to move house** déménager [**45**] ▷ *We're moving in July.* Nous allons déménager en juillet.
move forward *vb* avancer [**12**]
move in *vb* emménager [**45**] ▷ *They're moving in next week.* Ils emménagent la semaine prochaine.
move over *vb* se pousser [**28**] ▷ *Could you move over a bit?* Est-ce que vous pouvez vous pousser un peu?
movement *n* mouvement *m*
movie *n* film *m*; **the movies** le cinéma ▷ *Let's go to the movies!* Si on allait au cinéma?
moving *adj* ❶ *(not stationary)* en marche ▷ *a moving bus* un bus en marche ❷ *(touching)* touchant(e) ▷ *a moving story* une histoire touchante
MP *n* député *m* ▷ *She's an MP.* Elle est député.
mph *abbr* (= *miles per hour*) km/h (= *kilomètres-heure*) ▷ *to drive at 50 mph* rouler à 80 km/h

In France, speed is expressed in kilometres per hour. 50 mph is about 80 km/h.

Mr *n* ❶ Monsieur (*pl* Messieurs) ❷ *(in address)* M. (*pl* MM.)
Mrs *n* ❶ Madame (*pl* Mesdames) ❷ *(in address)* Mme (*pl* Mmes)
MS *n* (= *multiple sclerosis*) sclérose en plaques *f* ▷ *She's got MS.* Elle a la sclérose en plaques.
Ms *n* ❶ Madame (*pl* Mesdames) ❷ *(in address)* Mme (*pl* Mmes)

There isn't a direct equivalent of 'Ms' in French. If you are writing to somebody and don't know whether she is married, use **Madame**.

much *adj, adv, pron* ❶ *(with verb)* beaucoup ▷ *Do you go out much?* Tu sors beaucoup? ▷ *I don't like sport much.* Je n'aime pas beaucoup le sport. ▷ *I feel much better now.* Je me sens beaucoup mieux maintenant. ❷ *(with noun)* beaucoup de ▷ *I haven't got much money.* Je n'ai pas beaucoup d'argent. ▷ *I don't want much rice.* Je ne veux pas beaucoup de riz.; **very much** **(1)** *(with verb)* beaucoup ▷ *I enjoyed the film very much.* J'ai beaucoup apprécié le film. ▷ *Thank you very much.* Merci beaucoup. **(2)** *(followed by noun)* beaucoup de ▷ *I haven't got very much money.* Je n'ai pas beaucoup d'argent.; **not much** **(1)** pas beaucoup ▷ *Have you got a lot of luggage? — No, not much.* As-tu beaucoup de bagages? — Non, pas beaucoup. **(2)** pas grand-chose ▷ *What's on TV? — Not much.* Qu'est-ce qu'il y a à la télé? — Pas grand-chose. ▷ *What did you think of it? — Not much.* Qu'est-ce que tu en as pensé? — Pas grand-chose.; **How much?** Combien? ▷ *How much do you want?* Tu en veux combien? ▷ *How much time have you got?* Tu as combien de temps? ▷ *How much is it? (cost)* Combien est-ce que ça coûte?; **too much** trop ▷ *That's too much!* C'est trop! ▷ *It costs too much.* Ça coûte trop cher. ▷ *They give us too much homework.* Ils nous donnent trop de devoirs.; **so much** autant ▷ *I didn't think it would cost so much.* Je ne pensais pas que ça coûterait autant. ▷ *I've never seen so much traffic.* Je n'ai jamais vu autant de circulation.

mud *n* boue *f*

muddle *n* désordre *m* ▷ *The photos are in a muddle.* Les photos sont en désordre.

muddle up *vb (people)* confondre [**69**] ▷ *He muddles me up with my sister.* Il me confond avec ma sœur.; **to get muddled up** s'embrouiller [**28**] ▷ *I'm getting muddled up.* Je m'embrouille.

muddy *adj* boueux (*f* boueuse)

muesli *n* muesli *m*

mug *n* grande tasse *f* ▷ *Do you want a cup or a mug?* Est-ce que vous voulez une tasse normale ou une grande tasse?
▶ *vb* agresser [**28**] ▷ *He was mugged in the city centre.* Il s'est fait agresser au centre-ville.

mugging *n* agression *f*

multiple choice test *n* QCM *m* (= *le questionnaire à choix multiples*)

multiplication *n* multiplication *f*

multiply *vb* multiplier [**19**] ▷ *to multiply 6 by 3* multiplier six par trois

mum *n*

> You use **mère** in most cases, except when you are talking to your mother or using it as her name, then you would use **maman**.

❶ mère *f* ▷ *my mum* ma mère ▷ *her mum* sa mère ❷ maman *f* ▷ *Mum!* Maman! ▷ *I'll ask Mum.* Je vais demander à maman.

mummy *n* ❶ *(mum)* maman *f* ▷ *Mummy says I can go.* Maman dit que je peux y aller. ❷ *(Egyptian)* momie *f*

mumps *n* oreillons *mpl*

murder *n* meurtre *m*
▶ *vb* assassiner [**28**] ▷ *He was murdered.* Il a été assassiné.

murderer *n* assassin *m*

muscle *n* muscle *m*

museum *n* musée *m*

mushroom *n* champignon *m* ▷ *a mushroom omelette* une omelette aux champignons

music *n* musique *f*

musical *adj* doué pour la musique (*f* douée pour la musique) ▷ *I'm not musical.* Je ne suis pas doué pour la musique.; **a musical instrument** un instrument de musique
▶ *n* comédie musicale *f*

musician *n* musicien *m*, musicienne *f*

Muslim *n* musulman *m*, musulmane *f* ▷ *He's a Muslim.* Il est musulman.

mussel *n* moule *f*

must *vb*

> When 'must' means that you assume or suppose something, use **devoir**; when it means it's necessary to do something, eg 'I must buy some presents', use **il faut que ...**, which comes from the verb **falloir** and is followed by a verb in the subjunctive.

❶ *(I suppose)* devoir [**26**] ▷ *You must be tired.* Tu dois être fatigué. ▷ *They must have plenty of money.* Ils doivent avoir beaucoup d'argent. ▷ *There must be some problem.* Il doit y avoir un problème. ❷ il faut que ▷ *I must buy some presents.* Il faut que j'achète des cadeaux. ▷ *I really must go now.* Il faut que j'y aille.; **You mustn't forget to send her a card.** N'oublie surtout pas de lui envoyer une carte.; **You must come and see us.** *(invitation)* Venez donc nous voir.

mustard *n* moutarde *f*

mustn't *vb* = **must not**

my *adj* mon *m* ▷ *my father* mon père ma *f* ▷ *my aunt* ma tante mes *pl* ▷ *my parents* mes parents

> **ma** becomes **mon** before a vowel sound.

my friend (1) *(male)* mon ami **(2)** *(female)* mon amie

> Do not use **mon/ma/mes** with parts of the body.

▷ *I want to wash my hair.* Je voudrais me laver les cheveux. ▷ *I'm going to clean my teeth.* Je vais me brosser les dents. ▷ *I've hurt my foot.* Je me suis fait mal au pied.

myself *pron* ❶ me ▷ *I've hurt myself.* Je me suis fait mal. ▷ *I really enjoyed myself.* Je me suis vraiment bien amusé. ▷ *... when I look at myself in the mirror.* ... quand je me regarde dans la glace. ❷ moi ▷ *I don't like talking about myself.* Je n'aime pas parler de moi. ❸ moi-même ▷ *I made it myself.* Je l'ai fait moi-même.; **by myself** tout seul ▷ *I don't like travelling by myself.* Je n'aime pas voyager tout seul.

mysterious *adj* mystérieux (*f* mystérieuse)

mystery *n* mystère *m*; **a murder mystery** *(novel)* un roman policier

myth *n* ❶ *(legend)* mythe *m* ▷ *a Greek myth* un mythe grec ❷ *(untrue idea)* idée reçue *f* ▷ *That's a myth.* C'est une idée reçue.

nag *vb (scold)* harceler [**43**] ▷ *She's always nagging me.* Elle me harcèle constamment.

nail *n* ❶ *(on finger, toe)* ongle *m* ▷ *Don't bite your nails!* Ne te ronge pas les ongles! ❷ *(made of metal)* clou *m*

nailbrush *n* brosse à ongles *f*

nailfile *n* lime à ongles *f*

nail scissors *npl* ciseaux à ongles *mpl*

nail varnish *n* vernis à ongles *m*; **nail varnish remover** le dissolvant

naked *adj* nu(e)

name *n* nom *m*; **What's your name?** Comment vous appelez-vous?

nanny *n* garde d'enfants *f* ▷ *She's a nanny.* C'est une garde d'enfants.

napkin *n* serviette *f*

nappy *n* couche *f*
narrow *adj* étroit(e)
nasty *adj* ❶ *(bad)* mauvais(e) ▷ *a nasty cold* un mauvais rhume ❷ *(unfriendly)* méchant(e) ▷ *He gave me a nasty look.* Il m'a regardé d'un air méchant.
nation *n* nation *f*
national *adj* national(e) (*mpl* nationaux) ▷ *He's the national champion.* C'est le champion national.; **the national elections** les élections législatives
national anthem *n* hymne national *m*
nationality *n* nationalité *f*
National Lottery *n* Loterie nationale *f*
national park *n* parc national *m* (*pl* parcs nationaux)
natural *adj* naturel (*f* naturelle)
naturally *adv* naturellement ▷ *Naturally, we were very disappointed.* Nous avons naturellement été très déçus.
nature *n* nature *f*
naughty *adj* vilain(e) ▷ *Don't be naughty!* Ne fais pas le vilain!
navy *n* marine *f* ▷ *He's in the navy.* Il est dans la marine.
navy-blue *adj* bleu marine ▷ *a navy-blue skirt* une jupe bleu marine
near *adj* proche ▷ *It's fairly near.* C'est assez proche.; **It's near enough to walk.** On peut facilement y aller à pied.; **the nearest** le plus proche ▷ *The nearest shops were three kilometres away.* Les magasins les plus proches étaient à trois kilomètres.
▶ *prep, adv* près de ▷ *near my house* près de chez moi; **near here** près d'ici ▷ *Is there a bank near here?* Est-ce qu'il y a une banque près d'ici?; **near to** près de ▷ *It's very near to the school.* C'est tout près de l'école.
nearby *adv* à proximité ▷ *There's a supermarket nearby.* Il y a un supermarché à proximité.
▶ *adj* ❶ *(close)* proche ▷ *a nearby garage* un garage proche ❷ *(neighbouring)* voisin(e) ▷ *We went to the nearby village of Torrance.* Nous sommes allés à Torrance, le village voisin.
nearly *adv* presque ▷ *Dinner's nearly ready.* Le dîner est presque prêt. ▷ *I'm nearly 15.* J'ai presque quinze ans.; **I nearly missed the train.** J'ai failli rater le train.
neat *adj* soigné(e) ▷ *She has very neat writing.* Elle a une écriture très soignée.; **a neat whisky** un whisky sec
neatly *adv* soigneusement
necessarily *adv* **not necessarily** pas forcément
necessary *adj* nécessaire
neck *n* ❶ *(of body)* cou *m*; **a stiff neck** un torticolis ❷ *(of garment)* encolure *f* ▷ *a V-neck sweater* un pull avec une encolure en V
necklace *n* collier *m*
need *vb* avoir [8] besoin de ▷ *I need a bigger size.* J'ai besoin d'une plus grande taille.; **to need to do**

something avoir [**8**] besoin de faire quelque chose ▷ *I need to change some money.* J'ai besoin de changer de l'argent.
▶ *n* **There's no need to book.** Il n'est pas nécessaire de réserver.

needle *n* aiguille *f*

negative *n (photo)* négatif *m*
▶ *adj* négatif (*f* négative) ▷ *He's got a very negative attitude.* Il a une attitude très négative.

neglected *adj (untidy)* mal tenu(e) ▷ *The garden is neglected.* Le jardin est mal tenu.

negotiate *vb* négocier [**19**]

neighbour (*US* **neighbor**) *n* voisin *m*, voisine *f* ▷ *the neighbours' garden* le jardin des voisins

neighbourhood (*US* **neighborhood**) *n* quartier *m*

neither *pron, conj, adv* aucun des deux ▷ *Neither of them is coming.* Aucun des deux ne vient. ▷ *Carrots or peas? — Neither, thanks.* Des carottes ou des petits pois? — Aucun des deux merci.; aucune des deux ▷ *neither team* aucune des deux équipes; **neither ... nor ...** ni ... ni ... ▷ *Neither Sarah nor Tamsin is coming to the party.* Ni Sarah ni Tamsin ne viennent à la soirée.; **Neither do I.** Moi non plus. ▷ *I don't like him. — Neither do I!* Je ne l'aime pas. — Moi non plus!; **Neither have I.** Moi non plus. ▷ *I've never been to Spain. — Neither have I.* Je ne suis jamais allé en Espagne. — Moi non plus.

nephew *n* neveu *m* (*pl* neveux) ▷ *my nephew* mon neveu

nerve *n* ❶ nerf *m* ▷ *She sometimes gets on my nerves.* Elle me tape quelquefois sur les nerfs. ❷ *(cheek)* toupet *m* ▷ *He's got a nerve!* Il a du toupet!

nervous *adj (tense)* tendu(e) ▷ *I bite my nails when I'm nervous.* Je me ronge les ongles quand je suis tendu.; **to be nervous about something** appréhender [**28**] de faire quelque chose ▷ *I'm a bit nervous about flying to Paris by myself.* J'appréhende un peu d'aller toute seule en avion à Paris.

nest *n* nid *m*

Net *n* Net *m* ▷ *to surf the Net* surfer sur le Net

net *n* filet *m* ▷ *a fishing net* un filet de pêche

netball *n*
Netball is not played in France. Both sexes play basketball or volleyball instead.

Netherlands *npl* Pays-Bas *m*; **in the Netherlands** aux Pays-Bas

network *n* ❶ réseau *m* (*pl* réseaux) ❷ *(for mobile phone)* opérateur *m*

never *adv* ❶ jamais ▷ *Have you ever been to Germany? — No, never.* Est-ce que tu es déjà allé en Allemagne? — Non, jamais. ▷ *When are you going to phone him? — Never!* Quand est-ce que tu vas l'appeler? — Jamais! ❷ ne ... jamais
Add **ne** if the sentence contains a verb.
▷ *I never write letters.* Je n'écris jamais. ▷ *I have never been camping.*

Je n'ai jamais fait de camping. ▷ *Never leave valuables in your car.* Ne laissez jamais d'objets de valeur dans votre voiture.; **Never again!** Plus jamais!; **Never mind.** Ça ne fait rien.

new *adj* ❶ nouveau (*f* nouvelle, *mpl* nouveaux) ▷ *her new boyfriend* son nouveau copain ❷ *(brand new)* neuf (*f* neuve) ▷ *They've got a new car.* Ils ont une voiture neuve.

news *n* ❶ nouvelles *fpl* ▷ *I've had some bad news.* J'ai reçu de mauvaises nouvelles. ❷ *(single piece of news)* nouvelle *f* ▷ *That's wonderful news!* Quelle bonne nouvelle! ❸ *(on TV)* journal télévisé *m* ▷ *I watch the news every evening.* Je regarde le journal télévisé tous les soirs. ❹ *(on radio)* informations *fpl* ▷ *I listen to the news every morning.* J'écoute les informations tous les matins.

newsagent *n* marchand de journaux *m*

newspaper *n* journal *m* (*pl* journaux) ▷ *I deliver newspapers.* Je distribue des journaux.

newsreader *n* présentateur *m*, présentatrice *f*

New Year *n* Nouvel An *m* ▷ *to celebrate New Year* fêter le Nouvel An; **Happy New Year!** Bonne Année!; **New Year's Day** le Premier de l'an; **New Year's Eve** la Saint-Sylvestre

New Zealand *n* Nouvelle-Zélande *f*; **in New Zealand** en Nouvelle-Zélande

New Zealander *n* Néo-Zélandais *m*, Néo-Zélandaise *f*

next *adj, adv, prep* ❶ *(in time)* prochain(e) ▷ *next Saturday* samedi prochain ▷ *next year* l'année prochaine ▷ *next summer* l'été prochain ❷ *(in sequence)* suivant(e) ▷ *the next train* le train suivant ▷ *Next please!* Au suivant! ❸ *(afterwards)* ensuite ▷ *What shall I do next?* Qu'est-ce que je fais ensuite?; **next to** à côté de ▷ *next to the bank* à côté de la banque; **the next day** le lendemain ▷ *The next day we visited Versailles.* Le lendemain nous avons visité Versailles.; **the next time** la prochaine fois ▷ *the next time you see her* la prochaine fois que tu la verras; **next door** à côté ▷ *They live next door.* Ils habitent à côté.; **the next room** la pièce d'à côté

NHS *n* Sécurité sociale *f*

In France you have to pay for medical treatment when you receive it, and then claim it back from the **Sécurité sociale**.

nice *adj* ❶ *(kind)* gentil (*f* gentille) ▷ *Your parents are very nice.* Tes parents sont très gentils.; **to be nice to somebody** être [**35**] gentil avec quelqu'un ❷ *(pretty)* joli(e) ▷ *That's a nice dress!* Qu'est-ce qu'elle est jolie, cette robe! ❸ *(food)* bon (*f* bonne) ▷ *a nice cup of coffee* une bonne tasse de café; **Have a nice time!** Amuse-toi bien!; **nice weather** le beau temps; **It's a nice day.** Il fait beau.

nickname *n* surnom *m*
niece *n* nièce *f* ▷ *my niece* ma nièce
Nigeria *n* Nigéria *m*; **in Nigeria** au Nigéria
night *n* ❶ nuit *f* ▷ *I want a single room for two nights.* Je veux une chambre à un lit pour deux nuits.; **My mother works nights.** Ma mère travaille de nuit.; **at night** la nuit; **Goodnight!** Bonne nuit! ❷ *(evening)* soir *m* ▷ *last night* hier soir
nightie *n* chemise de nuit *f*
nightmare *n* cauchemar *m* ▷ *It was a real nightmare!* Ça a été un vrai cauchemar!; **to have a nightmare** faire [**36**] un cauchemar
nil *n* zéro *m* ▷ *We won one-nil.* Nous avons gagné un à zéro.
nine *num* neuf ▷ *She's nine.* Elle a neuf ans.
nineteen *num* dix-neuf ▷ *She's nineteen.* Elle a dix-neuf ans.
nineteenth *adj* dix-neuvième ▷ *the nineteenth floor* le dix-neuvième étage; **the nineteenth of August** le dix-neuf août
ninety *num* quatre-vingt-dix
ninth *adj* neuvième ▷ *the ninth floor* le neuvième étage; **the ninth of August** le neuf août
no *adv, adj* ❶ non ▷ *Are you coming? — No.* Est-ce que vous venez? — Non. ▷ *Would you like some more? — No thank you.* Vous en voulez encore? — Non merci. ❷ *(not any)* pas de ▷ *There's no hot water.* Il n'y a pas d'eau chaude. ▷ *There are no trains on Sundays.* Il n'y a pas de trains le dimanche. ▷ *No problem.* Pas de problème.; **I've got no idea.** Je n'en ai aucune idée.; **No way!** Pas question!; **'no smoking'** 'défense de fumer'
nobody *pron* ❶ personne ▷ *Who's going with you? — Nobody.* Qui t'accompagne? — Personne. ❷ ne ... personne

> Add **ne** if the sentence contains a verb.

▷ *There was nobody in the office.* Il n'y avait personne au bureau.; **Nobody likes him.** Personne ne l'aime.
nod *vb (in agreement)* acquiescer [**12**] d'un signe de tête; **to nod at somebody** *(as greeting)* saluer [**28**] quelqu'un d'un signe de tête
noise *n* bruit *m* ▷ *Please make less noise.* Faites moins de bruit s'il vous plaît.
noisy *adj* bruyant(e)
nominate *vb* ❶ *(appoint)* nommer [**28**] ▷ *She was nominated as director.* Elle a été nommée directrice. ❷ *(propose)* proposer [**28**] ▷ *I nominate Ian Alexander as president of the society.* Je propose Ian Alexander comme président de la société.; **He was nominated for an Oscar.** Il a été nominé pour un Oscar.
none *pron* ❶ aucun ▷ *What sports do you do? — None.* Qu'est-ce que tu fais comme sport? — Je n'en fais aucun.
aucune ▷ *How many sisters have you got? — None.* Tu as combien de

sœurs? — Aucune. ❷ aucun ... ne

> Add **ne** if the sentence contains a verb.

▷ *None of my friends wanted to come.* Aucun de mes amis n'a voulu venir.; **There's none left.** Il n'y en a plus.; **There are none left.** Il n'y en a plus.

nonsense *n* bêtises *fpl* ▷ *She talks a lot of nonsense.* Elle dit beaucoup de bêtises.

non-smoking *adj* non-fumeurs ▷ *a non-smoking carriage* une voiture non-fumeurs

non-stop *adj, adv* ❶ direct(e) ▷ *a non-stop flight* un vol direct ❷ sans arrêt ▷ *He talks non-stop.* Il parle sans arrêt.

noodles *npl* nouilles *fpl*

noon *n* midi *m* ▷ *at noon* à midi

no one *pron* ❶ personne ▷ *Who's going with you? — No one.* Qui t'accompagne? — Personne. ❷ ne ... personne

> Add **ne** if the sentence contains a verb.

▷ *There was no one in the office.* Il n'y avait personne au bureau.; **No one likes Christopher.** Personne n'aime Christopher.

nor *conj* **neither ... nor** ni ... ni ▷ *neither the cinema nor the swimming pool* ni le cinéma, ni la piscine; **Nor do I.** Moi non plus. ▷ *I didn't like the film. — Nor did I.* Je n'ai pas aimé le film. — Moi non plus.; **Nor have I.** Moi non plus. ▷ *I haven't seen him. — Nor have I.* Je ne l'ai pas vu. — Moi non plus.

normal *adj* ❶ *(usual)* habituel (*f* habituelle) ▷ *at the normal time* à l'heure habituelle ❷ *(standard)* normal(e) (*mpl* normaux) ▷ *a normal car* une voiture normale

normally *adv* ❶ *(usually)* généralement ▷ *I normally arrive at nine o'clock.* J'arrive généralement à neuf heures. ❷ *(as normal)* normalement ▷ *In spite of the strike, the airports are working normally.* Malgré la grève, les aéroports fonctionnent normalement.

Normandy *n* Normandie *f*; **in Normandy** en Normandie; **to Normandy** en Normandie

north *adj, adv* ❶ nord ▷ *the north coast* la côte nord; **a north wind** un vent du nord ❷ vers le nord ▷ *We were travelling north.* Nous allions vers le nord.; **north of** au nord de ▷ *It's north of London.* C'est au nord de Londres.

▶ *n* nord *m* ▷ *in the north* dans le nord

North America *n* Amérique du Nord *f*

northeast *n* nord-est *m* ▷ *in the northeast* au nord-est

northern *adj* **the northern part of the island** la partie nord de l'île; **Northern Europe** l'Europe du Nord

Northern Ireland *n* Irlande du Nord *f*; **in Northern Ireland** en Irlande du Nord; **to Northern Ireland** en Irlande du Nord; **I'm from Northern Ireland.** Je viens d'Irlande du Nord.

North Pole *n* pôle Nord *m*

North Sea *n* mer du Nord *f*
northwest *n* nord-ouest *m* ▷ *in the northwest* au nord-ouest
Norway *n* Norvège *f*; **in Norway** en Norvège
Norwegian *n* ❶ *(person)* Norvégien *m*, Norvégienne *f* ❷ *(language)* norvégien *m*
▶ *adj* norvégien (*f* norvégienne)
nose *n* nez *m* (*pl* nez)
nosebleed *n* **to have a nosebleed** saigner [**28**] du nez ▷ *I often get nosebleeds.* Je saigne souvent du nez.
nosy *adj* fouineur (*f* fouineuse)
not *adv* ❶ pas ▷ *Are you coming or not?* Est-ce que tu viens ou pas?; **not really** pas vraiment; **not at all** pas du tout; **not yet** pas encore ▷ *Have you finished? — Not yet.* As-tu fini? — Pas encore. ❷ ne ... pas

Add **ne** if the sentence contains a verb.

▷ *I'm not sure.* Je ne suis pas sûr. ▷ *It's not raining.* Il ne pleut pas. ▷ *You shouldn't do that.* Tu ne devrais pas faire ça. ▷ *They haven't arrived yet.* Ils ne sont pas encore arrivés. ❸ non ▷ *I hope not.* J'espère que non. ▷ *Can you lend me £10? — I'm afraid not.* Est-ce que tu peux me prêter dix livres? — Non, désolé.
note *n* ❶ note *f* ▷ *to take notes* prendre des notes ❷ *(letter)* mot *m* ▷ *I'll write her a note.* Je vais lui écrire un mot. ❸ *(banknote)* billet *m* ▷ *a £5 note* un billet de cinq livres
note down *vb* noter [**28**]
notebook *n* carnet *m*
notepad *n* bloc-notes *m* (*pl* blocs-notes)
nothing *n* ❶ rien ▷ *What's wrong? — Nothing.* Qu'est-ce qui ne va pas? — Rien. ▷ *nothing special* rien de particulier ❷ ne ... rien

Add **ne** if the sentence contains a verb.

▷ *He does nothing.* Il ne fait rien. ▷ *He ate nothing for breakfast.* Il n'a rien mangé au petit déjeuner.; **Nothing is open on Sundays.** Rien n'est ouvert le dimanche.
notice *n* *(sign)* panneau *m* (*pl* panneaux); **to put up a notice** mettre [**47**] un panneau; **a warning notice** un avertissement; **Don't take any notice of him!** Ne fais pas attention à lui!
▶ *vb* remarquer [**28**]
notice board *n* panneau d'affichage *m* (*pl* panneaux d'affichage)
nought *n* zéro *m*
noun *n* nom *m*
novel *n* roman *m*
novelist *n* romancier *m*, romancière *f*
November *n* novembre *m*; **in November** en novembre
now *adv, conj* maintenant ▷ *What are you doing now?* Qu'est-ce que tu fais maintenant?; **just now** en ce moment ▷ *I'm rather busy just now.* Je suis très occupé en ce moment.; **I did it just now.** Je viens de le faire.; **He should be there by now.** Il doit être arrivé à l'heure qu'il est.; **It should be ready by now.** Ça

devrait être déjà prêt.; **now and then** de temps en temps

nowhere *adv* nulle part ▷ *nowhere else* nulle part ailleurs

nuclear *adj* nucléaire ▷ *nuclear power* l'énergie nucléaire ▷ *a nuclear power station* une centrale nucléaire

nuisance *n* **It's a nuisance.** C'est très embêtant.; **Sorry to be a nuisance.** Désolé de vous déranger.

numb *adj* engourdi(e) ▷ *My leg's gone numb.* J'ai la jambe engourdie.; **numb with cold** engourdi par le froid

number *n* ❶ *(total amount)* nombre *m* ▷ *a large number of people* un grand nombre de gens ❷ *(of house, telephone, bank account)* numéro *m* ▷ *They live at number 5.* Ils habitent au numéro cinq. ▷ *What's your phone number?* Quel est votre numéro de téléphone? ▷ *You've got the wrong number.* Vous vous êtes trompé de numéro. ❸ *(figure, digit)* chiffre *m* ▷ *I can't read the second number.* Je n'arrive pas à lire le deuxième chiffre.

number plate *n* plaque d'immatriculation *f*

nun *n* religieuse *f* ▷ *She's a nun.* Elle est religieuse.

nurse *n* infirmier *m*, infirmière *f* ▷ *She's a nurse.* Elle est infirmière.

nursery *n* ❶ *(for children)* crèche *f* ❷ *(for plants)* pépinière *f*

nursery school *n* école maternelle *f*

The **école maternelle** is a state school for 2-6 year-olds.

nut *n* ❶ *(peanut)* cacahuète *f* ❷ *(hazelnut)* noisette *f* ❸ *(walnut)* noix *f* (*pl* noix) ❹ *(made of metal)* écrou *m*

nuts *adj* **He's nuts.** Il est dingue.

nylon *n* nylon *m*

oak *n* chêne *m* ▷ *an oak table* une table en chêne
oar *n* aviron *m*
oats *n* avoine *f*
obedient *adj* obéissant(e)
obey *vb* **to obey the rules** respecter [**28**] le règlement
object *n* objet *m* ▷ *a familiar object* un objet familier
objection *n* objection *f*
oboe *n* hautbois *m* ▷ *I play the oboe.* Je joue du hautbois.
obsessed *adj* obsédé(e) ▷ *He's obsessed with trains.* Il est obsédé par les trains.
obsession *n* obsession *f* ▷ *It's getting to be an obsession with you.* Ça devient une obsession chez toi.; **Football's an obsession of mine.** Le football est une de mes passions.
obtain *vb* obtenir [**83**]
obvious *adj* évident(e)
obviously *adv* ❶ *(of course)* évidemment ▷ *Do you want to pass the exam? — Obviously!* Tu veux être reçu à l'examen? — Évidemment!; **Obviously not!** Bien sûr que non! ❷ *(visibly)* manifestement ▷ *She was obviously exhausted.* Elle était manifestement épuisée.
occasion *n* occasion *f* ▷ *a special occasion* une occasion spéciale; **on several occasions** à plusieurs reprises
occasionally *adv* de temps en temps
occupation *n* profession *f*
occupy *vb* occuper [**28**] ▷ *That seat is occupied.* Cette place est occupée.
occur *vb (happen)* avoir [**8**] lieu ▷ *The accident occurred yesterday.* L'accident a eu lieu hier.; **It suddenly occurred to me that ...** Il m'est soudain venu à l'esprit que ...
ocean *n* océan *m*
o'clock *adv* **at four o'clock** à quatre heures; **It's five o'clock.** Il est cinq heures.
October *n* octobre *m*; **in October** en octobre
octopus *n* pieuvre *f*
odd *adj* ❶ bizarre ▷ *That's odd!* C'est bizarre! ❷ impair(e) ▷ *an odd number* un chiffre impair
of *prep* ❶ de ▷ *a boy of ten* un garçon de dix ans

de changes to **d'** before a vowel and most words beginning with 'h'.

d' ▷ *a kilo of oranges* un kilo d'oranges

de + **le** changes to **du**, and **de** + **les** changes to **des**.

du ▷ *the end of the film* la fin du film
des ▷ *the end of the holidays* la fin des vacances ❷ *(with quantity, amount)* en ▷ *Can I have half of that?* Je peux en avoir la moitié?; **three of us** trois d'entre nous; **a friend of mine** un de mes amis; **the 14th of September** le quatorze septembre; **That's very kind of you.** C'est très gentil de votre part.; **It's made of wood.** C'est en bois.

off *adv, prep, adj*

For other expressions with 'off', see the verbs 'get', 'take', 'turn' etc.

❶ *(heater, light, TV)* éteint(e) ▷ *All the lights are off.* Toutes les lumières sont éteintes. ❷ *(tap, gas)* fermé(e) ▷ *Are you sure the tap is off?* Tu es sûr que le robinet est fermé?
❸ *(cancelled)* annulé(e) ▷ *The match is off.* Le match est annulé.; **to be off sick** être [35] malade; **a day off** un jour de congé ▷ *to take a day off work* prendre un jour de congé; **She's off school today.** Elle n'est pas à l'école aujourd'hui.; **I must be off now.** Je dois m'en aller maintenant.; **I'm off.** Je m'en vais.

offence (*US* **offense**) *n (crime)* délit *m*

offer *n* proposition *f* ▷ *a good offer* une proposition intéressante; **'on special offer'** 'en promotion'
▶ *vb* proposer [28] ▷ *He offered to help me.* Il m'a proposé de m'aider.

office *n* bureau *m* (*pl* bureaux) ▷ *She works in an office.* Elle travaille dans un bureau.

officer *n* officier *m*

official *adj* officiel (*f* officielle)

off-licence *n* marchand de vins et spiritueux *m*

offside *adj (in football)* hors jeu

often *adv* souvent ▷ *It often rains.* Il pleut souvent. ▷ *How often do you go to the gym?* Tu vas souvent à la gym?

oil *n* ❶ *(for lubrication, cooking)* huile *f*; **an oil painting** une peinture à l'huile ❷ *(crude oil)* pétrole *m* ▷ *North Sea oil* le pétrole de la mer du Nord
▶ *vb* graisser [28]

oil rig *n* plateforme pétrolière *f* ▷ *He works on an oil rig.* Il travaille sur une plateforme pétrolière.

ointment *n* pommade *f*

okay *excl, adj (agreed)* d'accord ▷ *Could you call back later? — Okay!* Tu peux rappeler plus tard? — D'accord! ▷ *I'll meet you at six o'clock, okay?* Je te retrouve à six heures, d'accord? ▷ *Is that okay?* C'est d'accord?; **I'll do it tomorrow, if that's okay with you.** Je le ferai demain, si tu es d'accord.; **Are you okay?** Ça va?; **How was your holiday? — It was okay.** C'était comment tes vacances? — Pas mal.; **What's your teacher like? — He's okay.** Il est comment ton prof? — Il est sympa. *(informal)*

old *adj* ❶ vieux (*f* vieille, *mpl* vieux) ▷ *an old dog* un vieux chien ▷ *an old house* une vieille maison

> **vieux** changes to **vieil** before a vowel and most words beginning with 'h'.

vieil ▷ *an old man* un vieil homme; âgé(e)

> When talking about people it is more polite to use **âgé** instead of **vieux**.

▷ *old people* les personnes âgées ❷ *(former)* ancien (*f* ancienne) ▷ *my old English teacher* mon ancien professeur d'anglais; **How old are you?** Quel âge as-tu?; **He's ten years old.** Il a dix ans.; **my older brother** mon frère aîné ▷ *my older sister* ma sœur aînée; **She's two years older than me.** Elle a deux ans de plus que moi.; **I'm the oldest in the family.** Je suis l'aîné de la famille.

old age pensioner *n* retraité *m*, retraitée *f* ▷ *She's an old age pensioner.* Elle est retraitée.

old-fashioned *adj* ❶ démodé(e) ▷ *She wears old-fashioned clothes.* Elle porte des vêtements démodés. ❷ *(person)* vieux jeu ▷ *My parents are rather old-fashioned.* Mes parents sont plutôt vieux jeu.

olive *n* olive *f*

olive oil *n* huile d'olive *f*

Olympic *adj* olympique; **the Olympics** les Jeux olympiques *mpl*

omelette *n* omelette *f*

on *prep, adv*

> There are several ways of translating 'on'. Scan the examples to find one that is similar to what you want to say. For other expressions with 'on', see the verbs 'go', 'put', 'turn' etc.

❶ sur ▷ *on the table* sur la table ❷ à ▷ *on the left* à gauche ▷ *on the 2nd floor* au deuxième étage ▷ *I go to school on my bike.* Je vais à l'école à vélo.

> With days and dates 'on' is not translated.

▷ *on Friday* vendredi ▷ *on Fridays* le vendredi ▷ *on Christmas Day* le jour de Noël ▷ *on my birthday* le jour de mon anniversaire; **on TV** à la télé ▷ *What's on TV?* Qu'est-ce qu'il y a à la télé?; **on the radio** à la radio ▷ *I heard it on the radio.* Je l'ai entendu à la radio.; **on the bus** **(1)** *(by bus)* en bus ▷ *I go into town on the bus.* Je vais en ville en bus. **(2)** *(inside bus)* dans le bus ▷ *There were no empty seats on the bus.* Il n'y avait pas de places libres dans le bus.; **on holiday** en vacances ▷ *They're on holiday.* Ils sont en vacances.; **on strike** en grève ▶ *adj* ❶ *(heater, light, TV)* allumé(e) ▷ *I think I left the light on.* Je crois que j'ai laissé la lumière allumée. ❷ *(tap, gas)* ouvert(e) ▷ *Leave the tap on.* Laisse le robinet ouvert. ❸ *(machine)* en marche ▷ *Is the dishwasher on?* Est-ce que le lave-vaisselle est en marche?; **What's on at the cinema?** Qu'est-ce qui passe au cinéma?

once *adv* une fois ▷ *once a week* une fois par semaine ▷ *once more* encore une fois; **Once upon a time ...** Il était une fois ...; **at once** tout de suite; **once in a while** de temps en temps

one *num, pron*

> Use **un** for masculine nouns and **une** for feminine nouns.

❶ un ▷ *one day* un jour ▷ *Do you need a stamp? — No thanks, I've got one.* Est-ce que tu as besoin d'un timbre? — Non merci, j'en ai un. une ▷ *one minute* une minute ▷ *I've got one brother and one sister.* J'ai un frère et une sœur. ❷ *(impersonal)* on ▷ *One never knows.* On ne sait jamais.; **this one (1)** celui-ci *m* ▷ *Which foot is hurting? — This one.* Quel pied te fait mal? — Celui-ci. **(2)** celle-ci *f* ▷ *Which is the best photo? — This one.* Quelle est la meilleure photo? — Celle-ci.; **that one (1)** celui-là *m* ▷ *Which bag is yours? — That one.* Lequel est ton sac? — Celui-là. **(2)** celle-là *f* ▷ *Which seat do you want? — That one.* Quelle place voulez-vous? — Celle-là.

oneself *pron* ❶ se ▷ *to hurt oneself* se faire mal ❷ soi-même ▷ *It's quicker to do it oneself.* C'est plus rapide de le faire soi-même.

one-way *adj* **a one-way street** une impasse

onion *n* oignon *m* ▷ *onion soup* la soupe à l'oignon

online *adj, adv* en ligne

only *adv, adj, conj* ❶ seul(e) ▷ *Monday is the only day I'm free.* Le lundi est le seul jour où je suis libre. ▷ *French is the only subject I like.* Le français est la seule matière que j'aime. ❷ seulement ▷ *How much was it? — Only 10 euros.* Combien c'était? — Seulement dix euros. ❸ ne ... que ▷ *We only want to stay for one night.* Nous ne voulons rester qu'une nuit. ▷ *These books are only 3 euros.* Ces livres ne coûtent que trois euros. ❹ mais ▷ *I'd like the same sweater, only in black.* Je voudrais le même pull, mais en noir.; **an only child** un enfant unique

onwards *adv* à partir de ▷ *from July onwards* à partir de juillet

open *adj* ouvert(e) ▷ *The baker's is open on Sunday morning.* La boulangerie est ouverte le dimanche matin.; **in the open air** en plein air
▶ *vb* ❶ ouvrir **[55]** ▷ *Can I open the window?* Est-ce que je peux ouvrir la fenêtre? ▷ *What time do the shops open?* Les magasins ouvrent à quelle heure? ❷ s'ouvrir **[55]** ▷ *The door opens automatically.* La porte s'ouvre automatiquement.

opening hours *npl* heures d'ouverture *fpl*

opera *n* opéra *m*

operate *vb* ❶ fonctionner **[28]** ▷ *The lights operate on a timer.* Les lumières fonctionnent avec une minuterie. ❷ faire [**36**] fonctionner ▷ *How do you operate the camcorder?* Comment fait-on fonctionner le caméscope? ❸ *(perform surgery)* opérer [**34**]; **to operate on someone** opérer [**34**] quelqu'un

operation *n* opération *f* ▷ *a major operation* une grave opération; **to have an operation** se faire [**36**] opérer ▷ *I have never had an operation.* Je ne me suis jamais fait opérer.

opinion *n* avis *m* ▷ *in my opinion* à mon avis ▷ *He asked me my opinion.* Il m'a demandé mon avis.; **What's your opinion?** Qu'est-ce que vous en pensez?

opinion poll *n* sondage *m*

opponent *n* adversaire *mf*

opportunity *n* occasion *f*; **to have the opportunity to do something** avoir [**8**] l'occasion de faire quelque chose ▷ *I've never had the opportunity to go to France.* Je n'ai jamais eu l'occasion d'aller en France.

opposed *adj* **I've always been opposed to violence.** J'ai toujours été contre la violence.; **as opposed to** par opposition à

opposite *adj, adv, prep* ❶ opposé(e) ▷ *It's in the opposite direction.* C'est dans la direction opposée. ❷ en face ▷ *They live opposite.* Ils habitent en face. ❸ en face de ▷ *the girl sitting opposite me* la fille assise en face de moi; **the opposite sex** l'autre sexe

opposition *n* opposition *f*

optician *n* opticien *m*, opticienne *f* ▷ *She's an optician.* Elle est opticienne.

optimistic *adj* optimiste

option *n* ❶ *(choice)* choix *m* ▷ *I've got no option.* Je n'ai pas le choix. ❷ *(optional subject)* matière à option *f* ▷ *I'm doing geology as my option.* La géologie est ma matière à option.

or *conj* ❶ ou ▷ *Would you like tea or coffee?* Est-ce que tu veux du thé ou du café?

> Use **ni ... ni** in negative sentences.

▷ *I don't eat meat or fish.* Je ne mange ni viande, ni poisson. ❷ *(otherwise)* sinon ▷ *Hurry up or you'll miss the bus.* Dépêche-toi, sinon tu vas rater le bus.; **Give me the money, or else!** Donne-moi l'argent, sinon tu vas le regretter!

oral *adj* oral(e) *(mpl* oraux); **an oral exam** un oral
▶ *n* oral *m* (*pl* oraux) ▷ *I've got my French oral soon.* Je vais bientôt passer mon oral de français.

orange *n* orange *f*; **an orange juice** un jus d'orange
▶ *adj* orange

orchard *n* verger *m*

orchestra *n* orchestre *m* ▷ *I play in the school orchestra.* Je joue dans l'orchestre de l'école.

order *n* ❶ *(sequence)* ordre *m* ▷ *in alphabetical order* dans l'ordre alphabétique ❷ *(instruction)* commande *f* ▷ *The waiter took our order.* Le garçon a pris notre commande.; **in order to** pour ▷ *He*

does it in order to earn money. Il le fait pour gagner de l'argent.; **'out of order'** 'en panne'
▶ *vb* commander [**28**] ▷ *We ordered steak and chips.* Nous avons commandé un steak frites. ▷ *Are you ready to order?* Vous êtes prêt à commander?; **to order somebody about** donner [**28**] des ordres à quelqu'un ▷ *She liked to order him about.* Elle aimait lui donner des ordres.

ordinary *adj* ❶ ordinaire ▷ *an ordinary day* une journée ordinaire ❷ *(people)* comme les autres ▷ *an ordinary family* une famille comme les autres

organ *n (instrument)* orgue *m* ▷ *I play the organ.* Je joue de l'orgue.

organic *adj (vegetables, fruit)* biologique

organization *n* organisation *f*

organize *vb* organiser [**28**]

original *adj* original(e) *(mpl* originaux) ▷ *It's a very original idea.* C'est une idée très originale.; **Our original plan was to go camping.** À l'origine nous avions l'intention de faire du camping.

originally *adv* à l'origine

ornament *n* bibelot *m*

orphan *n* orphelin *m*, orpheline *f*

other *adj, pron* autre ▷ *Have you got these jeans in other colours?* Est-ce que vous avez ce jean dans d'autres couleurs? ▷ *on the other side of the street* de l'autre côté de la rue ▷ *the other day* l'autre jour; **the other one** l'autre ▷ *This one? — No, the other one.* Celui-ci? — Non, l'autre.; **the others** les autres ▷ *The others are going but I'm not.* Les autres y vont mais pas moi.

otherwise *adv, conj* ❶ *(if not)* sinon ▷ *Note down the number, otherwise you'll forget it.* Note le numéro, sinon tu vas l'oublier. ❷ *(in other ways)* à part ça ▷ *I'm tired, but otherwise I'm fine.* Je suis fatigué, mais à part ça, ça va.

ought *vb*

> To translate 'ought to' use the conditional tense of **devoir**.

▷ *I ought to phone my parents.* Je devrais appeler mes parents.

our *adj* notre (*pl* nos) ▷ *Our house is quite big.* Notre maison est plutôt grande.

ours *pron* le nôtre ▷ *Your garden is very big, ours is much smaller.* Votre jardin est très grand, le nôtre est beaucoup plus petit.
la nôtre ▷ *Your school is very different from ours.* Votre école est très différente de la nôtre.
les nôtres ▷ *Our teachers are strict. — Ours are too.* Nos professeurs sont sévères. — Les nôtres aussi.; **Is this ours?** C'est à nous? ▷ *This car is ours.* Cette voiture est à nous. ▷ *Whose is this? — It's ours.* C'est à qui? — À nous.

ourselves *pron* ❶ nous ▷ *We really enjoyed ourselves.* Nous nous sommes vraiment bien amusés. ❷ nous-mêmes ▷ *We built our garage ourselves.* Nous avons construit notre garage nous-mêmes.

out *adv, adj*

> There are several ways of translating 'out'. Scan the examples to find one that is similar to what you want to say. For other expressions with 'out', see the verbs 'go', 'put', 'turn' etc.

❶ *(outside)* dehors ▷ *It's cold out.* Il fait froid dehors. ❷ *(light, fire)* éteint(e) ▷ *All the lights are out.* Toutes les lumières sont éteintes.; **She's out.** Elle est sortie.; **She's out shopping.** Elle est sortie faire des courses.; **She's out for the afternoon.** Elle ne sera pas là de tout l'après-midi.; **out there** dehors ▷ *It's cold out there.* Il fait froid dehors.; **to go out** sortir **[79]** ▷ *I'm going out tonight.* Je sors ce soir.; **to go out with somebody** sortir **[79]** avec quelqu'un ▷ *I've been going out with him for two months.* Je sors avec lui depuis deux mois.; **out of (1)** dans ▷ *to drink out of a glass* boire dans un verre **(2)** sur ▷ *in 9 cases out of 10* dans neuf cas sur dix **(3)** en dehors de ▷ *He lives out of town.* Il habite en dehors de la ville.; **3 km out of town** à trois kilomètres de la ville; **out of curiosity** par curiosité; **out of work** sans emploi; **That is out of the question.** C'est hors de question.; **You're out!** *(in game)* Tu es éliminé!; **'way out'** 'sortie'

outdoor *adj* en plein air ▷ *an outdoor swimming pool* une piscine en plein air; **outdoor activities** les activités de plein air

outdoors *adv* au grand air

outfit *n* tenue *f* ▷ *She bought a new outfit for the wedding.* Elle a acheté une nouvelle tenue pour le mariage.; **a cowboy outfit** une panoplie de cowboy

outing *n* sortie *f* ▷ *to go on an outing* faire une sortie

outline *n* ❶ *(summary)* grandes lignes *fpl* ▷ *This is an outline of the plan.* Voici les grandes lignes du projet. ❷ *(shape)* contours *mpl* ▷ *We could see the outline of the mountain in the mist.* Nous distinguions les contours de la montagne dans la brume.

outside *n* extérieur *m*
▶ *adj, adv, prep* ❶ extérieur(e) ▷ *the outside walls* les murs extérieurs ❷ dehors ▷ *It's very cold outside.* Il fait très froid dehors. ❸ en dehors de ▷ *outside the school* en dehors de l'école ▷ *outside school hours* en dehors des heures de cours

outskirts *npl* banlieue *f* ▷ *on the outskirts of the town* dans les banlieues de la ville

outstanding *adj* remarquable

oval *adj* ovale

oven *n* four *m*

over *prep, adv, adj*

> When there is movement over something, use **par-dessus**; when something is located above something, use **au-dessus de**.

❶ par-dessus ▷ *The ball went over the wall.* Le ballon est passé par-dessus le mur. ❷ au-dessus de ▷ *There's a mirror over the washbasin.* Il y a une glace au-dessus du lavabo. ❸ *(more than)* plus de ▷ *It's over twenty kilos.* Ça pèse plus de vingt kilos. ▷ *The temperature was over thirty degrees.* Il faisait une température de plus de trente degrés. ❹ *(during)* pendant ▷ *over the holidays* pendant les vacances ❺ *(finished)* terminé(e) ▷ *I'll be happy when the exams are over.* Je serai content quand les examens seront terminés.; **over here** ici; **over there** là-bas; **all over Scotland** dans toute l'Écosse; **The baker's is over the road.** La boulangerie est de l'autre côté de la rue.; **I spilled coffee over my shirt.** J'ai renversé du café sur ma chemise.

overcast *adj* couvert(e) ▷ *The sky was overcast.* Le ciel était couvert.

overdose *n (of drugs)* overdose *f* ▷ *to take an overdose* faire une overdose

overdraft *n* découvert *m*; **to have an overdraft** être [**35**] à découvert

overseas *adv* à l'étranger ▷ *I'd like to work overseas.* J'aimerais travailler à l'étranger.

overtake *vb* dépasser [**58**]

overtime *n* heures supplémentaires *fpl* ▷ *to work overtime* faire des heures supplémentaires

overtook *vb see* **overtake**

overweight *adj* trop gros (*f* trop grosse)

owe *vb* devoir [**26**]; **to owe somebody something** devoir [**26**] quelque chose à quelqu'un ▷ *I owe you 50 euros.* Je te dois cinquante euros.

owing to *prep* en raison de ▷ *owing to bad weather* en raison du mauvais temps

owl *n* hibou *m* (*pl* hiboux)

own *adj* propre ▷ *I've got my own bathroom.* J'ai ma propre salle de bain.; **I'd like a room of my own.** J'aimerais avoir une chambre à moi.; **on his own** tout seul ▷ *on her own* toute seule
▶ *vb* posséder [**34**]

own up *vb* avouer [**28**]; **to own up to something** admettre [**47**] quelque chose

owner *n* propriétaire *mf*

oxygen *n* oxygène *m*

oyster *n* huître *f*

ozone layer *n* couche d'ozone *f*

p

Pacific *n* Pacifique *m*
pack *vb* faire [**36**] ses bagages ▷ *I'll help you pack.* Je vais t'aider à faire tes bagages.; **I've already packed my case.** J'ai déjà fait ma valise.; **Pack it in!** *(stop it)* Laisse tomber! ▶ *n* ❶ *(packet)* paquet *m* ▷ *a pack of cigarettes* un paquet de cigarettes ❷ *(of yoghurts, cans)* pack *m* ▷ *a six-pack* un pack de six; **a pack of cards** un jeu de cartes
package *n* paquet *m*; **a package holiday** un voyage organisé
packed *adj* bondé(e) ▷ *The cinema was packed.* Le cinéma était bondé.
packed lunch *n* repas froid *m* ▷ *I take a packed lunch to school.* J'apporte un repas froid à l'école.
packet *n* paquet *m* ▷ *a packet of cigarettes* un paquet de cigarettes
pad *n (notepad)* bloc-notes *m (pl* blocs-notes)
paddle *vb* ❶ *(canoe)* pagayer [**59**] ❷ *(in water)* faire [**36**] trempette ▶ *n (for canoe)* pagaie *f*; **to go for a paddle** faire [**36**] trempette
padlock *n* cadenas *m*
page *n (of book)* page *f* ▶ *vb* **to page somebody** faire [**36**] appeler quelqu'un
pain *n* douleur *f* ▷ *a terrible pain* une douleur insupportable; **I've got a pain in my stomach.** J'ai mal à l'estomac.; **to be in pain** souffrir [**54**] ▷ *She's in a lot of pain.* Elle souffre beaucoup.; **He's a real pain.** Il est vraiment pénible.
painful *adj* douloureux *(f* douloureuse) ▷ *to suffer from painful periods* souffrir de règles douloureuses; **Is it painful?** Ça te fait mal?
painkiller *n* analgésique *m*
paint *n* peinture *f* ▶ *vb* peindre [**60**] ▷ *to paint something green* peindre quelque chose en vert
paintbrush *n* pinceau *m (pl* pinceaux)
painter *n* peintre *m*
painting *n* ❶ peinture *f* ▷ *My hobby is painting.* Je fais de la peinture. ❷ *(picture)* tableau *m (pl* tableaux) ▷ *a painting by Picasso* un tableau de Picasso
pair *n* paire *f* ▷ *a pair of shoes* une paire de chaussures; **a pair of trousers** un pantalon; **a pair of jeans** un jean; **a pair of pants**

(1) *(briefs)* un slip **(2)** *(boxer shorts)* un caleçon **(3)** *(US: trousers)* un pantalon; **in pairs** deux par deux ▷ *We work in pairs.* On travaille deux par deux.

Pakistan *n* Pakistan *m*; **in Pakistan** au Pakistan; **to Pakistan** au Pakistan; **He's from Pakistan.** Il est pakistanais.

Pakistani *n* Pakistanais *m*, Pakistanaise *f*
▶ *adj* pakistanais(e)

palace *n* palais *m*

pale *adj* pâle ▷ *a pale blue shirt* une chemise bleu pâle

Palestine *n* Palestine *f*; **in Palestine** en Palestine

Palestinian *n* Palestinien *m*, Palestinienne *f*
▶ *adj* palestinien (*f* palestinienne)

palm *n* *(of hand)* paume *f*; **a palm tree** un palmier

pan *n* ❶ *(saucepan)* casserole *f* ❷ *(frying pan)* poêle *f*

pancake *n* crêpe *f*; **Pancake Day** mardi gras

Pancake Day is celebrated in France as well. Children dress up and eat **crêpes**.

panic *n* panique *f*
▶ *vb* s'affoler [**28**] **Don't panic!** Pas de panique!

panther *n* panthère *f*

pantomime *n* spectacle de Noël pour enfants *m*

pants *npl* ❶ *(briefs)* slip *msg* ▷ *a pair of pants* un slip ❷ *(boxer shorts)* caleçon *msg* ▷ *a pair of pants* un caleçon ❸ *(trousers: US)* pantalon *msg* ▷ *a pair of pants* un pantalon

pantyhose *npl (US)* collant *msg*

paper *n* ❶ papier *m* ▷ *a piece of paper* un morceau de papier; **a paper towel** une serviette en papier; **an exam paper** une épreuve écrite ❷ *(newspaper)* journal *m* (*pl* journaux) ▷ *I saw an advert in the paper.* J'ai vu une annonce dans le journal.

paperback *n* livre de poche *m*

paper clip *n* trombone *m*

paper round *n* tournée de distribution de journaux *f*

parachute *n* parachute *m*

parade *n* défilé *m*

paradise *n* paradis *m*

paragraph *n* paragraphe *m*

parallel *adj* parallèle

paralysed *adj* paralysé(e)

paramedic *n* auxiliaire médical *m*, auxiliaire médicale *f*

parcel *n* colis *m*

pardon *n* **Pardon?** Pardon?

parent *n* ❶ *(father)* père *m* ❷ *(mother)* mère *f*; **my parents** mes parents *mpl*

Paris *n* Paris *f*; **in Paris** à Paris; **to Paris** à Paris; **She's from Paris.** Elle est parisienne.

Parisian *n* Parisien *m*, Parisienne *f*
▶ *adj* parisien (*f* parisienne)

park *n* parc *m*; **a national park** un parc national; **a theme park** un parc à thème; **a car park** un parking
▶ *vb* ❶ garer [**28**] ▷ *Where can I park my car?* Où est-ce que je peux garer ma voiture? ❷ se garer [**28**] ▷ *We*

couldn't find anywhere to park. Nous avons eu du mal à nous garer.

parking *n* stationnement *m* ▷ *'no parking'* 'stationnement interdit'

Be careful not to translate **parking** by the French word **parking**.

parking lot *n (US)* parking *m*

parking meter *n* parcmètre *m*

parking ticket *n* p.-v. *m (informal)*

parliament *n* parlement *m*

parole *n* **on parole** en liberté conditionnelle

parrot *n* perroquet *m*

parsley *n* persil *m*

part *n* ❶ *(section)* partie *f* ▷ *The first part of the film was boring.* La première partie du film était ennuyeuse. ❷ *(component)* pièce *f* ▷ *spare parts* les pièces de rechange ❸ *(in play, film)* rôle *m*; **to take part in something** participer [**28**] à quelque chose ▷ *A lot of people took part in the demonstration.* Beaucoup de gens ont participé à la manifestation.

particular *adj* particulier *(f* particulière) ▷ *Are you looking for anything particular?* Est-ce que vous voulez quelque chose de particulier?; **nothing in particular** rien de particulier

particularly *adv* particulièrement

partly *adv* en partie

partner *n* ❶ *(in game)* partenaire *mf* ❷ *(in business)* associé *m*, associée *f* ❸ *(in dance)* cavalier *m*, cavalière *f* ❹ *(in relationship)* compagnon *m*, compagne *f*

part-time *adj, adv* à temps partiel ▷ *a part-time job* un travail à temps partiel ▷ *She works part-time.* Elle travaille à temps partiel.

party *n* ❶ fête *f* ▷ *a birthday party* une fête d'anniversaire ❷ *(more formal)* soirée *f* ▷ *I'm going to a party on Saturday.* Je vais à une soirée samedi. ❸ *(political)* parti *m* ▷ *the Conservative Party* le Parti conservateur ❹ *(group)* groupe *m* ▷ *a party of tourists* un groupe de touristes

pass *n* ❶ *(in mountains)* col *m* ▷ *The pass was blocked with snow.* Le col était enneigé. ❷ *(in football)* passe *f*; **to get a pass** *(in exam)* être [**35**] reçu ▷ *I got six passes.* J'ai été reçu dans six matières.; **a bus pass** une carte de bus

▶ *vb* ❶ *(exam)* être [**35**] reçu ▷ *Did you pass?* Tu as été reçu?; **to pass an exam** être [**35**] reçu à un examen

Be careful not to translate **to pass an exam** by **passer un examen**.

❷ passer [**58**] ▷ *Could you pass me the salt, please?* Est-ce que vous pourriez me passer le sel, s'il vous plaît? ▷ *The time has passed quickly.* Le temps a passé rapidement. ❸ passer [**58**] devant ▷ *I pass his house on my way to school.* Je passe devant chez lui en allant à l'école.

pass out *vb (faint)* s'évanouir [**38**]

passage *n* ❶ *(piece of writing)* passage *m* ▷ *Read the passage carefully.* Lisez attentivement le passage. ❷ *(corridor)* couloir *m*

passenger *n* passager *m*, passagère *f*

passion *n* passion *f*

passive *adj* passif (*f* passive); **passive smoking** le tabagisme passif

Passover *n* Pâque juive *f* ▷ *at Passover* à la Pâque juive

passport *n* passeport *m* ▷ *passport control* le contrôle des passeports

password *n* mot de passe *m*

past *adv, prep (beyond)* après ▷ *It's on the right, just past the station.* C'est sur la droite, juste après la gare.; **to go past (1)** passer [**58**] ▷ *The bus went past without stopping.* Le bus est passé sans s'arrêter. **(2)** passer [**58**] devant ▷ *The bus goes past our house.* Le bus passe devant notre maison.; **It's half past ten.** Il est dix heures et demie.; **It's quarter past nine.** Il est neuf heures et quart.; **It's ten past eight.** Il est huit heures dix.; **It's past midnight.** Il est minuit passé.
▶ *n* passé *m* ▷ *She lives in the past.* Elle vit dans le passé.; **in the past** *(previously)* autrefois ▷ *This was common in the past.* C'était courant autrefois.

pasta *n* pâtes *fpl* ▷ *Pasta is easy to cook.* Les pâtes sont faciles à préparer.

pasteurized *adj* pasteurisé(e)

pastry *n* pâte *f*; **pastries** les pâtisseries *fpl*

patch *n* ❶ pièce *f* ▷ *a patch of material* une pièce de tissu ❷ *(for flat tyre)* rustine *f*; **He's got a bald patch.** Il a le crâne dégarni.

path *n* ❶ *(footpath)* chemin *m* ❷ *(in garden, park)* allée *f*

pathetic *adj* lamentable ▷ *Our team was pathetic.* Notre équipe a été lamentable.

patience *n* ❶ patience *f* ▷ *He hasn't got much patience.* Il n'a pas beaucoup de patience. ❷ *(card game)* réussite *f* ▷ *to play patience* faire une réussite

patient *n* patient *m*, patiente *f*
▶ *adj* patient(e)

patio *n* patio *m*

patrol *n* patrouille *f*

patrol car *n* voiture de police *f*

pattern *n* motif *m* ▷ *a geometric pattern* un motif géométrique; **a sewing pattern** un patron

pause *n* pause *f*

pavement *n* trottoir *m*

paw *n* patte *f*

pay *n* salaire *m*
▶ *vb* ❶ payer [**59**] ▷ *They pay me more on Sundays.* Je suis payé davantage le dimanche. ❷ régler [**34**] ▷ *to pay by cheque* régler par chèque ▷ *to pay by credit card* régler par carte de crédit; **to pay for something** payer [**59**] quelque chose ▷ *I paid for my ticket.* J'ai payé mon billet. ▷ *I paid 50 euros for it.* Je l'ai payé cinquante euros.; **to pay extra for something** payer [**59**] un supplément pour quelque chose ▷ *You have to pay extra for breakfast.* Il faut payer un supplément pour le petit déjeuner.; **to pay attention**

faire [**36**] attention ▷ *Don't pay any attention to him!* Ne fais pas attention à lui!; **to pay somebody a visit** rendre [**7**] visite à quelqu'un ▷ *Paul paid us a visit last night.* Paul nous a rendu visite hier soir.; **to pay somebody back** rembourser [**28**] quelqu'un ▷ *I'll pay you back tomorrow.* Je te rembourserai demain.

payment *n* paiement *m*

payphone *n* téléphone public *m*

PC *n (= personal computer)* PC *m* ▷ *She typed the report on her PC.* Elle a tapé le rapport sur son PC.

PE *n* EPS *f* ▷ *We do PE twice a week.* Nous avons EPS deux fois par semaine.

pea *n* petit pois *m*

peace *n* ❶ *(after war)* paix *f* ❷ *(quietness)* calme *m*

peaceful *adj* ❶ *(calm)* paisible ▷ *a peaceful afternoon* un après-midi paisible ❷ *(not violent)* pacifique ▷ *a peaceful protest* une manifestation pacifique

peach *n* pêche *f*

peacock *n* paon *m*

peak *n (of mountain)* cime *f*; **the peak rate** le plein tarif ▷ *You pay the peak rate for calls at this time of day.* On paie le plein tarif quand on appelle à cette heure-ci.; **in peak season** en haute saison

peanut *n* cacahuète *f* ▷ *a packet of peanuts* un paquet de cacahuètes

peanut butter *n* beurre de cacahuètes *m* ▷ *a peanut-butter sandwich* un sandwich au beurre de cacahuètes

pear *n* poire *f*

pearl *n* perle *f*

pebble *n* galet *m* ▷ *a pebble beach* une plage de galets

peculiar *adj* bizarre ▷ *He's a peculiar person.* Il est bizarre. ▷ *It tastes peculiar.* Ça a un goût bizarre.

pedal *n* pédale *f*

pedestrian *n* piéton *m*

pedestrian crossing *n* passage pour piétons *m*

pee *n* **to have a pee** faire [**36**] pipi

peel *n (of orange)* écorce *f*
▸ *vb* ❶ éplucher [**28**] ▷ *Shall I peel the potatoes?* J'épluche les pommes de terre? ❷ peler [**43**] ▷ *My nose is peeling.* Mon nez pèle.

peg *n* ❶ *(for coats)* portemanteau *m* (*pl* portemanteaux) ❷ *(clothes peg)* pince à linge *f* ❸ *(tent peg)* piquet *m*

pelvis *n* bassin *m*

pen *n* stylo *m*

penalty *n* ❶ *(punishment)* peine *f*; **the death penalty** la peine de mort ❷ *(in football)* penalty *m* ❸ *(in rugby)* pénalité *f*; **a penalty shoot-out** les tirs au but

pence *npl* pence *mpl*

pencil *n* crayon *m*; **in pencil** au crayon

pencil case *n* trousse *f*

pencil sharpener *n* taille-crayon *m* (*pl* taille-crayons)

pendant *n* pendentif *m*

penfriend *n* correspondant *m*, correspondante *f*

penguin *n* pingouin *m*

penicillin *n* pénicilline *f*

penis *n* pénis *m*
penknife *n* canif *m*
penny *n* penny *m* (*pl* pence)
pension *n* retraite *f*
pensioner *n* retraité *m*, retraitée *f*
people *npl* ❶ gens *mpl* ▷ *a lot of people* beaucoup de gens ❷ (*individuals*) personnes *fpl* ▷ *six people* six personnes; **How many people are there in your family?** Vous êtes combien dans votre famille?; **French people** les Français; **People say that ...** On dit que ...
pepper *n* ❶ (*spice*) poivre *m* ▷ *Pass the pepper, please.* Passez-moi le poivre, s'il vous plaît. ❷ (*vegetable*) poivron *m* ▷ *a green pepper* un poivron vert
peppermill *n* moulin à poivre *m*
peppermint *n* (*sweet*) pastille de menthe *f*; **peppermint chewing gum** le chewing-gum à la menthe
per *prep* par ▷ *per day* par jour ▷ *per week* par semaine; **30 miles per hour** trente miles à l'heure
per cent *adv* pour cent ▷ *fifty per cent* cinquante pour cent
percentage *n* pourcentage *m*
percussion *n* percussion *f* ▷ *I play percussion.* Je joue des percussions.
perfect *adj* parfait(e) ▷ *Chantal speaks perfect English.* Chantal parle un anglais parfait.
perfectly *adv* parfaitement
perform *vb* (*act, play*) jouer [**28**]
performance *n* ❶ (*show*) spectacle *m* ▷ *The performance lasts two hours.* Le spectacle dure deux heures. ❷ (*acting*) interprétation *f* ▷ *his performance as Hamlet* son interprétation d'Hamlet ❸ (*results*) performance *f* ▷ *the team's poor performance* la médiocre performance de l'équipe
perfume *n* parfum *m*
perhaps *adv* peut-être ▷ *Perhaps he's ill.* Il est peut-être malade.; **perhaps not** peut-être pas
period *n* ❶ période *f* ▷ *for a limited period* pour une période limitée ❷ (*in history*) époque *f* ▷ *the Victorian period* l'époque victorienne ❸ (*menstruation*) règles *fpl* ▷ *I'm having my period.* J'ai mes règles. ❹ (*lesson time*) cours *m* ▷ *Each period lasts forty minutes.* Chaque cours dure quarante minutes.
perm *n* permanente *f* ▷ *She's got a perm.* Elle a une permanente.; **to have a perm** se faire [**36**] faire une permanente
permanent *adj* permanent(e)
permission *n* permission *f* ▷ *Could I have permission to leave early?* Pourrais-je avoir la permission de partir plus tôt?
permit *n* permis *m* ▷ *a fishing permit* un permis de pêche
persecute *vb* persécuter [**28**]
person *n* personne *f* ▷ *She's a very nice person.* C'est une personne très sympathique.; **in person** en personne
personal *adj* personnel (*f* personnelle); **personal column** les annonces personnelles *fpl*

personality *n* personnalité *f*
personally *adv* personnellement ▷ *I don't know him personally.* Je ne le connais pas personnellement.
personal stereo *n* Walkman® *m*
perspiration *n* transpiration *f*
persuade *vb* persuader [**28**]; **to persuade somebody to do something** persuader [**28**] quelqu'un de faire quelque chose ▷ *She persuaded me to go with her.* Elle m'a persuadé de l'accompagner.
pessimistic *adj* pessimiste
pest *n (person)* casse-pieds *mf* ▷ *He's a real pest!* C'est un vrai casse-pieds!
pester *vb* importuner [**28**]
pet *n* animal familier *m* ▷ *Have you got a pet?* Est-ce que tu as un animal familier?; **She's the teacher's pet.** C'est la chouchoute de la maîtresse.
petrol *n* essence *f*; **unleaded petrol** l'essence sans plomb

Be careful not to translate **petrol** by **pétrole**.

petrol station *n* station-service *f* (*pl* stations-service)
pharmacy *n* pharmacie *f*

Pharmacies in France are identified by a special green cross outside the shop.

pheasant *n* faisan *m*
philosophy *n* philosophie *f*
phobia *n* phobie *f*
phone *n* téléphone *m* ▷ *Where's the phone?* Où est le téléphone?; **by phone** par téléphone; **to be on the phone** être [**35**] au téléphone ▷ *She's on the phone at the moment.* Elle est au téléphone en ce moment.; **Can I use the phone, please?** Est-ce que je peux téléphoner, s'il vous plaît?
▸ *vb* appeler [**4**] ▷ *I'll phone the station.* Je vais appeler la gare.
phone bill *n* facture de téléphone *f*
phone book *n* annuaire *m*
phone box *n* cabine téléphonique *f*
phone call *n* appel *m* ▷ *There's a phone call for you.* Il y a un appel pour vous.; **to make a phone call** téléphoner [**28**] ▷ *Can I make a phone call?* Est-ce que peux téléphoner?
phonecard *n* carte de téléphone *f*
phone number *n* numéro de téléphone *m*
photo *n* photo *f*; **to take a photo** prendre [**65**] une photo; **to take a photo of somebody** prendre [**65**] quelqu'un en photo
photocopier *n* photocopieuse *f*
photocopy *n* photocopie *f*
▸ *vb* photocopier [**19**]
photograph *n* photo *f*; **to take a photograph** prendre [**65**] une photo; **to take a photograph of somebody** prendre [**65**] quelqu'un en photo
▸ *vb* photographier [**19**]
photographer *n* photographe *mf* ▷ *She's a photographer.* Elle est photographe.
photography *n* photo *f* ▷ *My hobby is photography.* Je fais de la photo.
phrase *n* expression *f*

phrase book *n* guide de conversation *m*

physical *adj* physique
▶ *n (US)* examen médical *m*

physicist *n* physicien *m*, physicienne *f* ▷ *He's a physicist.* Il est physicien.

physics *n* physique *f* ▷ *She teaches physics.* Elle enseigne la physique.

physiotherapist *n* kinésithérapeute *mf*

physiotherapy *n* kinésithérapie *f*

pianist *n* pianiste *mf*

piano *n* piano *m* ▷ *I play the piano.* Je joue du piano. ▷ *I have piano lessons.* Je prends des leçons de piano.

pick *n* **Take your pick!** Faites votre choix!
▶ *vb* ❶ *(choose)* choisir [**38**] ▷ *I picked the biggest piece.* J'ai choisi le plus gros morceau. ❷ *(for team)* sélectionner [**28**] ▷ *I've been picked for the team.* J'ai été sélectionné pour faire partie de l'équipe. ❸ *(fruit, flowers)* cueillir [**22**]

pick on *vb* harceler [**43**] ▷ *She's always picking on me.* Elle me harcèle constamment.

pick out *vb* choisir [**38**] ▷ *I like them all — it's difficult to pick one out.* Ils me plaisent tous — c'est difficile d'en choisir un.

pick up *vb* ❶ *(collect)* venir [**89**] chercher ▷ *We'll come to the airport to pick you up.* Nous viendrons vous chercher à l'aéroport. ❷ *(from floor)* ramasser [**28**] ▷ *Could you help me pick up the toys?* Tu peux m'aider à ramasser les jouets? ❸ *(learn)* apprendre [**65**] ▷ *I picked up some Spanish during my holiday.* J'ai appris quelques mots d'espagnol pendant mes vacances.

pickpocket *n* pickpocket *m*

picnic *n* pique-nique *m*; **to have a picnic** pique-niquer [**28**] ▷ *We had a picnic on the beach.* Nous avons pique-niqué sur la plage.

picture *n* ❶ illustration *f* ▷ *Children's books have lots of pictures.* Il y a beaucoup d'illustrations dans les livres pour enfants. ❷ photo *f* ▷ *My picture was in the paper.* Ma photo était dans le journal. ❸ *(painting)* tableau *m* (*pl* tableaux) ▷ *a famous picture* un tableau célèbre; **to paint a picture of something** peindre [**60**] quelque chose ❹ *(drawing)* dessin *m*; **to draw a picture of something** dessiner [**28**] quelque chose; **the pictures** *(cinema)* le cinéma ▷ *Shall we go to the pictures?* On va au cinéma?

picture messaging *n* envoi de photos par MMS *m*

pie *n* tourte *f* ▷ *an apple pie* une tourte aux pommes

piece *n* morceau *m* (*pl* morceaux) ▷ *A small piece, please.* Un petit morceau, s'il vous plaît.; **a piece of furniture** un meuble; **a piece of advice** un conseil

pier *n* jetée *f*

pierce *vb* percer [**12**] ▷ *She's going to have her ears pierced.* Elle va se faire percer les oreilles.

pierced *adj* percé(e) ▷ *I've got pierced*

ears. J'ai les oreilles percées.

piercing *n* piercing *m* ▷ *She has several piercings.* Elle a plusieurs piercings.

pig *n* cochon *m*

pigeon *n* pigeon *m*

piggy bank *n* tirelire *f*

pigtail *n* natte *f*

pile *n* ❶ *(untidy heap)* tas *m* ❷ *(tidy stack)* pile *f*

pill *n* pilule *f*; **to be on the pill** prendre [**65**] la pilule

pillow *n* oreiller *m*

pilot *n* pilote *m* ▷ *He's a pilot.* Il est pilote.

pimple *n* bouton *m*

PIN *n (= personal identification number)* code confidentiel *m*

pin *n* épingle *f*; **I've got pins and needles.** J'ai des fourmis dans les jambes.

pinball *n* flipper *m* ▷ *to play pinball* jouer au flipper; **a pinball machine** un flipper

pinch *vb* ❶ pincer [**12**] ▷ *He pinched me!* Il m'a pincé! ❷ *(informal: steal)* piquer [**28**] ▷ *Who's pinched my pen?* Qui est-ce qui m'a piqué mon stylo?

pine *n* pin *m* ▷ *a pine table* une table en pin

pineapple *n* ananas *m*

pink *adj* rose

pint *n* pinte *f*

In France measurements are in litres and centilitres. A pint is about 0.6 litres.

a pint of milk un demi-litre de lait; **to have a pint** boire [**10**] une bière ▷ *He's gone out for a pint.* Il est parti boire une bière.

pipe *n* ❶ *(for water, gas)* conduite *f* ▷ *The pipes froze.* Les conduites d'eau ont gelé. ❷ *(for smoking)* pipe *f* ▷ *He smokes a pipe.* Il fume la pipe.; **the pipes** *(bagpipes)* la cornemuse ▷ *He plays the pipes.* Il joue de la cornemuse.

pirate *n* pirate *m*

pirated *adj* pirate ▷ *a pirated DVD* un DVD pirate

Pisces *n* Poissons *m* ▷ *I'm Pisces.* Je suis Poissons.

pistol *n* pistolet *m*

pitch *n* terrain *m* ▷ *a football pitch* un terrain de football

▶ *vb (tent)* dresser [**28**] ▷ *We pitched our tent near the beach.* Nous avons dressé notre tente près de la plage.

pity *n* pitié *f*; **What a pity!** Quel dommage!

▶ *vb* plaindre [**17**]

pizza *n* pizza *f*

place *n* ❶ *(location)* endroit *m* ▷ *It's a quiet place.* C'est un endroit tranquille. ❷ *(space)* place *f* ▷ *a parking place* une place de parking ▷ *a university place* une place à l'université; **to change places** changer [**45**] de place ▷ *Tamsin, change places with Delphine!* Tamsin, change de place avec Delphine!; **to take place** avoir [**8**] lieu; **at your place** chez toi ▷ *Shall we meet at your place?* On se retrouve chez toi?; **to my place** chez moi ▷ *Do you want to come round to my place?* Tu veux venir chez moi?

a b c d e f g h i j k l m n o p q r s t u v w x y z

▶ *vb* ❶ poser [**28**] ▷ *He placed his hand on hers.* Il a posé la main sur la sienne. ❷ *(in competition, contest)* classer [**28**]

placement *n* stage *m*; **to do a work placement** faire [**36**] un stage en entreprise

plain *n* plaine *f*
▶ *adj, adv* ❶ *(not patterned)* uni(e) ▷ *a plain carpet* un tapis uni ❷ *(not fancy)* simple ▷ *a plain white blouse* un chemisier blanc simple

plain chocolate *n* chocolat à croquer *m*

plait *n* natte *f* ▷ *She wears her hair in a plait.* Elle a une natte.

plan *n* ❶ projet *m* ▷ *What are your plans for the holidays?* Quels sont tes projets pour les vacances? ▷ *to make plans* faire des projets; **Everything went according to plan.** Tout s'est passé comme prévu. ❷ *(map)* plan *m* ▷ *a plan of the campsite* un plan du terrain de camping; **my essay plan** le plan de ma dissertation
▶ *vb* ❶ *(make plans for)* préparer [**28**] ▷ *We're planning a trip to France.* Nous préparons un voyage en France. ❷ *(make schedule for)* planifier [**19**] ▷ *Plan your revision carefully.* Planifiez vos révisions avec soin.; **to plan to do something** avoir [**8**] l'intention de faire quelque chose ▷ *I'm planning to get a job in the holidays.* J'ai l'intention de trouver un job pour les vacances.

plane *n* avion *m* ▷ *by plane* en avion

planet *n* planète *f*

plant *n* ❶ plante *f* ▷ *to water the plants* arroser les plantes ❷ *(factory)* usine *f*
▶ *vb* planter [**28**]

plaster *n* ❶ *(sticking plaster)* pansement adhésif *m* ▷ *Have you got a plaster, by any chance?* Vous n'auriez pas un pansement adhésif, par hasard? ❷ *(for fracture)* plâtre *m* ▷ *Her leg's in plaster.* Elle a la jambe dans le plâtre.

plastic *n* plastique *m* ▷ *It's made of plastic.* C'est en plastique.
▶ *adj* en plastique ▷ *a plastic bag* un sac en plastique

plate *n (for food)* assiette *f*

platform *n* ❶ *(at station)* quai *m* ▷ *on platform 7* sur le quai numéro sept ❷ *(for performers)* estrade *f*

play *n* pièce *f* ▷ *a play by Shakespeare* une pièce de Shakespeare; **to put on a play** monter [**48**] une pièce
▶ *vb* ❶ jouer [**28**] ▷ *He's playing with his friends.* Il joue avec ses amis. ▷ *What sort of music do they play?* Quel genre de musique jouent-ils? ❷ *(against person, team)* jouer [**28**] contre ▷ *France will play Scotland next month.* La France jouera contre l'Écosse le mois prochain. ❸ *(sport, game)* jouer [**28**] à ▷ *I play hockey.* Je joue au hockey. ▷ *Can you play pool?* Tu sais jouer au billard américain? ❹ *(instrument)* jouer [**28**] de ▷ *I play the guitar.* Je joue de la guitare. ❺ *(CD, music)* écouter [**28**] ▷ *She's always playing that song.* Elle écoute tout le temps cette chanson.

play down *vb* dédramatiser [**28**] ▷ *He tried to play down his illness.* Il a essayé de dédramatiser sa maladie.

player *n* ❶ *(of sport)* joueur *m*, joueuse *f* ▷ *a football player* un joueur de football ❷ *(of instrument)* musicien *m*, musicienne *f*; **a piano player** un pianiste; **a saxophone player** un saxophoniste

playground *n* ❶ *(at school)* cour de récréation *f* ❷ *(in park)* aire de jeux *f*

playgroup *n* garderie *f*

playing card *n* carte à jouer *f*

playing field *n* terrain de sport *m*

playtime *n* récréation *f*

pleasant *adj* agréable

please *excl* ❶ *(polite form)* s'il vous plaît ▷ *Two coffees, please.* Deux cafés, s'il vous plaît. ❷ *(familiar form)* s'il te plaît ▷ *Please write back soon.* Réponds vite, s'il te plaît.

pleased *adj* content(e) ▷ *My mother's not going to be very pleased.* Ma mère ne va pas être contente du tout.; **Pleased to meet you!** Enchanté!

pleasure *n* plaisir *m* ▷ *I read for pleasure.* Je lis pour le plaisir.

plenty *n* largement assez ▷ *I've got plenty.* J'en ai largement assez. ▷ *That's plenty, thanks.* Ça suffit largement, merci.; **plenty of (1)** *(a lot)* beaucoup de ▷ *I've got plenty of things to do.* J'ai beaucoup de choses à faire. **(2)** *(enough)* largement assez de ▷ *I've got plenty of money.* J'ai largement assez d'argent. ▷ *We've got plenty of time.* Nous avons largement le temps.

pliers *npl* pince *fsg*; **a pair of pliers** une pince

plot *n* ❶ *(of story, play)* intrigue *f* ❷ *(against somebody)* conspiration *f* ▷ *a plot against the president* une conspiration contre le président ❸ *(of land)* carré *m* ▷ *a vegetable plot* un carré de légumes
▶ *vb* comploter [**28**] ▷ *They were plotting to kill him.* Ils complotaient de le tuer.

plough *n* charrue *f*
▶ *vb* labourer [**28**]

plug *n* ❶ *(electrical)* prise de courant *f* ▷ *The plug is faulty.* La prise est défectueuse. ❷ *(for sink)* bouchon *m*

plug in *vb* brancher [**28**] ▷ *Is it plugged in?* Est-ce que c'est branché?

plum *n* prune *f* ▷ *plum jam* la confiture de prunes

plumber *n* plombier *m* ▷ *He's a plumber.* Il est plombier.

plump *adj* dodu(e)

plural *n* pluriel *m*

plus *prep, adj* plus ▷ *4 plus 3 equals 7.* Quatre plus trois égalent sept. ▷ *three children plus a dog* trois enfants plus un chien; **I got a B plus.** J'ai eu un Bien.

p.m. *abbr* **at 8 p.m.** à huit heures du soir; **at 2 p.m.** à quatorze heures

In France times are often given using the 24-hour clock.

pneumonia *n* pneumonie *f*

poached *adj* **a poached egg** un œuf poché

pocket *n* poche *f*; **pocket money** l'argent de poche *m* ▷ *£8 a week pocket money* huit livres d'argent de poche par semaine

podcast *n* podcast *m*; **to download a podcast** télécharger [**45**] un podcast

poem *n* poème *m*

poet *n* poète *m*

poetry *n* poésie *f*

point *n* ❶ *(spot, score)* point *m* ▷ *a point on the horizon* un point à l'horizon ▷ *They scored 5 points.* Ils ont marqué cinq points. ❷ *(comment)* remarque *f* ▷ *He made some interesting points.* Il a fait quelque remarques intéressantes. ❸ *(tip)* pointe *f* ▷ *a pencil with a sharp point* un crayon à la pointe aiguisée ❹ *(in time)* moment *m* ▷ *At that point, we decided to leave.* À ce moment-là, nous avons décidé de partir.; **a point of view** un point de vue; **to get the point** comprendre [**65**] ▷ *Sorry, I don't get the point.* Désolé, je ne comprends pas.; **That's a good point!** C'est vrai!; **There's no point.** Cela ne sert à rien. ▷ *There's no point in waiting.* Cela ne sert à rien d'attendre.; **What's the point?** À quoi bon? ▷ *What's the point of leaving so early?* À quoi bon partir si tôt?; **Punctuality isn't my strong point.** La ponctualité n'est pas mon fort.; **two point five (2.5)** deux virgule cinq (2,5) ▶ *vb* montrer [**28**] du doigt ▷ *Don't point!* Ne montre pas du doigt!; **to point at somebody** montrer [**28**] quelqu'un du doigt ▷ *She pointed at Anne.* Elle a montré Anne du doigt.; **to point a gun at somebody** braquer [**28**] un revolver sur quelqu'un

point out *vb* ❶ *(show)* montrer [**28**] ▷ *The guide pointed out Notre-Dame to us.* Le guide nous a montré Notre-Dame. ❷ *(mention)* signaler [**28**] ▷ *I should point out that ...* Je dois vous signaler que ...

pointless *adj* inutile ▷ *It's pointless to argue.* Il est inutile de discuter.

poison *n* poison *m* ▶ *vb* empoisonner [**28**]

poisonous *adj* ❶ *(snake)* venimeux (*f* venimeuse) ❷ *(plant, mushroom)* vénéneux (*f* vénéneuse) ❸ *(gas)* toxique

poke *vb* **He poked the ground with his stick.** Il tapotait le sol avec sa canne.; **She poked me in the ribs.** Elle m'a enfoncé le doigt dans les côtes.

poker *n* poker *m* ▷ *I play poker.* Je joue au poker.

Poland *n* Pologne *f*; **in Poland** en Pologne; **to Poland** en Pologne

polar bear *n* ours blanc *m*

Pole *n* Polonais *m*, Polonaise *f*

pole *n* poteau *m* (*pl* poteaux) ▷ *a telegraph pole* un poteau télégraphique; **a tent pole** un montant de tente; **a ski pole** un bâton de ski; **the North Pole** le pôle Nord; **the South Pole** le pôle Sud

police *npl* police *f* ▷ *We called the*

police. Nous avons appelé la police.; **a police car** une voiture de police; **a police station** un commissariat de police

policeman *n* policier *m*

police officer *n* ❶ policier *m* ❷ femme policier *f* ▷ *She's a police officer.* Elle est femme policier.

policewoman *n* femme policier *f*

Polish *n (language)* polonais *m*
▸ *adj* polonais(e)

polish *n* ❶ *(for shoes)* cirage *m* ❷ *(for furniture)* cire *f*
▸ *vb* ❶ *(shoes, furniture)* cirer **[28]** ❷ *(glass)* faire **[36]** briller

polite *adj* poli(e)

politely *adv* poliment

political *adj* politique

politician *n* ❶ homme politique *m* ❷ femme politique *f*

politics *npl* politique *fsg* ▷ *I'm not interested in politics.* La politique ne m'intéresse pas.

pollute *vb* polluer **[28]**

polluted *adj* pollué(e)

pollution *n* pollution *f*

polo-necked sweater *n* pull à col roulé *m*

polythene bag *n* sac en plastique *m*

pond *n* ❶ *(big)* étang *m* ❷ *(smaller)* mare *f* ❸ *(in garden)* bassin *m* ▷ *We've got a pond in our garden.* Nous avons un bassin dans notre jardin.

pony *n* poney *m*

ponytail *n* queue de cheval *f* ▷ *He's got a ponytail.* Il a une queue de cheval.

pony trekking *n* **to go pony trekking** faire **[36]** une randonnée à dos de poney

poodle *n* caniche *m*

pool *n* ❶ *(puddle)* flaque *f* ❷ *(pond)* étang *m* ❸ *(for swimming)* piscine *f* ❹ *(game)* billard américain *m* ▷ *Shall we have a game of pool?* Si on jouait au billard américain?; **the pools** *(football)* le loto sportif ▷ *to do the pools* jouer au loto sportif

poor *adj* ❶ pauvre ▷ *a poor family* une famille pauvre ▷ *Poor David, he's very unlucky!* Le pauvre David, il n'a vraiment pas de chance!; **the poor** les pauvres *m* ❷ *(bad)* médiocre ▷ *a poor mark* une note médiocre

pop *adj* pop ▷ *pop music* la musique pop ▷ *a pop star* une pop star

pop in *vb* passer **[58]** ▷ *I just popped in to say hello.* Je suis juste passé dire bonjour.

pop out *vb* sortir **[79]**

pop round *vb* passer **[58]**

popcorn *n* pop-corn *m*

pope *n* pape *m*

poppy *n* coquelicot *m*

popular *adj* populaire ▷ *She's a very popular girl.* C'est une fille très populaire.

population *n* population *f*

porch *n* porche *m*

pork *n* porc *m* ▷ *a pork chop* une côtelette de porc

porridge *n* porridge *m*

port *n* ❶ *(harbour)* port *m* ❷ *(wine)* porto *m* ▷ *a glass of port* un verre de porto

portable *adj* portable ▷ *a portable TV* un téléviseur portable

porter *n* ❶ *(in hotel)* portier *m* ❷ *(at station)* porteur *m*

portion *n* portion *f* ▷ *a large portion of chips* une grosse portion de frites

portrait *n* portrait *m*

Portugal *n* Portugal *m*; **in Portugal** au Portugal; **We went to Portugal.** Nous sommes allés au Portugal.

Portuguese *n* ❶ *(person)* Portugais *m*, Portugaise *f* ❷ *(language)* portugais *m* ▸ *adj* portugais(e)

posh *adj* chic ▷ *a posh hotel* un hôtel chic

position *n* position *f* ▷ *an uncomfortable position* une position inconfortable

positive *adj* ❶ *(good)* positif (*f* positive) ▷ *a positive attitude* une attitude positive ❷ *(sure)* certain(e) ▷ *I'm positive.* J'en suis certain.

possession *n* **Have you got all your possessions?** Est-ce tu as toutes tes affaires?

possibility *n* **It's a possibility.** C'est possible.

possible *adj* possible ▷ *as soon as possible* aussitôt que possible

possibly *adv (perhaps)* peut-être ▷ *Are you coming to the party? — Possibly.* Est-ce que tu viens à la soirée? — Peut-être.; **... if you possibly can.** ... si cela vous est possible.; **I can't possibly come.** Je ne peux vraiment pas venir.

post *n* ❶ *(letters)* courrier *m* ▷ *Is there any post for me?* Est-ce qu'il y a du courrier pour moi? ❷ *(pole)* poteau *m* (*pl* poteaux) ▷ *The ball hit the post.* Le ballon a heurté le poteau. ❸ *(on forum, blog)* post *m* ▸ *vb (also online)* poster [**28**] ▷ *I've got some cards to post.* J'ai quelques cartes à poster.

postbox *n* boîte aux lettres *f*

postcard *n* carte postale *f*

postcode *n* code postal *m*

poster *n* ❶ poster *m* ▷ *I've got posters on my bedroom walls.* J'ai des posters sur les murs de ma chambre. ❷ *(advertising)* affiche *f* ▷ *There are posters all over town.* Il y a des affiches dans toute la ville.

postman *n* facteur *m* ▷ *He's a postman.* Il est facteur.

post office *n* poste *f* ▷ *Where's the post office, please?* Où est la poste, s'il vous plaît?

postpone *vb* remettre [**47**] à plus tard ▷ *The match has been postponed.* Le match a été remis à plus tard.

postwoman *n* factrice *f* ▷ *She's a postwoman.* Elle est factrice.

pot *n* ❶ pot *m* ▷ *a pot of jam* un pot de confiture; **the pots and pans** les casseroles ❷ *(teapot)* théière *f* ❸ *(coffeepot)* cafetière *f* ❹ *(marijuana)* herbe *f* ▷ *to smoke pot* fumer de l'herbe

potato *n* pomme de terre *f* ▷ *potato salad* la salade de pommes de terre; **mashed potatoes** la purée; **boiled potatoes** les pommes vapeur; **a baked potato** une pomme de

terre en friche des champs
pottery *n* poterie *f*
pound *n (weight, money)* livre *f* ▷ *How many euros do you get for a pound?* Combien d'euros a-t-on pour une livre?

In France measurements are in grams and kilograms. One pound is about 450 grams.

▷ *a pound of carrots* un demi-kilo de carottes
pour *vb* ❶ *(liquid)* verser [**28**] ▷ *She poured some water into the pan.* Elle a versé de l'eau dans la casserole.; **She poured him a drink.** Elle lui a servi à boire.; **Shall I pour you a cup of tea?** Je vous sers une tasse de thé? ❷ *(rain)* pleuvoir [**63**] à verse ▷ *It's pouring.* Il pleut à verse.; **in the pouring rain** sous une pluie torrentielle
poverty *n* pauvreté *f*
powder *n* poudre *f*
power *n* ❶ *(electricity)* courant *m* ▷ *The power's off.* Le courant est coupé.; **a power cut** une coupure de courant; **a power point** une prise de courant; **a power station** une centrale électrique ❷ *(energy)* énergie *f* ▷ *nuclear power* l'énergie nucléaire ❸ *(authority)* pouvoir *m* ▷ *to be in power* être au pouvoir
powerful *adj* puissant(e)
practical *adj* pratique ▷ *a practical suggestion* un conseil pratique; **She's very practical.** Elle a l'esprit pratique.
practically *adv* pratiquement ▷ *It's practically impossible.* C'est pratiquement impossible.
practice *n (for sport)* entraînement *m* ▷ *football practice* l'entraînement de foot; **I've got to do my piano practice.** Je dois travailler mon piano.; **It's normal practice in our school.** C'est ce qui se fait dans notre école.; **in practice** en pratique; **a medical practice** un cabinet médical
practise (*US* **practice**) *vb* ❶ *(music, hobby)* s'exercer [**12**] ▷ *I ought to practise more.* Je devrais m'exercer davantage. ❷ *(instrument)* travailler [**28**] ▷ *I practise the flute every evening.* Je travaille ma flûte tous les soirs. ❸ *(language)* pratiquer [**28**] ▷ *I practised my French when we were on holiday.* J'ai pratiqué mon français pendant les vacances. ❹ *(sport)* s'entraîner [**28**] ▷ *I don't practise enough.* Je ne m'entraîne pas assez.
praise *vb* faire [**36**] l'éloge de ▷ *The teachers praised our work.* Les professeurs ont fait l'éloge de notre travail.
pram *n* landau *m*
prawn *n* crevette *f*
pray *vb* prier [**19**] ▷ *to pray for something* prier pour quelque chose
prayer *n* prière *f*
precious *adj* précieux (*f* précieuse)
precise *adj* précis(e) ▷ *at that precise moment* à cet instant précis
precisely *adv* précisément ▷ *Precisely!* Précisément!; **at 10 a.m. precisely** à dix heures précises

predict *vb* prédire [**27**]

prefect *n*

- French schools do not have prefects. You could explain what a prefect is using the example given.

My sister's a prefect. Ma sœur est en dernière année et est chargée de maintenir la discipline.

prefer *vb* préférer [**34**] ▷ *Which would you prefer?* Lequel préfères-tu? ▷ *I prefer French to chemistry.* Je préfère le français à la chimie.

pregnant *adj* enceinte ▷ *She's six months pregnant.* Elle est enceinte de six mois.

prejudice *n* ❶ préjugé *m* ▷ *That's just a prejudice.* C'est un préjugé. ❷ préjugés *mpl* ▷ *There's a lot of racial prejudice.* Il y a beaucoup de préjugés raciaux.

prejudiced *adj* **to be prejudiced against somebody** avoir [**8**] des préjugés contre quelqu'un

premature *adj* prématuré(e); **a premature baby** un prématuré

Premier League *n* première division *f* ▷ *in the Premier League* en première division

premises *npl* locaux *mpl* ▷ *They're moving to new premises.* Ils vont occuper de nouveaux locaux.

prep *n (homework)* devoirs *mpl* ▷ *history prep* les devoirs d'histoire

preparation *n* préparation *f*

prepare *vb* préparer [**28**] ▷ *She has to prepare lessons in the evening.* Elle doit préparer ses cours le soir.; **to prepare for something** se préparer [**28**] pour quelque chose ▷ *We're preparing for our skiing holiday.* Nous nous préparons pour nos vacances à la neige.

prepared *adj* **to be prepared to do something** être [**35**] prêt à faire quelque chose ▷ *I'm prepared to help you.* Je suis prêt à t'aider.

prep school *n* école primaire privée *f*

prescribe *vb* prescrire [**30**]

prescription *n* ordonnance *f* ▷ *You can't get it without a prescription.* On ne peut pas se le procurer sans ordonnance.

present *adj* ❶ *(in attendance)* présent(e) ▷ *He wasn't present at the meeting.* Il n'était pas présent à la réunion. ❷ *(current)* actuel (*f* actuelle) ▷ *the present situation* la situation actuelle; **the present tense** le présent

▸ *n* ❶ *(gift)* cadeau *m* (*pl* cadeaux) ▷ *I'm going to buy presents.* Je vais acheter des cadeaux.; **to give somebody a present** offrir [**54**] un cadeau à quelqu'un ❷ *(time)* présent *m* ▷ *up to the present* jusqu'à présent; **for the present** pour l'instant; **at present** en ce moment

▸ *vb* **to present somebody with something** *(prize, medal)* remettre [**47**] quelque chose à quelqu'un

presenter *n (on TV)* présentateur *m*, présentatrice *f*

president *n* président *m*, présidente *f*

press *n* presse *f*; **a press conference** une conférence de presse
▸ *vb* ❶ appuyer [**53**] ▹ *Don't press too hard!* N'appuie pas trop fort! ❷ appuyer [**53**] sur ▹ *He pressed the accelerator.* Il a appuyé sur l'accélérateur.

press-up *n* **to do press-ups** faire [**36**] des pompes ▹ *I do twenty press-ups every morning.* Je fais vingt pompes tous les matins.

pressure *n* pression *f* ▹ *He's under a lot of pressure at work.* Il est sous pression au travail.; **a pressure group** un groupe de pression
▸ *vb* faire [**36**] pression sur ▹ *My parents are pressuring me.* Mes parents font pression sur moi.

presume *vb* supposer [**28**] ▹ *I presume so.* Je suppose que oui.

pretend *vb* **to pretend to do something** faire [**36**] semblant de faire quelque chose ▹ *He pretended to be asleep.* Il faisait semblant de dormir.

Be careful not to translate **to pretend** by **prétendre**.

pretty *adj, adv* ❶ joli(e) ▹ *She's very pretty.* Elle est très jolie. ❷ *(rather)* plutôt ▹ *That film was pretty bad.* Ce film était plutôt mauvais.; **The weather was pretty awful.** Il faisait un temps minable.; **It's pretty much the same.** C'est pratiquement la même chose.

prevent *vb* empêcher [**28**]; **to prevent somebody from doing something** empêcher [**28**] quelqu'un de faire quelque chose ▹ *They try to prevent us from smoking.* Ils essaient de nous empêcher de fumer.

previous *adj* précédent(e)

previously *adv* auparavant

price *n* prix *m*

price list *n* liste des prix *f*

prick *vb* piquer [**28**] ▹ *I've pricked my finger.* Je me suis piqué le doigt.

pride *n* fierté *f*

priest *n* prêtre *m* ▹ *He's a priest.* Il est prêtre.

primarily *adv* principalement

primary *adj* principal(e) *(mpl* principaux)

primary school *n* école primaire *f* ▹ *She's still at primary school.* Elle est encore à l'école primaire.

prime minister *n* Premier ministre *m*

prince *n* prince *m* ▹ *the Prince of Wales* le prince de Galles

princess *n* princesse *f* ▹ *Princess Anne* la princesse Anne

principal *adj* principal(e) *(mpl* principaux)
▸ *n (of college)* principal *m (pl* principaux)

principle *n* principe *m*; **on principle** par principe

print *n* ❶ *(photo)* tirage *m* ▹ *colour prints* des tirages en couleur ❷ *(letters)* caractères *mpl* ▹ *in small print* en petits caractères ❸ *(fingerprint)* empreinte digitale *f* ❹ *(picture)* gravure *f* ▹ *a framed print* une gravure encadrée

printer *n (machine)* imprimante *f*

printout *n* tirage *m*
priority *n* priorité *f*
prison *n* prison *f*; **in prison** en prison
prisoner *n* prisonnier *m*, prisonnière *f*
private *adj* privé(e) ▷ *a private school* une école privée; **'private property'** 'propriété privée'; **'private'** *(on envelope)* 'personnel'; **a private bathroom** une salle de bain individuelle; **I have private lessons.** Je prends des cours particuliers.
prize *n* prix *m* ▷ *to win a prize* gagner un prix
prize-giving *n* distribution des prix *f*
prizewinner *n* gagnant *m*, gagnante *f*
pro *n* **the pros and cons** le pour et le contre ▷ *We weighed up the pros and cons.* Nous avons pesé le pour et le contre.
probability *n* probabilité *f*
probable *adj* probable
probably *adv* probablement ▷ *probably not* probablement pas
problem *n* problème *m* ▷ *No problem!* Pas de problème!
process *n* processus *m* ▷ *the peace process* le processus de paix; **to be in the process of doing something** être [**35**] en train de faire quelque chose ▷ *We're in the process of painting the kitchen.* Nous sommes en train de peindre la cuisine.
procession *n (religious)* procession *f*
produce *vb* ❶ *(manufacture)* produire [**23**] ❷ *(play, show)* monter [**48**]
producer *n (of play, show)* metteur en scène *m*
product *n* produit *m*
production *n* ❶ production *f* ▷ *They're increasing production of luxury models.* Ils augmentent la production des modèles de luxe. ❷ *(play, show)* mise en scène *f* ▷ *a production of 'Hamlet'* une mise en scène de 'Hamlet'
profession *n* profession *f*
professional *n* professionnel *m*, professionnelle *f*
▶ *adj (player)* professionnel (*f* professionnelle) ▷ *a professional musician* un musicien professionnel; **a very professional piece of work** un vrai travail de professionnel
professor *n* professeur d'université *m*; **He's the French professor.** Il est titulaire de la chaire de français.
profit *n* bénéfice *m*
profitable *adj* rentable
program *n* programme *m* ▷ *a computer program* un programme informatique; **a TV program** *(US)* une émission de télévision
▶ *vb (computer)* programmer [**28**]
programme *n* ❶ *(on TV, radio)* émission *f* ❷ *(of events)* programme *m*
programmer *n* programmeur *m*, programmeuse *f* ▷ *She's a programmer.* Elle est programmeuse.

progress *n* progrès *m* ▷ *You're making progress!* Vous faites des progrès!

prohibit *vb* interdire [**27**] ▷ *Smoking is prohibited.* Il est interdit de fumer.

project *n* ❶ *(plan)* projet *m* ▷ *a development project* un projet de développement ❷ *(research)* dossier *m* ▷ *I'm doing a project on education in France.* Je prépare un dossier sur l'éducation en France.

projector *n* projecteur *m*

promise *n* promesse *f* ▷ *He made me a promise.* Il m'a fait une promesse.; **That's a promise!** C'est promis! ▶ *vb* promettre [**47**] ▷ *She promised to write.* Elle a promis d'écrire.

promote *vb* **to be promoted** être [**35**] promu ▷ *She was promoted after six months.* Elle a été promue au bout de six mois.

promotion *n* promotion *f*

prompt *adj, adv* rapide ▷ *a prompt reply* une réponse rapide; **at eight o'clock prompt** à huit heures précises

pronoun *n* pronom *m*

pronounce *vb* prononcer [**12**] ▷ *How do you pronounce that word?* Comment est-ce qu'on prononce ce mot?

pronunciation *n* prononciation *f*

proof *n* preuve *f*

proper *adj* ❶ *(genuine)* vrai(e) ▷ *proper French bread* du vrai pain français; **It's difficult to get a proper job.** Il est difficile de trouver un travail correct. ❷ adéquat(e) ▷ *You have to have the proper equipment.* Il faut avoir l'équipement adéquat. ▷ *We need proper training.* Il nous faut une formation adéquate.; **If you had come at the proper time ...** Si tu étais venu à l'heure dite ...

properly *adv* ❶ *(correctly)* comme il faut ▷ *You're not doing it properly.* Tu ne t'y prends pas comme il faut. ❷ *(appropriately)* convenablement ▷ *Dress properly for your interview.* Habille-toi convenablement pour ton entretien.

property *n* propriété *f*; **'private property'** 'propriété privée'; **stolen property** les objets volés

propose *vb* proposer [**28**] ▷ *I propose a new plan.* Je propose un changement de programme.; **to propose to do something** avoir [**8**] l'intention de faire quelque chose ▷ *What do you propose to do?* Qu'est-ce que tu as l'intention de faire?; **to propose to somebody** *(for marriage)* demander [**28**] quelqu'un en mariage ▷ *He proposed to her at the restaurant.* Il l'a demandée en mariage au restaurant.

prosecute *vb* poursuivre [**81**] en justice ▷ *They were prosecuted for murder.* Ils ont été poursuivis en justice pour meurtre.; **'Trespassers will be prosecuted'** 'Défense d'entrer sous peine de poursuites'

prostitute *n* prostituée *f*; **a male prostitute** un prostitué

protect *vb* protéger [**66**]

protection *n* protection *f*
protein *n* protéine *f*
protest *n* protestation *f* ▷ *He ignored their protests.* Il a ignoré leurs protestations.; **a protest march** une manifestation
▶ *vb* protester [**28**]
Protestant *n* protestant *m*, protestante *f* ▷ *I'm a Protestant.* Je suis protestant.
▶ *adj* protestant(e) ▷ *a Protestant church* une église protestante
protester *n* manifestant *m*, manifestante *f*
proud *adj* fier (*f* fière) ▷ *Her parents are proud of her.* Ses parents sont fiers d'elle.
prove *vb* prouver [**28**] ▷ *The police couldn't prove it.* La police n'a pas pu le prouver.
proverb *n* proverbe *m*
provide *vb* fournir [**38**]; **to provide somebody with something** fournir [**38**] quelque chose à quelqu'un ▷ *They provided us with maps.* Ils nous ont fourni des cartes.
provide for *vb* subvenir [**89**] aux besoins de
provided *conj* à condition que
à condition que has to be followed by the subjunctive.
▷ *He'll play in the next match provided he's fit.* Il jouera dans le prochain match, à condition qu'il soit en forme.
prune *n* pruneau *m* (*pl* pruneaux)
psychiatrist *n* psychiatre *mf* ▷ *She's a psychiatrist.* Elle est psychiatre.
psychological *adj* psychologique
psychologist *n* psychologue *mf* ▷ *He's a psychologist.* Il est psychologue.
psychology *n* psychologie *f*
PTO *abbr* (= *please turn over*) T.S.V.P. (= *tournez, s'il vous plaît*)
pub *n* pub *m*
public *n* public *m* ▷ *open to the public* ouvert au public; **in public** en public
▶ *adj* public (*f* publique); **a public holiday** un jour férié; **public opinion** l'opinion publique *f*; **the public address system** les haut-parleurs
publicity *n* publicité *f*
public school *n* école privée *f*
public transport *n* transports en commun *mpl*
publish *vb* publier [**19**]
publisher *n* éditeur *m*
pudding *n* dessert *m* ▷ *What's for pudding?* Qu'est-ce qu'il y a comme dessert?; **rice pudding** le riz au lait; **black pudding** le boudin noir
puddle *n* flaque *f*
puff pastry *n* pâte feuilletée *f*
pull *vb* tirer [**28**] ▷ *Pull!* Tirez!; **He pulled the trigger.** Il a appuyé sur la gâchette.; **to pull a muscle** se froisser [**28**] un muscle ▷ *I pulled a muscle when I was training.* Je me suis froissé un muscle à l'entraînement.; **You're pulling my leg!** Tu me fais marcher!
pull down *vb* démolir [**38**]
pull out *vb* ❶ (*tooth, weed*) arracher [**28**] ❷ (*car*) déboîter [**28**] ▷ *The car*

pulled out to overtake. La voiture a déboîté pour doubler. ❸ *(withdraw)* se retirer [**28**] ▷ *She pulled out of the tournament.* Elle s'est retirée du tournoi.

pull through *vb* s'en sortir [**79**] ▷ *They think he'll pull through.* Ils pensent qu'il va s'en sortir.

pull up *vb (car)* s'arrêter [**28**] ▷ *A black car pulled up beside me.* Une voiture noire s'est arrêtée à côté de moi.

pullover *n* pull-over *m*

pulse *n* pouls *m* ▷ *The nurse felt his pulse.* L'infirmière a pris son pouls.

pump *n* ❶ pompe *f* ▷ *a bicycle pump* une pompe à vélo ▷ *a petrol pump* une pompe à essence ❷ *(shoe)* chausson de gym *m*
▶ *vb* pomper [**28**]

pump up *vb (tyre)* gonfler [**28**]

pumpkin *n* potiron *m*

punch *n* ❶ *(blow)* coup de poing *m* ▷ *He gave me a punch.* Il m'a donné un coup de poing. ❷ *(drink)* punch *m*
▶ *vb* ❶ *(hit)* donner [**28**] un coup de poing à ▷ *He punched me!* Il m'a donné un coup de poing! ❷ *(in ticket machine)* composter [**28**] ▷ *Punch your ticket before you get on the train.* Compostez votre billet avant de monter dans le train. ❸ *(by hand)* poinçonner [**28**] ▷ *He forgot to punch my ticket.* Il a oublié de poinçonner mon billet.

punctual *adj* ponctuel *(f* ponctuelle)

punctuation *n* ponctuation *f*

puncture *n* crevaison *f* ▷ *I had to mend a puncture.* J'ai dû réparer une crevaison.; **to have a puncture** crever [**43**] ▷ *I had a puncture on the motorway.* J'ai crevé sur l'autoroute.

punish *vb* punir [**38**]; **to punish somebody for something** punir [**38**] quelqu'un de quelque chose; **to punish somebody for doing something** punir [**38**] quelqu'un d'avoir fait quelque chose

punishment *n* punition *f*

punk *n (person)* punk *mf*; **a punk rock band** un groupe de punk rock

pupil *n* élève *mf*

puppet *n* marionnette *f*

puppy *n* chiot *m*

purchase *vb* acheter [**1**]

pure *adj* pur(e) ▷ *pure orange juice* du pur jus d'orange

purple *adj* violet *(f* violette)

purpose *n* but *m* ▷ *What is the purpose of these changes?* Quel est le but de ces changements?; **on purpose** exprès ▷ *He did it on purpose.* Il l'a fait exprès.

purr *vb* ronronner [**28**]

purse *n* ❶ porte-monnaie *m (pl* porte-monnaie) ❷ *(US: handbag)* sac à main *m*

pursue *vb* poursuivre [**81**]

push *n* **to give somebody a push** pousser [**28**] quelqu'un ▷ *He gave me a push.* Il m'a poussé.
▶ *vb* ❶ pousser [**28**] ▷ *Don't push!* Arrêtez de pousser! ❷ *(button)* appuyer [**53**] sur; **to push somebody to do something** pousser [**28**] quelqu'un à faire

a b c d e f g h i j k l m n o p q r s t u v w x y z

quelque chose ▷ *My parents are pushing me to go to university.* Mes parents me poussent à entrer à l'université.; **to push drugs** revendre [**88**] de la drogue; **Push off!** Dégage!

push around *vb* bousculer [**28**] ▷ *He likes pushing people around.* Il aime bien bousculer les gens.

push through *vb* se frayer [**59**] un passage

pushchair *n* poussette *f*

push-up *n* **to do push-ups** faire [**36**] des pompes

put *vb* ❶ *(place)* mettre [**47**] ▷ *Where shall I put my things?* Où est-ce que je peux mettre mes affaires? ▷ *She's putting the baby to bed.* Elle met le bébé au lit. ❷ *(write)* écrire [**30**] ▷ *Don't forget to put your name on the paper.* N'oubliez pas d'écrire votre nom sur la feuille.

put aside *vb* mettre [**47**] de côté ▷ *Can you put this aside for me till tomorrow?* Est-ce que vous pouvez mettre ça de côté pour moi jusqu'à demain?

put away *vb* ranger [**45**] ▷ *Can you put away the dishes, please?* Tu peux ranger la vaisselle, s'il te plaît?

put back *vb (replace)* remettre [**47**] en place ▷ *Put it back when you've finished with it.* Remets-le en place une fois que tu auras fini.

put down *vb* ❶ poser [**28**] ▷ *I'll put these bags down for a minute.* Je vais poser ces sacs une minute. ❷ *(in writing)* noter [**28**] ▷ *I've put down a few ideas.* J'ai noté quelques idées.; **to have an animal put down** faire [**36**] piquer un animal ▷ *We had to have our old dog put down.* Nous avons dû faire piquer notre vieux chien.

put forward *vb* ❶ *(clock)* avancer [**12**] ▷ *Don't forget to put the clocks forward.* N'oubliez pas d'avancer les pendules d'une heure. ❷ *(idea, argument)* proposer [**28**] ▷ *to put forward a suggestion* proposer une suggestion

put in *vb (install)* installer [**28**] ▷ *We're going to get central heating put in.* Nous allons faire installer le chauffage central.; **He has put in a lot of work on this project.** Il a fourni beaucoup de travail pour ce projet.

put off *vb* ❶ *(switch off)* éteindre [**60**] ▷ *Shall I put the light off?* Est-ce que j'éteins la lumière? ❷ *(postpone)* remettre [**47**] à plus tard ▷ *I keep putting it off.* Je n'arrête pas de remettre ça à plus tard. ❸ *(distract)* déranger [**45**] ▷ *Stop putting me off!* Arrête de me déranger! ❹ *(discourage)* décourager [**45**] ▷ *He's not easily put off.* Il ne se laisse pas facilement décourager.

put on *vb* ❶ *(clothes, lipstick, CD)* mettre [**47**] ▷ *I'll put my coat on.* Je vais mettre mon manteau. ❷ *(light, heater, TV)* allumer [**28**] ▷ *Shall I put the heater on?* J'allume le chauffage? ❸ *(play, show)* monter [**48**] ▷ *We're putting on 'Bugsy Malone'.* Nous sommes en train de monter 'Bugsy Malone'. ❹ mettre

[**47**] à cuire ▷ *I'll put the potatoes on.* Je vais mettre les pommes de terre à cuire.; **to put on weight** grossir [**38**] ▷ *He's put on a lot of weight.* Il a beaucoup grossi.

put out *vb (light, cigarette, fire)* éteindre [**60**] ▷ *It took them five hours to put out the fire.* Ils ont mis cinq heures à éteindre l'incendie.

put through *vb* passer [**58**] ▷ *Can you put me through to the manager?* Est-ce que vous pouvez me passer le directeur?; **I'm putting you through.** Je vous passe la communication.

put up *vb* ❶ *(pin up)* mettre [**47**] ▷ *I'll put the poster up on my wall.* Je vais mettre le poster sur mon mur. ❷ *(tent)* monter [**48**] ▷ *We put up our tent in a field.* Nous avons monté la tente dans un champ. ❸ *(price)* augmenter [**28**] ▷ *They've put up the price.* Ils ont augmenté le prix. ❹ *(accommodate)* héberger [**45**] ▷ *My friend will put me up for the night.* Mon ami va m'héberger pour la nuit.; **to put one's hand up** lever [**43**] la main ▷ *If you have any questions, put up your hand.* Si vous avez une question, levez la main.; **to put up with something** supporter [**28**] quelque chose ▷ *I'm not going to put up with it any longer.* Je ne vais pas supporter ça plus longtemps.

puzzle *n (jigsaw)* puzzle *m*

puzzled *adj* perplexe ▷ *You look puzzled!* Tu as l'air perplexe!

pyjamas *npl* pyjama *msg* ▷ *my pyjamas* mon pyjama ▷ *a pair of pyjamas* un pyjama; **a pyjama top** un haut de pyjama

pyramid *n* pyramide *f*

Pyrenees *npl* Pyrénées *fpl*; **in the Pyrenees** dans les Pyrénées; **We went to the Pyrenees.** Nous sommes allés dans les Pyrénées.

a b c d e f g h i j k l m n o p q r s t u v w x y z

q

qualification *n* diplôme *m* ▷ *to leave school without any qualifications* quitter l'école sans aucun diplôme; **vocational qualifications** des qualifications professionnelles

qualified *adj* ❶ *(trained)* qualifié(e) ▷ *a qualified driving instructor* un moniteur d'auto-école qualifié ❷ *(nurse, teacher)* diplômé(e) ▷ *a qualified nurse* une infirmière diplômée

qualify *vb* ❶ *(for job)* obtenir [**83**] son diplôme ▷ *She qualified as a teacher last year.* Elle a obtenu son diplôme de professeur l'année dernière. ❷ *(in competition)* se qualifier [**19**] ▷ *Our team didn't qualify.* Notre équipe ne s'est pas qualifiée.

quality *n* qualité *f* ▷ *a good quality of life* une bonne qualité de vie ▷ *She's got lots of good qualities.* Elle a beaucoup de qualités.

quantity *n* quantité *f*

quarantine *n* quarantaine *f* ▷ *in quarantine* en quarantaine

quarrel *n* dispute *f*
▶ *vb* se disputer [**28**]

quarry *n (for stone)* carrière *f*

quarter *n* quart *m*; **three quarters** trois quarts; **a quarter of an hour** un quart d'heure ▷ *three quarters of an hour* trois quarts d'heure; **a quarter past ten** dix heures et quart; **a quarter to eleven** onze heures moins le quart

quarter final *n* quart de finale *m*

quartet *n* quatuor *m* ▷ *a string quartet* un quatuor à cordes

quay *n* quai *m*

queen *n* ❶ reine *f* ▷ *Queen Elizabeth* la reine Élisabeth ❷ *(playing card)* dame *f* ▷ *the queen of hearts* la dame de cœur; **the Queen Mother** la reine mère

query *n* question *f*
▶ *vb* mettre [**47**] en question ▷ *No one queried my decision.* Personne n'a mis en question ma décision.

question *n* question *f* ▷ *Can I ask a question?* Est-ce que je peux poser une question? ▷ *That's a difficult question.* C'est une question difficile.; **It's out of the question.** C'est hors de question.
▶ *vb* interroger [**45**] ▷ *He was questioned by the police.* Il a été interrogé par la police.

question mark *n* point d'interrogation *m*
questionnaire *n* questionnaire *m*
queue *n* queue *f*
▶ *vb* faire [**36**] la queue; **to queue for something** faire [**36**] la queue pour avoir quelque chose ▷ *We had to queue for tickets.* Nous avons dû faire la queue pour avoir les billets.
quick *adj, adv* rapide ▷ *a quick lunch* un déjeuner rapide ▷ *It's quicker by train.* C'est plus rapide en train.; **Be quick!** Dépêche-toi!; **She's a quick learner.** Elle apprend vite.; **Quick, phone the police!** Téléphonez vite à la police!
quickly *adv* vite ▷ *It was all over very quickly.* Ça s'est passé très vite.
quiet *adj* ❶ *(not talkative or noisy)* silencieux (*f* silencieuse) ▷ *You're very quiet today.* Tu es bien silencieux aujourd'hui. ▷ *The engine's very quiet.* Le moteur est très silencieux. ❷ *(peaceful)* tranquille ▷ *a quiet weekend* un week-end tranquille; **Be quiet!** Tais-toi!; **Quiet!** Silence!
quietly *adv* ❶ *(speak)* doucement ▷ *'She's dead,' he said quietly.* 'Elle est morte' dit-il doucement. ❷ *(move)* silencieusement; **He quietly opened the door.** Il a ouvert la porte sans faire de bruit.
quilt *n (duvet)* couette *f*
quit *vb (place, premises, job)* quitter [**28**] ▷ *She's decided to quit her job.* Elle a décidé de quitter son emploi.; **I quit!** J'abandonne!
quite *adv* ❶ *(rather)* assez ▷ *It's quite warm today.* Il fait assez bon aujourd'hui. ❷ *(entirely)* tout à fait ▷ *I'm not quite sure.* Je n'en suis pas tout à fait sûr.; **quite good** pas mal; **I've been there quite a lot.** J'y suis allé pas mal de fois.; **quite a lot of money** pas mal d'argent; **It costs quite a lot to go abroad.** Ça coûte assez cher d'aller à l'étranger.; **It's quite a long way.** C'est assez loin.; **It was quite a shock.** Ça a été un sacré choc.; **There were quite a few people there.** Il y avait pas mal de gens.
quiz *n* jeu-concours *m*
quotation *n* citation *f* ▷ *a quotation from Shakespeare* une citation de Shakespeare
quote *n* citation *f* ▷ *a Shakespeare quote* une citation de Shakespeare; **quotes** *(quotation marks)* les guillemets *mpl* ▷ *in quotes* entre guillemets
▶ *vb* citer [**28**] ▷ *He's always quoting Shakespeare.* Il n'arrête pas de citer Shakespeare.

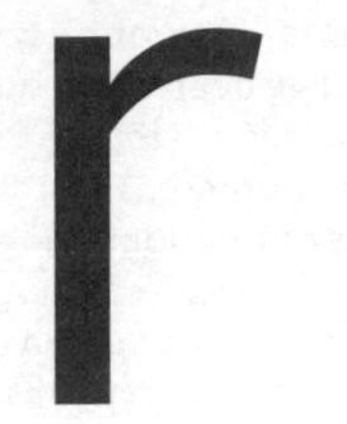

rabbi *n* rabbin *m*

rabbit *n* lapin *m*; **a rabbit hutch** un clapier

race *n* ❶ *(sport)* course *f* ▷ *a cycle race* une course cycliste ❷ *(species)* race *f* ▷ *the human race* la race humaine; **race relations** les relations interraciales *fpl*
▶ *vb* ❶ courir [16] ▷ *We raced to catch the bus.* Nous avons couru pour attraper le bus. ❷ *(have a race)* faire [36] la course; **I'll race you!** On fait la course!

racecourse *n* champ de courses *m*

racer *n (bike)* vélo de course *m*

racetrack *n* piste *f*

racial *adj* racial(e) *(mpl* raciaux) ▷ *racial discrimination* la discrimination raciale

racing car *n* voiture de course *f*

racing driver *n* pilote de course *m*

racism *n* racisme *m*

racist *adj* raciste
▶ *n* raciste *mf*

rack *n (for luggage)* porte-bagages *m (pl* porte-bagages)

racket *n* ❶ *(for sport)* raquette *f* ▷ *my tennis racket* ma raquette de tennis ❷ *(noise)* boucan *m* ▷ *They're making a terrible racket. (informal)* Ils font un boucan de tous les diables.

racquet *n* raquette *f*

radar *n* radar *m*

radiation *n* radiation *f*

radiator *n* radiateur *m*

radio *n* radio *f*; **on the radio** à la radio; **a radio station** une station de radio

radioactive *adj* radioactif *(f* radioactive)

radish *n* radis *m*

RAF *n (= Royal Air Force)* R.A.F. *f* ▷ *He's in the RAF.* Il est dans la R.A.F.

raffle *n* tombola *f* ▷ *a raffle ticket* un billet de tombola

raft *n* radeau *m (pl* radeaux)

rag *n* chiffon *m* ▷ *a piece of rag* un chiffon; **dressed in rags** en haillons

rage *n* rage *f* ▷ *mad with rage* fou de rage; **to be in a rage** être [35] furieux ▷ *She was in a rage.* Elle était furieuse.; **It's all the rage.** Ça fait fureur.

rail *n* ❶ *(on stairs)* rampe *f* ❷ *(on bridge, balcony)* balustrade *f* ▷ *Don't lean over the rail!* Ne vous penchez pas sur la balustrade! ❸ *(on railway line)* rail *m*; **by rail** en train

railcard *n* carte de chemin de fer *f* ▷ *a young person's railcard* une carte de chemin de fer tarif jeune
railroad *n (US)* chemin de fer *m*
railway *n* chemin de fer *m* ▷ *the privatization of the railways* la privatisation des chemins de fer; **a railway line** une ligne de chemin de fer; **a railway station** une gare
rain *n* pluie *f* ▷ *in the rain* sous la pluie ▶ *vb* pleuvoir [**63**] ▷ *It rains a lot here.* Il pleut beaucoup par ici.; **It's raining.** Il pleut.
rainbow *n* arc-en-ciel *m* (*pl* arcs-en-ciel)
raincoat *n* imperméable *m*
rainforest *n* forêt tropicale humide *f*
rainy *adj* pluvieux (*f* pluvieuse)
raise *vb* ❶ *(lift)* lever [**43**] ▷ *He raised his hand.* Il a levé la main. ❷ *(improve)* améliorer [**28**] ▷ *They want to raise standards in schools.* Ils veulent améliorer le niveau dans les écoles.; **to raise money** collecter [**28**] des fonds ▷ *The school is raising money for a new gym.* L'école collecte des fonds pour un nouveau gymnase.
raisin *n* raisin sec *m*
rake *n* râteau *m* (*pl* râteaux)
rally *n* ❶ *(of people)* rassemblement *m* ❷ *(sport)* rallye *m* ▷ *a rally driver* un pilote de rallye ❸ *(in tennis)* échange *m*
rambler *n* randonneur *m*, randonneuse *f*
ramp *n (for wheelchairs)* rampe d'accès *f*
ran *vb see* **run**
rang *vb see* **ring**
range *n* choix *m* ▷ *a wide range of colours* un grand choix de coloris; **a range of subjects** diverses matières ▷ *We study a range of subjects.* Nous étudions diverses matières.; **a mountain range** une chaîne de montagnes ▶ *vb* **to range from ... to** se situer [**28**] entre ... et ▷ *Temperatures in summer range from 20 to 35 degrees.* Les températures estivales se situent entre vingt et trente-cinq degrés.; **Tickets range from £2 to £20.** Les billets coûtent entre deux et vingt livres.
rap *n (music)* rap *m*
rape *n* viol *m* ▶ *vb* violer [**28**]
rapids *npl* rapides *mpl*
rare *adj* ❶ *(unusual)* rare ▷ *a rare plant* une plante rare ❷ *(steak)* saignant(e)
raspberry *n* framboise *f* ▷ *raspberry jam* la confiture de framboises
rat *n* rat *m*
rather *adv* plutôt ▷ *I was rather disappointed.* J'étais plutôt déçu. ▷ *£20! That's rather a lot!* Vingt livres! C'est plutôt cher!; **rather a lot of** pas mal de ▷ *I've got rather a lot of homework to do.* J'ai pas mal de devoirs à faire.; **rather than** plutôt que ▷ *We decided to camp, rather than stay at a hotel.* Nous avons décidé de camper plutôt que d'aller à l'hôtel.; **I'd rather ...** J'aimerais mieux ... ▷ *I'd rather stay in tonight.*

a b c d e f g h i j k l m n o p q r s t u v w x y z

J'aimerais mieux rester à la maison ce soir. ▷ *I'd rather have an apple than a banana.* J'aimerais mieux une pomme qu'une banane.

rattlesnake *n* serpent à sonnette *m*

rave *vb* s'extasier [**19**]
▶ *n (party)* rave *f*

ravenous *adj* **to be ravenous** avoir [**8**] une faim de loup ▷ *I'm ravenous!* J'ai une faim de loup!

raw *adj (food)* cru(e); **raw materials** les matières premières *fpl*

razor *n* rasoir *m* ▷ *some disposable razors* des rasoirs jetables; **a razor blade** une lame de rasoir

RE *n* éducation religieuse *f*

reach *n* **out of reach** hors de portée ▷ *The light switch was out of reach.* L'interrupteur était hors de portée.; **within easy reach of** à proximité de ▷ *The hotel is within easy reach of the town centre.* L'hôtel se trouve à proximité du centre-ville.
▶ *vb* ❶ arriver [**5**] à ▷ *We reached the hotel at 7 p.m.* Nous sommes arrivés à l'hôtel à sept heures du soir.; **We hope to reach the final.** Nous espérons aller en finale.
❷ *(decision)* parvenir [**89**] à ▷ *Eventually they reached a decision.* Ils sont finalement parvenus à une décision.; **He reached for his gun.** Il a tendu la main pour prendre son revolver.

reaction *n* réaction *f*

reactor *n* réacteur *m* ▷ *a nuclear reactor* un réacteur nucléaire

read *vb* lire [**44**] ▷ *I don't read much.* Je ne lis pas beaucoup. ▷ *Read the text out loud.* Lis le texte à haute voix.

read out *vb* lire [**44**] ▷ *He read out the article to me.* Il m'a lu l'article.; **to read out the results** annoncer [**12**] les résultats

reading *n* lecture *f* ▷ *Reading is one of my hobbies.* La lecture est l'une de mes activités favorites.

ready *adj* prêt(e) ▷ *She's nearly ready.* Elle est presque prête. ▷ *He's always ready to help.* Il est toujours prêt à rendre service.; **a ready meal** un plat cuisiné; **to get ready** se préparer [**28**] ▷ *She's getting ready to go out.* Elle est en train de se préparer pour sortir.; **to get something ready** préparer [**28**] quelque chose ▷ *He's getting the dinner ready.* Il est en train de préparer le dîner.

real *adj* ❶ vrai(e) ▷ *He wasn't a real police officer.* Ce n'était pas un vrai policier. ▷ *Her real name is Cordelia.* Son vrai nom est Cordelia.
❷ véritable ▷ *It's real leather.* C'est du cuir véritable. ▷ *It was a real nightmare.* C'était un véritable cauchemar.; **in real life** dans la réalité

realistic *adj* réaliste

reality *n* réalité *f*

realize *vb* **to realize that ...** se rendre [**7**] compte que ... ▷ *We realized that something was wrong.* Nous nous sommes rendu compte que quelque chose n'allait pas.

really *adv* vraiment ▷ *She's really nice.* Elle est vraiment sympathique. ▷ *Do you want to go? — Not really.* Tu veux y aller? — Pas vraiment.; **I'm learning German. — Really?** J'apprends l'allemand. — Ah bon?; **Do you really think so?** Tu es sûr?

realtor *n (US)* agent immobilier *m*

reason *n* raison *f* ▷ *There's no reason to think that ...* Il n'y a aucune raison de penser que ... ▷ *for security reasons* pour des raisons de sécurité; **That was the main reason I went.** C'est surtout pour ça que j'y suis allé.

reasonable *adj* ❶ *(sensible)* raisonnable ▷ *Be reasonable!* Sois raisonnable! ❷ *(not bad)* correct(e) ▷ *He wrote a reasonable essay.* Sa dissertation était correcte.

reasonably *adv* raisonnablement ▷ *The team played reasonably well.* L'équipe a joué raisonnablement bien.; **reasonably priced accommodation** un logement à un prix raisonnable

reassure *vb* rassurer **[28]**

reassuring *adj* rassurant(e)

rebellious *adj* rebelle

receipt *n* reçu *m*

receive *vb* recevoir **[67]**

receiver *n (of phone)* combiné *m*; **to pick up the receiver** décrocher **[28]**

recent *adj* récent(e)

recently *adv* ces derniers temps ▷ *I've been doing a lot of training recently.* Je me suis beaucoup entraîné ces derniers temps.

reception *n* réception *f* ▷ *Please leave your key at reception.* Merci de laisser votre clé à la réception. ▷ *The reception will be at a big hotel.* La réception aura lieu dans un grand hôtel.

receptionist *n* réceptionniste *mf*

recipe *n* recette *f*

reckon *vb* penser **[28]** ▷ *What do you reckon?* Qu'est-ce que tu en penses?

recognize *vb* reconnaître **[14]** ▷ *You'll recognize me by my red hair.* Vous me reconnaîtrez à mes cheveux roux.

recommend *vb* conseiller **[28]** ▷ *What do you recommend?* Qu'est-ce que vous me conseillez?

reconsider *vb* reconsidérer **[34]**

record *n* ❶ *(sport)* record *m* ▷ *the world record* le record du monde; **in record time** en un temps record ▷ *She finished the job in record time.* Elle a terminé le travail en un temps record. ❷ *(recording)* disque *m* ▷ *my favourite record* mon disque préféré; **a criminal record** un casier judiciaire ▷ *He's got a criminal record.* Il a un casier judiciaire.; **records** *(of police, hospital)* les archives *fpl* ▷ *I'll check in the records.* Je vais vérifier dans les archives.; **There is no record of your booking.** Il n'y a aucune trace de votre réservation.
▶ *vb (on film)* enregistrer **[28]** ▷ *They've just recorded their new album.* Ils viennent d'enregistrer leur nouveau disque.

recorded delivery *n* **to send something recorded delivery** envoyer [**33**] quelque chose en recommandé
recorder *n (instrument)* flûte à bec *f* ▷ *She plays the recorder.* Elle joue de la flûte à bec.; **a video recorder** un magnétoscope
recording *n* enregistrement *m*
record player *n* tourne-disque *m*
recover *vb* se remettre [**47**] ▷ *He's recovering from a knee injury.* Il se remet d'une blessure au genou.
recovery *n* rétablissement *m*; **Best wishes for a speedy recovery!** Meilleurs vœux de prompt rétablissement!
rectangle *n* rectangle *m*
rectangular *adj* rectangulaire
recycle *vb* recycler [**28**]
recycling *n* recyclage *m*
red *adj* ❶ rouge ▷ *a red rose* une rose rouge ▷ *red meat* la viande rouge; **a red light** *(traffic light)* un feu rouge ▷ *to go through a red light* brûler un feu rouge ❷ *(hair)* roux *(f* rousse) ▷ *Sam's got red hair.* Sam a les cheveux roux.
Red Cross *n* Croix-Rouge *f*
redcurrant *n* groseille *f*
redecorate *vb* ❶ *(with wallpaper)* retapisser [**28**] ❷ *(with paint)* refaire [**36**] les peintures
redo *vb* refaire [**36**]
reduce *vb* réduire [**23**] ▷ *at a reduced price* à prix réduit; **'reduce speed now'** 'ralentir'
reduction *n* réduction *f* ▷ *a 5% reduction* une réduction de cinq pour cent; **'huge reductions!'** 'prix sacrifiés!'
redundant *adj* **to be made redundant** être [**35**] licencié ▷ *He was made redundant yesterday.* Il a été licencié hier.
refer *vb* **to refer to** faire [**36**] allusion à ▷ *What are you referring to?* À quoi faites-vous allusion?
referee *n* arbitre *m*
reference *n* ❶ allusion *f* ▷ *He made no reference to the murder.* Il n'a fait aucune allusion au meurtre. ❷ *(for job application)* références *fpl* ▷ *Would you please give me a reference?* Pouvez-vous me fournir des références?; **a reference book** un ouvrage de référence
refill *vb* remplir [**38**] à nouveau ▷ *He refilled my glass.* Il a rempli mon verre à nouveau.
reflect *vb (light, image)* refléter [**34**]
reflection *n (in mirror)* reflet *m*
reflex *n* réflexe *m*
reflexive *adj* réfléchi(e) ▷ *a reflexive verb* un verbe réfléchi
refreshing *adj* rafraîchissant(e)
refreshments *npl* rafraîchissements *mpl*
refrigerator *n* réfrigérateur *m*
refuge *n* refuge *m*
refugee *n* réfugié *m*, réfugiée *f*
refund *n* remboursement *m* ▶ *vb* rembourser [**28**]
refuse *vb* refuser [**28**] ▶ *n* ordures *fpl*; **refuse collection** le ramassage des ordures
regain *vb* **to regain consciousness** reprendre [**65**] connaissance

regard *n* **Give my regards to Alice.** Transmettez mon bon souvenir à Alice.; **Louis sends his regards.** Vous avez le bonjour de Louis.; **'with kind regards'** 'bien cordialement'
▶ *vb* **to regard something as** considérer [**34**] quelque chose comme; **as regards ...** concernant ...
regiment *n* régiment *m*
region *n* région *f*
regional *adj* régional(e) (*mpl* régionaux)
register *n* (*in school*) registre d'absences *m*
▶ *vb* (*at school, college*) s'inscrire [**30**]
registered *adj* **a registered letter** une lettre recommandée
registration *n* ❶ (*roll call*) appel *m* ❷ (*of car*) numéro d'immatriculation *m*
regret *n* regret *m*; **I've got no regrets.** Je ne regrette rien.
▶ *vb* regretter [**28**] ▷ *Give me the money or you'll regret it!* Donne-moi l'argent, sinon tu vas le regretter!
regular *adj* ❶ régulier (*f* régulière) ▷ *at regular intervals* à intervalles réguliers ▷ *a regular verb* un verbe régulier; **to take regular exercise** faire [**36**] régulièrement de l'exercice ❷ (*average*) normal(e) (*mpl* normaux) ▷ *a regular portion of fries* une portion de frites normale
regularly *adv* régulièrement
regulation *n* règlement *m*
rehearsal *n* répétition *f*
rehearse *vb* répéter [**34**]
rein *n* rêne *f* ▷ *the reins* les rênes
reindeer *n* renne *m*
reject *vb* (*idea, suggestion*) rejeter [**41**] ▷ *We rejected that idea straight away.* Nous avons immédiatement rejeté cette idée.; **I applied but they rejected me.** J'ai posé ma candidature mais ils l'ont rejetée.
related *adj* (*people*) apparenté(e) ▷ *We're related.* Nous sommes apparentés.; **The two events were not related.** Il n'y avait aucun rapport entre les deux événements.
relation *n* ❶ (*person*) parent *m*, parente *f* ▷ *He's a distant relation.* C'est un parent éloigné. ▷ *my close relations* mes parents proches; **my relations** ma famille; **I've got relations in London.** J'ai de la famille à Londres. ❷ (*connection*) rapport *m* ▷ *It has no relation to reality.* Cela n'a aucun rapport avec la réalité.; **in relation to** par rapport à
relationship *n* relations *fpl* ▷ *We have a good relationship.* Nous avons de bonnes relations.; **I'm not in a relationship at the moment.** Je ne sors avec personne en ce moment.
relative *n* parent *m*, parente *f* ▷ *my close relatives* mes proches parents; **all her relatives** toute sa famille
relatively *adv* relativement
relax *vb* se détendre [**88**] ▷ *I relax listening to music.* Je me détends en écoutant de la musique.; **Relax! Everything's fine.** Ne t'en fais pas! Tout va bien.

relaxation *n* détente *f* ▷ *I don't have much time for relaxation.* Je n'ai pas beaucoup de moments de détente.

relaxed *adj* détendu(e)

relaxing *adj* reposant(e); **I find cooking relaxing.** Cela me détend de faire la cuisine.

relay *n* **a relay race** une course de relais

release *vb* ❶ *(prisoner)* libérer [**34**] ❷ *(report, news)* divulguer [**28**] ❸ *(CD, DVD)* sortir [**79**]
▶ *n (from prison)* libération *f* ▷ *the release of the prisoners* la libération des prisonniers; **the band's latest release** le dernier disque du groupe

relevant *adj (documents)* approprié(e); **That's not relevant.** Ça n'a aucun rapport.; **to be relevant to something** être [**35**] en rapport avec quelque chose ▷ *Education should be relevant to real life.* L'enseignement devrait être en rapport avec la réalité.

reliable *adj* fiable ▷ *a reliable car* une voiture fiable ▷ *He's not very reliable.* Il n'est pas très fiable.

relief *n* soulagement *m* ▷ *That's a relief!* Quel soulagement!

relieved *adj* soulagé(e) ▷ *I was relieved to hear ...* J'ai été soulagé d'apprendre ...

religion *n* religion *f* ▷ *What religion are you?* Quelle est votre religion?

religious *adj* ❶ religieux (*f* religieuse) ▷ *my religious beliefs* mes croyances religieuses ❷ croyant(e) ▷ *I'm not religious.* Je ne suis pas croyant.

reluctant *adj* **to be reluctant to do something** être [**35**] peu disposé à faire quelque chose ▷ *They were reluctant to help us.* Ils étaient peu disposés à nous aider.

reluctantly *adv* à contrecœur

rely on *vb* compter [**28**] sur ▷ *I'm relying on you.* Je compte sur toi.

remain *vb* rester [**71**]; **to remain silent** garder [**28**] le silence

remaining *adj* le reste de ▷ *the remaining ingredients* le reste des ingrédients

remark *n* remarque *f*

remarkable *adj* remarquable

remarkably *adv* remarquablement

remember *vb* se souvenir [**83**] de ▷ *I can't remember his name.* Je ne me souviens pas de son nom. ▷ *I don't remember.* Je ne m'en souviens pas.

> In French you often say 'don't forget' instead of 'remember'.

▷ *Remember your passport!* N'oublie pas ton passeport!

remind *vb* rappeler [**4**] ▷ *It reminds me of Scotland.* Cela me rappelle l'Écosse. ▷ *I'll remind you tomorrow.* Je te le rappellerai demain.

remote *adj* isolé(e) ▷ *a remote village* un village isolé

remote control *n* télécommande *f*

remotely *adv* **I'm not remotely interested.** Je ne suis absolument pas intéressé.; **Do you think it would be remotely possible?** Pensez-vous que cela serait éventuellement possible?

remove *vb* ❶ enlever [**43**] ▷ *Please remove your bag from my seat.* Est-ce que vous pouvez enlever votre sac de mon siège? ❷ *(stain)* faire [**36**] partir ▷ *Did you remove the stain?* Est-ce que tu as fait partir la tache?
renew *vb (passport, licence)* renouveler [**4**]
renewable *adj (energy, resource)* renouvelable
renovate *vb* rénover [**28**] ▷ *The building's been renovated.* Le bâtiment a été rénové.
rent *n* loyer *m*
▶ *vb* louer [**28**] ▷ *We rented a car.* Nous avons loué une voiture.
reorganize *vb* réorganiser [**28**]
rep *n (= representative)* représentant *m*, représentante *f*
repaid *vb see* **repay**
repair *vb* réparer [**28**]; **to get something repaired** faire [**36**] réparer quelque chose ▷ *I got the washing machine repaired.* J'ai fait réparer la machine à laver.
▶ *n* réparation *f*
repay *vb (money)* rembourser [**28**]
repeat *vb* répéter [**34**]
▶ *n* reprise *f* ▷ *There are too many repeats on TV.* Il y a trop de reprises à la télé.
repeatedly *adv* à plusieurs reprises
repetitive *adj (movement, work)* répétitif (*f* répétitive)
replace *vb* remplacer [**12**]
replay *n* **There will be a replay on Friday.** Le match sera rejoué vendredi.
▶ *vb (match)* rejouer [**28**]
reply *n* réponse *f*
▶ *vb* répondre [**69**]
report *n* ❶ *(of event)* compte rendu *m (pl* comptes rendus) ❷ *(news report)* reportage *m* ▷ *a report in the paper* un reportage dans le journal ❸ *(at school)* bulletin scolaire *m* ▷ *I got a good report this term.* J'ai un bon bulletin scolaire ce trimestre.
▶ *vb* ❶ signaler [**28**] ▷ *I reported the theft to the police.* J'ai signalé le vol au commissariat. ❷ se présenter [**28**] ▷ *Report to reception when you arrive.* Présentez-vous à la réception à votre arrivée.
reporter *n* reporter *m* ▷ *I'd like to be a reporter.* J'aimerais être reporter.
represent *vb* représenter [**28**]
representative *adj* représentatif (*f* représentative)
reptile *n* reptile *m*
republic *n* république *f*
reputation *n* réputation *f*
request *n* demande *f*
▶ *vb* demander [**28**]
require *vb* exiger [**45**] ▷ *The job requires good computational skills.* Cet emploi exige une bonne connaissance de l'informatique.; **What qualifications are required?** Quelles sont les diplômes requis?
rescue *vb* sauver [**28**]
▶ *n* ❶ sauvetage *m* ▷ *a rescue operation* une opération de sauvetage; **a mountain rescue team** une équipe de sauvetage en montagne ❷ secours *m* ▷ *the rescue services* les services de secours;

to come to somebody's rescue venir [**89**] au secours de quelqu'un ▷ *He came to my rescue.* Il est venu à mon secours.

research *n* ❶ *(experimental)* recherche *f* ▷ *He's doing research.* Il fait de la recherche. ❷ *(theoretical)* recherches *fpl* ▷ *She's doing some research in the library.* Elle fait des recherches à la bibliothèque.

resemblance *n* ressemblance *f*

resent *vb* être [**35**] contrarié par ▷ *I really resented your criticism.* J'ai été vraiment contrarié par tes critiques.

resentful *adj* plein de ressentiment (*f* pleine de ressentiment); **to feel resentful towards somebody** en vouloir [**93**] à quelqu'un

reservation *n (booking)* réservation *f* ▷ *I'd like to make a reservation for this evening.* J'aimerais faire une réservation pour ce soir.

reserve *n* ❶ *(place)* réserve *f* ▷ *a nature reserve* une réserve naturelle ❷ *(person)* remplaçant *m*, remplaçante *f* ▷ *I was reserve in the game last Saturday.* J'étais remplaçant dans le match de samedi dernier.
▶ *vb* réserver [**28**] ▷ *I'd like to reserve a table for tomorrow evening.* J'aimerais réserver une table pour demain soir.

reserved *adj* réservé(e) ▷ *a reserved seat* une place réservée ▷ *He's quite reserved.* Il est assez réservé.

resident *n* résident *m*, résidente *f*

residential *adj* résidentiel (*f* résidentielle) ▷ *a residential area* un quartier résidentiel

resign *vb* donner [**28**] sa démission

resit *vb* repasser [**28**] ▷ *I'm resitting the exam in December.* Je vais repasser l'examen en décembre.

resolution *n* résolution *f*; **Have you made any New Year's resolutions?** Tu as pris de bonnes résolutions pour la nouvelle année?

resort *n (at seaside)* station balnéaire *f* ▷ *It's a resort on the Costa del Sol.* C'est une station balnéaire sur la Costa del Sol.; **a ski resort** une station de ski; **as a last resort** en dernier recours

resource *n* ressource *f*

respect *n* respect *m*
▶ *vb* respecter [**28**]

respectable *adj* ❶ respectable ❷ *(standard, marks)* correct(e)

responsibility *n* responsabilité *f*

responsible *adj* ❶ *(in charge)* responsable; **to be responsible for something** être [**35**] responsable de quelque chose ▷ *He's responsible for booking the tickets.* Il est responsable de la réservation des billets.; **It's a responsible job.** C'est un poste à responsabilités. ❷ *(mature)* sérieux (*f* sérieuse) ▷ *You should be more responsible.* Tu devrais être un peu plus sérieux.

rest *n* ❶ *(relaxation)* repos *m* ▷ *five minutes' rest* cinq minutes de repos; **to have a rest** se reposer [**28**] ▷ *We stopped to have a rest.* Nous nous

sommes arrêtés pour nous reposer. ❷ *(remainder)* reste *m* ▷ *I'll do the rest.* Je ferai le reste. ▷ *the rest of the money* le reste de l'argent; **the rest of them** les autres ▷ *The rest of them went swimming.* Les autres sont allés nager.
▸ *vb* ❶ *(relax)* se reposer [**28**] ▷ *She's resting in her room.* Elle se repose dans sa chambre. ❷ *(not overstrain)* ménager [**45**] ▷ *He has to rest his knee.* Il doit ménager son genou. ❸ *(lean)* appuyer [**53**] ▷ *I rested my bike against the window.* J'ai appuyé mon vélo contre la fenêtre.

restaurant *n* restaurant *m* ▷ *We don't often go to restaurants.* Nous n'allons pas souvent au restaurant.; **a restaurant car** un wagon-restaurant

restless *adj* agité(e)

restore *vb (building, picture)* restaurer [**28**]

restrict *vb* limiter [**28**]

rest room *n (US)* toilettes *fpl*

result *n* résultat *m* ▷ *my exam results* mes résultats d'examen
▸ *vb* **to result in** occasionner [**28**]

resume *vb* reprendre [**65**] ▷ *They've resumed work.* Ils ont repris le travail.

Be careful not to translate **to resume** by **résumer**.

résumé *n (US)* curriculum vitae *m*

retire *vb* prendre [**65**] sa retraite ▷ *He retired last year.* Il a pris sa retraite l'an dernier.

retired *adj* retraité(e) ▷ *She's retired.* Elle est retraitée.; **a retired teacher** un professeur à la retraite

retirement *n* retraite *f*

return *n* ❶ retour *m* ▷ *after our return* à notre retour; **the return journey** le voyage de retour; **a return match** un match retour ❷ *(ticket)* aller retour *m* ▷ *A return to Avignon, please.* Un aller retour pour Avignon, s'il vous plaît.; **in return** en échange ▷ *... and I help her in return* ... et je l'aide en échange; **in return for** en échange de; **Many happy returns!** Bon anniversaire!
▸ *vb* ❶ *(come back)* revenir [**73**] ▷ *I've just returned from holiday.* Je viens de revenir de vacances.; **to return home** rentrer [**68**] à la maison ❷ *(go back)* retourner [**72**] ▷ *He returned to France the following year.* Il est retourné en France l'année suivante. ❸ *(give back)* rendre [**7**] ▷ *She borrows my things and doesn't return them.* Elle m'emprunte mes affaires et ne me les rend pas.

reunion *n* réunion *f*

reveal *vb* révéler [**34**]

revenge *n* vengeance *f* ▷ *in revenge* par vengeance; **to take revenge** se venger [**45**] ▷ *They planned to take revenge on him.* Ils voulaient se venger de lui.

reverse *vb (car)* faire [**36**] marche arrière ▷ *He reversed without looking.* Il a fait marche arrière sans regarder.; **to reverse the charges** *(telephone)* appeler [**4**] en PCV ▷ *I'd like to reverse the charges to Britain.* Je voudrais appeler la Grande-Bretagne en PCV.

▸ *adj* inverse ▹ *in reverse order* dans l'ordre inverse; **in reverse gear** en marche arrière

review *n (of book, film, programme)* critique *f* ▹ *The book had good reviews.* Ce livre a eu de bonnes critiques.

revise *vb* réviser [**28**] ▹ *I haven't started revising yet.* Je n'ai pas encore commencé à réviser.; **I've revised my opinion.** J'ai changé d'opinion.

revision *n* révisions *fpl* ▹ *Have you done a lot of revision?* Est-ce que tu as fait beaucoup de révisions?

revolting *adj* dégoûtant(e)

revolution *n* révolution *f*; **the French Revolution** la Révolution française

reward *n* récompense *f*

rewarding *adj* gratifiant(e) ▹ *a rewarding job* un travail gratifiant

rewind *vb* rembobiner [**28**] ▹ *to rewind a cassette* rembobiner une cassette

Rhine *n* Rhin *m*

rhinoceros *n* rhinocéros *m*

Rhone *n* Rhône *m*

rhubarb *n* rhubarbe *f* ▹ *a rhubarb tart* une tarte à la rhubarbe

rhythm *n* rythme *m*

rib *n* côte *f*

ribbon *n* ruban *m*

rice *n* riz *m*; **rice pudding** le riz au lait

rich *adj* riche; **the rich** les riches *mpl*

rid *vb* **to get rid of** se débarrasser [**28**] de ▹ *I want to get rid of some old clothes.* Je veux me débarrasser de vieux vêtements.

ridden *vb see* **ride**

ride *n* **to go for a ride (1)** *(on horse)* monter [**48**] à cheval **(2)** *(on bike)* faire [**36**] un tour en vélo ▹ *We went for a bike ride.* Nous sommes allés faire un tour en vélo.; **It's a short bus ride to the town centre.** Ce n'est pas loin du centre-ville en bus.

▸ *vb (on horse)* monter [**48**] à cheval ▹ *I'm learning to ride.* J'apprends à monter à cheval.; **to ride a bike** faire [**36**] du vélo ▹ *Can you ride a bike?* Tu sais faire du vélo?

rider *n* ❶ *(on horse)* cavalier *m*, cavalière *f* ▹ *She's a good rider.* C'est une bonne cavalière. ❷ *(on bike)* cycliste *mf*

ridiculous *adj* ridicule ▹ *Don't be ridiculous!* Ne sois pas ridicule!

riding *n* équitation *f*; **to go riding** faire [**36**] de l'équitation; **a riding school** une école d'équitation

rifle *n* fusil *m* ▹ *a hunting rifle* un fusil de chasse

right *adj, adv*

> There are several ways of translating 'right'. Scan the examples to find one that is similar to what you want to say.

❶ *(factually correct, suitable)* bon (*f* bonne) ▹ *the right answer* la bonne réponse ▹ *It isn't the right size.* Ce n'est pas la bonne taille. ▹ *We're on the right train.* Nous sommes dans le bon train.; **Is this the right road**

for Arles? Est-ce que c'est bien la route pour aller à Arles?
❷ *(correctly)* correctement ▷ *Am I pronouncing it right?* Est-ce que je prononce ça correctement?; **to be right (1)** *(person)* avoir [**8**] raison ▷ *You were right!* Tu avais raison! **(2)** *(statement, opinion)* être [**35**] vrai ▷ *That's right!* C'est vrai!
❸ *(accurate)* juste ▷ *Do you have the right time?* Est-ce que vous avez l'heure juste? ❹ *(morally correct)* bien ▷ *It's not right to behave like that.* Ce n'est pas bien d'agir comme ça.; **I think you did the right thing.** Je pense que tu as bien fait. ❺ *(not left)* droit(e) ▷ *my right hand* ma main droite ❻ *(turn, look)* à droite ▷ *Turn right at the traffic lights.* Tournez à droite aux prochains feux.; **Right! Let's get started.** Bon! On commence.; **right away** tout de suite ▷ *I'll do it right away.* Je vais le faire tout de suite.
▶ *n* ❶ droit *m*; **You've got no right to do that.** Vous n'avez pas le droit de faire ça. ❷ *(not left)* droite *f*; **on the right** à droite ▷ *Remember to drive on the right.* N'oubliez pas de conduire à droite.; **right of way** la priorité ▷ *It was our right of way.* Nous avions la priorité.

right-hand *adj* **the right-hand side** la droite ▷ *It's on the right-hand side.* C'est à droite.

right-handed *adj* droitier (*f* droitière)

rightly *adv* avec raison ▷ *She rightly decided not to go.* Elle a décidé, avec raison, de ne pas y aller.; **if I remember rightly** si je me souviens bien

ring *n* ❶ anneau *m* (*pl* anneaux) ▷ *a gold ring* un anneau en or
❷ *(with stones)* bague *f* ▷ *a diamond ring* une bague de diamants; **a wedding ring** une alliance
❸ *(circle)* cercle *m* ▷ *to stand in a ring* se mettre en cercle ❹ *(of bell)* coup de sonnette *m* ▷ *I was woken by a ring at the door.* J'ai été réveillé par un coup de sonnette.; **to give somebody a ring** appeler [**4**] quelqu'un ▷ *I'll give you a ring this evening.* Je t'appellerai ce soir.
▶ *vb* ❶ téléphoner [**28**] ▷ *Your mother rang this morning.* Ta mère a téléphoné ce matin.; **to ring somebody** appeler [**4**] quelqu'un ▷ *I'll ring you tomorrow morning.* Je t'appellerai demain matin.
❷ sonner [**28**] ▷ *The phone's ringing.* Le téléphone sonne.; **to ring the bell** *(doorbell)* sonner [**28**] à la porte ▷ *I rang the bell three times.* J'ai sonné trois fois à la porte.

ring back *vb* rappeler [**4**] ▷ *I'll ring back later.* Je rappellerai plus tard.

ring up *vb* **to ring somebody up** donner [**28**] un coup de fil à quelqu'un

ring binder *n* classeur *m*

rinse *vb* rincer [**12**]

riot *n* émeute *f*
▶ *vb* faire [**36**] une émeute

rip *vb* ❶ déchirer [**28**] ▷ *I've ripped my jeans.* J'ai déchiré mon jean. ❷ se déchirer [**28**] ▷ *My skirt's ripped.* Ma jupe s'est déchirée.

rip off *vb* arnaquer [**28**] ▷ *The hotel ripped us off.* L'hôtel nous a arnaqués.

rip up *vb* déchirer [**28**] ▷ *He read the note and then ripped it up.* Il a lu le mot, puis l'a déchiré.

ripe *adj* mûr(e)

rip-off *n* **It's a rip-off!** *(informal)* C'est de l'arnaque!

rise *n* ❶ *(in prices, temperature)* hausse *f* ▷ *a sudden rise in temperature* une hausse subite de température ❷ *(pay rise)* augmentation *f*
▶ *vb* ❶ *(increase)* augmenter [**28**] ▷ *Prices are rising.* Les prix augmentent. ❷ se lever [**43**] ▷ *The sun rises early in June.* Le soleil se lève tôt en juin.

risk *n* risque *m*; **to take risks** prendre [**65**] des risques; **It's at your own risk.** C'est à vos risques et périls.
▶ *vb* risquer [**28**] ▷ *You risk getting a fine.* Vous risquez de recevoir une amende.; **I wouldn't risk it if I were you.** À votre place, je ne prendrais pas ce risque.

rival *n* rival *m* (*pl* rivaux), rivale *f*
▶ *adj* ❶ rival(e) (*mpl* rivaux) ▷ *a rival gang* une bande rivale
❷ concurrent(e) ▷ *a rival company* une société concurrente

river *n* ❶ rivière *f* ▷ *The river runs alongside the canal.* La rivière longe le canal. ❷ *(major)* fleuve *m* ▷ *the rivers of France* les fleuves de France; **the river Seine** la Seine

road *n* ❶ route *f* ▷ *There's a lot of traffic on the roads.* Il y a beaucoup de circulation sur les routes.
❷ *(street)* rue *f* ▷ *They live across the road.* Ils habitent de l'autre côté de la rue.

road map *n* carte routière *f*

road rage *n* agressivité au volant *f*

road sign *n* panneau de signalisation *m* (*pl* panneaux de signalisation)

roadworks *npl* travaux *mpl*

roast *adj* rôti(e) ▷ *roast chicken* le poulet rôti; **roast pork** le rôti de porc; **roast beef** le rôti de bœuf

rob *vb* **to rob somebody** voler [**28**] quelqu'un ▷ *I've been robbed.* On m'a volé.; **to rob somebody of something** voler [**28**] quelque chose à quelqu'un ▷ *He was robbed of his wallet.* On lui a volé son portefeuille.; **to rob a bank** dévaliser [**28**] une banque

robber *n* voleur *m*; **a bank robber** un cambrioleur de banques

robbery *n* vol *m*; **a bank robbery** un hold-up; **armed robbery** le vol à main armée

robin *n* rouge-gorge *m*

robot *n* robot *m*

rock *n* ❶ *(substance)* roche *f* ▷ *They tunnelled through the rock.* Ils ont creusé un tunnel dans la roche.
❷ *(boulder)* rocher *m* ▷ *I sat on a rock.* Je me suis assis sur un rocher.
❸ *(stone)* pierre *f* ❹ *(music)* rock *m* ▷ *a rock concert* un concert de rock
❺ *(sweet)* sucre d'orge *m*

▸ *vb* ébranler [**28**] ▹ *The explosion rocked the building.* L'explosion a ébranlé le bâtiment.

rocket *n (firework, spacecraft)* fusée *f*

rocking horse *n* cheval à bascule *m* (*pl* chevaux à bascule)

rod *n (for fishing)* canne à pêche *f*

rode *vb see* **ride**

role *n* rôle *m*

role play *n* jeu de rôle *m* (*pl* jeux de rôles) ▹ *to do a role play* faire un jeu de rôle

roll *n* ❶ rouleau *m* (*pl* rouleaux) ▹ *a roll of tape* un rouleau de ruban adhésif ▹ *a toilet roll* un rouleau de papier hygiénique ❷ *(bread)* petit pain *m*

▸ *vb* rouler [**28**]; **to roll out the pastry** abaisser [**28**] la pâte

Rollerblade® *n* roller *m* ▹ *a pair of Rollerblades* une paire de rollers

rollercoaster *n* montagnes russes *fpl*

roller skates *npl* patins à roulettes *mpl*

roller-skating *n* patin à roulettes *m*; **to go roller-skating** faire [**36**] du patin à roulettes

Roman *adj, n (ancient)* romain(e) ▹ *a Roman villa* une villa romaine ▹ *the Roman empire* l'empire romain

Roman Catholic *n* catholique *mf* ▹ *He's a Roman Catholic.* Il est catholique.

romance *n* ❶ *(novels)* romans d'amour *mpl* ▹ *I read a lot of romance.* Je lis beaucoup de romans d'amour. ❷ *(glamour)* charme *m* ▹ *the romance of Paris* le charme de Paris; **a holiday romance** une idylle de vacances

Romania *n* Roumanie *f*; **in Romania** en Roumanie

Romanian *adj* roumain(e)

romantic *adj* romantique

roof *n* toit *m*

roof rack *n* galerie *f*

room *n* ❶ pièce *f* ▹ *the biggest room in the house* la plus grande pièce de la maison ❷ *(bedroom)* chambre *f* ▹ *She's in her room.* Elle est dans sa chambre.; **a single room** une chambre pour une personne; **a double room** une chambre pour deux personnes ❸ *(in school)* salle *f* ▹ *the music room* la salle de musique ❹ *(space)* place *f* ▹ *There's no room for that box.* Il n'y a pas de place pour cette boîte.

root *n* racine *f*

root around *vb* fouiller [**28**] ▹ *She started rooting around in her handbag.* Elle a commencé à fouiller dans son sac à main.

root out *vb* traquer [**28**] ▹ *They are determined to root out corruption.* Ils sont déterminés à traquer la corruption.

rope *n* corde *f*

rope in *vb* enrôler [**28**] ▹ *I was roped in to help with the refreshments.* J'ai été enrôlé pour servir les rafraîchissements.

rose *vb see* **rise**

▸ *n (flower)* rose *f*

rot *vb* pourrir [**38**]

rotten *adj (decayed)* pourri(e) ▹ *a rotten apple* une pomme pourrie; **rotten weather** un temps pourri; **That's a rotten thing to do.** Ce n'est vraiment pas gentil.; **to feel rotten** être [**35**] mal fichu *(informal)*

rough *adj* ❶ *(surface)* rêche ▷ *My hands are rough.* J'ai les mains rêches. ❷ *(game)* violent(e) ▷ *Rugby's a rough sport.* Le rugby est un sport violent. ❸ *(place)* difficile ▷ *It's a rough area.* C'est un quartier difficile. ❹ *(water)* houleux (*f* houleuse) ▷ *The sea was rough.* La mer était houleuse. ❺ approximatif (*f* approximative) ▷ *I've got a rough idea.* J'en ai une idée approximative.; **to feel rough** ne pas être [**35**] dans son assiette ▷ *I feel rough.* Je ne suis pas dans mon assiette.

roughly *adv* à peu près ▷ *It weighs roughly 20 kilos.* Ça pèse à peu près vingt kilos.

round *adj, adv, prep* ❶ rond(e) ▷ *a round table* une table ronde ❷ *(around)* autour de ▷ *We were sitting round the table.* Nous étions assis autour de la table.; **It's just round the corner.** *(very near)* C'est tout près.; **to go round to somebody's house** aller [**3**] chez quelqu'un ▷ *I went round to my friend's house.* Je suis allé chez mon ami.; **to have a look round** faire [**36**] un tour; **to go round a museum** visiter [**28**] un musée; **round here** près d'ici ▷ *Is there a chemist's round here?* Est-ce qu'il y a une pharmacie près d'ici?; **He lives round here.** Il habite dans les parages.; **all round** partout; **all year round** toute l'année; **round about** *(roughly)* environ ▷ *It costs round about £100.* Cela coûte environ cent livres. ▷ *round about 8 o'clock* à huit heures environ
▶ *n* ❶ *(of tournament)* manche *f* ❷ *(of boxing match)* round *m*; **a round of golf** une partie de golf; **a round of drinks** une tournée ▷ *He bought a round of drinks.* Il a offert une tournée.

round off *vb* terminer [**28**] ▷ *They rounded off the meal with liqueurs.* Ils ont terminé le repas par des liqueurs.

round up *vb* ❶ *(sheep, cattle, suspects)* rassembler [**28**] ❷ *(figure)* arrondir [**38**]

roundabout *n* ❶ *(at junction)* rond-point *m* (*pl* ronds-points) ❷ *(at funfair)* manège *m*

rounders *n* **Rounders is a bit like baseball.** Le 'rounders' ressemble un peu au base-ball.

Rounders is not played in France.

round trip *n (US)* aller et retour *m*

route *n* ❶ itinéraire *m* ▷ *We're planning our route.* Nous établissons notre itinéraire. ❷ *(of bus)* parcours *m*

routine *n* **my daily routine** mes occupations quotidiennes

row *n*

This word has two pronunciations. Make sure you choose the right translation.

❶ rangée *f* ▷ *a row of houses* une rangée de maisons ❷ *(of seats)* rang *m* ▷ *Our seats are in the front row.* Nos places se trouvent au premier rang.; **five times in a row** cinq fois d'affilée ❸ *(noise)* vacarme *m* ▷ *What's that terrible row?* Qu'est-ce que c'est que ce vacarme? ❹ *(quarrel)* dispute *f*; **to have a row** se disputer **[28]** ▷ *They've had a row.* Ils se sont disputés.
▶ *vb* ❶ ramer **[28]** ▷ *We took turns to row.* Nous avons ramé à tour de rôle. ❷ *(as sport)* faire **[36]** de l'aviron

rowboat *n (US)* bateau à rames *m*

rowing *n (sport)* aviron *m* ▷ *My hobby is rowing.* Je fais de l'aviron.; **a rowing boat** un bateau à rames

royal *adj* royal(e) (*mpl* royaux); **the royal family** la famille royale

rub *vb* ❶ *(stain)* frotter **[28]** ❷ *(part of body)* se frotter **[28]** ▷ *Don't rub your eyes!* Ne te frotte pas les yeux!; **to rub something out** effacer **[12]** quelque chose

rubber *n* ❶ caoutchouc *m* ▷ *rubber soles* des semelles en caoutchouc ❷ *(eraser)* gomme *f* ▷ *Can I borrow your rubber?* Je peux emprunter ta gomme?; **a rubber band** un élastique

rubbish *n* ❶ *(refuse)* ordures *fpl* ▷ *When do they collect the rubbish?* Quand est-ce qu'ils ramassent les ordures? ❷ *(junk)* camelote *f* ▷ *They sell a lot of rubbish at the market.* Ils vendent beaucoup de camelote au marché. ❸ *(nonsense)* bêtises *fpl* ▷ *Don't talk rubbish!* Ne dis pas de bêtises!; **That's a load of rubbish!** *(informal)* C'est vraiment n'importe quoi!; **a rubbish bin** une poubelle; **a rubbish dump** une décharge
▶ *adj* nul (*f* nulle) ▷ *They're a rubbish team!* Cette équipe est nulle!

rucksack *n* sac à dos *m*

rude *adj* ❶ *(impolite)* impoli(e) ▷ *It's rude to interrupt.* C'est impoli de couper la parole aux gens. ❷ *(offensive)* grossier (*f* grossière) ▷ *He was very rude to me.* Il a été très grossier avec moi.; **a rude word** un gros mot

rug *n* ❶ tapis *m* ▷ *a Persian rug* un tapis persan ❷ *(blanket)* couverture *f* ▷ *a tartan rug* une couverture écossaise

rugby *n* rugby *m* ▷ *I play rugby.* Je joue au rugby.

ruin *n* ruine *f* ▷ *the ruins of the castle* les ruines du château; **in ruins** en ruine
▶ *vb* ❶ abîmer **[28]** ▷ *You'll ruin your shoes.* Tu vas abîmer tes chaussures. ❷ gâcher **[28]** ▷ *It ruined our holiday.* Ça a gâché nos vacances. ❸ *(financially)* ruiner **[28]**

rule *n* ❶ règle *f* ▷ *the rules of grammar* les règles de grammaire; **as a rule** en règle générale ❷ *(regulation)* règlement *m* ▷ *It's against the rules.* C'est contre le règlement.

rule out *vb (possibility)* écarter **[28]**

ruler *n* règle *f* ▷ *Can I borrow your ruler?* Je peux emprunter ta règle?

rum *n* rhum *m*

rumour (*US* **rumor**) *n* rumeur *f*

▷ *It's just a rumour.* Ce n'est qu'une rumeur.

run *n (in cricket)* point *m* ▷ *to score a run* marquer un point; **to go for a run** courir [**16**] ▷ *I go for a run every morning.* Je cours tous les matins.; **I did a ten-kilometre run.** J'ai couru dix kilomètres.; **on the run** en fuite ▷ *The criminals are still on the run.* Les criminels sont toujours en fuite.; **in the long run** à long terme
▶ *vb* ❶ courir [**16**] ▷ *I ran five kilometres.* J'ai couru cinq kilomètres.; **to run a marathon** participer [**28**] à un marathon ❷ *(manage)* diriger [**45**] ▷ *He runs a large company.* Il dirige une grosse société. ❸ *(organize)* organiser [**28**] ▷ *They run music courses in the holidays.* Ils organisent des cours de musique pendant les vacances. ❹ *(water)* couler [**28**] ▷ *Don't leave the tap running.* Ne laisse pas couler le robinet.; **to run a bath** faire [**36**] couler un bain ❺ *(by car)* conduire [**23**] ▷ *I can run you to the station.* Je peux te conduire à la gare.

run away *vb* s'enfuir [**39**] ▷ *They ran away before the police came.* Ils se sont enfuis avant l'arrivée de la police.

run out *vb* **Time is running out.** Il ne reste plus beaucoup de temps.; **to run out of something** se trouver [**28**] à court de quelque chose ▷ *We ran out of money.* Nous nous sommes trouvés à court d'argent.

run over *vb* **to run somebody over** écraser [**28**] quelqu'un; **to get run over** se faire [**36**] écraser ▷ *Be careful, or you'll get run over!* Fais attention, sinon tu vas te faire écraser!

rung *vb see* **ring**

runner *n* coureur *m*, coureuse *f*

runner-up *n* second *m*, seconde *f*

running *n* course *f* ▷ *Running is my favourite sport.* La course est mon sport préféré.

run-up *n* **in the run-up to Christmas** pendant la période de préparation de Noël

runway *n* piste *f*

rush *n* hâte *f*; **in a rush** à la hâte
▶ *vb* ❶ *(run)* se précipiter [**28**] ▷ *Everyone rushed outside.* Tout le monde s'est précipité dehors. ❷ *(hurry)* se dépêcher [**28**] ▷ *There's no need to rush.* Ce n'est pas la peine de se dépêcher.

rush hour *n* heures de pointe *fpl* ▷ *in the rush hour* aux heures de pointe

Russia *n* Russie *f*; **in Russia** en Russie; **to Russia** en Russie

Russian *n* ❶ *(person)* Russe *mf* ❷ *(language)* russe *m*
▶ *adj* russe

rust *n* rouille *f*

rusty *adj* rouillé(e) ▷ *a rusty bike* un vélo rouillé ▷ *My French is very rusty.* Mon français est très rouillé.

rye *n* seigle *m*; **rye bread** le pain de seigle

S

Sabbath *n* ❶ *(Christian)* dimanche *m* ❷ *(Jewish)* sabbat *m*
sack *n* sac *m*; **to get the sack** être [**35**] mis à la porte
▸ *vb* **to sack somebody** mettre [**47**] quelqu'un à la porte ▹ *He was sacked.* On l'a mis à la porte.
sacred *adj* sacré(e)
sacrifice *n* sacrifice *m*
sad *adj* triste
saddle *n* selle *f*
saddlebag *n* sacoche *f*
safe *n* coffre-fort *m* (*pl* coffres-forts) ▹ *She put the money in the safe.* Elle a mis l'argent dans le coffre-fort.
▸ *adj* ❶ sans danger ▹ *Don't worry, it's perfectly safe.* Ne vous inquiétez pas, c'est absolument sans danger.; **Is it safe?** Ça n'est pas dangereux? ❷ *(machine, ladder)* sûr(e) ▹ *This car isn't safe.* Cette voiture n'est pas sûre. ❸ *(out of danger)* hors de danger ▹ *You're safe now.* Vous êtes hors de danger maintenant.; **to feel safe** se sentir [**77**] en sécurité; **safe sex** le sexe sans risques
safety *n* sécurité *f*; **a safety belt** une ceinture de sécurité; **a safety pin** une épingle de nourrice
Sagittarius *n* Sagittaire *mf* ▹ *I'm Sagittarius.* Je suis Sagittaire.
said *vb see* **say**
sail *n* voile *f*
▸ *vb* ❶ *(travel)* naviguer [**28**] ❷ *(set off)* prendre [**65**] la mer ▹ *The boat sails at eight o'clock.* Le bateau prend la mer à huit heures.
sailing *n* voile *f* ▹ *His hobby is sailing.* Son passe-temps, c'est la voile.; **to go sailing** faire [**36**] de la voile; **a sailing boat** un voilier; **a sailing ship** un grand voilier
sailor *n* marin *m* ▹ *He's a sailor.* Il est marin.
saint *n* saint *m*, sainte *f*
sake *n* **for the sake of** dans l'intérêt de
salad *n* salade *f*; **salad dressing** la vinaigrette
salami *n* salami *m*
salary *n* salaire *m*
sale *n (reductions)* soldes *mpl* ▹ *There's a sale on at Harrods.* Ce sont les soldes chez Harrods.; **on sale** en vente; **The factory's for sale.** L'usine est en vente.; **'for sale'** 'à vendre'
sales assistant *n* vendeur *m*,

vendeuse *f* ▷ *She's a sales assistant.* Elle est vendeuse.

salesman *n* ❶ *(sales rep)* représentant *m* ▷ *He's a salesman.* Il est représentant.; **a double-glazing salesman** un représentant en doubles vitrages ❷ *(sales assistant)* vendeur *m*

saleswoman *n* ❶ *(sales rep)* représentante *f* ▷ *She's a saleswoman.* Elle est représentante. ❷ *(sales assistant)* vendeuse *f*

salmon *n* saumon *m*

salon *n* salon *m* ▷ *a hair salon* un salon de coiffure

salt *n* sel *m*

salty *adj* salé(e)

Salvation Army *n* armée du Salut *f*

same *adj* même ▷ *at the same time* en même temps; **They're exactly the same.** Ils sont exactement pareils.; **It's not the same.** Ça n'est pas pareil.

sample *n* échantillon *m*

sand *n* sable *m*

sandal *n* sandale *f* ▷ *a pair of sandals* une paire de sandales

sand castle *n* château de sable *m* (*pl* châteaux de sable)

sandwich *n* sandwich *m* ▷ *a cheese sandwich* un sandwich au fromage

sang *vb see* **sing**

sanitary towel *n* serviette hygiénique *f*

sank *vb see* **sink**

Santa Claus *n* père Noël *m*

sarcastic *adj* sarcastique

sardine *n* sardine *f*

sat *vb see* **sit**

satchel *n* cartable *m*

satellite *n* satellite *m* ▷ *satellite television* la télévision par satellite; **a satellite dish** une antenne parabolique

satisfactory *adj* satisfaisant(e)

satisfied *adj* satisfait(e)

sat nav *n* GPS *m*

Saturday *n* samedi *m* ▷ *on Saturday* samedi ▷ *on Saturdays* le samedi ▷ *every Saturday* tous les samedis ▷ *last Saturday* samedi dernier ▷ *next Saturday* samedi prochain; **I've got a Saturday job.** Je travaille le samedi.

sauce *n* sauce *f*

saucepan *n* casserole *f*

saucer *n* soucoupe *f*

Saudi Arabia *n* Arabie Saoudite *f*; **in Saudi Arabia** en Arabie Saoudite

sausage *n* ❶ saucisse *f* ❷ *(salami)* saucisson *m*; **a sausage roll** un friand à la saucisse

save *vb* ❶ *(save up money)* mettre [**47**] de côté ▷ *I've saved £50 already.* J'ai déjà mis cinquante livres de côté. ❷ *(spend less)* économiser [**28**] ▷ *I saved £20 by waiting for the sales.* J'ai économisé vingt livres en attendant les soldes.; **to save time** gagner [**28**] du temps ▷ *We took a taxi to save time.* Nous avons pris un taxi pour gagner du temps. ▷ *It saved us time.* Ça nous a fait gagner du temps. ❸ *(rescue)* sauver [**28**] ▷ *Luckily, all the passengers were saved.* Heureusement, tous les passagers ont été sauvés. ❹ *(on* *computer)* sauvegarder [**28**] ▷ *Don't forget to save your work regularly.* N'oublie pas de sauvegarder ton travail régulièrement.

save up *vb* mettre [**47**] de l'argent de côté ▷ *I'm saving up for a new bike.* Je mets de l'argent de côté pour un nouveau vélo.

savings *npl* économies *fpl* ▷ *She spent all her savings on a computer.* Elle a dépensé toutes ses économies en achetant un ordinateur.

savoury *adj* salé(e) ▷ *Is it sweet or savoury?* C'est sucré ou salé?

saw *vb see* **see**
▶ *n* scie *f*

saxophone *n* saxophone *m* ▷ *I play the saxophone.* Je joue du saxophone.

say *vb* dire [**27**] ▷ *What did he say?* Qu'est-ce qu'il a dit? ▷ *Did you hear what she said?* Tu as entendu ce qu'elle a dit?; **Could you say that again?** Pourriez-vous répéter s'il vous plaît?; **That goes without saying.** Cela va sans dire.

saying *n* dicton *m* ▷ *It's just a saying.* C'est juste un dicton.

scale *n* ❶ *(of map)* échelle *f* ▷ *a large-scale map* une carte à grande échelle ❷ *(size, extent)* ampleur *f* ▷ *a disaster on a massive scale* un désastre d'une ampleur incroyable ❸ *(in music)* gamme *f*

scales *npl (in kitchen, shop)* balance *fsg*; **bathroom scales** le pèse-personne *sg*

scampi *npl* scampi *mpl*

scandal *n* ❶ *(outrage)* scandale *m* ▷ *It caused a scandal.* Ça a fait scandale. ❷ *(gossip)* ragots *mpl* ▷ *It's just scandal.* Ce ne sont que des ragots.

Scandinavia *n* Scandinavie *f*; **in Scandinavia** en Scandinavie

Scandinavian *adj* scandinave

scar *n* cicatrice *f*

scarce *adj* limité(e) ▷ *scarce resources* des ressources limitées; **Jobs are scarce these days.** Il y a peu de travail ces temps-ci.

scarcely *adv* à peine ▷ *I scarcely knew him.* Je le connaissais à peine.

scare *n* panique *f*; **a bomb scare** une alerte à la bombe
▶ *vb* **to scare somebody** faire [**36**] peur à quelqu'un ▷ *He scares me.* Il me fait peur.

scarecrow *n* épouvantail *m*

scared *adj* **to be scared** avoir [**8**] peur ▷ *I was scared stiff.* J'avais terriblement peur.; **to be scared of** avoir [**8**] peur de ▷ *Are you scared of him?* Est-ce que tu as peur de lui?

scarf *n* ❶ *(long)* écharpe *f* ❷ *(square)* foulard *m*

scary *adj* effrayant(e) ▷ *It was really scary.* C'était vraiment effrayant.

scene *n* ❶ *(place)* lieux *mpl* ▷ *the scene of the crime* les lieux du crime ❷ *(event, sight)* spectacle *m* ▷ *It was an amazing scene.* C'était un spectacle étonnant.; **to make a scene** faire [**36**] une scène

scenery *n (landscape)* paysage *m*

schedule *n* programme *m* ▷ *a busy schedule* un programme chargé; **on**

schedule comme prévu; **to be behind schedule** avoir [**8**] du retard
scheduled flight *n* vol régulier *m*
scheme *n* ❶ *(idea)* truc *m* ▷ *a crazy scheme he dreamed up* un truc farfelu qu'il a inventé ❷ *(project)* projet *m* ▷ *a council road-widening scheme* un projet municipal d'élargissement des routes
scholarship *n* bourse *f*
school *n* école *f*; **to go to school** aller [**3**] à l'école
schoolbag *n* cartable *m*
schoolbook *n* livre scolaire *m*
schoolboy *n* écolier *m*
schoolchildren *n* écoliers *mpl*
schoolgirl *n* écolière *f*
school uniform *n* uniforme scolaire *m*
science *n* science *f*
science fiction *n* science-fiction *f*
scientific *adj* scientifique
scientist *n* chercheur *m*, chercheuse *f*; **He trained as a scientist.** Il a une formation scientifique.
scissors *npl* ciseaux *mpl* ▷ *a pair of scissors* une paire de ciseaux
scooter *n* ❶ scooter *m* ❷ *(child's toy)* trottinette *f*
score *n* score *m* ▷ *The score was three nil.* Le score était trois à zéro.
▸ *vb* ❶ *(goal, point)* marquer [**28**] ▷ *to score a goal* marquer un but; **to score 6 out of 10** obtenir [**83**] un score de six sur dix ❷ *(keep score)* compter [**28**] les points ▷ *Who's going to score?* Qui va compter les points?
Scorpio *n* Scorpion *m* ▷ *I'm Scorpio.* Je suis Scorpion.
Scot *n* Écossais *m*, Écossaise *f*
Scotch tape® *n (US)* scotch® *m*
Scotland *n* Écosse *f*; **in Scotland** en Écosse; **to Scotland** en Écosse; **I'm from Scotland.** Je suis écossais.
Scots *adj* écossais(e) ▷ *a Scots accent* un accent écossais
Scotsman *n* Écossais *m*
Scotswoman *n* Écossaise *f*
Scottish *adj* écossais(e) ▷ *a Scottish accent* un accent écossais
scout *n* scout *m* ▷ *I'm in the Scouts.* Je suis scout.
scrambled eggs *npl* œufs brouillés *mpl*
scrap *n* ❶ bout *m* ▷ *a scrap of paper* un bout de papier ❷ *(fight)* bagarre *f*
▸ *vb (plan)* abandonner [**28**] ▷ *The idea was scrapped.* L'idée a été abandonnée.
scrapbook *n* album *m*
scratch *vb* se gratter [**28**] ▷ *Stop scratching!* Arrête de te gratter!
▸ *n (on skin)* égratignure *f*; **to start from scratch** partir [**57**] de zéro
scream *n* hurlement *m*
▸ *vb* hurler [**28**]
screen *n* écran *m*
screen-saver *n* économiseur d'écran *m*
screw *n* vis *f*
screwdriver *n* tournevis *m*
scribble *vb* griffonner [**28**]
scrub *vb* récurer [**28**] ▷ *to scrub a pan* récurer une casserole

sculpture *n* sculpture *f*
sea *n* mer *f*
seafood *n* fruits de mer *mpl* ▷ *I don't like seafood.* Je n'aime pas les fruits de mer.
seagull *n* mouette *f*
seal *n* ❶ *(animal)* phoque *m* ❷ *(on letter)* cachet *m*
▶ *vb* ❶ *(document)* sceller [**28**] ❷ *(letter)* coller [**28**]
seaman *n* marin *m*
search *vb* fouiller [**28**] ▷ *They searched the woods for her.* Ils ont fouillé les bois pour la trouver.; **to search for something** chercher [**28**] quelque chose ▷ *He searched for evidence.* Il cherchait des preuves.
▶ *n* fouille *f*
search party *n* expédition de secours *f*
seashore *n* bord de la mer *m* ▷ *on the seashore* au bord de la mer
seasick *adj* **to be seasick** avoir [**8**] le mal de mer
seaside *n* bord de la mer *m* ▷ *at the seaside* au bord de la mer
season *n* saison *f* ▷ *What's your favourite season?* Quelle est ta saison préférée?; **out of season** hors saison ▷ *It's cheaper to go there out of season.* C'est moins cher d'y aller hors saison.; **during the holiday season** en période de vacances; **a season ticket** une carte d'abonnement
seat *n* siège *m*
seat belt *n* ceinture de sécurité *f*
seaweed *n* algues *fpl*
second *adj* deuxième ▷ *on the second page* à la deuxième page; **to come second** *(in race)* arriver [**5**] deuxième; **the second of March** le deux mars
▶ *n* seconde *f* ▷ *It'll only take a second.* Ça va prendre juste une seconde.
secondary school *n* ❶ collège *m* ❷ lycée *m*

In France pupils go to a **collège** between the ages of 11 and 15, and then to a **lycée** until the age of 18.

second-class *adj, adv* ❶ *(ticket, compartment)* de seconde classe; **to travel second class** voyager [**45**] en seconde ❷ *(stamp, letter)* à tarif réduit ▷ *to send something second class* envoyer quelque chose à tarif réduit
secondhand *adj* d'occasion ▷ *a secondhand car* une voiture d'occasion
secondly *adv* deuxièmement; **firstly ... secondly ...** d'abord ... ensuite ... ▷ *Firstly, it's too expensive. Secondly, it wouldn't work anyway.* D'abord, c'est trop cher. Ensuite, ça ne marcherait pas de toute façon.
secret *adj* secret (*f* secrète) ▷ *a secret mission* une mission secrète
▶ *n* secret *m* ▷ *It's a secret.* C'est un secret. ▷ *Can you keep a secret?* Tu sais garder un secret?; **in secret** en secret
secretary *n* secrétaire *mf* ▷ *She's a secretary.* Elle est secrétaire.
secretly *n* secrètement

section *n* section *f*
security *n* sécurité *f* ▷ *a feeling of security* un sentiment de sécurité ▷ *a campaign to improve airport security* une campagne visant à améliorer la sécurité dans les aéroports; **job security** la sécurité de l'emploi
security guard *n* ❶ *(on guard)* garde chargé de la sécurité *m* ❷ *(transporting money)* un convoyeur de fonds
see *vb* voir [**92**] ▷ *I can't see.* Je n'y vois rien. ▷ *I saw him yesterday.* Je l'ai vu hier. ▷ *Have you seen him?* Est-ce que tu l'as vu?; **See you!** Salut!; **See you soon!** À bientôt!; **to see to something** s'occuper [**28**] de quelque chose ▷ *Can you see to the kids, please?* Tu peux t'occuper des enfants, s'il te plaît?
seed *n* graine *f* ▷ *sunflower seeds* des graines de tournesol
seek *vb* chercher [**28**]; **to seek help** chercher [**28**] de l'aide
seem *vb* avoir [**8**] l'air ▷ *She seems tired.* Elle a l'air fatiguée. ▷ *The shop seemed to be closed.* Le magasin avait l'air d'être fermé.; **That seems like a good idea.** Ce n'est pas une mauvaise idée.; **It seems that ...** Il paraît que ... ▷ *It seems she's getting married.* Il paraît qu'elle va se marier.; **There seems to be a problem.** Il semble y avoir un problème.
seen *vb see* **see**
seesaw *n* tapecul *m*
seldom *adv* rarement
select *vb* sélectionner [**28**]
selection *n* sélection *f*
self-catering *adj* **a self-catering apartment** un appartement de vacances
self-confidence *n* confiance en soi *f* ▷ *He hasn't got much self-confidence.* Il n'a pas très confiance en lui.
self-conscious *adj* **to be self-conscious (1)** *(embarrassed)* être [**35**] mal à l'aise ▷ *She was really self-conscious at first.* Elle était vraiment mal à l'aise au début. **(2)** *(shy)* manquer [**28**] d'assurance ▷ *He's always been rather self-conscious.* Il a toujours manqué un peu d'assurance.
self-defence (*US* **self-defense**) *n* autodéfense *f* ▷ *self-defence classes* les cours d'autodéfense; **She killed him in self-defence.** Elle l'a tué en légitime défense.
self-employed *adj* **to be self-employed** travailler [**28**] à son compte ▷ *He's self-employed.* Il travaille à son compte.; **the self-employed** les travailleurs indépendants
selfish *adj* égoïste ▷ *Don't be so selfish.* Ne sois pas si égoïste.
self-service *adj* **It's self-service.** *(café, shop)* C'est un self-service.; **a self-service restaurant** un restaurant self-service
sell *vb* vendre [**88**] ▷ *He sold it to me.* Il me l'a vendu.
sell off *vb* liquider [**28**]
sell out *vb* se vendre [**88**] ▷ *The*

tickets sold out in three hours. Les billets se sont tous vendus en trois heures. ▷ *The show didn't quite sell out.* Ce spectacle ne s'est pas très bien vendu.; **The tickets are all sold out.** Il ne reste plus de billets.

sell-by date *n* date limite de vente *f*

Sellotape® *n* scotch® *m*

semi *n* maison jumelée *f* ▷ *We live in a semi.* Nous habitons dans une maison jumelée.

semicircle *n* demi-cercle *m*

semicolon *n* point-virgule *m*

semi-detached house *n* maison jumelée *f* ▷ *We live in a semi-detached house.* Nous habitons dans une maison jumelée.

semi-final *n* demi-finale *f*

semi-skimmed milk *n* lait demi-écrémé *m*

send *vb* envoyer [**33**] ▷ *She sent me a birthday card.* Elle m'a envoyé une carte d'anniversaire.

send back *vb* renvoyer [**33**]

send off *vb* ❶ *(goods, letter)* envoyer [**33**] ❷ *(in sports match)* renvoyer [**33**] du terrain ▷ *He was sent off.* On l'a renvoyé du terrain.; **to send off for something (1)** *(free)* se faire [**36**] envoyer quelque chose ▷ *I've sent off for a brochure.* Je me suis fait envoyer une brochure. **(2)** *(paid for)* commander [**28**] quelque chose par correspondance ▷ *She sent off for a book.* Elle a commandé un livre par correspondance.

send out *vb* envoyer [**33**]; **to send out for** commander [**28**] par téléphone ▷ *Shall we send out for a pizza?* Et si on commandait une pizza par téléphone?

senior *adj* haut placé(e); **senior management** les cadres supérieurs; **senior school** le lycée; **senior pupils** les grandes classes

senior citizen *n* personne du troisième âge *f*

sensational *adj* sensationnel (*f* sensationnelle)

sense *n* ❶ *(wisdom)* bon sens *m* ▷ *Use your common sense!* Un peu de bon sens, voyons!; **It makes sense.** C'est logique.; **It doesn't make sense.** Ça n'a pas de sens. ❷ *(faculty)* sens *m* ▷ *the five senses* les cinq sens; **the sense of touch** le toucher; **the sense of smell** l'odorat *m*; **the sixth sense** le sixième sens; **sense of humour** le sens de l'humour ▷ *He's got no sense of humour.* Il n'a aucun sens de l'humour.

sensible *adj* raisonnable ▷ *Be sensible!* Sois raisonnable!

> Be careful not to translate **sensible** by the French word **sensible**.

sensitive *adj* sensible ▷ *She's very sensitive.* Elle est très sensible.

sent *vb see* **send**

sentence *n* ❶ phrase *f* ▷ *What does this sentence mean?* Que veut dire cette phrase? ❷ *(judgment)* condamnation *f* ❸ *(punishment)* peine *f* ▷ *the death sentence* la peine de mort; **He got a life sentence.**

Il a été condamné à la réclusion à perpétuité.
▶ *vb* condamner [**28**]; **to sentence somebody to life imprisonment** condamner [**28**] quelqu'un à la réclusion à perpétuité; **to sentence somebody to death** condamner [**28**] quelqu'un à mort

sentimental *adj* sentimental(e) (*mpl* sentimentaux)

separate *adj* séparé(e) ▷ *I wrote it on a separate sheet.* Je l'ai écrit sur une feuille séparée.; **The children have separate rooms.** Les enfants ont chacun leur chambre.; **on separate occasions** à différentes reprises
▶ *vb* ❶ séparer [**28**] ❷ *(married couple)* se séparer [**28**]

separately *adv* séparément

separation *n* séparation *f*

September *n* septembre *m*; **in September** en septembre

sequel *n (book, film)* suite *f*

sergeant *n* ❶ *(army)* sergent *m* ❷ *(police)* brigadier *m*

serial *n* feuilleton *m*

series *n* ❶ série *f* ▷ *a TV series* une série télévisée ❷ *(of numbers)* suite *f*

serious *adj* ❶ sérieux (*f* sérieuse) ▷ *You look very serious.* Tu as l'air sérieux.; **Are you serious?** Sérieusement? ❷ *(illness, mistake)* grave

seriously *adv* sérieusement ▷ *No, but seriously ...* Non, mais sérieusement ...; **to take somebody seriously** prendre [**65**] quelqu'un au sérieux; **seriously injured** gravement blessé; **Seriously?** Vraiment?

servant *n* domestique *mf*

serve *vb* ❶ servir [**78**] ▷ *Dinner is served.* Le dîner est servi. ▷ *It's Murray's turn to serve.* C'est à Murray de servir. ❷ *(prison sentence)* purger [**45**]; **to serve time** être [**35**] en prison; **It serves you right.** C'est bien fait pour toi.
▶ *n (tennis)* service *m*; **It's your serve.** C'est à toi de servir.

service *vb (car, washing machine)* réviser [**28**]
▶ *n* ❶ service *m* ▷ *Service is included.* Le service est compris. ❷ *(of car)* révision *f* ❸ *(church service)* office *m*; **the Fire Service** les sapeurs-pompiers; **the armed services** les forces armées

service charge *n* service *m* ▷ *There's no service charge.* Le service est compris.

service station *n* station-service *f* (*pl* stations-service)

serviette *n* serviette *f*

session *n* séance *f*

set *n* ❶ jeu *m* (*pl* jeux) ▷ *a set of keys* un jeu de clés ▷ *a chess set* un jeu d'échecs; **a train set** un train électrique ❷ *(in tennis)* set *m*
▶ *vb* ❶ *(alarm clock)* mettre [**47**] à sonner ▷ *I set the alarm for 7 o'clock.* J'ai mis le réveil à sonner pour sept heures. ❷ *(record)* établir [**38**] ▷ *The world record was set last year.* Le record du monde a été établi l'année dernière. ❸ *(sun)* se coucher [**28**] ▷ *The sun was setting.*

Le soleil se couchait.; **The film is set in Morocco.** L'action du film se déroule au Maroc.; **to set sail** prendre [**65**] la mer; **to set the table** mettre [**47**] le couvert

set off *vb* partir [**57**] ▷ *We set off for London at 9 o'clock.* Nous sommes partis pour Londres à neuf heures.

set out *vb* partir [**57**] ▷ *We set out for London at 9 o'clock.* Nous sommes partis pour Londres à neuf heures.

settee *n* canapé *m*

settle *vb* ❶ *(problem)* résoudre [**70**] ❷ *(argument, account)* régler [**34**]; **to settle on something** opter [**28**] pour quelque chose

settle down *vb (calm down)* se calmer [**28**]; **Settle down!** Du calme!

settle in *vb* s'installer [**28**]

seven *num* sept ▷ *She's seven.* Elle a sept ans.

seventeen *num* dix-sept ▷ *He's seventeen.* Il a dix-sept ans.

seventeenth *adj* dix-septième ▷ *her seventeenth birthday* son dix-septième anniversaire ▷ *the seventeenth floor* le dix-septième étage; **the seventeenth of August** le dix-sept août

seventh *adj* septième ▷ *the seventh floor* le septième étage; **the seventh of August** le sept août

seventy *num* soixante-dix

several *adj, pron* plusieurs ▷ *several schools* plusieurs écoles; **several of them** plusieurs ▷ *I've seen several of them.* J'en ai vu plusieurs.

sew *vb* coudre [**15**]

sew up *vb (tear)* recoudre [**15**]

sewing *n* couture *f* ▷ *I like sewing.* J'aime faire de la couture.; **a sewing machine** une machine à coudre

sewn *vb see* **sew**

sex *n* sexe *m*; **to have sex with somebody** coucher [**28**] avec quelqu'un; **sex education** l'éducation sexuelle *f*

sexism *n* sexisme *m*

sexist *adj* sexiste

sexual *adj* sexuel (*f* sexuelle) ▷ *sexual discrimination* la discrimination sexuelle ▷ *sexual harassment* le harcèlement sexuel

sexuality *n* sexualité *f*

sexy *adj* sexy

shabby *adj* miteux (*f* miteuse)

shade *n* ❶ ombre *f*; **in the shade** à l'ombre ▷ *It was 35 degrees in the shade.* Il faisait trente-cinq à l'ombre. ❷ *(colour)* nuance *f* ▷ *a shade of blue* une nuance de bleu

shadow *n* ombre *f*

shake *vb* ❶ secouer [**28**] ▷ *She shook the rug.* Elle a secoué le tapis. ❷ *(tremble)* trembler [**28**] ▷ *He was shaking with cold.* Il tremblait de froid.; **to shake one's head** *(in refusal)* faire [**36**] non de la tête; **to shake hands with somebody** serrer [**28**] la main à quelqu'un ▷ *They shook hands.* Ils se sont serré la main.

shaken *adj* secoué(e) ▷ *I was feeling a bit shaken.* J'étais un peu secoué.

shall *vb* **Shall I shut the window?** Vous voulez que je ferme la fenêtre?;

Shall we ask him to come with us? Si on lui demandait de venir avec nous?

shallow *adj (water, pool)* peu profond(e)

shambles *n* pagaille *f* ▷ *It's a complete shambles.* C'est la pagaille complète.

shame *n* honte *f* ▷ *The shame of it!* Quelle honte!; **What a shame!** Quel dommage!; **It's a shame that ...** C'est dommage que ...

> **c'est dommage que** has to be followed by a verb in the subjunctive.

▷ *It's a shame he isn't here.* C'est dommage qu'il ne soit pas ici.

shampoo *n* shampooing *m* ▷ *a bottle of shampoo* une bouteille de shampooing

shandy *n* panaché *m*

shape *n* forme *f*

share *n* ❶ *(in company)* action *f* ▷ *They've got shares in the company.* Ils ont des actions dans la société. ❷ part *f* ▷ *Everybody pays their share.* Tout le monde paie sa part.
▶ *vb* partager [**45**] ▷ *to share a room with somebody* partager une chambre avec quelqu'un

share out *vb* distribuer [**28**] ▷ *They shared the sweets out among the children.* Ils ont distribué les bonbons aux enfants.

shark *n* requin *m*

sharp *adj* ❶ *(razor, knife)* tranchant(e) ❷ *(spike, point)* pointu(e) ❸ *(clever)* intelligent(e) ▷ *She's very sharp.* Elle est très intelligente.; **at two o'clock sharp** à deux heures pile

shave *vb (have a shave)* se raser [**28**]; **to shave one's legs** se raser [**28**] les jambes

shaver *n* **an electric shaver** un rasoir électrique

shaving cream *n* crème à raser *f*

shaving foam *n* mousse à raser *f*

she *pron* elle ▷ *She's very nice.* Elle est très gentille.

shed *n* remise *f*

she'd = **she had**; **she would**

sheep *n* mouton *m*

sheepdog *n* chien de berger *m*

sheer *adj* pur(e) ▷ *It's sheer greed.* C'est de l'avidité pure.

sheet *n (on bed)* drap *m*; **a sheet of paper** une feuille de papier

shelf *n* ❶ *(in house)* étagère *f* ❷ *(in shop)* rayon *m*

shell *n* ❶ *(on beach)* coquillage *m* ❷ *(of egg, nut)* coquille *f* ❸ *(explosive)* obus *m*

she'll = **she will**

shellfish *n* fruits de mer *mpl*

shelter *n* **to take shelter** se mettre [**47**] à l'abri; **a bus shelter** un arrêt d'autobus

shelves *npl see* **shelf**

shepherd *n* berger *m*

sherry *n* xérès *m*

she's = **she is**; **she has**

shift *n* service *m* ▷ *His shift starts at 8 o'clock.* Il prend son service à huit heures. ▷ *the night shift* le service de nuit; **to do shift work** faire [**36**] les trois-huit
▶ *vb (move)* déplacer [**12**] ▷ *I couldn't*

shift the wardrobe on my own. Je n'ai pas pu déplacer l'armoire tout seul.; **Shift yourself!** *(informal)* Pousse-toi de là!

shin *n* tibia *m*

shine *vb* briller [**28**] ▷ *The sun was shining.* Le soleil brillait.

shiny *adj* brillant(e)

ship *n* ❶ bateau *m* (*pl* bateaux) ❷ *(warship)* navire *m*

shirt *n* ❶ *(man's)* chemise *f* ❷ *(woman's)* chemisier *m*

shiver *vb* frissonner [**28**]

shock *n* choc *m*; **to get a shock** **(1)** *(surprise)* avoir [**8**] un choc **(2)** *(electric)* recevoir [**67**] une décharge; **an electric shock** une décharge
▶ *vb* ❶ *(upset)* bouleverser [**28**] ▷ *They were shocked by the tragedy.* Ils ont été bouleversés par la tragédie. ❷ *(scandalize)* choquer [**28**] ▷ *I was rather shocked by her attitude.* J'ai été assez choqué par son attitude.

shocking *adj* choquant(e) ▷ *It's shocking!* C'est choquant!; **a shocking waste** un gaspillage épouvantable

shoe *n* chaussure *f*

shoelace *n* lacet *m*

shoe polish *n* cirage *m*

shoe shop *n* magasin de chaussures *m*

shone *vb* *see* **shine**

shook *vb* *see* **shake**

shoot *vb* ❶ *(kill)* abattre [**9**] ▷ *He was shot by a sniper.* Il a été abattu par un franc-tireur. ❷ *(execute)* fusiller [**28**] ▷ *He was shot at dawn.* Il a été fusillé à l'aube. ❸ *(gun)* tirer [**28**] ▷ *Don't shoot!* Ne tirez pas!; **to shoot at somebody** tirer [**28**] sur quelqu'un; **He shot himself with a revolver.** *(dead)* Il s'est suicidé d'un coup de revolver.; **He was shot in the leg.** *(wounded)* Il a reçu une balle dans la jambe.; **to shoot an arrow** envoyer [**33**] une flèche ❹ *(film)* tourner [**28**] ▷ *The film was shot in Prague.* Le film a été tourné à Prague. ❺ *(in football)* shooter [**28**]

shooting *n* ❶ coups de feu *mpl* ▷ *They heard shooting.* Ils ont entendu des coups de feu.; **a shooting** une fusillade ❷ *(hunting)* chasse *f* ▷ *to go shooting* aller à la chasse

shop *n* magasin *m* ▷ *a sports shop* un magasin de sports

shop assistant *n* vendeur *m*, vendeuse *f* ▷ *She's a shop assistant.* Elle est vendeuse.

shopkeeper *n* commerçant *m*, commerçante *f* ▷ *He's a shopkeeper.* Il est commerçant.

shoplifting *n* vol à l'étalage *m*

shopping *n* *(purchases)* courses *fpl* ▷ *Can you get the shopping from the car?* Tu peux aller chercher les courses dans la voiture?; **I love shopping.** J'adore faire du shopping.; **to go shopping** **(1)** *(for food)* faire [**36**] des courses **(2)** *(for pleasure)* faire [**36**] du shopping; **a shopping bag** un sac à provisions; **a shopping centre** un centre commercial

shop window *n* vitrine *f*

shore *n* rivage *m*; **on shore** à terre
short *adj* ❶ court(e) ▷ *a short skirt* une jupe courte ▷ *short hair* les cheveux courts; **too short** trop court ▷ *It was a great holiday, but too short.* C'étaient des vacances super, mais trop courtes.
❷ *(person, period of time)* petit(e) ▷ *She's quite short.* Elle est assez petite. ▷ *a short break* une petite pause ▷ *a short walk* une petite promenade; **to be short of something** être [**35**] à court de quelque chose ▷ *I'm short of money.* Je suis à court d'argent.; **at short notice** au dernier moment; **In short, the answer's no.** Bref, la réponse est non.
shortage *n* pénurie *f* ▷ *a water shortage* une pénurie d'eau
short cut *n* raccourci *m* ▷ *I took a short cut.* J'ai pris un raccourci.
shortly *adv* bientôt
shorts *npl* short *msg*; **a pair of shorts** un short
short-sighted *adj* myope
shot *vb see* **shoot**
▶ *n* ❶ *(gunshot)* coup de feu *m*
❷ *(photo)* photo *f* ▷ *a shot of Edinburgh Castle* une photo du château d'Édimbourg
❸ *(vaccination)* vaccin *m*
shotgun *n* fusil de chasse *m*
should *vb*

When 'should' means 'ought to', use **devoir**.

devoir [**26**] ▷ *You should take more exercise.* Vous devriez faire plus d'exercice. ▷ *That shouldn't be too hard.* Ça ne devrait pas être trop difficile.; **should have** avoir dû ▷ *I should have told you before.* J'aurais dû te le dire avant.

When 'should' means 'would', use the conditional tense.

▷ *I should go if I were you.* Si j'étais vous, j'irais. ▷ *I should be so lucky!* Ça serait trop beau!
shoulder *n* épaule *f*; **a shoulder bag** un sac à bandoulière
shouldn't = **should not**
shout *vb* crier [**19**] ▷ *Don't shout!* Ne criez pas! ▷ *'Go away!' he shouted.* 'Allez-vous-en!' a-t-il crié.
▶ *n* cri *m*
shovel *n* pelle *f*
show *n* ❶ *(performance)* spectacle *m*
❷ *(programme)* émission *f*
❸ *(exhibition)* salon *m*
▶ *vb* ❶ montrer [**28**]; **to show somebody something** montrer [**28**] quelque chose à quelqu'un ▷ *Have I shown you my new trainers?* Je t'ai montré mes nouvelles baskets? ❷ faire [**36**] preuve de ▷ *She showed great courage.* Elle a fait preuve de beaucoup de courage.; **It shows.** Ça se voit. ▷ *I've never been riding before. — It shows.* Je n'ai jamais fait de cheval. — Ça se voit.
show off *vb* frimer [**28**] *(informal)*
show up *vb (turn up)* se pointer [**28**] ▷ *He showed up late as usual.* Il s'est pointé en retard comme d'habitude.
shower *n* ❶ douche *f*; **to have a shower** prendre [**65**] une douche

⑪ (of rain) averse f
shown vb see **show**
show-off n frimeur m, frimeuse f
shrank vb see **shrink**
shriek vb hurler [**28**]
shrimps npl crevettes fpl
shrink vb (clothes, fabric) rétrécir [**38**]
Shrove Tuesday n mardi gras m
shrug vb **to shrug one's shoulders** hausser [**28**] les épaules
shrunk vb see **shrink**
shuffle vb **to shuffle the cards** battre [**9**] les cartes
shut vb fermer [**28**] ▷ *What time do you shut?* À quelle heure est-ce que vous fermez? ▷ *What time do the shops shut?* À quelle heure est-ce que les magasins ferment?
shut down vb fermer [**28**] ▷ *The cinema shut down last year.* Le cinéma a fermé l'année dernière.
shut up vb ❶ *(close)* fermer [**28**] ❷ *(be quiet)* se taire [**82**] ▷ *Shut up!* Tais-toi!
shuttle n navette f
shuttlecock n *(badminton)* volant m
shy adj timide
Sicily n Sicile f; **in Sicily** en Sicile; **to Sicily** en Sicile
sick adj ❶ *(ill)* malade ▷ *He was sick for four days.* Il a été malade pendant quatre jours. ❷ *(joke, humour)* de mauvais goût ▷ *That's really sick!* C'est vraiment de mauvais goût!; **to be sick** *(vomit)* vomir [**38**]; **I feel sick.** J'ai envie de vomir.; **to be sick of something** en avoir [**8**] assez de quelque chose ▷ *I'm sick of your jokes.* J'en ai assez de tes plaisanteries.
sickness n maladie f
side n ❶ *(of object, building, car)* côté m ▷ *He was driving on the wrong side of the road.* Il roulait du mauvais côté de la route. ❷ *(of pool, river, road)* bord m ▷ *by the side of the lake* au bord du lac ❸ *(of hill)* flanc m ❹ *(team)* équipe f; **He's on my side. (1)** *(on my team)* Il est dans mon équipe. **(2)** *(supporting me)* Il est de mon côté.; **side by side** côte à côte; **the side entrance** l'entrée latérale; **to take sides** prendre [**65**] parti ▷ *She always takes his side.* Elle prend toujours son parti.
sideboard n buffet m
side-effect n effet secondaire m
sidewalk n *(US)* trottoir m
sideways adv ❶ *(look, be facing)* de côté ❷ *(move)* de travers; **sideways on** de profil
sieve n passoire f
sigh n soupir m
▶ vb soupirer [**28**]
sight n ❶ vue f ▷ *to have poor sight* avoir une mauvaise vue; **to know somebody by sight** connaître [**14**] quelqu'un de vue ❷ spectacle m ▷ *It was an amazing sight.* C'était un spectacle étonnant.; **in sight** visible; **out of sight** hors de vue; **the sights** *(tourist spots)* les attractions touristiques; **to see the sights of London** visiter [**28**] Londres
sightseeing n tourisme m; **to go**

sightseeing faire [**36**] du tourisme

sign *n* ❶ *(notice)* panneau *m* *(pl* panneaux) ▷ *There was a big sign saying 'private'.* Il y avait un grand panneau indiquant 'privé'.; **a road sign** un panneau ❷ *(gesture, indication)* signe *m* ▷ *There's no sign of improvement.* Il n'y a aucun signe d'amélioration.; **What sign are you?** *(star sign)* Tu es de quel signe?
▶ *vb* signer [**28**]

sign on *vb* ❶ *(as unemployed)* s'inscrire [**30**] au chômage ❷ *(for course)* s'inscrire [**30**]

signal *n* signal *m* *(pl* signaux)
▶ *vb* **to signal to somebody** faire [**36**] un signe à quelqu'un

signature *n* signature *f*

significance *n* importance *f*

significant *adj* important(e)

sign language *n* langage des signes *m*

signpost *n* poteau indicateur *m*

silence *n* silence *m*

silent *adj* silencieux *(f* silencieuse)

silk *n* soie *f*
▶ *adj* en soie ▷ *a silk scarf* un foulard en soie

silky *adj* soyeux *(f* soyeuse)

silly *adj* bête

silver *n* argent *m* ▷ *a silver medal* une médaille d'argent

similar *adj* semblable; **similar to** semblable à

simple *adj* ❶ simple ▷ *It's very simple.* C'est très simple.
❷ *(simple-minded)* simplet *(f* simplette) ▷ *He's a bit simple.* Il est un peu simplet.

simply *adv* simplement ▷ *It's simply not possible.* Ça n'est tout simplement pas possible.

sin *n* péché *m*
▶ *vb* pécher [**28**]

since *prep, adv, conj* ❶ depuis ▷ *since Christmas* depuis Noël ▷ *since then* depuis ce moment-là ▷ *I haven't seen him since.* Je ne l'ai pas vu depuis.; **ever since** depuis ce moment-là ❷ depuis que ▷ *I haven't seen her since she left.* Je ne l'ai pas vue depuis qu'elle est partie.
❸ *(because)* puisque ▷ *Since you're tired, let's stay at home.* Puisque tu es fatigué, restons à la maison.

sincere *adj* sincère

sincerely *adv* **Yours sincerely ...** **(1)** *(in business letter)* Veuillez agréer l'expression de mes sentiments les meilleurs ... **(2)** *(in personal letter)* Cordialement ...

sing *vb* chanter [**28**] ▷ *He sang out of tune.* Il chantait faux.

singer *n* chanteur *m*, chanteuse *f*

singing *n* chant *m*

single *adj (unmarried)* célibataire; **a single room** une chambre pour une personne; **not a single thing** rien du tout
▶ *n (ticket)* aller simple *m* ▷ *A single to Toulouse, please.* Un aller simple pour Toulouse, s'il vous plaît.; **a CD single** un CD single

single parent *n* **She's a single parent.** Elle élève ses enfants toute seule.; **a single parent family** une famille monoparentale

singular *n* singulier *m* ▷ *in the singular* au singulier

sink *n* évier *m*
▶ *vb* couler [**28**]

sir *n* monsieur *m*; **Yes sir.** Oui, Monsieur.

siren *n* sirène *f*

sister *n* ❶ sœur *f* ▷ *my little sister* ma petite sœur ❷ *(nurse)* infirmière en chef *f*

sister-in-law *n* belle-sœur *f* (*pl* belles-sœurs)

sit *vb* s'asseoir [**6**]; **to sit on something** s'asseoir [**6**] sur quelque chose ▷ *She sat on the chair.* Elle s'est assise sur la chaise.; **to be sitting** être [**35**] assis; **to sit an exam** passer [**58**] un examen

sit down *vb* s'asseoir [**6**]

site *n* ❶ site *m* ▷ *an archaeological site* un site archéologique; **the site of the accident** le lieu de l'accident ❷ *(campsite)* camping *m*; **a building site** un chantier

sitting room *n* salon *m*

situation *n* situation *f*

six *num* six ▷ *He's six.* Il a six ans.

sixteen *num* seize ▷ *He's sixteen.* Il a seize ans.

sixteenth *adj* seizième ▷ *the sixteenth floor* le seizième étage; **the sixteenth of August** le seize août

sixth *adj* sixième ▷ *the sixth floor* le sixième étage; **the sixth of August** le six août

sixty *num* soixante

size *n* ❶ *(of object, clothing)* taille *f* ▷ *What size do you take?* Quelle taille est-ce que vous faites?; **I'm a size ten.** Je fais du trente-huit. ❷ *(of shoes)* pointure *f*; **I take size six.** Je fais du trente-neuf.

France uses the European system to show clothing and shoe sizes.

skate *vb* ❶ *(ice-skate)* faire [**36**] du patin à glace ❷ *(roller-skate)* faire [**36**] du patin à roulettes

skateboard *n* skateboard *m*

skateboarding *n* skateboard *m* ▷ *to go skateboarding* faire du skateboard

skates *n* patins *mpl*

skating *n* patin à glace *m* ▷ *to go skating* faire du patin à glace; **a skating rink** une patinoire

skeleton *n* squelette *m*

sketch *n (drawing)* croquis *m*
▶ *vb* **to sketch something** faire [**36**] un croquis de quelque chose

ski *n* ski *m*; **ski boots** les chaussures de ski *fpl*; **a ski lift** un remonte-pente; **ski pants** le fuseau *sg*; **a ski pole** un bâton de ski; **a ski slope** une piste de ski; **a ski suit** une combinaison de ski
▶ *vb* skier [**19**] ▷ *Can you ski?* Tu sais skier?

skid *vb* déraper [**28**]

skier *n* skieur *m*, skieuse *f*

skiing *n* ski *m*; **to go skiing** faire [**36**] du ski; **to go on a skiing holiday** aller [**3**] aux sports d'hiver

skilful *adj* adroit(e)

skill *n* talent *m* ▷ *He played with great skill.* Il a joué avec beaucoup de talent.

skilled *adj* **a skilled worker** un ouvrier spécialisé
skimmed milk *n* lait écrémé *m*
skin *n* peau *f* (*pl* peaux); **skin cancer** le cancer de la peau
skinhead *n* skinhead *mf*
skinny *adj* maigre
skip *n* (*container*) benne *f*
▸ *vb* sauter [**28**] ▹ *to skip a meal* sauter un repas; **to skip a lesson** sécher [**34**] un cours
skirt *n* jupe *f*
skive *vb* (*be lazy*) tirer [**28**] au flanc
skive off *vb* sécher [**34**] (*informal*) ▹ *to skive off school* sécher les cours
skull *n* crâne *m*
sky *n* ciel *m*
skyscraper *n* gratte-ciel *m* (*pl* gratte-ciel)
slam *vb* claquer [**28**] ▹ *The door slammed.* La porte a claqué. ▹ *She slammed the door.* Elle a claqué la porte.
slang *n* argot *m*
slap *n* claque *f*
▸ *vb* **to slap somebody** donner [**28**] une claque à quelqu'un
slate *n* ardoise *f*
sledge *n* luge *f*
sledging *n* **to go sledging** faire [**36**] de la luge
sleep *n* sommeil *m*; **I need some sleep.** J'ai besoin de dormir.; **to go to sleep** s'endormir [**29**]
▸ *vb* dormir [**29**] ▹ *I couldn't sleep last night.* J'ai mal dormi la nuit dernière.; **to sleep with somebody** coucher [**28**] avec quelqu'un
sleep around *vb* coucher [**28**] à droite et à gauche
sleep in *vb* ❶ (*accidentally*) ne pas se réveiller [**28**] ▹ *I'm sorry I'm late, I slept in.* Désolé d'être en retard: je ne me suis pas réveillé. ❷ (*on purpose*) faire [**36**] la grasse matinée
sleep together *vb* coucher [**28**] ensemble
sleeping bag *n* sac de couchage *m*
sleeping pill *n* somnifère *m*
sleepy *adj* **to feel sleepy** avoir [**8**] sommeil ▹ *I was feeling sleepy.* J'avais sommeil.; **a sleepy little village** un petit village tranquille
sleet *n* neige fondue *f*
▸ *vb* **It's sleeting.** Il tombe de la neige fondue.
sleeve *n* manche *f* ▹ *long sleeves* les manches longues
slept *vb see* **sleep**
slice *n* tranche *f*
▸ *vb* couper [**28**] en tranches
slide *n* ❶ (*in playground*) toboggan *m* ❷ (*photo*) diapositive *f* ❸ (*hair slide*) barrette *f*
▸ *vb* glisser [**28**]
slight *adj* léger (*f* légère) ▹ *a slight problem* un léger problème ▹ *a slight improvement* une légère amélioration
slightly *adv* légèrement
slim *adj* mince
▸ *vb* (*be on a diet*) faire [**36**] un régime ▹ *I'm slimming.* Je fais un régime.
sling *n* écharpe *f* ▹ *She had her arm in a sling.* Elle avait le bras en écharpe.

slip *n* ❶ *(mistake)* erreur *f* ❷ *(underskirt)* jupon *m* ❸ *(full-length underskirt)* combinaison *f*; **a slip of paper** un bout de papier; **a slip of the tongue** un lapsus
▸ *vb* glisser [**28**] ▷ *He slipped on the ice.* Il a glissé sur le verglas.

slip up *vb (make a mistake)* faire [**36**] une erreur

slipper *n* chausson *m*; **a pair of slippers** des chaussons

slippery *adj* glissant(e)

slip-up *n* erreur *f*

slope *n* pente *f*

slot *n* fente *f*

slot machine *n* ❶ *(for gambling)* machine à sous *f* ❷ *(vending machine)* distributeur automatique *m*

slow *adj, adv* ❶ lent(e) ▷ *We are behind a very slow lorry.* On est derrière un camion très lent.
❷ lentement ▷ *to go slow (person, car)* aller lentement ▷ *Drive slower!* Conduisez plus lentement!; **My watch is slow.** Ma montre retarde.

slow down *vb* ralentir [**38**]

slowly *adv* lentement

slug *n* limace *f*

slum *n* ❶ *(area)* quartier insalubre *m* ❷ *(house)* taudis *m*

smack *n* tape *f*
▸ *vb* **to smack somebody** donner [**28**] une tape à quelqu'un

small *adj* petit(e); **small change** la petite monnaie

smart *adj* ❶ *(elegant)* chic ❷ *(clever)* intelligent(e); **a smart idea** une idée astucieuse

smartphone *n* smartphone *m*

smashing *adj* formidable ▷ *I think he's smashing.* Je le trouve formidable.

smell *n* odeur *f*; **the sense of smell** l'odorat *m*
▸ *vb* ❶ sentir [**77**] mauvais ▷ *That old dog really smells!* Qu'est-ce qu'il sent mauvais, ce vieux chien!; **to smell of something** sentir [**77**] quelque chose ▷ *It smells of petrol.* Ça sent l'essence. ❷ *(detect)* sentir [**77**] ▷ *I can't smell anything.* Je ne sens rien.

smelly *adj* qui sent mauvais ▷ *He's got smelly feet.* Il a les pieds qui sentent mauvais.

smelt *vb see* **smell**

smile *n* sourire *m*
▸ *vb* sourire [**74**]

smiley *n* émoticon *m*

smoke *n* fumée *f*
▸ *vb* fumer [**28**] ▷ *I don't smoke.* Je ne fume pas.

smoker *n* fumeur *m*, fumeuse *f*

smoking *n* **to give up smoking** arrêter [**28**] de fumer; **Smoking is bad for you.** Le tabac est mauvais pour la santé.; **'no smoking'** 'défense de fumer'

smooth *adj* ❶ *(surface)* lisse ❷ *(person)* mielleux (*f* mielleuse)

SMS *n* SMS *m* ▷ *I'll send you an SMS.* Je t'enverrai un SMS.

smudge *n* bavure *f*

smuggle *vb (goods)* passer [**58**] en fraude ▷ *to smuggle cigarettes into a country* faire passer des cigarettes en fraude dans un pays; **They**

managed to smuggle him out of prison. Ils ont réussi à le faire sortir de prison clandestinement.

smuggler *n* contrebandier *m*, contrebandière *f*

smuggling *n* contrebande *f*

snack *n* en-cas *m* (*pl* en-cas); **to have a snack** prendre [**65**] un en-cas

snack bar *n* snack-bar *m*

snail *n* escargot *m*

snake *n* serpent *m*

snap *vb* (*break*) casser [**28**] net ▷ *The branch snapped.* La branche a cassé net.; **to snap one's fingers** faire [**36**] claquer ses doigts

snatch *vb* **to snatch something from somebody** arracher [**28**] quelque chose à quelqu'un ▷ *He snatched the keys from my hand.* Il m'a arraché les clés des mains.; **My bag was snatched.** On m'a arraché mon sac.

sneak *vb* **to sneak in** entrer [**32**] furtivement; **to sneak out** sortir [**79**] furtivement; **to sneak up on somebody** s'approcher [**28**] de quelqu'un sans faire de bruit

sneeze *vb* éternuer [**28**]

sniff *vb* ❶ renifler [**28**] ▷ *Stop sniffing!* Arrête de renifler! ❷ flairer [**28**] ▷ *The dog sniffed my hand.* Le chien m'a flairé la main.; **to sniff glue** sniffer [**28**] de la colle

snob *n* snob *mf*

snooker *n* billard *m* ▷ *to play snooker* jouer au billard

snooze *n* petit somme *m* ▷ *to have a snooze* faire un petit somme

snore *vb* ronfler [**28**]

snow *n* neige *f*

▶ *vb* neiger [**45**] ▷ *It's snowing.* Il neige.

snowball *n* boule de neige *f*

snowflake *n* flocon de neige *m*

snowman *n* bonhomme de neige *m* ▷ *to build a snowman* faire un bonhomme de neige

so *conj, adv* ❶ alors ▷ *The shop was closed, so I went home.* Le magasin était fermé, alors je suis rentré chez moi. ▷ *So, have you always lived in London?* Alors, vous avez toujours vécu à Londres?; **So what?** Et alors? ❷ (*so that*) donc ▷ *It rained, so I got wet.* Il pleuvait, donc j'ai été mouillé. ❸ (*very*) tellement ▷ *It was so heavy!* C'était tellement lourd! ▷ *He was talking so fast I couldn't understand.* Il parlait tellement vite que je ne comprenais pas.; **It's not so heavy!** Ça n'est pas si lourd que ça!; **How's your father? — Not so good.** Comment va ton père? — Pas très bien.; **so much** (*a lot*) tellement ▷ *I love you so much.* Je t'aime tellement.; **so much ...** tellement de ... ▷ *I've got so much work.* J'ai tellement de travail.; **so many ...** tellement de ... ▷ *I've got so many things to do today.* J'ai tellement de choses à faire aujourd'hui. ❹ (*in comparisons*) aussi ▷ *He's like his sister but not so clever.* Il est comme sa sœur mais pas aussi intelligent.; **so do I** moi aussi ▷ *I love horses. — So do I.* J'aime les chevaux. — Moi aussi.; **so have**

we nous aussi ▷ *I've been to France twice. — So have we.* Je suis allé en France deux fois. — Nous aussi.; **I think so.** Je crois.; **I hope so.** J'espère bien.; **That's not so.** Ça n'est pas le cas.; **so far** jusqu'à présent ▷ *It's been easy so far.* Ça a été facile jusqu'à présent.; **so far so good** jusqu'ici ça va; **ten or so people** environ dix personnes; **at five o'clock or so** à environ cinq heures

soak *vb* tremper [28]

soaking *adj* trempé(e) ▷ *By the time we got back we were soaking.* Nous sommes rentrés trempés.; **soaking wet** trempé ▷ *Your shoes are soaking wet.* Tes chaussures sont trempées.

soap *n* savon *m*

soap opera *n* feuilleton à l'eau de rose *m*

soap powder *n* lessive *f*

sob *vb* sangloter [28] ▷ *She was sobbing.* Elle sanglotait.

sober *adj* sobre

sober up *vb* dessoûler [28]

soccer *n* football *m* ▷ *to play soccer* jouer au football; **a soccer player** un joueur de football

social *adj* social(e) (*mpl* sociaux) ▷ *a social class* une classe sociale; **I have a good social life.** Je vois beaucoup de monde.

socialism *n* socialisme *m*

socialist *adj* socialiste ▶ *n* socialiste *mf*

social network *n* réseau social *m*

social security *n* ❶ *(money)* aide sociale *f*; **to be on social security** recevoir [67] de l'aide sociale ❷ *(organization)* sécurité sociale *f*

social worker *n* ❶ *(woman)* assistante sociale *f* ▷ *She's a social worker.* Elle est assistante sociale. ❷ *(man)* travailleur social *m* (*pl* travailleurs sociaux) ▷ *He's a social worker.* Il est travailleur social.

society *n* ❶ société *f* ▷ *We live in a multi-cultural society.* Nous vivons dans une société multiculturelle. ❷ club *m* ▷ *a drama society* un club de théâtre

sociology *n* sociologie *f*

sock *n* chaussette *f*

socket *n* prise de courant *f*

sofa *n* canapé *m*

soft *adj* ❶ *(fabric, texture)* doux (*f* douce) ❷ *(pillow, bed)* mou (*f* molle); **soft cheeses** les fromages à pâte molle ❸ *(hair)* fin(e); **to be soft on somebody** *(be kind to)* être [35] indulgent avec quelqu'un; **a soft drink** une boisson non alcoolisée; **soft drugs** les drogues douces *fpl*; **a soft option** une solution de facilité

software *n* logiciel *m*

soil *n* terre *f*

solar *adj* solaire; **a solar panel** un panneau solaire

solar power *n* énergie solaire *f*

sold *vb see* **sell**

soldier *n* soldat *m* ▷ *He's a soldier.* Il est soldat.

solicitor *n* ❶ *(for lawsuits)* avocat *m*, avocate *f* ▷ *He's a solicitor.* Il est avocat. ❷ *(for wills, property)* notaire *m* ▷ *She's a solicitor.* Elle est notaire.

solid *adj* ❶ *(not hollow)* massif (*f* massive) ▷ *solid gold* l'or massif ❷ solide ▷ *a solid wall* un mur solide; **for three hours solid** pendant trois heures entières

solo *n* solo *m* ▷ *a guitar solo* un solo de guitare

solution *n* solution *f*

solve *vb* résoudre **[70]**

some *adj, pron*

> When 'some' means 'a certain amount of', use **du**, **de la** or **des** according to the gender of the French noun that follows it. **du** and **de la** become **de l'** when they are followed by a noun starting with a vowel.

❶ du ▷ *Would you like some bread?* Voulez-vous du pain? de la ▷ *Would you like some beer?* Voulez-vous de la bière? de l' ▷ *Have you got some mineral water?* Avez-vous de l'eau minérale? des ▷ *I've got some Madonna albums.* J'ai des albums de Madonna.; **Some people say that ...** Il y a des gens qui disent que ...; **some day** un de ces jours; **some day next week** un jour la semaine prochaine ❷ *(some but not all)* certains (*f* certaines) ▷ *Are these mushrooms poisonous? — Only some.* Est-ce que ces champignons sont vénéneux? — Certains le sont.; **some of them** quelques-uns ▷ *I only sold some of them.* J'en ai seulement vendu quelques-uns.; **I only took some of it.** J'en ai seulement pris un peu.; **I'm going to buy some stamps. Do you want some too?** Je vais acheter des timbres. Tu en veux aussi?; **Would you like some coffee? — No thanks, I've got some.** Tu veux du café? — Non merci, j'en ai déjà.

somebody *pron* quelqu'un ▷ *Somebody stole my bag.* Quelqu'un a volé mon sac.

somehow *adv* **I'll do it somehow.** Je trouverai le moyen de le faire.; **Somehow I don't think he believed me.** Quelque chose me dit qu'il ne m'a pas cru.

someone *pron* quelqu'un

someplace *adv (US)* quelque part

something *pron* quelque chose ▷ *something special* quelque chose de spécial ▷ *That's really something!* C'est vraiment quelque chose! ▷ *It cost £100, or something like that.* Ça a coûté cent livres, ou quelque chose comme ça. ▷ *His name is Pierre or something.* Il s'appelle Pierre, ou quelque chose comme ça.

sometime *adv* un de ces jours ▷ *You must come and see us sometime.* Passez donc nous voir un de ces jours.; **sometime last month** dans le courant du mois dernier

sometimes *adv* quelquefois ▷ *Sometimes I think she hates me.* Quelquefois j'ai l'impression qu'elle me déteste.

somewhere *adv* quelque part ▷ *I left my keys somewhere.* J'ai laissé mes clés quelque part.

son *n* fils *m*
song *n* chanson *f*
son-in-law *n* gendre *m*
soon *adv* bientôt ▷ *very soon* très bientôt; **soon afterwards** peu après; **as soon as possible** aussitôt que possible
sooner *adv* plus tôt ▷ *Can't you come a bit sooner?* Tu ne peux pas venir un peu plus tôt?; **sooner or later** tôt ou tard
soprano *n (singer)* soprano *mf*
sorcerer *n* sorcier *m*
sore *adj* **My feet are sore.** J'ai mal aux pieds.; **It's sore.** Ça fait mal.; **That's a sore point.** C'est un point sensible.
▶ *n* plaie *f*
sorry *adj* désolé(e) ▷ *I'm really sorry.* Je suis vraiment désolé. ▷ *I'm sorry I'm late.* Je suis désolé d'être en retard.; **sorry!** pardon!; **I'm sorry about the noise.** Je m'excuse pour le bruit.; **You'll be sorry!** Tu le regretteras!; **to feel sorry for somebody** plaindre [17] quelqu'un
sort *n* sorte *f* ▷ *What sort of bike have you got?* Quelle sorte de vélo as-tu?
sort out *vb* ❶ *(objects)* ranger [45] ❷ *(problems)* résoudre [70]
sought *vb see* **seek** *vb*
soul *n* ❶ *(spirit)* âme *f* ❷ *(music)* soul *f*
sound *n* ❶ *(noise)* bruit *m* ▷ *Don't make a sound!* Pas un bruit! ▷ *the sound of footsteps* des bruits de pas ❷ son *m* ▷ *Can I turn the sound down?* Je peux baisser le son?
▶ *vb* **That sounds interesting.** Ça a l'air intéressant.; **It sounds as if she's doing well at school.** Elle a l'air de bien travailler à l'école.; **That sounds like a good idea.** C'est une bonne idée.
▶ *adj, adv* bon (*f* bonne) ▷ *That's sound advice.* C'est un bon conseil.; **sound asleep** profondément endormi
soundtrack *n* bande sonore *f*
soup *n* soupe *f* ▷ *vegetable soup* la soupe aux légumes
sour *adj* aigre
south *adj, adv* ❶ sud ▷ *the south coast* la côte sud ❷ vers le sud ▷ *We were travelling south.* Nous allions vers le sud.; **south of** au sud de ▷ *It's south of London.* C'est au sud de Londres.
▶ *n* sud *m* ▷ *in the south* dans le sud ▷ *the South of France* le sud de la France
South Africa *n* Afrique du Sud *f*; **in South Africa** en Afrique du Sud; **to South Africa** en Afrique du Sud
South America *n* Amérique du Sud *f*; **in South America** en Amérique du Sud; **to South America** en Amérique du Sud
South American *n* Sud-Américain *m*, Sud-Américaine *f*
▶ *adj* sud-américain(e)
southeast *n* sud-est *m* ▷ *southeast England* le sud-est de l'Angleterre
southern *adj* **the southern part of the island** la partie sud de l'île; **Southern England** le sud de l'Angleterre
South Pole *n* pôle Sud *m*

southwest *n* sud-ouest *m* ▷ *southwest France* le sud-ouest de la France

souvenir *n* souvenir *m*; **a souvenir shop** une boutique de souvenirs

Soviet *adj* **the former Soviet Union** l'ex-Union Soviétique *f*

soya *n* soja *m*

soy sauce *n* sauce de soja *f*

space *n* ❶ place *f* ▷ *There isn't enough space.* Il n'y a pas suffisamment de place.; **a parking space** une place de parking ❷ *(universe, gap)* espace *m* ▷ *Leave a space after your answer.* Laissez un espace après votre réponse.

spacecraft *n* engin spatial *m*

spade *n* pelle *f*; **spades** *(in cards)* le pique *sg* ▷ *the ace of spades* l'as de pique

Spain *n* Espagne *f*; **in Spain** en Espagne; **to Spain** en Espagne

Spaniard *n* Espagnol *m*, Espagnole *f*

spaniel *n* épagneul *m*

Spanish *n (language)* espagnol *m*; **the Spanish** les Espagnols ▶ *adj* espagnol(e) ▷ *She's Spanish.* Elle est espagnole.

spanner *n* clé anglaise *f*

spare *adj* de rechange ▷ *spare batteries* des piles de rechange ▷ *a spare part* une pièce de rechange; **a spare room** une chambre d'amis; **spare time** le temps libre ▷ *What do you do in your spare time?* Qu'est-ce que tu fais pendant ton temps libre?; **spare wheel** une roue de secours ▶ *vb* **Can you spare a moment?** Vous pouvez m'accorder un instant?; **I can't spare the time.** Je n'ai pas le temps.; **There's no room to spare.** Il n'y a plus de place.; **We arrived with time to spare.** Nous sommes arrivés en avance.
▶ *n* **a spare** un autre ▷ *I've lost my key. — Have you got a spare?* J'ai perdu ma clé. — Tu en as une autre?

sparkling *adj (water)* pétillant(e); **sparkling wine** le mousseux

sparrow *n* moineau *m* (*pl* moineaux)

spat *vb see* **spit**

speak *vb* parler **[28]** ▷ *Do you speak English?* Est-ce que vous parlez anglais?; **to speak to somebody** parler **[28]** à quelqu'un ▷ *Have you spoken to him?* Tu lui as parlé? ▷ *She spoke to him about it.* Elle lui en a parlé.

speak up *vb* parler **[28]** plus fort ▷ *Speak up, we can't hear you.* Parle plus fort, nous ne t'entendons pas.

speaker *n* ❶ *(loudspeaker)* enceinte *f* ❷ *(in debate)* intervenant *m*, intervenante *f*

special *adj* spécial(e) (*mpl* spéciaux)

specialist *n* spécialiste *mf*

speciality *n* spécialité *f*

specialize *vb* se spécialiser **[28]** ▷ *We specialize in skiing equipment.* Nous nous spécialisons dans les articles de ski.

specially *adv* ❶ spécialement ▷ *It's specially designed for teenagers.* C'est spécialement conçu pour les adolescents.; **not specially** pas spécialement ▷ *Do you like opera? — Not specially.* Tu aimes l'opéra? — Pas spécialement. ❷ surtout ▷ *It can be very cold here, specially in winter.* Il peut faire très froid ici, surtout en hiver.

species *n* espèce *f*

specific *adj* ❶ *(particular)* particulier (*f* particulière) ▷ *certain specific issues* certains problèmes particuliers ❷ *(precise)* précis(e) ▷ *Could you be more specific?* Est-ce que vous pourriez être plus précis?

specs, spectacles *npl* lunettes *fpl*

spectacular *adj* spectaculaire

spectator *n* spectateur *m*, spectatrice *f*

speech *n* discours *m* ▷ *to make a speech* faire un discours

speechless *adj* muet (*f* muette) ▷ *speechless with admiration* muet d'admiration; **I was speechless.** Je suis resté sans voix.

speed *n* vitesse *f* ▷ *a three-speed bike* un vélo à trois vitesses ▷ *at top speed* à toute vitesse

speed up *vb* accélérer [**34**]

speedboat *n* vedette *f*

speeding *n* excès de vitesse *m* ▷ *He was fined for speeding.* Il a reçu une contravention pour excès de vitesse.

speed limit *n* limitation de vitesse *f*; **to break the speed limit** faire [**36**] un excès de vitesse

spell *vb* ❶ *(in writing)* écrire [**30**] ▷ *How do you spell that?* Comment est-ce que ça s'écrit? ❷ *(out loud)* épeler [**4**] ▷ *Can you spell that please?* Est-ce que vous pouvez épeler, s'il vous plaît?; **I can't spell.** Je fais des fautes d'orthographe.

▸ *n* **to cast a spell on somebody** jeter [**41**] un sort à quelqu'un; **to be under somebody's spell** être [**35**] sous le charme de quelqu'un

spelling *n* orthographe *f* ▷ *My spelling is terrible.* Je fais beaucoup de fautes d'orthographe.; **a spelling mistake** une faute d'orthographe

spelt *vb see* **spell**

spend *vb* ❶ *(money)* dépenser [**28**] ❷ *(time)* passer [**58**] ▷ *He spent a month in France.* Il a passé un mois en France.

spice *n* épice *f*

spicy *adj* épicé(e)

spider *n* araignée *f*

spill *vb* ❶ *(tip over)* renverser [**28**] ▷ *He spilled his coffee over his trousers.* Il a renversé son café sur son pantalon. ❷ *(get spilt)* se répandre [**9**] ▷ *The soup spilled all over the table.* La soupe s'est répandue sur la table.

spinach *n* épinards *mpl*

spine *n* colonne vertébrale *f*

spire *n* flèche *f*

spirit *n* ❶ *(courage)* courage *m*; **to be in good spirits** être [**35**] de bonne humeur ❷ *(energy)* énergie *f*

spirits *npl* alcools forts *mpl* ▷ *I don't drink spirits.* Je ne bois pas d'alcools forts.

spiritual *adj* religieux (*f* religieuse) ▷ *the spiritual leader of Tibet* le chef religieux du Tibet

spit *n* salive *f*
▶ *vb* cracher [**28**]; **to spit something out** cracher [**28**] quelque chose

spite *n* **in spite of** malgré
▶ *vb* contrarier [**19**]

spiteful *adj* ❶ *(action)* méchant(e) ❷ *(person)* rancunier (*f* rancunière)

splash *vb* éclabousser [**28**] ▷ *Careful! Don't splash me!* Attention! Ne m'éclabousse pas!
▶ *n* plouf *m* ▷ *I heard a splash.* J'ai entendu un plouf.; **a splash of colour** une touche de couleur

splendid *adj* splendide

splinter *n* écharde *f*

split *vb* ❶ *(break apart)* fendre [**88**] ▷ *He split the wood with an axe.* Il a fendu le bois avec une hache. ❷ se fendre [**88**] ▷ *The ship hit a rock and split in two.* Le bateau a percuté un rocher et s'est fendu en deux. ❸ *(divide up)* partager [**45**] ▷ *They decided to split the profits.* Ils ont décidé de partager les bénéfices.

split up *vb* ❶ *(couple)* rompre [**75**] ▷ *My parents have split up.* Mes parents ont rompu. ❷ *(group)* se disperser [**28**]

spoil *vb* ❶ *(object)* abîmer [**28**] ❷ *(occasion)* gâcher [**28**] ❸ *(child)* gâter [**28**]

spoiled *adj* gâté(e) ▷ *a spoiled child* un enfant gâté

spoilsport *n* trouble-fête *mf*

spoilt *adj* gâté(e) ▷ *a spoilt child* un enfant gâté
▶ *vb see* **spoil**

spoken *vb see* **speak**

spokesman *n* porte-parole *m* (*pl* porte-parole)

spokeswoman *n* porte-parole *m* (*pl* porte-parole)

sponge *n* éponge *f*; **a sponge bag** une trousse de toilette; **a sponge cake** un biscuit de Savoie

sponsor *n* donateur *m*, donatrice *f*
▶ *vb* parrainer [**28**] ▷ *The festival was sponsored by ...* Le festival a été parrainé par ...

spontaneous *adj* spontané(e)

spooky *adj* ❶ *(eerie)* sinistre; **a spooky story** une histoire qui fait froid dans le dos ❷ *(strange)* étrange ▷ *a spooky coincidence* une étrange coïncidence

spoon *n* cuiller *f*

sport *n* sport *m* ▷ *What's your favourite sport?* Quel est ton sport préféré?; **a sports bag** un sac de sport; **a sports car** une voiture de sport; **a sports jacket** une veste sport; **Go on, be a sport!** Allez, sois sympa!

sportsman *n* sportif *m*

sportswear *n* vêtements de sport *mpl*

sportswoman *n* sportive *f*

sporty *adj* sportif (*f* sportive) ▷ *I'm not very sporty.* Je ne suis pas très sportif.

spot *n* ❶ *(mark)* tache *f* ▷ *There's a spot on your shirt.* Il y a une tache sur ta chemise. ❷ *(in pattern)* pois *m* ▷ *a red dress with white spots* une robe rouge à pois blancs ❸ *(pimple)* bouton *m* ▷ *He's covered in spots.* Il est couvert de boutons. ❹ *(place)*

coin *m* ▷ *It's a lovely spot for a picnic.* C'est un coin agréable pour un pique-nique.; **on the spot** **(1)** *(immediately)* sur-le-champ ▷ *They gave her the job on the spot.* Ils lui ont offert le poste sur-le-champ. **(2)** *(at the same place)* sur place ▷ *Luckily they were able to mend the car on the spot.* Heureusement ils ont pu réparer la voiture sur place.
▶ *vb* repérer **[34]** ▷ *I spotted a mistake.* J'ai repéré une faute.

spotless *adj* immaculé(e)

spotlight *n* projecteur *m* ▷ *The universities have been in the spotlight recently.* Les universités ont été sous le feu des projecteurs ces derniers temps.

spotty *adj (pimply)* boutonneux (*f* boutonneuse)

sprain *vb* **to sprain one's ankle** se faire **[36]** une entorse à la cheville
▶ *n* entorse *f* ▷ *It's just a sprain.* C'est juste une entorse.

spray *n (spray can)* bombe *f*
▶ *vb* ❶ vaporiser **[28]** ▷ *to spray perfume on one's hand* se vaporiser du parfum sur la main ❷ *(crops)* traiter **[28]** ❸ *(graffiti)* peindre **[60]** avec une bombe ▷ *Somebody had sprayed graffiti on the wall.* Quelqu'un avait peint des graffiti avec une bombe sur le mur.

spread *n* **chocolate spread** le chocolat à tartiner
▶ *vb* ❶ étaler **[28]** ▷ *to spread butter on a slice of bread* étaler du beurre sur une tranche de pain ❷ *(disease, news)* se propager **[45]** ▷ *The news spread rapidly.* La nouvelle s'est propagée rapidement.

spread out *vb (people)* se disperser **[28]**

spreadsheet *n (computer program)* tableur *m*

spring *n* ❶ *(season)* printemps *m*; **in spring** au printemps ❷ *(metal coil)* ressort *m* ❸ *(water hole)* source *f*

springtime *n* printemps *m*; **in springtime** au printemps

sprint *n* sprint *m*
▶ *vb* courir **[16]** à toute vitesse ▷ *She sprinted for the bus.* Elle a couru à toute vitesse pour attraper le bus.

sprouts *npl* **Brussels sprouts** les choux de Bruxelles *mpl*

spy *n* espion *m*, espionne *f*
▶ *vb* **to spy on somebody** espionner **[28]** quelqu'un

spying *n* espionnage *m*

square *n* ❶ carré *m* ▷ *a square and a triangle* un carré et un triangle ❷ place *f* ▷ *the town square* la place de l'hôtel de ville
▶ *adj* carré(e) ▷ *two square metres* deux mètres carrés; **It's 2 metres square.** Ça fait deux mètres sur deux.

squash *n (sport)* squash *m* ▷ *I play squash.* Je joue au squash.; **a squash court** un court de squash; **a squash racket** une raquette de squash; **orange squash** l'orangeade *f*; **lemon squash** la citronnade
▶ *vb* écraser **[28]** ▷ *You're squashing me.* Tu m'écrases.

squeak *vb* ❶ *(mouse, child)* pousser [**28**] un petit cri ❷ *(creak)* grincer [**12**]

squeeze *vb* ❶ *(fruit, toothpaste)* presser [**28**] ❷ *(hand, arm)* serrer [**28**]

squeeze in *vb* ❶ trouver [**28**] une petite place ▷ *It was a tiny car, but we managed to squeeze in.* La voiture était toute petite, mais nous avons réussi à trouver une petite place. ❷ *(for appointment)* caser [**28**] ▷ *I can squeeze you in at two o'clock.* Je peux vous caser demain à deux heures.

squirrel *n* écureuil *m*

stab *vb* poignarder [**28**]

stable *n* écurie *f*
▸ *adj* stable ▷ *a stable relationship* une relation stable

stack *n* pile *f* ▷ *a stack of books* une pile de livres

stadium *n* stade *m*

staff *n* ❶ *(in company)* personnel *m* ❷ *(in school)* professeurs *mpl*

staffroom *n* salle des professeurs *f*

stage *n* ❶ *(in plays)* scène *f* ❷ *(for speeches, lectures)* estrade *f*; **at this stage (1)** à ce stade ▷ *at this stage in the negotiations* à ce stade des négociations **(2)** pour l'instant ▷ *At this stage, it's too early to comment.* Pour l'instant, il est trop tôt pour se prononcer.; **to do something in stages** faire [**36**] quelque chose étape par étape

> Be careful not to translate **stage** by the French word **stage**.

stain *n* tache *f*
▸ *vb* tacher [**28**]

stainless steel *n* inox *m*

stair *n (step)* marche *f*

staircase *n* escalier *m*

stairs *npl* escalier *msg*

stale *adj (bread)* rassis (*f* rassie)

stalemate *n (in chess)* pat *m*

stall *n* stand *m* ▷ *He's got a market stall.* Il a un stand au marché.; **the stalls** *(in cinema, theatre)* l'orchestre *msg*

stammer *n* bégaiement *m*; **He's got a stammer.** Il bégaie.

stamp *vb (letter)* affranchir [**38**]; **to stamp one's foot** taper [**28**] du pied
▸ *n* ❶ timbre *m* ▷ *My hobby is stamp collecting.* Je collectionne les timbres.; **a stamp album** un album de timbres; **a stamp collection** une collection de timbres ❷ *(rubber stamp)* tampon *m*

stand *vb* ❶ *(be standing)* être [**35**] debout ▷ *He was standing by the door.* Il était debout à la porte. ❷ *(stand up)* se lever [**43**] ❸ *(tolerate, withstand)* supporter [**28**] ▷ *I can't stand all this noise.* Je ne supporte pas tout ce bruit.

stand for *vb* ❶ *(be short for)* être [**35**] l'abréviation de ▷ *'BT' stands for 'British Telecom'.* 'BT' est l'abréviation de 'British Telecom'. ❷ *(tolerate)* supporter [**28**] ▷ *I won't stand for it!* Je ne supporterai pas ça!; **to stand in for somebody** remplacer [**12**] quelqu'un

stand out *vb* se distinguer [**28**]

▷ *None of the candidates really stood out.* Aucun des candidats ne s'est distingué.; **She really stands out in that orange coat.** Tout le monde la remarque avec ce manteau orange.

stand up *vb (get up)* se lever [**43**]; **to stand up for** défendre [**88**] ▷ *Stand up for your rights!* Défendez vos droits!

standard *adj* ❶ courant(e) ▷ *standard French* le français courant ❷ *(equipment)* ordinaire; **the standard procedure** la procédure normale
▶ *n* niveau *m* (*pl* niveaux) ▷ *The standard is very high.* Le niveau est très haut.; **the standard of living** le niveau de vie; **She's got high standards.** Elle est très exigeante.

stands *npl (at sports ground)* tribune *fsg*

stank *vb see* **stink**

staple *n* agrafe *f*
▶ *vb* agrafer [**28**]

stapler *n* agrafeuse *f*

star *n* ❶ *(in sky)* étoile *f* ❷ *(celebrity)* vedette *f* ▷ *He's a TV star.* C'est une vedette de la télé.; **the stars** *(horoscope)* l'horoscope *m*
▶ *vb* être [**35**] la vedette ▷ *to star in a film* être la vedette d'un film; **The film stars Glenda Jackson.** Le film a pour vedette Glenda Jackson.; **... starring Johnny Depp** ... avec Johnny Depp

stare *vb* **to stare at something** fixer [**28**] quelque chose

start *n* ❶ début *m* ▷ *It's not much, but it's a start.* Ce n'est pas grand-chose, mais c'est un début.; **Shall we make a start on the washing-up?** On commence à faire la vaisselle? ❷ *(of race)* départ *m*
▶ *vb* ❶ commencer [**12**] ▷ *What time does it start?* À quelle heure est-ce que ça commence?; **to start doing something** commencer [**12**] à faire quelque chose ▷ *I started learning French three years ago.* J'ai commencé à apprendre le français il y a trois ans. ❷ *(organization)* créer [**18**] ▷ *He wants to start his own business.* Il veut créer sa propre entreprise. ❸ *(campaign)* organiser [**28**] ▷ *She started a campaign against drugs.* Elle a organisé une campagne contre la drogue. ❹ *(car)* démarrer [**28**] ▷ *He couldn't start the car.* Il n'a pas réussi à démarrer la voiture. ▷ *The car wouldn't start.* La voiture ne voulait pas démarrer.

start off *vb (leave)* partir [**57**] ▷ *We started off first thing in the morning.* Nous sommes partis en début de matinée.

starter *n (first course)* entrée *f*

starve *vb* mourir [**51**] de faim ▷ *People were literally starving.* Les gens mouraient littéralement de faim.; **I'm starving!** Je meurs de faim!

state *n* état *m*; **He was in a real state.** Il était dans tous ses états.; **the state** *(government)* l'État; **the States** *(USA)* les États-Unis *mpl*

▸ *vb* ❶ *(say)* déclarer [**28**] ▹ *He stated his intention to resign.* Il a déclaré son intention de démissionner. ❷ *(give)* donner [**28**] ▹ *Please state your name and address.* Veuillez donner vos nom et adresse.

statement *n* déclaration *f*

station *n (railway)* gare *f*; **the bus station** la gare routière; **a police station** un poste de police; **a radio station** une station de radio

stationer's *n* papeterie *f*

statue *n* statue *f*

stay *n* séjour *m* ▹ *my stay in France* mon séjour en France

▸ *vb* ❶ *(remain)* rester [**71**] ▹ *Stay here!* Reste ici! ❷ *(spend the night)* loger [**45**] ▹ *to stay with friends* loger chez des amis ▹ *Where are you staying?* Où est-ce que vous logez?; **to stay the night** passer [**58**] la nuit; **We stayed in Belgium for a few days.** Nous avons passé quelques jours en Belgique.

stay in *vb (not go out)* rester [**71**] à la maison

stay up *vb* rester [**71**] debout ▹ *We stayed up till midnight.* Nous sommes restés debout jusqu'à minuit.

steady *adj* ❶ régulier (*f* régulière) ▹ *steady progress* des progrès réguliers ❷ stable ▹ *a steady job* un emploi stable ❸ *(voice, hand)* ferme ❹ *(person)* calme; **a steady boyfriend** un copain; **a steady girlfriend** une copine

steak *n (beef)* steak *m* ▹ *steak and chips* un steak frites

steal *vb* voler [**28**]

steam *n* vapeur *f* ▹ *a steam engine* une locomotive à vapeur

steel *n* acier *m* ▹ *a steel door* une porte en acier

steep *adj (slope)* raide

steeple *n* clocher *m*

steering wheel *n* volant *m*

step *n* ❶ *(pace)* pas *m* ▹ *He took a step forward.* Il a fait un pas en avant. ❷ *(stair)* marche *f* ▹ *She tripped over the step.* Elle a trébuché sur la marche.

▸ *vb* **to step aside** faire [**36**] un pas de côté; **to step back** faire [**36**] un pas en arrière

stepbrother *n* demi-frère *m*

stepdaughter *n* belle-fille *f* (*pl* belles-filles)

stepfather *n* beau-père *m* (*pl* beaux-pères)

stepladder *n* escabeau *m* (*pl* escabeaux)

stepmother *n* belle-mère *f* (*pl* belles-mères)

stepsister *n* demi-sœur *f*

stepson *n* beau-fils *m* (*pl* beaux-fils)

stereo *n* chaîne stéréo *f* (*pl* chaînes stéréo)

sterling *adj* **£5 sterling** cinq livres sterling

stew *n* ragoût *m*

steward *n* steward *m*

stewardess *n* hôtesse de l'air *f*

stick *n* ❶ bâton *m* ❷ *(walking stick)* canne *f*

▸ *vb (with adhesive)* coller [**28**] ▹ *Stick the stamps on the envelope.*

Collez les timbres sur l'enveloppe.

stick out *vb (project)* sortir [**79**] ▷ *A pen was sticking out of his pocket.* Un stylo sortait de sa poche.; **Stick your tongue out and say 'ah'.** Tirez la langue et dites 'ah'.

sticker *n* autocollant *m*

stick insect *n* phasme *m*

sticky *adj* ❶ poisseux (*f* poisseuse) ▷ *to have sticky hands* avoir les mains poisseuses ❷ adhésif (*f* adhésive) ▷ *a sticky label* une étiquette adhésive

stiff *adj, adv (rigid)* rigide; **to have a stiff neck** avoir [**8**] un torticolis; **to feel stiff** avoir [**8**] des courbatures; **to be bored stiff** s'ennuyer [**53**] à mourir; **to be frozen stiff** être [**35**] mort de froid; **to be scared stiff** être [**35**] mort de peur

still *adv* ❶ encore ▷ *I still haven't finished.* Je n'ai pas encore fini. ▷ *Are you still in bed?* Tu es encore au lit?; **better still** encore mieux ❷ *(even so)* quand même ▷ *She knows I don't like it, but she still does it.* Elle sait que je n'aime pas ça, mais elle le fait quand même. ❸ *(after all)* enfin ▷ *Still, it's the thought that counts.* Enfin, c'est l'intention qui compte.
▶ *adj* **Keep still!** Ne bouge pas!; **Sit still!** Reste tranquille!

sting *n* piqûre *f* ▷ *a bee sting* une piqûre d'abeille
▶ *vb* piquer [**28**] ▷ *I've been stung.* J'ai été piqué.

stink *vb* puer [**28**] ▷ *It stinks!* Ça pue!
▶ *n* puanteur *f*

stir *vb* remuer [**28**]

stitch *vb (cloth)* coudre [**15**]
▶ *n* ❶ *(in sewing)* point *m* ❷ *(in wound)* point de suture *m* ▷ *I had five stitches.* J'ai eu cinq points de suture.

stock *n* ❶ *(supply)* réserve *f* ❷ *(in shop)* stock *m* ▷ *in stock* en stock; **out of stock** épuisé ❸ bouillon *m* ▷ *chicken stock* du bouillon de volaille
▶ *vb (have in stock)* avoir [**8**] ▷ *Do you stock camping stoves?* Vous avez des camping-gaz?

stock up *vb* s'approvisionner [**28**] ▷ *to stock up with something* s'approvisionner en quelque chose

stock cube *n* cube de bouillon *m*

stocking *n* bas *m*

stole, stolen *vb see* **steal**

stomach *n* estomac *m*

stomachache *n* **to have stomachache** avoir [**8**] mal au ventre

stone *n* ❶ *(rock)* pierre *f* ▷ *a stone wall* un mur en pierre ❷ *(in fruit)* noyau *m* (*pl* noyaux) ▷ *a peach stone* un noyau de pêche

In France, weight is expressed in kilos. A stone is about 6.3 kg.

I weigh eight stone. Je pèse cinquante kilos.

stood *vb see* **stand**

stool *n* tabouret *m*

stop *vb* ❶ arrêter [**28**] ▷ *a campaign to stop whaling* une campagne pour arrêter la chasse à la baleine ❷ s'arrêter [**28**] ▷ *The bus doesn't stop there.* Le bus ne s'arrête pas là. ▷ *I think the rain's going to stop.* Je

pense qu'il va s'arrêter de pleuvoir.; **to stop doing something** arrêter [**28**] de faire quelque chose ▷ *to stop smoking* arrêter de fumer; **to stop somebody doing something** empêcher [**28**] quelqu'un de faire quelque chose; **Stop!** Stop!
▶ *n* arrêt *m* ▷ *a bus stop* un arrêt de bus; **This is my stop.** Je descends ici.

stopwatch *n* chronomètre *m*

store *n* ❶ *(shop)* magasin *m* ▷ *a furniture store* un magasin de meubles ❷ *(stock, storeroom)* réserve *f*
▶ *vb* ❶ garder [**28**] ▷ *They store potatoes in the cellar.* Ils gardent des pommes de terre dans la cave. ❷ *(information)* enregistrer [**28**]

storey *n* étage *m* ▷ *a three-storey building* un immeuble à trois étages

storm *n* ❶ *(gale)* tempête *f* ❷ *(thunderstorm)* orage *m*

stormy *adj* orageux (*f* orageuse)

story *n* histoire *f*

stove *n* ❶ *(in kitchen)* cuisinière *f* ❷ *(camping stove)* réchaud *m*

straight *adj* ❶ droit(e) ▷ *a straight line* une ligne droite ❷ raide ▷ *straight hair* les cheveux raides ❸ *(heterosexual)* hétéro; **straight away** tout de suite; **straight on** tout droit

straightforward *adj* simple

strain *n* stress *m*; **It was a strain.** C'était éprouvant.
▶ *vb* se faire [**36**] mal à ▷ *I strained my back.* Je me suis fait mal au dos.; **to strain a muscle** se froisser [**28**] un muscle

strange *adj* bizarre ▷ *That's strange!* C'est bizarre!

stranger *n* inconnu *m*, inconnue *f* ▷ *Don't talk to strangers.* Ne parle pas aux inconnus.; **I'm a stranger here.** Je ne suis pas d'ici.

strangle *vb* étrangler [**28**]

strap *n* ❶ *(of bag, camera, suitcase)* courroie *f* ❷ *(of bra, dress)* bretelle *f* ❸ *(on shoe)* lanière *f* ❹ *(of watch)* bracelet *m*

straw *n* paille *f*; **That's the last straw!** Ça, c'est le comble!

strawberry *n* fraise *f* ▷ *strawberry jam* la confiture de fraises

stray *n* **a stray cat** un chat perdu

stream *n* ruisseau *m* (*pl* ruisseaux)

street *n* rue *f* ▷ *in the street* dans la rue

streetlamp *n* réverbère *m*

streetwise *adj* dégourdi(e)

strength *n* force *f*

stress *vb* souligner [**28**] ▷ *I would like to stress that ...* J'aimerais souligner que ...
▶ *n* stress *m*

stretch *vb* ❶ *(person, animal)* s'étirer [**28**] ▷ *The dog woke up and stretched.* Le chien s'est réveillé et s'est étiré. ❷ *(get bigger)* se détendre [**88**] ▷ *My sweater stretched when I washed it.* Mon pull s'est détendu au lavage. ❸ *(stretch out)* tendre [**88**] ▷ *They stretched a rope between two trees.* Ils ont tendu une corde entre deux arbres.; **to stretch out one's arms** tendre [**88**] les bras

stretcher *n* brancard *m*

stretchy *adj* élastique

strict *adj* strict(e)
strike *n* grève *f*; **to be on strike** être [35] en grève; **to go on strike** faire [36] grève
▶ *vb* ❶ *(clock)* sonner [28] ▷ *The clock struck three.* L'horloge a sonné trois heures. ❷ *(go on strike)* faire [36] grève ❸ *(hit)* frapper [28]; **to strike a match** frotter [28] une allumette
striker *n* ❶ *(person on strike)* gréviste *mf* ❷ *(footballer)* buteur *m*
string *n* ❶ ficelle *f* ▷ *a piece of string* un bout de ficelle ❷ *(of violin, guitar)* corde *f*
strip *vb (get undressed)* se déshabiller [28]
▶ *n* bande *f*; **a strip cartoon** une bande dessinée
stripe *n* rayure *f*
striped *adj* à rayures ▷ *a striped skirt* une jupe à rayures
stroke *vb* caresser [28]
▶ *n* attaque *f* ▷ *to have a stroke* avoir une attaque
stroll *n* **to go for a stroll** aller [3] faire une petite promenade
stroller *n (US)* poussette *f*
strong *adj* ❶ fort(e) ▷ *She's very strong.* Elle est très forte. ❷ *(material)* résistant(e)
strongly *adv* fortement ▷ *We recommend strongly that ...* Nous recommandons fortement que ...; **He smelt strongly of tobacco.** Il sentait fort le tabac.; **strongly built** solidement bâti; **I don't feel strongly about it.** Ça m'est égal.
struck *vb see* **strike**
struggle *vb (physically)* se débattre [9] ▷ *He struggled, but he couldn't escape.* Il s'est débattu, mais il n'a pas pu s'échapper.; **to struggle to do something (1)** *(fight)* se battre [9] pour faire quelque chose ▷ *He struggled to get custody of his daughter.* Il s'est battu pour obtenir la garde de sa fille. **(2)** *(have difficulty)* avoir [8] du mal à faire quelque chose
▶ *n (for independence, equality)* lutte *f*; **It was a struggle.** Ça a été laborieux.
stubborn *adj* têtu(e)
stuck *vb see* **stick**
▶ *adj (jammed)* coincé(e) ▷ *It's stuck.* C'est coincé.; **to get stuck** rester [71] coincé ▷ *We got stuck in a traffic jam.* Nous sommes restés coincés dans un embouteillage.
stuck-up *adj* coincé(e) *(informal)*
stud *n* ❶ *(earring)* boucle d'oreille *f* ❷ *(on football boots)* clou *m*
student *n* étudiant *m*, étudiante *f*
studio *n* studio *m* ▷ *a TV studio* un studio de télévision; **a studio flat** un studio
study *vb* ❶ *(at university)* faire [36] des études ▷ *I plan to study biology.* J'ai l'intention de faire des études de biologie. ❷ *(do homework)* travailler [28] ▷ *I've got to study tonight.* Je dois travailler ce soir.
stuff *n* ❶ *(substance)* truc *m* ▷ *I need some stuff for hay fever.* J'ai besoin d'un truc contre le rhume des foins. ❷ *(things)* trucs *mpl* ▷ *There's some stuff on the table for you.* Il y a des

trucs sur la table pour toi.
❸ *(possessions)* affaires *fpl* ▷ *Have you got all your stuff?* Est-ce que tu as toutes tes affaires?

stuffy *adj (room)* mal aéré(e); **It's really stuffy in here.** On étouffe ici.

stumble *vb* trébucher [**28**]

stung *vb see* **sting**

stunk *vb see* **stink**

stunned *adj (amazed)* sidéré(e) ▷ *I was stunned.* J'étais sidéré.

stunning *adj* superbe

stunt *n (in film)* cascade *f*

stuntman *n* cascadeur *m*

stupid *adj* stupide ▷ *a stupid joke* une plaisanterie stupide; **Me, go jogging? Don't be stupid!** Moi, faire du footing? Ne dis pas de bêtises!

stutter *vb* bégayer [**59**]
▸ *n* **He's got a stutter.** Il bégaie.

style *n* style *m* ▷ *That's not his style.* Ça n'est pas son style.

subject *n* ❶ sujet *m* ▷ *The subject of my project was the internet.* Le sujet de mon projet était l'Internet. ❷ *(at school)* matière *f* ▷ *What's your favourite subject?* Quelle est ta matière préférée?

subjunctive *n* subjonctif *m*

submarine *n* sous-marin *m*

subscription *n (to paper, magazine)* abonnement *m*; **to take out a subscription to something** s'abonner [**28**] à quelque chose

subsidy *n* subvention *f*

substance *n* substance *f*

substitute *n (person)* remplaçant *m*, remplaçante *f*
▸ *vb* substituer [**28**] ▷ *to substitute A for B* substituer A à B

subtitled *adj* sous-titré(e)

subtitles *npl* sous-titres *mpl* ▷ *a French film with English subtitles* un film français avec des sous-titres en anglais

subtle *adj* subtil(e)

subtract *vb* retrancher [**28**] ▷ *to subtract 3 from 5* retrancher trois de cinq

suburb *n* banlieue *f* ▷ *a suburb of Paris* une banlieue de Paris

subway *n (underpass)* passage souterrain *m*

succeed *vb* réussir [**38**] ▷ *to succeed in doing something* réussir à faire quelque chose

success *n* succès *m* ▷ *The play was a great success.* La pièce a eu beaucoup de succès.

successful *adj* réussi(e) ▷ *a successful attempt* une tentative réussie; **to be successful in doing something** réussir [**38**] à faire quelque chose; **He's a successful businessman.** Ses affaires marchent bien.

successfully *adv* avec succès

such *adj, adv* si ▷ *such nice people* des gens si gentils; **such a lot of** tellement de ▷ *such a lot of work* tellement de travail; **such as** *(like)* comme ▷ *hot countries, such as India* les pays chauds, comme l'Inde; **not as such** pas exactement ▷ *He's not an expert as such, but ...* Ce n'est pas exactement un expert, mais ...;

There's no such thing. Ça n'existe pas. ▷ *There's no such thing as the yeti.* Le yéti n'existe pas.
such-and-such *adj* tel ou tel (*f* telle ou telle) ▷ *such-and-such a place* tel ou tel endroit
suck *vb* sucer [**12**] ▷ *to suck one's thumb* sucer son pouce
sudden *adj* soudain(e) ▷ *a sudden change* un changement soudain; **all of a sudden** tout à coup
suddenly *adv* ❶ *(stop, leave, change)* brusquement ❷ *(die)* subitement ❸ *(at beginning of sentence)* soudain ▷ *Suddenly, the door opened.* Soudain, la porte s'est ouverte.
suede *n* daim *m* ▷ *a suede jacket* une veste en daim
suffer *vb* souffrir [**54**] ▷ *She was really suffering.* Elle souffrait beaucoup.; **to suffer from a disease** avoir [**8**] une maladie ▷ *I suffer from hay fever.* J'ai le rhume des foins.
suffocate *vb* suffoquer [**28**]
sugar *n* sucre *m* ▷ *Do you take sugar?* Est-ce que vous prenez du sucre?
suggest *vb* suggérer [**34**] ▷ *I suggested they set off early.* Je leur ai suggéré de partir de bonne heure.
suggestion *n* suggestion *f* ▷ *to make a suggestion* faire une suggestion
suicide *n* suicide *m*; **to commit suicide** se suicider [**28**]
suit *n* ❶ *(man's)* costume *m* ❷ *(woman's)* tailleur *m* ▶ *vb* ❶ *(be convenient for)* convenir [**89**] à ▷ *What time would suit you?* Quelle heure vous conviendrait?; **That suits me fine.** Ça m'arrange.; **Suit yourself!** Comme tu veux! ❷ *(look good on)* aller [**3**] bien à ▷ *That dress really suits you.* Cette robe te va vraiment bien.
suitable *adj* ❶ convenable ▷ *a suitable time* une heure convenable ❷ *(clothes)* approprié(e) ▷ *suitable clothing* des vêtements appropriés
suitcase *n* valise *f*
suite *n (of rooms)* suite *f*; **a bedroom suite** une chambre à coucher
sulk *vb* bouder [**28**]
sultana *n* raisin sec *m* (*pl* raisins secs)
sum *n* ❶ *(calculation)* calcul *m* ▷ *She's good at sums.* Elle est bonne en calcul. ❷ *(amount)* somme *f* ▷ *a sum of money* une somme d'argent
sum up *vb* résumer [**28**]
summarize *vb* résumer [**28**]
summary *n* résumé *m*
summer *n* été *m*; **in summer** en été; **summer clothes** les vêtements d'été; **the summer holidays** les vacances d'été; **a summer camp** *(US)* une colonie de vacances
summertime *n* été *m*; **in summertime** en été
summit *n* sommet *m*
sun *n* soleil *m* ▷ *in the sun* au soleil
sunbathe *vb* se bronzer [**28**]
sunblock *n* écran total *m*
sunburn *n* coup de soleil *m*

sunburnt *adj* **I got sunburnt.** J'ai attrapé un coup de soleil.

Sunday *n* dimanche *m* ▷ *on Sunday* dimanche ▷ *on Sundays* le dimanche ▷ *every Sunday* tous les dimanches ▷ *last Sunday* dimanche dernier ▷ *next Sunday* dimanche prochain

Sunday school *n* catéchisme *m*

le catéchisme, the French equivalent of 'Sunday school', takes place during the week after school rather than on a Sunday.

sunflower *n* tournesol *m*

sung *vb see* **sing**

sunglasses *npl* lunettes de soleil *fpl*

sunk *vb see* **sink**

sunlight *n* soleil *m*

sunny *adj* ensoleillé(e) ▷ *a sunny morning* une matinée ensoleillée; **It's sunny.** Il fait du soleil.; **a sunny day** une belle journée

sunrise *n* lever du soleil *m*

sunroof *n* toit ouvrant *m*

sunscreen *n* crème solaire *f*

sunset *n* coucher du soleil *m*

sunshine *n* soleil *m*

sunstroke *n* insolation *f* ▷ *to get sunstroke* attraper une insolation

suntan *n* bronzage *m*; **suntan lotion** le lait solaire; **suntan oil** l'huile solaire *f*

super *adj* formidable

supermarket *n* supermarché *m*

supernatural *adj* surnaturel (*f* surnaturelle)

superstitious *adj* superstitieux (*f* superstitieuse)

supervise *vb* surveiller [**28**]

supervisor *n* ❶ *(in factory)* surveillant *m*, surveillante *f* ❷ *(in department store)* chef de rayon *m*

supper *n* dîner *m*

supplement *n* supplément *m*

supplies *npl (food)* vivres *mpl*

supply *vb (provide)* fournir [**38**]; **to supply somebody with something** fournir [**38**] quelque chose à quelqu'un ▷ *The centre supplied us with all the equipment.* Le centre nous a fourni tout l'équipement.

▶ *n* provision *f* ▷ *a supply of paper* une provision de papier; **the water supply** *(to town)* l'approvisionnement en eau *m*

supply teacher *n* suppléant *m*, suppléante *f*

support *vb* ❶ soutenir [**83**] ▷ *My mum has always supported me.* Ma mère m'a toujours soutenu. ❷ être [**35**] supporter de ▷ *What team do you support?* Tu es supporter de quelle équipe? ❸ *(financially)* subvenir [**89**] aux besoins de ▷ *She had to support five children on her own.* Elle a dû subvenir toute seule aux besoins de cinq enfants.

Be careful not to translate **to support** by **supporter**.

▶ *n (backing)* soutien *m*

supporter *n* ❶ supporter *m* ▷ *a Liverpool supporter* un supporter de Liverpool ❷ sympathisant *m*, sympathisante *f* ▷ *a supporter of the Labour Party* un sympathisant du parti travailliste

suppose *vb* imaginer [**28**] ▷ *I suppose he's late.* J'imagine qu'il est en retard.; **I suppose so.** J'imagine.; **to be supposed to do something** être [**35**] censé faire quelque chose ▷ *You're supposed to show your passport.* On est censé montrer son passeport.

supposing *conj* si ▷ *Supposing you won the lottery ...* Si tu gagnais à la loterie ...

sure *adj* sûr(e) ▷ *Are you sure?* Tu es sûr?; **Sure!** Bien sûr!; **to make sure that ...** vérifier [**19**] que ... ▷ *I'm going to make sure the door's locked.* Je vais vérifier que la porte est fermée à clé.

surely *adv* **Surely you've been to London?** J'imagine que tu es allé à Londres, non?; **The shops are closed on Sundays, surely?** J'imagine que les magasins sont fermés le dimanche, non?

surf *n* ressac *m*
▶ *vb* surfer [**28**]; **to go surfing** faire [**36**] du surf; **to surf the Net** surfer [**28**] sur le Net

surface *n* surface *f*

surfboard *n* planche de surf *f*

surfing *n* surf *m* ▷ *to go surfing* faire du surf

surgeon *n* chirurgien *m* ▷ *She's a surgeon.* Elle est chirurgien.

surgery *n (doctor's surgery)* cabinet médical *m*; **surgery hours** les heures de consultation *fpl*

surname *n* nom de famille *m*

surprise *n* surprise *f*

surprised *adj* surpris(e) ▷ *I was surprised to see him.* J'ai été surpris de le voir.

surprising *adj* surprenant(e)

surrender *vb* capituler [**28**]

surrogate mother *n* mère porteuse *f*

surround *vb* encercler [**28**] ▷ *The police surrounded the house.* La police a encerclé la maison.; **surrounded by** entouré de ▷ *The house is surrounded by trees.* La maison est entourée d'arbres.

surroundings *npl* cadre *msg* ▷ *a hotel in beautiful surroundings* un hôtel situé dans un beau cadre

survey *n (research)* enquête *f*

survivor *n* survivant *m*, survivante *f* ▷ *There were no survivors.* Il n'y a pas eu de survivants.

suspect *vb* soupçonner [**28**]
▶ *n* suspect *m*, suspecte *f*

suspend *vb* ❶ *(from school, team)* exclure [**13**] ▷ *He's been suspended.* Il s'est fait exclure. ❷ *(from job)* suspendre [**88**]

suspense *n* ❶ *(waiting)* attente *f* ▷ *The suspense was terrible.* L'attente a été terrible. ❷ *(in story)* suspense *m* ▷ *a film with lots of suspense* un film avec beaucoup de suspense

suspicious *adj* ❶ méfiant(e) ▷ *He was suspicious at first.* Il était méfiant au début. ❷ *(suspicious-looking)* louche ▷ *a suspicious person* un individu louche

swallow *vb* avaler [**28**]

swam *vb see* **swim**

swan *n* cygne *m*

swap *vb* échanger [**45**] ▷ *to swap A*

for B échanger A contre B

swear *vb (make an oath, curse)* jurer [**28**]

swearword *n* gros mot *m*

sweat *n* transpiration *f*
▸ *vb* transpirer [**28**]

sweater *n* pull *m*

sweatshirt *n* sweat *m*

Swede *n (person)* Suédois *m*, Suédoise *f*

Sweden *n* Suède *f*; **in Sweden** en Suède; **to Sweden** en Suède

Swedish *n (language)* suédois *m*
▸ *adj* suédois(e) ▷ *She's Swedish.* Elle est suédoise.

sweep *vb* balayer [**59**]; **to sweep the floor** balayer [**59**]

sweet *n* ❶ *(candy)* bonbon *m* ▷ *a bag of sweets* un paquet de bonbons ❷ *(pudding)* dessert *m* ▷ *What sweet did you have?* Qu'est-ce que vous avez mangé comme dessert?
▸ *adj* ❶ *(not savoury)* sucré(e) ❷ *(kind)* gentil (*f* gentille) ▷ *That was really sweet of you.* C'était vraiment gentil de ta part. ❸ *(cute)* mignon (*f* mignonne) ▷ *Isn't she sweet?* Comme elle est mignonne!; **sweet and sour pork** le porc à la sauce aigre-douce

sweetcorn *n* maïs doux *m*

swept *vb see* **sweep**

swerve *vb* faire [**36**] une embardée ▷ *He swerved to avoid the cyclist.* Il a fait une embardée pour éviter le cycliste.

swim *n* **to go for a swim** aller [**3**] se baigner
▸ *vb* nager [**45**] ▷ *Can you swim?* Tu sais nager?; **She swam across the river.** Elle a traversé la rivière à la nage.

swimmer *n* nageur *m*, nageuse *f* ▷ *She's a good swimmer.* C'est une bonne nageuse.

swimming *n* natation *f* ▷ *Do you like swimming?* Tu aimes la natation?; **to go swimming** *(in a pool)* aller [**3**] à la piscine; **a swimming cap** un bonnet de bain; **a swimming costume** un maillot de bain; **a swimming pool** une piscine; **swimming trunks** le maillot de bain

swimsuit *n* maillot de bain *m*

swing *n (in playground, garden)* balançoire *f*
▸ *vb* ❶ se balancer [**12**] ▷ *A bunch of keys swung from his belt.* Un trousseau de clés se balançait à sa ceinture.; **Sam was swinging an umbrella as he walked.** Sam balançait son parapluie en marchant. ❷ virer [**28**] ▷ *The canoe swung round sharply.* Le canoë a viré brusquement.

Swiss *n (person)* Suisse *mf*; **the Swiss** les Suisses
▸ *adj* suisse ▷ *Sabine's Swiss.* Sabine est suisse.

switch *n (for light, radio etc)* bouton *m*
▸ *vb* changer [**45**] de ▷ *We switched partners.* Nous avons changé de partenaire.

switch off *vb* ❶ *(electrical appliance)* éteindre [**60**] ❷ *(engine, machine)* arrêter [**28**]

switch on *vb* ❶ *(electrical appliance)* allumer [**28**] ❷ *(engine, machine)* mettre [**47**] en marche

Switzerland *n* Suisse *f*; **in Switzerland** en Suisse

swollen *adj (arm, leg)* enflé(e)

swop *vb* échanger [**45**] ▷ *to swop A for B* échanger A contre B

sword *n* épée *f*

swore, sworn *vb see* **swear**

swot *n* bûcheur *m*, bûcheuse *f* ▶ *vb* bosser [**28**] dur ▷ *I'll have to swot for my maths exam.* Je vais devoir bosser dur pour mon examen de maths.

swum *vb see* **swim**

swung *vb see* **swing**

syllabus *n* programme *m* ▷ *on the syllabus* au programme

symbol *n* symbole *m*

sympathetic *adj* compréhensif (*f* compréhensive)

> Be careful not to translate **sympathetic** by **sympathique**.

sympathize *vb* **to sympathize with somebody** comprendre [**65**] quelqu'un

sympathy *n* compassion *f*

symptom *n* symptôme *m*

syringe *n* seringue *f*

system *n* système *m*

t

table *n* table *f* ▷ *to lay the table* mettre la table

tablecloth *n* nappe *f*

tablespoon *n* grande cuillère *f*; **two tablespoons of sugar** deux cuillerées à soupe de sucre

tablet *n* ❶ *(medicine)* comprimé *m* ❷ *(computer)* tablette *f*

table tennis *n* ping-pong *m* ▷ *to play table tennis* jouer au ping-pong

tact *n* tact *m*

tactful *adj* plein de tact (*f* pleine de tact)

tactics *npl* tactique *fsg*

tadpole *n* têtard *m*

tag *n (label)* étiquette *f*

tail *n* queue *f*; **Heads or tails?** Pile ou face?

tailor *n* tailleur *m*

take *vb* ❶ prendre [**65**] ▷ *Are you*

taking your new camera? Tu prends ton nouvel appareil photo? ▷ *He took a plate from the cupboard.* Il a pris une assiette dans le placard. ▷ *It takes about an hour.* Ça prend environ une heure. ❷ *(person)* emmener [**43**] ▷ *When will you take me to London?* Quand est-ce que tu vas m'emmener à Londres?; **to take something somewhere** emporter [**28**] quelque chose quelque part ▷ *Do you take your exercise books home?* Vous emportez vos cahiers chez vous? ▷ *Don't take anything valuable with you.* N'emportez pas d'objets de valeur. ▷ *I'm going to take my coat to the cleaner's.* Je vais donner mon manteau à nettoyer. ❸ *(effort, skill)* demander [**28**] ▷ *That takes a lot of courage.* Cela demande beaucoup de courage.; **It takes a lot of money to do that.** Il faut beaucoup d'argent pour faire ça. ❹ *(tolerate)* supporter [**28**] ▷ *He can't take being criticized.* Il ne supporte pas d'être critiqué. ❺ *(exam, test)* passer [**58**] ▷ *Have you taken your driving test yet?* Est-ce que tu as déjà passé ton permis de conduire? ❻ *(subject)* faire [**36**] ▷ *I decided to take French instead of German.* J'ai décidé de faire du français au lieu de l'allemand.

take after *vb* ressembler [**28**] à ▷ *She takes after her mother.* Elle ressemble à sa mère.

take apart *vb* **to take something apart** démonter [**28**] quelque chose

take away *vb* ❶ *(object)* emporter [**28**] ❷ *(person)* emmener [**43**]; **to take something away** *(confiscate)* confisquer [**28**] quelque chose; **hot meals to take away** des plats chauds à emporter

take back *vb* rapporter [**28**] ▷ *I took it back to the shop.* Je l'ai rapporté au magasin.; **I take it all back!** Je n'ai rien dit!

take down *vb* ❶ *(poster, sign)* enlever [**43**] ❷ *(painting, curtains)* décrocher [**28**] ❸ *(tent, scaffolding)* démonter [**28**] ❹ *(make a note of)* prendre [**65**] en note ▷ *He took down the details in his notebook.* Il a pris tous les détails en note dans son carnet.

take in *vb (understand)* comprendre [**65**] ▷ *I didn't really take it in.* Je n'ai pas bien compris.

take off *vb* ❶ *(plane)* décoller [**28**] ▷ *The plane took off twenty minutes late.* L'avion a décollé avec vingt minutes de retard. ❷ *(clothes)* enlever [**43**] ▷ *Take your coat off.* Enlevez votre manteau.

take out *vb (from container, pocket)* sortir [**79**]; **He took her out to the theatre.** Il l'a emmenée au théâtre.

take over *vb* prendre [**65**] la relève ▷ *I'll take over now.* Je vais prendre la relève.; **to take over from somebody** remplacer [**12**] quelqu'un

takeaway *n (meal)* plat à emporter *m*; **a Chinese takeaway** un restaurant chinois qui vend des plats à emporter

taken *vb see* **take**
takeoff *n (of plane)* décollage *m*
tale *n (story)* conte *m*
talent *n* talent *m* ▷ *She's got lots of talent.* Elle a beaucoup de talent.; **to have a talent for something** être [**35**] doué pour quelque chose ▷ *He's got a real talent for languages.* Il est vraiment doué pour les langues.
talented *adj* **She's a talented pianist.** C'est une pianiste de talent.
talk *n* ❶ *(speech)* exposé *m* ▷ *She gave a talk on rock climbing.* Elle a fait un exposé sur la varappe. ❷ *(conversation)* conversation *f* ▷ *I had a talk with my Mum about it.* J'ai eu une petite conversation avec ma mère à ce sujet. ❸ *(gossip)* racontars *mpl* ▷ *It's just talk.* Ce sont des racontars.
▶ *vb* parler [**28**] ▷ *to talk about something* parler de quelque chose; **to talk something over with somebody** discuter [**28**] de quelque chose avec quelqu'un
talkative *adj* bavard(e)
tall *adj* ❶ *(person, tree)* grand(e); **to be 2 metres tall** mesurer [**28**] deux mètres ❷ *(building)* haut(e)
tame *adj (animal)* apprivoisé(e) ▷ *They've got a tame hedgehog.* Ils ont un hérisson apprivoisé.
tampon *n* tampon *m*
tan *n* bronzage *m* ▷ *She's got an amazing tan.* Elle a un bronzage superbe.
tangerine *n* mandarine *f*
tangle *n* ❶ *(ropes, cables)* enchevêtrement *m* ❷ *(hair)* nœud *m*; **to be in a tangle (1)** *(ropes, cables)* être [**35**] enchevêtré **(2)** *(hair)* être [**35**] emmêlé
tank *n* ❶ *(for water, petrol)* réservoir *m* ❷ *(military)* char d'assaut *m*; **a fish tank** un aquarium
tanker *n* ❶ *(ship)* pétrolier *m*; **an oil tanker** un pétrolier ❷ *(truck)* camion-citerne *m*; **a petrol tanker** un camion-citerne
tap *n* ❶ *(water tap)* robinet *m* ❷ *(gentle blow)* petite tape *f*
tap-dancing *n* claquettes *fpl* ▷ *I do tap-dancing.* Je fais des claquettes.
tape *vb (record)* enregistrer [**28**] ▷ *Did you tape that film last night?* As-tu enregistré le film hier soir?
▶ *n* ❶ cassette *f* ❷ *(sticky tape)* scotch® *m*
tape measure *n* mètre à ruban *m*
tape recorder *n* magnétophone *m*
target *n* cible *f*
tart *n* tarte *f* ▷ *an apple tart* une tarte aux pommes
tartan *adj* écossais(e) ▷ *a tartan scarf* une écharpe écossaise
task *n* tâche *f*
taste *n* goût *m* ▷ *It's got a really strange taste.* Ça a un goût vraiment bizarre. ▷ *a joke in bad taste* une plaisanterie de mauvais goût; **Would you like a taste?** Tu veux goûter?
▶ *vb* goûter [**28**] ▷ *Would you like to taste it?* Vous voulez y goûter?; **to taste of something** avoir [**8**] un goût de quelque chose ▷ *It tastes of*

fish. Ça a un goût de poisson.; **You can taste the garlic in it.** Ça a bien le goût d'ail.

tasty *adj* savoureux (*f* savoureuse)

tattoo *n* tatouage *m*

taught *vb see* **teach**

Taurus *n* Taureau *m* ▷ *I'm Taurus*. Je suis Taureau.

tax *n* ❶ *(on income)* impôts *mpl* ❷ *(on goods, alcohol)* taxe *f*

taxi *n* taxi *m*; **a taxi driver** un chauffeur de taxi

taxi rank *n* station de taxis *f*

TB *n* tuberculose *f*

tea *n* ❶ thé *m* ▷ *a cup of tea* une tasse de thé; **a tea bag** un sachet de thé ❷ *(evening meal)* dîner *m*; **We were having tea.** Nous étions en train de dîner.

teach *vb* ❶ apprendre [**65**] ▷ *My sister taught me to swim*. Ma sœur m'a appris à nager. ❷ *(in school)* enseigner [**28**] ▷ *She teaches physics*. Elle enseigne la physique.

teacher *n* ❶ *(in secondary school)* professeur *m* ▷ *a maths teacher* un professeur de maths ▷ *She's a teacher*. Elle est professeur. ❷ *(in primary school)* instituteur *m*, institutrice *f* ▷ *He's a primary school teacher*. Il est instituteur.

teaching assistant *n* aide-éducateur *m*, aide-éducatrice *f*

team *n* équipe *f* ▷ *a football team* une équipe de football

teapot *n* théière *f*

tear *n* larme *f* ▷ *She was in tears*. Elle était en larmes.
▶ *vb* ❶ déchirer [**28**] ▷ *Be careful or you'll tear the page*. Fais attention, tu vas déchirer la page. ❷ se déchirer [**28**] ▷ *It won't tear, it's very strong*. Ça ne se déchire pas, c'est très solide.

tear up *vb* déchirer [**28**] ▷ *He tore up the letter*. Il a déchiré la lettre.

tease *vb* ❶ *(unkindly)* tourmenter [**28**] ▷ *Stop teasing that poor animal!* Arrête de tourmenter cette pauvre bête! ❷ *(jokingly)* taquiner [**28**] ▷ *He's teasing you*. Il te taquine.; **I was only teasing.** Je plaisantais.

teaspoon *n* petite cuillère *f*; **two teaspoons of sugar** deux cuillerées à café de sucre

teatime *n (in evening)* heure du dîner *f* ▷ *It was nearly teatime*. C'était presque l'heure du dîner.; **Teatime!** À table!

tea towel *n* torchon *m*

technical *adj* technique; **a technical college** un lycée technique

technician *n* technicien *m*, technicienne *f*

technological *adj* technologique

technology *n* technologie *f*

teddy bear *n* nounours *m*

teenage *adj* ❶ pour les jeunes ▷ *a teenage magazine* un magazine pour les jeunes ❷ *(boys, girls)* adolescent(e) ▷ *She has two teenage daughters*. Elle a deux filles adolescentes.

teenager *n* adolescent *m*, adolescente *f*

teens *npl* **She's in her teens.** C'est une adolescente.

tee-shirt *n* tee-shirt *m*
teeth *npl* dents *fpl*
telephone *n* téléphone *m* ▷ *on the telephone* au téléphone; **a telephone box** une cabine téléphonique; **a telephone call** un coup de téléphone; **the telephone directory** l'annuaire *m*; **a telephone number** un numéro de téléphone
telescope *n* télescope *m*
television *n* télévision *f*; **on television** à la télévision; **a television licence** une redevance de télévision; **a television programme** une émission de télévision
tell *vb* dire [**27**]; **to tell somebody something** dire [**27**] quelque chose à quelqu'un ▷ *Did you tell your mother?* Tu l'as dit à ta mère? ▷ *I told him that I was going on holiday.* Je lui ai dit que je partais en vacances.; **to tell somebody to do something** dire [**27**] à quelqu'un de faire quelque chose ▷ *He told me to wait a moment.* Il m'a dit d'attendre un moment.; **to tell lies** dire [**27**] des mensonges; **to tell a story** raconter [**28**] une histoire; **I can't tell the difference between them.** Je n'arrive pas à les distinguer.
tell off *vb* gronder [**28**]
telly *n* télé *f* ▷ *to watch telly* regarder la télé; **on telly** à la télé
temper *n* caractère *m* ▷ *He's got a terrible temper.* Il a un sale caractère.; **to be in a temper** être [**35**] en colère; **to lose one's temper** se mettre [**47**] en colère ▷ *I lost my temper.* Je me suis mis en colère.
temperature *n (of oven, water, person)* température *f*; **The temperature was 30 degrees.** Il faisait trente degrés.; **to have a temperature** avoir [**8**] de la fièvre
temple *n* temple *m*
temporary *adj* temporaire
temptation *n* tentation *f*
tempting *adj* tentant(e)
ten *num* dix ▷ *She's ten.* Elle a dix ans.
tend *vb* **to tend to do something** avoir [**8**] tendance à faire quelque chose ▷ *He tends to arrive late.* Il a tendance à arriver en retard.
tennis *n* tennis *m* ▷ *Do you play tennis?* Vous jouez au tennis?; **a tennis ball** une balle de tennis; **a tennis court** un court de tennis; **a tennis racket** une raquette de tennis
tennis player *n* joueur de tennis *m*, joueuse de tennis *f* ▷ *He's a tennis player.* Il est joueur de tennis.
tenor *n* ténor *m*
tenpin bowling *n* bowling *m* ▷ *to go tenpin bowling* jouer au bowling
tense *adj* tendu(e)
▶ *n* **the present tense** le présent; **the future tense** le futur
tension *n* tension *f*
tent *n* tente *f*; **a tent peg** un piquet de tente; **a tent pole** un montant de tente
tenth *adj* dixième ▷ *the tenth floor* le dixième étage; **the tenth of August** le dix août

term *n* ❶ *(at school)* trimestre *m* ❷ terme *m* ▷ *a short-term solution* une solution à court terme; **to come to terms with something** accepter [**28**] quelque chose

terminal *adj (illness, patient)* incurable
▶ *n (of computer)* un terminal; **an oil terminal** un terminal pétrolier; **an air terminal** une aérogare

terminally *adv* **to be terminally ill** être [**35**] condamné

terrace *n* ❶ *(patio)* terrasse *f* ❷ *(row of houses)* rangée de maisons *f*; **the terraces** *(at stadium)* les gradins *mpl*

terraced *adj* **a terraced house** une maison mitoyenne

terrible *adj* épouvantable ▷ *My French is terrible.* Mon français est épouvantable.

terribly *adv* ❶ terriblement ▷ *He suffers terribly.* Il souffre terriblement. ❷ vraiment ▷ *I'm terribly sorry.* Je suis vraiment désolé.

terrific *adj (wonderful)* super ▷ *That's terrific!* C'est super!; **You look terrific!** Tu es superbe!

terrified *adj* terrifié(e) ▷ *I was terrified!* J'étais terrifié!

terrorism *n* terrorisme *m*

terrorist *n* terroriste *mf*; **a terrorist attack** un attentat terroriste

test *n* ❶ *(at school)* interrogation *f* ▷ *I've got a test tomorrow.* J'ai une interrogation demain. ❷ *(trial, check)* essai *m* ▷ *nuclear tests* les essais nucléaires ❸ *(medical)* analyse *f* ▷ *a blood test* une analyse de sang ▷ *They're going to do some more tests.* Ils vont faire d'autres analyses.; **driving test** l'examen du permis de conduire ▷ *He's got his driving test tomorrow.* Il passe son permis de conduire demain.
▶ *vb* ❶ essayer [**59**] ▷ *to test something out* essayer quelque chose ❷ *(class)* interroger [**45**] ▷ *He tested us on the vocabulary.* Il nous a interrogés sur le vocabulaire.; **She was tested for drugs.** On lui a fait subir un contrôle antidopage.

test tube *n* éprouvette *f*

text *n* ❶ texte *m* ❷ *(on mobile phone)* SMS *m*
▶ *vb* **to text someone** envoyer [**33**] un SMS à quelqu'un

textbook *n* manuel *m* ▷ *a French textbook* un manuel de français

text message *n* SMS *m*

Thames *n* Tamise *f*

than *conj* que ▷ *She's taller than me.* Elle est plus grande que moi.; **more than ten years** plus de dix ans; **more than once** plus d'une fois

thank *vb* remercier [**19**] ▷ *Don't forget to write and thank them.* N'oublie pas de leur écrire pour les remercier.; **thank you** merci; **thank you very much** merci beaucoup

thanks *excl* merci!; **thanks to** grâce à ▷ *Thanks to him, everything went OK.* Grâce à lui, tout s'est bien passé.

that *adj, pron, conj*

> Use **ce** when 'that' is followed by a masculine noun, and **cette** when 'that' is followed by a feminine noun. **ce** changes to **cet** before a vowel and before most words beginning with 'h'.

❶ ce ▷ *that book* ce livre; cet ▷ *that man* cet homme; cette ▷ *that woman* cette femme ▷ *that road* cette route; **THAT road** cette route-là; **that one (1)** celui-là *m* ▷ *This man? — No, that one.* Cet homme-ci? — Non, celui-là. **(2)** celle-là *f* ▷ *Do you like this photo? — No, I prefer that one.* Tu aimes cette photo? — Non, je préfère celle-là. ❷ ça ▷ *You see that?* Tu vois ça?; **What's that?** Qu'est-ce que c'est?; **Who's that?** Qui est-ce?; **Is that you?** C'est toi?; **That's ...** C'est ... ▷ *That's my teacher.* C'est mon prof. ▷ *That's what he said.* C'est ce qu'il a dit.

> In relative phrases use **qui** when 'that' refers to the subject of the sentence, and **que** when it refers to the object.

❸ qui ▷ *the man that saw us* l'homme qui nous a vus ▷ *the man that spoke to us* l'homme qui nous a parlé ❹ que ▷ *the man that we saw* l'homme que nous avons vu ▷ *the man that we spoke to* l'homme à qui nous avons parlé

> **que** changes to **qu'** before a vowel and before most words beginning with 'h'.

▷ *the dog that she bought* le chien qu'elle a acheté ▷ *He thought that Henri was ill.* Il pensait qu'Henri était malade. ▷ *I know that she likes chocolate.* Je sais qu'elle aime le chocolat.; **It was that big.** Il était grand comme ça.; **It's about that high.** C'est à peu près haut comme ça.; **It's not that difficult.** Ça n'est pas si difficile que ça.

the *art*

> Use **le** with a masculine noun, and **la** with a feminine noun. Use **l'** before a vowel and most words beginning with 'h'. For plural nouns always use **les**.

le ▷ *the boy* le garçon; l' ▷ *the man* l'homme *m* ▷ *the air* l'air *m* ▷ *the habit* l'habitude *f*; la ▷ *the girl* la fille; les ▷ *the children* les enfants

theatre (*US* **theater**) *n* théâtre *m*

theft *n* vol *m*

their *adj* leur (*pl* leurs) ▷ *their house* leur maison ▷ *their parents* leurs parents

theirs *pron* le leur ▷ *It's not our garage, it's theirs.* Ce n'est pas notre garage, c'est le leur. la leur ▷ *It's not our car, it's theirs.* Ce n'est pas notre voiture, c'est la leur. les leurs ▷ *They're not our ideas, they're theirs.* Ce ne sont pas nos idées, ce sont les leurs.; **Is this theirs? (1)** *(masculine owners)* C'est à eux? **(2)** *(feminine owners)* C'est à elles? ▷ *This car is theirs.* Cette voiture est à eux.

them *pron* ❶ les ▷ *I didn't see them.* Je

ne les ai pas vus.

Use **leur** when 'them' means 'to them'.

❷ leur ▷ *I told them the truth.* Je leur ai dit la vérité.

Use **eux** or **elles** after a preposition.

❸ eux *mpl* ▷ *It's for them.* C'est pour eux.; elles *fpl* ▷ *Ann and Sophie came — Graham was with them.* Ann et Sophie sont venues — Graham était avec elles.

theme park *n* parc d'attractions *m*

themselves *pron* ❶ se ▷ *Did they hurt themselves?* Est-ce qu'ils se sont fait mal? ❷ eux-mêmes *m*, elles-mêmes *f* ▷ *They did it themselves.* Ils l'ont fait eux-mêmes.

then *adv, conj* ❶ *(next)* ensuite ▷ *I get dressed. Then I have breakfast.* Je m'habille. Ensuite je prends mon petit déjeuner. ❷ *(in that case)* alors ▷ *My pen's run out. — Use a pencil then!* Il n'y a plus d'encre dans mon stylo. — Alors utilise un crayon! ❸ *(at that time)* à l'époque ▷ *There was no electricity then.* Il n'y avait pas l'électricité à l'époque.; **now and then** de temps en temps ▷ *Do you play chess? — Now and then.* Vous jouez aux échecs? — De temps en temps.; **By then it was too late.** Il était déjà trop tard.

there *adv* ❶ là ▷ *Put it there, on the table.* Mets-le là, sur la table.; **over there** là-bas; **in there** là; **on there** là; **up there** là-haut; **down there** là-bas; **There he is!** Le voilà! ❷ y ▷ *He went there on Friday.* Il y est allé vendredi.; **There is ...** Il y a ... ▷ *There's a factory near my house.* Il y a une usine près de chez moi.; **There are ...** Il y a ... ▷ *There are five people in my family.* Il y a cinq personnes dans ma famille.; **There has been an accident.** Il y a eu un accident.

therefore *adv* donc

there's = **there is**; **there has**

thermometer *n* thermomètre *m*

these *adj, pron* ❶ ces ▷ *these shoes* ces chaussures; **THESE shoes** ces chaussures-ci ❷ ceux-ci *m* ▷ *I want these!* Je veux ceux-ci!; celles-ci *f* ▷ *I'm looking for some sandals. Can I try these?* Je cherche des sandales. Je peux essayer celles-ci?

they *pron*

Check if 'they' stands for a masculine or feminine noun.

ils ▷ *Are there any tickets left? — No, they're all sold.* Est-ce qu'il reste des billets? — Non, ils sont tous vendus.

elles ▷ *Do you like those shoes? — No, they're horrible.* Tu aimes ces chaussures? — Non, elles sont affreuses.; **They say that ...** On dit que ...

they'd = **they had**; **they would**

they'll = **they will**

they're = **they are**

they've = **they have**

thick *adj* ❶ *(not thin)* épais *(f* épaisse); **The walls are one metre thick.** Les murs font un mètre d'épaisseur. ❷ *(stupid)* bête

thief *n* voleur *m*, voleuse *f*; **Stop thief!** Au voleur!

thigh *n* cuisse *f*

thin *adj* ❶ *(person, slice)* mince ❷ *(skinny)* maigre

thing *n* ❶ chose *f* ▷ *beautiful things* de belles choses ❷ *(thingy)* truc *m* ▷ *What's that thing called?* Comment s'appelle ce truc?; **my things** *(belongings)* mes affaires *fpl*; **You poor thing!** Mon pauvre!

think *vb* ❶ *(believe)* penser [**28**] ▷ *I think you're wrong.* Je pense que vous avez tort. ▷ *What do you think about the war?* Que pensez-vous de la guerre? ❷ *(spend time thinking)* réfléchir [**38**] ▷ *Think carefully before you reply.* Réfléchis bien avant de répondre. ▷ *I'll think about it.* Je vais y réfléchir.; **What are you thinking about?** À quoi tu penses? ❸ *(imagine)* imaginer [**28**] ▷ *Think what life would be like without cars.* Imaginez la vie sans voitures.; **I think so.** Oui, je crois.; **I don't think so.** Je ne crois pas.; **I'll think it over.** Je vais y réfléchir.

third *adj* troisième ▷ *the third day* le troisième jour ▷ *the third time* la troisième fois ▷ *I came third.* Je suis arrivé troisième.; **the third of March** le trois mars
▸ *n* tiers *m* ▷ *a third of the population* un tiers de la population

thirdly *adv* troisièmement

Third World *n* tiers-monde *m*

thirst *n* soif *f*

thirsty *adj* **to be thirsty** avoir [**8**] soif

thirteen *num* treize ▷ *I'm thirteen.* J'ai treize ans.

thirteenth *adj* treizième ▷ *her thirteenth birthday* son treizième anniversaire ▷ *the thirteenth floor* le treizième étage; **the thirteenth of August** le treize août

thirty *num* trente

this *adj, pron*

> Use **ce** when 'this' is followed by a masculine noun, and **cette** when 'this' is followed by a feminine noun. **ce** changes to **cet** before a vowel and before most words beginning with 'h'.

❶ ce ▷ *this book* ce livre; cet ▷ *this man* cet homme; cette ▷ *this woman* cette femme ▷ *this road* cette route; **THIS road** cette route-ci; **this one (1)** celui-ci *m* ▷ *Pass me that pen. — This one?* Passe-moi ce stylo. — Celui-ci? **(2)** celle-ci *f* ▷ *Of the two photos, I prefer this one.* Des deux photos, c'est celle-ci que je préfère. ❷ ça ▷ *You see this?* Tu vois ça?; **What's this?** Qu'est-ce que c'est?; **This is my mother.** *(introduction)* Je te présente ma mère.; **This is Gavin speaking.** *(on the phone)* C'est Gavin à l'appareil.

thistle *n* chardon *m*

thorough *adj* minutieux (*f* minutieuse) ▷ *She's very thorough.* Elle est très minutieuse.

those *adj, pron* ❶ ces ▷ *those shoes* ces chaussures; **THOSE shoes** ces chaussures-là ❷ ceux-là *m* ▷ *I want those!* Je veux ceux-là!

celles-là *f* ▷ *I'm looking for some sandals. Can I try those?* Je cherche des sandales. Je peux essayer celles-là?

though *conj, adv* bien que ▷ *Though it's raining* ... Bien qu'il pleuve ...

bien que has to be followed by a verb in the subjunctive.

He's a nice person, though he's not very clever. Il est sympa, mais pas très malin.

thought *vb see* **think**

▶ *n (idea)* idée *f* ▷ *I've just had a thought.* Je viens d'avoir une idée.; **It was a nice thought, thank you.** C'est gentil de ta part, merci.

thoughtful *adj* ❶ *(deep in thought)* pensif (*f* pensive) ▷ *You look thoughtful.* Tu as l'air pensif. ❷ *(considerate)* prévenant(e) ▷ *She's very thoughtful.* Elle est très prévenante.

thoughtless *adj* **He's completely thoughtless.** Il ne pense absolument pas aux autres.

thousand *num* **a thousand** mille ▷ *a thousand euros* mille euros; **£2000** deux mille livres; **thousands of people** des milliers de personnes

thousandth *adj, n* millième *m*

thread *n* fil *m*

threat *n* menace *f*

threaten *vb* menacer **[12]** ▷ *to threaten to do something* menacer de faire quelque chose

three *num* trois ▷ *She's three.* Elle a trois ans.

threw *vb see* **throw**

thrilled *adj* **I was thrilled.** *(pleased)* J'étais absolument ravi.

thriller *n* thriller *m*

thrilling *adj* palpitant(e)

throat *n* gorge *f* ▷ *to have a sore throat* avoir mal à la gorge

through *prep, adj, adv* ❶ par ▷ *through the window* par la fenêtre; **to go through a tunnel** traverser **[28]** un tunnel ❷ à travers ▷ *through the crowd* à travers la foule; **a through train** un train direct; **'no through road'** 'impasse'

throughout *prep* **throughout Britain** dans toute la Grande-Bretagne; **throughout the year** pendant toute l'année

throw *vb* lancer **[12]** ▷ *He threw the ball to me.* Il m'a lancé le ballon.; **to throw a party** organiser **[28]** une soirée; **That really threw him.** Ça l'a décontenancé.

throw away *vb* ❶ *(rubbish)* jeter **[41]** ❷ *(chance)* perdre **[61]**

throw out *vb* ❶ *(throw away)* jeter **[41]** ❷ *(person)* mettre **[47]** à la porte ▷ *I threw him out.* Je l'ai mis à la porte.

throw up *vb* vomir **[38]**

thumb *n* pouce *m*

thumb tack *n (US)* punaise *f*

thump *vb* **to thump somebody** donner **[28]** un coup de poing à quelqu'un

thunder *n* tonnerre *m*

thunderstorm *n* orage *m*

Thursday *n* jeudi *m* ▷ *on Thursday* jeudi ▷ *on Thursdays* le jeudi ▷ *every Thursday* tous les jeudis ▷ *last*

Thursday jeudi dernier ▷ *next Thursday* jeudi prochain

tick *n* ❶ *(mark)* coche *f* ❷ *(of clock)* tic-tac *m*; **I'll be back in a tick.** J'en ai pour une seconde.
▸ *vb* ❶ cocher [**28**] ▷ *Tick the appropriate box.* Cochez la case correspondante. ❷ *(clock)* faire [**36**] tic-tac

tick off *vb* ❶ *(check)* cocher [**28**] ▷ *He ticked off our names on the list.* Il a coché nos noms sur la liste. ❷ *(tell off)* passer [**58**] un savon à ▷ *She ticked me off for being late.* Elle m'a passé un savon à cause de mon retard.

ticket *n*

> Be careful to choose correctly between **le ticket** and **le billet**.

❶ *(for bus, tube, cinema, museum)* ticket *m* ▷ *an underground ticket* un ticket de métro ❷ *(for plane, train, theatre, concert)* billet *m*; **a parking ticket** un p.-v. *(informal)*

ticket inspector *n* contrôleur *m*, contrôleuse *f*

ticket office *n* guichet *m*

tickle *vb* chatouiller [**28**]

tide *n* marée *f*; **high tide** la marée haute; **low tide** la marée basse

tidy *adj* ❶ *(room)* bien rangé(e) ▷ *Your room's very tidy.* Ta chambre est bien rangée. ❷ *(person)* ordonné(e) ▷ *She's very tidy.* Elle est très ordonnée.
▸ *vb* ranger [**45**] ▷ *Go and tidy your room.* Va ranger ta chambre.

tidy up *vb* ranger [**45**] ▷ *Don't forget to tidy up afterwards.* N'oubliez pas de ranger après.

tie *n (necktie)* cravate *f*; **It was a tie.** *(in sport)* Ils ont fait match nul.
▸ *vb* ❶ *(ribbon, shoelaces)* nouer [**28**]; **to tie a knot in something** faire [**36**] un nœud à quelque chose ❷ *(in sport)* faire [**36**] match nul ▷ *They tied three all.* Ils ont fait match nul, trois à trois.

tie up *vb* ❶ *(parcel)* ficeler [**4**] ❷ *(dog, boat)* attacher [**28**] ❸ *(prisoner)* ligoter [**28**]

tiger *n* tigre *m*

tight *adj* ❶ *(tight-fitting)* moulant(e) ▷ *tight clothes* les vêtements moulants ❷ *(too tight)* juste ▷ *This dress is a bit tight.* Cette robe est un peu juste.

tighten *vb* ❶ *(rope)* tendre [**88**] ❷ *(screw)* resserrer [**28**]

tightly *adv (hold)* fort

tights *npl* collant *msg*

tile *n* ❶ *(on roof)* tuile *f* ❷ *(on wall, floor)* carreau *m (pl* carreaux)

till *n* caisse *f*
▸ *prep, conj* ❶ jusqu'à ▷ *I waited till ten o'clock.* J'ai attendu jusqu'à dix heures.; **till now** jusqu'à présent; **till then** jusque-là ❷ avant

> Use **avant** if the sentence you want to translate contains a negative such as 'not' or 'never'.

▷ *It won't be ready till next week.* Ça ne sera pas prêt avant la semaine prochaine.

time *n* ❶ *(on clock)* heure *f* ▷ *What time is it?* Quelle heure est-il? ▷ *What time do you get up?* À quelle heure tu te lèves?; **on time** à l'heure

▷ *He never arrives on time.* Il n'arrive jamais à l'heure. ❷ *(amount of time)* temps *m* ▷ *I'm sorry, I haven't got time.* Je suis désolé, je n'ai pas le temps.; **from time to time** de temps en temps; **in time** à temps ▷ *We arrived in time for lunch.* Nous sommes arrivés à temps pour le déjeuner.; **just in time** juste à temps; **in no time** en un rien de temps ▷ *It was ready in no time.* Ça a été prêt en un rien de temps.; **It's time to go.** Il est temps de partir.; **a long time** longtemps ▷ *Have you lived here for a long time?* Vous habitez ici depuis longtemps? ❸ *(moment)* moment *m* ▷ *This isn't a good time to ask him.* Ce n'est pas le bon moment pour lui demander.; **for the time being** pour le moment ❹ *(occasion)* fois *f* ▷ *this time* cette fois-ci ▷ *next time* la prochaine fois ▷ *two at a time* deux à la fois; **How many times?** Combien de fois?; **at times** parfois; **in a week's time** dans une semaine ▷ *I'll come back in a month's time.* Je reviendrai dans un mois.; **Come and see us any time.** Venez nous voir quand vous voulez.; **to have a good time** bien s'amuser [**28**] ▷ *Did you have a good time?* Vous vous êtes bien amusés?; **2 times 2 is 4** deux fois deux égalent quatre

time off *n* temps libre *m*

timetable *n* ❶ *(for train, bus)* horaire *m* ❷ *(at school)* emploi du temps *m*

tin *n* ❶ boîte *f* ▷ *a tin of soup* une boîte de soupe ▷ *a biscuit tin* une boîte à biscuits ❷ boîte de conserve *f* ▷ *The bin was full of tins.* La poubelle était pleine de boîtes de conserve. ❸ *(type of metal)* étain *m*

tin opener *n* ouvre-boîte *m*

tiny *adj* minuscule

tip *n* ❶ *(money)* pourboire *m* ▷ *Shall I give him a tip?* Je lui donne un pourboire? ❷ *(advice)* tuyau *m* (*pl* tuyaux) ▷ *a useful tip* un bon tuyau *(informal)* ❸ *(end)* bout *m* ▷ *It's on the tip of my tongue.* Je l'ai sur le bout de la langue.; **a rubbish tip** une décharge; **This place is a complete tip!** Quel fouillis!
▸ *vb* donner [**28**] un pourboire à ▷ *Don't forget to tip the taxi driver.* N'oubliez pas de donner un pourboire au chauffeur de taxi.

tipsy *adj* pompette

tiptoe *n* **on tiptoe** sur la pointe des pieds

tired *adj* fatigué(e) ▷ *I'm tired.* Je suis fatigué.; **to be tired of something** en avoir [**8**] assez de quelque chose

tiring *adj* fatigant(e)

tissue *n* kleenex® *m* ▷ *Have you got a tissue?* Tu as un kleenex?®

title *n* titre *m*

to *prep*

> **à** + **le** changes to **au**. **à** + **les** changes to **aux**.

❶ à ▷ *to go to Paris* aller à Paris ▷ *to go to school* aller à l'école ▷ *a letter to his mother* une lettre à sa mère ▷ *the answer to the question* la réponse à la question; au ▷ *to go to the theatre* aller au théâtre; aux ▷ *We said goodbye to the neighbours.* Nous avons dit au revoir aux voisins.; **ready to go** prêt à partir; **ready to eat** prêt à manger; **It's easy to do.** C'est facile à faire.; **something to drink** quelque chose à boire; **I've got things to do.** J'ai des choses à faire.; **from ... to ...** de ... à ... ▷ *from nine o'clock to half past three* de neuf heures à trois heures et demie ❷ de ▷ *the train to London* le train de Londres ▷ *the road to Edinburgh* la route d'Édimbourg ▷ *the key to the front door* la clé de la porte d'entrée; **It's difficult to say.** C'est difficile à dire.; **It's easy to criticize.** C'est facile de critiquer.

> When referring to someone's house, shop or office, use **chez**.

❸ chez ▷ *to go to the doctor's* aller chez le docteur ▷ *to go to the butcher's* aller chez le boucher ▷ *Let's go to Anne's house.* Si on allait chez Anne?

> When 'to' refers to a country which is feminine, use **en**; when the country is masculine, use **au**.

❹ en ▷ *to go to France* aller en France; au ▷ *to go to Portugal* aller au Portugal ❺ *(up to)* jusqu'à ▷ *to count to ten* compter jusqu'à dix ❻ *(in order to)* pour ▷ *I did it to help you.* Je l'ai fait pour vous aider. ▷ *She's too young to go to school.* Elle est trop jeune pour aller à l'école.

toad *n* crapaud *m*

toast *n* ❶ pain grillé *m* ▷ *a piece of toast* une tranche de pain grillé ❷ *(speech)* toast *m* ▷ *to drink a toast to somebody* porter un toast à quelqu'un

toaster *n* grille-pain *m* (*pl* grille-pain)

toastie *n* sandwich chaud *m*; **a cheese and ham toastie** un croque-monsieur

tobacco *n* tabac *m*

tobacconist's *n* bureau de tabac *m* (*pl* bureaux de tabac)

today *adv* aujourd'hui ▷ *What did you do today?* Qu'est-ce que tu as fait aujourd'hui?

toddler *n* bambin *m*

toe *n* doigt de pied *m*

toffee *n* caramel *m*

together *adv* ❶ ensemble ▷ *Are they still together?* Ils sont toujours ensemble? ❷ *(at the same time)* en même temps ▷ *Don't all speak together!* Ne parlez pas tous en même temps!; **together with** *(with person)* avec

toilet *n* toilettes *fpl*

toilet paper *n* papier hygiénique *m*

toiletries *npl* articles de toilette *mpl*

toilet roll *n* rouleau de papier hygiénique *m* (*pl* rouleaux de papier hygiénique)

told *vb see* **tell**

toll *n (on bridge, motorway)* péage *m*

tomato *n* tomate *f* ▷ *tomato sauce* la sauce tomate ▷ *tomato soup* la soupe à la tomate

tomorrow *adv* demain ▷ *tomorrow morning* demain matin ▷ *tomorrow night* demain soir; **the day after tomorrow** après-demain

ton *n* tonne *f* ▷ *That old bike weighs a ton.* Ce vieux vélo pèse une tonne.

In France measurements are in metric tonnes rather than tons. A ton is slightly more than a **tonne**.

tongue *n* langue *f*; **to say something tongue in cheek** dire [**27**] quelque chose en plaisantant

tonic *n (tonic water)* Schweppes® *m*; **a gin and tonic** un gin tonic

tonight *adv* ❶ *(this evening)* ce soir ▷ *Are you going out tonight?* Tu sors ce soir? ❷ *(during the night)* cette nuit ▷ *I'll sleep well tonight.* Je dormirai bien cette nuit.

tonsillitis *n* angine *f*

tonsils *npl* amygdales *fpl*

too *adv* ❶ *(as well)* aussi ▷ *My sister came too.* Ma sœur est venue aussi. ❷ *(excessively)* trop ▷ *The water's too hot.* L'eau est trop chaude. ▷ *We arrived too late.* Nous sommes arrivés trop tard.; **too much** **(1)** *(with noun)* trop de ▷ *too much noise* trop de bruit **(2)** *(with verb)* trop ▷ *At Christmas we always eat too much.* À Noël nous mangeons toujours trop. **(3)** *(too expensive)* trop cher ▷ *Fifty euros? That's too much.* Cinquante euros? C'est trop cher.; **too many** trop de ▷ *too many hamburgers* trop de hamburgers; **Too bad!** Tant pis!

took *vb see* **take**

tool *n* outil *m*; **a tool box** une boîte à outils

tooth *n* dent *f*

toothache *n* mal de dents *m* ▷ *to have toothache* avoir mal aux dents

toothbrush *n* brosse à dents *f*

toothpaste *n* dentifrice *m*

top *n* ❶ *(of page, ladder, garment)* haut *m* ▷ *at the top of the page* en haut de la page; **a bikini top** un haut de bikini ❷ *(of mountain)* sommet *m* ❸ *(of table)* dessus *m*; **on top of** *(on)* sur ▷ *on top of the fridge* sur le frigo; **There's a surcharge on top of that.** Il y a un supplément en plus.; **from top to bottom** de fond en comble ▷ *I searched the house from top to bottom.* J'ai fouillé la maison de fond en comble. ❹ *(of box, jar)* couvercle *m* ❺ *(of bottle)* bouchon *m*

▶ *adj (first-class)* grand(e) ▷ *a top surgeon* un grand chirurgien; **a top model** un top model; **He always gets top marks in French.** Il a toujours d'excellentes notes en français.; **the top floor** le dernier étage ▷ *on the top floor* au dernier étage

topic *n* sujet *m* ▷ *The essay can be on any topic.* Cette dissertation peut être sur n'importe quel sujet.

torch *n* lampe de poche *f*

tore, torn *vb see* **tear**

tortoise *n* tortue *f*

torture *n* torture *f* ▷ *It was pure torture.* C'était une vraie torture.

▶ *vb* torturer [**28**] ▷ *Stop torturing*

that poor animal! Arrête de torturer cette pauvre bête!

total *adj* total(e) (*mpl* totaux); **the total amount** le total
▸ *n* total *m* (*pl* totaux); **the grand total** le total

totally *adv* complètement ▹ *He's totally useless.* Il est complètement nul.

touch *n* **to get in touch with somebody** prendre [**65**] contact avec quelqu'un; **to keep in touch with somebody** ne pas perdre [**61**] contact avec quelqu'un; **Keep in touch!** Donne-moi de tes nouvelles!; **to lose touch** se perdre [**61**] de vue; **to lose touch with somebody** perdre [**61**] quelqu'un de vue
▸ *vb* toucher [**28**]; **Don't touch that!** N'y touche pas!

touchpad *n* pavé tactile *m*

tough *adj* ❶ dur(e) ▹ *It was tough, but I managed OK.* C'était dur, mais je m'en suis tiré. ▹ *It's a tough job.* C'est dur.; **The meat's tough.** La viande est coriace. ❷ *(strong)* solide ▹ *She's tough. She can take it.* Elle est solide. Elle tiendra le coup. ❸ *(rough, violent)* dangereux (*f* dangereuse); **He thinks he's a tough guy.** Il se prend pour un gros dur.; **Tough luck!** C'est comme ça!

tour *n* ❶ *(of town, museum)* visite *f* ▹ *We went on a tour of the city.* Nous avons visité la ville.; **a package tour** un voyage organisé ❷ *(by singer, group)* tournée *f* ▹ *on tour* en tournée; **to go on tour** faire [**36**] une tournée
▸ *vb* **Robbie Williams is touring Europe.** Robbie Williams est en tournée en Europe.

tourism *n* tourisme *m*

tourist *n* touriste *mf*; **tourist information office** l'office du tourisme *m*

towards *prep* ❶ *(in the direction of)* vers ▹ *He came towards me.* Il est venu vers moi. ❷ *(of attitude)* envers ▹ *my feelings towards him* mes sentiments envers lui

towel *n* serviette *f*

tower *n* tour *f*; **a tower block** une tour

town *n* ville *f* ▹ *a town plan* un plan de ville; **the town centre** le centre-ville; **the town hall** la mairie

tow truck *n (US)* dépanneuse *f*

toy *n* jouet *m* ▹ *a toy shop* un magasin de jouets; **a toy car** une petite voiture

trace *n* trace *f* ▹ *There was no trace of the robbers.* Il n'y avait pas de trace des voleurs.
▸ *vb (draw)* décalquer [**28**]

tracing paper *n* papier calque *m*

track *n* ❶ *(dirt road)* chemin *m* ❷ *(railway line)* voie ferrée *f* ❸ *(in sport)* piste *f* ▹ *two laps of the track* deux tours de piste ❹ *(song)* chanson *f* ▹ *This is my favourite track.* C'est ma chanson préférée. ❺ *(trail)* traces *fpl* ▹ *They followed the tracks for miles.* Ils ont suivi les traces pendant des kilomètres.

track down *vb* **to track somebody down** retrouver [**28**]

quelqu'un ▷ *The police never tracked down the killer.* La police n'a jamais retrouvé l'assassin.
tracksuit *n* jogging *m*
tractor *n* tracteur *m*
trade *n (skill, job)* métier *m* ▷ *to learn a trade* apprendre un métier
trade union *n* syndicat *m*
tradition *n* tradition *f*
traditional *adj* traditionnel (*f* traditionnelle)
traffic *n* circulation *f* ▷ *The traffic was terrible.* Il y avait une circulation épouvantable.
traffic circle *n (US)* rond-point *m* (*pl* ronds-points)
traffic jam *n* embouteillage *m*
traffic lights *npl* feux *mpl*
traffic warden *n* contractuel *m*, contractuelle *f*
tragedy *n* tragédie *f*
tragic *adj* tragique
trailer *n* ❶ *(vehicle)* remorque *f* ❷ *(film advert)* bande-annonce *f*
train *n* ❶ train *m* ❷ *(on underground)* rame *f*
▶ *vb (sport)* s'entraîner [**28**] ▷ *to train for a race* s'entraîner pour une course; **to train as a teacher** suivre [**81**] une formation d'enseignant; **to train an animal to do something** dresser [**28**] un animal à faire quelque chose
trained *adj* **She's a trained nurse.** Elle est infirmière diplômée.
trainee *n* ❶ *(in profession)* stagiaire *mf* ▷ *She's a trainee.* Elle est stagiaire. ❷ *(apprentice)* apprenti *m*, apprentie *f* ▷ *a trainee plumber* un apprenti plombier
trainer *n* ❶ *(sports coach)* entraîneur *m* ❷ *(of animals)* dompteur *m*, dompteuse *f*
trainers *npl* baskets *fpl* ▷ *a pair of trainers* une paire de baskets
training *n* ❶ formation *f* ▷ *a training course* un stage de formation ❷ *(sport)* entraînement *m*
tram *n* tramway *m*
tramp *n* clochard *m*, clocharde *f*
trampoline *n* trampoline *m*
transfer *n (sticker)* décalcomanie *f*
transit *n* transit *m* ▷ *in transit* en transit
transit lounge *n* salle de transit *f*
translate *vb* traduire [**23**] ▷ *to translate something into English* traduire quelque chose en anglais
translation *n* traduction *f*
translator *n* traducteur *m*, traductrice *f* ▷ *Anita's a translator.* Anita est traductrice.
transparent *adj* transparent(e)
transplant *n* greffe *f* ▷ *a heart transplant* une greffe du cœur
transport *n* transport *m* ▷ *public transport* les transports en commun
▶ *vb* transporter [**28**]
trap *n* piège *m*
trash *n (US)* ordures *fpl*; **the trash can** la poubelle
travel *n* voyages *mpl*
▶ *vb* voyager [**45**] ▷ *I prefer to travel by train.* Je préfère voyager en train.; **I'd like to travel round the world.** J'aimerais faire le tour du

monde.; **We travelled over 800 kilometres.** Nous avons fait plus de huit cents kilomètres.; **News travels fast!** Les nouvelles circulent vite!

travel agency *n* agence de voyages *f*

travel agent *n* **She's a travel agent.** Elle travaille dans une agence de voyages.

traveller (*US* **traveler**) *n* ❶ *(on bus, train, plane)* voyageur *m*, voyageuse *f* ❷ *(gypsy)* nomade *mf*

traveller's cheque (*US* **traveler's check**) *n* chèque de voyage *m*

travelling (*US* **traveling**) *n* **I love travelling.** J'adore les voyages.

travel sickness *n* mal des transports *m*

tray *n* plateau *m* (*pl* plateaux)

tread *vb* marcher [**28**] ▷ *to tread on something* marcher sur quelque chose

treasure *n* trésor *m*

treat *n* ❶ *(present)* petit cadeau *m* (*pl* petits cadeaux) ❷ *(food)* gâterie *f*; **to give somebody a treat** faire [**36**] plaisir à quelqu'un
▸ *vb (well, badly)* traiter [**28**]; **to treat somebody to something** offrir [**54**] quelque chose à quelqu'un ▷ *He treated us to an ice cream.* Il nous a offert une glace.

treatment *n* traitement *m*

treble *vb* tripler [**28**] ▷ *The cost of living there has trebled.* Le coût de la vie là-bas a triplé.

tree *n* arbre *m*

tremble *vb* trembler [**28**]

tremendous *adj* énorme ▷ *a tremendous success* un succès énorme

trend *n (fashion)* mode *f*

trendy *adj* branché(e)

trial *n (in court)* procès *m*

triangle *n* triangle *m*

tribe *n* tribu *f*

trick *n* ❶ tour *m* ▷ *to play a trick on somebody* jouer un tour à quelqu'un ❷ *(knack)* truc *m* ▷ *It's not easy: there's a trick to it.* Ce n'est pas facile: il y a un truc.
▸ *vb* **to trick somebody** rouler [**28**] quelqu'un

tricky *adj* délicat(e)

tricycle *n* tricycle *m*

trip *n* voyage *m* ▷ *to go on a trip* faire un voyage; **a day trip** une excursion d'une journée
▸ *vb (stumble)* trébucher [**28**]

triple *adj* triple

triplets *npl* triplés *mpl*, triplées *fpl*

trivial *adj* insignifiant(e)

trod, trodden *vb see* **tread**

trolley *n* chariot *m*

trombone *n* trombone *m* ▷ *I play the trombone.* Je joue du trombone.

troops *npl* troupes *mpl* ▷ *British troops* les troupes britanniques

trophy *n* trophée *m* ▷ *to win a trophy* gagner un trophée

tropical *adj* tropical(e) ▷ *The weather was tropical.* Il faisait une chaleur tropicale.

trouble *n* problème *m* ▷ *The trouble is, it's too expensive.* Le problème, c'est que c'est trop cher.; **to be in trouble** avoir [**8**] des ennuis;

What's the trouble? Qu'est-ce qui ne va pas?; **stomach trouble** troubles gastriques; **to take a lot of trouble over something** se donner [**28**] beaucoup de mal pour quelque chose; **Don't worry, it's no trouble.** Mais non, ça ne me dérange pas du tout.

troublemaker *n* élément perturbateur *m*

trousers *npl* pantalon *msg*

trout *n* truite *f*

truant *n* **to play truant** faire [**36**] l'école buissonnière

truck *n* camion *m*; **a truck driver** un camionneur ▷ *He's a truck driver.* Il est camionneur.

true *adj* vrai(e); **That's true.** C'est vrai.; **to come true** se réaliser [**28**] ▷ *I hope my dream will come true.* J'espère que mon rêve se réalisera.; **true love** le grand amour

truly *adv* vraiment ▷ *It was a truly remarkable victory.* C'était vraiment une victoire remarquable.; **Yours truly.** Je vous prie d'agréer mes salutations distinguées.

trumpet *n* trompette *f* ▷ *She plays the trumpet.* Elle joue de la trompette.

trunk *n* ❶ *(of tree)* tronc *m* ❷ *(of elephant)* trompe *f* ❸ *(luggage)* malle *f* ❹ *(US: of car)* coffre *m*

trunks *npl* **swimming trunks** le maillot de bain

trust *n* confiance *f* ▷ *to have trust in somebody* avoir confiance en quelqu'un
▶ *vb* **to trust somebody** faire [**36**] confiance à quelqu'un ▷ *Don't you trust me?* Tu ne me fais pas confiance?

truth *n* vérité *f*

try *n* essai *m* ▷ *his third try* son troisième essai; **to have a try** essayer [**59**]; **It's worth a try.** Ça vaut la peine d'essayer.; **to give something a try** essayer [**59**] quelque chose
▶ *vb* ❶ *(attempt)* essayer [**59**] ▷ *to try to do something* essayer de faire quelque chose; **to try again** refaire [**36**] un essai ❷ *(taste)* goûter [**28**] ▷ *Would you like to try some?* Voulez-vous goûter?

try on *vb (clothes)* essayer [**59**]

try out *vb* essayer [**59**]

T-shirt *n* tee-shirt *m*

tube *n* tube *m*; **the Tube** *(underground)* le métro

tuberculosis *n* tuberculose *f*

Tuesday *n* mardi *m* ▷ *on Tuesday* mardi ▷ *on Tuesdays* le mardi ▷ *every Tuesday* tous les mardis ▷ *last Tuesday* mardi dernier ▷ *next Tuesday* mardi prochain; **Shrove Tuesday** *(Pancake Tuesday)* le mardi gras

tuition *n* cours *mpl*; **private tuition** les cours particuliers

tulip *n* tulipe *f*

tumble dryer *n* sèche-linge *m* (*pl* sèche-linge)

tummy *n* ventre *m*

tuna *n* thon *m*

tune *n (melody)* air *m*; **to play in tune** jouer [**28**] juste; **to sing out of tune** chanter [**28**] faux

Tunisia *n* Tunisie *f*; **in Tunisia** en Tunisie
tunnel *n* tunnel *m*; **the Channel Tunnel** le tunnel sous la Manche
Turk *n* Turc *m*, Turque *f*
Turkey *n* Turquie *f*; **in Turkey** en Turquie; **to Turkey** en Turquie
turkey *n* ❶ *(meat)* dinde *f* ❷ *(live bird)* dindon *m*
Turkish *n (language)* turc *m*
▶ *adj* turc (*f* turque)
turn *n* ❶ *(bend in road)* tournant *m*; **'no left turn'** 'défense de tourner à gauche' ❷ *(go)* tour *m* ▷ *It's my turn!* C'est mon tour!
▶ *vb* ❶ tourner **[28]** ▷ *Turn right at the lights.* Tournez à droite aux feux. ❷ *(become)* devenir **[25]** ▷ *to turn red* devenir rouge; **to turn into something** se transformer **[28]** en quelque chose ▷ *The frog turned into a prince.* La grenouille s'est transformée en prince.
turn back *vb* faire **[36]** demi-tour ▷ *We turned back.* Nous avons fait demi-tour.
turn down *vb* ❶ *(offer)* refuser **[28]** ❷ *(radio, TV, heating)* baisser **[28]** ▷ *Shall I turn the heating down?* Je baisse le chauffage?
turn off *vb* ❶ *(light, radio)* éteindre **[60]** ❷ *(tap)* fermer **[28]** ❸ *(engine)* arrêter **[28]**
turn on *vb* ❶ *(light, radio)* allumer **[28]** ❷ *(tap)* ouvrir **[55]** ❸ *(engine)* mettre **[47]** en marche
turn out *vb* **It turned out to be a mistake.** Il s'est avéré que c'était une erreur.; **It turned out that she was right.** Il s'est avéré qu'elle avait raison.
turn round *vb* ❶ *(car)* faire **[36]** demi-tour ❷ *(person)* se retourner **[72]**
turn up *vb* ❶ *(arrive)* arriver **[5]** ❷ *(heater)* monter **[48]**; **Could you turn up the radio?** Tu peux monter le son de la radio?
turning *n* **It's the third turning on the left.** C'est la troisième à gauche.; **We took the wrong turning.** Nous n'avons pas tourné au bon endroit.
turnip *n* navet *m*
turquoise *adj (colour)* turquoise
turtle *n* tortue *f*
tutor *n (private teacher)* professeur particulier *m*
TV *n* télé *f*
tweezers *npl* pince à épiler *fsg*
twelfth *adj* douzième ▷ *the twelfth floor* le douzième étage; **the twelfth of August** le douze août
twelve *num* douze ▷ *She's twelve.* Elle a douze ans.; **twelve o'clock (1)** *(midday)* midi **(2)** *(midnight)* minuit
twentieth *adj* vingtième ▷ *the twentieth time* la vingtième fois; **the twentieth of May** le vingt mai
twenty *num* vingt ▷ *He's twenty.* Il a vingt ans.
twice *adv* deux fois; **twice as much** deux fois plus ▷ *He gets twice as much pocket money as me.* Il a deux fois plus d'argent de poche que moi.
twin *n* jumeau *m* (*mpl* jumeaux), jumelle *f*; **my twin brother** mon

frère jumeau; **her twin sister** sa sœur jumelle; **identical twins** les vrais jumeaux; **a twin room** une chambre à deux lits

twinned *adj* jumelé(e) ▷ *Stroud is twinned with Châteaubriant.* Stroud est jumelée avec Châteaubriant.

twist *vb* ❶ *(bend)* tordre [**49**] ❷ *(distort)* déformer [**28**] ▷ *You're twisting my words.* Tu déformes ce que j'ai dit.

two *num* deux ▷ *She's two.* Elle a deux ans.

type *n* type *m* ▷ *What type of camera have you got?* Quel type d'appareil photo as-tu?
▶ *vb* taper [**28**] à la machine ▷ *Can you type?* Tu sais taper à la machine?; **to type a letter** taper [**28**] une lettre

typewriter *n* machine à écrire *f*

typical *adj* typique ▷ *That's just typical!* C'est typique!

tyre *n* pneu *m*; **the tyre pressure** la pression des pneus

U

UFO *n* OVNI *m* (= *objet volant non identifié*)

ugly *adj* laid(e)

UK *n* (= *United Kingdom*) Royaume-Uni *m*; **from the UK** du Royaume-Uni; **in the UK** au Royaume-Uni; **to the UK** au Royaume-Uni

ulcer *n* ulcère *m*; **a mouth ulcer** un aphte

Ulster *n* Irlande du Nord *f*; **in Ulster** en Irlande du Nord

umbrella *n* ❶ parapluie *m* ❷ *(for sun)* parasol *m*

umpire *n* ❶ *(in cricket)* arbitre *m* ❷ *(in tennis)* juge de chaise *m*

UN *n* (= *United Nations*) ONU *f* (= *Organisation des Nations Unies*)

unable *adj* **to be unable to do something** ne pas pouvoir [**64**]

faire quelque chose ▷ *I was unable to come.* Je n'ai pas pu venir.
unanimous *adj* unanime ▷ *a unanimous decision* une décision unanime
unavoidable *adj* inévitable
unbearable *adj* insupportable
unbelievable *adj* incroyable
unbreakable *adj* incassable
uncertain *adj* incertain(e) ▷ *The future is uncertain.* L'avenir est incertain.; **to be uncertain about something** ne pas être [**35**] sûr de quelque chose
uncle *n* oncle *m* ▷ *my uncle* mon oncle
uncomfortable *adj* pas confortable ▷ *The seats are rather uncomfortable.* Les sièges ne sont pas très confortables.
unconscious *adj* sans connaissance
uncontrollable *adj* incontrôlable
under *prep* ❶ sous ▷ *The cat's under the table.* Le chat est sous la table. ▷ *The tunnel goes under the Channel.* Le tunnel passe sous la Manche.; **under there** là-dessous ▷ *What's under there?* Qu'est-ce qu'il y a là-dessous? ❷ *(less than)* moins de ▷ *under 20 people* moins de vingt personnes ▷ *children under 10* les enfants de moins de dix ans
underage *adj* **He's underage.** Il n'a pas l'âge réglementaire.
underground *adj, adv* ❶ souterrain(e) ▷ *an underground car park* un parking souterrain ❷ sous terre ▷ *Moles live underground.* Les taupes vivent sous terre.
▶ *n* métro *m* ▷ *Is there an underground in Lille?* Est-ce qu'il y a un métro à Lille?
underline *vb* souligner [**28**]
underneath *prep, adv* ❶ sous ▷ *underneath the carpet* sous la moquette ❷ dessous ▷ *I got out of the car and looked underneath.* Je suis descendu de la voiture et j'ai regardé dessous.
underpants *npl* slip *msg*
underpass *n* ❶ *(for people)* passage souterrain *m* ❷ *(for cars)* passage inférieur *m*
undershirt *n (US)* maillot de corps *m*
understand *vb* comprendre [**65**] ▷ *Do you understand?* Vous comprenez? ▷ *I don't understand this word.* Je ne comprends pas ce mot. ▷ *Is that understood?* C'est compris?
understanding *adj* compréhensif (*f* compréhensive) ▷ *She's very understanding.* Elle est très compréhensive.
understood *vb see* **understand**
undertaker *n* entrepreneur des pompes funèbres *m*
underwater *adj, adv* sous l'eau ▷ *This sequence was filmed underwater.* Cette séquence a été filmée sous l'eau.; **an underwater camera** un appareil photographique de plongée; **underwater photography** la photographie subaquatique
underwear *n* sous-vêtements *mpl*

undo *vb* ❶ *(buttons, knot)* défaire [**36**] ❷ *(parcel)* déballer [**28**]
undress *vb (get undressed)* se déshabiller [**28**] ▷ *The doctor told me to undress.* Le médecin m'a dit de me déshabiller.
unemployed *adj* au chômage ▷ *He's unemployed.* Il est au chômage.; **the unemployed** les chômeurs *mpl*
unemployment *n* chômage *m*
unexpected *adj* inattendu(e) ▷ *an unexpected visitor* un visiteur inattendu
unexpectedly *adv* à l'improviste ▷ *They arrived unexpectedly.* Ils sont arrivés à l'improviste.
unfair *adj* injuste ▷ *It's unfair to girls.* C'est injuste pour les filles.
unfamiliar *adj* **I heard an unfamiliar voice.** J'ai entendu une voix que je ne connaissais pas.
unfashionable *adj* démodé(e)
unfit *adj* **I'm rather unfit.** Je ne suis pas en très bonne condition physique.
unfold *vb* déplier [**19**] ▷ *She unfolded the map.* Elle a déplié la carte.
unforgettable *adj* inoubliable
unfortunately *adv* malheureusement ▷ *Unfortunately, I arrived late.* Malheureusement, je suis arrivé en retard.
unfriendly *adj* pas aimable ▷ *The waiters are a bit unfriendly.* Les serveurs ne sont pas très aimables.
ungrateful *adj* ingrat(e)
unhappy *adj* malheureux (*f* malheureuse) ▷ *He was very unhappy as a child.* Il était très malheureux quand il était petit.; **to look unhappy** avoir [**8**] l'air triste
unhealthy *adj* ❶ *(person)* maladif (*f* maladive) ❷ *(place, habit)* malsain(e) ❸ *(food)* pas sain(e)
uni *n (university)* fac *f* ▷ *to go to uni* aller à la fac
uniform *n* uniforme *m* ▷ *school uniform* l'uniforme scolaire
uninhabited *adj* inhabité(e)
union *n (trade union)* syndicat *m*
Union Jack *n* drapeau du Royaume-Uni *m*
unique *adj* unique
unit *n* ❶ unité *f* ▷ *a unit of measurement* une unité de mesure ❷ *(piece of furniture)* élément *m* ▷ *a kitchen unit* un élément de cuisine
United Kingdom *n* Royaume-Uni *m*
United Nations *n* Nations Unies *fpl*
United States *n* États-Unis *mpl*; **in the United States** aux États-Unis; **to the United States** aux États-Unis
universe *n* univers *m*
university *n* université *f* ▷ *She's at university.* Elle va à l'université. ▷ *Do you want to go to university?* Tu veux aller à l'université?
unleaded petrol *n* essence sans plomb *f*
unless *conj* **unless he leaves** à moins qu'il ne parte ▷ *I won't come unless you phone me.* Je ne viendrai

pas à moins que tu ne me téléphones.

unlikely *adj* peu probable ▷ *It's possible, but unlikely.* C'est possible, mais peu probable.

unload *vb* décharger [**45**] ▷ *We unloaded the car.* Nous avons déchargé la voiture. ▷ *The lorries go there to unload.* Les camions y vont pour être déchargés.

unlock *vb* ouvrir [**55**] ▷ *He unlocked the door of the car.* Il a ouvert la portière de la voiture.

unlucky *adj* **to be unlucky** **(1)** *(number, object)* porter [**28**] malheur ▷ *They say thirteen is an unlucky number.* On dit que le nombre treize porte malheur. **(2)** *(person)* ne pas avoir [**8**] de chance ▷ *Did you win? — No, I was unlucky.* Vous avez gagné? — Non, je n'ai pas eu de chance.

unmarried *adj (person)* célibataire ▷ *an unmarried mother* une mère célibataire; **an unmarried couple** un couple non marié

unnatural *adj* pas naturel (*f* pas naturelle)

unnecessary *adj* inutile

unpack *vb* ❶ défaire [**36**] ▷ *I unpacked my suitcase.* J'ai défait ma valise. ❷ déballer [**28**] ses affaires ▷ *I went to my room to unpack.* Je suis allé dans ma chambre pour déballer mes affaires. ▷ *I haven't unpacked my clothes yet.* Je n'ai pas encore déballé mes affaires.

unpleasant *adj* désagréable

unplug *vb* débrancher [**28**]

unpopular *adj* impopulaire

unrealistic *adj* peu réaliste

unreasonable *adj* pas raisonnable ▷ *Her attitude was completely unreasonable.* Son attitude n'était pas du tout raisonnable.

unreliable *adj (car, machine)* pas fiable ▷ *It's a nice car, but a bit unreliable.* C'est une belle voiture, mais elle n'est pas très fiable.; **He's completely unreliable.** On ne peut pas du tout compter sur lui.

unroll *vb* dérouler [**28**]

unscrew *vb* dévisser [**28**] ▷ *She unscrewed the top of the bottle.* Elle a dévissé le bouchon de la bouteille.

unsuccessful *adj (attempt)* vain(e); **to be unsuccessful in doing something** ne pas réussir [**38**] à faire quelque chose ▷ *an unsuccessful artist* un artiste qui n'a pas réussi

unsuitable *adj (clothes, equipment)* inapproprié(e)

untidy *adj* ❶ en désordre ▷ *My bedroom's always untidy.* Ma chambre est toujours en désordre. ❷ *(appearance, person)* débraillé(e) ▷ *He's always untidy.* Il est toujours débraillé. ❸ *(in character)* désordonné(e) ▷ *He's a very untidy person.* Il est très désordonné.

untie *vb* ❶ *(knot, parcel)* défaire [**36**] ❷ *(animal)* détacher [**28**]

until *prep, conj* ❶ jusqu'à ▷ *I waited until ten o'clock.* J'ai attendu jusqu'à dix heures.; **until now** jusqu'à présent ▷ *It's never been a problem* *until now.* Ça n'a jamais été un problème jusqu'à présent.; **until then** jusque-là ▷ *Until then I'd never been to France.* Jusque-là je n'étais jamais allé en France. ❷ avant

> Use **avant** if the sentence you want to translate contains a negative, such as 'not' or 'never'

▷ *It won't be ready until next week.* Ça ne sera pas prêt avant la semaine prochaine.

unusual *adj* ❶ insolite ▷ *an unusual shape* une forme insolite ❷ rare ▷ *It's unusual to get snow at this time of year.* Il est rare qu'il neige à cette époque de l'année.

unwilling *adj* **to be unwilling to do something** ne pas être [**35**] disposé à faire quelque chose ▷ *He was unwilling to help me.* Il n'était pas disposé à m'aider.

unwrap *vb* déballer [**28**] ▷ *After the meal we unwrapped the presents.* Après le repas nous avons déballé les cadeaux.

up *prep, adv*

> For other expressions with 'up', see the verbs 'go', 'come', 'put', 'turn' etc.

en haut ▷ *up on the hill* en haut de la colline; **up here** ici; **up there** là-haut; **up north** dans le nord; **to be up** *(out of bed)* être [**35**] levé ▷ *We were up at 6.* Nous étions levés à six heures. ▷ *He's not up yet.* Il n'est pas encore levé.; **What's up?** Qu'est-ce qu'il y a? ▷ *What's up with her?* Qu'est-ce qu'elle a?; **to get up** *(in the morning)* se lever [**43**] ▷ *What time do you get up?* À quelle heure est-ce que tu te lèves?; **to go up** monter [**48**] ▷ *The bus went up the hill.* Le bus a monté la colline.; **to go up to somebody** s'approcher [**28**] de quelqu'un ▷ *She came up to me.* Elle s'est approchée de moi.; **up to** *(as far as)* jusqu'à ▷ *to count up to fifty* compter jusqu'à cinquante ▷ *up to now* jusqu'à présent; **It's up to you.** C'est à vous de décider.

uphill *adv* **to go uphill** monter [**48**]

upper *adj* supérieur(e) ▷ *on the upper floor* à l'étage supérieur

upper sixth *n* **the upper sixth** la terminale ▷ *She's in the upper sixth.* Elle est en terminale.

upright *adj* **to stand upright** se tenir [**83**] droit

upset *n* **a stomach upset** une indigestion
▶ *adj* contrarié(e) ▷ *She's still a bit upset.* Elle est encore un peu contrariée.; **I had an upset stomach.** J'avais l'estomac dérangé.
▶ *vb* **to upset somebody** contrarier [**19**] quelqu'un

upside down *adv* à l'envers ▷ *That painting is upside down.* Ce tableau est à l'envers.

upstairs *adv* en haut ▷ *Where's your coat? — It's upstairs.* Où est ton manteau? — Il est en haut.; **to go upstairs** monter [**48**]

up-to-date *adj* ❶ *(car, stereo)* moderne ❷ *(information)* à jour ▷ *an up-to-date timetable* un horaire à jour; **to bring something up to**

date moderniser [**28**] quelque chose

upwards *adv* vers le haut ▷ *to look upwards* regarder vers le haut

urgent *adj* urgent(e) ▷ *Is it urgent?* C'est urgent?

US *n* USA *mpl*

us *pron* nous ▷ *They helped us.* Ils nous ont aidés.

USA *n* USA *mpl*

use *n* **It's no use.** Ça ne sert à rien. ▷ *It's no use shouting, she's deaf.* Ça ne sert à rien de crier, elle est sourde.; **It's no use, I can't do it.** Il n'y a rien à faire, je n'y arrive pas.; **to make use of something** utiliser [**28**] quelque chose
▶ *vb* utiliser [**28**] ▷ *Can we use a dictionary in the exam?* Est-ce qu'on peut utiliser un dictionnaire à l'examen?; **Can I use your phone?** Je peux téléphoner?; **to use the toilet** aller [**3**] aux W.C.; **I used to live in London.** J'habitais à Londres autrefois.; **I used not to like maths, but now ...** Avant, je n'aimais pas les maths, mais maintenant ...; **to be used to something** avoir [**8**] l'habitude de quelque chose ▷ *He wasn't used to driving on the right.* Il n'avait pas l'habitude de conduire à droite. ▷ *Don't worry, I'm used to it.* Ne t'inquiète pas, j'ai l'habitude.; **a used car** une voiture d'occasion

use up *vb* ❶ finir [**38**] ▷ *We've used up all the paint.* Nous avons fini la peinture. ❷ *(money)* dépenser [**28**]

useful *adj* utile

useless *adj* nul (*f* nulle) ▷ *This map is just useless.* Cette carte est vraiment nulle. ▷ *You're useless!* Tu es nul!; **It's useless!** Ça ne sert à rien!

user *n* utilisateur *m*, utilisatrice *f*

user-friendly *adj* facile à utiliser

username *n* nom d'utilisateur *m*

usual *adj* habituel (*f* habituelle); **as usual** comme d'habitude

usually *adv* ❶ *(generally)* en général ▷ *I usually get to school at about half past eight.* En général, j'arrive à l'école vers huit heures et demie. ❷ *(when making a contrast)* d'habitude ▷ *Usually I don't wear make-up, but today is a special occasion.* D'habitude je ne me maquille pas, mais aujourd'hui c'est spécial.

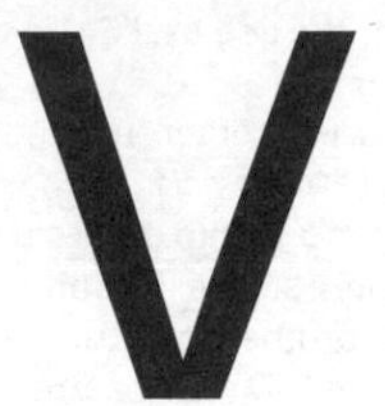

vacancy *n* ❶ *(job)* poste vacant *m* ❷ *(room in hotel)* chambre disponible *f*; **'no vacancies'** *(on sign)* 'complet'
vacant *adj* libre
vacation *n (US)* vacances *fpl* ▷ *to be on vacation* être en vacances ▷ *to take a vacation* prendre des vacances
vaccinate *vb* vacciner [**28**]
vacuum *vb* passer [**58**] l'aspirateur ▷ *to vacuum the hall* passer l'aspirateur dans le couloir
vacuum cleaner *n* aspirateur *m*
vagina *n* vagin *m*
vague *adj* vague
vain *adj* vaniteux (*f* vaniteuse) ▷ *He's so vain!* Qu'est-ce qu'il est vaniteux!; **in vain** en vain
Valentine card *n* carte de la Saint-Valentin *f*
Valentine's Day *n* Saint-Valentin *f*
valid *adj* valable ▷ *This ticket is valid for three months.* Ce billet est valable trois mois.
valley *n* vallée *f*
valuable *adj* ❶ de valeur ▷ *a valuable picture* un tableau de valeur ❷ précieux (*f* précieuse) ▷ *valuable help* une aide précieuse
value *n* valeur *f*
van *n* camionnette *f*
vandal *n* vandale *mf*
vandalism *n* vandalisme *m*
vandalize *vb* saccager [**45**]
vanilla *n* vanille *f* ▷ *vanilla ice cream* la glace à la vanille
vanish *vb* disparaître [**56**]
variety *n* variété *f*
various *adj* plusieurs ▷ *We visited various villages in the area.* Nous avons visité plusieurs villages de la région.
vary *vb* varier [**19**]
vase *n* vase *m*
VAT *n (= value added tax)* TVA *f (= taxe sur la valeur ajoutée)*
VCR *n (= video cassette recorder)* magnétoscope *m*
VDU *n (= visual display unit)* moniteur *m*
veal *n* veau *m*
vegan *n* végétalien *m*, végétalienne *f* ▷ *I'm a vegan.* Je suis végétalien.
vegetable *n* légume *m* ▷ *vegetable soup* la soupe aux légumes
vegetarian *adj* végétarien (*f* végétarienne) ▷ *I'm vegetarian.* Je suis végétarien. ▷ *vegetarian*

lasagne les lasagnes végétariennes *fpl*
▶ *n* végétarien *m*, végétarienne *f* ▷ *I'm a vegetarian.* Je suis végétarien.

vehicle *n* véhicule *m*

vein *n* veine *f*

velvet *n* velours *m*

vending machine *n* distributeur automatique *m*

verb *n* verbe *m*

verdict *n* verdict *m*

vertical *adj* vertical(e) (*mpl* verticaux)

vertigo *n* vertige *m* ▷ *I get vertigo.* J'ai le vertige.

very *adv* très ▷ *very tall* très grand ▷ *not very interesting* pas très intéressant; **very much** beaucoup

vest *n* ❶ (*underclothing*) maillot de corps *m* ❷ (*US: waistcoat*) gilet *m*

vet *n* vétérinaire *mf* ▷ *She's a vet.* Elle est vétérinaire.

via *prep* en passant par ▷ *We went to Paris via Boulogne.* Nous sommes allés à Paris en passant par Boulogne.

vicar *n* pasteur *m* ▷ *He's a vicar.* Il est pasteur.

vicious *adj* ❶ brutal(e) (*mpl* brutaux) ▷ *a vicious attack* une agression brutale ❷ (*dog, person*) méchant(e); **a vicious circle** un cercle vicieux

victim *n* victime *f* ▷ *He was the victim of a mugging.* Il a été victime d'une agression.

victory *n* victoire *f*

video *vb* ❶ (*from TV*) enregistrer **[28]** ❷ (*with video camera*) filmer **[28]**
▶ *n* ❶ (*film*) vidéo *f* ▷ *to watch a video* regarder une vidéo ▷ *a video of my family on holiday* une vidéo de ma famille en vacances ❷ (*video cassette*) cassette vidéo *f* ▷ *She lent me a video.* Elle m'a prêté une cassette vidéo. ❸ (*video recorder*) magnétoscope *m*; **a video camera** une caméra vidéo; **a video game** un jeu vidéo ▷ *He likes playing video games.* Il aime les jeux vidéo.; **a video recorder** un magnétoscope; **a video shop** un vidéoclub

Vietnam *n* Viêt-Nam *m*; **in Vietnam** au Viêt-Nam

Vietnamese *adj* vietnamien (*f* vietnamienne)

view *n* ❶ vue *f* ▷ *There's an amazing view.* Il y a une vue extraordinaire. ❷ (*opinion*) avis *m* ▷ *in my view* à mon avis

viewer *n* téléspectateur *m*, téléspectatrice *f*

viewpoint *n* point de vue *m*

vile *adj* (*smell, food*) dégoûtant(e)

villa *n* villa *f*

village *n* village *m*

vine *n* vigne *f*

vinegar *n* vinaigre *m*

vineyard *n* vignoble *m*

viola *n* alto *m* ▷ *I play the viola.* Je joue de l'alto.

violence *n* violence *f*

violent *adj* violent(e)

violin *n* violon *m* ▷ *I play the violin.* Je joue du violon.

violinist *n* violoniste *mf*

virgin *n* vierge *f* ▷ *to be a virgin* être vierge

Virgo *n* Vierge *f* ▷ *I'm Virgo.* Je suis Vierge.
virtual reality *n* réalité virtuelle *f*
virus *n (also computing)* virus *m*
visa *n* visa *m*
visible *adj* visible
visit *n* ❶ *(to museum)* visite *f* ❷ *(to country)* séjour *m* ▷ *Did you enjoy your visit to France?* Ton séjour en France s'est bien passé?; **my last visit to my grandmother** la dernière fois que je suis allé voir ma grand-mère
▶ *vb* ❶ *(person)* rendre [**7**] visite à ▷ *to visit somebody* rendre visite à quelqu'un ❷ *(place)* visiter [**28**] ▷ *We'd like to visit the castle.* Nous voudrions visiter le château.
visitor *n* ❶ *(tourist)* visiteur *m*, visiteuse *f* ❷ *(guest)* invité *m*, invitée *f*; **to have a visitor** avoir [**8**] de la visite
visual *adj* visuel (*f* visuelle)
vital *adj* vital(e) (*mpl* vitaux)
vitamin *n* vitamine *f*
vivid *adj (colour)* vif (*f* vive); **to have a vivid imagination** avoir [**8**] une imagination débordante
vocabulary *n* vocabulaire *m*
vocational *adj* professionnel (*f* professionnelle); **a vocational course** un stage de formation professionnelle
vodka *n* vodka *f*
voice *n* voix *f* (*pl* voix)
voice mail *n* boîte vocale *f*
volcano *n* volcan *m*
volleyball *n* volley-ball *m* ▷ *to play volleyball* jouer au volley-ball
voluntary *adj (contribution, statement)* volontaire; **to do voluntary work** travailler [**28**] bénévolement
volunteer *n* volontaire *mf*
▶ *vb* **to volunteer to do something** se proposer [**28**] pour faire quelque chose
vomit *vb* vomir [**38**]
vote *vb* voter [**28**]
voucher *n* bon *m* ▷ *a gift voucher* un bon d'achat
vowel *n* voyelle *f*
vulgar *adj* vulgaire

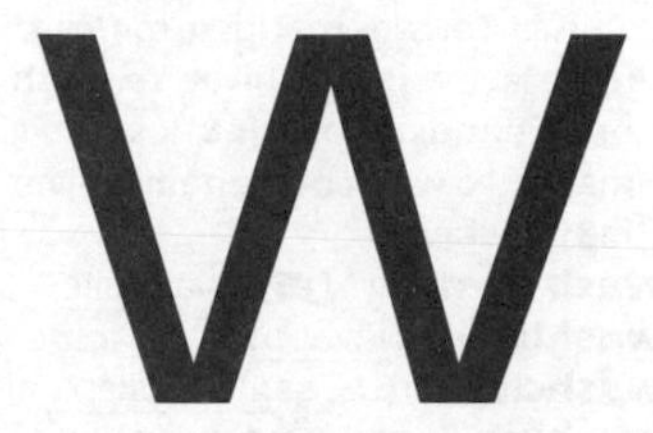

wage *n* salaire *m* ▷ *He collected his wages.* Il a retiré son salaire.

waist *n* taille *f*

waistcoat *n* gilet *m*

wait *vb* attendre [7]; **to wait for something** attendre [7] quelque chose; **to wait for somebody** attendre [7] quelqu'un ▷ *I'll wait for you.* Je t'attendrai.; **Wait for me!** Attends-moi!; **Wait a minute!** Attends!; **to keep somebody waiting** faire [36] attendre quelqu'un ▷ *They kept us waiting for hours.* Ils nous ont fait attendre pendant des heures.; **I can't wait for the holidays.** J'ai hâte d'être en vacances.; **I can't wait to see him again.** J'ai hâte de le revoir.

wait up *vb* attendre [7] pour se coucher

waiter *n* serveur *m*; **Waiter!** Excusez-moi!

waiting list *n* liste d'attente *f*

waiting room *n* salle d'attente *f*

waitress *n* serveuse *f*

wake up *vb* se réveiller [28] ▷ *I woke up at six o'clock.* Je me suis réveillé à six heures.; **to wake somebody up** réveiller [28] quelqu'un ▷ *Please would you wake me up at seven o'clock?* Pourriez-vous me réveiller à sept heures?

Wales *n* pays de Galles *m*; **in Wales** au pays de Galles; **to Wales** au pays de Galles; **I'm from Wales.** Je suis gallois.; **the Prince of Wales** le prince de Galles

walk *vb* ❶ marcher [28] ▷ *He walks fast.* Il marche vite. ❷ *(go on foot)* aller [3] à pied ▷ *We walked 10 kilometres.* Nous avons fait dix kilomètres à pied.; **to walk the dog** promener [43] le chien
▸ *n* promenade *f* ▷ *to go for a walk* faire une promenade; **It's 10 minutes' walk from here.** C'est à dix minutes d'ici à pied.

walkie-talkie *n* talkie-walkie *m*

walking *n* randonnée *f* ▷ *I did some walking in the Alps last summer.* J'ai fait de la randonnée dans les Alpes l'été dernier.

walking stick *n* canne *f*

wall *n* mur *m*

wallet *n* portefeuille *m*

wallpaper *n* ❶ papier peint *m* ❷ *(for phone, PC)* fond d'écran *m*

walnut *n* noix *f* (*pl* noix)

wander *vb* **to wander around**

flâner [**28**] ▷ *I just wandered around for a while.* J'ai flâné un peu.

want *vb* vouloir [**93**] ▷ *Do you want some cake?* Tu veux du gâteau?; **to want to do something** vouloir [**93**] faire quelque chose ▷ *I want to go to the cinema.* Je veux aller au cinéma.

war *n* guerre *f*

ward *n (room in hospital)* salle *f*

wardrobe *n (piece of furniture)* armoire *f*

warehouse *n* entrepôt *m*

warm *adj* ❶ chaud(e) ▷ *warm water* l'eau chaude; **It's warm in here.** Il fait chaud ici.; **to be warm** *(person)* avoir [**8**] chaud ▷ *I'm too warm.* J'ai trop chaud. ❷ chaleureux (*f* chaleureuse) ▷ *a warm welcome* un accueil chaleureux

warm up *vb* ❶ *(for sport)* s'échauffer [**28**] ❷ *(food)* réchauffer [**28**] ▷ *I'll warm up some lasagne for you.* Je vais te réchauffer des lasagnes.

warn *vb* prévenir [**89**] ▷ *Well, I warned you!* Je t'avais prévenu!; **to warn somebody to do something** conseiller [**28**] à quelqu'un de faire quelque chose

warning *n* avertissement *m*

wart *n* verrue *f*

was *vb see* **be**

wash *n* **to have a wash** se laver [**28**] ▷ *I had a wash.* Je me suis lavé.; **to give something a wash** laver [**28**] quelque chose ▷ *He gave the car a wash.* Il a lavé la voiture.
▶ *vb* ❶ laver [**28**] ▷ *to wash something* laver quelque chose ❷ *(have a wash)* se laver [**28**] ▷ *Every morning I get up, wash and get dressed.* Tous les matins je me lève, je me lave et je m'habille.; **to wash one's hands** se laver [**28**] les mains; **to wash one's hair** se laver [**28**] les cheveux

wash up *vb* faire [**36**] la vaisselle

washbasin *n* lavabo *m*

washcloth *n (US)* gant de toilette *m*

washing *n* linge *m* ▷ *dirty washing* du linge sale; **Have you got any washing?** Tu as du linge à laver?; **to do the washing** faire [**36**] la lessive

washing machine *n* machine à laver *f*

washing powder *n* lessive *f*

washing-up *n* **to do the washing-up** faire [**36**] la vaisselle

washing-up liquid *n* produit à vaisselle *m*

wasn't = **was not**

wasp *n* guêpe *f*

waste *n* ❶ gaspillage *m* ▷ *It's such a waste!* C'est vraiment du gaspillage!; **It's a waste of time.** C'est une perte de temps. ❷ *(rubbish)* déchets *mpl* ▷ *nuclear waste* les déchets nucléaires
▶ *vb* gaspiller [**28**] ▷ *I don't like wasting money.* Je n'aime pas gaspiller de l'argent.; **to waste time** perdre [**61**] du temps ▷ *There's no time to waste.* Il n'y a pas de temps à perdre.

wastepaper basket *n* corbeille à papier *f*

watch *n* montre *f*
▶ *vb* ❶ regarder [**28**] ▷ *to watch television* regarder la télévision ▷ *Watch me!* Regarde-moi! ❷ *(keep a watch on)* surveiller [**28**] ▷ *The police were watching the house.* La police surveillait la maison.

watch out *vb* faire [**36**] attention; **Watch out!** Attention!

water *n* eau *f*
▶ *vb* arroser [**28**] ▷ *He was watering his tulips.* Il arrosait ses tulipes.

waterfall *n* cascade *f*

watering can *n* arrosoir *m*

watermelon *n* pastèque *f*

waterproof *adj* imperméable ▷ *Is this jacket waterproof?* Ce blouson est-il imperméable?; **a waterproof watch** une montre étanche

water-skiing *n* ski nautique *m* ▷ *to go water-skiing* faire du ski nautique

wave *n* ❶ *(in water)* vague *f* ❷ *(of hand)* signe *m* ▷ *We gave him a wave.* Nous lui avons fait signe.
▶ *vb* faire [**36**] un signe de la main ▷ *to wave at somebody* faire un signe de la main à quelqu'un; **to wave goodbye** faire [**36**] au revoir de la main ▷ *I waved her goodbye.* Je lui ai fait au revoir de la main.

wax *n* cire *f*

way *n* ❶ *(manner)* façon *f* ▷ *She looked at me in a strange way.* Elle m'a regardé d'une façon étrange.; **This book tells you the right way to do it.** Ce livre explique comment il faut faire.; **You're doing it the wrong way.** Ce n'est pas comme ça qu'il faut faire.; **in a way ...** dans un sens ...; **a way of life** un mode de vie ❷ *(route)* chemin *m* ▷ *I don't know the way.* Je ne connais pas le chemin.; **on the way** en chemin ▷ *We stopped on the way.* Nous nous sommes arrêtés en chemin.; **It's a long way.** C'est loin. ▷ *Paris is a long way from London.* Paris est loin de Londres.; **Which way is it?** C'est par où?; **The supermarket is this way.** Le supermarché est par ici.; **Do you know the way to the station?** Vous savez comment aller à la gare?; **He's on his way.** Il arrive.; **'way in'** 'entrée'; **'way out'** 'sortie'; **by the way ...** au fait ...

we *pron* nous ▷ *We're staying here for a week.* Nous restons une semaine ici.

weak *adj* faible

wealthy *adj* riche

weapon *n* arme *f*

wear *vb (clothes)* porter [**28**] ▷ *She was wearing a hat.* Elle portait un chapeau.; **She was wearing black.** Elle était en noir.

weather *n* temps *m* ▷ *What was the weather like?* Quel temps a-t-il fait? ▷ *The weather was lovely.* Il a fait un temps magnifique.

weather forecast *n* météo *f*

web *n* ❶ *(spider)* toile *f* ❷ *(World Wide Web)* web *m*

web address *n* adresse web *f*

web browser *n* navigateur *m*

webcam *n* webcam *f*

website *n* site web *m*

we'd = **we had**; **we would**

wedding *n* mariage *m*; **wedding**

anniversary l'anniversaire de mariage *m*; **wedding dress** la robe de mariée

Wednesday *n* mercredi *m* ▷ *on Wednesday* mercredi ▷ *on Wednesdays* le mercredi ▷ *every Wednesday* tous les mercredis ▷ *last Wednesday* mercredi dernier ▷ *next Wednesday* mercredi prochain

weed *n* mauvaise herbe *f* ▷ *The garden's full of weeds.* Le jardin est plein de mauvaises herbes.

week *n* semaine *f* ▷ *last week* la semaine dernière ▷ *every week* toutes les semaines ▷ *next week* la semaine prochaine ▷ *in a week's time* dans une semaine; **a week on Friday** vendredi en huit

weekday *n* **on weekdays** en semaine

weekend *n* week-end *m* ▷ *at weekends* le week-end ▷ *last weekend* le week-end dernier ▷ *next weekend* le week-end prochain

weigh *vb* peser [**43**] ▷ *How much do you weigh?* Combien est-ce que tu pèses?; **to weigh oneself** se peser [**43**]

weight *n* poids *m*; **to lose weight** maigrir [**38**]; **to put on weight** grossir [**38**]

weightlifting *n* haltérophilie *f*

weird *adj* bizarre

welcome *n* accueil *m* ▷ *They gave her a warm welcome.* Ils lui ont fait un accueil chaleureux.; **Welcome!** Bienvenue! ▷ *Welcome to France!* Bienvenue en France!
▶ *vb* **to welcome somebody** accueillir [**22**] quelqu'un; **Thank you! — You're welcome!** Merci! — De rien!

well *adj, adv* ❶ bien ▷ *You did that really well.* Tu as très bien fait ça.; **to do well** réussir [**38**] bien ▷ *She's doing really well at school.* Elle réussit vraiment bien à l'école.; **to be well** *(in good health)* aller [**3**] bien ▷ *I'm not very well at the moment.* Je ne vais pas très bien en ce moment.; **get well soon!** remets-toi vite!; **well done!** bravo! ❷ enfin ▷ *It's enormous! Well, quite big anyway.* C'est énorme! Enfin, c'est assez grand.; **as well** aussi ▷ *I decided to have dessert as well.* J'ai décidé de prendre aussi un dessert. ▷ *We went to Chartres as well as Paris.* Nous sommes allés à Paris et à Chartres aussi.
▶ *n* puits *m* (*pl* puits)

we'll = **we will**

well-behaved *adj* sage

wellingtons *npl* bottes en caoutchouc *fpl*

well-known *adj* célèbre ▷ *a well-known film star* une vedette de cinéma célèbre

well-off *adj* aisé(e)

Welsh *n (language)* gallois *m*
▶ *adj* gallois(e) ▷ *She's Welsh.* Elle est galloise.; **Welsh people** les Gallois *mpl*

Welshman *n* Gallois *m*

Welshwoman *n* Galloise *f*

went *vb see* **go**

were *vb see* **be**

we're = **we are**

weren't = **were not**

west *n* ouest *m* ▷ *in the west* dans l'ouest
▶ *adj, adv* ❶ ouest ▷ *the west coast* la côte ouest; **west of** à l'ouest de ▷ *Stroud is west of Oxford.* Stroud est à l'ouest d'Oxford. ❷ vers l'ouest ▷ *We were travelling west.* Nous allions vers l'ouest.; **the West Country** le sud-ouest de l'Angleterre

westbound *adj* **The truck was westbound on the M5.** Le camion roulait sur la M5 en direction de l'ouest.; **Westbound traffic is moving very slowly.** La circulation en direction de l'ouest est très ralentie.

western *n (film)* western *m*
▶ *adj* **the western part of the island** la partie ouest de l'île; **Western Europe** l'Europe de l'Ouest

West Indian *n (person)* Antillais *m*, Antillaise *f*
▶ *adj* antillais(e) ▷ *She's West Indian.* Elle est antillaise.

West Indies *npl* Antilles *fpl*; **in the West Indies** aux Antilles

wet *adj* mouillé(e) ▷ *wet clothes* les vêtements mouillés; **to get wet** se faire [36] mouiller; **dripping wet** trempé; **wet weather** le temps pluvieux; **It was wet all week.** Il a plu toute la semaine.

wetsuit *n* combinaison de plongée *f*

we've = **we have**

whale *n* baleine *f*

what *adj, pron* ❶ *(which)* quel *(f* quelle) ▷ *What colour is it?* C'est de quelle couleur? ▷ *What's the capital of Finland?* Quelle est la capitale de la Finlande? ▷ *What a mess!* Quel fouillis! ❷ qu'est-ce que ▷ *What are you doing?* Qu'est-ce que vous faites? ▷ *What did you say?* Qu'est-ce que vous avez dit? ▷ *What is it?* Qu'est-ce que c'est? ▷ *What's the matter?* Qu'est-ce qu'il y a?
❸ qu'est-ce qui ▷ *What happened?* Qu'est-ce qui s'est passé?

> In relative phrases use **ce qui** or **ce que** depending on whether 'what' refers to the subject or the object of the sentence.

❹ *(subject)* ce qui ▷ *I saw what happened.* J'ai vu ce qui est arrivé.; *(object)* ce que ▷ *Tell me what you did.* Dites-moi ce que vous avez fait.; **What?** *(what did you say)* Comment?

wheat *n* blé *m*

wheel *n* roue *f*; **the steering wheel** le volant

wheelchair *n* fauteuil roulant *m*

when *adv, conj* quand ▷ *When did he go?* Quand est-ce qu'il est parti? ▷ *She was reading when I came in.* Elle lisait quand je suis entré.

where *adv, conj* où ▷ *Where's Emma today?* Où est Emma aujourd'hui? ▷ *Where do you live?* Où habites-tu?

whether *conj* si ▷ *I don't know whether to go or not.* Je ne sais pas si je dois y aller ou non.

which *adj, pron* ❶ quel *(f* quelle) ▷ *Which flavour do you want?* Quel parfum est-ce que tu veux?

> When asking 'which one' use **lequel** or **laquelle**, depending on whether the noun is masculine or feminine.

I know his brother. — Which one? Je connais son frère. — Lequel?; **I know his sister. — Which one?** Je connais sa sœur. — Laquelle?; **Which would you like?** Lequel est-ce que vous voulez?; **Which of these are yours?** Lesquels sont à vous?

> In relative phrases use **qui** or **que** depending on whether 'which' refers to the subject or the object of the sentence.

❷ *(subject)* qui ▷ *the CD which is playing now* le CD qui passe maintenant; *(object)* que ▷ *the CD which I bought yesterday* le CD que j'ai acheté hier

while *conj* ❶ pendant que ▷ *You hold the torch while I look inside.* Tiens la lampe électrique pendant que je regarde à l'intérieur. ❷ alors que ▷ *Isobel is very dynamic, while Kay is more laid-back.* Isobel est très dynamique, alors que Kay est plus relax.
▶ *n* moment *m* ▷ *after a while* au bout d'un moment; **a while ago** il y a un moment ▷ *He was here a while ago.* Il était là il y a un moment.; **for a while** pendant quelque temps ▷ *I lived in London for a while.* J'ai vécu à Londres pendant quelque temps.; **quite a while** longtemps ▷ *quite a while ago* il y a longtemps

whip *n* fouet *m*
▶ *vb* ❶ *(person, animal)* fouetter **[28]** ❷ *(eggs)* battre **[9]**

whipped cream *n* crème fouettée *f*

whiskers *npl* moustaches *fpl*

whisky *n* whisky *m* (*pl* whiskies)

whisper *vb* chuchoter **[28]**

whistle *n* sifflet *m*; **The referee blew his whistle.** L'arbitre a sifflé.
▶ *vb* siffler **[28]**

white *adj* blanc (*f* blanche) ▷ *He's got white hair.* Il a les cheveux blancs.; **white wine** le vin blanc; **white bread** le pain blanc; **white coffee** le café au lait; **a white man** un Blanc; **a white woman** une Blanche; **white people** les Blancs

whiteboard *n* tableau blanc *m*

Whitsun *n* Pentecôte *f*

who *pron* ❶ qui ▷ *Who said that?* Qui a dit ça?

> In relative phrases use **qui** or **que** depending on whether 'who' refers to the subject or the object of the verb.

❷ *(subject)* qui ▷ *the man who saw us* l'homme qui nous a vus; *(object)* que ▷ *the man who we saw* l'homme que nous avons vu

whole *adj* tout(e) ▷ *the whole class* toute la classe ▷ *the whole afternoon* tout l'après-midi; **a whole box of chocolates** toute une boîte de chocolats; **the whole world** le monde entier
▶ *n* **The whole of Wales was affected.** Le pays de Galles tout entier a été touché.; **on the whole** dans l'ensemble

wholemeal *adj* complet (*f* complète); **wholemeal bread** le pain complet

wholewheat *adj (US)* complet (*f* complète)

whom *pron* qui ▷ *Whom did you see?* Qui avez-vous vu? ▷ *the man to whom I spoke* l'homme à qui j'ai parlé

whose *pron, adj* ❶ à qui ▷ *Whose is this?* À qui est-ce? ▷ *I know whose it is.* Je sais à qui c'est. ❷ *(after noun)* dont ▷ *the girl whose picture was in the paper* la jeune fille dont la photo était dans le journal

why *adv* pourquoi ▷ *Why did you do that?* Pourquoi avez-vous fait ça? ▷ *That's why he did it.* Voilà pourquoi il a fait ça. ▷ *Tell me why.* Dis-moi pourquoi.; **I've never been to France. — Why not?** Je ne suis jamais allé en France. — Pourquoi?; **All right, why not?** D'accord, pourquoi pas?

wicked *adj* ❶ *(evil)* méchant(e) ❷ *(really great)* génial(e) (*mpl* géniaux)

wide *adj, adv* large ▷ *a wide road* une route large; **wide open** grand ouvert ▷ *The door was wide open.* La porte était grande ouverte.; **wide awake** complètement réveillé

widow *n* veuve *f* ▷ *She's a widow.* Elle est veuve.

widower *n* veuf *m* ▷ *He's a widower.* Il est veuf.

width *n* largeur *f*

wife *n* femme *f* ▷ *She's his wife.* C'est sa femme.

Wi-Fi *n* wifi *m*

wig *n* perruque *f*

wild *adj* ❶ *(not tame)* sauvage ▷ *a wild animal* un animal sauvage ❷ *(crazy)* fou (*f* folle) ▷ *She's a bit wild.* Elle est un peu folle.

wildlife *n* nature *f* ▷ *I'm interested in wildlife.* Je m'intéresse à la nature.

will *n* testament *m* ▷ *He left me some money in his will.* Il m'a laissé de l'argent dans son testament.
▸ *vb* **I'll show you your room.** Je vais te montrer ta chambre.; **I'll give you a hand.** Je vais t'aider.

> Use the French future tense when referring to the more distant future.

I will finish it tomorrow. Je le finirai demain.; **It won't take long.** Ça ne prendra pas longtemps.; **Will you wash up? — No, I won't.** Est-ce que tu peux faire la vaisselle? — Non.; **Will you help me?** Est-ce que tu peux m'aider?; **Will you be quiet!** Voulez-vous bien vous taire!; **That will be the postman.** Ça doit être le facteur.

willing *adj* **to be willing to do something** être [**35**] prêt à faire quelque chose

win *vb* gagner [**28**] ▷ *Did you win?* Est-ce que tu as gagné?; **to win a prize** remporter [**28**] un prix
▸ *n* victoire *f*

wind *vb* ❶ *(rope, wool, wire)* enrouler [**28**] ❷ *(river, path)* serpenter [**28**] ▷ *The road winds through the valley.* La route serpente à travers la vallée.

▸ *n* vent *m* ▹ *There was a strong wind.* Il y avait beaucoup de vent.; **a wind instrument** un instrument à vent; **wind power** l'énergie éolienne *f*

window *n* ❶ *(of building)* fenêtre *f* ❷ *(in car, train)* vitre *f*; **a shop window** une vitrine ❸ *(window pane)* carreau *m* (*pl* carreaux) ▹ *to break a window* casser un carreau ▹ *a broken window* un carreau cassé

windscreen *n* pare-brise *m* (*pl* pare-brise)

windscreen wiper *n* essuie-glace *m* (*pl* essuie-glace)

windshield *n (US)* pare-brise *m* (*pl* pare-brise)

windshield wiper *n (US)* essuie-glace *m* (*pl* essuie-glace)

windy *adj (place)* venteux (*f* venteuse); **It's windy.** Il y a du vent.

wine *n* vin *m* ▹ *a bottle of wine* une bouteille de vin ▹ *a glass of wine* un verre de vin; **white wine** le vin blanc; **red wine** le vin rouge; **a wine bar** un bar à vin; **a wine glass** un verre à vin; **the wine list** la carte des vins

wing *n* aile *f*

wink *vb* **to wink at somebody** faire [**36**] un clin d'œil à quelqu'un ▹ *He winked at me.* Il m'a fait un clin d'œil.

winner *n* gagnant *m*, gagnante *f*

winning *adj* **the winning team** l'équipe gagnante; **the winning goal** le but décisif

winter *n* hiver *m*; **in winter** en hiver

wipe *vb* essuyer [**53**]; **to wipe one's feet** s'essuyer [**53**] les pieds ▹ *Wipe your feet!* Essuie-toi les pieds!

wipe up *vb* essuyer [**53**]

wire *n* fil de fer *m*

wisdom tooth *n* dent de sagesse *f*

wise *adj* sage

wish *vb* **to wish for something** souhaiter [**28**] quelque chose ▹ *What more could you wish for?* Que pourrais-tu souhaiter de plus?; **to wish to do something** désirer [**28**] faire quelque chose ▹ *I wish to make a complaint.* Je désire porter plainte.; **I wish you were here!** Si seulement tu étais ici!; **I wish you'd told me!** Si seulement tu m'en avais parlé!

▸ *n* vœu *m* (*pl* vœux) ▹ *to make a wish* faire un vœu; **'best wishes'** *(on greetings card)* 'meilleurs vœux'; **'with best wishes, Kathy'** 'bien amicalement, Kathy'

wit *n (humour)* esprit *m*

with *prep* ❶ avec ▹ *Come with me.* Venez avec moi. ▹ *He walks with a stick.* Il marche avec une canne.; **a woman with blue eyes** une femme aux yeux bleus ❷ *(at the home of)* chez ▹ *We stayed with friends.* Nous avons logé chez des amis. ❸ de ▹ *green with envy* vert de jalousie ▹ *to shake with fear* trembler de peur ▹ *Fill the jug with water.* Remplis la carafe d'eau.

without *prep* sans ▹ *without a coat* sans manteau ▹ *without speaking* sans parler

witness *n* témoin *m* ▹ *There were no*

witnesses. Il n'y avait pas de témoins.

witty *adj* spirituel (*f* spirituelle)

wives *npl see* **wife**

woke up, woken up *vb see* **wake up**

wolf *n* loup *m*

woman *n* femme *f* ▷ *a woman doctor* une femme médecin

won *vb see* **win**

wonder *vb* se demander [**28**] ▷ *I wonder why she said that.* Je me demande pourquoi elle a dit ça. ▷ *I wonder what that means.* Je me demande ce que ça veut dire. ▷ *I wonder where Caroline is.* Je me demande où est Caroline.

wonderful *adj* formidable

won't = **will not**

wood *n (timber, forest)* bois *m* ▷ *It's made of wood.* C'est en bois. ▷ *We went for a walk in the wood.* Nous sommes allés nous promener dans le bois.

wooden *adj* en bois ▷ *a wooden chair* une chaise en bois

woodwork *n* menuiserie *f* ▷ *My hobby is woodwork.* Je fais de la menuiserie.

wool *n* laine *f* ▷ *It's made of wool.* C'est en laine.

word *n* mot *m* ▷ *a difficult word* un mot difficile; **What's the word for 'shop' in French?** Comment dit-on 'shop' en français?; **in other words** en d'autres termes; **to have a word with somebody** parler [**28**] avec quelqu'un; **the words** *(lyrics)* les paroles *fpl* ▷ *I really like the words of this song.* J'adore les paroles de cette chanson.

word processing *n* traitement de texte *m*

word processor *n* machine de traitement de texte *f*

wore *vb see* **wear**

work *n* travail *m (pl* travaux) ▷ *She's looking for work.* Elle cherche du travail. ▷ *He's at work at the moment.* Il est au travail en ce moment.; **It's hard work.** C'est dur.; **to be off work** *(sick)* être [**35**] malade ▷ *He's been off work for a week.* Il est malade depuis une semaine.; **He's out of work.** Il est sans emploi. ▶ *vb* ❶ *(person)* travailler [**28**] ▷ *She works in a shop.* Elle travaille dans un magasin. ▷ *to work hard* travailler dur ❷ *(machine, plan)* marcher [**28**] ▷ *The heating isn't working.* Le chauffage ne marche pas. ▷ *My plan worked perfectly.* Mon plan a marché impeccablement.

work out *vb* ❶ *(exercise)* faire [**36**] de l'exercice ▷ *I work out twice a week.* Je fais de l'exercice deux fois par semaine. ❷ *(turn out)* marcher [**28**] ▷ *In the end it worked out really well.* Au bout du compte, ça a très bien marché. ❸ *(figure out)* arriver [**5**] à comprendre ▷ *I just couldn't work it out.* Je n'arrivais pas du tout à comprendre.; **It works out at £10 each.** Ça fait dix livres chacun.

worker *n (in factory)* ouvrier *m*, ouvrière *f*; **He's a factory worker.** Il est ouvrier.; **She's a good worker.** Elle travaille bien.

work experience *n* stage *m* ▷ *I'm going to do work experience in a factory.* Je vais faire un stage dans une usine.

working-class *adj* ouvrier (*f* ouvrière) ▷ *a working-class family* une famille ouvrière

workman *n* ouvrier *m*

worksheet *n* feuille d'exercices *f*

workshop *n* atelier *m* ▷ *a drama workshop* un atelier de théâtre

workspace *n (computing)* espace de travail *m*

workstation *n* poste de travail *m*

world *n* monde *m*; **He's the world champion.** Il est champion du monde.

worm *n* ver *m*

worn *vb see* **wear**

▸ *adj* usé(e) ▷ *The carpet is a bit worn.* La moquette est un peu usée.; **worn out** *(tired)* épuisé(e)

worried *adj* inquiet (*f* inquiète) ▷ *She's very worried.* Elle est très inquiète.; **to be worried about something** s'inquiéter [**34**] pour quelque chose ▷ *I'm worried about the exams.* Je m'inquiète pour les examens.; **to look worried** avoir [**8**] l'air inquiet ▷ *She looks a bit worried.* Elle a l'air un peu inquiète.

worry *vb* s'inquiéter [**34**]; **Don't worry!** Ne t'inquiète pas!

worse *adj, adv* ❶ pire ▷ *It was even worse than that.* C'était encore pire que ça. ❷ plus mal ▷ *I'm feeling worse.* Je me sens plus mal.

worst *adj* **the worst** le plus mauvais ▷ *He got the worst mark in the whole class.* Il a eu la plus mauvaise note de toute la classe.; **my worst enemy** mon pire ennemi; **Maths is my worst subject.** Je suis vraiment nul en maths.

▸ *n* pire *m* ▷ *The worst of it is that ...* Le pire c'est que ...; **at worst** au pire; **if the worst comes to the worst** au pire

worth *adj* **to be worth** valoir [**87**] ▷ *It's worth a lot of money.* Ça vaut très cher. ▷ *How much is it worth?* Ça vaut combien?; **It's worth it.** Ça vaut la peine. ▷ *Is it worth it?* Est-ce que ça vaut la peine? ▷ *It's not worth it.* Ça ne vaut pas la peine.

would *vb* **Would you like a biscuit?** Vous voulez un biscuit?; **Would you like to go and see a film?** Est-ce que tu veux aller voir un film?; **Would you close the door please?** Vous pouvez fermer la porte, s'il vous plaît?; **I'd like ...** J'aimerais ... ▷ *I'd like to go to America.* J'aimerais aller en Amérique.; **I said I would do it.** J'ai dit que je le ferais.; **If you asked him he'd do it.** Si vous le lui demandiez, il le ferait.; **If you had asked him he would have done it.** Si vous le lui aviez demandé, il l'aurait fait.

wouldn't = **would not**

wound *n* blessure *f*

▸ *vb* blesser [**28**] ▷ *He was wounded in the leg.* Il a été blessé à la jambe.

wrap *vb* emballer [**28**] ▷ *She's wrapping her Christmas presents.* Elle est en train d'emballer ses cadeaux de Noël.; **Can you wrap it for me please?** *(in shop)* Vous pouvez me faire un papier cadeau, s'il vous plaît?

wrap up *vb* emballer [**28**]

wrapping paper *n* papier cadeau *m*

wreck *n* ❶ *(vehicle, machine)* tas de ferraille *m* ▷ *That car is a wreck!* Cette voiture est un tas de ferraille! ❷ *(person)* loque *f* ▷ *After the exams I was a complete wreck.* Après les examens j'étais une véritable loque.
▶ *vb* ❶ *(building, vehicle)* démolir [**38**] ▷ *The explosion wrecked the whole house.* L'explosion a démoli toute la maison. ❷ *(plan, holiday)* ruiner [**28**] ▷ *The trip was wrecked by bad weather.* Le voyage a été ruiné par le mauvais temps.

wrestler *n* lutteur *m*, lutteuse *f*

wrestling *n* lutte *f*

wrinkled *adj* ridé(e)

wrist *n* poignet *m*

write *vb* écrire [**30**] ▷ *to write a letter* écrire une lettre; **to write to somebody** écrire [**30**] à quelqu'un ▷ *I'm going to write to her in French.* Je vais lui écrire en français.

write down *vb* noter [**28**] ▷ *I wrote down the address.* J'ai noté l'adresse.; **Can you write it down for me, please?** Vous pouvez me l'écrire, s'il vous plaît?

writer *n* écrivain *m* ▷ *She's a writer.* Elle est écrivain.

writing *n* écriture *f* ▷ *I can't read your writing.* Je n'arrive pas à lire ton écriture.; **in writing** par écrit

written *vb see* **write**

wrong *adj, adv* ❶ *(incorrect)* faux *(f* fausse) ▷ *The information they gave us was wrong.* Les renseignements qu'ils nous ont donnés étaient faux.; **the wrong answer** la mauvaise réponse; **You've got the wrong number.** Vous vous êtes trompé de numéro. ❷ *(morally bad)* mal ▷ *I think hunting is wrong.* Je trouve que c'est mal de chasser.; **to be wrong** *(mistaken)* se tromper [**28**] ▷ *You're wrong about that.* Tu te trompes.; **to do something wrong** se tromper [**28**] ▷ *You've done it wrong.* Tu t'es trompé.; **to go wrong** *(plan)* mal tourner [**28**] ▷ *The robbery went wrong and they got caught.* Le cambriolage a mal tourné et ils ont été pris.; **What's wrong?** Qu'est-ce qu'il y a?; **What's wrong with her?** Qu'est-ce qu'elle a?

wrote *vb see* **write**

WWW *n (= World Wide Web)* Web *m*

Xmas *n* (= *Christmas*) Noël

X-ray *vb* **to X-ray something** faire [**36**] une radio de quelque chose ▷ *They X-rayed my arm.* Ils ont fait une radio de mon bras.
▶ *n* radio *f* ▷ *to have an X-ray* passer une radio

yacht *n* ❶ *(sailing boat)* voilier *m* ❷ *(luxury motorboat)* yacht *m*

yawn *vb* bâiller [**28**]

year *n* an *m* ▷ *last year* l'an dernier ▷ *next year* l'an prochain; **to be 15 years old** avoir [**8**] quinze ans; **an eight-year-old child** un enfant de huit ans

In French secondary schools, years are counted from the **sixième** (youngest) to **première** and **terminale** (oldest).

▷ *year 7* la sixième ▷ *year 8* la cinquième ▷ *year 9* la quatrième ▷ *year 10* la troisième ▷ *year 11* la seconde; **She's in year 11.** Elle est en seconde.; **He's a first-year.** Il est en sixième.

yell *vb* hurler [**28**]

yellow *adj* jaune

yes *adv* ❶ oui ▷ *Do you like it? — Yes.* Tu aimes ça? — Oui.; **Would you like a cup of tea? — Yes please.** Voulez-vous une tasse de thé? — Je veux bien. ❷ si

Use **si** when answering negative questions.

▷ *Don't you like it? — Yes!* Tu n'aimes pas ça? — Si! ▷ *You're not Swiss, are you? — Yes I am!* Tu n'es pas suisse, si? — Si!

yesterday *adv* hier ▷ *yesterday morning* hier matin ▷ *yesterday afternoon* hier après-midi ▷ *yesterday evening* hier soir ▷ *all day yesterday* toute la journée d'hier

yet *adv* encore; **not yet** pas encore ▷ *It's not finished yet.* Ce n'est pas encore fini.; **not as yet** pas encore ▷ *There's no news as yet.* Nous n'avons pas encore de nouvelles.; **Have you finished yet?** Vous avez fini?

yoghurt *n* yaourt *m*

yolk *n* jaune d'œuf *m*

you *pron*

Only use **tu** when speaking to one person of your own age or younger. If in doubt use **vous**.

❶ *(polite form or plural)* vous ▷ *Do you like football?* Est-ce que vous aimez le football? ▷ *Can I help you?* Est-ce que je peux vous aider? ▷ *It's for you.* C'est pour vous. ❷ *(familiar singular)* tu ▷ *Do you like football?* Tu aimes le football?

vous never changes, but **tu** has different forms. When 'you' is the object of the sentence use **te** not **tu**. **te** becomes **t'** before a vowel sound.

❸ te ▷ *I know you.* Je te connais. t' ▷ *I saw you.* Je t'ai vu. ❹ toi

toi is used instead of **tu** after a preposition and in comparisons.

▷ *It's for you.* C'est pour toi. ▷ *She's younger than you.* Elle est plus jeune que toi.

young *adj* jeune; **young people** les jeunes

younger *adj* plus jeune ▷ *He's younger than me.* Il est plus jeune que moi.; **my younger brother** mon frère cadet; **my younger sister** ma sœur cadette

youngest *adj* plus jeune ▷ *my youngest brother* mon plus jeune frère ▷ *She's the youngest.* C'est la plus jeune.

your *adj*

Only use **ton/ta/tes** when speaking to one person of your own age or younger. If in doubt use **votre/vos**.

❶ *(polite form or plural)* votre ▷ *your house* votre maison
vos *pl* ▷ *your seats* vos places
❷ *(familiar singular)* ton *m* ▷ *your brother* ton frère
ta *f* ▷ *your sister* ta sœur
tes *pl* ▷ *your parents* tes parents

ta becomes **ton** before a vowel sound

your friend (1) *(male)* ton ami **(2)** *(female)* ton amie

Do not use **votre/vos** or **ton/ta/tes** with parts of the body.

a b c d e f g h i j k l m n o p q r s t u v w x y z

▷ *Would you like to wash your hands?* Est-ce que vous voulez vous laver les mains?

yours *pron*

> Only use **le tien/la tienne/les tiens/les tiennes** when talking to one person of your own age or younger. If in doubt use **le vôtre/la vôtre/les vôtres**. The same applies to **à toi** and **à vous**.

❶ le vôtre ▷ *I've lost my pen. Can I use yours?* J'ai perdu mon stylo. Je peux utiliser le vôtre?
la vôtre ▷ *I like that car. Is it yours?* J'aime cette voiture-là. C'est la vôtre?
les vôtres ▷ *my parents and yours* mes parents et les vôtres; **Is this yours?** C'est à vous? ▷ *This book is yours.* Ce livre est à vous. ▷ *Whose is this? — It's yours.* C'est à qui? — À vous.; **Yours sincerely ...** Veuillez agréer l'expression de mes sentiments les meilleurs ... ❷ le tien ▷ *I've lost my pen. Can I use yours?* J'ai perdu mon stylo. Je peux utiliser le tien?
la tienne ▷ *I like that car. Is it yours?* J'aime cette voiture-là. C'est la tienne?
les tiens ▷ *my parents and yours* mes parents et les tiens
les tiennes ▷ *My hands are dirty, yours are clean.* Mes mains sont sales, les tiennes sont propres.; **Is this yours?** C'est à toi? ▷ *This book is yours.* Ce livre est à toi. ▷ *Whose is this? — It's yours.* C'est à qui? — À toi.

yourself *pron*

> Only use **te** when talking to one person of your own age or younger; use **vous** to everyone else. If in doubt use **vous**.

❶ *(polite form)* vous ▷ *Have you hurt yourself?* Est-ce que vous vous êtes fait mal? ▷ *Tell me about yourself!* Parlez-moi de vous! ❷ *(familiar form)* te ▷ *Have you hurt yourself?* Est-ce que tu t'es fait mal?
❸ *(familiar form)* toi

> After a preposition, use **toi** instead of **te**.

▷ *Tell me about yourself!* Parle-moi de toi! ❹ toi-même ▷ *Do it yourself!* Fais-le toi-même! ❺ vous-même ▷ *Do it yourself!* Faites-le vous-même!

yourselves *pron* ❶ vous ▷ *Did you enjoy yourselves?* Vous vous êtes bien amusés? ❷ vous-mêmes ▷ *Did you make it yourselves?* Vous l'avez fait vous-mêmes?

youth club *n* centre de loisirs *m*

youth hostel *n* auberge de jeunesse *f*

Yugoslavia *n* Yougoslavie *f*; **in the former Yugoslavia** en ex-Yougoslavie

Z

zany *adj* loufoque
zebra *n* zèbre *m*
zebra crossing *n* passage clouté *m*
zero *n* zéro *m*
zip *n* fermeture éclair® *f* (*pl* fermetures éclair®)
zip code *n (US)* code postal *m*
zipper *n (US)* fermeture éclair® *f* (*pl* fermetures éclair®)
zodiac *n* zodiaque *m* ▷ *the signs of the zodiac* les signes du zodiaque
zone *n* zone *f*
zoo *n* zoo *m*
zoom lens *n* zoom *m*
zucchini *n (US)* courgette *f*

VERB TABLES

Introduction

The verb tables in the following section contain 93 tables of French verbs (some regular and some irregular) in alphabetical order. Each table shows you the following form:

Present	*eg* je fais = **I do** *or* **I'm doing**
Present Subjunctive	*eg* je fasse = **I do**
Perfect	*eg* j'ai fait = **I did** *or* **I have done**
Imperfect	*eg* je faisais = **I was doing** *or* **I did**
Future	*eg* je ferai = **I will do**
Conditional	*eg* je ferais = **I would do**
Imperative	*eg* fais = **do**
Past Participle	*eg* fait = **done**
Present Participle	*eg* faisant = **doing**

On the both sides of the dictionary, all the French verbs are followed by a number (eg: **donner** [**28**] *vb* to give). This number corresponds to a page number in the Verb Tables. All the French verbs in this dictionary follow the pattern of one of these 93 verbs (eg: '**aimer** [**28**] vb **to love**' follows the same pattern as **donner**, shown on page **28**).

In order to help you use the verbs shown in the Verb Tables correctly, there are also a number of example phrases at the bottom of each page to show the verb as it is used in context.

Remember:

je/j'	=	I
tu	=	you (*to one person you know well*)
il	=	he/it
elle	=	she/it
on	=	we/one
nous	=	we
vous	=	you (*polite form or plural*)
ils/elles	=	they

to buy acheter

PRESENT

j'	achète
tu	achètes
il/elle/on	achète
nous	achetons
vous	achetez
ils/elles	achètent

PRESENT SUBJUNCTIVE

j'	achète
tu	achètes
il/elle/on	achète
nous	achetions
vous	achetiez
ils/elles	achètent

PERFECT

j'	ai acheté
tu	as acheté
il/elle/on	a acheté
nous	avons acheté
vous	avez acheté
ils/elles	ont acheté

IMPERFECT

j'	achetais
tu	achetais
il/elle/on	achetait
nous	achetions
vous	achetiez
ils/elles	achetaient

FUTURE

j'	achèterai
tu	achèteras
il/elle/on	achètera
nous	achèterons
vous	achèterez
ils/elles	achèteront

CONDITIONAL

j'	achèterais
tu	achèterais
il/elle/on	achèterait
nous	achèterions
vous	achèteriez
ils/elles	achèteraient

IMPERATIVE

achète / achetons / achetez

PAST PARTICIPLE

acheté

PRESENT PARTICIPLE

achetant

EXAMPLE PHRASES

J'ai acheté des gâteaux à la pâtisserie.	*I bought some cakes at the cake shop.*
Qu'est-ce que tu lui **as acheté** pour son anniversaire?	*What did you buy him for his birthday?*
Je **n'achète** jamais de chips.	*I never buy crisps.*

acquérir *to acquire*

PRESENT		PRESENT SUBJUNCTIVE	
j'	acquiers	j'	acquière
tu	acquiers	tu	acquières
il/elle/on	acquiert	il/elle/on	acquière
nous	acquérons	nous	acquérions
vous	acquérez	vous	acquériez
ils/elles	acquièrent	ils/elles	acquièrent

PERFECT		IMPERFECT	
j'	ai acquis	j'	acquérais
tu	as acquis	tu	acquérais
il/elle/on	a acquis	il/elle/on	acquérait
nous	avons acquis	nous	acquérions
vous	avez acquis	vous	acquériez
ils/elles	ont acquis	ils/elles	acquéraient

FUTURE		CONDITIONAL	
j'	acquerrai	j'	acquerrais
tu	acquerras	tu	acquerrais
il/elle/on	acquerra	il/elle/on	acquerrait
nous	acquerrons	nous	acquerrions
vous	acquerrez	vous	acquerriez
ils/elles	acquerront	ils/elles	acquerraient

IMPERATIVE
acquiers / acquérons / acquérez

PAST PARTICIPLE
acquis

PRESENT PARTICIPLE
acquérant

EXAMPLE PHRASES

Elle **a acquis** la nationalité française en 2013.	*She acquired French nationality in 2013.*

to go **aller**

PRESENT

je	vais
tu	vas
il/elle/on	va
nous	allons
vous	allez
ils/elles	vont

PRESENT SUBJUNCTIVE

j'	aille
tu	ailles
il/elle/on	aille
nous	allions
vous	alliez
ils/elles	aillent

PERFECT

je	suis allé(e)
tu	es allé(e)
il/elle/on	est allé(e)
nous	sommes allé(e)s
vous	êtes allé(e)(s)
ils/elles	sont allé(e)s

IMPERFECT

j'	allais
tu	allais
il/elle/on	allait
nous	allions
vous	alliez
ils/elles	allaient

FUTURE

j'	irai
tu	iras
il/elle/on	ira
nous	irons
vous	irez
ils/elles	iront

CONDITIONAL

j'	irais
tu	irais
il/elle/on	irait
nous	irions
vous	iriez
ils/elles	iraient

IMPERATIVE

va / allons / allez

PAST PARTICIPLE

allé

PRESENT PARTICIPLE

allant

EXAMPLE PHRASES

Vous **allez** au cinéma?	*Are you going to the cinema?*
Je **suis allé** à Londres.	*I went to London.*
Est-ce que tu **es** déjà **allé** en Allemagne?	*Have you ever been to Germany?*

Table 4

appeler *to call*

PRESENT

j'	appelle
tu	appelles
il/elle/on	appelle
nous	appelons
vous	appelez
ils/elles	appellent

PRESENT SUBJUNCTIVE

j'	appelle
tu	appelles
il/elle/on	appelle
nous	appelions
vous	appeliez
ils/elles	appellent

PERFECT

j'	ai appelé
tu	as appelé
il/elle/on	a appelé
nous	avons appelé
vous	avez appelé
ils/elles	ont appelé

IMPERFECT

j'	appelais
tu	appelais
il/elle/on	appelait
nous	appelions
vous	appeliez
ils/elles	appelaient

FUTURE

j'	appellerai
tu	appelleras
il/elle/on	appellera
nous	appellerons
vous	appellerez
ils/elles	appelleront

CONDITIONAL

j'	appellerais
tu	appellerais
il/elle/on	appellerait
nous	appellerions
vous	appelleriez
ils/elles	appelleraient

IMPERATIVE

appelle / appelons / appelez

PAST PARTICIPLE

appelé

PRESENT PARTICIPLE

appelant

EXAMPLE PHRASES

Elle **a appelé** le médecin.	*She called the doctor.*
J'**ai appelé** Richard à Londres.	*I called Richard in London.*
Comment tu **t'appelles**?	*What's your name?*

- *Note that **s'appeler** follows the same pattern, but takes **être** in the perfect tense. For an example of a reflexive verb in full, see verb table **6 s'asseoir**.*

to arrive **arriver**

PRESENT

j'	arrive
tu	arrives
il/elle/on	arrive
nous	arrivons
vous	arrivez
ils/elles	arrivent

PRESENT SUBJUNCTIVE

j'	arrive
tu	arrives
il/elle/on	arrive
nous	arrivions
vous	arriviez
ils/elles	arrivent

PERFECT

je	suis arrivé(e)
tu	es arrivé(e)
il/elle/on	est arrivé(e)
nous	sommes arrivé(e)s
vous	êtes arrivé(e)(s)
ils/elles	sont arrivé(e)s

IMPERFECT

j'	arrivais
tu	arrivais
il/elle/on	arrivait
nous	arrivions
vous	arriviez
ils/elles	arrivaient

FUTURE

j'	arriverai
tu	arriveras
il/elle/on	arrivera
nous	arriverons
vous	arriverez
ils/elles	arriveront

CONDITIONAL

j'	arriverais
tu	arriverais
il/elle/on	arriverait
nous	arriverions
vous	arriveriez
ils/elles	arriveraient

IMPERATIVE

arrive / arrivons / arrivez

PAST PARTICIPLE

arrivé

PRESENT PARTICIPLE

arrivant

EXAMPLE PHRASES

J'**arrive** à l'école à huit heures. — *I arrive at school at 8 o'clock.*
Le prof n'**est** pas encore **arrivé**. — *The teacher hasn't arrived yet.*
Qu'est-ce qui **est arrivé** à Aurélie? — *What happened to Aurélie?*

s'asseoir *to sit down*

PRESENT

je	m'assieds/m'assois
tu	t'assieds/t'assois
il/elle/on	s'assied/s'assoit
nous	nous asseyons/nous assoyons
vous	vous asseyez/vous assoyez
ils/elles	s'asseyent/s'assoient

PRESENT SUBJUNCTIVE

je	m'asseye
tu	t'asseyes
il/elle/on	s'asseye
nous	nous asseyions
vous	vous asseyiez
ils/elles	s'asseyent

PERFECT

je	me suis assis(e)
tu	t'es assis(e)
il/elle/on	s'est assis(e)
nous	nous sommes assis(es)
vous	vous êtes assis(e(s))
ils/elles	se sont assis(es)

IMPERFECT

je	m'asseyais
tu	t'asseyais
il/elle/on	s'asseyait
nous	nous asseyions
vous	vous asseyiez
ils/elles	s'asseyaient

FUTURE

je	m'assiérai
tu	t'assiéras
il/elle/on	s'assiéra
nous	nous assiérons
vous	vous assiérez
ils/elles	s'assiéront

CONDITIONAL

je	m'assiérais
tu	t'assiérais
il/elle/on	s'assiérait
nous	nous assiérions
vous	vous assiériez
ils/elles	s'assiéraient

IMPERATIVE

assieds-toi / asseyons-nous / asseyez-vous

PAST PARTICIPLE

assis

PRESENT PARTICIPLE

s'asseyant

EXAMPLE PHRASES

Assieds-toi, Nicole.	*Sit down Nicole.*
Asseyez-vous, les enfants.	*Sit down children.*
Je peux **m'asseoir**?	*May I sit down?*
Je **me suis assise** sur un chewing-gum!	*I've sat on some chewing gum!*

to wait **attendre**

PRESENT

j'	attends
tu	attends
il/elle/on	attend
nous	attendons
vous	attendez
ils/elles	attendent

PRESENT SUBJUNCTIVE

j'	attende
tu	attendes
il/elle/on	attende
nous	attendions
vous	attendiez
ils/elles	attendent

PERFECT

j'	ai attendu
tu	as attendu
il/elle/on	a attendu
nous	avons attendu
vous	avez attendu
ils/elles	ont attendu

IMPERFECT

j'	attendais
tu	attendais
il/elle/on	attendait
nous	attendions
vous	attendiez
ils/elles	attendaient

FUTURE

j'	attendrai
tu	attendras
il/elle/on	attendra
nous	attendrons
vous	attendrez
ils/elles	attendront

CONDITIONAL

j'	attendrais
tu	attendrais
il/elle/on	attendrait
nous	attendrions
vous	attendriez
ils/elles	attendraient

IMPERATIVE

attends / attendons / attendez

PAST PARTICIPLE

attendu

PRESENT PARTICIPLE

attendant

EXAMPLE PHRASES

Attends-moi!	*Wait for me!*
Tu **attends** depuis longtemps?	*Have you been waiting long?*
Je l'**ai attendu** à la poste.	*I waited for him at the post office.*
Je **m'attends** à ce qu'il soit en retard.	*I expect he'll be late.*

- *Note that **s'attendre** follows the same pattern, but take **être** in the perfect tense. For an example of a reflexive verb in full, see verb table **6 s'asseoir**.*

Table 8

avoir *to have*

PRESENT

j'	ai
tu	as
il/elle/on	a
nous	avons
vous	avez
ils/elles	ont

PRESENT SUBJUNCTIVE

j'	aie
tu	aies
il/elle/on	ait
nous	ayons
vous	ayez
ils/elles	aient

PERFECT

j'	ai eu
tu	as eu
il/elle/on	a eu
nous	avons eu
vous	avez eu
ils/elles	ont eu

IMPERFECT

j'	avais
tu	avais
il/elle/on	avait
nous	avions
vous	aviez
ils/elles	avaient

FUTURE

j'	aurai
tu	auras
il/elle/on	aura
nous	aurons
vous	aurez
ils/elles	auront

CONDITIONAL

j'	aurais
tu	aurais
il/elle/on	aurait
nous	aurions
vous	auriez
ils/elles	auraient

IMPERATIVE

aie / ayons / ayez

PAST PARTICIPLE

eu

PRESENT PARTICIPLE

ayant

EXAMPLE PHRASES

Il **a** les yeux bleus.	*He's got blue eyes.*
Quel âge **as**-tu?	*How old are you?*
Il **a eu** un accident.	*He's had an accident.*
J'**avais** faim.	*I was hungry.*
Il y **a** beaucoup de monde.	*There are lots of people.*

to beat **battre**

PRESENT

je	bats
tu	bats
il/elle/on	bat
nous	battons
vous	battez
ils/elles	battent

PRESENT SUBJUNCTIVE

je	batte
tu	battes
il/elle/on	batte
nous	battions
vous	battiez
ils/elles	battent

PERFECT

j'	ai battu
tu	as battu
il/elle/on	a battu
nous	avons battu
vous	avez battu
ils/elles	ont battu

IMPERFECT

je	battais
tu	battais
il/elle/on	battait
nous	battions
vous	battiez
ils/elles	battaient

FUTURE

je	battrai
tu	battras
il/elle/on	battra
nous	battrons
vous	battrez
ils/elles	battront

CONDITIONAL

je	battrais
tu	battrais
il/elle/on	battrait
nous	battrions
vous	battriez
ils/elles	battraient

IMPERATIVE

bats / battons / battez

PAST PARTICIPLE

battu

PRESENT PARTICIPLE

battant

EXAMPLE PHRASES

On les **a battus** deux à un.	*We beat them 2-1.*
J'ai le cœur qui **bat**!	*My heart's beating (fast)!*
Arrêtez de **vous battre**!	*Stop fighting!*

- *Note that* ***se battre*** *follows the same pattern, but takes* ***être*** *in the perfect tense. For an example of a reflexive verb in full, see verb table* ***82 se taire****.*

boire *to drink*

PRESENT

je	bois
tu	bois
il/elle/on	boit
nous	buvons
vous	buvez
ils/elles	boivent

PRESENT SUBJUNCTIVE

je	boive
tu	boives
il/elle/on	boive
nous	buvions
vous	buviez
ils/elles	boivent

PERFECT

j'	ai bu
tu	as bu
il/elle/on	a bu
nous	avons bu
vous	avez bu
ils/elles	ont bu

IMPERFECT

je	buvais
tu	buvais
il/elle/on	buvait
nous	buvions
vous	buviez
ils/elles	buvaient

FUTURE

je	boirai
tu	boiras
il/elle/on	boira
nous	boirons
vous	boirez
ils/elles	boiront

CONDITIONAL

je	boirais
tu	boirais
il/elle/on	boirait
nous	boirions
vous	boiriez
ils/elles	boiraient

IMPERATIVE

bois / buvons / buvez

PAST PARTICIPLE

bu

PRESENT PARTICIPLE

buvant

EXAMPLE PHRASES

Qu'est-ce que tu veux **boire**?	*What would you like to drink?*
Il ne **boit** jamais d'alcool.	*He never drinks alcohol.*
J'**ai bu** un litre d'eau.	*I drank a litre of water.*

PRESENT

je	bous
tu	bous
il/elle/on	bout
nous	bouillons
vous	bouillez
ils/elles	bouillent

PRESENT SUBJUNCTIVE

je	bouille
tu	bouilles
il/elle/on	bouille
nous	bouillions
vous	bouilliez
ils/elles	bouillent

PERFECT

j'	ai bouilli
tu	as bouilli
il/elle/on	a bouilli
nous	avons bouilli
vous	avez bouilli
ils/elles	ont bouilli

IMPERFECT

je	bouillais
tu	bouillais
il/elle/on	bouillait
nous	bouillions
vous	bouilliez
ils/elles	bouillaient

FUTURE

je	bouillirai
tu	bouilliras
il/elle/on	bouillira
nous	bouillirons
vous	bouillirez
ils/elles	bouilliront

CONDITIONAL

je	bouillirais
tu	bouillirais
il/elle/on	bouillirait
nous	bouillirions
vous	bouilliriez
ils/elles	bouilliraient

IMPERATIVE

bous / bouillons / bouillez

PAST PARTICIPLE

bouilli

PRESENT PARTICIPLE

bouillant

EXAMPLE PHRASES

L'eau **bout**. — *The water's boiling.*

Tu peux mettre de l'eau à **bouillir**? — *Can you boil some water?*

commencer *to begin*

PRESENT

je	commence
tu	commences
il/elle/on	commence
nous	commençons
vous	commencez
ils/elles	commencent

PRESENT SUBJUNCTIVE

je	commence
tu	commences
il/elle/on	commence
nous	commencions
vous	commenciez
ils/elles	commencent

PERFECT

j'	ai commencé
tu	as commencé
il/elle/on	a commencé
nous	avons commencé
vous	avez commencé
ils/elles	ont commencé

IMPERFECT

je	commençais
tu	commençais
il/elle/on	commençait
nous	commencions
vous	commenciez
ils/elles	commençaient

FUTURE

je	commencerai
tu	commenceras
il/elle/on	commencera
nous	commencerons
vous	commencerez
ils/elles	commenceront

CONDITIONAL

je	commencerais
tu	commencerais
il/elle/on	commencerait
nous	commencerions
vous	commenceriez
ils/elles	commenceraient

IMPERATIVE

commence / commençons / commencez

PAST PARTICIPLE

commencé

PRESENT PARTICIPLE

commençant

EXAMPLE PHRASES

Il **a commencé** à pleuvoir. — *It started to rain.*

Les cours **commencent** à neuf heures. — *Lessons start at 9 o'clock.*

Tu **as** déjà **commencé** de réviser pour les examens? — *Have you started revising for the exams?*

to conclude conclure

PRESENT

je	conclus
tu	conclus
il/elle/on	conclut
nous	concluons
vous	concluez
ils/elles	concluent

PRESENT SUBJUNCTIVE

je	conclue
tu	conclues
il/elle/on	conclue
nous	concluions
vous	concluiez
ils/elles	concluent

PERFECT

j'	ai conclu
tu	as conclu
il/elle/on	a conclu
nous	avons conclu
vous	avez conclu
ils/elles	ont conclu

IMPERFECT

je	concluais
tu	concluais
il/elle/on	concluait
nous	concluions
vous	concluiez
ils/elles	concluaient

FUTURE

je	conclurai
tu	concluras
il/elle/on	conclura
nous	conclurons
vous	conclurez
ils/elles	concluront

CONDITIONAL

je	conclurais
tu	conclurais
il/elle/on	conclurait
nous	conclurions
vous	concluriez
ils/elles	concluraient

IMPERATIVE

conclus / concluons / concluez

PAST PARTICIPLE

conclu

PRESENT PARTICIPLE

concluant

EXAMPLE PHRASES

Ils **ont conclu** un marché.	*They concluded a deal.*
J'en **ai conclu** qu'il était parti.	*I concluded that he had gone.*
Je **conclurai** par ces mots...	*I will conclude with these words...*

connaître *to know*

PRESENT		PRESENT SUBJUNCTIVE	
je	connais	je	connaisse
tu	connais	tu	connaisses
il/elle/on	connaît	il/elle/on	connaisse
nous	connaissons	nous	connaissions
vous	connaissez	vous	connaissiez
ils/elles	connaissent	ils/elles	connaissent

PERFECT		IMPERFECT	
j'	ai connu	je	connaissais
tu	as connu	tu	connaissais
il/elle/on	a connu	il/elle/on	connaissait
nous	avons connu	nous	connaissions
vous	avez connu	vous	connaissiez
ils/elles	ont connu	ils/elles	connaissaient

FUTURE		CONDITIONAL	
je	connaîtrai	je	connaîtrais
tu	connaîtras	tu	connaîtrais
il/elle/on	connaîtra	il/elle/on	connaîtrait
nous	connaîtrons	nous	connaîtrions
vous	connaîtrez	vous	connaîtriez
ils/elles	connaîtront	ils/elles	connaîtraient

IMPERATIVE
connais / connaissons / connaissez

PAST PARTICIPLE
connu

PRESENT PARTICIPLE
connaissant

EXAMPLE PHRASES

Je ne **connais** pas du tout cette région.	*I don't know the area at all.*
Vous **connaissez** M Amiot?	*Do you know Mr Amiot?*
Il n'**a** pas **connu** son grand-père.	*He never knew his grandad.*
Ils **se sont connus** à Rouen.	*They first met in Rouen.*

- *Note that **se connaître** follows the same pattern, but takes **être** in the perfect tense. For an example of a reflexive verb in full, see verb table **82 se taire**.*

to sew **coudre**

PRESENT

je	couds
tu	couds
il/elle/on	coud
nous	cousons
vous	cousez
ils/elles	cousent

PRESENT SUBJUNCTIVE

je	couse
tu	couses
il/elle/on	couse
nous	cousions
vous	cousiez
ils/elles	cousent

PERFECT

j'	ai cousu
tu	as cousu
il/elle/on	a cousu
nous	avons cousu
vous	avez cousu
ils/elles	ont cousu

IMPERFECT

je	cousais
tu	cousais
il/elle/on	cousait
nous	cousions
vous	cousiez
ils/elles	cousaient

FUTURE

je	coudrai
tu	coudras
il/elle/on	coudra
nous	coudrons
vous	coudrez
ils/elles	coudront

CONDITIONAL

je	coudrais
tu	coudrais
il/elle/on	coudrait
nous	coudrions
vous	coudriez
ils/elles	coudraient

IMPERATIVE

couds / cousons / cousez

PAST PARTICIPLE

cousu

PRESENT PARTICIPLE

cousant

EXAMPLE PHRASES

Tu sais **coudre**? — *Can you sew?*

Elle **a cousu** elle-même son costume. — *She made her costume herself.*

Table 16

courir *to run*

PRESENT

je	cours
tu	cours
il/elle/on	court
nous	courons
vous	courez
ils/elles	courent

PRESENT SUBJUNCTIVE

je	coure
tu	coures
il/elle/on	coure
nous	courions
vous	couriez
ils/elles	courent

PERFECT

j'	ai couru
tu	as couru
il/elle/on	a couru
nous	avons couru
vous	avez couru
ils/elles	ont couru

IMPERFECT

je	courais
tu	courais
il/elle/on	courait
nous	courions
vous	couriez
ils/elles	couraient

FUTURE

je	courrai
tu	courras
il/elle/on	courra
nous	courrons
vous	courrez
ils/elles	courront

CONDITIONAL

je	courrais
tu	courrais
il/elle/on	courrait
nous	courrions
vous	courriez
ils/elles	courraient

IMPERATIVE

cours / courons / courez

PAST PARTICIPLE

couru

PRESENT PARTICIPLE

courant

EXAMPLE PHRASES

Je ne **cours** pas très vite. — *I can't run very fast.*
Elle est sortie en **courant**. — *She ran out.*
Ne **courez** pas dans le couloir. — *Don't run in the corridor.*
J'**ai couru** jusqu'à l'école. — *I ran all the way to school.*

to fear **craindre**

PRESENT

je	crains
tu	crains
il/elle/on	craint
nous	craignons
vous	craignez
ils/elles	craignent

PRESENT SUBJUNCTIVE

je	craigne
tu	craignes
il/elle/on	craigne
nous	craignions
vous	craigniez
ils/elles	craignent

PERFECT

j'	ai craint
tu	as craint
il/elle/on	a craint
nous	avons craint
vous	avez craint
ils/elles	ont craint

IMPERFECT

je	craignais
tu	craignais
il/elle/on	craignait
nous	craignions
vous	craigniez
ils/elles	craignaient

FUTURE

je	craindrai
tu	craindras
il/elle/on	craindra
nous	craindrons
vous	craindrez
ils/elles	craindront

CONDITIONAL

je	craindrais
tu	craindrais
il/elle/on	craindrait
nous	craindrions
vous	craindriez
ils/elles	craindraient

IMPERATIVE

crains / craignons / craignez

PAST PARTICIPLE

craint

PRESENT PARTICIPLE

craignant

EXAMPLE PHRASES

Tu n'as rien à **craindre**. — *You've got nothing to fear.*
Je **crains** le pire. — *I fear the worst.*

Table 18

créer *to create*

PRESENT

je	crée
tu	crées
il/elle/on	crée
nous	créons
vous	créez
ils/elles	créent

PRESENT SUBJUNCTIVE

je	crée
tu	crées
il/elle/on	crée
nous	créions
vous	créiez
ils/elles	créent

PERFECT

j'	ai créé
tu	as créé
il/elle/on	a créé
nous	avons créé
vous	avez créé
ils/elles	ont créé

IMPERFECT

je	créais
tu	créais
il/elle/on	créait
nous	créions
vous	créiez
ils/elles	créaient

FUTURE

je	créerai
tu	créeras
il/elle/on	créera
nous	créerons
vous	créerez
ils/elles	créeront

CONDITIONAL

je	créerais
tu	créerais
il/elle/on	créerait
nous	créerions
vous	créeriez
ils/elles	créeraient

IMPERATIVE

crée / créons / créez

PAST PARTICIPLE

créé

PRESENT PARTICIPLE

créant

EXAMPLE PHRASES

Il **a créé** une nouvelle invention.	*He's created a new invention.*
Ce virus **crée** des difficultés dans le monde entier.	*This virus is creating difficulties all over the world.*
Le gouvernement **créera** deux mille emplois supplémentaires.	*The government will create an extra 2000 jobs.*

to shout **crier**

PRESENT

je	crie
tu	cries
il/elle/on	crie
nous	crions
vous	criez
ils/elles	crient

PRESENT SUBJUNCTIVE

je	crie
tu	cries
il/elle/on	crie
nous	criions
vous	criiez
ils/elles	crient

PERFECT

j'	ai crié
tu	as crié
il/elle/on	a crié
nous	avons crié
vous	avez crié
ils/elles	ont crié

IMPERFECT

je	criais
tu	criais
il/elle/on	criait
nous	criions
vous	criiez
ils/elles	criaient

FUTURE

je	crierai
tu	crieras
il/elle/on	criera
nous	crierons
vous	crierez
ils/elles	crieront

CONDITIONAL

je	crierais
tu	crierais
il/elle/on	crierait
nous	crierions
vous	crieriez
ils/elles	crieraient

IMPERATIVE

crie / crions / criez

PAST PARTICIPLE

crié

PRESENT PARTICIPLE

criant

EXAMPLE PHRASES

Ne **crie** pas comme ça! — *Don't shout!*
Elle **a crié** au secours. — *She cried for help.*
Il **criait** de plus en plus fort. — *He shouted louder and louder.*

croire *to believe*

PRESENT

je	crois
tu	crois
il/elle/on	croit
nous	croyons
vous	croyez
ils/elles	croient

PRESENT SUBJUNCTIVE

je	croie
tu	croies
il/elle/on	croie
nous	croyions
vous	croyiez
ils/elles	croient

PERFECT

j'	ai cru
tu	as cru
il/elle/on	a cru
nous	avons cru
vous	avez cru
ils/elles	ont cru

IMPERFECT

je	croyais
tu	croyais
il/elle/on	croyait
nous	croyions
vous	croyiez
ils/elles	croyaient

FUTURE

je	croirai
tu	croiras
il/elle/on	croira
nous	croirons
vous	croirez
ils/elles	croiront

CONDITIONAL

je	croirais
tu	croirais
il/elle/on	croirait
nous	croirions
vous	croiriez
ils/elles	croiraient

IMPERATIVE

crois / croyons / croyez

PAST PARTICIPLE

cru

PRESENT PARTICIPLE

croyant

EXAMPLE PHRASES

Je ne te **crois** pas. — *I don't believe you.*
J'**ai cru** que tu n'allais pas venir. — *I thought you weren't going to come.*
Elle **croyait** encore au père Noël. — *She still believed in Santa.*

to grow **croître**

PRESENT

je	croîs
tu	croîs
il/elle/on	croît
nous	croissons
vous	croissez
ils/elles	croissent

PRESENT SUBJUNCTIVE

je	croisse
tu	croisses
il/elle/on	croisse
nous	croissions
vous	croissiez
ils/elles	croissent

PERFECT

j'	ai crû
tu	as crû
il/elle/on	a crû
nous	avons crû
vous	avez crû
ils/elles	ont crû

IMPERFECT

je	croissais
tu	croissais
il/elle/on	croissait
nous	croissions
vous	croissiez
ils/elles	croissaient

FUTURE

je	croîtrai
tu	croîtras
il/elle/on	croîtra
nous	croîtrons
vous	croîtrez
ils/elles	croîtront

CONDITIONAL

je	croîtrais
tu	croîtrais
il/elle/on	croîtrait
nous	croîtrions
vous	croîtriez
ils/elles	croîtraient

IMPERATIVE

croîs / croissons / croissez

PAST PARTICIPLE

crû (NB: crue, crus, crues)

PRESENT PARTICIPLE

croissant

EXAMPLE PHRASES

Les ventes **croissent** de 6% par an. — *Sales are growing by 6% per year.*

C'est une plante qui **croît** dans les pays chauds. — *This plant grows in hot countries.*

Table 22

cueillir *to pick*

PRESENT

je	cueille
tu	cueilles
il/elle/on	cueille
nous	cueillons
vous	cueillez
ils/elles	cueillent

PRESENT SUBJUNCTIVE

je	cueille
tu	cueilles
il/elle/on	cueille
nous	cueillions
vous	cueilliez
ils/elles	cueillent

PERFECT

j'	ai cueilli
tu	as cueilli
il/elle/on	a cueilli
nous	avons cueilli
vous	avez cueilli
ils/elles	ont cueilli

IMPERFECT

je	cueillais
tu	cueillais
il/elle/on	cueillait
nous	cueillions
vous	cueilliez
ils/elles	cueillaient

FUTURE

je	cueillerai
tu	cueilleras
il/elle/on	cueillera
nous	cueillerons
vous	cueillerez
ils/elles	cueilleront

CONDITIONAL

je	cueillerais
tu	cueillerais
il/elle/on	cueillerait
nous	cueillerions
vous	cueilleriez
ils/elles	cueilleraient

IMPERATIVE

cueille / cueillons / cueillez

PAST PARTICIPLE

cueilli

PRESENT PARTICIPLE

cueillant

EXAMPLE PHRASES

J'**ai cueilli** quelques fraises dans le jardin. — *I've picked a few strawberries in the garden.*

Il est interdit de **cueillir** des fleurs sauvages dans la montagne. — *It's forbidden to pick wild flowers in the mountains.*

PRESENT

je	cuis
tu	cuis
il/elle/on	cuit
nous	cuisons
vous	cuisez
ils/elles	cuisent

PRESENT SUBJUNCTIVE

je	cuise
tu	cuises
il/elle/on	cuise
nous	cuisions
vous	cuisiez
ils/elles	cuisent

PERFECT

j'	ai cuit
tu	as cuit
il/elle/on	a cuit
nous	avons cuit
vous	avez cuit
ils/elles	ont cuit

IMPERFECT

je	cuisais
tu	cuisais
il/elle/on	cuisait
nous	cuisions
vous	cuisiez
ils/elles	cuisaient

FUTURE

je	cuirai
tu	cuiras
il/elle/on	cuira
nous	cuirons
vous	cuirez
ils/elles	cuiront

CONDITIONAL

je	cuirais
tu	cuirais
il/elle/on	cuirait
nous	cuirions
vous	cuiriez
ils/elles	cuiraient

IMPERATIVE

cuis / cuisons / cuisez

PAST PARTICIPLE

cuit

PRESENT PARTICIPLE

cuisant

EXAMPLE PHRASES

Je les **ai cuits** au beurre.	*I cooked them in butter.*
En général, je **cuis** les légumes à la vapeur.	*I usually steam vegetables.*
Ce gâteau prend environ une heure à **cuire**.	*This cake takes about an hour to bake.*

descendre *to go down*

PRESENT

je	descends
tu	descends
il/elle/on	descend
nous	descendons
vous	descendez
ils/elles	descendent

PRESENT SUBJUNCTIVE

je	descende
tu	descendes
il/elle/on	descende
nous	descendions
vous	descendiez
ils/elles	descendent

PERFECT

je	suis descendu(e)
tu	es descendu(e)
il/elle/on	est descendu(e)
nous	sommes descendu(e)(s)
vous	êtes descendu(e)(s)
ils/elles	sont descendu(e)s

IMPERFECT

je	descendais
tu	descendais
il/elle/on	descendait
nous	descendions
vous	descendiez
ils/elles	descendaient

FUTURE

je	descendrai
tu	descendras
il/elle/on	descendra
nous	descendrons
vous	descendrez
ils/elles	descendront

CONDITIONAL

je	descendrais
tu	descendrais
il/elle/on	descendrait
nous	descendrions
vous	descendriez
ils/elles	descendraient

IMPERATIVE

descends / descendons / descendez

PAST PARTICIPLE

descendu

PRESENT PARTICIPLE

descendant

EXAMPLE PHRASES

Descendez la rue jusqu'au rond-point.	*Go down the street to the roundabout.*
Reste en bas: je **descends**!	*Stay downstairs – I'm coming down!*
Nous **sommes descendus** à la station Trocadéro.	*We got off at the Trocadéro station.*
Vous pouvez **descendre** ma valise, s'il vous plaît?	*Can you get my suitcase down, please?*

- *Note that **descendre** takes **avoir** in the perfect tense when it is used with a direct object.*

PRESENT

je	deviens
tu	deviens
il/elle/on	devient
nous	devenons
vous	devenez
ils/elles	deviennent

PRESENT SUBJUNCTIVE

je	devienne
tu	deviennes
il/elle/on	devienne
nous	devenions
vous	deveniez
ils/elles	deviennent

PERFECT

je	suis devenu(e)
tu	es devenu(e)
il/elle/on	est devenu(e)
nous	sommes devenu(e)s
vous	êtes devenu(e)(s)
ils/elles	sont devenu(e)s

IMPERFECT

je	devenais
tu	devenais
il/elle/on	devenait
nous	devenions
vous	deveniez
ils/elles	devenaient

FUTURE

je	deviendrai
tu	deviendras
il/elle/on	deviendra
nous	deviendrons
vous	deviendrez
ils/elles	deviendront

CONDITIONAL

je	deviendrais
tu	deviendrais
il/elle/on	deviendrait
nous	deviendrions
vous	deviendriez
ils/elles	deviendraient

IMPERATIVE

deviens / devenons / devenez

PAST PARTICIPLE

devenu

PRESENT PARTICIPLE

devenant

EXAMPLE PHRASES

Il **est devenu** médecin.	*He became a doctor.*
Ça **devient** de plus en plus difficile.	*It's becoming more and more difficult.*
Qu'est-ce qu'elle **est devenue**?	*What has become of her?*

devoir *to have to; to owe*

PRESENT

je	dois
tu	dois
il/elle/on	doit
nous	devons
vous	devez
ils/elles	doivent

PRESENT SUBJUNCTIVE

je	doive
tu	doives
il/elle/on	doive
nous	devions
vous	deviez
ils/elles	doivent

PERFECT

j'	ai dû
tu	as dû
il/elle/on	a dû
nous	avons dû
vous	avez dû
ils/elles	ont dû

IMPERFECT

je	devais
tu	devais
il/elle/on	devait
nous	devions
vous	deviez
ils/elles	devaient

FUTURE

je	devrai
tu	devras
il/elle/on	devra
nous	devrons
vous	devrez
ils/elles	devront

CONDITIONAL

je	devrais
tu	devrais
il/elle/on	devrait
nous	devrions
vous	devriez
ils/elles	devraient

IMPERATIVE

dois / devons / devez

PAST PARTICIPLE

dû (NB: due, dus, dues)

PRESENT PARTICIPLE

devant

EXAMPLE PHRASES

Je **dois** aller faire les courses ce matin.	*I have to do the shopping this morning.*
À quelle heure est-ce que tu **dois** partir?	*What time do you have to leave?*
Il **a dû** faire ses devoirs hier soir.	*He had to do his homework last night.*
Il **devait** prendre le train pour aller travailler.	*He had to go to work by train.*

PRESENT

je	dis
tu	dis
il/elle/on	dit
nous	disons
vous	dites
ils/elles	disent

PRESENT SUBJUNCTIVE

je	dise
tu	dises
il/elle/on	dise
nous	disions
vous	disiez
ils/elles	disent

PERFECT

j'	ai dit
tu	as dit
il/elle/on	a dit
nous	avons dit
vous	avez dit
ils/elles	ont dit

IMPERFECT

je	disais
tu	disais
il/elle/on	disait
nous	disions
vous	disiez
ils/elles	disaient

FUTURE

je	dirai
tu	diras
il/elle/on	dira
nous	dirons
vous	direz
ils/elles	diront

CONDITIONAL

je	dirais
tu	dirais
il/elle/on	dirait
nous	dirions
vous	diriez
ils/elles	diraient

IMPERATIVE

dis / disons / dites

PAST PARTICIPLE

dit

PRESENT PARTICIPLE

disant

EXAMPLE PHRASES

Qu'est-ce qu'elle **dit**?	*What is she saying?*
"Bonjour!", **a**-t-il **dit**.	*"Hello!" he said.*
Ils m'**ont dit** que le film était nul.	*They told me that the film was rubbish.*
Comment ça **se dit** en anglais?	*How do you say that in English?*

- *Note that **se dire** follows the same pattern, but takes **être** in the perfect tense. For an example of a reflexive verb in full, see verb table **82 se taire**.*

Table 28

donner *to give*

PRESENT

je	donne
tu	donnes
il/elle/on	donne
nous	donnons
vous	donnez
ils/elles	donnent

PRESENT SUBJUNCTIVE

je	donne
tu	donnes
il/elle/on	donne
nous	donnions
vous	donniez
ils/elles	donnent

PERFECT

j'	ai donné
tu	as donné
il/elle/on	a donné
nous	avons donné
vous	avez donné
ils/elles	ont donné

IMPERFECT

je	donnais
tu	donnais
il/elle/on	donnait
nous	donnions
vous	donniez
ils/elles	donnaient

FUTURE

je	donnerai
tu	donneras
il/elle/on	donnera
nous	donnerons
vous	donnerez
ils/elles	donneront

CONDITIONAL

je	donnerais
tu	donnerais
il/elle/on	donnerait
nous	donnerions
vous	donneriez
ils/elles	donneraient

IMPERATIVE

donne / donnons / donnez

PAST PARTICIPLE

donné

PRESENT PARTICIPLE

donnant

EXAMPLE PHRASES

Donne-moi la main.	*Give me your hand.*
Est-ce que je t'**ai donné** mon adresse?	*Did I give you my address?*
L'appartement **donne** sur la place.	*The flat overlooks the square.*

to sleep dormir

PRESENT

je	dors
tu	dors
il/elle/on	dort
nous	dormons
vous	dormez
ils/elles	dorment

PRESENT SUBJUNCTIVE

je	dorme
tu	dormes
il/elle/on	dorme
nous	dormions
vous	dormiez
ils/elles	dorment

PERFECT

j'	ai dormi
tu	as dormi
il/elle/on	a dormi
nous	avons dormi
vous	avez dormi
ils/elles	ont dormi

IMPERFECT

je	dormais
tu	dormais
il/elle/on	dormait
nous	dormions
vous	dormiez
ils/elles	dormaient

FUTURE

je	dormirai
tu	dormiras
il/elle/on	dormira
nous	dormirons
vous	dormirez
ils/elles	dormiront

CONDITIONAL

je	dormirais
tu	dormirais
il/elle/on	dormirait
nous	dormirions
vous	dormiriez
ils/elles	dormiraient

IMPERATIVE

dors / dormons / dormez

PAST PARTICIPLE

dormi

PRESENT PARTICIPLE

dormant

EXAMPLE PHRASES

Tu **as** bien **dormi**? — *Did you sleep well?*

Nous **dormons** dans la même chambre. — *We sleep in the same bedroom.*

À 9 heures, il **dormait** déjà. — *He was already asleep by nine.*

Table 30

écrire *to write*

PRESENT

j'	écris
tu	écris
il/elle/on	écrit
nous	écrivons
vous	écrivez
ils/elles	écrivent

PRESENT SUBJUNCTIVE

j'	écrive
tu	écrives
il/elle/on	écrive
nous	écrivions
vous	écriviez
ils/elles	écrivent

PERFECT

j'	ai écrit
tu	as écrit
il/elle/on	a écrit
nous	avons écrit
vous	avez écrit
ils/elles	ont écrit

IMPERFECT

j'	écrivais
tu	écrivais
il/elle/on	écrivait
nous	écrivions
vous	écriviez
ils/elles	écrivaient

FUTURE

j'	écrirai
tu	écriras
il/elle/on	écrira
nous	écrirons
vous	écrirez
ils/elles	écriront

CONDITIONAL

j'	écrirais
tu	écrirais
il/elle/on	écrirait
nous	écririons
vous	écririez
ils/elles	écriraient

IMPERATIVE

écris / écrivons / écrivez

PAST PARTICIPLE

écrit

PRESENT PARTICIPLE

écrivant

EXAMPLE PHRASES

Tu **as écrit** à ta correspondante récemment? — *Have you written to your penfriend lately?*

Elle **écrit** des romans. — *She writes novels.*

Comment ça **s'écrit**, "brouillard"? — *How do you spell "brouillard"?*

*Note that **s'écrire** follows the same pattern, but take **être** in the perfect tense. For an example of a reflexive verb in full, see verb table **6 s'asseoir**.*

to move **émouvoir**

PRESENT

j'	émeus
tu	émeus
il/elle/on	émeut
nous	émouvons
vous	émouvez
ils/elles	émeuvent

PRESENT SUBJUNCTIVE

j'	émeuve
tu	émeuves
il/elle/on	émeuve
nous	émouvions
vous	émouviez
ils/elles	émeuvent

PERFECT

j'	ai ému
tu	as ému
il/elle/on	a ému
nous	avons ému
vous	avez ému
ils/elles	ont ému

IMPERFECT

j'	émouvais
tu	émouvais
il/elle/on	émouvait
nous	émouvions
vous	émouviez
ils/elles	émouvaient

FUTURE

j'	émouvrai
tu	émouvras
il/elle/on	émouvra
nous	émouvrons
vous	émouvrez
ils/elles	émouvront

CONDITIONAL

j'	émouvrais
tu	émouvrais
il/elle/on	émouvrait
nous	émouvrions
vous	émouvriez
ils/elles	émouvraient

IMPERATIVE

émeus / émouvons / émouvez

PAST PARTICIPLE

ému

PRESENT PARTICIPLE

émouvant

EXAMPLE PHRASES

Ce film nous **a ému**. — *This film moved us.*

Cette histoire m'**émeut** toujours beaucoup. — *This story always moves me to tears.*

Table 32

entrer *to enter*

PRESENT

j'	entre
tu	entres
il/elle/on	entre
nous	entrons
vous	entrez
ils/elles	entrent

PRESENT SUBJUNCTIVE

j'	entre
tu	entres
il/elle/on	entre
nous	entrions
vous	entriez
ils/elles	entrent

PERFECT

je	suis entré(e)
tu	es entré(e)
il/elle/on	est entré(e)
nous	sommes entré(e)s
vous	êtes entré(e)(s)
ils/elles	sont entré(e)s

IMPERFECT

j'	entrais
tu	entrais
il/elle/on	entrait
nous	entrions
vous	entriez
ils/elles	entraient

FUTURE

j'	entrerai
tu	entreras
il/elle/on	entrera
nous	entrerons
vous	entrerez
ils/elles	entreront

CONDITIONAL

j'	entrerais
tu	entrerais
il/elle/on	entrerait
nous	entrerions
vous	entreriez
ils/elles	entreraient

IMPERATIVE

entre / entrons / entrez

PAST PARTICIPLE

entré

PRESENT PARTICIPLE

entrant

EXAMPLE PHRASES

Je peux **entrer**?	*Can I come in?*
Essuie-toi les pieds en **entrant**.	*Wipe your feet as you come in.*
Ils **sont** tous **entrés** dans la maison.	*They all went into the house.*

to send **envoyer**

PRESENT

j'	envoie
tu	envoies
il/elle/on	envoie
nous	envoyons
vous	envoyez
ils/elles	envoient

PRESENT SUBJUNCTIVE

j'	envoie
tu	envoies
il/elle/on	envoie
nous	envoyions
vous	envoyiez
ils/elles	envoient

PERFECT

j'	ai envoyé
tu	as envoyé
il/elle/on	a envoyé
nous	avons envoyé
vous	avez envoyé
ils/elles	ont envoyé

IMPERFECT

j'	envoyais
tu	envoyais
il/elle/on	envoyait
nous	envoyions
vous	envoyiez
ils/elles	envoyaient

FUTURE

j'	enverrai
tu	enverras
il/elle/on	enverra
nous	enverrons
vous	enverrez
ils/elles	enverront

CONDITIONAL

j'	enverrais
tu	enverrais
il/elle/on	enverrait
nous	enverrions
vous	enverriez
ils/elles	enverraient

IMPERATIVE

envoie / envoyons / envoyez

PAST PARTICIPLE

envoyé

PRESENT PARTICIPLE

envoyant

EXAMPLE PHRASES

J'**ai envoyé** une carte postale à ma tante.	*I sent my aunt a postcard.*
Envoie-moi un e-mail.	*Send me an email.*
Je t'**enverrai** ton cadeau par la poste.	*I'll send you your present by post.*

Table 34

espérer *to hope*

PRESENT

j'	espère
tu	espères
il/elle/on	espère
nous	espérons
vous	espérez
ils/elles	espèrent

PRESENT SUBJUNCTIVE

j'	espère
tu	espères
il/elle/on	espère
nous	espérions
vous	espériez
ils/elles	espèrent

PERFECT

j'	ai espéré
tu	as espéré
il/elle/on	a espéré
nous	avons espéré
vous	avez espéré
ils/elles	ont espéré

IMPERFECT

j'	espérais
tu	espérais
il/elle/on	espérait
nous	espérions
vous	espériez
ils/elles	espéraient

FUTURE

j'	espérerai
tu	espéreras
il/elle/on	espérera
nous	espérerons
vous	espérerez
ils/elles	espéreront

CONDITIONAL

j'	espérerais
tu	espérerais
il/elle/on	espérerait
nous	espérerions
vous	espéreriez
ils/elles	espéreraient

IMPERATIVE

espère / espérons / espérez

PAST PARTICIPLE

espéré

PRESENT PARTICIPLE

espérant

EXAMPLE PHRASES

J'**espère** que tu vas bien.	*I hope you're well.*
Il **espérait** pouvoir venir.	*He was hoping he'd be able to come.*
Tu penses réussir tes examens? – J'**espère** bien!	*Do you think you'll pass your exams? – I hope so!*

to be être

PRESENT

je	suis
tu	es
il/elle/on	est
nous	sommes
vous	êtes
ils/elles	sont

PRESENT SUBJUNCTIVE

je	sois
tu	sois
il/elle/on	soit
nous	soyons
vous	soyez
ils/elles	soient

PERFECT

j'	ai été
tu	as été
il/elle/on	a été
nous	avons été
vous	avez été
ils/elles	ont été

IMPERFECT

j'	étais
tu	étais
il/elle/on	était
nous	étions
vous	étiez
ils/elles	étaient

FUTURE

je	serai
tu	seras
il/elle/on	sera
nous	serons
vous	serez
ils/elles	seront

CONDITIONAL

je	serais
tu	serais
il/elle/on	serait
nous	serions
vous	seriez
ils/elles	seraient

IMPERATIVE

sois / soyons / soyez

PAST PARTICIPLE

été

PRESENT PARTICIPLE

étant

EXAMPLE PHRASES

Mon père **est** professeur.	*My father's a teacher.*
Quelle heure **est**-il? – Il **est** dix heures.	*What time is it? – It's 10 o'clock.*
Ils ne **sont** pas encore arrivés.	*They haven't arrived yet.*

Table 36

faire *to do; to make*

PRESENT

je	fais
tu	fais
il/elle/on	fait
nous	faisons
vous	faites
ils/elles	font

PRESENT SUBJUNCTIVE

je	fasse
tu	fasses
il/elle/on	fasse
nous	fassions
vous	fassiez
ils/elles	fassent

PERFECT

j'	ai fait
tu	as fait
il/elle/on	a fait
nous	avons fait
vous	avez fait
ils/elles	ont fait

IMPERFECT

je	faisais
tu	faisais
il/elle/on	faisait
nous	faisions
vous	faisiez
ils/elles	faisaient

FUTURE

je	ferai
tu	feras
il/elle/on	fera
nous	ferons
vous	ferez
ils/elles	feront

CONDITIONAL

je	ferais
tu	ferais
il/elle/on	ferait
nous	ferions
vous	feriez
ils/elles	feraient

IMPERATIVE

fais / faisons / faites

PAST PARTICIPLE

fait

PRESENT PARTICIPLE

faisant

EXAMPLE PHRASES

Qu'est-ce que tu **fais**?	*What are you doing?*
Qu'est-ce qu'il **a fait**?	*What has he done?* or *What did he do?*
J'**ai fait** un gâteau.	*I've made a cake* or *I made a cake.*
Il **s'est fait** couper les cheveux.	*He's had his hair cut.*

- *Note that **se faire** follows the same pattern, but takes **être** in the perfect tense. For an example of a reflexive verb in full, see verb table **82 se taire**.*

PRESENT

il faut

PRESENT SUBJUNCTIVE

il faille

PERFECT

il a fallu

IMPERFECT

il fallait

FUTURE

il faudra

CONDITIONAL

il faudrait

IMPERATIVE

not used

PAST PARTICIPLE

fallu

PRESENT PARTICIPLE

not used

EXAMPLE PHRASES

Il **faut** se dépêcher!	*We have to hurry up!*
Il me **fallait** de l'argent.	*I needed money.*
Il **faudra** que tu sois là à 8 heures.	*You'll have to be there at 8.*

Table 38

finir *to finish*

PRESENT

je	finis
tu	finis
il/elle/on	finit
nous	finissons
vous	finissez
ils/elles	finissent

PRESENT SUBJUNCTIVE

je	finisse
tu	finisses
il/elle/on	finisse
nous	finissions
vous	finissiez
ils/elles	finissent

PERFECT

j'	ai fini
tu	as fini
il/elle/on	a fini
nous	avons fini
vous	avez fini
ils/elles	ont fini

IMPERFECT

je	finissais
tu	finissais
il/elle/on	finissait
nous	finissions
vous	finissiez
ils/elles	finissaient

FUTURE

je	finirai
tu	finiras
il/elle/on	finira
nous	finirons
vous	finirez
ils/elles	finiront

CONDITIONAL

je	finirais
tu	finirais
il/elle/on	finirait
nous	finirions
vous	finiriez
ils/elles	finiraient

IMPERATIVE

finis / finissons / finissez

PAST PARTICIPLE

fini

PRESENT PARTICIPLE

finissant

EXAMPLE PHRASES

Finis ta soupe!	*Finish your soup!*
J'ai **fini**!	*I've finished!*
Je **finirai** mes devoirs demain.	*I'll finish my homework tomorrow.*

PRESENT

je	fuis
tu	fuis
il/elle/on	fuit
nous	fuyons
vous	fuyez
ils/elles	fuient

PRESENT SUBJUNCTIVE

je	fuie
tu	fuies
il/elle/on	fuie
nous	fuyions
vous	fuyiez
ils/elles	fuient

PERFECT

j'	ai fui
tu	as fui
il/elle/on	a fui
nous	avons fui
vous	avez fui
ils/elles	ont fui

IMPERFECT

je	fuyais
tu	fuyais
il/elle/on	fuyait
nous	fuyions
vous	fuyiez
ils/elles	fuyaient

FUTURE

je	fuirai
tu	fuiras
il/elle/on	fuira
nous	fuirons
vous	fuirez
ils/elles	fuiront

CONDITIONAL

je	fuirais
tu	fuirais
il/elle/on	fuirait
nous	fuirions
vous	fuiriez
ils/elles	fuiraient

IMPERATIVE

fuis / fuyons / fuyez

PAST PARTICIPLE

fui

PRESENT PARTICIPLE

fuyant

EXAMPLE PHRASES

Ils **ont fui** leur pays.	*They fled their country.*
Le robinet **fuit**.	*The tap is dripping.*

haïr *to hate*

PRESENT

je	hais
tu	hais
il/elle/on	hait
nous	haïssons
vous	haïssez
ils/elles	haïssent

PRESENT SUBJUNCTIVE

je	haïsse
tu	haïsses
il/elle/on	haïsse
nous	haïssions
vous	haïssiez
ils/elles	haïssent

PERFECT

j'	ai haï
tu	as haï
il/elle/on	a haï
nous	avons haï
vous	avez haï
ils/elles	ont haï

IMPERFECT

je	haïssais
tu	haïssais
il/elle/on	haïssait
nous	haïssions
vous	haïssiez
ils/elles	haïssaient

FUTURE

je	haïrai
tu	haïras
il/elle/on	haïra
nous	haïrons
vous	haïrez
ils/elles	haïront

CONDITIONAL

je	haïrais
tu	haïrais
il/elle/on	haïrait
nous	haïrions
vous	haïriez
ils/elles	haïraient

IMPERATIVE

hais / haïssons / haïssez

PAST PARTICIPLE

haï

PRESENT PARTICIPLE

haïssant

EXAMPLE PHRASES

Je te **hais**!	*I hate you!*
Elle **haïssait** tout le monde.	*She hated everyone.*
Ils **se haïssent**.	*They hate each other.*

- *Note that **se haïr** follows the same pattern, but takes **être** in the perfect tense. For an example of a reflexive verb in full, see verb table **82 se taire**.*

PRESENT

je	jette
tu	jettes
il/elle/on	jette
nous	jetons
vous	jetez
ils/elles	jettent

PRESENT SUBJUNCTIVE

je	jette
tu	jettes
il/elle/on	jette
nous	jetions
vous	jetiez
ils/elles	jettent

PERFECT

j'	ai jeté
tu	as jeté
il/elle/on	a jeté
nous	avons jeté
vous	avez jeté
ils/elles	ont jeté

IMPERFECT

je	jetais
tu	jetais
il/elle/on	jetait
nous	jetions
vous	jetiez
ils/elles	jetaient

FUTURE

je	jetterai
tu	jetteras
il/elle/on	jettera
nous	jetterons
vous	jetterez
ils/elles	jetteront

CONDITIONAL

je	jetterais
tu	jetterais
il/elle/on	jetterait
nous	jetterions
vous	jetteriez
ils/elles	jetteraient

IMPERATIVE

jette / jetons / jetez

PAST PARTICIPLE

jeté

PRESENT PARTICIPLE

jetant

EXAMPLE PHRASES

Ne **jette** pas tes vêtements par terre. — *Don't throw your clothes on the floor.*

Elle **a jeté** son chewing-gum par la fenêtre. — *She threw her chewing gum out of the window.*

Ils ne **jettent** jamais rien. — *They never throw anything away.*

Table 42

joindre *to join*

PRESENT

je	joins
tu	joins
il/elle/on	joint
nous	joignons
vous	joignez
ils/elles	joignent

PRESENT SUBJUNCTIVE

je	joigne
tu	joignes
il/elle/on	joigne
nous	joignions
vous	joigniez
ils/elles	joignent

PERFECT

j'	ai joint
tu	as joint
il/elle/on	a joint
nous	avons joint
vous	avez joint
ils/elles	ont joint

IMPERFECT

je	joignais
tu	joignais
il/elle/on	joignait
nous	joignions
vous	joigniez
ils/elles	joignaient

FUTURE

je	joindrai
tu	joindras
il/elle/on	joindra
nous	joindrons
vous	joindrez
ils/elles	joindront

CONDITIONAL

je	joindrais
tu	joindrais
il/elle/on	joindrait
nous	joindrions
vous	joindriez
ils/elles	joindraient

IMPERATIVE

joins / joignons / joignez

PAST PARTICIPLE

joint

PRESENT PARTICIPLE

joignant

EXAMPLE PHRASES

Où est-ce qu'on peut te **joindre** ce week-end? — *Where can we contact you this weekend?*

On **a joint** les deux tables. — *We put the two tables together.*

to lift **lever**

PRESENT		PRESENT SUBJUNCTIVE	
je	lève	je	lève
tu	lèves	tu	lèves
il/elle/on	lève	il/elle/on	lève
nous	levons	nous	levions
vous	levez	vous	leviez
ils/elles	lèvent	ils/elles	lèvent

PERFECT		IMPERFECT	
j'	ai levé	je	levais
tu	as levé	tu	levais
il/elle/on	a levé	il/elle/on	levait
nous	avons levé	nous	levions
vous	avez levé	vous	leviez
ils/elles	ont levé	ils/elles	levaient

FUTURE		CONDITIONAL	
je	lèverai	je	lèverais
tu	lèveras	tu	lèverais
il/elle/on	lèvera	il/elle/on	lèverait
nous	lèverons	nous	lèverions
vous	lèverez	vous	lèveriez
ils/elles	lèveront	ils/elles	lèveraient

IMPERATIVE

lève / levons / levez

PAST PARTICIPLE

levé

PRESENT PARTICIPLE

levant

EXAMPLE PHRASES

Lève la tête.	*Lift your head up.*
Levez la main!	*Put your hand up!*
Je **me lève** tous les jours à sept heures.	*I get up at 7 every day.*

- *Note that* ***se lever*** *follows the same pattern, but takes* ***être*** *in the perfect tense. For an example of a reflexive verb in full, see verb table* ***82 se taire****.*

Table 44

lire *to read*

PRESENT

je	lis
tu	lis
il/elle/on	lit
nous	lisons
vous	lisez
ils/elles	lisent

PRESENT SUBJUNCTIVE

je	lise
tu	lises
il/elle/on	lise
nous	lisions
vous	lisiez
ils/elles	lisent

PERFECT

j'	ai lu
tu	as lu
il/elle/on	a lu
nous	avons lu
vous	avez lu
ils/elles	ont lu

IMPERFECT

je	lisais
tu	lisais
il/elle/on	lisait
nous	lisions
vous	lisiez
ils/elles	lisaient

FUTURE

je	lirai
tu	liras
il/elle/on	lira
nous	lirons
vous	lirez
ils/elles	liront

CONDITIONAL

je	lirais
tu	lirais
il/elle/on	lirait
nous	lirions
vous	liriez
ils/elles	liraient

IMPERATIVE

lis / lisons / lisez

PAST PARTICIPLE

lu

PRESENT PARTICIPLE

lisant

EXAMPLE PHRASES

Vous **avez lu** "Madame Bovary"? — *Have you read "Madame Bovary"?*
Je le **lirai** dans l'avion. — *I'll read it on the plane.*
Elle lui **lisait** une histoire. — *She was reading him a story.*

to eat **manger**

PRESENT

je	mange
tu	manges
il/elle/on	mange
nous	mangeons
vous	mangez
ils/elles	mangent

PRESENT SUBJUNCTIVE

je	mange
tu	manges
il/elle/on	mange
nous	mangions
vous	mangiez
ils/elles	mangent

PERFECT

j'	ai mangé
tu	as mangé
il/elle/on	a mangé
nous	avons mangé
vous	avez mangé
ils/elles	ont mangé

IMPERFECT

je	mangeais
tu	mangeais
il/elle/on	mangeait
nous	mangions
vous	mangiez
ils/elles	mangeaient

FUTURE

je	mangerai
tu	mangeras
il/elle/on	mangera
nous	mangerons
vous	mangerez
ils/elles	mangeront

CONDITIONAL

je	mangerais
tu	mangerais
il/elle/on	mangerait
nous	mangerions
vous	mangeriez
ils/elles	mangeraient

IMPERATIVE

mange / mangeons / mangez

PAST PARTICIPLE

mangé

PRESENT PARTICIPLE

mangeant

EXAMPLE PHRASES

Nous ne **mangeons** pas souvent ensemble.	*We don't often eat together.*
Tu **as** assez **mangé**?	*Have you had enough to eat?*
Je **mangerai** plus tard.	*I'll eat later on.*

Table 46

maudire *to curse*

PRESENT

je	maudis
tu	maudis
il/elle/on	maudit
nous	maudissons
vous	maudissez
ils/elles	maudissent

PRESENT SUBJUNCTIVE

je	maudisse
tu	maudisses
il/elle/on	maudisse
nous	maudissions
vous	maudissiez
ils/elles	maudissent

PERFECT

j'	ai maudit
tu	as maudit
il/elle/on	a maudit
nous	avons maudit
vous	avez maudit
ils/elles	ont maudit

IMPERFECT

je	maudissais
tu	maudissais
il/elle/on	maudissait
nous	maudissions
vous	maudissiez
ils/elles	maudissaient

FUTURE

je	maudirai
tu	maudiras
il/elle/on	maudira
nous	maudirons
vous	maudirez
ils/elles	maudiront

CONDITIONAL

je	maudirais
tu	maudirais
il/elle/on	maudirait
nous	maudirions
vous	maudiriez
ils/elles	maudiraient

IMPERATIVE

maudis / maudissons / maudissez

PAST PARTICIPLE

maudit

PRESENT PARTICIPLE

maudissant

EXAMPLE PHRASES

Ils **maudissent** leurs ennemis. *They curse their enemies.*
Ce **maudit** stylo ne marche pas! *This blasted pen doesn't work!*

PRESENT		**PRESENT SUBJUNCTIVE**	
je	mets	je	mette
tu	mets	tu	mettes
il/elle/on	met	il/elle/on	mette
nous	mettons	nous	mettions
vous	mettez	vous	mettiez
ils/elles	mettent	ils/elles	mettent

PERFECT		**IMPERFECT**	
j'	ai mis	je	mettais
tu	as mis	tu	mettais
il/elle/on	a mis	il/elle/on	mettait
nous	avons mis	nous	mettions
vous	avez mis	vous	mettiez
ils/elles	ont mis	ils/elles	mettaient

FUTURE		**CONDITIONAL**	
je	mettrai	je	mettrais
tu	mettras	tu	mettrais
il/elle/on	mettra	il/elle/on	mettrait
nous	mettrons	nous	mettrions
vous	mettrez	vous	mettriez
ils/elles	mettront	ils/elles	mettraient

IMPERATIVE

mets / mettons / mettez

PAST PARTICIPLE

mis

PRESENT PARTICIPLE

mettant

EXAMPLE PHRASES

Mets ton manteau!	*Put your coat on!*
Où est-ce que tu **as mis** les clés?	*Where have you put the keys?*
J'**ai mis** le livre sur la table.	*I put the book on the table.*
Elle **s'est mise** à pleurer.	*She started crying.*

- *Note that **se mettre** follows the same pattern, but takes **être** in the perfect tense. For an example of a reflexive verb in full, see verb table **82 se taire**.*

Table 48

monter *to go up*

PRESENT

je	monte
tu	montes
il/elle/on	monte
nous	montons
vous	montez
ils/elles	montent

PRESENT SUBJUNCTIVE

je	monte
tu	montes
il/elle/on	monte
nous	montions
vous	montiez
ils/elles	montent

PERFECT

je	suis monté(e)
tu	es monté(e)
il/elle/on	est monté(e)
nous	sommes monté(e)s
vous	êtes monté(e)(s)
ils/elles	sont monté(e)s

IMPERFECT

je	montais
tu	montais
il/elle/on	montait
nous	montions
vous	montiez
ils/elles	montaient

FUTURE

je	monterai
tu	monteras
il/elle/on	montera
nous	monterons
vous	monterez
ils/elles	monteront

CONDITIONAL

je	monterais
tu	monterais
il/elle/on	monterait
nous	monterions
vous	monteriez
ils/elles	monteraient

IMPERATIVE

monte / montons / montez

PAST PARTICIPLE

monté

PRESENT PARTICIPLE

montant

EXAMPLE PHRASES

Je **suis montée** tout en haut de la tour.	*I went all the way up the tower.*
Monte dans la voiture, je t'emmène.	*Get into the car, I'll take you there.*
Il s'est tordu la cheville en **montant** à une échelle.	*He twisted his ankle going up a ladder.*

- *Note that **monter** takes **avoir** in the perfect tense when it is used with a direct object.*
- *The verb **surmonter** follows the same pattern as **monter**, but takes **avoir** in the perfect tense.*

to bite **mordre**

PRESENT

je	mords
tu	mords
il/elle/on	mord
nous	mordons
vous	mordez
ils/elles	mordent

PRESENT SUBJUNCTIVE

je	morde
tu	mordes
il/elle/on	morde
nous	mordions
vous	mordiez
ils/elles	mordent

PERFECT

j'	ai mordu
tu	as mordu
il/elle/on	a mordu
nous	avons mordu
vous	avez mordu
ils/elles	ont mordu

IMPERFECT

je	mordais
tu	mordais
il/elle/on	mordait
nous	mordions
vous	mordiez
ils/elles	mordaient

FUTURE

je	mordrai
tu	mordras
il/elle/on	mordra
nous	mordrons
vous	mordrez
ils/elles	mordront

CONDITIONAL

je	mordrais
tu	mordrais
il/elle/on	mordrait
nous	mordrions
vous	mordriez
ils/elles	mordraient

IMPERATIVE

mords / mordons / mordez

PAST PARTICIPLE

mordu

PRESENT PARTICIPLE

mordant

EXAMPLE PHRASES

Le chien m'**a mordu**.	*The dog bit me.*
Il ne va pas te **mordre**!	*He won't bite!*

Table 50

moudre *to grind*

PRESENT

je	mouds
tu	mouds
il/elle/on	moud
nous	moulons
vous	moulez
ils/elles	moulent

PRESENT SUBJUNCTIVE

je	moule
tu	moules
il/elle/on	moule
nous	moulions
vous	mouliez
ils/elles	moulent

PERFECT

j'	ai moulu
tu	as moulu
il/elle/on	a moulu
nous	avons moulu
vous	avez moulu
ils/elles	ont moulu

IMPERFECT

je	moulais
tu	moulais
il/elle/on	moulait
nous	moulions
vous	mouliez
ils/elles	moulaient

FUTURE

je	moudrai
tu	moudras
il/elle/on	moudra
nous	moudrons
vous	moudrez
ils/elles	moudront

CONDITIONAL

je	moudrais
tu	moudrais
il/elle/on	moudrait
nous	moudrions
vous	moudriez
ils/elles	moudraient

IMPERATIVE

mouds / moulons / moulez

PAST PARTICIPLE

moulu

PRESENT PARTICIPLE

moulant

EXAMPLE PHRASES

J'**ai moulu** du café pour demain matin. — *I've ground some coffee for tomorrow morning.*

PRESENT

je	meurs
tu	meurs
il/elle/on	meurt
nous	mourons
vous	mourez
ils/elles	meurent

PRESENT SUBJUNCTIVE

je	meure
tu	meures
il/elle/on	meure
nous	mourions
vous	mouriez
ils/elles	meurent

PERFECT

je	suis mort(e)
tu	es mort(e)
il/elle/on	est mort(e)
nous	sommes mort(e)s
vous	êtes mort(e)(s)
ils/elles	sont mort(e)s

IMPERFECT

je	mourais
tu	mourais
il/elle/on	mourait
nous	mourions
vous	mouriez
ils/elles	mouraient

FUTURE

je	mourrai
tu	mourras
il/elle/on	mourra
nous	mourrons
vous	mourrez
ils/elles	mourront

CONDITIONAL

je	mourrais
tu	mourrais
il/elle/on	mourrait
nous	mourrions
vous	mourriez
ils/elles	mourraient

IMPERATIVE

meurs / mourons / mourez

PAST PARTICIPLE

mort

PRESENT PARTICIPLE

mourant

EXAMPLE PHRASES

Elle **est morte** en 2005.	*She died in 2005.*
Ils **sont morts**.	*They're dead.*
On **meurt** de froid ici!	*We're freezing to death in here!*

naître *to be born*

PRESENT		PRESENT SUBJUNCTIVE	
je	nais	je	naisse
tu	nais	tu	naisses
il/elle/on	naît	il/elle/on	naisse
nous	naissons	nous	naissions
vous	naissez	vous	naissiez
ils/elles	naissent	ils/elles	naissent

PERFECT		IMPERFECT	
je	suis né(e)	je	naissais
tu	es né(e)	tu	naissais
il/elle/on	est né(e)	il/elle/on	naissait
nous	sommes né(e)s	nous	naissions
vous	êtes né(e)(s)	vous	naissiez
ils/elles	sont né(e)s	ils/elles	naissaient

FUTURE		CONDITIONAL	
je	naîtrai	je	naîtrais
tu	naîtras	tu	naîtrais
il/elle/on	naîtra	il/elle/on	naîtrait
nous	naîtrons	nous	naîtrions
vous	naîtrez	vous	naîtriez
ils/elles	naîtront	ils/elles	naîtraient

IMPERATIVE

nais / naissons / naissez

PAST PARTICIPLE

né

PRESENT PARTICIPLE

naissant

EXAMPLE PHRASES

Je **suis née** le 12 février.	*I was born on 12 February.*
Le bébé de Delphine **naîtra** en mars.	*Delphine is going to have a baby in March.*
Quand est-ce que tu **es né**?	*When were you born?*

PRESENT

je	nettoie
tu	nettoies
il/elle/on	nettoie
nous	nettoyons
vous	nettoyez
ils/elles	nettoient

PRESENT SUBJUNCTIVE

je	nettoie
tu	nettoies
il/elle/on	nettoie
nous	nettoyions
vous	nettoyiez
ils/elles	nettoient

PERFECT

j'	ai nettoyé
tu	as nettoyé
il/elle/on	a nettoyé
nous	avons nettoyé
vous	avez nettoyé
ils/elles	ont nettoyé

IMPERFECT

je	nettoyais
tu	nettoyais
il/elle/on	nettoyait
nous	nettoyions
vous	nettoyiez
ils/elles	nettoyaient

FUTURE

je	nettoierai
tu	nettoieras
il/elle/on	nettoiera
nous	nettoierons
vous	nettoierez
ils/elles	nettoieront

CONDITIONAL

je	nettoierais
tu	nettoierais
il/elle/on	nettoierait
nous	nettoierions
vous	nettoieriez
ils/elles	nettoieraient

IMPERATIVE

nettoie / nettoyons / nettoyez

PAST PARTICIPLE

nettoyé

PRESENT PARTICIPLE

nettoyant

EXAMPLE PHRASES

Richard **a nettoyé** tout l'appartement.	*Richard has cleaned the whole flat.*
Elle **nettoyait** le sol en écoutant la radio.	*She was cleaning the floor while listening to the radio.*
Je ne **nettoie** pas souvent mes lunettes.	*I don't clean my glasses very often.*

Table 54

offrir *to offer*

PRESENT

j'	offre
tu	offres
il/elle/on	offre
nous	offrons
vous	offrez
ils/elles	offrent

PRESENT SUBJUNCTIVE

j'	offre
tu	offres
il/elle/on	offre
nous	offrions
vous	offriez
ils/elles	offrent

PERFECT

j'	ai offert
tu	as offert
il/elle/on	a offert
nous	avons offert
vous	avez offert
ils/elles	ont offert

IMPERFECT

j'	offrais
tu	offrais
il/elle/on	offrait
nous	offrions
vous	offriez
ils/elles	offraient

FUTURE

j'	offrirai
tu	offriras
il/elle/on	offrira
nous	offrirons
vous	offrirez
ils/elles	offriront

CONDITIONAL

j'	offrirais
tu	offrirais
il/elle/on	offrirait
nous	offririons
vous	offririez
ils/elles	offriraient

IMPERATIVE

offre / offrons / offrez

PAST PARTICIPLE

offert

PRESENT PARTICIPLE

offrant

EXAMPLE PHRASES

On lui **a offert** un poste de secrétaire.	*They offered her a secreterial post.*
Offre-lui des fleurs.	*Give her some flowers.*
Viens, je t'**offre** à boire.	*Come on, I'll buy you a drink.*
Je **me suis offert** un nouveau stylo.	*I treated myself to a new pen.*

- *Note that **s'offrir** follows the same pattern, but takes **être** in the perfect tense. For an example of a reflexive verb in full, see verb table **6 s'asseoir**.*

PRESENT		PRESENT SUBJUNCTIVE	
j'	ouvre	j'	ouvre
tu	ouvres	tu	ouvres
il/elle/on	ouvre	il/elle/on	ouvre
nous	ouvrons	nous	ouvrions
vous	ouvrez	vous	ouvriez
ils/elles	ouvrent	ils/elles	ouvrent

PERFECT		IMPERFECT	
j'	ai ouvert	j'	ouvrais
tu	as ouvert	tu	ouvrais
il/elle/on	a ouvert	il/elle/on	ouvrait
nous	avons ouvert	nous	ouvrions
vous	avez ouvert	vous	ouvriez
ils/elles	ont ouvert	ils/elles	ouvraient

FUTURE		CONDITIONAL	
j'	ouvrirai	j'	ouvrirais
tu	ouvriras	tu	ouvrirais
il/elle/on	ouvrira	il/elle/on	ouvrirait
nous	ouvrirons	nous	ouvririons
vous	ouvrirez	vous	ouvririez
ils/elles	ouvriront	ils/elles	ouvriraient

IMPERATIVE
ouvre / ouvrons / ouvrez

PAST PARTICIPLE
ouvert

PRESENT PARTICIPLE
ouvrant

EXAMPLE PHRASES

Elle **a ouvert** la porte.	*She opened the door.*
Est-ce que tu pourrais **ouvrir** la fenêtre?	*Could you open the window?*
Je me suis coupé en **ouvrant** une boîte de conserve.	*I cut myself opening a tin.*
La porte **s'est ouverte**.	*The door opened.*

- *Note that **s'ouvrir** follows the same pattern, but takes **être** in the perfect tense. For an example of a reflexive verb in full, see verb table **6 s'asseoir**.*

Table 56

paraître *to appear*

PRESENT

je	parais
tu	parais
il/elle/on	paraît
nous	paraissons
vous	paraissez
ils/elles	paraissent

PRESENT SUBJUNCTIVE

je	paraisse
tu	paraisses
il/elle/on	paraisse
nous	paraissions
vous	paraissiez
ils/elles	paraissent

PERFECT

j'	ai paru
tu	as paru
il/elle/on	a paru
nous	avons paru
vous	avez paru
ils/elles	ont paru

IMPERFECT

je	paraissais
tu	paraissais
il/elle/on	paraissait
nous	paraissions
vous	paraissiez
ils/elles	paraissaient

FUTURE

je	paraîtrai
tu	paraîtras
il/elle/on	paraîtra
nous	paraîtrons
vous	paraîtrez
ils/elles	paraîtront

CONDITIONAL

je	paraîtrais
tu	paraîtrais
il/elle/on	paraîtrait
nous	paraîtrions
vous	paraîtriez
ils/elles	paraîtraient

IMPERATIVE

parais / paraissons / paraissez

PAST PARTICIPLE

paru

PRESENT PARTICIPLE

paraissant

EXAMPLE PHRASES

Elle **paraissait** fatiguée.	*She seemed tired.*
Gisèle **paraît** plus jeune que son âge.	*Gisèle doesn't look her age.*
Il **paraît** qu'il fait chaud toute l'année là-bas.	*Apparently it's hot all year round over there.*

- *Note that the verb **apparaître** follows the same pattern as **paraître**, but takes **être** in the perfect tense.*

PRESENT

je	pars
tu	pars
il/elle/on	part
nous	partons
vous	partez
ils/elles	partent

PRESENT SUBJUNCTIVE

je	parte
tu	partes
il/elle/on	parte
nous	partions
vous	partiez
ils/elles	partent

PERFECT

je	suis parti(e)
tu	es parti(e)
il/elle/on	est parti(e)
nous	sommes parti(e)s
vous	êtes parti(e)(s)
ils/elles	sont parti(e)s

IMPERFECT

je	partais
tu	partais
il/elle/on	partait
nous	partions
vous	partiez
ils/elles	partaient

FUTURE

je	partirai
tu	partiras
il/elle/on	partira
nous	partirons
vous	partirez
ils/elles	partiront

CONDITIONAL

je	partirais
tu	partirais
il/elle/on	partirait
nous	partirions
vous	partiriez
ils/elles	partiraient

IMPERATIVE

pars / partons / partez

PAST PARTICIPLE

parti

PRESENT PARTICIPLE

partant

EXAMPLE PHRASES

On **part** en vacances le 15 août. — *We're going on holiday on 15 August.*
Ne **partez** pas sans moi! — *Don't leave without me!*
Elle **est partie** tôt ce matin. — *She left early this morning.*

passer *to pass*

PRESENT

je	passe
tu	passes
il/elle/on	passe
nous	passons
vous	passez
ils/elles	passent

PRESENT SUBJUNCTIVE

je	passe
tu	passes
il/elle/on	passe
nous	passions
vous	passiez
ils/elles	passent

PERFECT

j'	ai passé
tu	as passé
il/elle/on	a passé
nous	avons passé
vous	avez passé
ils/elles	ont passé

IMPERFECT

je	passais
tu	passais
il/elle/on	passait
nous	passions
vous	passiez
ils/elles	passaient

FUTURE

je	passerai
tu	passeras
il/elle/on	passera
nous	passerons
vous	passerez
ils/elles	passeront

CONDITIONAL

je	passerais
tu	passerais
il/elle/on	passerait
nous	passerions
vous	passeriez
ils/elles	passeraient

IMPERATIVE

passe / passons / passez

PAST PARTICIPLE

passé

PRESENT PARTICIPLE

passant

EXAMPLE PHRASES

Les mois **ont passé**.	*Months passed.*
Il **a passé** son examen en juin.	*He took his exam in June.*
Elle y **a passé** deux mois.	*She spent two months there.*
Elle **est passée** me dire bonjour.	*She came by to say hello.*
L'histoire **se passe** au Mexique.	*The story takes place in Mexico.*

- *Note that **passer** can also take **être** in the perfect tense when it means "to call in" or "to go through"*
- *Note that **se passer** follows the same pattern, but takes **être** in the perfect tense. For an example of a reflexive verb in full, see verb table **6 s'asseoir**.*

to pay payer

PRESENT

je	paye
tu	payes
il/elle/on	paye
nous	payons
vous	payez
ils/elles	payent

PRESENT SUBJUNCTIVE

je	paye
tu	payes
il/elle/on	paye
nous	payions
vous	payiez
ils/elles	payent

PERFECT

j'	ai payé
tu	as payé
il/elle/on	a payé
nous	avons payé
vous	avez payé
ils/elles	ont payé

IMPERFECT

je	payais
tu	payais
il/elle/on	payait
nous	payions
vous	payiez
ils/elles	payaient

FUTURE

je	paierai
tu	paieras
il/elle/on	paiera
nous	paierons
vous	paierez
ils/elles	paieront

CONDITIONAL

je	paierais
tu	paierais
il/elle/on	paierait
nous	paierions
vous	paieriez
ils/elles	paieraient

IMPERATIVE

paye / payons / payez

PAST PARTICIPLE

payé

PRESENT PARTICIPLE

payant

EXAMPLE PHRASES

Tu l'**as payé** combien? — *How much did you pay for it?*
Ma patronne me **paiera** demain. — *My boss will pay me tomorrow.*
Les étudiants **payent** moitié prix. — *Students pay half price.*

Table 60

peindre *to paint*

PRESENT

je	peins
tu	peins
il/elle/on	peint
nous	peignons
vous	peignez
ils/elles	peignent

PRESENT SUBJUNCTIVE

je	peigne
tu	peignes
il/elle/on	peigne
nous	peignions
vous	peigniez
ils/elles	peignent

PERFECT

j'	ai peint
tu	as peint
il/elle/on	a peint
nous	avons peint
vous	avez peint
ils/elles	ont peint

IMPERFECT

je	peignais
tu	peignais
il/elle/on	peignait
nous	peignions
vous	peigniez
ils/elles	peignaient

FUTURE

je	peindrai
tu	peindras
il/elle/on	peindra
nous	peindrons
vous	peindrez
ils/elles	peindront

CONDITIONAL

je	peindrais
tu	peindrais
il/elle/on	peindrait
nous	peindrions
vous	peindriez
ils/elles	peindraient

IMPERATIVE

peins / peignons / peignez

PAST PARTICIPLE

peint

PRESENT PARTICIPLE

peignant

EXAMPLE PHRASES

On **a peint** l'entrée en bleu clair. — *We painted the hall light blue.*
Ce tableau **a été peint** en 1913. — *This picture was painted in 1913.*

to lose **perdre**

PRESENT

je	perds
tu	perds
il/elle/on	perd
nous	perdons
vous	perdez
ils/elles	perdent

PRESENT SUBJUNCTIVE

je	perde
tu	perdes
il/elle/on	perde
nous	perdions
vous	perdiez
ils/elles	perdent

PERFECT

j'	ai perdu
tu	as perdu
il/elle/on	a perdu
nous	avons perdu
vous	avez perdu
ils/elles	ont perdu

IMPERFECT

je	perdais
tu	perdais
il/elle/on	perdait
nous	perdions
vous	perdiez
ils/elles	perdaient

FUTURE

je	perdrai
tu	perdras
il/elle/on	perdra
nous	perdrons
vous	perdrez
ils/elles	perdront

CONDITIONAL

je	perdrais
tu	perdrais
il/elle/on	perdrait
nous	perdrions
vous	perdriez
ils/elles	perdraient

IMPERATIVE

perds / perdons / perdez

PAST PARTICIPLE

perdu

PRESENT PARTICIPLE

perdant

EXAMPLE PHRASES

J'**ai perdu** mon porte-monnaie dans le métro.	*I lost my purse on the underground.*
L'Italie **a perdu** un à zéro.	*Italy lost one-nil.*
Si tu **te perds**, appelle-moi.	*Call me if you get lost.*

- *Note that **se perdre** follows the same pattern, but takes **être** in the perfect tense. For an example of a reflexive verb in full, see verb table **82 se taire**.*

Table 62

plaire *to please*

PRESENT

je	plais
tu	plais
il/elle/on	plaît
nous	plaisons
vous	plaisez
ils/elles	plaisent

PRESENT SUBJUNCTIVE

je	plaise
tu	plaises
il/elle/on	plaise
nous	plaisions
vous	plaisiez
ils/elles	plaisent

PERFECT

j'	ai plu
tu	as plu
il/elle/on	a plu
nous	avons plu
vous	avez plu
ils/elles	ont plu

IMPERFECT

je	plaisais
tu	plaisais
il/elle/on	plaisait
nous	plaisions
vous	plaisiez
ils/elles	plaisaient

FUTURE

je	plairai
tu	plairas
il/elle/on	plaira
nous	plairons
vous	plairez
ils/elles	plairont

CONDITIONAL

je	plairais
tu	plairais
il/elle/on	plairait
nous	plairions
vous	plairiez
ils/elles	plairaient

IMPERATIVE

plais / plaisons / plaisez

PAST PARTICIPLE

plu

PRESENT PARTICIPLE

plaisant

EXAMPLE PHRASES

Le menu ne me **plaît** pas.	*I don't like the menu.*
Ça te **plairait** d'aller à la mer?	*Would you like to go to the seaside?*
Ça t'**a plu**, le film?	*Did you like the film?*
s'il te **plaît**	*please*
s'il vous **plaît**	*please*

PRESENT

il pleut

PRESENT SUBJUNCTIVE

il pleuve

PERFECT

il a plu

IMPERFECT

il pleuvait

FUTURE

il pleuvra

CONDITIONAL

il pleuvrait

IMPERATIVE

not used

PRESENT PARTICIPLE

not used

PAST PARTICIPLE

plu

EXAMPLE PHRASES

Il **a plu** toute la journée. *It rained all day long.*
Il **pleut** beaucoup à Glasgow. *It rains a lot in Glasgow.*
J'espère qu'il ne **pleuvra** pas demain. *I hope it won't be raining tomorrow.*

Table 64

pouvoir *to be able*

PRESENT

je	peux
tu	peux
il/elle/on	peut
nous	pouvons
vous	pouvez
ils/elles	peuvent

PRESENT SUBJUNCTIVE

je	puisse
tu	puisses
il/elle/on	puisse
nous	puissions
vous	puissiez
ils/elles	puissent

PERFECT

j'	ai pu
tu	as pu
il/elle/on	a pu
nous	avons pu
vous	avez pu
ils/elles	ont pu

IMPERFECT

je	pouvais
tu	pouvais
il/elle/on	pouvait
nous	pouvions
vous	pouviez
ils/elles	pouvaient

FUTURE

je	pourrai
tu	pourras
il/elle/on	pourra
nous	pourrons
vous	pourrez
ils/elles	pourront

CONDITIONAL

je	pourrais
tu	pourrais
il/elle/on	pourrait
nous	pourrions
vous	pourriez
ils/elles	pourraient

IMPERATIVE

not used

PAST PARTICIPLE

pu

PRESENT PARTICIPLE

pouvant

EXAMPLE PHRASES

Je **peux** t'aider, si tu veux.	*I can help you if you like.*
J'ai fait tout ce que j'**ai pu**.	*I did all I could.*
Je ne **pourrai** pas venir samedi.	*I won't be able to come on Saturday.*

to take **prendre**

PRESENT

je	prends
tu	prends
il/elle/on	prend
nous	prenons
vous	prenez
ils/elles	prennent

PRESENT SUBJUNCTIVE

je	prenne
tu	prennes
il/elle/on	prenne
nous	prenions
vous	preniez
ils/elles	prennent

PERFECT

j'	ai pris
tu	as pris
il/elle/on	a pris
nous	avons pris
vous	avez pris
ils/elles	ont pris

IMPERFECT

je	prenais
tu	prenais
il/elle/on	prenait
nous	prenions
vous	preniez
ils/elles	prenaient

FUTURE

je	prendrai
tu	prendras
il/elle/on	prendra
nous	prendrons
vous	prendrez
ils/elles	prendront

CONDITIONAL

je	prendrais
tu	prendrais
il/elle/on	prendrait
nous	prendrions
vous	prendriez
ils/elles	prendraient

IMPERATIVE

prends / prenons / prenez

PAST PARTICIPLE

pris

PRESENT PARTICIPLE

prenant

EXAMPLE PHRASES

J'**ai pris** plein de photos.	*I took lots of pictures.*
N'oublie pas de **prendre** ton passeport.	*Don't forget to take your passport.*
Il **prendra** le train de 8h20.	*He'll take the 8.20 train.*
Pour qui est-ce qu'il **se prend**?	*Who does he think he is?*

- *Note that **se prendre** follows the same pattern, but takes **être** in the perfect tense. For an example of a reflexive verb in full, see verb table **82 se taire**.*

Table 66

protéger *to protect*

PRESENT

je	protège
tu	protèges
il/elle/on	protège
nous	protégeons
vous	protégez
ils/elles	protègent

PRESENT SUBJUNCTIVE

je	protège
tu	protèges
il/elle/on	protège
nous	protégions
vous	protégiez
ils/elles	protègent

PERFECT

j'	ai protégé
tu	as protégé
il/elle/on	a protégé
nous	avons protégé
vous	avez protégé
ils/elles	ont protégé

IMPERFECT

je	protégeais
tu	protégeais
il/elle/on	protégeait
nous	protégions
vous	protégiez
ils/elles	protégeaient

FUTURE

je	protégerai
tu	protégeras
il/elle/on	protégera
nous	protégerons
vous	protégerez
ils/elles	protégeront

CONDITIONAL

je	protégerais
tu	protégerais
il/elle/on	protégerait
nous	protégerions
vous	protégeriez
ils/elles	protégeraient

IMPERATIVE

protège / protégeons / protégez

PAST PARTICIPLE

protégé

PRESENT PARTICIPLE

protégeant

EXAMPLE PHRASES

Il **protège** sa petite sœur à l'école. — *He protects his little sister at school.*

Protège ton livre de la pluie. — *Protect your book from the rain.*

Le champ **est protégé** du vent par la colline. — *The field is sheltered from the wind by the hill.*

PRESENT

je	reçois
tu	reçois
il/elle/on	reçoit
nous	recevons
vous	recevez
ils/elles	reçoivent

PRESENT SUBJUNCTIVE

je	reçoive
tu	reçoives
il/elle/on	reçoive
nous	recevions
vous	receviez
ils/elles	reçoivent

PERFECT

j'	ai reçu
tu	as reçu
il/elle/on	a reçu
nous	avons reçu
vous	avez reçu
ils/elles	ont reçu

IMPERFECT

je	recevais
tu	recevais
il/elle/on	recevait
nous	recevions
vous	receviez
ils/elles	recevaient

FUTURE

je	recevrai
tu	recevras
il/elle/on	recevra
nous	recevrons
vous	recevrez
ils/elles	recevront

CONDITIONAL

je	recevrais
tu	recevrais
il/elle/on	recevrait
nous	recevrions
vous	recevriez
ils/elles	recevraient

IMPERATIVE

reçois / recevons / recevez

PAST PARTICIPLE

reçu

PRESENT PARTICIPLE

recevant

EXAMPLE PHRASES

Elle **a reçu** une lettre de Charlotte.	*She received a letter from Charlotte.*
Je ne **reçois** jamais de courrier.	*I never get any mail.*
Elle **recevra** une réponse la semaine prochaine.	*She'll get an answer next week.*

Table **68**

rentrer *to go back; to go in*

PRESENT		PRESENT SUBJUNCTIVE	
je	rentre	je	rentre
tu	rentres	tu	rentres
il/elle/on	rentre	il/elle/on	rentre
nous	rentrons	nous	rentrions
vous	rentrez	vous	rentriez
ils/elles	rentrent	ils/elles	rentrent

PERFECT		IMPERFECT	
je	suis rentré(e)	je	rentrais
tu	es rentré(e)	tu	rentrais
il/elle/on	est rentré(e)	il/elle/on	rentrait
nous	sommes rentré(e)s	nous	rentrions
vous	êtes rentré(e)(s)	vous	rentriez
ils/elles	sont rentré(e)s	ils/elles	rentraient

FUTURE		CONDITIONAL	
je	rentrerai	je	rentrerais
tu	rentreras	tu	rentrerais
il/elle/on	rentrera	il/elle/on	rentrerait
nous	rentrerons	nous	rentrerions
vous	rentrerez	vous	rentreriez
ils/elles	rentreront	ils/elles	rentreraient

IMPERATIVE
rentre / rentrons / rentrez

PAST PARTICIPLE
rentré

PRESENT PARTICIPLE
rentrant

EXAMPLE PHRASES

Ne **rentre** pas trop tard.	*Don't come home too late.*
Ils **sont rentrés** dans le magasin.	*They went into the shop.*
À quelle heure est-ce qu'elle **est rentrée**?	*What time did she get in?*
Je **rentre** déjeuner à midi.	*I go home for lunch.*
Il **a** déjà **rentré** la voiture dans le garage.	*He's already brought the car into the garage.*

- *Note that **rentrer** takes **avoir** in the perfect tense when it is used with a direct object.*

to answer **répondre**

PRESENT

je	réponds
tu	réponds
il/elle/on	répond
nous	répondons
vous	répondez
ils/elles	répondent

PRESENT SUBJUNCTIVE

je	réponde
tu	répondes
il/elle/on	réponde
nous	répondions
vous	répondiez
ils/elles	répondent

PERFECT

j'	ai répondu
tu	as répondu
il/elle/on	a répondu
nous	avons répondu
vous	avez répondu
ils/elles	ont répondu

IMPERFECT

je	répondais
tu	répondais
il/elle/on	répondait
nous	répondions
vous	répondiez
ils/elles	répondaient

FUTURE

je	répondrai
tu	répondras
il/elle/on	répondra
nous	répondrons
vous	répondrez
ils/elles	répondront

CONDITIONAL

je	répondrais
tu	répondrais
il/elle/on	répondrait
nous	répondrions
vous	répondriez
ils/elles	répondraient

IMPERATIVE

réponds / répondons / répondez

PAST PARTICIPLE

répondu

PRESENT PARTICIPLE

répondant

EXAMPLE PHRASES

Lisez le texte et **répondez** aux questions.	*Read the text and answer the questions.*
C'est elle qui **a répondu** au téléphone.	*She answered the phone.*
Ça ne **répond** pas.	*There's no reply.*

résoudre *to solve*

PRESENT

je	résous
tu	résous
il/elle/on	résout
nous	résolvons
vous	résolvez
ils/elles	résolvent

PRESENT SUBJUNCTIVE

je	résolve
tu	résolves
il/elle/on	résolve
nous	résolvions
vous	résolviez
ils/elles	résolvent

PERFECT

j'	ai résolu
tu	as résolu
il/elle/on	a résolu
nous	avons résolu
vous	avez résolu
ils/elles	ont résolu

IMPERFECT

je	résolvais
tu	résolvais
il/elle/on	résolvait
nous	résolvions
vous	résolviez
ils/elles	résolvaient

FUTURE

je	résoudrai
tu	résoudras
il/elle/on	résoudra
nous	résoudrons
vous	résoudrez
ils/elles	résoudront

CONDITIONAL

je	résoudrais
tu	résoudrais
il/elle/on	résoudrait
nous	résoudrions
vous	résoudriez
ils/elles	résoudraient

IMPERATIVE

résous / résolvons / résolvez

PAST PARTICIPLE

résolu

PRESENT PARTICIPLE

résolvant

EXAMPLE PHRASES

J'**ai résolu** le problème. — *I've solved the problem.*

La violence ne **résout** rien. — *Violence doesn't solve anything.*

- *Note that the verb **dissoudre** follows the same pattern as **résoudre**, except for its past participle which is **dissous** (m), **dissoute** (f).*

to remain **rester**

PRESENT

je	reste
tu	restes
il/elle/on	reste
nous	restons
vous	restez
ils/elles	restent

PRESENT SUBJUNCTIVE

je	reste
tu	restes
il/elle/on	reste
nous	restions
vous	restiez
ils/elles	restent

PERFECT

je	suis resté(e)
tu	es resté(e)
il/elle/on	est resté(e)
nous	sommes resté(e)s
vous	êtes resté(e)(s)
ils/elles	sont resté(e)s

IMPERFECT

je	restais
tu	restais
il/elle/on	restait
nous	restions
vous	restiez
ils/elles	restaient

FUTURE

je	resterai
tu	resteras
il/elle/on	restera
nous	resterons
vous	resterez
ils/elles	resteront

CONDITIONAL

je	resterais
tu	resterais
il/elle/on	resterait
nous	resterions
vous	resteriez
ils/elles	resteraient

IMPERATIVE

reste / restons / restez

PAST PARTICIPLE

resté

PRESENT PARTICIPLE

restant

EXAMPLE PHRASES

Cet été, je **reste** en Écosse.	*I'm staying in Scotland this summer.*
Ils ne **sont** pas **restés** très longtemps.	*They didn't stay very long.*
Il leur **restait** encore un peu d'argent.	*They still had some money left.*

retourner *to return*

PRESENT

je	retourne
tu	retournes
il/elle/on	retourne
nous	retournons
vous	retournez
ils/elles	retournent

PRESENT SUBJUNCTIVE

je	retourne
tu	retournes
il/elle/on	retourne
nous	retournions
vous	retourniez
ils/elles	retournent

PERFECT

je	suis retourné(e)
tu	es retourné(e)
il/elle/on	est retourné(e)
nous	sommes retourné(e)s
vous	êtes retourné(e)(s)
ils/elles	sont retourné(e)s

IMPERFECT

je	retournais
tu	retournais
il/elle/on	retournait
nous	retournions
vous	retourniez
ils/elles	retournaient

FUTURE

je	retournerai
tu	retourneras
il/elle/on	retournera
nous	retournerons
vous	retournerez
ils/elles	retourneront

CONDITIONAL

je	retournerais
tu	retournerais
il/elle/on	retournerait
nous	retournerions
vous	retourneriez
ils/elles	retourneraient

IMPERATIVE

retourne / retournons / retournez

PAST PARTICIPLE

retourné

PRESENT PARTICIPLE

retournant

EXAMPLE PHRASES

Tu **es retournée** à Londres? — *Have you been back to London?*
J'aimerais bien **retourner** en Italie un jour. — *I'd like to go back to Italy one day.*
Elle **a retourné** la carte pour vérifier. — *She turned the card over to check.*
Zoë, **retourne-toi**! — *Turn around Zoë!*

- *Note that **retourner** takes **avoir** in the perfect tense when it is used with a direct object.*
- *Note that **se retourner** follows the same pattern, and takes **être** in the perfect tense. For an example of a reflexive verb in full, see verb table **82 se taire**.*

to come back **revenir**

PRESENT

je	reviens
tu	reviens
il/elle/on	revient
nous	revenons
vous	revenez
ils/elles	reviennent

PRESENT SUBJUNCTIVE

je	revienne
tu	reviennes
il/elle/on	revienne
nous	revenions
vous	reveniez
ils/elles	reviennent

PERFECT

je	suis revenu(e)
tu	es revenu(e)
il/elle/on	est revenu(e)
nous	sommes revenu(e)s
vous	êtes revenu(e)(s)
ils/elles	sont revenu(e)s

IMPERFECT

je	revenais
tu	revenais
il/elle/on	revenait
nous	revenions
vous	reveniez
ils/elles	revenaient

FUTURE

je	reviendrai
tu	reviendras
il/elle/on	reviendra
nous	reviendrons
vous	reviendrez
ils/elles	reviendront

CONDITIONAL

je	reviendrais
tu	reviendrais
il/elle/on	reviendrait
nous	reviendrions
vous	reviendriez
ils/elles	reviendraient

IMPERATIVE

reviens / revenons / revenez

PAST PARTICIPLE

revenu

PRESENT PARTICIPLE

revenant

EXAMPLE PHRASES

Mon chat n'**est** toujours pas **revenu**. — *My cat still hasn't come back.*

Je **reviens** dans cinq minutes! — *I'll be back in five minutes!*

Ça me **revient**! — *It's coming back to me now!*

rire *to laugh*

PRESENT

je	ris
tu	ris
il/elle/on	rit
nous	rions
vous	riez
ils/elles	rient

PRESENT SUBJUNCTIVE

je	rie
tu	ries
il/elle/on	rie
nous	riions
vous	riiez
ils/elles	rient

PERFECT

j'	ai ri
tu	as ri
il/elle/on	a ri
nous	avons ri
vous	avez ri
ils/elles	ont ri

IMPERFECT

je	riais
tu	riais
il/elle/on	riait
nous	riions
vous	riiez
ils/elles	riaient

FUTURE

je	rirai
tu	riras
il/elle/on	rira
nous	rirons
vous	rirez
ils/elles	riront

CONDITIONAL

je	rirais
tu	rirais
il/elle/on	rirait
nous	ririons
vous	ririez
ils/elles	riraient

IMPERATIVE

ris / rions / riez

PAST PARTICIPLE

ri

PRESENT PARTICIPLE

riant

EXAMPLE PHRASES

On **a** bien **ri**.	*We had a good laugh.*
Ne **ris** pas, ce n'est pas drôle!	*Don't laugh, it's not funny!*
C'était juste pour **rire**.	*It was only for a laugh.*

PRESENT

je	romps
tu	romps
il/elle/on	rompt
nous	rompons
vous	rompez
ils/elles	rompent

PRESENT SUBJUNCTIVE

je	rompe
tu	rompes
il/elle/on	rompe
nous	rompions
vous	rompiez
ils/elles	rompent

PERFECT

j'	ai rompu
tu	as rompu
il/elle/on	a rompu
nous	avons rompu
vous	avez rompu
ils/elles	ont rompu

IMPERFECT

je	rompais
tu	rompais
il/elle/on	rompait
nous	rompions
vous	rompiez
ils/elles	rompaient

FUTURE

je	romprai
tu	rompras
il/elle/on	rompra
nous	romprons
vous	romprez
ils/elles	rompront

CONDITIONAL

je	romprais
tu	romprais
il/elle/on	romprait
nous	romprions
vous	rompriez
ils/elles	rompraient

IMPERATIVE

romps / rompons / rompez

PAST PARTICIPLE

rompu

PRESENT PARTICIPLE

rompant

EXAMPLE PHRASES

Elle **a rompu** le silence. — *She broke the silence.*

Paul et Jo **ont rompu**. — *Paul and Jo have split up.*

savoir *to know*

PRESENT

je	sais
tu	sais
il/elle/on	sait
nous	savons
vous	savez
ils/elles	savent

PRESENT SUBJUNCTIVE

je	sache
tu	saches
il/elle/on	sache
nous	sachions
vous	sachiez
ils/elles	sachent

PERFECT

j'	ai su
tu	as su
il/elle/on	a su
nous	avons su
vous	avez su
ils/elles	ont su

IMPERFECT

je	savais
tu	savais
il/elle/on	savait
nous	savions
vous	saviez
ils/elles	savaient

FUTURE

je	saurai
tu	sauras
il/elle/on	saura
nous	saurons
vous	saurez
ils/elles	sauront

CONDITIONAL

je	saurais
tu	saurais
il/elle/on	saurait
nous	saurions
vous	sauriez
ils/elles	sauraient

IMPERATIVE

sache / sachons / sachez

PAST PARTICIPLE

su

PRESENT PARTICIPLE

sachant

EXAMPLE PHRASES

Tu **sais** ce que tu vas faire l'année prochaine?	*Do you know what you're doing next year?*
Je ne **sais** pas.	*I don't know.*
Elle ne **sait** pas nager.	*She can't swim.*
Tu **savais** que son père était pakistanais?	*Did you know her father was Pakistani?*

to smell; to feel **sentir**

PRESENT

je	sens
tu	sens
il/elle/on	sent
nous	sentons
vous	sentez
ils/elles	sentent

PRESENT SUBJUNCTIVE

je	sente
tu	sentes
il/elle/on	sente
nous	sentions
vous	sentiez
ils/elles	sentent

PERFECT

j'	ai senti
tu	as senti
il/elle/on	a senti
nous	avons senti
vous	avez senti
ils/elles	ont senti

IMPERFECT

je	sentais
tu	sentais
il/elle/on	sentait
nous	sentions
vous	sentiez
ils/elles	sentaient

FUTURE

je	sentirai
tu	sentiras
il/elle/on	sentira
nous	sentirons
vous	sentirez
ils/elles	sentiront

CONDITIONAL

je	sentirais
tu	sentirais
il/elle/on	sentirait
nous	sentirions
vous	sentiriez
ils/elles	sentiraient

IMPERATIVE

sens / sentons / sentez

PAST PARTICIPLE

senti

PRESENT PARTICIPLE

sentant

EXAMPLE PHRASES

Ça **sentait** mauvais. — *It smelt bad.*
Je n'**ai** rien **senti**. — *I didn't feel a thing.*
Elle ne **se sent** pas bien. — *She's not feeling well.*

- *Note that **se sentir** follows the same pattern, but takes **être** in the perfect tense. For an example of a reflexive verb in full, see verb table **82 se taire**.*

servir *to serve*

PRESENT

je	sers
tu	sers
il/elle/on	sert
nous	servons
vous	servez
ils/elles	servent

PRESENT SUBJUNCTIVE

je	serve
tu	serves
il/elle/on	serve
nous	servions
vous	serviez
ils/elles	servent

PERFECT

j'	ai servi
tu	as servi
il/elle/on	a servi
nous	avons servi
vous	avez servi
ils/elles	ont servi

IMPERFECT

je	servais
tu	servais
il/elle/on	servait
nous	servions
vous	serviez
ils/elles	servaient

FUTURE

je	servirai
tu	serviras
il/elle/on	servira
nous	servirons
vous	servirez
ils/elles	serviront

CONDITIONAL

je	servirais
tu	servirais
il/elle/on	servirait
nous	servirions
vous	serviriez
ils/elles	serviraient

IMPERATIVE

sers / servons / servez

PAST PARTICIPLE

servi

PRESENT PARTICIPLE

servant

EXAMPLE PHRASES

On vous **sert**?	*Are you being served?*
Ça **sert** à quoi ce bouton?	*What is this button for?*
Servez-vous en viande.	*Help yourself to meat.*

- *Note that **se servir** follows the same pattern, but takes **être** in the perfect tense. For an example of a reflexive verb in full, see verb table **82 se taire**.*

to go out **sortir**

PRESENT

je	sors
tu	sors
il/elle/on	sort
nous	sortons
vous	sortez
ils/elles	sortent

PRESENT SUBJUNCTIVE

je	sorte
tu	sortes
il/elle/on	sorte
nous	sortions
vous	sortiez
ils/elles	sortent

PERFECT

je	suis sorti(e)
tu	es sorti(e)
il/elle/on	est sorti(e)
nous	sommes sorti(e)s
vous	êtes sorti(e)(s)
ils/elles	sont sorti(e)s

IMPERFECT

je	sortais
tu	sortais
il/elle/on	sortait
nous	sortions
vous	sortiez
ils/elles	sortaient

FUTURE

je	sortirai
tu	sortiras
il/elle/on	sortira
nous	sortirons
vous	sortirez
ils/elles	sortiront

CONDITIONAL

je	sortirais
tu	sortirais
il/elle/on	sortirait
nous	sortirions
vous	sortiriez
ils/elles	sortiraient

IMPERATIVE

sors / sortons / sortez

PAST PARTICIPLE

sorti

PRESENT PARTICIPLE

sortant

EXAMPLE PHRASES

Je ne **suis** pas **sortie** ce week-end.	*I didn't go out this weekend.*
Aurélie **sort** avec Bruno.	*Aurélie is going out with Bruno.*
Elle **est sortie** de l'hôpital hier.	*She came out of hospital yesterday.*
Je n'**ai** pas **sorti** le chien parce qu'il pleuvait.	*I didn't take the dog out for a walk because it was raining.*

• *Note that **sortir** takes **avoir** in the perfect tense when it is used with a direct object.*

suffire *to be enough*

PRESENT

je	suffis
tu	suffis
il/elle/on	suffit
nous	suffisons
vous	suffisez
ils/elles	suffisent

PRESENT SUBJUNCTIVE

je	suffise
tu	suffises
il/elle/on	suffise
nous	suffisions
vous	suffisiez
ils/elles	suffisent

PERFECT

j'	ai suffi
tu	as suffi
il/elle/on	a suffi
nous	avons suffi
vous	avez suffi
ils/elles	ont suffi

IMPERFECT

je	suffisais
tu	suffisais
il/elle/on	suffisait
nous	suffisions
vous	suffisiez
ils/elles	suffisaient

FUTURE

je	suffirai
tu	suffiras
il/elle/on	suffira
nous	suffirons
vous	suffirez
ils/elles	suffiront

CONDITIONAL

je	suffirais
tu	suffirais
il/elle/on	suffirait
nous	suffirions
vous	suffiriez
ils/elles	suffiraient

IMPERATIVE

suffis / suffisons / suffisez

PAST PARTICIPLE

suffi

PRESENT PARTICIPLE

suffisant

EXAMPLE PHRASES

Ça te **suffira**, 10 euros?	*Will 10 euros be enough?*
Ça **suffit**!	*That's enough!*
Il **suffisait** de me le demander.	*You only had to ask.*

- *Note that the verb **frire** follows the same pattern as **suffire**, but that it is used mainly in the present singular and in compound tenses such as the perfect tense. Its past participle is **frit**.*

to follow suivre

PRESENT

je	suis
tu	suis
il/elle/on	suit
nous	suivons
vous	suivez
ils/elles	suivent

PRESENT SUBJUNCTIVE

je	suive
tu	suives
il/elle/on	suive
nous	suivions
vous	suiviez
ils/elles	suivent

PERFECT

j'	ai suivi
tu	as suivi
il/elle/on	a suivi
nous	avons suivi
vous	avez suivi
ils/elles	ont suivi

IMPERFECT

je	suivais
tu	suivais
il/elle/on	suivait
nous	suivions
vous	suiviez
ils/elles	suivaient

FUTURE

je	suivrai
tu	suivras
il/elle/on	suivra
nous	suivrons
vous	suivrez
ils/elles	suivront

CONDITIONAL

je	suivrais
tu	suivrais
il/elle/on	suivrait
nous	suivrions
vous	suivriez
ils/elles	suivraient

IMPERATIVE

suis / suivons / suivez

PAST PARTICIPLE

suivi

PRESENT PARTICIPLE

suivant

EXAMPLE PHRASES

Mon chat me **suit** partout dans la maison.	*My cat follows me everywhere around the house.*
Il **a suivi** un cours d'allemand pendant six mois.	*He did a German course for 6 months.*
Elles n'arrivent pas à **suivre** en maths.	*They can't keep up in maths.*

se taire *to stop talking*

PRESENT

je	me tais
tu	te tais
il/elle/on	se tait
nous	nous taisons
vous	vous taisez
ils/elles	se taisent

PRESENT SUBJUNCTIVE

je	me taise
tu	te taises
il/elle/on	se taise
nous	nous taisions
vous	vous taisiez
ils/elles	se taisent

PERFECT

je	me suis tu(e)
tu	t'es tu(e)
il/elle/on	s'est tu(e)
nous	nous sommes tu(e)s
vous	vous êtes tu(e)(s)
ils/elles	se sont tu(e)s

IMPERFECT

je	me taisais
tu	te taisais
il/elle/on	se taisait
nous	nous taisions
vous	vous taisiez
ils/elles	se taisaient

FUTURE

je	me tairai
tu	te tairas
il/elle/on	se taira
nous	nous tairons
vous	vous tairez
ils/elles	se tairont

CONDITIONAL

je	me tairais
tu	te tairais
il/elle/on	se tairait
nous	nous tairions
vous	vous tairiez
ils/elles	se tairaient

IMPERATIVE

tais-toi / taisons-nous / taisez-vous

PAST PARTICIPLE

tu

PRESENT PARTICIPLE

se taisant

EXAMPLE PHRASES

Il **s'est tu**.	*He stopped talking.*
Taisez-vous!	*Be quiet!*
Sophie, **tais-toi**!	*Be quiet Sophie!*

to hold **tenir**

PRESENT

je	tiens
tu	tiens
il/elle/on	tient
nous	tenons
vous	tenez
ils/elles	tiennent

PRESENT SUBJUNCTIVE

je	tienne
tu	tiennes
il/elle/on	tienne
nous	tenions
vous	teniez
ils/elles	tiennent

PERFECT

j'	ai tenu
tu	as tenu
il/elle/on	a tenu
nous	avons tenu
vous	avez tenu
ils/elles	ont tenu

IMPERFECT

je	tenais
tu	tenais
il/elle/on	tenait
nous	tenions
vous	teniez
ils/elles	tenaient

FUTURE

je	tiendrai
tu	tiendras
il/elle/on	tiendra
nous	tiendrons
vous	tiendrez
ils/elles	tiendront

CONDITIONAL

je	tiendrais
tu	tiendrais
il/elle/on	tiendrait
nous	tiendrions
vous	tiendriez
ils/elles	tiendraient

IMPERATIVE

tiens / tenons / tenez

PAST PARTICIPLE

tenu

PRESENT PARTICIPLE

tenant

EXAMPLE PHRASES

Tiens-moi la main.	*Hold my hand.*
Elle **tenait** beaucoup à son chat.	*She was really attached to her cat.*
Tiens, prends mon stylo.	*Here, have my pen.*
Tiens-toi droit!	*Sit up straight!*

- *Note that* ***se tenir*** *follows the same pattern, but takes* ***être*** *in the perfect tense. For an example of a reflexive verb in full, see verb table* ***82 se taire***.

Table 84

tomber *to fall*

PRESENT

je	tombe
tu	tombes
il/elle/on	tombe
nous	tombons
vous	tombez
ils/elles	tombent

PRESENT SUBJUNCTIVE

je	tombe
tu	tombes
il/elle/on	tombe
nous	tombions
vous	tombiez
ils/elles	tombent

PERFECT

je	suis tombé(e)
tu	es tombé(e)
il/elle/on	est tombé(e)
nous	sommes tombé(e)s
vous	êtes tombé(e)(s)
ils/elles	sont tombé(e)s

IMPERFECT

je	tombais
tu	tombais
il/elle/on	tombait
nous	tombions
vous	tombiez
ils/elles	tombaient

FUTURE

je	tomberai
tu	tomberas
il/elle/on	tombera
nous	tomberons
vous	tomberez
ils/elles	tomberont

CONDITIONAL

je	tomberais
tu	tomberais
il/elle/on	tomberait
nous	tomberions
vous	tomberiez
ils/elles	tomberaient

IMPERATIVE

tombe / tombons / tombez

PAST PARTICIPLE

tombé

PRESENT PARTICIPLE

tombant

EXAMPLE PHRASES

Attention, tu vas **tomber**! — *Be careful, you'll fall!*

Nicole **est tombée** de cheval. — *Nicole fell off her horse.*

Elle s'est faite mal en **tombant** dans l'escalier. — *She hurt herself falling down the stairs.*

to milk **traire**

PRESENT

je	trais
tu	trais
il/elle/on	trait
nous	trayons
vous	trayez
ils/elles	traient

PRESENT SUBJUNCTIVE

je	traie
tu	traies
il/elle/on	traie
nous	trayions
vous	trayiez
ils/elles	traient

PERFECT

j'	ai trait
tu	as trait
il/elle/on	a trait
nous	avons trait
vous	avez trait
ils/elles	ont trait

IMPERFECT

je	trayais
tu	trayais
il/elle/on	trayait
nous	trayions
vous	trayiez
ils/elles	trayaient

FUTURE

je	trairai
tu	trairas
il/elle/on	traira
nous	trairons
vous	trairez
ils/elles	trairont

CONDITIONAL

je	trairais
tu	trairais
il/elle/on	trairait
nous	trairions
vous	trairiez
ils/elles	trairaient

IMPERATIVE

trais / trayons / trayez

PAST PARTICIPLE

trait

PRESENT PARTICIPLE

trayant

EXAMPLE PHRASES

À la ferme, on a appris à **traire** les vaches. — *We learnt to milk cows on the farm.*

Elle **trait** les vaches à six heures du matin. — *She milks the cows at 6 am.*

Table 86

vaincre *to defeat*

PRESENT

je	vaincs
tu	vaincs
il/elle/on	vainc
nous	vainquons
vous	vainquez
ils/elles	vainquent

PRESENT SUBJUNCTIVE

je	vainque
tu	vainques
il/elle/on	vainque
nous	vainquions
vous	vainquiez
ils/elles	vainquent

PERFECT

j'	ai vaincu
tu	as vaincu
il/elle/on	a vaincu
nous	avons vaincu
vous	avez vaincu
ils/elles	ont vaincu

IMPERFECT

je	vainquais
tu	vainquais
il/elle/on	vainquait
nous	vainquions
vous	vainquiez
ils/elles	vainquaient

FUTURE

je	vaincrai
tu	vaincras
il/elle/on	vaincra
nous	vaincrons
vous	vaincrez
ils/elles	vaincront

CONDITIONAL

je	vaincrais
tu	vaincrais
il/elle/on	vaincrait
nous	vaincrions
vous	vaincriez
ils/elles	vaincraient

IMPERATIVE

vaincs / vainquons / vainquez

PAST PARTICIPLE

vaincu

PRESENT PARTICIPLE

vainquant

EXAMPLE PHRASES

L'armée **a été vaincue**. — *The army was defeated.*

La France **a vaincu** la Corée trois buts à deux. — *France beat Korea 3 goals to 2.*

to be worth **valoir**

PRESENT

je	vaux
tu	vaux
il/elle/on	vaut
nous	valons
vous	valez
ils/elles	valent

PRESENT SUBJUNCTIVE

je	vaille
tu	vailles
il/elle/on	vaille
nous	valions
vous	valiez
ils/elles	vaillent

PERFECT

j'	ai valu
tu	as valu
il/elle/on	a valu
nous	avons valu
vous	avez valu
ils/elles	ont valu

IMPERFECT

je	valais
tu	valais
il/elle/on	valait
nous	valions
vous	valiez
ils/elles	valaient

FUTURE

je	vaudrai
tu	vaudras
il/elle/on	vaudra
nous	vaudrons
vous	vaudrez
ils/elles	vaudront

CONDITIONAL

je	vaudrais
tu	vaudrais
il/elle/on	vaudrait
nous	vaudrions
vous	vaudriez
ils/elles	vaudraient

IMPERATIVE

vaux / valons / valez

PAST PARTICIPLE

valu

PRESENT PARTICIPLE

valant

EXAMPLE PHRASES

Ça **vaut** combien?	*How much is it worth?*
Ça **vaudrait** la peine d'essayer.	*It would be worth a try.*
Il **vaut** mieux ne pas y penser.	*It's best not to think about it.*

vendre *to sell*

PRESENT

je	vends
tu	vends
il/elle/on	vend
nous	vendons
vous	vendez
ils/elles	vendent

PRESENT SUBJUNCTIVE

je	vende
tu	vendes
il/elle/on	vende
nous	vendions
vous	vendiez
ils/elles	vendent

PERFECT

j'	ai vendu
tu	as vendu
il/elle/on	a vendu
nous	avons vendu
vous	avez vendu
ils/elles	ont vendu

IMPERFECT

je	vendais
tu	vendais
il/elle/on	vendait
nous	vendions
vous	vendiez
ils/elles	vendaient

FUTURE

je	vendrai
tu	vendras
il/elle/on	vendra
nous	vendrons
vous	vendrez
ils/elles	vendront

CONDITIONAL

je	vendrais
tu	vendrais
il/elle/on	vendrait
nous	vendrions
vous	vendriez
ils/elles	vendraient

IMPERATIVE

vends / vendons / vendez

PAST PARTICIPLE

vendu

PRESENT PARTICIPLE

vendant

EXAMPLE PHRASES

Il m'**a vendu** son vélo pour 50 euros.	*He sold me his bike for 50 euros.*
Est-ce que vous **vendez** des piles?	*Do you sell batteries?*
Elle voudrait **vendre** sa voiture.	*She would like to sell her car.*

to come **venir**

PRESENT

je	viens
tu	viens
il/elle/on	vient
nous	venons
vous	venez
ils/elles	viennent

PRESENT SUBJUNCTIVE

je	vienne
tu	viennes
il/elle/on	vienne
nous	venions
vous	veniez
ils/elles	viennent

PERFECT

je	suis venu(e)
tu	es venu(e)
il/elle/on	est venu(e)
nous	sommes venu(e)s
vous	êtes venu(e)(s)
ils/elles	sont venu(e)s

IMPERFECT

je	venais
tu	venais
il/elle/on	venait
nous	venions
vous	veniez
ils/elles	venaient

FUTURE

je	viendrai
tu	viendras
il/elle/on	viendra
nous	viendrons
vous	viendrez
ils/elles	viendront

CONDITIONAL

je	viendrais
tu	viendrais
il/elle/on	viendrait
nous	viendrions
vous	viendriez
ils/elles	viendraient

IMPERATIVE

viens / venons / venez

PAST PARTICIPLE

venu

PRESENT PARTICIPLE

venant

EXAMPLE PHRASES

Elle ne **viendra** pas cette année.	*She won't be coming this year.*
Fatou et Malik **viennent** du Sénégal.	*Fatou and Malik come from Senegal.*
Je **viens** de manger.	*I've just eaten.*

- *Note that the verbs **convenir** and **prévenir** follow the same pattern as **venir**, but take **avoir** in the perfect tense.*

Table 90

vêtir *to dress*

PRESENT

je	vêts
tu	vêts
il/elle/on	vêt
nous	vêtons
vous	vêtez
ils/elles	vêtent

PRESENT SUBJUNCTIVE

je	vête
tu	vêtes
il/elle/on	vête
nous	vêtions
vous	vêtiez
ils/elles	vêtent

PERFECT

j'	ai vêtu
tu	as vêtu
il/elle/on	a vêtu
nous	avons vêtu
vous	avez vêtu
ils/elles	ont vêtu

IMPERFECT

je	vêtais
tu	vêtais
il/elle/on	vêtait
nous	vêtions
vous	vêtiez
ils/elles	vêtaient

FUTURE

je	vêtirai
tu	vêtiras
il/elle/on	vêtira
nous	vêtirons
vous	vêtirez
ils/elles	vêtiront

CONDITIONAL

je	vêtirais
tu	vêtirais
il/elle/on	vêtirait
nous	vêtirions
vous	vêtiriez
ils/elles	vêtiraient

IMPERATIVE

vêts / vêtons / vêtez

PAST PARTICIPLE

vêtu

PRESENT PARTICIPLE

vêtant

EXAMPLE PHRASES

Il **était vêtu** d'un pantalon et d'un pull. — *He was wearing trousers and a jumper.*

Il faut se lever, se laver et **se vêtir** en 10 minutes. — *You have to get up, get washed and get dressed in 10 minutes.*

- *Note that **se vêtir** follows the same pattern, but takes **être** in the perfect tense. For an example of a reflexive verb in full, see verb table **82 se taire**.*

PRESENT

je	vis
tu	vis
il/elle/on	vit
nous	vivons
vous	vivez
ils/elles	vivent

PRESENT SUBJUNCTIVE

je	vive
tu	vives
il/elle/on	vive
nous	vivions
vous	viviez
ils/elles	vivent

PERFECT

j'	ai vécu
tu	as vécu
il/elle/on	a vécu
nous	avons vécu
vous	avez vécu
ils/elles	ont vécu

IMPERFECT

je	vivais
tu	vivais
il/elle/on	vivait
nous	vivions
vous	viviez
ils/elles	vivaient

FUTURE

je	vivrai
tu	vivras
il/elle/on	vivra
nous	vivrons
vous	vivrez
ils/elles	vivront

CONDITIONAL

je	vivrais
tu	vivrais
il/elle/on	vivrait
nous	vivrions
vous	vivriez
ils/elles	vivraient

IMPERATIVE

vis / vivons / vivez

PAST PARTICIPLE

vécu

PRESENT PARTICIPLE

vivant

EXAMPLE PHRASES

Ma sœur **vit** en Espagne.	*My sister lives in Spain.*
Il **a vécu** dix ans à Lyon.	*He lived in Lyons for 10 years.*
Les gorilles **vivent** surtout dans la forêt.	*Gorillas mostly live in the forest.*

Table 92

voir *to see*

PRESENT

je	vois
tu	vois
il/elle/on	voit
nous	voyons
vous	voyez
ils/elles	voient

PRESENT SUBJUNCTIVE

je	voie
tu	voies
il/elle/on	voie
nous	voyions
vous	voyiez
ils/elles	voient

PERFECT

j'	ai vu
tu	as vu
il/elle/on	a vu
nous	avons vu
vous	avez vu
ils/elles	ont vu

IMPERFECT

je	voyais
tu	voyais
il/elle/on	voyait
nous	voyions
vous	voyiez
ils/elles	voyaient

FUTURE

je	verrai
tu	verras
il/elle/on	verra
nous	verrons
vous	verrez
ils/elles	verront

CONDITIONAL

je	verrais
tu	verrais
il/elle/on	verrait
nous	verrions
vous	verriez
ils/elles	verraient

IMPERATIVE

vois / voyons / voyez

PAST PARTICIPLE

vu

PRESENT PARTICIPLE

voyant

EXAMPLE PHRASES

Venez me **voir** demain.	*Come and see me tomorrow.*
Je ne **vois** rien sans mes lunettes.	*I can't see anything without my glasses.*
Est-ce que tu l'**as vu**?	*Did you see him?* OR *Have you seen him?*
Est-ce que cette tache **se voit**?	*Does that stain show?*

- *Note that **se voir** follows the same pattern, but takes **être** in the perfect tense. For an example of a reflexive verb in full, see verb table **82 se taire**.*
- *The verb **prévoir** follows the same pattern as **voir**, except for the future tense (**je prévoirai**, etc) and the conditional (**je prévoirais**, etc).*

PRESENT

je	veux
tu	veux
il/elle/on	veut
nous	voulons
vous	voulez
ils/elles	veulent

PRESENT SUBJUNCTIVE

je	veuille
tu	veuilles
il/elle/on	veuille
nous	voulions
vous	vouliez
ils/elles	veuillent

PERFECT

j'	ai voulu
tu	as voulu
il/elle/on	a voulu
nous	avons voulu
vous	avez voulu
ils/elles	ont voulu

IMPERFECT

je	voulais
tu	voulais
il/elle/on	voulait
nous	voulions
vous	vouliez
ils/elles	voulaient

FUTURE

je	voudrai
tu	voudras
il/elle/on	voudra
nous	voudrons
vous	voudrez
ils/elles	voudront

CONDITIONAL

je	voudrais
tu	voudrais
il/elle/on	voudrait
nous	voudrions
vous	voudriez
ils/elles	voudraient

IMPERATIVE

veuille / veuillons / veuillez

PAST PARTICIPLE

voulu

PRESENT PARTICIPLE

voulant

EXAMPLE PHRASES

Elle **veut** un vélo pour Noël.	*She wants a bike for Christmas.*
Ils **voulaient** aller au cinéma.	*They wanted to go to the cinema.*
Tu **voudrais** une tasse de thé?	*Would you like a cup of tea?*